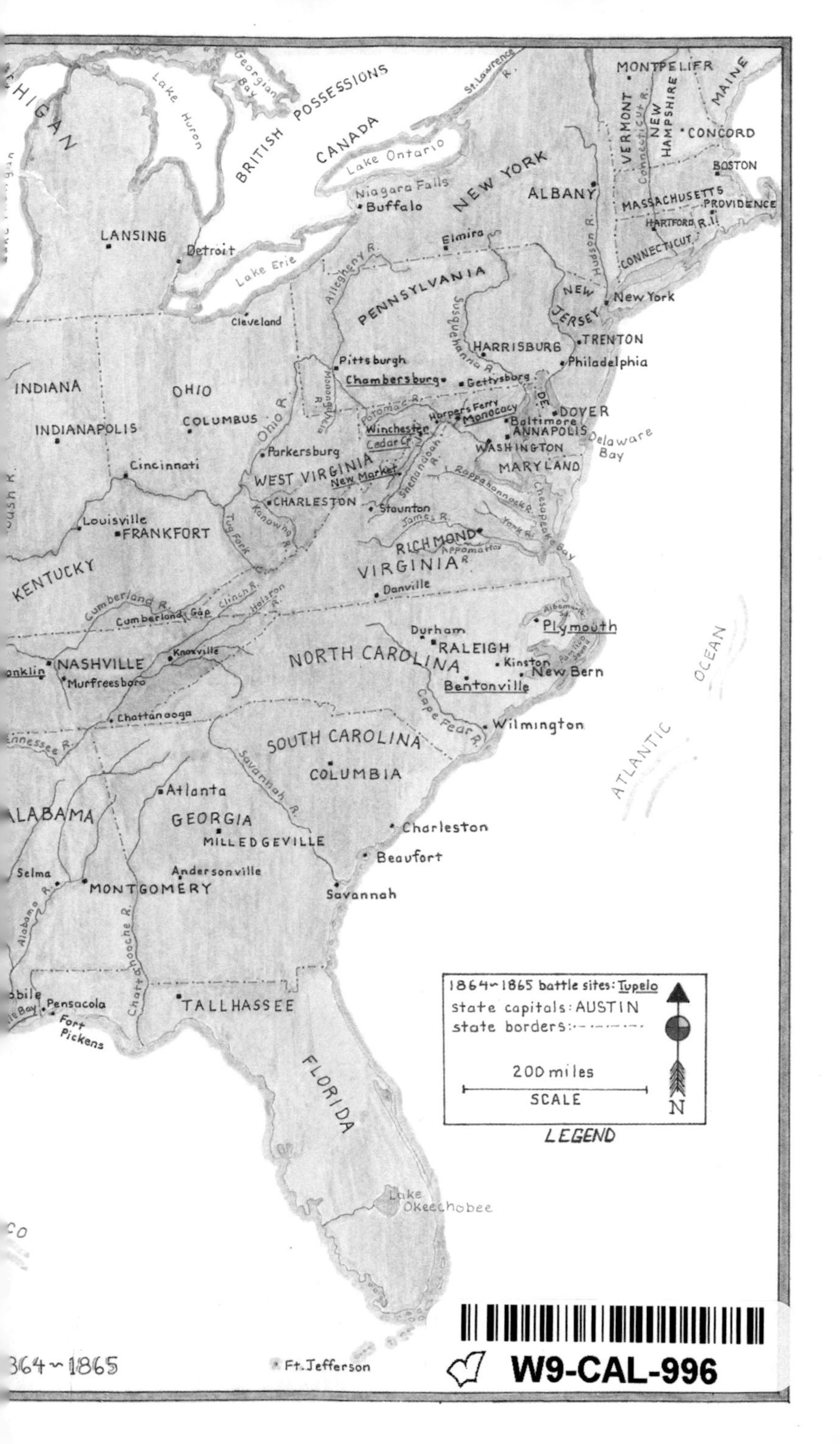

BRITISH POSSESSIONS
CANADA
Lake Huron
Georgian Bay
Lake Ontario
Lake Erie
St. Lawrence R.
Niagara Falls
Buffalo
NEW YORK
ALBANY
MONTPELIER
VERMONT
NEW HAMPSHIRE
MAINE
CONCORD
BOSTON
MASSACHUSETTS
PROVIDENCE
HARTFORD
R.I.
CONNECTICUT
Connecticut R.
Hudson R.
New York
NEW JERSEY
TRENTON
Philadelphia
LANSING
Detroit
Cleveland
Elmira
Allegheny R.
PENNSYLVANIA
Susquehanna R.
HARRISBURG
Pittsburgh
Chambersburg
Gettysburg
Monongahela R.
INDIANA
OHIO
INDIANAPOLIS
COLUMBUS
Ohio R.
Potomac R.
Harpers Ferry
Monocacy
Baltimore
DE.
DOVER
ANNAPOLIS
Winchester
Cedar Cr.
WASHINGTON
Delaware Bay
MARYLAND
Parkersburg
Cincinnati
WEST VIRGINIA
New Market
Shenandoah R.
Rappahannock R.
CHARLESTON
Staunton
Kanawha R.
Tug Fork
Louisville
FRANKFORT
James R.
York R.
Chesapeake Bay
RICHMOND
Appomattox R.
VIRGINIA
KENTUCKY
Danville
Cumberland R.
Cumberland Gap
Clinch R.
Holston R.
Albemarle Sd.
Plymouth
Durham
RALEIGH
NORTH CAROLINA
Kinston
New Bern
Pamlico Sound
Bentonville
NASHVILLE
Murfreesboro
Knoxville
Chattanooga
Cape Fear R.
Wilmington
SOUTH CAROLINA
COLUMBIA
Savannah R.
ATLANTIC OCEAN
Atlanta
ALABAMA
GEORGIA
MILLEDGEVILLE
Charleston
Beaufort
Selma
Alabama R.
MONTGOMERY
Andersonville
Savannah
Chattahoochee R.
Pensacola
Fort Pickens
TALLHASSEE
FLORIDA
Lake Okeechobee
Ft. Jefferson
1864~1865 battle sites: Tupelo
state capitals: AUSTIN
state borders:
200 miles
SCALE
N
LEGEND

THE CIVIL WAR

THE FINAL YEAR

The Civil War

THE FINAL YEAR TOLD BY THOSE WHO LIVED IT

Aaron Sheehan-Dean, editor

THE LIBRARY OF AMERICA

See Note on the Texts on page 791 for further information.

The paper used in this publication meets the
minimum requirements of the American National Standard for
Information Sciences—Permanence of Paper for Printed
Library Materials, ANSI Z39.48—1984.

Distributed to the trade in the United States
by Penguin Group (USA) Inc.
and in Canada by Penguin Books Canada Ltd.

Library of Congress Control Number: 2013941526
ISBN 978-1-59853-294-4

First Printing
The Library of America—250

Manufactured in the United States of America

The Civil War:
The Final Year Told by Those Who Lived It
is published with support from

THE ANDREW W. MELLON FOUNDATION

and

THE NATIONAL ENDOWMENT
FOR THE HUMANITIES

The Civil War: The Final Year Told by Those Who Lived It
is kept in print in memory of

THE BERKLEY FOUNDATION

the Guardians of American Letters Fund,
established by The Library of America
to ensure that every volume in the series
will be permanently available.

Contents

Preface

> "Has there ever been another historical crisis of the magnitude of 1861–65 in which so many people were so articulate?"
> —Edmund Wilson

THIS Library of America volume is the last in a four-volume series bringing together memorable and significant writing by participants in the American Civil War. Each volume in the series covers approximately one year of the conflict, from the election of Abraham Lincoln in November 1860 to the end of the war in the spring of 1865, and presents a chronological selection of documents from the broadest possible range of authoritative sources—diaries, letters, speeches, military reports, newspaper articles, memoirs, poems, and public papers. Drawing upon an immense and unique body of American writing, the series offers a narrative of the war years that encompasses military and political events and their social and personal reverberations. Created by persons of every class and condition, the writing included here captures the American nation and the American language in the crucial period of their modern formation. Selections have been chosen for their historical significance, their literary quality, and their narrative energy, and are printed from the best available sources. The goal has been to shape a narrative that is both broad and balanced in scope, while at the same time doing justice to the number and diversity of voices and perspectives preserved for us in the writing of the era.

Introduction

On March 8, 1864, Ulysses S. Grant arrived in Washington, D.C., to take command of the armies of the United States, but before he could lead them against the Confederacy, he needed to be introduced to the capital. After meeting President Lincoln for the first time, Grant found himself the center of attention at a White House reception. By the end of the night the modest rumpled man who had been working as a store clerk when the war began was standing on a sofa so that onlookers could catch a glimpse of the general they hoped would save the nation's military fortunes. Grant's victories at Vicksburg and Chattanooga had made him the preeminent Union commander of the war, but he had yet to prove his mettle against Robert E. Lee and his formidable Army of Northern Virginia. Nor was it certain that President Lincoln would be reelected in the fall of 1864, or if he was defeated, that his successor would be willing, or able, to continue the conflict. As the sundered nation began its fourth year of war, both sides could still find reasons to hope that their faith in victory might be rewarded in the months ahead.

The previous year had not begun well for the Union. After its disastrous defeat at Fredericksburg under Ambrose Burnside in December 1862, the Army of the Potomac had suffered from widespread demoralization, alarming desertion rates, and intrigues among its senior generals. Lincoln's decision in January 1863 to replace Burnside with Joseph Hooker helped restore the army's morale, but Hooker's offensive across the Rappahannock River in May ended in a humiliating repulse at Chancellorsville. Confronted by a numerically superior opponent, Lee demonstrated his characteristic audacity by dividing his army and launching a series of counterattacks that drove Hooker back across the river. Although Chancellorsville cost the Confederacy 13,000 men killed, wounded, or missing, the battle bolstered Lee's already high confidence in the ability of his troops. Determined to seize the strategic initiative in the east, Lee invaded Pennsylvania in June in the hope of gaining a third consecutive victory over the Army of the Potomac. When Hooker's successor, George G. Meade, defeated him at Gettysburg in July, Lee managed to escape back across the Potomac into Virginia, where the two opposing commanders maneuvered inconclusively for the remainder of the year. While Lee was aware that the Gettysburg campaign had proved a costly failure, many Southerners considered the battle to have been a draw, while many Northerners—especially President Lincoln—understood that defensive victories alone would not win the war in the east.

By the end of 1863 there was no uncertainty regarding the ability of the Union to win offensive victories in the western theater. After spending the winter engaged in a series of futile attempts to reach the Confederate stronghold at Vicksburg through the rivers and bayous of the Mississippi Delta, Grant had shown a willingness to take risks equal to Lee's. Crossing the Mississippi well below Vicksburg at the beginning of May, Grant had marched his army northeast to Jackson, then turned west to attack his main objective from the rear. Vicksburg's surrender on July 4, the day after the failure of Lee's final assault at Gettysburg, gave the Union control of the entire length of the Mississippi and effectively cut Texas, western Louisiana, and Arkansas off from the rest of the Confederacy. "The Father of Waters," Lincoln gratefully observed, "again goes unvexed to the sea." During the summer of 1863 William S. Rosecrans also succeeded in gaining control of Middle Tennessee for the Union, skillfully maneuvering Braxton Bragg out of a series of defensive positions and forcing him to retreat into northwestern Georgia. Reinforced by Confederate troops from Virginia and Mississippi, Bragg turned on Rosecrans in September and defeated his Army of the Cumberland at Chickamauga. The victory rallied Confederate spirits but proved short-lived. Union forces under Grant broke Bragg's siege of Chattanooga, and in November they drove the Confederates off Missionary Ridge and forced them back into northwestern Georgia.

Union forces faced military, political, and humanitarian challenges as they advanced deeper into southern territory. The need to occupy towns and cities, and to guard railroads and bridges against Confederate guerrillas and cavalry raiders, drew troops away from the main northern armies. In fighting guerrillas, Union soldiers increasingly showed less restraint in exercising the "hard war" policies first adopted in 1862, burning farms, imprisoning or expelling civilians suspected of disloyalty, and often summarily executing captured "bushwhackers," actions that only increased the hatred most white Southerners felt toward the northern occupiers. The question of how civilian governments were to be reconstructed in the South became a potential source of division between President Lincoln and the Radical Republicans in Congress. And both the Union army and the various civilian aid agencies that assisted it found themselves hard-pressed to care for the thousands of former slaves who came into the Union lines each month.

Despite the success of the Union armies, dissension and violence would mark 1863 in the North. When Clement L. Vallandigham, one of the leading Democratic opponents of emancipation and the draft, declared in May that "a wicked, cruel and unnecessary" war was being waged "for the purpose of crushing out liberty and erecting a despotism; a war for the freedom of the blacks, and the enslavement of the whites," Burnside had him arrested and tried by a military commission in Ohio. Burnside's actions stirred up a hornet's nest of controversy over free speech and the permissible boundaries of wartime dissent that continued well after Lincoln banished Vallandigham into Confederate-held territory. In July the enforcement of the draft sent rioters, many of them Irish and German immigrants, rampaging through the streets of New York. Mobs, angry over the draft and emancipation, turned on black New Yorkers, lynching at least eleven African Americans and attacking the homes and businesses of prominent Republicans. The final toll of 105 dead made the New York draft riots the worst act of urban violence in the United States during the nineteenth century. In the meantime, Vallandigham had escaped to Canada, where he campaigned from exile as the Democratic candidate for governor of Ohio. His overwhelming defeat in the fall of 1863 raised Republican hopes for success in the 1864 elections, yet few supporters of the administration expected that it would be reelected if the coming year failed to produce decisive battlefield victories.

Jefferson Davis could take little solace from considering

Lincoln's trials. In the spring of 1863 a series of food riots in southern cities, including the famous Richmond Bread Riot of early April, demonstrated a new militancy on the part of white southern women as they took to the streets to protest rising prices and the Confederate government's failure to organize effective relief. Often identifying themselves as soldiers' wives, these hungry women parlayed their sacrifices in sending sons, husbands, brothers, and fathers off to war to win legislative support for an unprecedented public welfare program that proved only partially successful in alleviating hunger and scarcity in the Confederacy. Confederate conscription efforts also met with violent resistance from armed draft evaders and deserters who took refuge in remote regions of the South.

While white Southerners expressed discontent with the demands of war, black Southerners challenged slavery at every level. Every slaveholder could report evidence of what he considered disrespectful behavior, if not outright rebellion. In rare cases, enslaved people committed acts of violence and destruction against former masters. More often, wherever the opportunity presented itself, slaves fled. Gathering family members, they escaped on foot, on horseback, or by boat to the nearest Union outpost. In the opening months of the war, Union commanders had possessed considerable leeway to return runaway slaves, and Democratic generals, especially George B. McClellan, had drawn the scorn of Republicans in Congress and the press for their willingness to protect slaveholders' rights. But the Emancipation Proclamation, along with legislation passed by Congress in 1862, had turned the Union army into a giant engine for emancipation. In areas such as coastal Georgia and Florida and the Mississippi Valley, the Union army organized expeditions whose main purpose was to free slaves, some of whom were then recruited for service in the rapidly expanding U.S. Colored Troops.

During 1863 the Union army's use of black soldiers began to have a major impact upon the war. The heroic efforts of African American troops at Port Hudson, Milliken's Bend, and Fort Wagner helped change northern attitudes about race. Although many Democrats continued to vigorously oppose black enlistment, a sizable number of skeptical white Northerners came to respect the willingness of black men to die for the Union, while the manpower advantage the North gained by turning slaves (and free black men) into soldiers could not be ignored in the Confederacy. In January 1864 Patrick Cleburne, a Confederate division commander with an outstanding battle record, asked his fellow generals in the Army of Tennessee to consider emancipating slaves and enlisting them in the Confederate forces. A copy of his address was sent to Jefferson Davis, who ordered it suppressed. At the same time, the Davis administration continued to refuse to exchange black prisoners, a policy that had contributed to the breakdown of the exchange cartel during 1863 and increased death and hardship among prisoners of war on both sides.

By the beginning of 1864 mass death and suffering had become a permanent presence in the American psyche. The battle of Gettysburg alone had killed about seven thousand men outright, and several thousand more would eventually die of their wounds or be maimed for life. Northerners and Southerners alike contended with the shock of seeing men without arms or legs, disfigured by shrapnel, or ravaged by disease. Still the war continued, as soldiers and civilians on both sides accepted the necessity of a fourth year of fighting with a mixture of determination and resignation. Many in the North expected that Grant would quickly defeat Lee in the spring and capture Richmond, while Confederate hopes focused on the gradual exhaustion of the northern will to fight and the defeat of the Lincoln administration at the polls. As spring came, both sides would plunge again into the maelstrom of battle.

Aaron Sheehan-Dean

"YANKEE WICKEDNESS": NORTH CAROLINA, MARCH 1864

Catherine Edmondston: Diary, March 8, 1864

In July 1862 the Union and Confederate armies negotiated an agreement on prisoner exchanges. The cartel began to collapse in the summer of 1863 because the Confederates refused to treat black soldiers and their officers as prisoners of war. Union officials insisted that black and white prisoners be treated equally under the cartel, and later protested when men paroled at Vicksburg returned to the Confederate ranks without being properly exchanged. By February 1864 some 5,000 Union prisoners were being held in Richmond, where they suffered from hunger, disease, and exposure. Brigadier General Judson Kilpatrick, a division commander in the Army of the Potomac's cavalry corps, gained approval from President Lincoln and Secretary of War Edwin M. Stanton for a raid on the Confederate capital aimed at freeing the prisoners. On February 28 Kilpatrick and 3,500 men crossed the Rapidan River sixty miles north of Richmond, then split up the next day. The main force under Kilpatrick encountered unexpectedly strong resistance when it reached the northern outskirts of the city on March 1, while a smaller body of 460 men led by Colonel Ulric Dahlgren was unable to cross the James River and attack Richmond from the south. While Kilpatrick and most of his command reached the Union lines on the Virginia Peninsula, Dahlgren was killed in an ambush on March 2. In papers found on his body Dahlgren wrote that once the prisoners were released and the city captured, "it must be destroyed and Jeff Davis and Cabinet killed." (Kilpatrick would later deny having given or received orders to burn the city or to kill Confederate leaders.) The papers were given to Jefferson Davis on March 4 and published in the Richmond press the next day. Catherine Edmondston followed reports of the raid from her plantation home in Halifax County, North Carolina.

MARCH 8, 1864

News last night which makes the blood of all true hearted Confederates boil in their veins at this new instance of Yankee wickedness & meanness. Lieut Pollard Comdg Company H of the 9th Va Cavelry, aided by some Home guards & a small detachment from Lieut Col Robbin's Command, followed a large party of the Yankee Cavalry, harrassing their rear all day Wednesday, crossing the Mattapony after them. The Enemy under Col Dahlgren's command took the fork of the road leading to Walkertown when Lieut Pollard, hastily dividing his force, left a small body in pursuit & taking the other fork succeeding in a circuit, & having been joined by the forces above named, appeared on their front about eleven at night; Dahlgren ordered a charge—& in the act was shot through the head. A fight then ensued in which he took 90 prisoners, 35 negroes, & 150 horses & the rest of the enemy dispersed in the darkness in wild flight through the woods. On Col Dahlgren's person was found memoranda & orders disclosing a most diabolical plan in which, God be praised, he was defeated. He was to cross to the South side of the James about thirty miles above Richmond with one Squadron, keeping the other on the North side, signalling each other as they went. That on the South side was to seize the bridges at Richmond, release the prisoners on Belle Isle, arming them from waggons which they carried loaded with small arms for the purpose & supplying them with oakum balls soaked in tar with which they were all well provided for the purpose of destroying the city by fire.

The North side party was to destroy the Arsenal etc. at Bellona & the two Squadrons making a junction in the city were to seize Mr Davis & his Cabinet, *hang them* immediately, join the prisoners in setting the city on fire, & by daybreak be across the Pamunky in full retreat, leaving murder, rapine, & a city in ashes behind them. But God ordained otherwise. A negroe whom they seized for a guide brought them, doubtless in good faith to them, to a point on the James where he told them they could cross; but the River being higher than he was aware of, when they reached the place, they were unable to do so, whereupon they instantly hanged him. This, however, disconcerted their plans and meeting with a stouter resistance than they thought, they were forced to retreat without so much as entering Richmond. Are our enemies civilized? Do they even *profess* the doctrines of Christ? What sort of a return is this for the way our troops acted towards them in their last summer's campaign into Penn? We respected all private rights, horses only excepted, & not *one* private dwelling in ashes marked the footsteps of our army. One only was molested & that by three men, Mississippians, who had all of them had their own houses burned by the enemy & their wives & children driven out homeless. They dared not *burn* it in retaliation, for they feared the smoke would betray them & that Gen Lee in stern justice would visit on them the penalty of a violated Order, so they only hacked & hewed the furniture to peices, & tell me how many thousand of our Southern homes have been thus and worse treated? Blood thirsty tho it appears, our Government ought to adopt a different course with men captured on such an expedition. It is not regular warfare & they are not entitled to the privileges of prisoners of war. It is mockery to insist that they are. Dahlgren is the son of the Commodore now in command before Charleston. The one aids in the infamous attempt to destroy a whole city & to hurry thousands of non-combattants incapable of resistance to a dreadful death. The other is even worse; at the head of a gang of picked ruffians armed with fire balls, his deliberate purpose is to turn loose upon innocent women a mixed multitude, a mob of prisoners, without even the show of an authority to command them, with orders to pillage, burn, destroy, murder; in short, do all that their evil passions prompt them, whilst he himself a commissioned officer of the U S hangs without trial the heads of a Government whose meanest soldier his Government has admitted to the rights of a belligerant. Talk of Punic Faith no more! hence forth let it be "Yankee faith." Like father like son. Dahlgren and Kilpatrick's paths are marked with desolation, vide some of the particulars marked D.

Ellen Renshaw House: Diary, March 9–11, 19, 1864

In a referendum held on June 8, 1861, Tennessee voters had endorsed leaving the Union by 104,913 to 47,238. Secession was opposed by 70 percent of the voters in East Tennessee, a mountainous region with relatively few slaveholders that would remain bitterly divided between secessionists and unionists. Ellen Renshaw House had moved with her family from Marietta, Georgia, to Knoxville shortly before the war. She remained in the city after it was occupied by Union troops on September 2, 1863, and during the subsequent siege by Confederate forces under Lieutenant General James Longstreet from November 17 to December 4. "God grant it is not so. It is so," House wrote in her diary after Longstreet abandoned his attempt to retake Knoxville. By March 1864 one of House's brothers was a prisoner of war on Johnson's Island in Lake Erie, while another brother was serving with the Confederate army at Mobile, Alabama.

March 9. Wednesday. I felt so worried all night about poor Leo, I could not sleep, and got up before daylight, and went down to see him, poor dog. He did not know me, he was dying. Oh! I felt so badly about it got father to go for Dr Rogers. He could not come, then for Will. By the time he got here he was dead. It seems more like a human being had died than a dog. It even bought tears to Will's eyes. I expect it made him think of the baby, & he used to be so fond of him. I have been crying nearly the whole day. I cant help it. My heart aches when I think of his being dead. Will sent a man round to bury him. Dr R. came after he was dead. Said he thought he had probably been shot.

This afternoon father said Lieut Shaw had told him there were sixty prisoners in the jail, and sister & I thought we would go see them. When we went to the office the clerk Jim said there was only one man besides the Indians. I dont know why they have not been sent north with the other prisoners. While I was standing by the door talking, an Officer came up with a Confederate Lieut. I asked Lieut Shaw if I could speak to him. He said certainly. The officers who came with him very pertly said Oh! yes you can look at & talk to him as much as you like. I turned to him and asked in my very pleasantest manner, Where were you captured Lt. He looked slightly sneaking & replied "I was not captured at all." (I know my face was in a blaze. I would liked to see some one slap his face) "You came in" I asked. He said "yes" the contemptable rascal. I turned round as fast and walked off in a hurry. The Yankee Officers laughed. I know Lt Shaw told him that I was the D——t rebel he ever saw.

From there we went to see Mrs French & Mrs McClannahan. Not long after we came home Capt Whitman came with a Capt McAlister to get board for himself, wife & child. Of course mother had to say they could come. I hate the idea of Yankee woman & children in the house. We have whipped them above here at Panther Springs. Letter from Johnnie & I answered it.

March 10. Thursday. It rained heavily last night. Capt McAlister came this morning. He is the nephew of old Col McAlister of Sav. and studied law there. Knows a great many of fathers friends as does his wife, who seems very much of a Lady. They arrived two days since & have been staying at Gen Carters. The Capt & I got at it tonight. He said he heard of me before he came here. Father, he says, is considered a good Union man, Mother a very proper person, but one of the daughters was an outrageous rebel. I told him I was perfectly willing for them to consider me so, and if I thought there was any chance of them sending me South I would cut up some anticks most certainly. I am glad to hear they consider father a good Union man, as long as he has taken the oath, for that being the case they will not make him responsible for any thing I may do, and I expect sometime I will do something devilish—that is just the word, though not a lady like one.

Poor Leo. I miss him so much, turn round expecting to see him every time I hear a noise. I did not think any one could love a dumb animal as much as I did him, and miss him as sadly. Mrs. Currey came over this morning & took tea. I hear that there is a report in town that Mrs Kain went to head Quarters after she had received her orders and begged to be allowed to take the oath. Said she was a northern woman & had always been a Union woman but had never dared to say so. How on earth such a thing could have been started I cant imagine, at least could not till I heard the fountain from which it emanated was Mrs Longward. Of course I wondered no longer. She like her father needs not the slightest foundation for any structure, however elaborate or gigantic. I wonder what Mrs K could say if she could hear it.

March 11. Friday. No news of any importance today. I am told the pickets were run in last night two miles above here. Some say our saints were that near to Knoxville. Capt McAlister told me tonight that he had seen Gen Carter and had quite a long talk with him, during which he (Gen C) had requested him to caution me, as I would certainly be sent South if I were not more prudent. That I had been very active &c, and the military here had from my actions and conversations been led to believe me a very violent rebel, one who would sell her soul and body for the benefit of the Confederates. I told him I certainly would lay down my life willingly did I know by so doing I would do the Confederacy the least good. That I had never done any thing I would not do again or said any thing I would not say over under the same circumstances. The only thing I have ever done was to wave to our poor fellows as they were going north to prison, and there I forgot for the moment I was not free but was living under a despotism. That if they sent me south they would not punish me very much. I'd have been there long ago if father & mother had not been so much opposed to it &c &c. Gen Carter is foolish if he thinks he is going to frighten me. I am not afraid of him or any other Yankee living or dead. The Capt says Capt Whitman told him the same thing about me.

One of his clerks named Price told Lusie he shot my dog, the triffling rascal. Oh! wont I have an opportunity some time to pay off a few of the debts I owe to the miserable wretches, and wont I do it with a good will. Capt McA told mother Gen Carter was very much surprised to hear she was a relation of

Admiral Renshaw. I suppose she should have gone and informed him of the fact on his first arrival in Knoxville. He (Gen C) is an old navy officer.

March 19. Saturday. I felt so badly this morning I did not get up till after breakfast. There has been a fight up the road in which the Yanks did not whip and they have fallen back twenty five miles. Yankee rumor says to that there has been an attack made on the train below in which the Rebels were driven back. Dr. Piggott was in this morning. He says all the sick are getting along very well with one exception. He does not know when he will be sent out, says he is afraid he will take root in East Tenn. Capt McAlister and himself had quite an argument in which the Capt did not get much the best. He is so abominably self-opinionated, so fond of talking about his family being a ruling one for so many years, and about his loving the Southern people so, and his being a christian—and having his hands clean, that he used all his influence to prevent the war and all that kind of stuff—and the next minute says the Southern people must & will be exterminated rather than the Union be destroyed. I do believe it would afford him sincere pleasure to see the whole scale lynching of the rebels which he advocated so strongly carried into execution before his own eyes.

Oh! I do get furious to hear him talk. It seems to me sometimes that I feel perfectly reckless of what I say or do. It is growing on me every day. As long as I could keep out of the way of the vile creatures I did it, and got along very well, but since I cant turn round without seeing one, and have them eternally in our sitting room, always introducing the subject, I cant contain myself. I say all sorts of things about all their officers & men, abuse Carter or any of them, and say every thing impudent that comes into my head. If Gen Longstreet dont come soon goodness only knows where it will end.

I hear that Gen Carter says Col Keith ought to have put Mrs Hamilton in prison because she said she gloried in being a Rebel, and if he had her in his power again he would certainly do it. Maj Gratz says Mrs Hamilton told him the reason she did not want to go south was that Sam H. and herself were to be married as soon as he returned from the North. This afternoon what did Capt & Mrs McA. have to do but go to see Mrs Brownlow—rather reversing the order of things. She told them that she never had done any work in her life and it came very hard now, as she has lost a servant and had to do it. Nothing like telling a good one, and she also said that there were many ladies here who would do themselves the pleasure of calling on her as soon as they knew she was here, was sorry she had not known it sooner. If the tory women come here I'll insult them certain and sure.

NORTHERN INDUSTRY:
PENNSYLVANIA, MARCH 1864

Scientific American: *New Rolling Mills in Pittsburgh*

March 26, 1864

A survey of the American iron industry published in 1859 recorded 202 active rolling mills in the United States, only nineteen of which were located in states that later joined the Confederacy. During the war three additional mills went into operation in the Confederate states, while twelve entirely new mills were opened in the North; in addition, many existing northern ironworks expanded their facilities during the conflict. The increased productive capacity of several works in Pittsburgh was detailed by *Scientific American* at a time when the southern iron industry was struggling with shortages of crude iron and skilled workers and the loss of several manufacturing facilities in Tennessee.

QUITE a number of new rolling mills have been put up by Pittsburgh manufacturers during the past year. Messrs. Lyon & Shorb, of the Sligo Works, have put up a mill two hundred feet in length by one hundred and four feet in width, capable of turning out armor plates of the largest size; the firm has also erected a sheet mill ninety feet long by eighty feet wide. The Messrs. McKnight, of the Birmingham Works, have erected a new sheet-iron and armor-plate mill, the buildings of which are sixty by eighty feet. The plate mill has a capacity of fifty tuns per week, and is constructed with a view to the rolling of sheet-iron, for the production of which it has a capacity of one thousand tuns a year. The Messrs. Jones & Laughlins, of the American Works, have erected a building two hundred by one hundred and twenty-five feet, within which is constructed two sheet mills, and a twelve-inch train for bar, and three eight-inch trains for small iron and hoops; three heating furnaces and two annealing furnaces. The capacity of these mills is thirty tuns per day. Messrs. Reese, Graff & Dull have built a forge, a plate mill and a sheet mill, occupying a building two hundred and five by one hundred and five feet. The plate mill is constructed for rolling armor plates for naval uses, ten feet long and from one to one and a half inches thick, weighing from one thousand six hundred pounds to a tun each. The plate mill has a capacity of one hundred tuns, the sheet mills a capacity of fifteen tuns, and the forge of two hundred and ten tuns a week. They have also erected a hoop mill of two trains with a capacity of eighty tuns per week, the mill building of which is one hundred and twenty by seventy-five feet. Messrs. Kloman & Philipps, and Messrs. Wharton, Brothers & Co. have each put up a new mill.

OPENING A FREEDMEN'S SCHOOL: VIRGINIA, MARCH 1864

Harriet Ann Jacobs and Louisa M. Jacobs to Lydia Maria Child

In the summer of 1862 Harriet Ann Jacobs, the author of *Incidents in the Life of a Slave Girl*, had begun relief work among the former slaves who had fled to Alexandria, Virginia. She was joined there in November 1863 by her daughter Louisa Matilda Jacobs, and together they established the Jacobs Free School, located at Pitt and Oronoco streets in Alexandria. Harriet and Louisa Jacobs wrote about the school to the abolitionist Lydia Maria Child, who had edited *Incidents*, in a letter that appeared in the *National Anti-Slavery Standard* on April 16, 1864.

ALEXANDRIA, March 26, 1864.

DEAR MRS. CHILD:

When I went to the North, last Fall, the Freedmen here were building a schoolhouse, and I expected it would have been finished by the time I returned. But when we arrived, we found it uncompleted. Their funds had got exhausted, and the work was at a stand-still for several weeks. This was a disappointment; but the time did not hang idle on our hands, I assure you. We went round visiting the new homes of the Freedmen, which now dot the landscape, built with their first earnings as free laborers. Within the last eight months seven hundred little cabins have been built, containing from two to four rooms. The average cost was from one hundred to two hundred and fifty dollars. In building school-houses or shelters for the old and decrepid, they have received but little assistance. They have had to struggle along and help themselves as they could. But though this has been discouraging, at times, it teaches them self reliance; and that is good for them, as it is for everybody. We have over seven thousand colored refugees in this place, and, including the hospitals, less than four hundred rations are given out. This shows that they are willing to earn their own way, and generally capable of it. Indeed, when I look back on the condition in which I first found them, and compare it with their condition now, I am convinced they are not so far behind other races as some people represent them. The two rooms we occupy were given to me by the Military Governor, to be appropriated to the use of decrepid women, when we leave them.

When we went round visiting the homes of these people, we found much to commend them for. Many of them showed marks of industry, neatness, and natural refinement. In others, chaos reigned supreme. There was nothing about them to indicate the presence of a wifely wife, or a motherly mother. They bore abundant marks of the half-barbarous, miserable condition of Slavery, from which the inmates had lately come. It made me sad to see their shiftlessness and discomfort; but I was hopeful for the future. The consciousness of working for themselves, and of having a character to gain, will inspire them with energy and enterprise, and a higher civilization will gradually come.

Children abounded in these cabins. They peeped out from every nook and corner. Many of them were extremely pretty and bright-looking. Some had features and complexions purely Anglo-Saxon; showing plainly enough the slaveholder's horror of amalgamation. Some smiled upon us, and were very ready to be friends. Others regarded us with shy, suspicious looks, as is apt to be the case with children who have had a cramped childhood. But they all wanted to accept our invitation to go to school, and so did all the parents for them.

In the course of our rounds, we visited a settlement which had received no name. We suggested to the settlers that it would be proper to name it for some champion of Liberty. We told them of the Hon. Chas. Sumner, whose large heart and great mind had for years been devoted to the cause of the poor slaves. We told how violent and cruel slaveholders had nearly murdered him for standing up so manfully in defense of Freedom. His claim to their gratitude was at once recognized, and the settlement was called Sumnerville.

Before we came here, a white lady, from Chelsea, Mass., was laboring as a missionary among the Refugees; and a white teacher, sent by the Educational Commission of Boston, accompanied us. One of the freedmen, whose cabin consisted of two rooms, gave it up to us for our school. We soon found that the clamor of little voices begging for admittance far exceeded the narrow limits of this establishment.

Friends at the North had given us some articles left from one of the Fairs. To these we added what we could, and got up a little Fair here, to help them in the completion of the school-house. By this means we raised one hundred and fifty dollars, and they were much gratified by the result. With the completion of the school-house our field of labor widened, and we were joyful over the prospect of extended usefulness. But some difficulties occurred, as there always do in the settlement of such affairs. A question arose whether the white teachers or the colored teachers should be superintendents. The freedmen had built the school-house for their children, and were Trustees of the school. So, after some discussion, it was decided that it would be best for them to hold a meeting, and settle the question for themselves. I wish you could have been at that meeting. Most of the people were slaves, until quite recently, but they talked sensibly, and I assure you that they put the question to vote in quite parliamentary style. The result was a decision that the colored teachers should have charge of the school. We were gratified by this result, because our sympathies are closely linked with our oppressed race. These people, born and bred in slavery, had always been so accustomed to look upon the white race as their natural superiors and masters, that we had some doubts whether they could easily throw off the habit; and the fact of their giving preference to colored teachers, as managers of the establishment, seemed to us to indicate that even their brief possession of freedom had begun to inspire them with respect for their race.

On the 11th of January we opened school in the new school-house, with seventy-five scholars. Now, we have two hundred and twenty-five. Slavery has not crushed out the animal spirits of these children. Fun lurks in the corners of their eyes, dimples their mouths, tingles at their fingers' ends, and is, like a torpedo, ready to explode at the slightest touch. The war-spirit has a powerful hold upon them. No one turns the other cheek for a second blow. But they evince a generous nature. They never allow an older and stronger scholar to impose upon a younger and weaker one; and when they happen to have any little delicacies, they are very ready to share them with others. The task of regulating them is by no means an easy one; but we put heart, mind, and strength freely into the work, and only regret that we have not more physical strength. Their ardent desire to learn is very encouraging, and the improvement they make consoles us for many trials. You would be astonished at the progress many of them have made in this short time. Many who less than three months ago scarcely knew the A.B.C. are now reading and spelling in words of two or three syllables. When I look at these bright little boys, I often wonder whether there is not some Frederick Douglass among them, destined to do honor to his race in the future. No one can predict, now-a-days, how rapidly the wheels of progress will move on.

There is also an evening-school here, chiefly consisting of adults and largely attended; but with that I am not connected.

On the 10th of this month, there was considerable excitement here. The bells were rung in honor of the vote to abolish slavery in Virginia. Many did not know what was the cause of such a demonstration. Some thought it was an alarm of fire; others supposed the rebels had made a raid, and were marching down King st. We were, at first, inclined to the latter opinion; for, looking up that street we saw a company of the most woe-begone looking horsemen. It was raining hard, and some of them had dismounted, leading their poor jaded skeletons of horses. We soon learned that there were a portion of Kilpatrick's cavalry, on their way to Culpepper. Poor fellows! They had had a weary tramp, and must still tramp on, through mud and rain, till they reached their journey's end. What hopeless despondency would take possession of our hearts, if we looked only on the suffering occasioned by this war, and not on the good already accomplished, and the still grander results shadowed forth in the future. The slowly-moving ambulance often passes by, with low beat of the drum, as the soldiers convey some comrade to his last resting-place. Buried on strange soil, far away from mother, wife, and children! Poor fellows! But they die the death of brave men in a noble cause. The Soldier's Burying Ground here is well cared for, and is a beautiful place.

How nobly are the colored soldiers fighting and dying in the cause of freedom! Our hearts are proud of the manhood they evince, in spite of the indignities heaped upon them. They are kept constantly on fatigue duty, digging trenches, and unloading vessels. Look at the Massachusetts Fifty-Fourth! Every man of them a hero! marching so boldly and steadily to victory or death, for the freedom of their race, and the salvation of their country! *Their* country! It makes my blood run warm to think how that country treats her colored sons, even the bravest and the best. If merit deserves reward, surely the 54th regiment is worthy of shoulder-straps. I have lately heard, from a friend in Boston, that the rank of second-lieutenant has been conferred. I am thankful there is a beginning. I am full of hope for the future. A Power mightier than man is guiding this revolution; and though justice moves slowly, it will come at last. The American people will outlive this mean prejudice against complexion. Sooner or later, they will learn that "a man's a man for a' that."

We went to the wharf last Tuesday, to welcome the emigrants returned from Hayti. It was a bitter cold day, the snow was falling, and they were barefooted and bareheaded, with scarcely rags enough to cover them. They were put in wagons and carried to Green Heights. We did what we could for them. I went to see them next day, and found that three had died during the night. I was grieved for their hard lot; but I comforted myself with the idea that this would put an end to colonization projects. They are eight miles from here, but I shall go to see them again to-morrow. I hope to obtain among them some recruits for the Massachusetts Cavalry. I am trying to help Mr. Downing and Mr. Remond; not for money, but because I want to do all I can to strengthen the hands of those who are battling for Freedom.

Thank you for your letter. I wish you could have seen the happy group of faces round me, at our little Fair, while I read it to them. The memory of the grateful hearts I have found among these freed men and women, will cheer me all my life. Yours truly,

H. JACOBS and L. JACOBS.

“MY IRONS WERE TAKEN OFF”: TENNESSEE, MARCH 1864

Jim Heiskell: Statement Regarding His Escape from Slavery

President Lincoln had exempted Tennessee from the states covered by the Emancipation Proclamation in an attempt to strengthen the unionist government established in Nashville by Andrew Johnson in 1862. While the Union army encouraged the slaves of Confederate owners in Tennessee to escape, government policy toward slaves owned by unionists was often ambiguous. Jim Heiskell was owned by William Heiskell, a unionist in Knoxville who served as an agent of the Treasury Department. After running away from a farm outside the city, Jim Heiskell was captured in Knoxville in late March 1864 and then escaped again with the help of his brother Bob. His case aroused controversy when it was alleged by the *New-York Daily Tribune* that Brigadier General Samuel P. Carter, the provost marshal of Knoxville, had sent soldiers to help guard Jim Heiskell after his capture. (Legislation passed by Congress in 1862 prohibited Union officers from returning any fugitive slave, regardless of the loyalty of the owner.) Carter denied the charge and claimed that he had sent the guards to defend the Heiskell house against Bob Heiskell, who reportedly had armed himself with a revolver, threatened William Heiskell's life, and called his wife “a d—d old freckle faced bitch.” On March 28, 1864, Major General John M. Schofield, the commander of the Army of the Ohio, ordered that Bob and Jim Heiskell be declared “free from the control of their late master, Mr. William Heiskell,” and placed “under the protection of the United States Government.” Jim Heiskell gave a statement for the record two days later.

Statement of “Jim” Heiskell

My name is Jim; I have been living on Bull run, with a man by the name of Pierce; they called him Cromwell Pierce. I run off from him nearly two months ago, because he treated me so mean: he half starved and whipped me. I was whipped three or four times a week, sometimes with a cowhide, and sometimes with a hickory. He put so much work on me, I could not do it;

chopping & hauling wood and lumber logs. I am about thirteen years old. I got a pretty good meal at dinner, but he only gave us a half pint of milk for breakfast and supper, with cornbread. I ran away to town; I had a brother "Bob" living in Knoxville, and other boys I knew. I would have staid on the plantation if I had been well used. I wanted also to see some pleasure in town. I hired myself to Capt. Smith as a servant, and went to work as a waiter in Quarter Master Winslow's office as a waiter for the mess. After Capt. Winslow went home, I went to live with Bob, helping him.

Last Friday just after dinner, I saw Pierce Mr. Heiskell's overseer. He caught me on Gay street, he ran after me, and carried me down Cumberland street to Mr. Heiskell's house. Mr. Heiskell, his wife and two sons, and a daughter were in the house. Mr. Heiskell asked me what made me run away; he grabbed me by the back of the ears, and jerked me down on the floor on my face; Mr. Pierce held me & Mr. Heiskell put irons on my legs. Mr. Heiskell took me by the hair of my head, and Mr. Pierce took me around my body, they carried me upstairs, and then Mr. Heiskell dagged me into a room by my hair. They made me stand up, and then they laid me down on my belly & pulled off my breeches as far as they could, and turned my shirt and jacket up over my head. (I heard Mr Heiskell ask for the cowhide before he started with me upstairs.) Mr. Pierce held my legs, and Mr. Heiskell got a straddle of me, and whipped me with the rawhide on my back & legs. Mr. Pierce is a large man, and very strong. Mr. Heiskell rested two or three times, and begun again. I hollowed—"O, Lord" all the time. They whipped me, it seemed to me, half an hour. They then told me to get up and dress, and said if I did'nt behave myself up there they would come up again and whip me again at night. The irons were left on my legs. Mr. Heiskell came up at dark and asked me what that "yallow nigger was talking to me about". He meant my brother Bob, who had been talking to me opposite the house. I was standing up and when he (Mr. Heiskell) asked me about the "yaller nigger", he kicked me with his right foot on my hip and knocked me over on the floor, as the irons were on my feet, I could not catch myself. I knew my brother Bob was around the house trying to get me out. About one hour by sun two soldiers came to the house, one staid & the other went away. I saw them through the window. They had sabres. I thought they had come to guard me to keep Bob from getting me. I heard Bob whisling, and I went to the window and looked through the curtain. Bob told me to hoist the window, put something under it & swing out of the window. I did as my brother told me, and hung by my hands. Bob said "Drop," but I said I was afraid I would hurt myself. Bob said "Wait a minute and I will get a ladder". He brought a ladder and put it against the house, under the window. I got halfway down before they hoisted the window; I fell & Bob caught me and run off with me in his arms. I saw Mr. Pierce sitting at the window, he had a double-barreled gun in his hands. By the time I could count three I heard a gun fired two or three times, quick, I heard Mr. Pierce call "Jim" "Jim" and the guards hollered "halt; halt!" I had no hat or shoes on. We both hid, and laid flat on the ground. I saw the guard, running around there hunting for us. After lying there until the guards had gone away, we got up and Bob carried me to a friend's house. I had the irons on my legs. I got some supper and staid there until next day. My irons were taken off by a colored man, who carried me to the hospital. I am now employed working in the hospital No. 1.

his
–signed– Jim × Heiskell–
mark

March 30, 1864

HUNGRY FAMILIES: NORTH CAROLINA, APRIL 1864

Susan C. Woolker to Zebulon B. Vance

In February 1863 the North Carolina legislature appropriated $1 million for the relief of indigent wives and families of soldiers and directed the county courts to distribute the aid. Several weeks later food riots broke out in several southern cities, including Salisbury and High Point in North Carolina, as groups of women, many of them soldiers' wives, invaded and looted shops they believed were charging unfair prices. The privations suffered by soldiers' families contributed to the peace movement that emerged in the state during the summer of 1863, when speakers at more than a hundred public meetings called for a negotiated end to the war. Susan C. Woolker, a resident of Davie County, wrote about the food situation in the spring of 1864 to Governor Zebulon B. Vance, a critic of the Davis administration who supported continued prosecution of the war.

Hillsdale N.C.
Apr. the 3 rd /64

Sir I write you a feiw lines to inform you how we are treated about something to eat truly hopeing you will have things changed from what they are now I will inform you what I am alowed per month I am only alowed $10.00 for my self and one child a woman with two childrens only alowed $13.00 per month to get meat and bread with grain is from $20.00 to $30.00 per bushel bacon from $3. to $5.00 per pound and we cant get it for the money the men that has it to sell wont have the money for it and there is aplenty both meat and bread and molases in the country for us all to have plenty but those men that has it wont let the soldiers familys have it they send one load of privisian to the factory after another to get spun cotton and the soldiers familys may suffer while their men are in the army fighting for them and what they have my husband and father has been in the survis over two years Ma is left with three children and is only alowed $13.00 per month and you well know that wont half support her the way evry thing is selling I know some men that has plenty of molases and wont sell them for any thing but grain and that is what soldiers familys has not got I dont know how they can expect the No Ca soldiers to fight and their familys treated as they are. I never have tried to discourage my husband any at all—I try to encourage him all I can I am willing to work for every thing to eat I can but I cant live with my work and what I get from Mr A Reid I sent to him for something to eat yesterday and he sent me word his orders was not to let any of us have any thing untill May court and I have not had any thing at all in over a month and I am very unhealthy not able to do much work and I dont know what I will do and many others that is left in my situation unless you will have this matter attended to in a short time I beg you to have things arranged better for if you dont the soldiers will get disheartened and come home and I dont want them to have to come home without an honerable peace and ef they will find me plenty to eat my husband will fight through this war if he is spaired to live before he will quit and come home but you think yourself of this matter if you was in the army and was to hear your wife and children was suffiring and could not get anything to eat I think you would be very much tempted to start home and you knew there was plenty for them and they was not allowed have it pleas fix this as soon as you can I hope you will send and press this provisions from those men that has it for if you dont I am afraid the women will have it to do and I dont want to press any thing if I can help it they have got spun cotton out our reach it is $80.00 per bunch in Greensborough that will take nearly eight month wages that a soldier gets to get one bunch cotton I will close this by saying pleas provide for us

yours truly
SUSAN C WOOLKER

PLANNING THE SPRING CAMPAIGN:
WASHINGTON, D.C., APRIL 1864

Ulysses S. Grant to William T. Sherman

Ulysses S. Grant arrived in Washington, D.C., on March 8, 1864, and was appointed general-in-chief of the Union armies on March 10. That same day he visited Major General George G. Meade in northern Virginia. Grant left Washington the next day, having decided to make his headquarters in the field with the Army of the Potomac while keeping Meade as its commander. He conferred in Nashville and Cincinnati with William T. Sherman, who would succeed him as commander of the Union armies between the Alleghenies and the Mississippi, before returning to Washington on March 22. Grant wrote to Sherman about his plans after presenting them to President Lincoln, who expressed his approval of Grant's intention to use all of the Union forces available by saying, "Those not skinning can hold a leg."

Private & Confidential

Washington, D.C., Apl. 4th *1864*.

MAJ. GEN. W. T. SHERMAN,
COMD.G MIL. DIV. OF THE MISS.
GENERAL,

It is my design, if the enemy keep quiet and allow me to take the initiative in the Spring Campaign to work all parts of the Army to-gether, and, somewhat, towards a common center. For your information I now write you my programme as at present determined upon.

I have sent orders to Banks, by private messenger, to finish up his present expedition against Schrievesport with all dispatch. To turn over the defence of the Red River to Gen. Steele and the Navy and return your troops to you and his own to New Orleans. To abandon all of Texas, except the Rio Grande and to hold that with not to exceed four thousand men. To reduce the number of troops on the Miss. to the lowest number necessary to hold it and to collect from his command not less than twenty-five thousand men. To this I will add five thousand from Mo. With this force he is to commence operations against Mobile as soon as he can. It will be impossible for him to commence too early.

Gilmore joins Butler with ten thousand men and the two operate against Richmond from the south side of James River. This will give Butler thirty-three thousand men to operate with, W. F. Smith commanding the right wing of his forces and Gilmore the left wing. I will stay with the Army of the Potomac increased by Burnsides Corps of not less than 25.000 effective men, and operate directly against Lee's Army wherever it may be found. Sigel collects all his available force in two columns, one under Ord & Averell to start from Beverly Va. and the other under Crook to start from Charleston on the Kanawphy to move against the Va. & Ten. rail-road. Crook will have all Cavalry and will endeavor to get in about Saltville and move East from there to join Ord. His force will be all cavalry whilst Ord will have from ten to twelve thousand men of all arms. You I propose to move against Johnston's Army, to break it up and to get into the interior of the enemy's country as far as you can, inflicting all the damage you can against their War resources.

I do not propose to lay down for you a plan of Campaign but simply to lay down the work it is desirable to have done and leave you free to execute in your own way. Submit to me however as early as you can your plan of operation.

As stated Banks is ordered to commence operations as soon as he can. Gilmore is ordered to report at Fortress Monroe by the 18th inst, or as soon thereafter as practicable. Sigel is concentrating now. None will move from their places of rendezvous until I direct, except Banks. I want to be ready to move by the 25th inst, if possible. But all I can now direct is that you get ready as soon as possible I know you will have difficulties to encounter getting through the mountains to where supplies are abundant, but I believe you will accomplish it.

From the expedition from the Dept. of West Va. I do not calculate on very great results. But it is the only way I can take troops from there. With the long line of rail-road Sigel has to protect he can spare no troops except to move directly to his front. In this way he must get through to inflict great damage on the enemy, or the enemy must detach from one of his armies a large force to prevent it. In other words if Sigel cant skin himself he can hold a leg whilst some one else skins.

I am General, very respectfully
your obt. svt.
U. S. GRANT
Lt. Gen.

"A TEAR OF SOROW": LOUISIANA, APRIL 1864

William Winters to Harriet Winters

In March 1864 about 30,000 Union troops under Major General Nathaniel P. Banks began advancing up the Red River into northwest Louisiana with the objective of capturing Shreveport, the headquarters of the Confederate Trans-Mississippi Department. Although Grant considered the campaign a needless diversion from the goal of seizing Mobile, the Red River expedition was strongly supported by President Lincoln, who hoped that it would extend Union control over all of Louisiana and Arkansas, make possible the occupation of East Texas, and restrain French actions in Mexico. Sergeant William Winters of the 67th Indiana Infantry, a saddle and harness maker from Bartholomew County who had fought in the Vicksburg campaign, was among the soldiers taking part in the expedition. His regiment left Alexandria, Louisiana, on March 28 and marched northwest to Natchitoches. On April 7 Winters reached Pleasant Hill, where his brigade was ordered to reinforce the cavalry leading the advance. The next day Major General Richard Taylor and 8,800 Confederates attacked the head of the Union column near Mansfield, thirty-five miles south of Shreveport, and drove it back to Pleasant Hill. Union losses in the battle of Mansfield (also known as Sabine Crossroads) were reported as 113 killed, 581 wounded, and 1,541 missing. Among the missing was William Winters, who was later declared to have been killed in action on April 8, 1864. His place of burial is unknown.

---

in camp at Nachitoches,
Louisiana, April 4th, 1864

Mrs. H. J. Winter

Dear wife, I just received six letters, and I almost jumped up and down when I got them into my hands. I am so glad to hear that you and the children are well, and I hope that you and they will not be visited with either of those fell diseases that is scourgeing the country, and, ma, oh, do take care of our litle girls, for I cant loose them.

We are in camp here and have been for a couple of days but are ready to be called out at any moment, for we have drove the enemy before us for several days before we halted, and they are waiting to engage us at Pleasant hill, some thirty five miles above us on the road to shreveport and expect to give us a whiping there, they say, but they have not got the men to do it with. But they will no doubt fight us there.

this place is quite a nice town with a large convent called the Sacred heart of Jesus. There is quite a number of nuns and children that are put here to go to school for fear of the influences of hereticks. I was through a grave yard of theirs with tom Eaton and picked some myrtle flowers, and I will put them in this. The country here and between here and Alexandria is considerably hilley and rolling and covered with pitch pine, and as we marched through it I thought of the pine clad hills of my boyhood home and how oft I had rambled through them in chaseing the nimble squirrill and rabbit, and then I thought of my own litle ones, and a tear of sorow stole down my cheek that I turned aside and wiped away. The country is lovly and rich but mostly catholic. The town of Nachitoches is situated on what they call old river or old red river, the bed of what is red river proper, but the river runs some four miles from here now through a new chanell.

We expect to go forward in a day or two and are liable to be sent at any time. we have not been paid off yet, and I canot tell when we will be paid.

I got a letter from wes. He seems to think that lando might of given more than he did and Jim a litle less, but I guess he is not following a verey honorable calling, or he would not have quite so mutch mony to spend as he apears to have. I got a letter from Bell and one from Mary Jane. Wes wrote that he was agoing to sell out his furniture and move back to the gate and keep house for Aleck. All good enough. vine wrote that she was agoing to the city to keep house for Jim awhile. From what was wrote, Aus and his wife have both joined christy chappell, a blessing to his family if he will only stick to it.

well, hat, we have about a hundred miles more to march to shreveport, and perhaps we may have a couple of fights before we get there, but I hope not, but if we do we will be at Shrevesport before you receive this and it may be in eternity, some of us, but we are all in the best of spirits and health and spirits and ready for all that is our duty to do as soldiers and hope to have the pleasure of seeing our homes, friends, and dear ones after our trials and deprivations are over and this cruel war is at an end.

The weather is butifull, and everything is growing and spreading its buties and oders to all, heeding not the preasence of an invading armey. Some of the fair ones of this country take pleasure in abuseing us in unmeasured terms for comeing into their country and homes and say that we had better stay at home and attend to our business and come to disgrace their homes with our yankey preasence. But we cant help what they think about us. We are all well. My own health is as good as it ever was in my life, and I hope that it may continue to be so for the balance of my term, if I am compeled to serve it out. well, hat, if I had the time I would write you more, if I had time to do so, but will have to conclude with this, as the mail goes out in a few minutes, and it may be the only chance to write before we get to Shreveport, and I would not miss sending this to you, as I know that you want to know where I am. Hopeing that this will find you all well, I remain yours as ever, William Winters

FREEDOM AND SLAVERY: VIRGINIA, APRIL 1864

Wilbur Fisk to The Green Mountain Freeman

Private Wilbur Fisk of the 2nd Vermont Infantry began writing letters in December 1861 to *The Green Mountain Freeman* of Montpelier under the pen name "Anti-Rebel." Fisk fought in the Seven Days' Battles before being hospitalized with chronic diarrhea in September 1862. He returned to his regiment in March 1863, fought in the Chancellorsville campaign, and was posted to a reserve position at Gettysburg. He wrote to the *Freeman* as the Army of the Potomac awaited the opening of its third spring campaign.

Camp near Brandy Station, Va.
April 7, 1864

We have just had what is here known as a general inspection. The inspection occupied but very few minutes, and as it takes the place of our regular drill this afternoon we shall have nothing further to do till night. The pleasantest way that I can think of to spend these idle moments is to pen a few lines to the *Freeman*, though I am afraid it is almost imposing upon good nature to attempt to offer anything for entertainment when the times are as dull as now. I have been tolerated so long that my self-confident assurance has grown immensely, and if I keep on writing I don't know but that my habit of writing for the *Freeman* will by and by become seated and incurable. But I cannot help it. When I know that the readers of the *Freeman* include but very few sneering copperheads if any at all, and that all are interested in the soldier's welfare, and interested in the cause for which we are here, it is very easy and pleasant to write, and I cannot resist the temptation, and I will not try.

The signs of an advance movement begin to thicken. Sutlers have been ordered away, and there is now, I understand, an order at headquarters for the men to pack up, to be sent off, every article that we do not need, such as extra clothing, overcoats, blankets, and the like, as has been our custom every spring. These are only preliminary movements and really indicate nothing immediate, but so far as we know, the army may be ordered to move within a week. We have had considerable wet rainy weather of late, which will doubtless retard operations some. A few that are prone to prophesy say that it is doubtful if we move from here before May. But we soldiers trust this matter is in wiser hands than ours, and when they consider that the proper time has arrived for action, and order us forward, we shall go cheerfully and confidently, whether the time be sooner or later. It seems to be the prevailing opinion here in the army, that we are at last to have a campaign that will for once be really "short, sharp, and decisive," and I will add, victorious. Great confidence is felt in the plans that General Grant will adopt, and the means that he will have to use in crushing the last vestige of this Heaven accursed rebellion. Having authority that extends from the Atlantic to the Mississippi, from Mobile to Washington, we may reasonably expect a concert of action in the coming campaigns that will ensure us success and victory. God grant that we may not be disappointed.

Success and victory! whose heart does not beat quicker at the thought? What consequences will have been achieved when this great rebellion shall have been forever humbled. It is not merely that this terrible war may be ended, and we safely at liberty again, that we hope to conquer our enemies and be once more at peace, but that the great principles of a free government, whose worth no mind short of Infinite Wisdom can estimate, and which even after the world has stood so long is still considered an experiment, may not be overthrown, and the progress of civilization and freedom may not be rolled back for ages, or receive a blow from which they may never recover. We are anxious of course to get out of this war, for we long most earnestly to return to the almost sacred hills and valleys of old Vermont, but we are not so anxious for this, as we are that the faith of the world in the intelligence and virtue of the common people, and their ability to govern themselves and maintain national unity without being rent asunder by internal strife and discord—a faith that despots the world over profess to sneer at, and hold to be a delusion, and which stimulates the noblest energies of the masses of mankind—that this may be maintained, increased and perpetuated. If these principles succeed, Slavery must fall, and fall forever. The two are so antagonistical that, even if both are right, or neither of them, men embracing each could not possibly live together in peace, unless we are to suppose that God has given them a larger spirit of forbearance than is vouchsafed to humanity in general. There never was a real unity between them, and there never can be. Slavery is a relic of the darkest ages, and the poorest government on earth is better in principle than that. If we are going to have a free government at all, let us have it all free, or else we had better give up the name. Slavery has fostered an aristocracy of the rankest kind, and this aristocracy is the bitterest foe that a really free government can have. Slavery and despotism have challenged war with us, and by it she must abide. Slavery was jealous of the comelier strength that Freedom possessed; and maliciously envied her irresistible march onward to a higher destiny. Slavery drew the sword, and would have stabbed Freedom to the heart, had not God denied her the strength. She could not bear that her more righteous neighbor should be prospered, while she herself was accursed, and in her foolish madness she has tried to rend the Union in twain. With that institution it is success or death. Compromise with Slavery, and restore the Union with Slavery in it still! As well might Jehovah compromise with Satan and give him back part of Heaven.

There never before was a rebellion like this one. Generally a rebellion has been the outbreak of the people against the tyranny of a few. Their cause has usually been the cause of liberty, and more or less just. Knit together by the idea of freeing themselves from an odious despotism, and armed with justice, and backed by numbers, they have often succeeded, and history has applauded their bravery. In this war it has been different. The people have not rebelled against the few, but the few have rebelled against the people. Our government is the people's, and against this government the proud slaveholder has rebelled. With Slavery for a corner stone they hope to rob our government of her honor, and erect within our borders a rival government, which every attribute of the Almighty must detest. Can they succeed? Is the glory of our nation to be destroyed forever? Is the great experiment which our forefathers have made, and which has been our pride and boast so long, to be a failure after all? If the North will do her duty, we answer, Never! And the North *will* do her duty. She knows what it is, and she does not fear it. Never in a war before did the rank and file feel a more resolute earnestness for a just cause, and a more invincible determination to succeed, than in this war; and what the rank and file are determined to do everybody knows will surely be done. We mean to be thorough about it too. We are not going to destroy the military power of the dragon Confederacy and not destroy its fangs also. We have as a nation yielded to their rapacious demands times enough. We have cringed before Slavery as long as we will.

"Far better die in such a strife,
Than still to Slavery's claims concede,
Than crouch beneath her frown for life,
Far better in the field to bleed:
To live thus wage a life-long shame,
To die is victory and fame."

I almost lose my temper sometimes (what little I have got) when I hear men that really ought to know better, call this war a mere crusade to free the negroes, "a nigger war" and nothing more. But even if I was fighting to free the negroes simply, I don't know why I should be acting from a motive that I need be ashamed of. I verily believe that He who when He was on the earth healed foul leprosy, gave sight to the blind beggars, and preached the gospel to the poor, would not be ashamed to act from such a motive. And if he would not, why should I? Fighting to free the "niggers!" Why yes, my dear fellow, we are doing just that and a great deal more. But, sir, I am going to tell you, you would not speak of that so contemptuously, if you had not all your life long fed your soul upon motives so small, so mean, and so selfish, that the sublimer motives of sacrificing blood and treasure to elevate a degraded and downtrodden race, is entirely beyond your comprehension. Should such an event, however, rather help than hinder the success of this war, we trust that you will acquiesce in the result, and when the future of this country shall have become by this means more glorious than the past has ever been, we shall hope that you will find that your own liberty and happiness has not been at all infringed upon by giving the same liberty and happiness to a few ignorant and despised sons of Africa.

But I have prolonged this discussion till my space is full, and I have no room for general news, if any had been needed. The weather has been pleasant since the snow and rainstorms of Saturday and Monday, but just now another storm is threatened. We are to have three drills each day till further orders, two in the forenoon, and one in the afternoon, and this with our other duties, getting wood, and the like, will leave us rather a short allowance of time for idleness.

AN EXPULSION ORDER: TENNESSEE, APRIL 1864

Ellen Renshaw House: Diary, April 8, 1864

From January to November 1864 Brigadier General Samuel P. Carter, the provost marshal of Knoxville, ordered the expulsion of more than fifty Confederate sympathizers, the majority of them women. The expulsions were encouraged by Knoxville's leading unionist, the newspaper editor William G. (Parson) Brownlow, who denounced "*she* rebels" as "brazen as the devil" in his *Knoxville Whig and Rebel Ventilator*. Among those banished into Confederate-held territory was Ellen Renshaw House, who was expelled along with Susan Ramsey, the sixteen-year-old daughter of a prominent secessionist. House crossed the lines in northeastern Tennessee and spent the summer in Abingdon, Virginia, before settling in Eatonton, Georgia, in September 1864.

April 8. Friday. Well it has come at last. I am ordered to leave on Monday for the South. My orders came about ten. Mother is perfectly furious about it. At first she said she would come too, but we told her that would never do, so she said sister should come with me. I declare she thinks I am a baby and not fit to take care of myself. She went with sister to ask permission for her to come too. Old Gratz objected, said they did want to send her. She had been very prudent. Said he would have to see Schofield about it &c. Mother told him she would like to know why I had been sent out. He would not tell her for some time. At last he said they had a great many charges against me and they had been thinking of sending me South for some time, but the immediate cause was my insulting Mrs McAlister. It is about the only thing they could accuse me of that I have never done & I never have done that. I almost wish I had now. He said it was reported by a third person, and when Capt McA was asked about it he was a gentleman and was obliged to acknowledge it. Also that Parson Brownlow heard it and urged the matter till Gen Carter ordered me out, that they would have the charges written out by afternoon & I could have them. I wish I could get them but no one would go for them for me. I have a great mind to go after them myself.

Some time after Sister came home, her permission came too. Father takes it very quietly. When I told him all he asked was if I was well supplied with thick shoes. He thinks them essential to my health. When Mr Wilson came home I opened on him. Told him I had received my orders to go South thanks to him. I suppose the charge was my insulting Mrs McA, and reported by a third person, that third person must be him & he had reported what he knew to be false. He said I was very much mistaken. He was very sorry I had been ordered out and had never said anything about me. I replied I was not sorry to go, but glad to find out he was more of a gentleman than I had taken him to be. Cordie Fletcher came over and offered to help me. I have a great many things to get, & am very much afraid I will forget many things I need. One thing is certain. I am going to take my derringer and Johnnies's Uniform &c to a dead most certainty. Reported fight down at Cleveland. The Yankees here say that Joe Johnson is nothing for miles of that place.

"A PROUD DAY": WASHINGTON, D.C., APRIL 1864

Lois Bryan Adams to the Detroit Advertiser and Tribune

Proposals to end slavery by amending the Constitution were introduced in the House of Representatives by Republican congressmen James M. Ashley of Ohio and James F. Wilson of Iowa on December 14, 1863, and in the Senate by Missouri Unionist John B. Henderson on January 11, 1864. Illinois Republican Lyman Trumbull, the chairman of the Senate Judiciary Committee, drew on these proposals to give the Thirteenth Amendment its final form. In a speech in the Senate on March 28, Trumbull admitted that the confiscation acts passed by Congress in 1861 and 1862 and the Emancipation Proclamation were "ineffectual to the destruction of slavery" because their effects did not extend to all slave-owners and to all of the slave states. The proposed amendment, Trumbull said, would ensure that slavery could "never be reestablished by State authority" and would "restore to a whole race that freedom which is theirs by the gift of God, but which we for generations have wickedly denied them." An experienced journalist who had moved from Michigan to Washington in 1863, Lois Bryan Adams worked as a clerk for the recently established Department of Agriculture while contributing regular letters to the *Detroit Advertiser and Tribune*. She wrote about the Senate debate on the amendment in dispatches that appeared on April 15 and 19, 1864.

Letter from Washington

IN THE SENATE | REVERDY JOHNSON | GEORGE THOMPSON AT THE CAPITOL | AMENDMENT OF THE CONSTITUTION | SCENE IN THE SENATE

From Our Own Correspondent

Washington, April 9, 1864

The first week of April has been an eventful one at the capital. It was led off in the Senate by the Hon. Reverdy Johnson of Maryland in a noble and thoroughly antislavery speech; followed up in the House by the reception and speech of George

Thompson of England and crowned in the Senate by the passage of a vote to amend the Constitution by inserting a clause abolishing slavery and prohibiting it in the United States henceforth and forever.

Mr. Johnson's speech was one of peculiar interest, and was listened to with more than usual attention by the Senate. It was in explanation and justification of the vote he intended to give on the amendment of the Constitution. He carefully reviewed and refuted the theories advanced by some that the power to abolish slavery lay with the Chief Executive of the nation, or that Congress had the power of enacting laws for the purpose. Neither proclamation nor acts of Congress, he said, could affect slaves not actually under the jurisdiction of the laws of the United States. Except as a war measure, Congress and the President could not move in the matter at all, and the war power conferred upon them could not be exerted against loyal States; therefore, Maryland, Kentucky, and Missouri would be slave states still, though the institution were abolished in all others. He said that whatever his previous opinions had been, he was now convinced that no permanent peace could be established without the utter extinction of slavery. Involuntary servitude and a republican government were totally incompatible; if we would save the one we must destroy the other. It was a clear, calm, logical, and truly patriotic speech, one that it did the hearts of the Republican Senators good to hear, and the stern, incontrovertible truths of which fell heavily on the heads of the few hapless Copperheads present.

Mr. Johnson is an old man with thin white hair, but with a goodly plumpness of body, a freshness of complexion and a depth and strength of voice betokening anything but feebleness, of either mind or body. His face is of an oval cast, guiltless of beard or mustache, and his eyes are remarkably prominent, in fact "pop-eyed" is the only word that can properly describe them. The expression of his face is rather sour and forbidding; he seldom smiles, or appears to let himself down upon a common social level with other mortals, preserving, apparently, a sort of stoical dignity of indifference which seems always to be saying "I am the Honorable Reverdy Johnson, of Maryland." But whether this is only in appearance or not, it is very certain the world can afford to let him look as he pleases, so long as he will give it such hopeful, encouraging words as fell from his lips on Tuesday last.

The announcement that the House of Representatives had voted the use of their hall for Wednesday evening to the noted abolition lecturer, George Thompson of England was a terrible shock to the failing and sensitive nerves of the District slave aristocracy. Alas, they said, what is Washington coming to! Not only are the rail-splitters of the West and the mudsills of the East in our White House, and in our halls of legislation, thronging our Department and swarming our streets, but here they have invited to speak in our capitol, and against our institutions, that, to us, most odious of all human compounds, an Anglo-American Abolitionist. Not many years ago he was mobbed and beaten, and driven from one city to another, and finally from the country; now he is welcomed back, toasted and honored, and taken into the capitol to consummate his triumph.

Yes, it was a triumph, and as such the friends of freedom and free speech felt it. Mr. Thompson's welcome was most enthusiastic. The lecture was given under the auspices of the Washington Young Men's Association, and though the tickets for floor seats were one dollar each, and for the galleries 50 cents, both floor and galleries were early crowded to their utmost capacity. The President and most of his cabinet, as well as many Senators and members, were present. Vice President Hamlin presided, and after a few appropriate words of introduction, presented Mr. Thompson to the audience. The prolonged and hearty cheering which greeted him as he rose, affected him almost to tears. It was some moments before he could control his emotion, or give volume enough to his voice to make it heard across the room.

Washington, the old Washington, has been fairly dazed of late by witnessing events "significant of the times"; it is beginning to understand that there are signs in these times which do not all fail, and events which mark the giant strides of progress in such a way that there can be no retracing them in the future. This event, the mere admission of the speaker to the place where he stood by the invitation of the national Representatives, was one of marked significance; and still more so, if possible, were the shouts of applause and cheers of approval breaking from that great multitude, as from one heart, and raining down from the gilded ceilings like glad omens to the doctrines of universal liberty and human rights. What a change from a few years past, and what a triumph!

Slowly and sullenly the dark clouds of barbarism are rolling away, and quick and bright the sunshine follows. Some of those long dwelling in darkness are sorely hurt and troubled by the light. It blinds and bewilders them: poor creatures, how they struggle and gasp, and stretch out their arms in vain endeavors to bring the cloud back again. Such a spectacle was witnessed in the Senate on Friday, when the resolution to amend the Constitution was before that body. Speeches had been made during the week by Senators Hale and Clark, of New Hampshire, and others, all bearing upon the great question of the amendment, and all in turn snarled, growled, yelped and whined at by Powell, Saulsbury, Davis, and McDougal. Friday, Charles Sumner spoke, and it was understood that the vote was to be taken before the Senate adjourned. Long before Mr. Sumner sat down, it was easy to see how the wrath of Powell, Davis & Co. was working, and the moment his last word was said, Powell was upon his feet, flushed, excited, angry. With all the vehemence of his portly body concentrated in his red face, and quivering, out-stretched hand, he proceeded to denounce the Senators who were so anxious to meddle with what did not belong to them; he sneered at Yankee patriotism as altogether mercenary, and multiplied taunts and invectives on Sumner's head, till his voice grew thick and hoarse, and his arms must have ached from the violence with which it cut the empty air. The honorable Senators, however, at whom he launched his thunderbolts, seemed to feel them as little as the air did his strokes. All were busy attending to little matters of their own, some writing letters, some looking over the piled-up papers on his desk, some with heads bent together, earnestly talking, some glancing over the columns of the newspapers, and not one with the attitude or countenance of a listener. Sumner now and then glanced up from his papers with a quiet smile, as much as to say, "Rave on if it please you; such words are powerless in this chamber now." And he did rave, denounce and protest till, finding he could not disturb the quiet indifference of the Senators, he dropped into his seat, and was succeeded by the mattered growlings of Saulsbury, who wanted to make compromises and peace-offerings; the piping yelps of little old Garrett Davis, who "considered that his niggers belonged to him the same as his horses did, and he wanted compensation for them," and the egotistic, whinings of McDougal, who, while glorifying himself, maintained his perpendicular with some difficulty by holding fast to the two desks between which he stood.

And so, with rage, and whine, and whimper the time wore on, and it was 5 o'clock before the vote was taken. But the Senators knew they could afford to be patient. When the yeas and nays were at last called, the resolution for the amendment passed by a vote of 37 to 6!
L.

Our Washington Letter

A Day in the Senate | Scenes on the Floor and in the Galleries | Passage of the Amendment Resolution
From Our Own Correspondent
Washington, April 9, 1864

"'Twere worth whole years of peaceful life, / One glance at their array."

Friday, the 8th of April, was a proud day in the Senate, and a proud one for our country. It was the day on which the vote for the amendment of the Constitution was to be taken, and it was a pleasant sight to look down from the galleries upon the men who had the task in hand, and who were moving on steadily and unitedly to its consummation. The resolution has been referred to the Judiciary committee, by them thoroughly considered, and the demand of millions embodied in words approved by the committee, was now waiting the final action of the Senate before being sent to the House, and from thence to the Legislatures of the several States for their ratification.

Satisfaction, security, triumph, may be seen on almost every face in the Senate chamber today; not the mere triumph of man over man, the security based on numerical strength, or the soulless satisfaction of having gained a point simply for the defeat of an opposition. No; there is something better, nobler, grander in the faces of these men today; something that speaks of purpose based on principle, of deep and earnest thought, and self-reliant action for the right; there is a consciousness of responsibility appropriate to the occasion, and who shall blame them if they blend with this an air of confidence as they compare their position now with what it was in the long, dark, stormy days of southern rule and republican minority. They can speak now like freemen, and there is not a sneaking assassin at hand with knife or bludgeon to strike down the defenders of liberty. So Johnson and Howard and Hale and Clark and others have been speaking during the week that has passed, as so Sumner has been speaking today—speaking for humanity against the legalized tyranny of a slave aristocracy.

Is it to be wondered at that the feeble half dozen defenders of a dead faith, the few lingering relics of a once powerful class of graduates from the institution whose chief cornerstone is barbarism brutalized, should writhe under the truths they are forced to hear, should struggle as with a death agony against the mighty power that is crushing them between the ruins of their own bloody Molock? They do writhe and struggle in the impotence of their rage, and if the calm, confident giants only smile and bend to their task with still more resolute energy, can they be called merciless, unkind?

The world and the future will not call them so. Neither does the great, true heart of the present. With a warm, throbbing amen, in the name of humanity it bids them God speed, till these floors shall no longer be desecrated by the slaveholders' tread, or these walls echo back words that are libels alike on God and Man.

Such words Powell, maddened to desperation, is shouting in the ears of Senators, who hear as if they heard not, or only in the magnanimity of their approaching triumph, permit him to speak unchecked. In the same breath he boasts of what he calls "the staunch, true patriotism of the glorious Old Commonwealth of Kentucky," kills New England with a sneer, buries her with a grimace, accuses the Administration of unprecedented and unlimited corruption, tells us that this war is all for a brute race, who have not in them the elements of manhood, and that, so help him God, he will oppose now and forever every measure that would give them freedom. He raves till his face is like scarlet, and his tongue runs through all the degrees of abuse admissible in Congressional courtesy to find invectives bitter enough to vent his wrath against the Senator from Massachusetts. But sneers, taunts, mockery, and derision, are alike powerless from such a source now. His only attentive listeners are Saulsbury of Delaware who, with hands clenched under his coat tails, walks restlessly up and down his accustomed beat; Garret Davis of Kentucky who, with his little body in one chair, nurses his little feet on the cushions of another, and with a little smile on his little face, drinks in to the extent of his little capacity the wonderful words of his big brother Senator; and McDougal of California who should know better, but who sits open-mouthed to swallow all, that he may dole it out again in his maudlin way, diluted by the nauseous fumes and amber juices that scent his breath and stain his beard. These, after the speaker takes his seat, give back successively a characteristic echo of his words and sentiments.

But stay; there are other listeners, though not many now, in the galleries. A little while ago, when Sumner spoke, all these seats were full, but one by one, and dozens by dozens, the occupants have gone, all but the few scattered here and there, who are resolved to wait till dark, and after, if they must, to hear the vote. These, however, are waiting, rather than listening; for, in little groups, they are softly talking to each other; or, singly, smiling at the futile efforts of the slave-quartette below, to ward off as long as they may the blow that they know must come, and soon. But these are not all. Directly opposite us, and not far from the diplomatic gallery, is a long seat occupied by people who are evidently deeply interested witnesses of every word and act of the Senators upon the floor. They came early, were ushered into that seat by the door-keeper, and, unlike most gallery visitants, have kept their places quietly, and watched with intense and absorbing interest the proceedings of the day. They have attracted some friendly and some angry glances from below. I think Garret Davis would like to pierce them through and through with those little, stiletto-like eyes of his; and I know Saulsbury would be delighted to annihilate them with that terrible frown with which he clouds his brow when his "gentlemanly instincts" are disturbed. See how he scowls over his shoulder and compresses his lips in scorn. Do they see it, or know it, or care for it, those three men and three women in that distant seat? They are the best behaved people in the gallery today; they are handsomely and neatly dressed in black silks and broadcloths, and—their skins are almost black.

But now the pygmies have worried themselves quiet; and the giants are gathering up their strength. For the last hour they have been loitering about, apparently unconscious of the storm they had raised, or of the work yet to be done: now they come up from the corners where they had been gathered in little groups, from the side sofas where they had been stretching their limbs to rest, from anti rooms, from reading of newspapers and from writing at desks—they come, they are ready. Nearly all are standing now. The yeas and nays are called. They are no feeble, half-uttered, half-meant responses that come up and are recorded on that list of names which should be the roll of honor for the present age. There is a heart in every "aye" of the thirty-eight. The six short, sullen "noes" are as soulless as they are powerless.

The work is done, and the giants are men again, smiling and shaking hands amidst the hum and buzz of hearty congratulating voices. So we leave them.

L.

THE FORT PILLOW MASSACRE:
TENNESSEE, APRIL 1864

Achilles V. Clark to Judith Porter and Henrietta Ray

Major General Nathan Bedford Forrest, a wealthy plantation owner and former slave trader who would later become the first Grand Wizard of the Ku Klux Klan, led 2,300 men from his cavalry command in an attack on Fort Pillow, Tennessee, on April 12, 1864. The outpost, located on a bluff overlooking the Mississippi River forty miles north of Memphis, was defended by about 600 Union soldiers, 305 from the 6th U.S. Colored Heavy Artillery and 2nd U.S. Colored Light Artillery and at least 277 from the 13th Tennessee Cavalry, a regiment of white unionists that included deserters from the Confederate army. Sergeant Achilles V. Clark of the Confederate 20th Tennessee Cavalry wrote about the assault on the fort to his sisters, both of whom were married to slaveholding Confederate soldiers (the end of the letter is missing).

Camp near Brownsville
April 14th 1864

My Dear Sisters,

I write you a few hurried lines to inform you that I am quite well and have just passed safely through the most terrible ordeal of my whole life. I guess that you know what I mean as you doubtless have before this heard of the taking of Fort Pillow. In as much as I am a member of Forrest's Cavalry modesty would direct that I should say nothing in our praise nor will I but will tell you in as few words as possible what was done and leave you to judge whether or not we acted well or ill. If you remember we left Paris Wednesday morning from which point we proceeding immediately to Eaton Gibson County where we found Col. Bell's camp. Saturday we prepared five days rations in antisipain of a move to some place we knew not where. Sunday evening directly after supper the bugle sounded to saddle. at twelve o'clock we marched off in the direction of

Brownsville. We camped just at daybreak on the north side and about two miles from South Forked Deer river where we rested one hour. Mounting our horses we crossed the above mentioned stream and one mile this side took the Fort Pillow road. From this time we rightly supposed that we were going to attack that place. At 10 A.M. (Monday) we stopped to feed and were detained about one hour and a half. At 3 P.M. we stopped again and rested until six. From this time on we were in our saddles until we reached a point one and a half miles this side of the Fort where we dismounted to fight (this was about 7 A.M. Tuesday) leaving every fourth man to hold horses, we marched on foot in sight of the fortifications which were said to be manned by about seven hundred renegade Tennesseans and negroes commanded by Major Boothe of the Negro regiment Major Bradford of the 13th Tenn. U.S.V. being second in command. Our brigade filed round to the right of the fort Chalmer's command to the left. Skirmishers were deployed and we advanced very slowly it is true but surely toward the enemy. Just here it would be proper to describe the fort which I shall attempt to do. It is a very strong earthwork situated on a high bluff inside the works erected by Gen. Pillow in 1861. It is formed by an irregular trench being dug somewhat in the shape of a half circle the edge of the bluff being the diameter. The fort is quite small just about large enough to hold a thousand men in two ranks. The ditch is eight feet deep and six wide and the dirt thrown from the ditch on the inside formed a bank five feet high making from the bottom of the ditch to the top of the breast work thirteen feet up which we had to climb. By two o'clock P.M. we had approached within fifty yards of the fort on all sides. A part of our regiment was in twenty steps of it. Strange to say after five hours constant firing the Yankees had not killed a single one of our men and wounded only a very few among whom I am sorry to name the gallant Capt. Wilson of our regiment who fell in twenty steps of the fort shot through the lungs dangerously though tis greatly to be hoped not mortally wounded. At 2 P.M. Gen. Forrest demanded a surrender and gave twenty minutes to consider. The Yankees refused threatening that if we charged their breast works to show no quarter. The bugle sounded the charge and in less than ten minutes we were in the fort hurling the cowardly villains howling down the bluff. Our men were so exasperated by the Yankees' threats of no quarter that they gave but little. The slaughter was awful. Words cannot describe the scene. The poor deluded negroes would run up to our men fall upon their knees and with uplifted hands scream for mercy but they were ordered to their feet and then shot down. The whitte men fared but little better. Their fort turned out to be a great slaughter pen. Blood, human blood stood about in pools and brains could have been gathered up in any quantity. I with several others tried to stop the butchery and at one time had partially succeeded. but Gen. Forrest ordered them shot down like dogs. and the carnage continued. Finally our men became sick of blood and the firing ceased. The result. The report kept in the Post Adjutants office shows that there were seven hundred and ninty men for duty on the morning of the fight. We brought away about one hundred and sixty white men and about seventy five negroes. Two transports came down the morning after the fight and took off the badly wounded Yankees and negroes about thirty or forty in all. The remainder were thrown into the trench before which two hours previous they had stood and bade open defiance to Forrest and all his ragged hounds, and were covered up about two feet deep. We captured seven hundred stands of small arms, six pieces of the finest artillery I ever saw, a large amount of quarter masters and commissary stores. Our loss as compared to that of the enemy were small yet we deeply mourn the loss of ten or fifteen as brave men as ever pulled a trigger. Those from our Regt. John Beard of our company a bright minded moral young man who fell on top of the breast work close to my side. [ ]

PREDICTING UNION PLANS: VIRGINIA, APRIL 1864

Robert E. Lee to Jefferson Davis

The Army of the Potomac and the Army of Northern Virginia had gone into winter quarters on opposite sides of the Rapidan River in December 1863 following the inconclusive Mine Run campaign, which ended without a major battle being fought. During the winter and early spring of 1864 General Robert E. Lee tried to anticipate Union plans while confronting serious shortages of men, food, and forage. "There is nothing to be had in this section for man or animals," he wrote to Jefferson Davis from his headquarters at Orange Court House on April 12. Lee shared his appraisal of the overall military situation with Davis three days later.

Headquarters
April 15, 1864

Mr. President:

The reports of the scouts are still conflicting as to the character of the reinforcements to the Army of the Potomac, & the composition of that at Annapolis under Genl Burnside. I think it probably that the 8th Corps, which embraces the troops who have heretofore guarded the line of the B & O Rr, the entrenchments around Washington, & Alexandria, &c., have been moved up to the Rappahannock, & that an equivalent has been sent to Annapolis from Genl Meade. Lt Col Mosby states that the 11th & 12th Corps, consolidated, have been also sent to Genl Burnside. But whatever doubt there may be on these points, I think it certain that the enemy is organizing a large army on the Rappahannock, & another at Annapolis, & that the former is intended to move directly on Richmond, while the latter is intended to take it in flank or rear. I think we may also reasonably suppose that the Federal troops that have so long besieged Charleston will, with a portion of their iron clad steamers, be transferred to the James River. I consider that the suspension of the attack on that city was virtually declared when Genl Gillmore transferred his operations to the St. John's River. It can only be continued during the summer months by the fleet. The expedition of the enemy up Red River has so diminished his forces about New Orleans & Mobile that I think no attack upon the latter city need be apprehended soon, especially as we have reason to hope that he will return from his expedition in a shattered condition. I have thought therefore that Genl Johnston might draw something from Mobile during the summer to strengthen his hands, & that Genl Beauregard with a portion of his troops might move into North Carolina to oppose Genl Burnside should he resume his old position in that State, or be ready to advance to the James River should that route be taken. I do not know what benefit Genl Buckner can accomplish in his present position. If he is able to advance into Tennessee, reoccupy Knoxville, or unite with Genl Johnston, great good may be accomplished, but if he can only hold Bristol, I think he had better be called for a season to Richmond. We shall have to glean troops from every quarter to oppose the apparent combination of the enemy. If Richmond could be held secure against the attack from the east, I would propose that I draw Longstreet to me & move right against the enemy on the Rappahannock. Should God give us a crowning victory there, all their plans would be dissipated, & their troops now collecting on the waters of the Chesapeake will be recalled to the defence of Washington. But to make this move I must have provisions & forage. I am not yet able to call to me the cavalry or artillery. If I am obliged to retire from this line, either by a flank movement of the enemy or the want of supplies, great injury will befall us. I have ventured to throw out these suggestions to Your Excellency in order that in surveying the whole field of operations you may consider all the circumstances bearing on the question. Should you determine it is better to divide this army & fall back towards Richmond I am ready to do so. I however see no better plan for the defence of Richmond than that I have proposed.

I am with great respect, your
obt servt

R. E. LEE
Genl

The New York Times: *The Black Flag*

April 16, 1864

Of the 585 Union soldiers known to have been at Fort Pillow on April 12, 1864, 277 were killed or died from their wounds in Union hospitals—82 from the 13th Tennessee Cavalry and 195 from the 6th U.S. Colored Heavy Artillery and the 2nd U.S. Colored Light Artillery. On April 13 the Confederates paroled several dozen wounded men and allowed them to be evacuated under flag of truce to Memphis and Cairo, Illinois. A report on the massacre from Cairo appeared in *The New York Times* on April 16, the same day stories about Fort Pillow ran in the *New York Herald*, *New-York Tribune*, *Chicago Tribune*, *Cincinnati Gazette*, and *St. Louis Missouri Democrat.*

THE BLACK FLAG.

Horrible Massacre by the Rebels.
Fort Pillow Captured After a Desperate Fight.
Four Hundred of the Garrison Brutally Murdered.
Wounded and Unarmed Men Bayoneted and Their Bodies Burned.
White and Black Indiscriminately Butchered.
Devilish Atrocities of the Insatiate Fiends.

FROM CAIRO.

CAIRO, Thursday, April 14.

On Tuesday morning the rebel Gen. FORREST attacked Fort Pillow. Soon after the attack FORREST sent a flag of truce demanding the surrender of the fort and garrison, meanwhile disposing of his force so as to gain the advantage. Our forces were under command of Major BOOTH, of the Thirteenth Tennessee (U.S.) Heavy Artillery, formerly of the First Alabama Cavalry.

The flag of truce was refused, and fighting resumed. Afterward a second flag came in, which was also refused.

Both flags gave the rebels advantage of gaining new positions.

The battle was kept up until 3 P.M., when Major BOOTH was killed, and Major BRADFORD took command.

The rebels now came in swarms over our troops, compelling them to surrender.

Immediately upon the surrender ensued a scene which utterly baffles description. Up to that time, comparatively few of our men had been killed; but, insatiate as fiends, bloodthirsty as devils incarnate, the Confederates commenced an indiscriminate butchery of the whites and blacks, including those of both colors who had been previously wounded.

The black soldiers, becoming demoralized, rushed to the rear, the white officers having thrown down their arms.

Both white and black were bayoneted, shot or sabred; even dead bodies were horribly mutilated, and children of seven and eight years and several negro women killed in cold blood. Soldiers unable to speak from wounds were shot dead, and their bodies rolled down the banks into the river. The dead and wounded negroes were piled in heaps and burned, and several citizens who had joined our forces for protection were killed or wounded.

Out of the garrison of six hundred, only two hundred remained alive.

Among our dead officers are Capt. BRADFORD, Lieuts. BARR, ACKERSSTROM, WILSON, REVEL and Major BOOTH, all of the Thirteenth Tennessee Cavalry.

Capt. POSTON and Lieut. LYON, Thirteenth Tennessee Cavalry, and Capt. YOUNG, Twenty-fourth Missouri, Acting-Provost-Marshal, were taken prisoners.

Maj. BRADFORD was also captured, but is said to have escaped; it is feared, however, that he has been killed.

The steamer *Platte Valley* came up at about half-past 3 o'clock, and was hailed by the rebels under a flag of truce. Men were sent ashore to bury the dead, and take aboard such of the wounded as the enemy had allowed to live. Fifty-seven were taken aboard, including seven or eight colored. Eight died on the way up. The steamer arrived here this evening, and was immediately sent to the Mound City Hospital, to discharge her suffering cargo.

Among our wounded officers of colored troops are Capt. PORTER, Lieut. LIBBERTS and Adjt. LEMMING.

Six guns were captured by the rebels, and carried off, including two ten-pound Parrotts and two twelve-pound howitzers. A large amount of stores was destroyed or carried away.

The intention of the rebels seemed to be to evacuate the place, and move on toward Memphis.

LATER.

CAIRO, Thursday, April 15.

Two negro soldiers, wounded at Fort Pillow, were buried by the rebels, but afterward worked themselves out of their graves. They were among those brought up in the *Platte Valley*, and are now in hospital at Mound City.

The officers of the *Platte Valley* receive great credit from the military authorities for landing at Fort Pillow, at eminent risk, and taking our wounded on board, and for their kind attentions on the way up.

REPORTS FROM ST. LOUIS.

ST. LOUIS, Friday, April 15.

The correspondent of the *Union*, who was on board the steamer *Platte Valley* at Fort Pillow, gives even a more appalling description of the fiendishness of the rebels than our Cairo dispatches.

Many of our wounded were shot in the hospital. The remainder were driven out, and the hospital was burned.

On the morning after the battle the rebels went over the field, and shot the negroes who had not died from their wounds.

Several of the guns captured by FORREST at Fort Pillow were spiked before falling into his hands. Others were turned upon gunboat No. 7, which, having fired some 300 rounds and exhausted her ammunition, was compelled to withdraw. Although a tinclad, she received but slight injury.

Gen. LEE arrived and assumed the command at the beginning of the battle. Previous to which Gen. CHALMERS directed the movements. FORREST, with the main force, retired after the fight to Brownsville, taking with him the captured funds.

While the steamer *Platte Valley* lay under flag of truce, taking on board our wounded, some of the rebel officers, and among them Gen. CHALMERS, went on board, and some of our officers showed them great deference, drinking with them, and showing them other marks of courtesy.

Many of those who had escaped from the works and hospital, who desired to be treated as prisoners of war, as the rebels said, were ordered to fall into line, and when they had formed, were inhumanly shot down.

Of 350 colored troops not more than 56 escaped the massacre, and not one officer that commanded them survives. Only four officers of the Thirteenth Tennessee escaped death.

The loss of the Thirteenth Tennessee is 800 killed. The remainder were wounded and captured.

Gen. CHALMER told this correspondent that, although it was against the policy of his Government to spare negro soldiers or their officers, he had done all in his power to stop the carnage. At the same time he believed it was right.

Another officer said our white troops would have been protected had they not been found on duty with negroes.

While the rebels endeavored to conceal their loss, it was evident that they suffered severely. Col. REED, commanding a Tennessee regiment, was mortally wounded. There were two or three well filled hospitals at a short distance in the country.

DEFINING LIBERTY AND CONSIDERING RETRIBUTION: MARYLAND, APRIL 1864

Abraham Lincoln: Address at Baltimore Sanitary Fair

Lincoln spoke at the opening ceremonies of the Baltimore Sanitary Fair, held in the great hall of the Maryland Institute to raise funds for the U.S. Christian and U.S. Sanitary Commissions, the two major relief organizations aiding Union soldiers.

April 18, 1864

Ladies and Gentlemen—Calling to mind that we are in Baltimore, we can not fail to note that the world moves. Looking upon these many people, assembled here, to serve, as they best may, the soldiers of the Union, it occurs at once that three years ago, the same soldiers could not so much as pass through Baltimore. The change from then till now, is both great, and gratifying. Blessings on the brave men who have wrought the change, and the fair women who strive to reward them for it.

But Baltimore suggests more than could happen within Baltimore. The change within Baltimore is part only of a far wider change. When the war began, three years ago, neither party, nor any man, expected it would last till now. Each looked for the end, in some way, long ere to-day. Neither did any anticipate that domestic slavery would be much affected by the war. But here we are; the war has not ended, and slavery has been much affected—how much needs not now to be recounted. So true is it that man proposes, and God disposes.

But we can see the past, though we may not claim to have directed it; and seeing it, in this case, we feel more hopeful and confident for the future.

The world has never had a good definition of the word liberty, and the American people, just now, are much in want of one. We all declare for liberty; but in using the same *word* we do not all mean the same *thing*. With some the word liberty may mean for each man to do as he pleases with himself, and the product of his labor; while with others the same word may mean for some men to do as they please with other men, and the product of other men's labor. Here are two, not only different, but incompatable things, called by the same name—liberty. And it follows that each of the things is, by the respective parties, called by two different and incompatable names—liberty and tyranny.

The shepherd drives the wolf from the sheep's throat, for which the sheep thanks the shepherd as a *liberator*, while the wolf denounces him for the same act as the destroyer of liberty, especially as the sheep was a black one. Plainly the sheep and the wolf are not agreed upon a definition of the word liberty; and precisely the same difference prevails to-day among us human creatures, even in the North, and all professing to love liberty. Hence we behold the processes by which thousands are daily passing from under the yoke of bondage, hailed by some as the advance of liberty, and bewailed by others as the destruction of all liberty. Recently, as it seems, the people of Maryland have been doing something to define liberty; and thanks to them that, in what they have done, the wolf's dictionary, has been repudiated.

It is not very becoming for one in my position to make speeches at great length; but there is another subject upon which I feel that I ought to say a word. A painful rumor, true I fear, has reached us of the massacre, by the rebel forces, at Fort Pillow, in the West end of Tennessee, on the Mississippi river, of some three hundred colored soldiers and white officers, who had just been overpowered by their assailants. There seems to be some anxiety in the public mind whether the government is doing its duty to the colored soldier, and to the service, at this point. At the beginning of the war, and for some time, the use of colored troops was not contemplated; and how the change of purpose was wrought, I will not now take time to explain. Upon a clear conviction of duty I resolved to turn that element of strength to account; and I am responsible for it to the American people, to the christian world, to history, and on my final account to God. Having determined to use the negro as a soldier, there is no way but to give him all the protection given to any other soldier. The difficulty is not in stating the principle, but in practically applying it. It is a mistake to suppose the government is indifferent to this matter, or is not doing the best it can in regard to it. We do not to-day *know* that a colored soldier, or white officer commanding colored soldiers, has been massacred by the rebels when made a prisoner. We fear it, believe it, I may say, but we do not *know* it. To take the life of one of their prisoners, on the assumption that they murder ours, when it is short of certainty that they do murder ours, might be too serious, too cruel a mistake. We are having the Fort-Pillow affair thoroughly investigated; and such investigation will probably show conclusively how the truth is. If, after all that has been said, it shall turn out that there has been no massacre at Fort-Pillow, it will be almost safe to say there has been none, and will be none elsewhere. If there has been the massacre of three hundred there, or even the tenth part of three hundred, it will be conclusively proved; and being so proved, the retribution shall as surely come. It will be matter of grave consideration in what exact course to apply the retribution; but in the supposed case, it must come.

R.H.C. to The Christian Recorder

April 30, 1864

Two weeks after the Fort Pillow massacre *The Christian Recorder*, a weekly newspaper published in Philadelphia by the African Methodist Episcopal Church, printed a letter signed "R.H.C." It may have been written by Richard Harvey Cain, an African Methodist Episcopal minister in Brooklyn, New York, who moved to South Carolina after the war and was elected to Congress during Reconstruction.

FORT PILLOW.

MR. EDITOR:—Still we press forward in the great march of mind and matter: winds still blow; and the southern breezes bring a wail of horror from the devoted "Fort. Pillow." Kentucky, that "virago" in the community of States, whose scoldings have retarded the progress of "civilization," in these war times more than any other, is now drinking the cup of secession wrath, which is a just retribution meted out to her. But, the dying groans of those butchered men, the desolate hearthstones, cry against, and the widowed mothers and orphans, will hold her accountable for their murdered kindred. Yet, through this bloody sea lies the land of liberty; and although we may have to pour out rivers of blood, liberty is not attainable without it. The brutality which prompted the slaughter of that garrison of brave men, is but a preface to the great book of scaled crimes which this abominable system of slavery has been perpetrating upon our race for two hundred and forty-five years. None but the blacks of this land, have heretofore realized the hateful nature of the beast: but now, white men are beginning to feel, and to realize what its beauties are. This fell spirit was the main spring of this rebellion; it has dictated all the movements in the attempt to destroy the government; it moved the schemers to assassinate President Lincoln, on his passage to Washington; it has murdered all colored soldiers captured by the rebels.

While we deplore the loss of these brave men, we feel that, from their ashes will rise thousands to avenge their deaths. We accept the alternative, and believe that the 54th and 55th Mass., 20th and 26th U.S. troops, in connection with the 1st, 4th, and all the other colored men in the service, will receive this news with defiance sparkling in every eye. The terrors of death should not affright them from the resolve to fight the battles of freedom. We all know, that in the destruction of slavery is the safety of the nation, and the hope of the race. We know that, when we enlisted, threats had been made, and we expected them to be fulfilled; and this butchery is not a new thing to us—we have had experiences before to-day. With slaveholders, this is only *an act on a grander scale*, than those thousands of similar ones performed daily by the lords of the lash, before this rebellion—and, instead of daunting our courage, should only nerve us to do and dare more in this struggle for human rights and universal liberty.

We now call on our noble brethren in the army, to swear anew never to cease fighting, until they shall have made a rebel to bite the dust for every hair of those three hundred of our brethren massacred in Fort Pillow; and, whenever you may be called upon to measure arms or bayonets, with the rebel horde, give no quarter; take no prisoners; make it dangerous to take the life of a black soldier by these barbarians; then, they will respect your manhood, and you will be treated as you deserve at the hands of those who have made you outlaws. If there be a complaint that you are savage, you can with justice point to forts Wagoner, Hudson, Pillow, and to Milliken's bend, and remember the deeds of cruelty there inflicted upon the innocent. Warriors! remember that you fight for liberty! Remember the wives and children you have left behind! Remember, you from New York, the *July riots!* You from the South, who are soldiers of the Republic, remember your old gray-haired mothers, who are yet within the lines of rebeldom; remember your wives and little ones, robbed and maltreated by ruffians and "Legrees;" remember your daughters, dishonored by those red-handed murderers of your race! Remember, that for two hundred and fifty years, your people have been sold and bartered like so many beasts, and then bow down before God, and swear anew to uphold your country's cause, and the cause of universal liberty: for, in the maintenance of liberty on this continent is the hope of all European nations. Think not that the blood you shed will avail nothing: if you fall in this mighty struggle; you will leave a name that shall live, after you have passed away; and the generations following will rise up and call you blessed. Your children will, undoubtedly, enjoy more liberty, and, the same spirit which animates you to do and dare in this fearful crisis, will fall upon them in double proportion, and they shall rise up to a position honorable among mankind.

No people can hope to be lifted up entirely by the labors or benevolence of others. We must not look for sympathy; we must not ask for pity; we must rise above this condition. So long as we are pensioners on other people's pity, we will be subject to their insults; but the moment we assume our rights, and maintain them by every lawful means; so soon as it appears to the world that we are not mendicants, but men ready to make any sacrifice for liberty and untrammelled freedom, then, the world will recognize in us more than mere objects of pity.

While our kindred are battling in the field, we who are at home, must not forget that we have duties to perform to those whom they have left behind. We should cheer their hearts by speaking words of comfort; and, if need be, contribute to their wants. Further, the leading minds must look after the interests of the soldiers; see that no injustice be done them by subordinates of the government, for it is by this class they suffer more than any other. And now that there is a great progressive movement on hand, let not any man among us stop, in his efforts to elevate and honor his race. Let those in civil life be on their guard, let them forward the education of the rising generation, and help forward every enterprise which tends to refine, mould, and fashion the future course of our kindred.

R.H.C.

DEBATING RETALIATION: WASHINGTON, D.C., MAY 1864

Gideon Welles: Diary, May 3, 5–6, 1864

In a proclamation issued in December 1862, Jefferson Davis had ordered that former slaves captured while fighting in the Union army be turned over to state authorities to be tried for the capital offense of insurrection. In May 1863 his policy was extended by the Confederate Congress to apply to free blacks from the North. In practice, captured black soldiers were either summarily executed, returned or sold into slavery, or used for forced labor by the Confederate army. President Lincoln responded on July 30, 1863, issuing an order declaring that "for every soldier of the United States killed in violation of the laws of war, a rebel soldier shall be executed," and that for every one enslaved, "a rebel soldier shall be placed at hard labor on the public works." Despite reports that Confederate troops continued to kill and mistreat black prisoners, no retaliatory measures had been undertaken by the time of the assault on Fort Pillow. Secretary of the Navy Gideon Welles recorded the discussions held by the cabinet in early May as the congressional Joint Committee on the Conduct of the War prepared to release its report on the massacre. The inconclusive deliberations resulted in no further action, and no Confederate officer was ever charged in connection with the killings at Fort Pillow.

Tuesday 3. At the Cabinet meeting the President requested each member to give him an opinion as to what course the Government should pursue in relation to the recent massacre at Fort Pillow. The committee from Congress who have visited the scene returned yesterday and will soon report. All the reported horrors are said to be verified. The President wishes to be prepared to act as soon as the subject is brought to his notice officially, and hence Cabinet advice in advance.

The subject is one of great responsibility and great embarrassment especially before we are in possession of the facts and evidence of the committee. There must be something in these terrible reports, but I distrust Congressional committees. They exaggerate.

Mrs. W. and Edgar left to-day for New York. She is to spend a few days at Irvington—Edgar to complete his college course.

Tom is filled with unrestrained zeal to go to the army. It is much of it boyish fervor but none the less earnest.

Thursday 5. I have written a letter to the President in relation to the Fort Pillow massacre, but it is not satisfactory to me, nor can I make it so without the evidence of what was done, nor am I certain that even then I could come to a conclusion on so grave and important a question. The idea of retaliation—killing man for man which is the popular noisy demand is barbarous, and I cannot assent to or advise it. The leading officers should be held accountable and punished but how. The policy of killing negro soldiers after they have surrendered must not be permitted, and the Rebel leaders should be called upon to avow or disavow it. But how is this to be done? Shall we go to Jeff Davis and his government, or apply to General Lee. If they will give us no answer, or declare they will kill the negroes, or justify Forrest, shall we take innocent Rebel officers as hostages. The whole subject is beset with difficulties. I cannot yield to any inhuman scheme of retaliation. Must wait the publication of the testimony.

Friday 6. At the Cabinet meeting each of the members read his opinion. There had, I think been some concert between Seward and Stanton and probably Chase—that is they had talked on the subject, although there was not coincidence of views on all respects. Although I was dissatisfied with my own, it was as well as most others.

Between Mr. Bates and Mr. Blair a suggestion came out that met my views better than anything that had previously occurred. It is, that the President should, by proclamation declare the officers who had command at the massacre are outlaws, and require any of our officers who may capture them, to detain them in custody and not exchange them, but hold them to punishment. The thought was not very distinctly enunciated. In a conversation that followed the reading of our papers, I expressed myself in favor of this new suggestion which relieved the subject of much of the difficulty. It avoids communication with the Rebel authorities. Takes the matter in our own hands. We get rid of the barbarity of retaliation.

Stanton fell in with my suggestion, so far as to propose that should Forrest, or Chalmers, or any officer conspicuous in this butchery be captured, that he should be turned over for trial for the murders at Fort Pillow. I sat beside Chase and mentioned to him some of the advantages of this course, and he said it made a favorable impression. I urged him to say so, for it appeared to me that the President and Seward did not appreciate it.

We get no tidings from the front. There is an impression that we are on the eve of a great battle and that it may already have commenced.

PROTESTING SLAVE IMPRESSMENT: ALABAMA, MAY 1864

Petition from the Slaveholders of Randolph County, Alabama

From the beginning of the war the impressment of slaves for military labor by the Confederate army met with widespread resistance from southern slaveholders, who protested the loss of needed labor and feared that their impressed slaves might die, escape, or lose respect for their owners' authority. The Confederate Congress passed legislation in March 1863 intended to make impressment more equitable, but small slaveholders continued to object that the regulations favored large planters. On May 6, 1864, forty-six slaveowners from Randolph County in northeastern Alabama petitioned Jefferson Davis for relief from an assessment levied by Colonel Frederick S. Blount, the impressment agent for the Department of Alabama, Mississippi, and East Louisiana. Blount subsequently wrote on May 14 to Henry M. Gay, the impressment agent for the county, requisitioning fifty slaves for labor service. After Gay responded on June 1 that he would be able to furnish only five slaves, Blount agreed to exempt Randolph County from the impressment.

Wesabulga Randolph Co Ala May 6th 1864

To his Excellency Jefferson Davis The undersigned citizens & Slaveholders of the county of Randolph & State of Alabama would respectfully represent to your Excellency That Col Blount impressing agt of Slaves Stationed at Mobile Ala; has recently ordered an impressment of 33⅓ per cent of the able bodied Slaves of this County; when in adjoining counties where the Slave population is greater only from 5 to 10 per cent have been taken— This we think to be unjust, & *not* in accordance with the intentions of the act. We think that an uniform rate should be levied in the whole State; or so much of it as is now within our lines; So that the burden Should fall uniformly on all; But he appears to order an arbitrary number from each county without refferance to the number of Slaves in the County. He thus levies a percentage which is uniform in the county, but does not bear any proportion to the levies in adjoining Counties— He also counts *in* all the women that are within the ages of 17 to 50 & takes one third of the *total number in men* between the ages of 17 to 50.

Randolph is a poor & mountainous County with the largest population of any in the State. There are only 300 negroes (women & men) within the prescribed ages in the county & he takes one Hundred   Seventy five per cent of the White Males are now in the Service; leaving the great majority of their wives & children to be Supported by the remainder   There are numbers of widows & orphans of the Soldiers who have perished by the casualities of war to be also Supported by public funds—

The County does not in ordinary times produce more than a Sufficiency of food for its population; last year there was a deficit of over 40000 bushels; of corn about one half of which has been provided from the tax in Kind; the ballance has to be purchased in the Canebrake; transported a distance of 125 miles on R.R, & hauled thence in waggons from 30 to 50 miles to reach the various points of distribution in the county—

There are now on the rolls of the Probate court, 1600 indigent families to be Supported; they average 5 to each family; making a grand total of 8000 persons   Deaths from Starvation have absolutely occurred; notwithstanding the utmost efforts that we have been able to make; & now many of the women & children are seeking & feeding upon the bran from the mills

Women riots have taken place in Several parts of the County in which Govt wheat & corn has been seized to prevent Starvation of themselves & families; Where it will end unless relief is afforded we cannot tell

We have entered into these details that your Excellency may See the deplorable condition of things in this County, & aid us if in your power & the exigencies of the Service permit—

To take the Negroes *now* from the fields when the crop is just planted & ready for cultivation would inevitably cause the loss of a portion of the crops So essential to feed the County   we have appealed to Col Blount asking that the impressment be delayed or abandoned; but without effect & we now appeal to your Excellency as our last resource under God to give us Such measure of assistance as you can. If you refuse us—we must Submit & take our chance—do our duty & trust to

Almighty Providence for the result under all the circumstances we therefore pray your Excellency.

That Randolph County be exempt from the operations of the impressment act. If, however the Case is so urgent & the hands are so essential to save Mobile; then we ask that the impressment be delayed until fall when the crops are gathered; In case neither of these prayers can be granted we pray that the rate be made uniform in the Whole State—& that *we* be not punished for our poverty— we would Humbly Suggest to your Excellency that there are large numbers of negroes about our towns & cities (used for the pleasure of their owners; or idling about; a curse to the community—*consumers not producers*) that we think might be exhausted before the agricultural labour of the county is interfered with.

Hoping that your Excellency may favourably consider our humble prayer—we remain as ever your Excellencies devoted Servants

"OUR RIGHT CAUSE": VIRGINIA, MAY 1864

Samuel W. Fiske to the Springfield Republican

A company commander in the 14th Connecticut Infantry, Captain Samuel W. Fiske had joined his regiment in August 1862 and fought at Antietam, Chancellorsville, Gettysburg, and Bristoe Station. On the day before the Army of the Potomac began crossing the Rapidan, he sent one of his regular letters to the *Springfield* (Massachusetts) *Republican*, written under the pen name Dunn Browne. Fiske was shot on the morning of May 6 while fighting along the Orange Plank Road in the Wilderness as part of the Third Brigade, Second Division, Second Corps. Wounded in the right lung, he was taken to a Union army hospital in Fredericksburg, Virginia, where he died on May 22, 1864, the day after this letter appeared in the *Republican*.

Dunn Browne's Parting Grumble and Advice

Camp on the Rapidan, Va.
May 3, 1864

A Tempest In Camp

Dear Republican: Stepping out of my tent yesterday for a moment, I saw a huge red cloud sweeping over Pony mountain with tremendous rapidity and fury, and before we had half done wondering whether it was some stray aurora borealis shooting across Virginia, one of the boys exclaimed, "That's genuine Virginia mud taking to itself wings"; and sure enough, our whole eastern horizon was darkened with a tornado of dust, and we sprang to our houses to keep them from breaking their connection with the hillside on which we are located. What a time we did have, to be sure! The principle of gravitation was nowhere. The "star of empire" never took its way westward with half the velocity with which the barrels from our chimneys, the hats from our heads and the canvas from our huts started on a tour towards the Rocky mountains. We could readily believe that the earth was whirling from west to east as rapidly as the astronomers tell us, and moreover that she evidently meant to leave us behind, this trip at least. The many trees that had been left standing in and about our camp couldn't withstand the blast for a moment, but broke like pipe stems before the first rush of the tempest; and woe to the luckless log hut that happened to be squatted in the path of its fall. A huge pine made kindling wood of the stately mansion of our colonel, grinding to splinters the tender young pines that composed its walls as ruthlessly as the porcine mother sometimes devours her offspring. Well for the colonel that he was out of his hut at the time on a tour of picket duty, or there would have been a likely chance for promotion to somebody in our regiment. I have heard of nobody that was injured, at least seriously, but the "scare" was considerable, and the dust that filled our houses and covered our beds and clothes and food, something like the cloud of ashes that buried Pompeii. Our oldest sailors said they never saw anything like it. The tempest soon blew itself over, however, and the rain that succeeded it was not much more than enough to lay the dust. So we speedily repaired damages and settled into our pristine "quiet along the Rapidan."

A Razee Of Our Houses

To-day, nevertheless, an order from division headquarters has done what the tornado didn't half accomplish, namely, has unroofed all our houses and leveled them to the ground. "Going to move," are we? Oh no, not at all. But the fact is we are getting altogether too effeminate for soldiers. Why should we lie in comfortable dry huts, on bunks raised from the ground, when thousands of acres of sacred Virginia soil lie all around us, on which (with the slight trouble of tearing our houses down) we may extend ourselves? Why indulge in chimneys when it is so much more soldierly to gather round a smoky fire out of doors to cook our food and warm ourselves? Why interfere with the providential design of these searching spring rains and withering winds by remaining behind plastered log barriers and under tight roofs, when so little work will enable us to return to nature's wild simplicity? Some of our foolish boys murmur at these orders emanating from comfortable, luxurious headquarters, and think we might as well have remained in our tight little cabins the few days we have yet to stay, as to catch colds all of us by lying on the ground before we commence our summer's marchings. But it is well known that soldiers will grumble at the kindest provisions made for their comfort, and of course we shall go on with our wholesome sanitary arrangements regardless of any such talk.

The Ration Question

Why, actually, some of these ungrateful boys object to the bill Senator Wilson is introducing, cutting down their ration to the old standard; and declare that with the present ration (marching), they used last summer frequently to eat the ten crackers allowed per day at a single meal, and wonder what they will do if it is reduced. Now it is well known (to all the people that stay at home and read the newspapers) that no man can possibly eat the whole of the bountiful ration that Uncle Sam allows his soldiers; and it is well known to the heads of the war bureaus at Washington (as we see by an order issued on the subject last year) that it is perfectly easy for the soldier to carry 12 days' rations on his person on the march, and even, in case of necessity, where the beef is driven on the hoof, and there is some green corn to be obtained, 24 or 30 days' rations. In face of these well known facts, then, how absurd for a soldier to set up the statement that he does, as a matter of fact, often eat a whole day's marching ration at a single meal and call for more, and that no soldier ever did carry on his back more than what he ate in six days! How preposterous to mention the circumstance that nineteen out of twenty of the enlisted men spend their whole pay in purchasing additions to this same extravagantly liberal allowance of Uncle Sam, and that after a three days' march, on a supply of (it may be) 11 days' rations, the usual price of hard tack is a dime a piece! I have seen hundreds of times a dollar offered for half a dozen hard breads, or for a day's ration, although of course a true soldier will scorn to take money from a comrade for anything to eat that he may happen to have over.

Does it ever occur to anyone who is thinking of the liberal rations of our government, to ask whether the soldier, as a matter of fact, gets that full allowance? It is true that if the soldier had all the beans, rice, molasses, potatoes, dried apples, pickles, hominy, &c., &c., that the regulations allow him, and time and skill to cook them properly, he would be able to satisfy his appetite very reasonably, and even often have something over. But when we come to the marches, the hard work of the soldier, his ration is ten crackers a day (a short pound) and three-fourths of a pound of pork or one and one-quarter pounds of fresh beef of the poorest and boniest kind, and nothing else except a small allowance of sugar and coffee. This hard bread is frequently spoiled by wet, and some part of it unfit to eat by reason of bugs and worms. Now I affirm, in spite of Gen. Wilson, or Gen. Halleck, or anybody else, that this is a short ration for a hearty man on a hard march, and that when the extra of "small rations," as they are called (beans, rice, &c.), are not issued, at least 12 or 14 crackers a day should be issued to make the ration good. If the soldier obtained the money value of these articles to which he is entitled, but which are not issued, as the regulations say he shall, in his company fund, the matter would be better, but in practice he seldom or never does.

The Boys Like To Be Talked To

There are several things which I could suggest as measures likely to benefit the boys of our army, but as my turn has not yet come to take command of the forces, they may not be at present adopted. I think, for instance, that they ought to be talked to a little more. All the great generals of ancient times, and of modern times, too, have stirred the enthusiasms of their troops on the eve of battle by rousing speeches. Xenophon, Hannibal, Scipio, Caesar, everybody who wanted to get some great exploits out of the troops under his command, has told them what he wanted them to do, appealed to their patriotism, their religion, their love of glory, or whatever motive might most excite them to lofty action. Cromwell stirred up the religious enthusiasm of his troops till no foe of equal numbers could resist their grim onset. Napoleon, with a few fiery sentences, roused his Frenchmen to the most exalted spirit of courage and devotion. Now no soldiers under heaven ever came to war from a more intelligent spirit of patriotism than ours; none with a clearer sense of the principles which lay at the basis of the contest in which they are engaged; none more capable of being encouraged and roused to enthusiasm by the lofty enthusiasms of a generous leader. And our nation, of all others, has been a nation of perpetual public gatherings and speech makings. But our generals have said never a word (I speak in a general way) to encourage the troops, to keep alive their patriotism and regard for the cause, to cherish that living sympathy which should ever exist between a leader and his troops—have seemed desirous, on the whole, to make their men mere machines, going into battle without knowing anything where the pinch of the contest was, or precisely what was required of them—save to go forward at the order "forward" and fire at the order "fire."

I believe a good deal more might be made by a different course of proceeding, that our boys are something more than shooting machines, or if machines, that there are strings and pulleys and wheels in them that mere military orders don't reach, and yet which might have much effect in deciding battles—these great and terrible battles that are to decide this opening campaign, and probably bring the war to an end—these coming successes (as we devoutly hope) that are to atone for the disgraceful reverses our arms have this spring sustained in every quarter where they have been engaged. Oh for power to speak a word that might thrill the breast of every Union soldier and rouse in him that holy enthusiasm for our right cause, which should make every blow struck irresistible, and carry our arms victorious right into the citadel of rebellion, and conquer a right peace. One or two of Meade's modest, earnest orders, published to the army near the Gettysburg times, had a wonderfully happy effect. I trust more may be issued, and that every opportunity may be taken to inspire the patriotism and enthusiasm of our troops, and keep before their minds the great principles which first sent them forth from their peaceful homes to fight for endangered liberty and republican government, for God and freedom throughout the world.

Yours truly,

DUNN BROWNE

BATTLE OF THE WILDERNESS:
VIRGINIA, MAY 1864

Theodore Lyman: Journal, May 4–7, 1864

The Army of the Potomac crossed the Rapidan River on May 4, 1864, the day before Benjamin F. Butler began his waterborne advance up the James River toward Richmond. At the same time, Franz Sigel was leading Union troops south in the Shenandoah Valley, while forces under George Crook and William W. Averell were conducting raids in southwestern Virginia as part of Grant's overall plan to prevent reinforcements from reaching Lee's army. Once across the Rapidan, the Army of the Potomac would have to make its way through the Wilderness of Spotsylvania, an area of scrub woods and dense undergrowth where much of the battle of Chancellorsville had been fought the year before. Grant and Meade hoped their troops would quickly reach more open country, forcing Lee either to retreat or to fight on ground where the Union's numerical superiority in men and artillery could be fully exploited. A wealthy Bostonian, Lieutenant Colonel Theodore Lyman had spent the first two years of the war touring Europe before becoming an aide on Meade's staff in September 1863. Lyman's notebook journal for the period May 3 to June 16, 1864, bears the notation that the "notes in this book were not written herein on the spot, but taken from letters home & from memoranda written at the time and afterwards enlarged when I wrote out the notes of the Campaign for Gen. Meade's Report. This book was not begun till June 1865." In the sketch maps Lyman drew in his notebook, Union corps are indicated by their respective badges: for the Second Corps, commanded by Major General Winfield Scott Hancock, a three-leaf clover; for the Fifth Corps (Major General Gouverneur K. Warren), a Maltese cross; for the Sixth Corps (Major General John Sedgwick), a Greek cross; for the Ninth Corps (Major General Ambrose Burnside), an anchor. The designations "Q," "R," and "S" indicate the order in which the maps appear in Lyman's notebook.

May 4, 1864, Wednesday.

We all were up by star-light; a warm, clear night; had our breakfast by daybreak, and at 5.25 A.M. turned our backs on our little village of the last six months, and the grove about it, dear even in its desolation! The columns had been moving a good part of the night and we cut a part of the 6th Corps, just at Brandy Station, beyond which point the road was full of waggons and troops. Beyond Stevensburg the road-side was full of violets, and the little leaves of the wood trees were just beginning to unfold, the size of a mouse's ear perhaps. 7 A.M. The General unluckily came up with a cavalry waggon train, out of place; the worst thing for his temper! He sent me after its Quartermaster, Capt. Luddington, whom he gave awful dressing to, and ordered him to get his whole train out of the road and to halt till the other trains had passed. The sun getting well up made the temperature much warmer, as was testified by the castaway packs & blankets with which troops will often at the outset encumber themselves. 8 A.M. Arrived near Germanna Ford and halted just where we had camped the night of the withdrawal from Mine Run. *Sapristi*, it was cold that night! Though here was green grass in place of an half inch of ice, Griffin's division was over and his ammunition was then crossing. 8.30 A.M. News from Hancock that he was crossing, Gregg having had no opposition and having seen only videttes.— Roads everywhere excellent. 9.30. We crossed. There were two pontoons, a wooden & a canvass, the ascent up the opposite high & steep bank was bad, with a difficult turn near the top. We halted just on the other side and Grant & his staff arrived some time after. 12.15 P.M. All the 5th Corps, with its artillery and wheeled vehicles across.— It began at 6.30 A.M. The 6th Corps began to cross at 12.40 and was all over at 5.20 and the canvas pontoon was taken up. A good part of the time, say ½, only one pontoon could be used, because the troops were moving in single column. We may then estimate 15 hours for the passage of 46,000 infantry, with one half of their ambulances and ammunition and intrenching waggons and the whole of their artillery, over a single bridge, with steep, bad approaches on each side; i.e. a little over 3,000 men an hour, with their artillery and wheels. The latter took a good deal of the time because of the delay in getting them up the steep ascent. Sat on the bank and watched the steady stream, as it came over. That eve took a bath in the Rapid Ann and thought that might come sometime to bathe in the James!

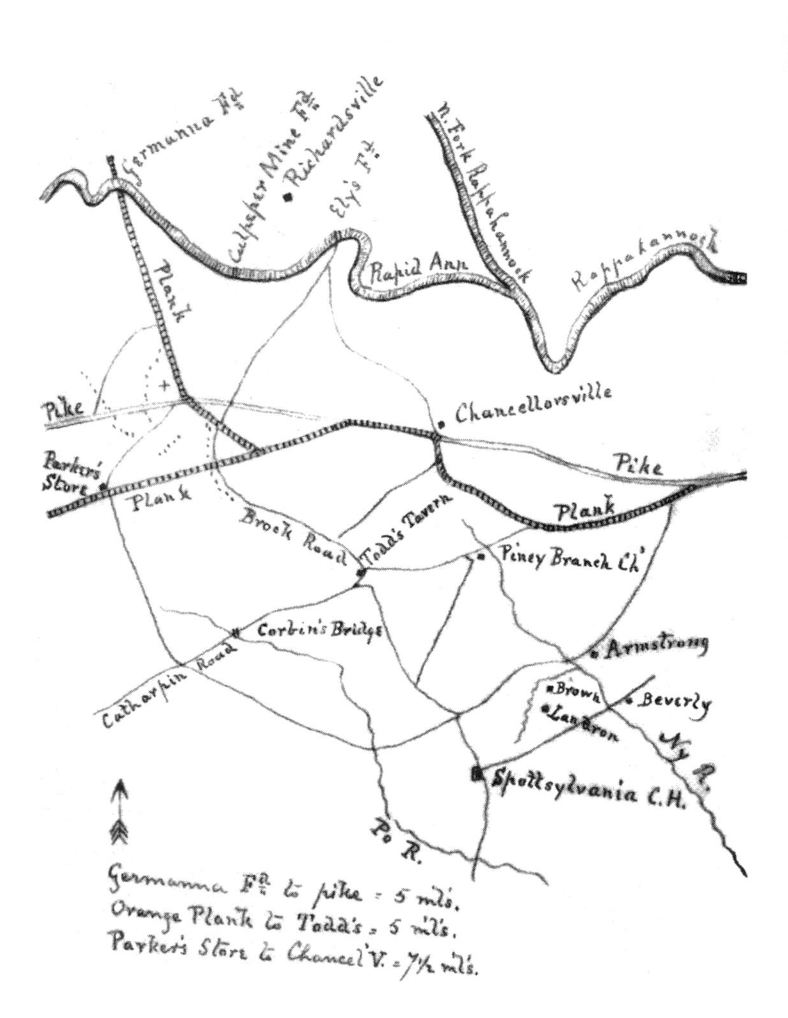

Germanna Fd.
Culpeper Mine Fd.
Richardsville
Ely's Fd.
N. Fork Rappahannock
Rapid Ann
Rappahannock
Plank
Pike
Chancellorsville
Parker's Store
Plank
Pike
Plank
Brock Road
Todd's Tavern
Piney Branch Ch.
Corbin's Bridge
Catharpin Road
Armstrong
Brown
Beverly
Landron
Ny R.
Spottsylvania C.H.
Po R.
Germanna Fd. to pike = 5 mls.
Orange Plank to Todd's = 5 mls.
Parker's Store to Chancel'V. = 7½ mls.

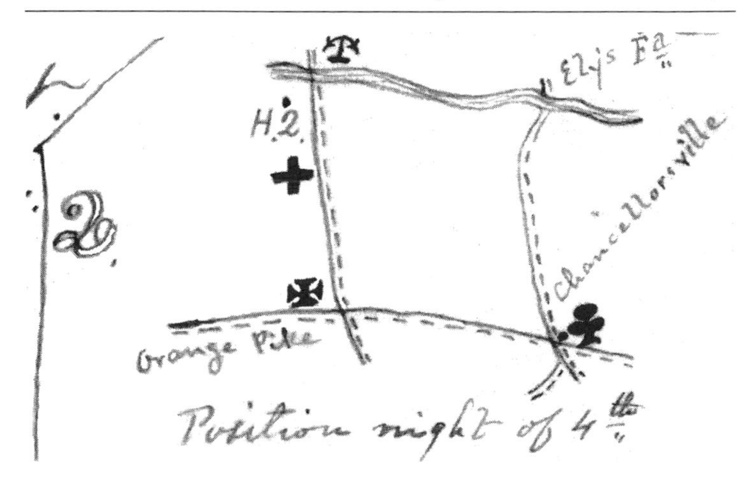

Our cook, little M. Mercier, came to grief, having been spirited away by the provost guard of the 2d Corps, as a straggler or spy; so our supper was got up by the waiter boy, Marshall. Our camp was near the river, and Grant's was close to us. Some of his officers; Duff & old Jerry Dent e.g. were very flippant and regarded Grant as already routing Lee and utterly breaking up the rebellion!—not so the more sober.—There arrived Gen. Seymour, the unlucky man of Olustee, dark bearded and over given to talk and write; but of well known valor. He was assigned to a brigade 3d Div. 6th Corps, where his command was destined to be of the shortest.

May 5, Thursday.

The head of the 9th Corps got last night as far as Germanna Ford; but the troops extended thence far back. Order of march (epitome) for May 5. (Of course this was but partially carried out, owing to the battle.) Sheridan, with Gregg's and Torbert's Divisions, to attack enemy's cavalry at Hamilton's crossing (towards Fredericksburg). Wilson's Cav. Div. to move out at 5 A.M. to Craig's Meeting House, on Catharpin road, and to throw out on the Catharpin & Pamunkey roads and on the Orange Plank & Pike, &c. 2d Corps move at 5 to Shady Grove Church, and extend its right towards the 5th Corps at Parker's Store. 5th Corps at 5, to Parker's Store and extend its right to

6th Corps at Wilderness Tavern. 6th Corps to Wilderness Tavern, leaving one Div. at Germanna Fd. till Burnside had got over troops enough to hold it. Reserve Artillery to Corbin's Bridge. Trains to near Todd's Tavern. Headq'rs on Orange Plank near to 5th Corps. When in position the army will be held ready to advance. Right & left flanks to be well watched and pickets thrown well out. (Note. In the first of this order, may be seen already Sheridan's budding ambition for personal and independent distinction. He wanted to do something *separate*, though the interests of the service were plainly against the scattering of forces. The order was countermanded.)— We rode some 4½ miles and arrived at 7.10 A.M. at Old Wilderness Tavern, on the right of the road and near the Orange Pike. Here were Generals Warren & Sedgwick. The 5th Corps was marching past and the 6th was in its rear. Was greeted by Bill Thorndike, Surgeon in the 39th Mass. of Robinson's Div. Told him that Griffin reported the enemy on the Orange Pike, 2 miles west of the Germanna Plank. Wright was ordered to move S.W. from the Germanna Plank and feel for Griffin's right. 10.30 A.M. The 5th New York cavalry, holding the Orange Plank at Parker's store, has been attacked by infantry and driven in, with loss. Enemy reported at Frederickshall, south of the N. Anna (idle story).— 10.45 Getty's Div. of 6th Corps ordered to proceed at once to junction of the cross-road (continuation of the Brock Road) and the Orange Plank, and hold it. One division of Burnside reported across. All expected over by night. Headq'rs move to a piney knoll on the right of the Orange Pike and opposite the Maj. Lacy house. There was a good space of open country just here extending on both sides of the pike, though chiefly on the left; but, about a mile up the road were pine woods, wherein was Griffin's division going south along the Germanna Plank, the low woods began near the junction of the Brock cross-road with this. 12.10. Ordered to go to Gen. Getty and explain to him the position of the army and direct him to seek roads to the right and join with Crawford's left. At the beginning of the cross-road found Gen. Eustis' brigade going into the woods;—told him the orders, and he said he would send 3 regiments instead of 2, to feel to the right. Found Getty sitting on the ground, near the Plank Road, but on the cross-road. He said the whole of Hill's Corps was coming down the plank, and the skirmishers were within 300 yards. They had been fighting, and two or three bodies lay near us, and a wounded man occasionally passed. Getty told me to tell Gen. Meade that he had but 3 brigades, having been ordered to leave one behind. 12.50. Reported back at Headq'rs. Just at this moment, heavy musketry from Griffin and some apparently from Wright, also from Wadsworth on Griffin's left. It lasted, rising & falling, for about 1½ hours. 1.50. Ordered to go to 5th N.Y. Cav. & direct them, as soon as filled up with ammunition, to proceed down the Brock Road and open communication with Gen. Hancock, who was moving up. Found the regiment to the rear of the Germanna Plank; men distributing cartridges; the Colonel having somewhat cooked. Ordered him to report to Gen. Getty, as above. 2. Sent again to countermand the above order, as Hancock was nearly in junction with Getty's left. Returning to Headq'rs found the pike blocked with ambulances and with wounded on foot, who continually enquired "How far to the 5th Corps Hospital?" They were chiefly from Griffin's Div. and also many from Wadsworth's. Met Joe Hayes, supported by Dalton, and by a servant on his horse. He was talking wildly and the blood streamed down his face! A dangerous wound to look at—shot in the head. There we were three classmates together!— Helped him along till assured he had enough assistance, when left him with Dalton. 2.45. Griffin comes in, followed by his mustering officer, Geo. Barnard. He is stern & angry. Says in a loud voice that he drove back the enemy, Ewell, ¾ of a mile, but got no support on the flanks, and had to retreat—the regulars much cut up. Implies censure on Wright and apparently also on his corps commander, Warren. Wadsworth also driven back.— Rawlins got very angry, considered the language mutinous and wished him put in arrest.— Grant seemed of the same mind and asked Meade; "who is this Gen. *Gregg*? You ought to arrest him!" Meade said "It's Griffin, not Gregg; and it's only his way of talking."— Rawlins asked me what he had done; told him his reputation as an officer was good. In this charge Bartlett's brigade, the first line commanded by Hayes, broke and drove the enemy, handsomely.— Bartlett's horse was killed and he badly hurt in the head by his fall. There is little doubt that Wright made slow work in his advance. 3 P.M. Burnside ordered up. 3.15. Sent with a written order to Getty to attack (& Hancock to go in too); but to attack alone if Hancock was not ready. Delivered it at 3.25. Getty in the same spot—very cool—evidently did not think it good strategy to attack till more of the 2d Corps was up; but promptly sent aides to Eustis & Wheaton directing them to prepare at once to advance. 4.15. Ordered to take with me orderlies; report to Hancock and send back reports of progress from time to time. Reported at 4.45 to Hancock, who sat on his horse at the crossing of the Brock and Plank roads. He told me to write to Gen. Meade that it was hard to bring up troops in this wood—only part of corps up, but would do as well as he could.— All this time heavy musketry in our front and stray balls coming over. The country a "Wilderness" indeed!—a thick cover of sapplings, from 15 to 30 feet high with a close under-growth of bushes. Now rides up an officer—Maj. Mundy—"Sir! Gen. Getty is hard pressed and his ammunition nearly out"—"Tell him to hold on, & Gen. Gibbon will be up to help him!" Another officer, from the left, comes up; "Sir! Gen. Mott's division has broken, and is coming back!"—"Tell him to stop them!" roared Hancock, and galloped towards the left and began rallying the retreating troops in the Brock road. "Maj. Mitchell, go to Gen. Gibbon and tell him to come up on the double-quick!" (The bad conduct of this division of Mott's, once renowned as the 2d Division of the 3d Corps, Hooker's old command, was an instance of demoralization. Commanded successively by the dull Prince, the dancing master Carr, and by Mott, a cool, gallant man but without capacity for a large body of troops, its morale was further shaken by the breaking up of the Third Corps and its transfer to the 2d. In this, and the fights just after, its conduct was doubtless on the whole, disgraceful. When reduced to a brigade, under old McAllister, it did once more, good fighting at the Battle of Hatcher's Run &c.) Hancock rode then off to the left. I was in the "cross-road" (continuation of the Brock) when Carroll's & Hay's brigades came up, the former leading (or Hays perhaps was already there and only sent some regiments to assist.)— At any rate Carroll's men formed in the cross-road, and faced left to the front. They were blown by the double-quick. One of their Colonels said; "Now I don't want any hollering;—that's

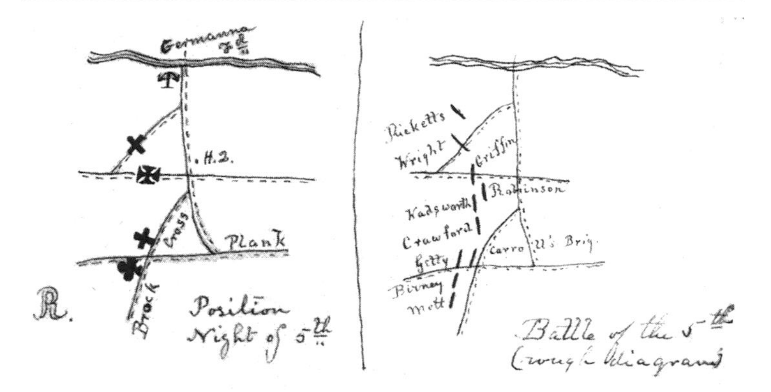

childish!"— Then, prime! Forward!— Soon after heard that Carroll was shot through the arm, and then that Hays was killed. The musketry continued, but the fresh troops had saved the day. Just as the sun was declining Gen. Hays was carried past me, on a stretcher borne on the shoulders of four men. He was shot straight through the head, but still had a mechanical respiration. At dark the fight was a drawn one; the line extending, as before, along the Brock and west of the cross-road. Portions of the 5th, 6th & 2d Corps had been opposed to Hill's & Ewell's Corps. It was after dark when got to Headq'rs, the tents being pitched in a dusty field, east of the Germanna Plank. Had frequently sent reports during the day, as ordered. Wilson's cavalry got cut off today between Parker's Store & Catharpin Road, and had to cut their way through to Sheridan. Grant ordered a general attack tomorrow at 4.30 A.M. but postponed it to 5, because they suggested Burnside would not be up till that time. "He won't be up—I know him well!" said Duane (who hates B.) and so it turned out.

May 6, Friday.

All hands up before daylight. Sunrise was at about 4.50. The General was in the saddle in the gray of the morning. As he sat in the hollow by the Germanna Plank, up comes Capt. Hutton of B's staff and says only one division was up and the road blocked with artillery (part of which was then passing us).— The General uttered some exclamation, and H said: "if you will authorize me sir, I will take the responsibility of ordering the artillery out of the road, and bring up the infantry at once."—"No Sir" said M flatly. "I have no command over Gen. Burnside." And here was the first mishap—the fight would have been better if Grant had not been there, for Meade knew B well and would have got him on the march at an earlier hour. B had been up the night before and had said "Well then my troops shall break camp by half past two." (I think)—But he had a genius of slowness. 5.15. Ordered to ride to Gen. Hancock, remain there during the day, and report back by orderlies. There was skirmishing already and, as rode down the cross road, the volleys began. Found H at join of the Brock and Plank. "Tell Gen. Meade" he cried, "we are driving them most beautifully. Birney has gone in and he is just cleaning them out beautifully." I said I was ordered to report only one division of Burnside up; but he would attack as soon as he could.—"I knew it! Just what I expected!" cried Hancock. "If he could attack *now*, we could smash A.P. Hill all to pieces!!"—The musketry was receding.—Squads of prisoners were coming in. We had taken the rifle-pits they had made in the night and now we were straightening the line, previous to pushing on. The fire therefore slackened. 6.45. Gen. Getty rode past me, in the cross-road, looking pale; to my enquiry, he said; "I am shot through the shoulder; I don't know how badly"—a man of indomitable courage and coolness!— One of his aides (the fair haired), shot through the arm, the other with his horse shot. Immortal fighting did that valiant 2d Division 6th Corps, on these two bloody days!— About 7 A.M. Webb's brigade moved up the Brock and wheeled into the plank to support Birney. Waved my hand to Abbott, as he rode past at the head of the 20th, smiling gaily. 7.45. Stevenson up with one brigade of his division, sent to reinforce Hancock. The other brigade had lost the road, but was expected soon. There was Charlie Mills, and Stevie Weld, Lt. Col. of the 56th. Told them we were driving them, and they had only to go in & finish up the rebs. 7.50 A.M. One of Barlow's brigades is to go in along the incomplete railroad cut and strike the enemy in flank. 9. Column reported coming up the Brock road and deploying skirmishers. This, in the event, proved only a lot of cavalry, but these demonstrations had a most paralysing effect on our left, and seriously affected the fight. Gibbon was stampeded and

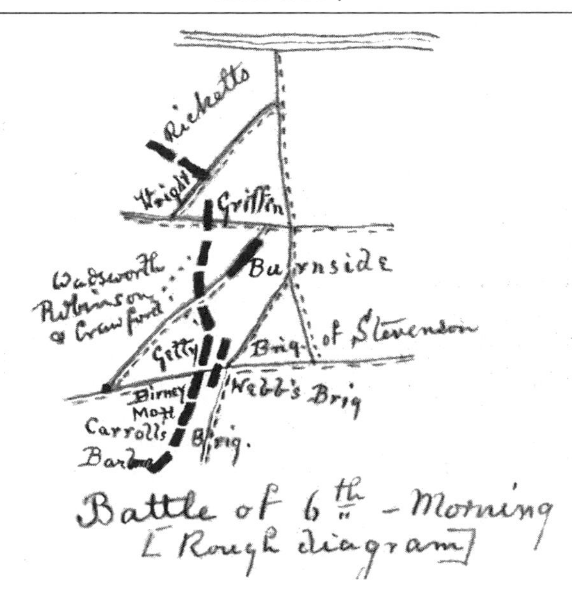

made no vigorous handling of Barlow's division and of Carroll's brigade.— Hancock complained after, that Gibbon's feeble command of the left wing of his corps changed the face of the day. 10. These rebel cavalry were beaten by ours, on the Brock road. It must have been about this time that a prisoner of *Longstreet's Corps* was brought to me! This showed the presence of these troops, who had not before been in the fight, being on the march from Orange C. H. Reported this at once to Gen. Meade.— Macy was shot through the leg about this time, the 20th being heavily engaged on the right of the plank. He told me (after) that Gen. Wadsworth was back & forth there a great deal ordering him to the *left* of the plank, whereas Webb had put him where he was. 11. Abbott mortally wounded. Maj. Angel told me he saw him lying on the line; his eyes fixed. There is a great likeness between Angel & Maj. Norval, both Staff officers of 2d Corps; the former being Engineer at Headq'rs. 11.10. The first grand break—said, by the officer who came, to be first the right of Barlow, but think it was the left of Mott. Longstreet had struck heavily there, diagonally towards the Plank (as would appear from rebel accounts).— For a long time the wounded had been coming back rapidly along the road; at one period 2 light twelves had, by order of Gen. Birney, been placed on the plank and had fired solid shot over our men. Gibbon too had opened a battery on the left, but it ceased firing on information that the shot struck in our own lines. The attack became general on the whole front. Stevenson's brigade of raw "Veterans," broke after being under a severe fire for 10 minutes. Col. Griswold of the 56th was killed. Col. Bartlett, of the 57th, wounded, Gen. Stevenson, nearly surrounded, escaped by the right. A large part of the whole line came back, slowly but mixed up—a hopeless sight! American soldiers, in this condition are enough to sink one's heart! They have no craven terror—they have their arms; but, for the moment, they will not fight, nor even rally. Drew my sword and tried to stop them, but with small success, at the partial rifle-pit that ran along the road. There was no danger, the enemy did not follow. 12. Rode in and reported the state of the case in person to Gen. Meade. Gen. Patrick went out with his brigade, and, as the stream of stragglers came up the cross-road, he stopped them in the open fields & rapidly reorganized them. Artillery had been planted on the ridge near Headq'rs pointing S.W. The General told me to remain a little. Grant, who was smoking stoically under a pine, expressed himself annoyed and surprised that Burnside did not attack, especially as Comstock was with him as engineer & staff officer, to show him the way. 1 P.M. Trains ordered to fall back towards Ely's Ford, as a precautionary measure. 1.15 (about)—Back to Hancock. He alone, in rear of Brock Road; and there he asked me to sit down under the trees, as he was very tired indeed. All his staff were away to set in order the troops. They had now constructed a tolerable rifle-pit extending along the Brock and to the head of the cross-road. He said that his troops were rallied but very tired and mixed up, and not in a condition to advance. He had given orders to have the utmost exertions put forth in putting regiments in order, but many of the field officers were killed & wounded, and it was hard. At 2 P.M. Burnside, after going almost to Parker's Store and again back, made a short attack with loud musketry. Ventured to urge Hancock (who was very pleasant & talkative) to try and attack too, but he said with much regret that it would be to hazard too much, though there was nothing in his immediate front, which had been swept by Stevenson's other brigade, which marched from left to right. He spoke highly of the commander of this brigade. There presently came a note from Gen. Meade that Burnside had attacked and taken a small breastwork, and could Hancock attack also?—Burnside's success was, after all, trifling, if anything. Potter told me (after) that his division like the rest in that corps, was mostly of raw men, that they made a very good rush at first, but were presently driven back as fast as they came. Gen. Wadsworth today was mortally wounded and left in the hands of the enemy, near the Plank Road. The attacks of Griffin and of Sedgwick's two divisions, on the right amounted to nothing. Flint saw (May '65) the place where the 6th Corps charged, and said there were no marks of very hard fighting, but on the left, along the Plank Road, there were places in front of the rebel pits, where the entire growth of saplings was cut down by musketry. Concerning this fight on the Plank Road there has been the greatest discussion between Webb's brigade, Getty's division and the division of Birney and of Wadsworth, especially the two latter. Wadsworth's people, and Cope, of Gen. Warren's staff, state that they drove back the rebels, and got a footing on the Plank Road (attacking the rebel left in that part of the field) and that one brigade swept the whole front of the 2d Corps and came out on the other side, while the 2d Corps were lying behind breastworks doing nothing! Birney's people *per contra* say that Wadsworth's attack amounted to nothing and he was driven back, though personally he came on the Plank Road and interfered with the order of battle, while they did all the successful fighting! The two accounts are entirely unreconcilable, but are not astonishing in a desperate fight in a thick cover, where no one can see 100 feet, and every one is liable to get turned round. Macy told me that, though he lost over ¼ of his men killed and wounded he *never saw a rebel*! In truth this whole Battle of the Wilderness was a scientific "bushwhack" of 200,000 men! 3.15 P.M. All being quiet got permission of Hancock to go back to 2d Corps Hospital & look after Abbott. (The hospital was some 2 miles back on a cleared farm, approachable only by a winding wood road, south of the plank. It was excellently arranged, particularly for the small means, but a ghastly sight indeed! Arms & legs lay outside the operating tents, and each table had a bleeding man on it, insensible from ether, and with the surgeons at work on him. As I entered a large tent and asked "Is Maj. Abbott here?"—"Here he is, sir," said a servant.— I should not have recognized the white face & uprolled eyes! He was unconscious and dying fast. Lifted Macy up, and we stood there till he was gone—Macy shedding tears. Took his valuables in charge and a lock of his hair, and got the promise that his body should go home, if possible.— In the embalming place (a negro house) there lay already the body of a Captain of Infantry; the assistant had just cut down on the femoral artery.) Abbott died about 4. As was riding again towards the front, about 4.30, the artillery on Gibbon's left suddenly opened heavily, followed by a sharp musketry. Immediately rode up the Germanna Plank to Gen. Meade, reported the fact and asked if he could not get Burnside ordered in to attack and help Hancock. In spite of this Gen. Meade seemed sceptical of the severity of the attack. Burnside did of his own accord, put in a division, with good effect. "The best thing old Burn' did during the day," said the General afterwards. 5.20 P.M. Rode back to join Gen. H but on the road met Maj. Hancock (I think) who said the enemy had broken through at the plank, and there was no communication with the left wing! Found Birney in the cross-road, and he said the same; upon which sent back a note which stampeded the General. All wrong on Birney's part—along came Saunders (I believe) & we rode together down the road & found all open, and that the enemy had only broken through in one small place, but had been driven out, leaving over 50 dead on that spot. Presently found Hancock and remained till about sunset with him. 7 P.M. While at dinner heard a little scattered musketry and presently up gallops Capt. Beaumont, followed by Lt. Col. Kent—in great flurry, saying the 6th Corps was broken and driven back, the enemy on the Germanna Plank & Orange Pike, and that we had better look out not to be captured. They both were quite out of their heads. "And where" said Gen. M calmly, are Upton's & Shaler's brigades, that Sedgwick said he could spare me, this morning?"—"I don't know Sir."— "Do you mean to tell me that the 6th Corps is not to do any more fighting this campaign?"—"I am fearful not Sir!" quoth

Kent. Orders were sent at once for the Pennsylvania Reserves to move to the support, by the Germanna Plank. There were the wildest reports that Gen. Sedgwick was taken &c. &c. Capt. Cadwalader who rode up the plank towards Germanna Ford, was fired on, sure enough, by some rebs! About 7.30 P.M. Ordered to take over a statement of the case to Gen. Grant, in the hollow hard by. He seemed more disturbed than Meade about it, and they afterwards consulted together. In truth they (the enemy) had no idea of their success. They made a dash with Edw. Johnson's division about dusk, or somewhat before, and surprised completely Ricketts' shaky division, which fled at once; but most, or the whole of the first division (and perhaps part of the 3d) stood firm; and the rebels were more than content to get Gens. Seymour & Shaler, and some other prisoners, and a lot of muskets & camp equipage. In consequence of this mishap the right was ordered swung back, so as to slant towards Germanna Plank. That poor 93d N.Y.—the "bloodless," so long the headquarter guard, even from McClellan's day! Today they went in and are bloody enough now; 15 or 16 officers hit in these two days, and men in proportion. Lost my sword today from its scabbard, while galloping in the woods. Some means should be devised to hold in the swords of mounted officers, the number lost is very great. Col. Walker found it & gave it to me; he, by the way, had lost his. Old Washburn, senator & the great friend of Grant, is a companion of the campaign. He came down entirely confident that Grant would at once swallow and annihilate Lee; but he wears another face now! Griffin lost a couple of guns yesterday.— We took some colors today. Grant told Meade that Joe Johnston would have retreated after two such days' punishment. He recognizes the difference of the Western rebel fighting. During this day Sheridan defended our flanks & rear, with considerable fighting.

May 7, Saturday.

When we rose this morn we were pretty uncertain what the enemy was about, whether working on our flanks, or fallen back, or stationary.—All was quiet.— 5 A.M. Ferrero's negro div. of the 9th Corps was up and massed in a hollow in the direction of the Lacy house. It made me sad to see them.—Can

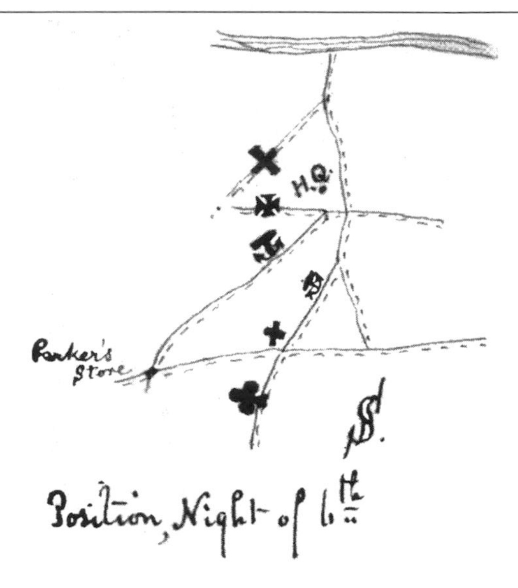

we not fight our own battles? The General rode through them on his way to Grant. 5.30. Ordered, to write to Gen. Sedgwick and direct him to hold all the ground the enemy would let him; and keep his cavalry & pickets well out. 9. Hancock reports nothing in his immediate front; Wright, from the other wing, reports nothing just in front of him, apparently. Warren reports a force in his front, though perhaps fallen back. 10. Warren sends out a reconnaissance of 1,000 men along the pike, from Griffin.—Heavy skirmish in that direction, and some artillery. 10.45 Ordered to ride out to Griffin and ask the result of the reconnaissance. Rode out to our breastworks on the pike, and found our artillery firing in the road and the enemy firing back, though rather wildly, for the most part. Some shooting in the heavy pine woods in front. There were a good many deep hollows hereabout, quite hilly as compared with the plank-road. Did not find Griffin, but Capt. Martin, his Chief of Artillery, told me the result of the reconnaissance was not yet reported. Rode to the left, then to the rear to Gen. Warren's Headq'rs where stopped and sent a written report to our Headq'rs. Two or three shells fell in the hollow hard by; the place was the Lacy house. 2 P.M. Had returned to

Headq'rs.—Meade in an ill humor, had read what Warren sent—"the enemy's shells fall near my Headquarters."—"Well, can't I see that? What's *that* to do with it?" says the General. Was rejoiced & surprised to find tent-mate "Rosie," who had ridden across country, all the way from Rappahannock Station, in company of Mr. Dana, Assist. Sec. of War, a large man, a combination of scholar and newspaper editor, with a dab of amiability, a large dab of conceit, and another large dab of ultraism. He was to be another civil companion of Grant. Rosie was equipped, from Washington, with what we supposed to be a huge field-glass, but which turned out to be a large case-bottle, which banged his ribs whenever he galloped! A scout was now to go through to Rappahannock. Sent (through McGregor, correspondent of the Associated Press) by his hand a telegram to Mimi. 3. The 22d N.Y. Cav., somewhere by Germanna ford, got a shell thrown at them and rushed in wild confusion down the road, led off by the Colonel, an abominable coward and scoundrel. The regiment itself was raw. Meade arrested him and put the Major in his place, remarking tartly, "I don't believe he's a bit better!" Wounded ordered sent to Rappahannock Station. Butler yesterday occupied suddenly City Point. Went into a hollow behind our knoll, where was a field hospital. There were some rebel wounded there lying. They were loading the wounded in ambulances, to go north, only leaving a few very badly hurt. Now however, came notice that the rebel infantry and cavalry were advancing along the river bank, to occupy all the fords, including Ely's. The cavalry officer who sent this in ought to have been shot! The force the enemy sent along there is pretty known now to have been most trifling and nothing prevented us from driving them off. Alas! for the poor wounded! The train of them was already far on its way, when Gen. Meade had to send word to halt, and subsequently to face it towards Fredericksburg. What delay & suffering! How many men whose vital force was just sufficient to have brought them safely to Washington, were killed by this protraction of their trials! This day Sheridan concentrated near Todd's Tavern and attacked and severely beat Stuart's cavalry. The order of march for eve of May 7th. Reserve Artillery at 7 P.M. via Chancellorsville and Aldrich's to crossing of Alsop and Piney Branch Church roads, 5th Corps to Spottsylvania C.H., via Brock road and by Todd's Tavern. 6th Corps by pike & plank to Chancellorsville and escort trains to cross of Piney Branch & Block house roads. 9th Corps follow 6th. 2d follows 5th to Todd's Tavern. As Grant sat under a pine tree, he said, in his short way: "Tonight Lee will be retreating south!" This showed that he did not yet fully take in Lee's obstinacy & the goodness of his army. Although his remark about Johnston showed that he already began to appreciate them. At 8.45 P.M. we left Headquarters. All the afternoon there had been commotion among the baggage waggons, and the heavy artillery were moving too. The dust was in fine clouds as we rode down the cross-road and halted at Hancock's near the junction of the plank. The General bade us ride on and stop for him at Gibbon's whom we found on the Brock, at a little house. It was a picturesque sight the infantry closely huddled asleep, under the breastwork that followed the road. On top it and outside were sentries with their muskets ready. The officers paced up and down; all were prepared for instant action. We got some iced water from Gibbon, and lay down to take a nap in the dust. By & bye came the General, with a following of all that cavalry of Gen. Patrick's, which raised such a dust as well nigh to suffocate us. We rode on by the Brock road; then got wrong, in passing some batteries in position; then got straight again. The General told me to make the cavalry in rear go ahead of us; which did, at expense of tearing my blouse to pieces, for the road was narrow with woods each side and was full of cavalry. Could see nobody, so dark was it. At last we struck a cavalry outpost, and, soon after, got to Todd's Tavern, at the crossing of the roads. It is an ordinary old building, of moderate size. There were some women & negroes there. Gen. Gregg came out to welcome us. They have had successful fighting round here for 3 days.

“THE DISASTER CAME”: VIRGINIA, MAY 1864

Wilbur Fisk to The Green Mountain Freeman

Wilbur Fisk served in the 2nd Vermont Infantry, one of five Vermont regiments that made up the Second Brigade, Second Division, Sixth Corps. On May 5 his division, led by Brigadier General George W. Getty, was ordered to occupy and hold the junction of the Brock Road and the Orange Plank Road. In the fighting that followed, the 2nd Vermont, which had crossed the Rapidan with about 700 men in its ranks, lost 297 men killed, wounded, or missing.

On the Battle-Field
May 9, 1864

I presume you have heard, before this, all the incidents worth relating of the present bloody campaign, so that any further account will be only a repetition of the same or similar scenes, such as we all have witnessed. Being one of that fortunate number that lives to "tell the tale," I am inclined, however, to run the risk and do so, though so completely worn out and exhausted as I find myself to-day, I should give a very tame account of what I have seen and experienced, for I have hardly life enough left to tell where I have been or what I have seen. Of course, no one of us can give much of an account of anything that has happened beyond his own range of vision, for it is difficult to get much of an idea beyond that ourselves.

On the morning of the 4th of May we left our old camp at early dawn, and took the war path once more. The morning was bright and clear, the air cool and refreshing, as we bid adieu to our winter's home, and started on what we knew to be the most perilous campaign of the war. We took the same line of march that we did last fall, marching direct to Germanna Ford, and halting for the night two or three miles beyond.

At daylight next morning we took the plank road, and marched out to its junction with the plank road that runs from

Fredericksburg to Gordonsville. We saw nothing of the enemy, and heard nothing of them until just before we reached the latter point, when our column unexpectedly came up on a column of rebel troops coming this way. After a little skirmishing, the rebels fell back. Here was a high point of land where the roads cross at right angles, and it is in the midst of an endless wilderness—"a wilderness of woe," as the boys call it. The troops massed in here in considerable numbers, and after some moments got into working order. Our regiment crossed the Fredericksburg road, and filed into the woods with other troops in line in our rear and front. Pretty soon the order came to advance. We marched in line of battle on the left side of the Fredericksburg road, in the same direction that the road runs, and we soon came upon the enemy. There was one line ahead of us. We followed close to them, and were equally exposed. The rebels gave us a warm reception. They poured their bullets into us so fast that we had to lie down to load and fire. The front line gave way, and we were obliged to take their places. We were under their fire over three hours, before we were relieved. We were close on to them, and their fire was terribly effective. Our regiment lost 264 men in killed and wounded. Just a little to the rear of where our line was formed, where the bullets swept close to the ground, every bush and twig was cut and splintered by the leaden balls. The woods was a dense thicket of small trees about the size of hop poles, and they stood three times as numerous as they are usually set in a hop yard; but along the whole length of the line I doubt if a single tree could have been found that had not been pierced several times with bullets, and all were hit about breast high. Had the rebels fired a little lower, they would have annihilated the whole line; they nearly did it as it was. Our Colonel was killed, our Lieut. Colonel and acting Major wounded, and only three captains were with us after the fight. We all had our hairbreadth escapes to tell of. My propensity for boasting has already been discovered. I could say that I had a bullet pass through my clothes on each side, one of them giving me a pretty smart rap, and one ball split the crown of my cap into two, knocking it off my head as neatly as it could have been done by the most scientific boxer.

Another line marched up to take our places, and we fell back to the road and that night we threw up breastworks the best we could, considering that we had to dig among roots and stumps with but few tools and poor ones at that. The firing stopped at dark without our having gained an inch on the enemy. We were called up in the morning before light. Our hours of sleep were few and brief. At half past four o'clock we were ordered to advance into the same place again. There were pale and anxious faces in our regiment when that order was given. We had had very insufficient rest for the two nights previous, and the terrible nervous exhaustion of fighting had left us in hardly a fit condition to endure another such an ordeal so soon. There was so many men missing from our number that it hardly seemed like the same regiment. But the order was forward, and I do not know that a single man failed to take his place. We advanced directly down to the same place where we fought the day before. Our dead comrades lay on the ground, just as they had fallen, many of whom we recognized. We would gladly have fallen out to give them a decent burial, but we had no time to think of that. We drove the enemy this time and captured some prisoners. The prisoners were mostly North Carolinians, and some of them came into our lines swinging their hats and saying "the tar heels wouldn't stand that morning!" We advanced about a mile and a half, I should think, when our left flank was furiously attacked and a division of the Second Corps miserably gave way, leaving us in a most perilous and exposed position. We were in the point of the letter V, and the rebels were fast closing up the sides. On they came, double quick, elated with the prospect of capturing a fine lot of Yankees. I do not know how well they succeeded. My legs saved me abundantly. We had to leave our dead and wounded, and without much ceremony, or order retreat out of that place, leaving all that we had gained in the hands of the enemy. The front lines became considerably disorganized, but the rear lines held the enemy in check. Oh how discouraging it is to lose ground before the enemy. So much hard fighting, and so many killed and wounded for nothing. We had lost over fifty men in this fight. One of my comrades was shot dead there. I was lying at the time as close to the ground as I could to load and fire, while he, less timid than myself, had raised himself up, and was loading and firing as fast as possible. The ball struck near his heart. He exclaimed, I am killed and attempted to step to the rear, but fell on to me and immediately died. Just then we were obliged to retreat, and leave him where he fell. He was a new recruit but he had shown himself to be a brave soldier. He gave his life for his country, and those of us that have served the longest can do no more.

There was considerable disorder and confusion in our hasty retreat, and the regiment was more or less broken up. There was no chance for us when the left gave away but to run or be taken prisoner. We were between two fires, and the enemy had every advantage. The road was to be the rallying point in case of disaster. The disaster came, and every man that had good legs was in duty bound to use them. I found myself with a squad belonging to the division that broke and caused the defeat—decidedly bad company to be in. Some of their officers drew their swords and revolvers and tried their utmost to rally them again. They might as well have appealed to the winds. When I got back to the road there was considerable excitement. Generals and their aides were giving and carrying orders in all directions. They thought the enemy were coming in overwhelming force. I had got among a lot of stragglers, and I began to consider myself a straggler, too. At any rate I was shamelessly demoralized. I didn't know where my regiment had gone to, and to be candid about it, I didn't care. I was tired almost to death, and as hungry as a wolf. I had been fighting to the best of my ability for Uncle Sam's Constitution, and now I thought it of about as much importance to me individually, to pay a little attention to my own. They tried to halt us at the first line of breastworks, but I saw fresh troops coming that hadn't been in the fight at all, and I thought they might as well hold the line as me. My object was to find a safe place in the rear, and in spite of revolvers, or swords, entreaties, or persuasions, I found it. A Colonel's horse stepped on my foot and crushed off my shoe, and being barefooted, and lame, of course, I had but little difficulty in accomplishing my purpose. I should have been ashamed of such conduct at any other time, but just then all I thought of was a cup of coffee, and a dinner of hard tack. The regiment might have been ordered into another battle, and every man of them been killed, and I shouldn't have been ashamed that I wasn't with them. My patriotism was well nigh used up, and so was I, till I had had some refreshments. I made a deep impression on my haversack, which nourished my fighting qualities so that I could return to my regiment. I found the regiment had moved to the right, a little on the line, and were stationed behind a rude breastwork preparing to defend it against an attack from the enemy, which was momentarily expected. No serious attack, however, was made directly in our front, but to the left, where we advanced in the first place, they tried to break our lines and they tried it hard. They charged clear up to the breastwork, and fairly planted the colors on the top of it, but they did not live to hold them there long. The ground in front of the works was literally covered with the rebel dead after they left. One Colonel lay dead clear up to the breastwork. Two were shot on the top of the breastwork, and fell over on our side. I believe I have never heard such a murderous roar of musketry as was made to repel that charge. The rebels fell back and did not renew the attack.

The next day there was no fighting of any consequence. I was on picket. The picket line was advanced farther out than we had been before. We discovered nothing but a few sharpshooters who retreated as we advanced, until we came upon their line of breastworks. They opened on us with artillery, and having no support we had to fall back. We had been assigned to the second Corps, under General Hancock, during this fighting, and that afternoon we went back to our own Corps.

Such is an off-hand description of what we did during the first few days of this campaign. How much we have accomplished, I cannot tell. You never need to ask a private soldier for general information. He is the last man to get that. His circle of observation is very limited. He sees but little of what is going on, and takes a part in still less. I have told what I saw, which you will please take for what it is worth. If Providence spares my life, and the rebels don't pick me off, I hope before many days to be able to chronicle a decided and glorious victory here.

"ANOTHER STRUGGLE WITH DEATH": VIRGINIA, MAY 1864

J.F.J. Caldwell: from The History of a Brigade of South Carolinians

When Lee learned on May 4 that Grant was crossing the Rapidan, he ordered his infantry corps commanders, Richard Ewell, A. P. Hill, and James Longstreet, to march east from their camps around Orange Court House and Gordonsville. The next morning Lee decided to engage Grant's army before it could move through the Wilderness. He directed Ewell to continue his advance along the Orange Turnpike and Hill to move along the Orange Plank Road three miles to the south, hoping that they would be able to hold the Union forces in position long enough for James Longstreet to attack Grant's open left flank from the south. Lieutenant James F. J. Caldwell served in Company B of the 1st South Carolina Infantry in McGowan's Brigade, which was assigned to Wilcox's Division in A. P. Hill's Third Corps. On the afternoon of May 5 the brigade was posted to the Chewning farm, about a mile from the Orange Plank Road, shortly before Union forces (including Wilbur Fisk and the 2nd Vermont Infantry) counterattacked Hill's advance troops. Caldwell wrote about the fighting that followed in an 1866 brigade history.

About 4 o'clock P. M., when we arrived at Wilderness run, we heard a rambling skirmish fire in front, not far off. We filed to the left and passed through an open field. There were several pieces of artillery here, and near them General Lee and General Stuart, on foot. The battle was evidently not distant, but we flattered ourselves that it was *rather* late in the day for much to be done towards a general engagement. We were carried nearly a mile farther, through a body of woods, and halted on a clear, commanding ridge. Having been marching right in front, we were countermarched by regiments, so as to face the enemy by the front rank. Ewell's corps was engaged at some distance on our left. Rev. Mr. Mullaly, chaplain of Orr's regiment of Rifles, held prayers with his regiment. It was one of the most impressive scenes I ever witnessed. On the left thundered the dull battle; on the right the sharp crack of rifles gradually swelled to equal importance; above was the blue, placid heavens; around us a varied landscape of forest and fields, green with the earliest foliage of spring; and here knelt hirsute and browned veterans shriving for another struggle with death.

In the midst of the prayer, a harsh, rapid fire broke out right on the plank-road we had left; the order was issued to face about and forward; and then we went, sometimes in quick-time, sometimes at the double-quick, towards the constantly increasing battle. The roar of muskets became continuous, augmented occasionally by the report of cannon, and always by the ringing rebel cheer. Heth's division, the only one at this point, was engaged, and we knew that we were going to reinforce them. Just as we reached the plank-road, two or three shell fell among us, but I believe no one was struck in the brigade. The road was crowded with non-combatants, artillery and ordnance wagons. Here and there lay a dead man. The firing in front waxed fiercer, if possible, than ever. The First regiment lead the march. They, with the Rifles, were filed across the road and fronted. The three remaining regiments were formed with their right resting on the road. The following was the order of arrangement, from right to left: First regiment, Orr's Rifles, on the right of the road; Twelfth regiment, Thirteenth regiment, Fourteenth regiment, on the left of the road.

Lane's and Thomas's brigades had been left about the position which I have just described, on the left of and near a mile from the plank-road. We entered the conflict alone. As soon as the line was formed and dressed, the order to advance was given. Balls fired at Heth's division, in front of us, fell among us at the beginning of our advance. We pressed on, guide left, through the thick undergrowth, until we reached Heth's line, now much thinned and exhausted. We had very imprudently begun to cheer before this. We passed over this line cheering. There was no use of this. We should have charged without uttering a word until within a few yards of the Federal line. As it was, we drew upon ourselves a terrific volley of musketry. The advance was greatly impeded by the matted growth of saplings and bushes, and in the delay a scattering fire commenced along our line. The fighting of the brigade cannot be described, as a whole, from this time.

The pressure was greatest on the right of the brigade; for, in addition to the worst conceivable ground for marching, and the demoralizing spectacle of another division lying down, and, after we had passed them, firing through our ranks, the enemy's line extended far to the right of ours. The first regiment was the extreme right regiment on this part of the Confederate line. All idea of a charge had to be abandoned. The First and Rifle regiments halted, and set to firing industriously. The Rifles suffered a peculiar disadvantage in halting upon high ground where the enemy's balls told fearfully. So great indeed was the slaughter that followed the first round or two, that they were forced to retire for a time. The First regiment was now entirely alone. There were no troops, as I said before, on the right of them, on the same line, and on the left was the gap left by at least four hundred men—at least one hundred and fifty yards. The fire of the enemy was not very accurate at first, being much too high; but after a time it became fatally close. Many a life must have been saved by the dense growth of oak saplings. Scarcely a man in that regiment but was struck by a ball during the evening. Lieut. Col. Shooter commanded this regiment with singular gallantry and composure, fighting for an hour everything that could be brought against him.

On the left of the road the advance was carried farther than on the right. It must be admitted, in justice to the regiments on the right, that the fire on the left was not so heavy, at the outset, as that they met. The three regiments pushed forward intrepidly. The Twelfth behaved with their accustomed gallantry. They continued the advance, until they broke the enemy's line, which they followed up, killing large numbers and capturing more. Their charge was too impetuous, if anything. They pushed ahead until they lost the connection with the rest of the brigade, and found themselves almost entirely surrounded by the enemy. They captured, among other prisoners, a brigadier-general, whose sword a friend of mine has to this day. Finding themselves thus outflanked by their own exertions, they faced about, put their prisoners before them, and drove back for our line. They succeeded in cutting out, with a small loss. The two remaining regiments, the Thirteenth and

Fourteenth, continued the advance, though less rapidly, until the fire of the enemy became so severe on their left, (where there were no troops of ours at this time,) that Gen. McGowan deemed it necessary to withdraw the whole brigade a short distance to the rear. Capt. L. C. Haskell and Lieut. G. A. Wardlaw had their horses shot under them. Our loss was heavy.

Orr's regiment of Rifles returned to the attack on the right of the road, but it and the First regiment had to be withdrawn somewhat, for the want of troops on their right. Scales' brigade was sent in to assist them, but they never reached the point of our extreme advance; so that the enemy almost enfiladed the line of these two regiments.

Now the pressure became fearful on both flanks. Our line (I mean the Confederate line) was, as I have once or twice said, miserably short. For a time, we had a front of but a single brigade. I do not judge any one; but I think it was the shortest, most huddled, most ineffective line-of-battle I ever saw. But for the gallantry of our troops, which even surpassed itself, all must have been lost. The balls of the enemy, at one point, crossed the road from each side. Still they pressed on us, filling the air with shouts and the roll of arms, and sweeping the woods with balls. At one time they drove so furiously on the right of the road, that men had to be ranged *along* the road to keep them back, or, rather, to support the meagre line that held them in check. On the extreme left, the pressure was considerably relieved by the putting in of Thomas's brigade. Still a great gap was open on his left, which skirmishers had to be thrown out to protect. It began to look like every man would have to be his own general. The open space on the left, and the presence of artillery on the eminence I before described as the place we met Lee and Stuart, deterred the Federals from any determined advance, otherwise so easily made.

Our whole brigade, after the establishment of Scales' brigade on the right, was moved to the left of the road, where they fought until night. A portion of us went to the extreme left and remained with Thomas's brigade, while the rest occupied a position rather farther back and resting on the road.

Of course, there was some confusion in the command. The difficulties were even greater than I have been able to describe—greater than any one, who has not fought in such a place, can at all understand. Such woods, if you have one line which is to remain stationary and on the defence, are an advantage; but if you attack, (as we always did by countercharge, if not by the first charge,) or if you must relieve one line with another, it is the worst place in the world. It is impossible to keep even a regiment well dressed. Then the enemy open fire on you. Some men will invariably return this fire. Gradually all join in it; and once the whole roar of battle opens, there is an end of unison of action. We did remarkably well. I could not see anything distinctly, on account of the bushes, the smoke of our line and that of the Federal; but other men professed to see the enemy constantly relieving. It has been currently stated, on our side, that two corps and two divisions were engaged on the part of the Federals. We had the two smallest divisions in Lee's army to meet them.

Night came at last, putting an end to actual battle, but, in fact, increasing the confusion and danger of the scene. It was confidently expected that Longstreet, with Kershaw's, Field's, and Anderson's divisions, would relieve us by daylight; and therefore it was not considered necessary to re-form the lines. Besides, the nature of the ground, the intense darkness, and the close proximity of the enemy, rendered it almost impracticable. Moreover, certain persons, high in office, decided that Grant would not renew the attack in the morning!

We lay upon our arms—a portion of the brigade out with Gen. Thomas, on the left and at the extreme front, the larger part with Gen. McGowan, on the plank-road. There was occasional firing among the pickets, but the enemy did not venture upon an attack. Rations of bacon and "hard tack" were issued to us after a fashion.

The night passed and the morning came; still no Blucher. At dawn, General McGowan formed the brigade on the left of the road, about where we had commenced the charge the day before. This was the 6th of May.

Our right rested on the road; Thomas's brigade was immediately on the right of the road. A part of his command had spent the night there, the rest were joined with them at daylight. The line of our brigade struck the road at an acute angle, making a salient with Thomas's brigade. Besides the latter brigade, there were no troops in line on the right of the road, as far as I have been able to learn, except, perhaps, Scales' brigade. Lane's brigade was not disposed, and Heth's division lay—I know not how, but not in line of battle, if all I have heard is correct. *We had reckoned too confidently on the coming of the War Horse!*

Longstreet was early on the way. He had been despatched to execute a grand movement on the left flank of the enemy, as Ewell had done the day before on his right. Longstreet had had to march from Gordonsville, which, of course, delayed him; and then he was recalled when on his way around Grant's left, which must delay his coming to us still more. Indeed, he did well to reach us when he did. But more of this hereafter.

The enemy moved upon us in full force, at sunrise. Our battalion of sharpshooters were deployed as skirmishers, in our front. The Twelfth regiment occupied the right of the brigade, the Fourteenth was next them, the First next them, the Thirteenth next them. Orr's Rifles were disconnected from us and on the extreme left.

The enemy moved up carefully, without noise or disorder. They first engaged our sharpshooters. The latter, though unavoidably, were in the worst position possible, being in a ravine between the elevation over which the enemy approached and the eminence we occupied. They retired slowly on the main line of battle. In the mean time, the Federals advanced along the right side of the road, on Thomas's brigade. For some reason or other, that brigade broke. The enemy may have struck their flank, or overlapped them, or they may not have been well in line. At all events, they gave way, at a distance on the right of the road. The first intimation we had of the state of affairs was the mass of disorganized men who rushed up the road. The enemy, naturally, pushed forward. Soon no troops were left to oppose their advance on that side of the road. The angle made by our lines on each side of the road being a salient, the enemy, by pressing in, came almost square upon the flank of McGowan's brigade. The Twelfth regiment stood firm in spite of the panic on their right, until the Federal line swept up to them, and not only enfiladed them, but threatened to cut them off from the rear. The regiment was even called upon to surrender, but it replied by firing on the confident enemy.

The enemy now advanced in front as well as on the right flank. The pressure was irresistible. The Twelfth regiment doubled back and retired. The movement continued up the line until all the regiments of the brigade, except the Rifles, (who were on the extreme left and disconnected from us,) gave way. There was no panic and no great haste; the men seemed to fall back from a deliberate conviction that it was impossible to hold the ground, and, of course, foolish to attempt it. It was mortifying, but it was only what every veteran has experienced.

We retired upon Poagne's artillery, which was in position, with a low temporary breastwork in front, on the summit of the open hill, about two hundred yards in rear of our original line. Here the brigade was halted at once and reformed along the line of the artillery. General Lee and General Hill were here, evidently excited and chagrined. The former expressed himself rather roughly to us, especially to us unfortunate file-closers; but I am not sure but his anger implied a sort of compliment to our past performances. But let that pass.

We were now informed that Lieutenant-General Longstreet was near at hand, with 25,000 fresh men. This was good matter to rally on. We were marched to the plank-road by special order of General Hill; but, just as we were crossing it, we received an order to return to the left. We saw General Longstreet riding down the road towards us, followed by his column of troops. The fire of the enemy, of late rather scattering, now became fierce and incessant, and we could hear a reply to it from our side. Kershaw's South Carolina brigade, of McLaws', afterwards Kershaw's division, had met them. The fire on both sides of the road increased to a continuous roar. Kershaw's brigade was extended across the road, and received the grand charge of the Federals. Members of that brigade have told me that the enemy rushed upon them at the double-quick, huzzahing loudly. The woods were filled with Confederate fugitives. Three brigades, of Wilcox's division, and all of Heth's, were driven more or less rapidly, crowded together in hopeless disorder, and only to be wondered at, when any of them attempted to make a stand.

Yet Kershaw's brigade bore themselves with illustrious gallantry. Some of the regiments had not only to deploy under fire, but, when they were formed, to force their way through crowds of flying men, and re-establish their line. They met Grant's legions, opened a cool and murderous fire upon them, and continued it so steadily and resolutely that the latter were compelled to give back. Here, I honestly believe, the Army of Northern Virginia was saved! That brigade sustained a heavy loss, beginning with many patient, gallant spirits in the ranks and culminating in Nance, Galliard and Doby.

The bulk of Longstreet's three divisions was now thrown into action. The enemy checked, they charged them, and followed up the advantage, until they drove them far through the wilderness of woods. The principal contest was just along the plank-road. Poagne's artillery, on the left of the road, had a few shots at the enemy, but these soon retired before the well-directed canister. At this place it was that General Lee put himself at the head of a brigade, to lead the charge. He was finally induced to return to the rear, the men imploring him to go back, as they could do all the fighting without him. The charge was gallantly pushed by Longstreet's line, the old ground was retrieved, and the Federals crowded up in most distressing perplexity. General Longstreet was, unfortunately, wounded, just as the tide of victory fairly set in in our favor. Brigadier-General Jenkins, of South Carolina, was killed at the same time.

McGowan's brigade was moved to the left, to the position first occupied by us the evening before, in an open field, about a mile from the road. As we filed out of the woods into this field, our sharpshooters, who were deployed as skirmishers on the right flank, saw and opened upon the skirmishers of the enemy. We were soon fronted and ordered to cross the field and occupy the ridge, some two or three hundred yards distant. We did so, at the double-quick, cheering as we went. The skirmishers of the enemy gave way at once before us. We halted on the ridge designated, expecting to receive the fire of a Federal line of battle, but they did not advance upon us. A scattering fire was kept up by them from the jungle below, and a few casualties resulted in our ranks, but this seemed quite unimportant after the last eighteen hours' work. We were, after a few minutes, retired a hundred or two hundred yards, where we piled up rails for breastworks, and lay during the remainder of the day.

The firing and cheering continued on the right, in the

direction of the plank-road. Both armies were crowding all their energies there. On the left, Ewell was still bending back Grant's right wing, and the firing indicated considerable earnestness on both sides; but the great tumult was along Longstreet's line, and we could see columns of troops moved from Grant's right to re-inforce that point. The artillery posted with us amused themselves by firing into these columns, at long range, and scattering them with shell. We were not disturbed—our position was too strong. It would have been a great relief to chastise somebody in reparation of our morning's misfortune.

We lay quiet for the rest of that day and night. On the afternoon of the next day, the 7th, we were moved to the woods in our front, thereby shortening our line a good deal. There was no fighting, this day, on any part of the line. Fires swept the forests for miles around, obscuring the sun with smoke, and filling the air with stench. We were ordered to erect defences; but we had scarcely begun to collect rails and logs of wood, when we were ordered to desist. At dusk we were ordered to prepare for the march.

We were moved a few hundred yards to the right, and there rested until morning. While we were closing up here, a pace at a time, the grandest vocal exhibition took place that I have ever heard. Far up on the right of the Confederate line a shout was raised. Gradually it was taken up and passed down, until it reached us. We lifted it, as our turn came, and handed it to the left, where it went echoing to the remotest corner of Ewell's corps. This was done once with powerful effect. Then rumors of various things, but always speaking of good fortune that had befallen the Confederates, sped along the line with characteristic swiftness. Again the shout arose on the right—again it rushed down upon us from a distance of perhaps two miles—again we caught it and flung it joyously to the left, where it only ceased when the last post had huzzahed. And yet a third time this mighty wave of sound rang along the Confederate lines. The effect was beyond expression. It seemed to fill every heart with new life, to inspire every nerve with might never known before. Men seemed fairly convulsed with the fierce enthusiasm; and I believe that if at that instant the advance of the whole army upon Grant could have been ordered, we should have swept it into the very Rappahannock. As it was, there was a story prevalent, next day, of the stampeding of a Federal corps. I doubt the entire accuracy of the account; but I know that we gathered an immense amount of private plunder on our front.

Horace Porter: from Campaigning with Grant

By nightfall on May 6 the battle of the Wilderness had ended in a stalemate, and on May 7 the opposing armies skirmished while for the most part remaining behind hastily built earthworks. Union losses in the Wilderness were reported as 17,666 men killed, wounded, or missing, while Confederate casualties are estimated to have totaled about 11,000. The Union casualties exceeded those of the battle of Chancellorsville in May 1863, which had ended with the Army of the Potomac under Joseph Hooker retreating across the Rappahannock River. Determined to continue the campaign until Lee was defeated, Grant issued orders on the morning of May 7 for the army to march that night to the crossroads at Spotsylvania Court House, ten miles to the southeast. Lieutenant Colonel Horace Porter was a West Point graduate who had joined Grant's staff in April 1864. He recalled the beginning of the march to Spotsylvania in an 1897 memoir.

All preparations for the night march had now been completed. The wagon-trains were to move at 4 P.M., so as to get a start of the infantry, and then go into park and let the troops pass them. The cavalry had been thrown out in advance; the infantry began the march at 8:30 P.M. Warren was to proceed along the Brock road toward Spottsylvania Court-house, moving by the rear of Hancock, whose corps was to remain in its position during the night to guard against a possible attack by the enemy, and afterward to follow Warren. Sedgwick was to move by way of Chancellorsville and Piney Branch Church. Burnside was to follow Sedgwick, and to cover the trains which moved on the roads that were farthest from the enemy.

Soon after dark, Generals Grant and Meade, accompanied by their staffs, after having given personal supervision to the starting of the march, rode along the Brock road toward Hancock's headquarters, with the intention of waiting there till Warren's troops should reach that point. While moving close to Hancock's line, there occurred an unexpected demonstration on the part of the troops, which created one of the most memorable scenes of the campaign. Notwithstanding the darkness of the night, the form of the commander was recognized, and word was passed rapidly along that the chief who had led them through the mazes of the Wilderness was again moving forward with his horse's head turned toward Richmond. Troops know but little about what is going on in a large army, except the occurrences which take place in their immediate vicinity; but this night ride of the general-in-chief told plainly the story of success, and gave each man to understand that the cry was to be "On to Richmond!" Soldiers weary and sleepy after their long battle, with stiffened limbs and smarting wounds, now sprang to their feet, forgetful of their pains, and rushed forward to the roadside. Wild cheers echoed through the forest, and glad shouts of triumph rent the air. Men swung their hats, tossed up their arms, and pressed forward to within touch of their chief, clapping their hands, and speaking to him with the familiarity of comrades. Pine-knots and leaves were set on fire, and lighted the scene with their weird, flickering glare. The night march had become a triumphal procession for the new commander. The demonstration was the emphatic verdict pronounced by the troops upon his first battle in the East. The excitement had been imparted to the horses, which soon became restive, and even the general's large bay, over which he possessed ordinarily such perfect control, became difficult to manage. Instead of being elated by this significant ovation, the general, thoughtful only of the practical question of the success of the movement, said: "This is most unfortunate. The sound will reach the ears of the enemy, and I fear it may reveal our movement." By his direction, staff-officers rode forward and urged the men to keep quiet so as not to attract the enemy's attention; but the demonstration did not really cease until the general was out of sight.

Herman Melville: The Armies of the Wilderness

"The Armies of the Wilderness" first appeared in *Battle-Pieces and Aspects of the War*, published in August 1866. In an endnote in *Battle-Pieces* to the poem "Chattanooga," Melville described the "enthusiasm" and "elation" with which Union troops had captured Missionary Ridge in November 1863, and then wrote: "General Grant, at Culpepper, a few weeks prior to crossing the Rapidan for the Wilderness, expressed to a visitor his impression of the impulse and the spectacle: Said he, 'I never saw any thing like it:' language which seems curiously undertoned, considering its application; but from the taciturn Commander it was equivalent to a superlative or hyperbole from the talkative." The "visitor" was Melville, who had traveled to Virginia in April 1864 to visit his cousin, Lieutenant Colonel Henry Gansevoort of the 13th New York Cavalry, and then met Grant at his headquarters in Culpeper.

The Armies of the Wilderness.
(1863–4.)

I.

Like snows the camps on Southern hills
  Lay all the winter long,
Our levies there in patience stood—
  They stood in patience strong.
On fronting slopes gleamed other camps
  Where faith as firmly clung:
Ah, froward kin! so brave amiss—
  The zealots of the Wrong.

In this strife of brothers
  (God, hear their country call),
However it be, whatever betide,
  Let not the just one fall.

Through the pointed glass our soldiers saw
  The base-ball bounding sent;
They could have joined them in their sport
  But for the vale's deep rent.
And others turned the reddish soil,
  Like diggers of graves they bent:
The reddish soil and trenching toil
    Begat presentiment.

Did the Fathers feel mistrust?
  Can no final good be wrought?
Over and over, again and again
  Must the fight for the Right be fought?

They lead a Gray-back to the crag:
  "Your earth-works yonder—tell us, man!"
"A prisoner—no deserter, I,
  Nor one of the tell-tale clan."
His rags they mark: "True-blue like you
  Should wear the color—your Country's, man!"
He grinds his teeth: "However that be,
  Yon earth-works have their plan."

Such brave ones, foully snared
  By Belial's wily plea,
Were faithful unto the evil end—
  Feudal fidelity.

"Well, then, your camps—come, tell the names!"
  Freely he leveled his finger then:
"Yonder—see—are our Georgians; on the crest,
  The Carolinians; lower, past the glen,
Virginians—Alabamians—Mississippians—Kentuckians
  (Follow my finger)—Tennesseeans; and the ten
Camps *there*—ask your grave-pits; they'll tell.
  Halloa! I see the picket-hut, the den
Where I last night lay." "Where's Lee?"
  "In the hearts and bayonets of all yon men!"

The tribes swarm up to war
As in ages long ago,
Ere the palm of promise leaved
And the lily of Christ did blow.

Their mounted pickets for miles are spied
Dotting the lowland plain,
The nearer ones in their veteran-rags—
Loutish they loll in lazy disdain.
But ours in perilous places bide
With rifles ready and eyes that strain
Deep through the dim suspected wood
Where the Rapidan rolls amain.

The Indian has passed away,
But creeping comes another—
Deadlier far. Picket,
Take heed—take heed of thy brother!

From a wood-hung height, an outpost lone,
Crowned with a woodman's fort,
The sentinel looks on a land of dole,
Like Paran, all amort.
Black chimneys, gigantic in moor-like wastes,
The scowl of the clouded sky retort;
The hearth is a houseless stone again—
Ah! where shall the people be sought?

Since the venom such blastment deals,
The South should have paused, and thrice,
Ere with heat of her hate she hatched
The egg with the cockatrice.

A path down the mountain winds to the glade
Where the dead of the Moonlight Fight lie low;
A hand reaches out of the thin-laid mould
As begging help which none can bestow.
But the field-mouse small and busy ant
Heap their hillocks, to hide if they may the woe:

By the bubbling spring lies the rusted canteen,
  And the drum which the drummer-boy dying let go.

Dust to dust, and blood for blood—
  Passion and pangs! Has Time
Gone back? or is this the Age
  Of the world's great Prime?

The wagon mired and cannon dragged
  Have trenched their scar; the plain
Tramped like the cindery beach of the damned—
  A site for the city of Cain.
And stumps of forests for dreary leagues
  Like a massacre show. The armies have lain
By fires where gums and balms did burn,
  And the seeds of Summer's reign.

Where are the birds and boys?
  Who shall go chestnutting when
October returns? The nuts—
  O, long ere they grow again.

They snug their huts with the chapel-pews,
  In court-houses stable their steeds—
Kindle their fires with indentures and bonds,
  And old Lord Fairfax's parchment deeds;
And Virginian gentlemen's libraries old—
  Books which only the scholar heeds—
Are flung to his kennel. It is ravage and range,
  And gardens are left to weeds.

Turned adrift into war
  Man runs wild on the plain,
Like the jennets let loose
  On the Pampas—zebras again.

Like the Pleiads dim, see the tents through the storm—
  Aloft by the hill-side hamlet's graves,
On a head-stone used for a hearth-stone there

The water is bubbling for punch for our braves.
What if the night be drear, and the blast
Ghostly shrieks? their rollicking staves
Make frolic the heart; beating time with their swords,
What care they if Winter raves?

Is life but a dream? and so,
In the dream do men laugh aloud?
So strange seems mirth in a camp,
So like a white tent to a shroud.

II.

The May-weed springs; and comes a Man
And mounts our Signal Hill;
A quiet Man, and plain in garb—
Briefly he looks his fill,
Then drops his gray eye on the ground,
Like a loaded mortar he is still:
Meekness and grimness meet in him—
The silent General.

Were men but strong and wise,
Honest as Grant, and calm,
War would be left to the red and black ants,
And the happy world disarm.

That eve a stir was in the camps,
Forerunning quiet soon to come
Among the streets of beechen huts
No more to know the drum.
The weed shall choke the lowly door,
And foxes peer within the gloom,
Till scared perchance by Mosby's prowling men,
Who ride in the rear of doom.

Far West, and farther South,
Wherever the sword has been,
Deserted camps are met,
And desert graves are seen.

The livelong night they ford the flood;
With guns held high they silent press,
Till shimmers the grass in their bayonets' sheen—
On Morning's banks their ranks they dress;
Then by the forests lightly wind,
Whose waving boughs the pennons seem to bless,
Borne by the cavalry scouting on—
Sounding the Wilderness.

Like shoals of fish in spring
That visit Crusoe's isle,
The host in the lonesome place—
The hundred thousand file.

The foe that held his guarded hills
Must speed to woods afar;
For the scheme that was nursed by the Culpepper hearth
With the slowly-smoked cigar—
The scheme that smouldered through winter long
Now bursts into act—into war—
The resolute scheme of a heart as calm
As the Cyclone's core.

The fight for the city is fought
In Nature's old domain;
Man goes out to the wilds,
And Orpheus' charm is vain.

In glades they meet skull after skull
Where pine-cones lay—the rusted gun,
Green shoes full of bones, the mouldering coat
And cuddled-up skeleton;
And scores of such. Some start as in dreams,
And comrades lost bemoan:
By the edge of those wilds Stonewall had charged—
But the Year and the Man were gone.

At the height of their madness
The night winds pause,

Recollecting themselves;
But no lull in these wars.

A gleam!—a volley! And who shall go
Storming the swarmers in jungles dread?
No cannon-ball answers, no proxies are sent—
They rush in the shrapnel's stead.
Plume and sash are vanities now—
Let them deck the pall of the dead;
They go where the shade is, perhaps into Hades,
Where the brave of all times have led.

There's a dust of hurrying feet,
Bitten lips and bated breath,
And drums that challenge to the grave,
And faces fixed, forefeeling death.

What husky huzzahs in the hazy groves—
What flying encounters fell;
Pursuer and pursued like ghosts disappear
In gloomed shade—their end who shall tell?
The crippled, a ragged-barked stick for a crutch,
Limp to some elfin dell—
Hobble from the sight of dead faces—white
As pebbles in a well.

Few burial rites shall be;
No priest with book and band
Shall come to the secret place
Of the corpse in the foeman's land.

Watch and fast, march and fight—clutch your gun!
Day-fights and night-fights; sore is the stress;
Look, through the pines what line comes on?
Longstreet slants through the hauntedness!
'Tis charge for charge, and shout for yell:
Such battles on battles oppress—
But Heaven lent strength, the Right strove well,
And emerged from the Wilderness.

Emerged, for the way was won;
But the Pillar of Smoke that led
Was brand-like with ghosts that went up
Ashy and red.

None can narrate that strife in the pines,
A seal is on it—Sabæan lore!
Obscure as the wood, the entangled rhyme
But hints at the maze of war—
Vivid glimpses or livid through peopled gloom,
And fires which creep and char—
A riddle of death, of which the slain
Sole solvers are.

Long they withhold the roll
Of the shroudless dead. It is right;
Not yet can we bear the flare
Of the funeral light.

Ulysses S. Grant to Edwin M. Stanton and to Henry W. Halleck

On May 7 Lee anticipated that Grant would leave the Wilderness and ordered Richard Anderson, the new commander of Longstreet's corps, to move to Spotsylvania. Marching overnight, Anderson's men outpaced the southward Union advance and blocked it at Laurel Hill on May 8. The next day both armies extended their lines, skirmished, and entrenched. On May 10 Grant launched a series of attacks that either failed to break through the Confederate lines or had to be abandoned for lack of reinforcements. The following morning he assessed the progress of the campaign in two letters that were carried to Washington by his friend and political patron, Illinois congressman Elihu B. Washburne. Grant's letter to Stanton was widely printed in the northern press and became famous for its closing sentence.

Head Qrs. in the Field, Va
8 AM May 11th 1864.

HON. E. M. STANTON,
SEC. OF WAR. WASHINGTON D. C.

We have now entered the sixth day of very hard fighting. The result to this time is much in our favor. Our losses have been heavy as well as those of the enemy. I think the loss of the enemy must be greater. We have taken over five thousand prisoners, in battle, while he has taken from us but few except stragglers. I propose to fight it out on this line if it takes all summer.

U. S. GRANT
Lieut. Gen. Comdg Armies

Near Spotsylvania C. H. Va.
May 11th 1864. 8.30 A.M.

MAJ. GEN. HALLECK,
CHIEF OF STAFF OF ARMY,
GENERAL,

We have now ended the sixth day of very heavy fighting. The result to this time is much in our favor. But our losses have been heavy as well as those of the enemy. We have lost to this time eleven General officers killed, wounded or missing, and probably twenty thousand men. I think the loss of the enemy must be greater we having taken over four thousand prisoners, in battle, whilst he has taken from us but few except stragglers. I am now sending back to Belle Plaines all my wagons for a fresh supply of provisions, and Ammunition, and propose to fight it out on this line if it takes all Summer.

The arrival of reinforcements here will be very encouraging to the men and I hope they will be sent as fast as possible and in as great numbers. My object in having them sent to Belle Plaines was to use them as an escort to our supply train. If it is more convenient to send them out by train to march from the rail-road to Belle Plain or Fredericksburg send them so.

I am satisfied the enemy are very shaky and are only kept up to the mark by the greatest exertion on the part of their officers, and by keeping them entrenched in every position they take.

Up to this time there is no indication of any portion of Lee's Army being detached for the defence of Richmond.

Very respectfully
your obt. svt.
U. S. GRANT
Lt. Gen.

BATTLE OF SPOTSYLVANIA: VIRGINIA, MAY 1864

Charles Harvey Brewster to Martha Brewster and to Mary Brewster

Lieutenant Charles Harvey Brewster, the adjutant of the 10th Massachusetts Infantry, had seen action at the siege of Yorktown, Fair Oaks, Oak Grove, Malvern Hill, Chancellorsville, and Rappahannock Station. His regiment was assigned to the Fourth Brigade, Second Division, Sixth Corps, and fought in the Wilderness along the Orange Plank Road before marching to Spotsylvania. He wrote to his mother and his sister Mary about the fighting in the Wilderness, at Laurel Hill on May 8, and at the "Bloody Angle" on May 12.

Head Quarters 10th Mass Vols May 11th 1864

Dear Mother,

I have squatted on the ground in the hot sun to commence a letter to you although whether I shall ever finish it or ever have a chance to send it is more than I can tell. We started from our camp at Brandy Station at 4 o'clock on the morning of May 4th and crossed the Rapidan before night and bivouacked on the heights on this side that night. The next day we moved a short distance into the wilderness where we saw the usual signs of a pending fight. we went into line of battle and waited, or rather moved round from place to place, until about 4 o'clock PM It was thick woods and a man could hardly make his way through. At 4 o'clock we moved forward in line of battle and soon came upon the enemy who opened fire upon us. We fought them in our usual style, and in a very short time the old 10th lost one Officer killed + 4 wounded and 15 men killed + 86 wounded. The names of the Officers are Lt Ashley Co I killed Lt Graves (K) Lt Midgely (H) Lt Eaton (F) Lt Eldridge (E) we were relieved and the fight went on and our forces drove the scamps about half a mile and it then became dark. we went back to the road and replenished our ammunition and went back again. We lay down without blanket and shivered through the night and were aroused about 4 o'clock by the roar of musketry and had to fall in without any breakfast. The battle soon became general and lasted all day neither side gaining much advantage but both losing thousands of men. This day we did not get into the front line and lost but 3 or 4 men and Capt Shurtleff wounded in the arm. Night came on and we lay down and we thought to have a nights rest, but I had only just lain down when an order came to fall in and away we went to join the 1st + 3rd Divisions of our Corps. We had been detached as usual to do some fighting with other Corps. The next day we started at 4 o'clock AM and spent the day maneuvering round and marching in the hot sun but did not get any fighting.

At 8 o'clock PM we started and marched all night, arriving at Chancellorsville in the morning shortly after sunrise. Our Corps had lost up to this time 8000 men. After a halt of about 5 minutes we were started on the Spottsylvania C H road and marched until about 2 o'clock PM when we were halted and expected to sleep all night, but very soon we were ordered to fall in and marched off on to a range of hills where we saw the usual signs of battle in mangled men brought to the rear on stretchers and the woods each side of the road filled with the mingled bodies of dead Rebels and Union soldiers.

We were halted and lay down in the woods a short time when we were assigned our position, first to support a battery and then to form part of a storming party and to take some hills on our front. Our Regt and the 2nd RI formed the left of the line and had to cross a swamp of tangled briers and mud knee deep and before we could reach our position, the first line advanced and we took our places in the 2nd and advanced as well as we could through a dense thicket, but we could not keep up our connection with the rest of the line, and as the attempt failed we being on lower swampy ground did not see when the rest fell back, and consequently were left far in advance of the rest of the Division. We did not hear the orders to fall back and we would not fall back without, and soon found out that we had no communication with the rest of the Army.

It was almost dark and we knew not which way to go, so we concluded to make the best of it and stay where we were all night. It soon became so dark that we could not see a thing and the enemy advanced came down the hill into this hole. We kept quiet until they were under our very noses and then poured a volley into them, when they broke and disapeared like the work of Magic.

We soon became aware of a line of battle approaching in our rear and now the question was whether they were friends or enemies and none could answer. So I went back towards them and as I approached they cocked thier pieces and I began to think it was all over with me and my poor Regiment.

I hailed them, "What troops are those?" "Who be you?" was the reply. I replied United States thinking it best to settle the question at once. Come into the lines then said they. I went in as I knew it was of no use to run as I should bring thier whole fire upon my Regiment if I did. Judge how glad I was to find they were the 77th New York! but I had hard work to convince them that I was not a terrible Rebel in disguise, but I finally succeed and now I saw more trouble, for I knew that if the Rebels advanced again they would open fire and our Regt would catch it both ways. Time was precious, as the Rebs might come again at any moment and we must get our Regiment into the same line with them. When do you think the cowards would not allow it. That is when we proposed the arrangement they insinuated that we were afraid to stay in the front line.

Well it was finally agreed upon that they should uncap thier pieces and we would hold the front. Pretty soon the Rebs did advance again and sure enough a lot of the cowardly devils did blaze away, and there we were between two fires, but we succeeded in stopping them and they probably held thier pieces so high that they did not do us or anybody else any damage, but if we had not got them to uncap thier pieces we should have been destroyed.

As it was we lost 1 killed and 8 wounded, but I cannot tell you the half or tenth part of the terrors of that horrid night. How I got again taken prisoner by the 61st Penn Regt in the same line and lots of other things which I cannot write about that you cannot understand when I tell you.

About six o'clock that morning we were ordered out of that place and came back and joined the rest of the Brigades when the Army began to build breast works, and here we lie in the same place we came to that morning. we are well fortified and the Rebels are all along our front also fortified and fighting is going on all the time. Our losses are enormous and so are the Rebels. We captured in our first fight May 5th we captured 2500 prisoners and yesterday 3400 and every day between more or less. we have been without communication with the rest of the world since we started but I understand that our wounded have finally been carried to Fredericksburg, and communication opened with Washington but we have received no mail nor sent any since we started. Our Division General (Getty) was wounded in the fight May 5th. Gen Hayes + Gen Wadsworth were killed Gen Shaler was captured. And Oh greatest of all losses our beloved Sedgwick was killed by a sharpshooter day before yesterday. His Corps weeps. He was our Uncle John and we shall never see his equal his loss to the country at this time is irreparable. Gen Eustis has gone to command a Brigade in the 1st Division and Col Edwards is commanding ours which is another misery as he does not know anything and we have another fool somebody Neil to command the Division [ ] before we get to Richmond. As an offset to all this we hear that Longstreet is seriously wounded. he was to the Rebel Army what Sedgwick was to ours. It is reported this morning that Gen Augur has arrived with the 8th Corps 27000 strong to reinforce us and I hope it is true.

At the 2nd days fight Burnsides Corps came up and the 57th Veterans of Mass who broke and ran at the very first fire as might be expected the 56th + 58th did not do much better and thier performances together with part of the 2nd Corps came very near finishing the business for the Army. Our Regiment was out all day yesterday and all last night as support for the picket line of our Brigade.

The fighting was terrible all day long on different parts of the line, and thousands must have been killed and wounded on both sides but in our immediate front nothing was done but heavy skirmishing which we had 5 wounded.

I am lying just inside the Breastworks and every little while a sharpshooters bullet from the other side of the line goes humming past my head and smack into a tree or the ground out while out on the skirmish line is the continual popping of the opposing lines which may at any moment break out into the terrible war of the line of battle and the thunder of Artillery but the day is given up to rest on our side if the enemy does not attack and if he attacks us in our fortifications Lord have mercy on him.

It is said that the loss of this Corps is greater than any in the Army and greatest in our Division of the Corps. Our Brigade has lost up to this morning 541 in killed and wounded, the Vt Brigade is almost all used up it is reported this morning that there are but 900 left of it fit for duty. Bill Robinson was wounded twice but not seriously. Our wounded after the 1st + 2nd days battle were brought along in ambulances except such as could walk and there were not enough ambulances + empty wagons for all of them so some had to be left at Chancellorsville which consists of one or two houses and no inhabitants.

It was mighty hard to have to come away and leave them. there were from our Regt and there were lots of wounded Rebels left at the same time many of the Ambulances had wounded Rebels in them and it created great indignation that they were not put out and ours brought off on as many as could be after we got back of Fredericksburg and communication was established the wounded who could walk were started off on foot ahead of the Ambulances and escort of cavalry, and in arriving at Fredericksburg it is reported the citizens armed a lot of boys and marched them off to Richmond as prisoners and yet I do not suppose this blessed government will ever retaliate upon them for it. we are so excessively merciful I have moved about ¾ of a mile since I commenced this letter, and am now sitting under a tree that much farther to the right in the line of battle. the reason is that the Brigade on our right has gone to support another Division which is about to make an assault and we have to extend our front so as to occupy thiers and our own. Just at this moment everything is perfectly still and in a few moments I presume the very air will be rent with the roar of musketry and Artillery.

At Chancellorsville we passed over the battle ground of last year there were lots of human skulls and bones lying top of the ground and we left plenty more dead bodies there to decay and bleach to keep thier grim company. the woods we have fought over both there and here are strewn with the dead bodies of both parties who lay as they fell unburied, but I cannot give you an idea of half the horrors I have witnessed and yet so common have they become that they do not excite a feeling of horror.

Word has just come that letters sent in 5 minutes will go to night so I wind up abruptly. Love to all

Your aff son
Charlie

PS Col P is well.

Head Quarters 10th Mass Vols May 13th 1864

Dear Mary,

I wrote to Mother day before yesterday since which time we had fought another terrible battle. We went in at six o'clock yesterday morning and came out about the same time this morning. I am writing this seated in the mud covered with blood + dirt and powder I have not time to give you the particulars much but yesterday morning some of our troops charged the enemys works in the rain before or at daylight and captured 20 guns and any quantity of prisoners including Maj Gen Johnson + 2 Brig Generals. we went up to hold the enemys rifle pits and redoubts and had not been there long before the enemy charged them. our Regiment was the right of our Brigade and on the right of us was the 2nd Brig of the 1st Div who broke and ran like sheep without firing a gun. the Rebels came into the same rifle pit with us and commenced an enfilading fire before we knew they were there and we had any quantity of men killed and wounded in much less time than it takes to tell of it. Capt Weatherill was hit as were Capt Knight Capt Johnson Capt Gilmore + Geo Bigelow also Major Parker and his horse was riddled with bullets + killed.

Lieut Munyan was also wounded but I think not seriously. Geo Bigelow's wound did not disable him and he is still on duty, a bullet grazed his throat I do not know how many men we have lost yet as we have not got but about 30 muskets with us this morning and some of the Officers are missing yet. both flagstaffs were hit three times and the state flag was cut short off.

We staid there what part of us did not break when the Rebels flanked us and fought until 4 o'clock PM and staid there in the mud without sleep in the mud until about 6 o'clock this morning. I cannot begin to tell you the horrors I have seen, but I must wait to tell you about this campaign when I get home there is to much of it, the incidence crowd upon me so and I have but a little time and it is commencing to rain our men fought the Rebels close to the other side of the breast works and knocked thier guns aside, and jumped up on the work and shot them down. I saw this morning the other side of the pit and the Rebels are piled up in heaps 3 or 4 deep and the pit is filled with them piled up dead and wounded together I saw one completely trodded in the mud so as to look like part of it and yet he was breathing and gasping. it was bad enough on our side of the breast work but on thiers it was awful. some of the wounded were groaning and some praying but I cannot write more this morning. I just wrote a line to let you know that I am safe so far. So is Col P. Have not heard from home yet since the campaign commenced we have had no mails. Love to all

Yours
Charlie.

Head Quarters 10th Mass Vols May 15th 1864

Dear Mother

I wrote to Mary day before yesterday the day after our last battle but when I got it done I directed it to you and as I had but that one envelope I had to let it go so. It is Sunday to day and as we are waiting here in line of battle and throwing up rifle pits, I thought I would commence a letter to you although I do not know that we shall remain here ten minutes. We started yesterday morning about 2 o'c from near our last battle field and marched to the Bowling Green Turnpike striking at some 12 miles from Fredericksburg marching there until about 4 or 5 o'clock PM and then started on and came out into the fields and formed on the left of the 5th Corps preparatory to a grand charge upon the enemy. we have got into a comparatively open country and it was a grand sight to see six lines of battle stretching across the hills and through the vales. we are right upon the banks of the river Po and the men were cautioned to hold up thier cartridge boxes when they crossed the river. some batteries were brought up and threw about 150 shells over onto the opposite hills but got no reply. the Johnies had skeedadled so we were spared one great fight and in the night two which was a great relief to us I can tell you.

But previous to all this in the afternoon a Brigade of the 1st Div of our Corps had crossed alone and the Rebels charged upon them putting them to flight and capturing a large proportion of them. After the performance, we lay down here and had a good nights sleep. it was the most quiet night we have had since we started upon this campaign. Our Regiment suffered terribly in the fight the other day losing 6 Officers wounded and 8 men killed + 34 wounded that we know of besides probably a good many that we do not know of and from 12 to 20 taken prisoners. this makes a grand total of 13 Officers killed + wounded and 24 men killed 135 wounded + 46 missing making 218 Officers + men in 12 days the Regiment is reduced to 150 muskets and at this rate there will be none of us left to see Richmond. Sidney Williams 1st Sergt of Co C is missing since the battle and his company all think he is taken prisoner, although it is possible that he might have been hit and wandered off into the woods. if you tell his people any thing about it you must say that he is taken prisoner without doubt I think he is. Lieut Munyans wound is quite serious and it is feared he will lose his leg. Major Parker also they say will have to lose his right fore arm. Capt Knight was shot in the side, and is in a very critical condition.

We had plenty of rumors yesterday that Richmond was taken but do not place any confidence in them. we have not seen a paper nor recieved any mail since we started. we have had a general order announcing Gen Shermans victories at Tunnell Hill and Dalton and that Gen Butler had captured Petersburgh, also a communication from Gen Sheridan commanding the cavalry, that he has turned the enemys right and got into thier rear, destroyed 10 or 12 miles of the Orange Railroad and expects to fight the enemys cavalry of the South Anna River. They have destroyed a large Depot of supplies of the enemys at Beaver Dam, and recaptured 500 of our men who were taken prisoner by the enemy.

We are being largely reenforced by fresh troops and there is need enough of it, as we should not have any army left by the time we should get to Richmond at the present rate. Our Division started with nearly 9000 men and we have lost about ⅔ of them we seem to get into every fight that takes place. We are tired sleepy and worn out but if we could believe that everything was working out all right we should be satisfied.

We took in the fight of Wednesday 8000 prisoners, 18 guns, 22 colors + 2 General Officers. the field hospitals are full all the time and the Ambulances and empty wagons are kept constantly going with the wounded to Fredericksburgh. I wish it might end soon for it is dreadful to be kept in a constant state of excitement like this. you must remember that we have been 11 days under fire more or less every day and almost every night.

I wish the cowards at home who snear at the noble Army of the Potomac, might be forced out here to take thier share of the luxuries of the Officers Confound them. it is outrageous and abominable that the Army must be slandered and abused by the cowards that stay at home and cannot be coaxed or forced out here at any event. Now that the business seems almost winding up it seems almost as though a government that could not draft its own subjects to fight its battles, is hardly worth volunteering to fight for. I get enraged every time I think of it.

We are encamped on a splendid plantation and the corn and wheat is growing finely or rather was before we came but I am afraid the crops will be very small this year. We have not seen our Wagons since we started, and I am getting sadly delapidated. my rear is entirely unprotected I having worn the seat of my pants and drawers entirely off.

The most terrible sight I ever saw was the Rebel side of the breast work we fought over the other day. there was one point on a ridge where the storm of bullets never ceased for 24 hours and the dead were piled in heaps upon heaps and the wounded men were intermixed with them, held fast by thier dead companions who fell upon them continually adding to the ghastly pile. The breast works were on the edge of a heavy oak woods and large trees 18 inches or more in diameter were worn and cut completely off by the storm of bullets and fell upon the dead and wounded Rebels. those that lay upon our side in the night when the trees fell said that thier howlings were awful when these trees came down upon them. when I looked over in the morning there was one Rebel sat up praying at the top of his voice and others were gibbering in insanity others were groaning and whining at the greatest rate while during the whole of it I did not hear one of our wounded make any fuss other than once in a while one would sing out Oh! when he was hit. but it is a terrible terrible business to make the best of it.

Some of our cavalry the other day took a squad of Rebel prisoners a few days ago and among them was a deserter from our ranks. he was shot without ceremony. that is not much ceremony. I don't know whether he was tried or not but a square was formed and he was to be hung but we were all marching for battle and there was no time to hang him so he was shot. I don't know what Regt he belonged to. we were marching by at the time.

I shall enclose in this a list of names and wounded which you have better have published if there has been none. you can hand it to the Gazzette and they can do as they have a mind to. I don't know when you will get this however as I do not know as any mail is going to day. this is the third letter I have written since I started from camp you must be sure and let me know if you get them. There is a tremendous mail for the Army but nobody can stop to assort consequently we are kept without it I don't know where it is but I suppose at Fredericksburg. Give my respects to all the neighbors, and love to Mary Matt + Thomas reserving a large share for yourself from

Your aff son
Charlie.

THE BLOODY ANGLE: VIRGINIA, MAY 1864

J.F.J. Caldwell: from The History of a Brigade of South Carolinians

On May 8 the South Carolina brigade commanded by Samuel McGowan left the Wilderness and began marching toward Spotsylvania. James F. J. Caldwell later described the battlefield where the brigade had lost 481 men killed, wounded, or missing in two days of fighting: "From a thick wilderness of stunted saplings, unbroken by a hog-path, the place had become a charred, torn, open woods, cut up with numerous narrow wagon-roads. Every tree seemed to be riddled with balls. Small arms, mostly broken or bent, strewed the ground, with every conceivable damaged article of accoutrement or clothing, and graves filled with the dead of both armies, were fearfully frequent. Horses lay unburied. The stench of burning vegetable matter and clothing, and the gases streaming up through the thin covering of the graves, almost suffocated me in the hot, close air of the forest." McGowan's Brigade reached Spotsylvania the next day and was posted to the Confederate right. At dawn on May 12 nearly 20,000 Union soldiers attacked and overran the apex of a large salient near the center of the Confederate line, beginning a close-quarters struggle that lasted for more than twenty-two hours. Although the initial assault captured 3,000 prisoners, the Union troops became disorganized and were soon driven back by Confederate counterattacks. Both sides sent reinforcements to the salient, where the most intense fighting took place on its northwestern side along 200 yards of fieldworks known as the Bloody Angle. The battle for the "Mule Shoe" salient cost the Union about 6,000 men killed, wounded, or missing and the Confederates about 8,000, including 451 men from McGowan's Brigade.

THE 12TH OF MAY broke cool and cloudy. Soon after dawn a fine mist set in, which sometimes increased to a hard shower, but never entirely ceased, for twenty-four hours. McGowan's brigade was moved still farther to the left. Firing could be heard on our left, although, on account of the thick growth and irregular surface of the country, we could not determine where or in what force. We could see the enemy moving troops through a cleared space rather northwest of our position. The skirmishers on both sides fired from time to time. After a while, the artillery between us and the Court House opened on the enemy. They replied; and there was a pretty sharp duel for a time. A battery of theirs, considerably on our left, and, apparently, about a salient in our line, almost enfiladed the works we occupied. But we had good traverses, and there were few, if any, casualties in the brigade. I remember seeing only one man (a North Carolinian who had straggled in among us) struck. He made wry faces and not a little noise, but soon recovered.

About ten o'clock, our brigade was suddenly ordered out of the works, detached from the rest of the division, and marched back from the line, but bearing towards the left. The fields were soft and muddy, the rains quite heavy. Nevertheless, we hurried on, often at the double-quick. Before long, shells passed over our heads, and musketry became plainly audible in front. Our pace was increased to a run. Turning to the right, as we struck an interior line of works, we bore directly for the firing.

We were now along Ewell's line. The shell came thicker and nearer, frequently striking close at our feet, and throwing mud and water high into the air. The rain continued. As we panted up the way, Maj. Gen. Rodes, of Ewell's corps, walked up to the road-side, and asked what troops we were. "McGowan's South Carolina brigade," was the reply. "There are no better soldiers in the world than these!" cried he to some officers about him. We hurried on, thinking more of him and more of ourselves than ever before.

Reaching the summit of an open hill, where stood a little old house and its surrounding naked orchard, we were fronted and ordered forward on the left of the road. The Twelfth regiment was on the right of our line, then the First, then the Thirteenth, then the Rifles, then the Fourteenth. Now we entered the battle. There were two lines of works before us: the first, or inner line, from a hundred and fifty to two hundred yards from us, the second, or outer line, perhaps a hundred yards beyond it, and parallel with it. There were troops in the outer line, but in the inner one only what appeared to be masses without organization. The enemy were firing in front of the extreme right of the brigade, and their balls came obliquely down our line; but we could not discover, on account of the woods about the point of firing, under what circumstances the battle was held. There was a good deal of doubt as to how far we should go, or in what direction. At first it was understood that we should throw ourselves into the woods, where the musketry was; but, somehow, this idea changed to the impression that we were to move straight forward—which would bring only about the extreme right regiment to the chief point of attack. The truth is, the road by which we had come was not at all straight, which made the right of the line front much farther north than the rest, and the fire was too hot for us to wait for the long, loose column to close up, so as to make an entirely orderly advance. More than all this, there was a death-struggle ahead, which must be met instantly.

We advanced at the double-quick, cheering loudly, and entered the inner works. Whether by order or tacit understanding, we halted here, except the Twelfth regiment, which was the right of the brigade. That moved at once to the outer line, and threw itself with its wonted impetuosity, into the heart of the battle. Let us pause a moment to describe the state of affairs here.

Major General Edward Johnson's division had held the outer line of works on the night of the 11th. These works, at one point of the line, ran out into a sharp salient. This was on a ridge; but before it was a dense pine thicket, up to the very works. About parallel with the works, and varying from thirty to seventy-five yards from them, was a hollow, which the enemy could crawl up without being perceived, and, by lying down just at the crest of the ridge, have almost as secure a place for firing as was afforded by the Confederate works. An attack was apprehended at this weak point, and a large quantity of artillery was placed there, a strong infantry line was put in, powerful protections against small arms, by means of log-piles in front and traverses on the flank, were erected, and, in fine, perfect preparation, it was thought, made to receive the attack. Just at daylight, however, on the 12th, Grant's massed lines flung themselves against the point, swept over the astonished Confederates, captured about twenty pieces of field-artillery, and near two thousand prisoners, (General Johnson among them,) and broke the very keystone of our arch.

An effort was made, as speedily as possible, to recapture the works. The enemy pressed on to the inner line. What troops were sent against them I do not know, except that among them were some of Anderson's old division. General Abner Perrin charged brilliantly with his brigade, beat away the enemy from the interior line, jumped his horse over the works, and was leading the final charge upon the exterior line, when he was shot through and killed. Here the Confederate movement stopped short. Our brigade was sent to General Ewell to carry it through.

The demoralization of the troops that had been about this point was deplorable. They seemed to feel that Grant had all the hosts of hell in assault upon us.

To resume: the brigade advanced upon the works. About the time we reached the inner line, General McGowan was wounded by a Minie ball, in the right arm, and forced to quit the field. Colonel Brockman, senior colonel present, was also wounded, and Colonel J. N. Brown, of the Fourteenth regiment, assumed command, then or a little later. The four regiments—First, Thirteenth, Fourteenth and Rifles (the Twelfth had passed on to the outer line)—closed up and arranged their lines. Soon the order was given to advance to the outer line. We did so, with a cheer and at the double-quick, plunging through mud knee-deep, and getting in as best we could. Here, however, lay Harris' Mississippi brigade. We were ordered to close to the right. We moved by the flank up the works, under the fatally accurate fire of the enemy, and ranged ourselves along the intrenchment. The sight we encountered was not calculated to encourage us. The trenches, dug on the inner side, were almost filled with water. Dead men lay on the surface of the ground and in the pools of water. The wounded bled and groaned, stretched or huddled in every attitude of pain. The water was crimsoned with blood. Abandoned knapsacks, guns and accoutrements, with ammunition boxes, were scattered all around. In the rear, disabled caissons stood and limbers of guns. The rain poured heavily, and an incessant fire was kept upon us from front and flank. The enemy still held the works on the right of the angle, and fired across the traverses. Nor were these foes easily seen. They barely raised their heads above the logs, at the moment of firing. It was plainly a question of bravery and endurance now.

We entered upon the task with all our might. Some fired at the line lying in front, on the edge of the ridge before described; others kept down the enemy lodged in the traverses on the right. At one or two places, Confederates and Federals were only separated by the works, and the latter not a few times reached their guns over and fired right down upon the heads of the former.

So continued the painfully unvarying battle for perhaps two hours. At the end of that time a rumor arose that the enemy were desirous to come in and surrender. Col. Brown gives the following account of it in his official report:—"About two o'clock, P.M., the firing ceased along the line, and I observed the enemy standing up in our front, their colors flying and arms pointing upward. I called to them to lay down their arms and come in. An officer answered, that he was awaiting our surrender—that we had raised a white flag, whereupon he had ceased firing. I replied that 'I commanded here; and if any flag was raised it was without authority, and unless he came in, firing would be resumed.' He begged a conference, which was granted, and a subordinate officer advanced near the breastwork and informed me that a white flag was flying on my right. He was informed that unless his commander surrendered, the firing would be continued. He started back to his lines, and, failing to exhibit his flag of truce, was shot down midway between the lines, which were not more than twenty yards apart at this point. The firing again commenced with unabated fury."

Farther on the left of the brigade, where nothing was known of this conference, there was an opinion that the light-colored flag (that of Connecticut, I believe) displayed by the enemy was intended for a truce. A Babel of tongues succeeded—officers ordering the resumption of the firing; men calling out to the Federal line, questioning each other, imploring for the fire to be held and the enemy allowed to come in. To those who reflected a moment, it should have been plain that we were deceiving ourselves. The idea of that solid line of men, with arms in their hands, coming in to surrender to us was preposterous. But a general infatuation prevailed—a silly infatuation, if it had not involved so much. So the two lines stood, bawling, gesticulating, arguing, and what not. At length a gun was fired, perhaps the one Colonel Brown mentions. All of both lines joined in, and the roar of battle was renewed, sounding like pleasant music to many of us now.

The Twelfth regiment suffered most heavily. They entered the point of greatest danger—just at the break—and received a concentrated fire of artillery that crashed through the works, and the fusilade of infantry from the front and across the traverses on the right flank. Men just across the works would, in places, thrust over their pieces and discharge them in their faces. They lost fearfully, but they fought nobly. Sometimes, they would have to give way to the left, but they always rallied and fought at the nearest footing.

The firing was astonishingly accurate all along the line. No man could raise his shoulders above the works without danger of immediate death. Some of the enemy lay against our works in front. I saw several of them jump over and surrender during relaxations of firing. An ensign of a Federal regiment came right up to us during the "peace negotiations," and demanded our surrender. Lieutenant Carlisle, of the Thirteenth regiment, replied that we would not surrender. Then the ensign insisted that, as he had come under a false impression, he should be allowed to return to his command. Lieutenant Carlisle, pleased with his composure, consented. But, as he went back, a man, from another part of the line, shot him through the face, and he came and jumped over to us.

This was the place to test individual courage. Some ordinarily good soldiers did next to nothing, others excelled themselves. The question became, pretty plainly, whether one was willing to meet death, not merely to run the chances of it. Two men, particularly, attracted my attention. I regret, exceedingly, that I have not been able to ascertain their names, for I am anxious that they should have what little fame may be derived from distinguished mention in these pages.

The first of these belonged, I think, to the Fourteenth regiment. He was a tall, well-formed man, apparently just arrived at maturity. He was a private. He would load his piece with the greatest care, rise to his full height, (which exposed at least half of his person,) and, after a long, steady aim, deliver his fire. Then he would kneel and reload. Sometimes he would aim, but take down his piece and watch again for his mark, then aim again and fire. The balls flew round him like hail, from front and flank. I saw him fire at least a hundred times between noon and dark. Finally, late in the evening, I saw him rise and single out his man, in the grass in front, and draw down upon him. Then, appearing not to be satisfied, he recovered his piece, remaining erect and watching. After, perhaps, half a minute, he raised his rifle and aimed. Just as his finger touched the trigger, I heard the crash of a ball, and, looking at him, saw a stream of blood gush from his left breast. He fell and died without a struggle.

Another soldier, of probably not more than eighteen years, interested me early in the fight. Although scarcely so deliberate as the other, he fired with great perseverance and coolness, until just after the death of the other. He was a handsome boy, tall and slender, with eyes as tender as a woman's, and a smooth, fair cheek, just darkening with the first downy beard. Seeming to be weary, about sunset, he sat down in the cross-trench to rest. He was hardly down, when a ball glanced from a tree and struck him just behind the right ear. He struggled up and shook with a brief convulsion. Some one caught him in his arms. He raised his eyes, with the sweetest, saddest smile I think I ever saw on earth, and died almost on the instant. It was a strange wound. I could see nothing but a small, red blister where the ball struck him.

A lad in Harris's brigade was shot down among us, early in the fight—a little, smooth-faced fellow, very out of place in this carnage. He fell at once in death agonies, but he cried out to his comrades, "Boys, I'm killed; but tell mother I died a Christian!"

Lieutenant-Colonel Shooter, of the First regiment, was shot as we entered the works. Some of his regiment stopped to assist him. But he bade them go forward and leave him, adding, "I know that I am a dead man; but I die with my eyes fixed on victory!"

We lay five or six deep, closing constantly to the right, and thus losing all distinct organization. A good part of Harris's Mississippians were with us. There was no farther cessation of fire after the pause before described. Every now and then a regular volley would be hurled at us from what we supposed a fresh line of Federals, but it would gradually tone down to the slow, particular, fatal firing of a siege. The prisoners, who ran in to us now and then, informed us that Grant's whole energies were directed against this point. They represented the wood on their side as filled with dead, wounded, fighters and skulkers. A Confederate officer, a prisoner among them at the time, has since told me that he saw many thousand troops, in many successive lines, moving against the bloody angle until night. "Whiskey," he added, "was forwarded by the barrel to the front, and provost-guard drove up, with merciless fidelity, those whom drink failed to bring to the mark." We were told that if we would hold the place till dark we should be relieved. Dark came, but no relief. The water became a deeper crimson; the corpses grew more numerous. Every tree about us, for thirty feet from the ground, was barked by balls. Just before sunset, a tree of six or eight inches diameter, just behind the works, was cut down by the bullets of the enemy. We noticed, at the same time, a large oak hacked and torn in a manner never before seen. Some predicted its fall during the night, but the most of us considered that out of the question. But, about ten o'clock, it did fall forward upon the works, wounding some men and startling a great many more. An officer, who afterwards measured this tree, informed me that it was twenty-two inches in diameter! This was entirely the work of rifle-balls. Midnight came; still no relief, no cessation of the firing. Numbers of the troops sank, overpowered, into the muddy trenches and slept soundly. The rain continued.

Just before daylight, we were ordered, in a whisper, which was passed along the line, to retire slowly and noiselessly from the works. We did so, and either we conducted it so well that the enemy were not aware of the movement, or else, (as I think most likely,) they had become so dispirited by our stubborn resistance of eighteen hours, that they had left only a skirmish line to keep up appearances. At all events, they did not attempt to pursue us. Day dawned as the evacuation was completed. A second line of works, or rather a third, had been thrown up some five hundred yards in our rear, and in this, as we passed over, we found troops of Longstreet's corps, ready for the enemy. They were not called upon to meet him. He entered, but did not hold, the line we had left; much less did he attempt the second one.

WHIPPING A SLAVEMASTER: VIRGINIA, MAY 1864

Edward A. Wild to Robert S. Davis

A homeopathic physician before the war, Edward A. Wild lost an arm while leading the 35th Massachusetts Infantry at South Mountain in September 1862. He returned to duty in 1863 as a brigadier general and in April 1864 was given command of a brigade of black soldiers in the Eighteenth Corps. On May 11 his division commander, Brigadier General Edward W. Hinks, ordered Wild to report on the shooting of a civilian by his troops and the whipping of a civilian prisoner in his custody. Wild refused to reply to Hinks and addressed his response instead to Major Robert S. Davis, assistant adjutant general to Major General Benjamin F. Butler, the commander of the Department of Virginia and North Carolina. Hinks brought charges against Wild in connection with the whipping incident, but they were later withdrawn.

Wilson's Wharf, James River May 12th 64

Sir— Not being in the habit of accepting rebuke for acts not committed, and feeling that I can judge of "the qualities becoming to a man or a Soldier" quite as well as I can be informed by Brig. Genl. Edwd. W. Hinks in *such a letter* as the *above*, I have the honor to forward it, together with this, my protest, through Division Hd. qrs. for the consideration of the Major General Commanding the Department—

I protest against the whole tone of the above letter, as unbecoming and unjust; as being full of harsh rebuke, administered before even making any inquiry; and therefore, as *pre*-judging cases against me, and taking for granted, that "acts perpetrated" by me are necessarily "barbarous and cruel" not admitting the possibility of any justification; nor the probability of any excuse—

I have the honor to submit the following statement of facts—

On Friday May 6th I sent a party to surprise a Rebel Signal Station at Sandy Point. The party at the Station numbered *10* men, on being driven from the house they run into a swamp, directly upon one of my detachments, forming part of the trap— after considerable resistance, the Capture was complete, *5* Rebels were Killed, 3 wounded and *2* Caught, the dead were properly buried on the spot, the wounded and Prisoners were brought into camp and afterwards sent down to Fortress Monroe. The *10* guns were brought into camp, according to the nicest discrimination they were classed thus—*8* Soldiers and *2* citizens of whom *1* citizen was killed and 1 wounded. In this affair great credit is due to Capt. Eagle and Lt. Price 1st U.S.C.T. for skillfully carrying out the Plans.

On Monday Morning May 9th before daylight I sent a party to surprise a Squad of Rebel's who had been playing the *Guerrilla*, and attacked us three times, learning that they were passing the night at a Certain house I sent thither to take them; but being misinformed as to the distance, my party did not arrive till day. The Rebels *11* in number, made a stand, in good order under an officer in uniform, (said to be an adjutant) Our mounted advance party consisting only of *5* charged upon the *11* killed one, wounded another, run them into a bit of a swamp, and then waited for the main body to come up, but the rebels had passed through the swamp, and in two Boats crossed the Chicahominy, The Citizen Killed proved luckily to be Wilcox, the owner of the house, and the Enrolling Officer of the District. He was properly buried in the Yard, His house was burned. In this affair Major Cook 22d U.S.C.T. deserves credit for his boldness, and especially I would mention Henry Harris a Colored Sergeant of Capt. Choate's 2d U.S.C. Baty. for the daring he displayed, I wish it to be distinctly understood by Brig. Genl. Hinks that I shall continue to Kill *Guerrillas*, and Rebels offering armed resistance Whether they style themselves Citizens or Soldiers—

On Tuesday May 10th William H. Clopton, was brought in by the Pickets. He had been actively disloyal so that I held him as Prisoner of War, and have sent him as such to Fortress Monroe. He has acquired a notoriety as the most cruel Slave Master in this region, but in my presence he put on the character of a Snivelling Saint. I found half a dozen *women* among our refugees, whom he had often whipped unmercifully, even baring their whole persons for the purpose in presence of *Whites and Blacks.* I laid him bare and putting the whip into the hands of the Women, three of Whom took turns in settling some old scores on their masters back. A black Man, whom he had abused finished the administration of Poetical justice, and even in this scene the superior humanity of the Blacks over their white master was manifest in their moderation and backwardness. I wish that his back had been as deeply scarred as those of the women, but I abstained and left it to them—I wish it to be distinctly understood by Brig. Genl. Hinks that I shall do the same thing again under similar circumstances. I forgot to state that this Clopton is a high minded Virginia Gentleman, living for many years next door to the late John Tyler ExPresident of the U.S. and then and still intimate with his family.

And now as this is the second time that Brig. Genl. Hinks, has invoked the rules of Civilized warfare, and enjoined upon us the excercise of magnanimity and forbearance, I would respectfully inquire, for my own information and Guidance, whether it has been definitely arranged that Black Troops shall exchange courtesies with Rebel Soldiers? and if so on which side, such courtesies are expected to commence, and whether any guaranties have been offered on the part of the Rebels calculated to prove satisfactory and reassuring to the African Mind? Very Respectfully Your Obt. Sert

(Signed) Edwd. A. Wild

BATTLE OF RESACA: GEORGIA, MAY 1864

James A. Connolly to Mary Dunn Connolly

On May 7 Major General William T. Sherman began his campaign in northern Georgia by advancing toward Dalton along the railroad line from Chattanooga to Atlanta. Sherman commanded about 100,000 men, divided among the Army of the Cumberland (60,000) under Major General George H. Thomas, the Army of the Tennessee (25,000) under Major General James B. McPherson, and the Army of the Ohio (13,000) under Major General John M. Schofield. He was opposed by General Joseph E. Johnston, who commanded about 50,000 men in the Army of Tennessee. While Thomas and Schofield probed the Confederate defenses on Rocky Face Ridge west of Dalton, Sherman sent McPherson on a flanking march to the south toward the railroad at Resaca. When McPherson failed to take the town, Sherman began moving the rest of his army south as well, forcing Johnston to retreat from Dalton to Resaca on the night of May 12. Major James A. Connolly had served with the 123rd Illinois Infantry before joining the staff of Absalom Baird, commander of the Third Division, Fourteenth Corps, in the Army of the Cumberland.

Near Resaca, Ga., May 15, 1864.

Dear wife:

Just as I had written the date above, I said: "Hello, the enemy are shelling us." This exclamation was called out by the fact of a shell from the enemy's battery exploding very near our headquarters. It is now about nine o'clock at night, the moon is shining with a misty light through the battle smoke that is slowly settling down like a curtain, over these hills and valleys; the mournful notes of a whippoorwill, near by, mingle in strange contrast with the exultant shouts of our soldiers—the answering yells of the rebels—the rattling fire of the skirmish line, and the occasional bursting of a shell. To-day we have done nothing but shift positions and keep up a heavy skirmish fire. Yesterday our Division and Judah's Division of Scofield's Corps, had some hard fighting. We drove the enemy about a mile and entirely within his fortifications, several of our regiments planting their colors on his fortifications, but were compelled to withdraw under a terrible fire. We, however, fell back but a short distance to the cover of the woods, where we still are, and the enemy have not ventured outside their works since. A report has just reached us that Hooker drove the enemy about a mile to-day. We will probably be engaged to-morrow, and we may be engaged yet to-night, for the enemy may take a notion to come out of his works under cover of the darkness, and attack us. I hope he wont, for I don't want to be disturbed after I get to sleep, and then I don't like fighting in the night anyhow. We have men enough here to whip Johnston, and if he don't escape pretty soon he never will. I presume "you all," as the Southern people say, feel very much elated over Grant's success. Well, you will hear something from this army, some of these days that will be a full match for anything Grant or any other man can do with the Potomac army, and I begin to have hope that the only large armies of the rebellion will be shattered, if not destroyed, by the 4th of July. We have the railroad in running order to Tilton, which is several miles south of Dalton, and are having no trouble about supplies. The weather is fine, the roads fairly good, our men flushed with success, and I hope we push right on, day and night, though we be ragged, dirty, tired and hungry, until we exterminate these battalions of treason. Good night.

Your husband.

Kingston, Ga., May 20, 1864.

Dear wife:

If you will look at a map you will see that "we all" are still pushing southward, but a look at the map will give you little idea of the country we are passing through—will fail to point out to you the fields that are being reddened by the blood of our soldiers, and the hundreds of little mounds that are rising by the wayside day by day, as if to mark the footprints of the God of War as he stalks along through this beautiful country. This point is where the railroad from Rome forms a junction with the main line from Chattanooga to Atlanta. Rome is in our possession, and such has been the extraordinary rapidity with which the railroad has been repaired, as we have pushed along, that a train from Chattanooga ran into Kingston this morning about daylight, while at the same time a rebel train from Atlanta was whistling on the same road, and only two miles distant, but it is now about 9 o'clock in the morning, and the last whistle of the rebel train, north of the Etowah River, sounded some hours ago, the last rebel has undoubtedly crossed the river, the bridge across the river has been burned, I suppose, and the rebel army is wending its way, weary and dispirited, toward that mythical ditch of which we have heard so much.

Two hours later. Just at this point in this pencilled letter, about two hours ago I was interrupted, and the whole Division startled, by a cavalryman rushing up to headquarters, his horse covered with foam, and reporting that he had just seen the rebels, in line of battle, about one fourth of a mile distant, and advancing on us. In a jiffy this unfinished letter was thrust in my pocket, my horse saddled, and I was ordered by the General to go back with the cavalryman the way he had come, and ascertain the truth of his report, for cavalry reports are much like rebel money—don't pass at their face value. I went out through our pickets and cautiously moved along until I had gone about a mile to the front when I came to a strong line of breastworks, constructed by the rebels last night, but this morning they are deserted. I crossed these breastworks and went on until I came to another line of works, but they too are deserted this morning. I crossed this second line and went on a short distance, when I saw some mounted rebels ahead and they saw me; they fired a couple of shots which fell far short, and seeing I was out of their reach, I stood still with my cavalryman, but the rebs started toward me, and, not wishing to have a difficulty with them, I "fell back in good order" until they fired again, set up a yell and started after me on a run when I accelerated the pace of my "Rosinante" and *advanced to the rear* at a rapid pace and got safely inside our picket line; the cavalryman who accompanied me dodged off to one side and hid in the brush when the chase began. He came in a few moments ago, all right, but is not able to explain why he made his scare report. I reported to the General and all is quiet again, but if you find this letter all crumpled up, remember I had it in its unfinished state in my pocket during that chase, and as I can't get at my desk, paper is scarce, and I can't afford to begin it again. Beautiful country, beautiful weather, and everything going well with the Yankees in Georgia. You may still address me at Ringgold.

Your husband.

“THESE SAD FIELDS”: GEORGIA, MAY 1864

Alpheus S. Williams to Mary Williams

The opposing armies skirmished near Resaca on May 13 and then fought inconclusively for the next two days. When Johnston learned that Union troops had crossed the Oostanaula River downstream from Resaca, he abandoned the town and withdrew across the Oostanaula on the night of May 15. The battle of Resaca cost the Union more than 2,700 men killed, wounded, or missing, and the Confederates about 2,800. Johnston's army continued to retreat until May 20, when it crossed the Etowah River thirty miles south of Resaca. Brigadier General Alpheus S. Williams had fought at Cedar Mountain, Second Bull Run, Antietam, Chancellorsville, and Gettysburg before joining the Army of the Cumberland, where he commanded the First Division in the Twentieth Corps. He wrote to his daughter about the fighting at Resaca (the end of the letter is missing).

Camp near Cassville, Georgia,
May 20, 1864.

My Dear Daughter:

For the life of me, I cannot recollect whether I have written you since I left Trickum Post Office or not. I scribbled a short pencil note from that place. Since then my mind has been so full of constant duties, responsibilities, and cares, and events have followed in such rapid and varied succession that my recollections are a jumble. Day and night we may be said to be on duty and under anxieties. No one who has not had the experience can fancy how the mind is fatigued and deranged (as well as the body) by these days and nights of constant labor and care.

We left Trickum Post Office on the night of the 9th after much reconnoitering and skirmishing toward Buzzard's Roost and reached the entrance of Snake Creek Gap in the Chattanooga Mountains in the morning. The whole march, as everywhere, through woods, with hardly a clearing. On the 12th, moved the division through the gap about six miles and encamped. On the 13th moved towards Resaca, under arms always from daylight and lying ready for a fight all night. I carry nothing for myself and staff of a dozen but four tent flies and one wall tent for an office. All private baggage is left behind. The wagon with the tent flies is seldom up and consequently we roll ourselves in overcoats and what we can carry on our horses and take shelter under trees every night. The days are hot and the nights quite cold and foggy. Most of us have been without a change of clothing for nearly three weeks.

On the 14th we moved through thickets and underbrush to the rear and in support of Butterfield's division, and in the afternoon received a hurried order to move rapidly farther to the left to support Stanley's division of the 4th Corps. I reached the ground just in time to deploy one (3rd) brigade and to repulse the Rebels handsomely. They had broken one brigade of Stanley's division and were pressing it with yells and were already near one battery (5th Indiana, Capt. Simonson, Lt. Morrison commanding) when I astonished the exultant rascals by pushing a brigade from the woods directly across the battery, which was in a small "open" in a small valley. They "skedaddled" as fast as they had advanced, hardly exchanging a half-dozen volleys. They were so surprised that they fired wildly and didn't wound a dozen men. I was much complimented for the affair and Gen. Howard, commander of the 4th Corps, came and thanked me.

On the 15th we had a more serious engagement. Butterfield's division attacked their entrenched positions on the hills, short steep hills with narrow ravines. I was supporting. While his attack was in progress, information was brought to me that the Rebels were moving towards our left in force. I changed front and in luck had plenty of time to form my line and place my batteries in position before they attacked. They came on in masses and evidently without expectation of what was before them. All at once, when within fair range, my front line and the batteries (one of which I had with much work got on the ridge of a high hill) opened upon them with a tremendous volley. The rascals were evidently astounded, and they were tremendously punished. They kept up the attack, however, for an hour or so, bringing up fresh troops, but finally gave way in a hurry.

We captured one battle flag and the colonel of the 38th

Alabama, several other officers, and several hundred prisoners. The flag was a gaudy one and covered with the names of battles in which the regiment had been engaged. It was the only flag taken during the day. But that I was not advised of any supports on the left, I could have charged them with great success. As it was, I did a good thing, and the division behaved splendidly. Not a man left the ranks unless wounded. In the language of a private of the 27th Indiana (one of my old regiments) we had a "splendid fight," and he added, "'Old pap' (that is I) was right amongst us."

The fight ended about dusk and in the morning there was no enemy in front. I went out over the field in our front, not out of curiosity but to see what was in advance. There were scores of dead Rebels lying in the woods all along our front, and I confess a feeling of pity as I saw them. One old grey-headed man proved to be a chaplain of the Rebel regiment, and it is rather a singular coincidence that one of our own chaplains (3rd Wisconsin) was seriously wounded directly in front of where he was found dead. Early in the war I had a curiosity to ride over a battlefield. Now I feel nothing but sorrow and compassion, and it is with reluctance that I go over these sad fields. Especially so, when I see a "blue jacket" lying stretched in the attitude that nobody can mistake who has seen the dead on a battlefield. These "boys" have been so long with me that I feel as if a friend had fallen, though I recognize no face that I can recollect to have seen before. But I think of some sorrowful heart at home and oh, Minnie, how sadly my heart sinks with the thought.

I put parties to bury the dead Rebels but was ordered away before half were collected over the mile and a half in our front. I fear many were left unburied, though I left detachments to gather up all they could find. As I marched away, I was obliged to go along the line where my own dead were being collected by their comrades and interred in graves carefully marked with name, rank, and company. It is interesting to see how tenderly and solemnly they gather together their dead comrades in some chosen spot, and with what sorrowful countenances they lay them in their last resting place. There is much that is beautiful as well as sad in these bloody events. I lost in this battle between four and five hundred killed and wounded. [ ]

BATTLE OF PICKETT'S MILL: GEORGIA, MAY 1864

Samuel T. Foster: Diary, May 23–28, 1864

After crossing the Etowah River Johnston withdrew to a strong position at Allatoona Pass. Sherman decided to outflank the Confederate defenses by leaving the railroad, marching to Dallas, fourteen miles southwest of Allatoona, and then heading east toward Marietta. When Union troops began crossing the Etowah on May 23, Johnston anticipated Sherman's maneuver and moved his army toward Dallas. The two sides fought at New Hope Church, four miles northeast of Dallas, on May 25, and then continued to skirmish. Captain Samuel T. Foster led a company in the 24th Texas Cavalry (Dismounted) and had fought at Chickamauga before being wounded at Chattanooga. His regiment was assigned to Brigadier General Hiram B. Granbury's Texas brigade in Major General Patrick R. Cleburne's division. On May 27 Cleburne's division defended the extreme right of the Confederate line against a flanking attack by a division from the Army of the Cumberland. The battle of Pickett's Mill cost the Union 1,600 men killed, wounded, or missing, and the Confederates about 500.

MAY 23—Still here—no move. I had an opportunity to draw a pair of shoes last night but had to take a pair of No 8s because there were none smaller to be had. It was these or none. About 10 OClock this morning the order came to march.

We travel in a south west direction, but none of us have any idea where we are going to. Traveled about 10 miles, and stoped, had a little rain this evening, just enough to lay the dust.

MAY 24th

Last night about 12 O'Clock (midnight) two days rations came to us and were issued, consisting of corn bread and bacon and by 3 O'Clock this morning we are marched off— We kept up the march until about 11 O'Clock AM, having traveled about 15 miles, direction still south west. There are a great many conjectures and guessing as to where we are going and what we are going for. Some say we are going to Florida and put in a pontoon bridge over to Cuba, and go over there. While others contend that some Yank would put a torpedo under it and blow it up.

MAY 25th

Remained in our camp last night until 3 O'clock AM, when we were marched back the same road we come along yesterday for about 4 miles— The Yanks are about again. Artillery and small arms, in hearing of us— We are halted here and told to hold ourselves in readiness to move at a moments notice. By 11 O'Clock AM we had all taken a good sleep, when one days rations comes in consisting of bacon and crackers. Later in the evening another days rations are issued. About dusk it commenced raining, and we were ordered to move off. Heavy firing all day in our front— We moved about 2 miles and are halted in the road. After standing in our places in the road for half an hour—an order came to get out one side of the road, make fires and go to sleep.

MAY 26

Remained in camp by the roadside the rest of the night. This morning we are marched off early, and go in the direction of where the heavy fireing was yesterday— We could hear the skirmish firing from the time we started and as we march, it gets louder and louder nearer and nearer. Now we can hear an occasional bullet whistling past, like it was on the hunt of some one. We are marched up in rear of the line of battle, and then follow the line to the right for about 2 miles where we are put in position as a reserve force— We don't know whether we are on the right left or centre of the army but the heavy firing has been on our left and front all day today. Some of our boys (our Brigade is separated from every body) go to the breastworks in front of us to see what soldiers are there, because they have no confidence in any of them except the Arkansas troops (who are nicknamed "Josh'es" and when ever a Texan meets an Ark. soldier, he says, how are you Josh. Or where are you going Josh &c. It is all the time Josh——). We find Georgia troops in our front; and our boys tell them that if they run that we will shoot them, and no mistake, and as soon as they find out that the Texans are in their rear, they believe we will shoot them sure enough——

MAY 27

Remained in our place all night, and this morning Genl Granbury called for a scout of 5 men to go around the Yankee Army. Col Wilkes ordered me to send them from my Company. They started out early in the day, and returned in the afternoon, and reported that they were massing their troops on the right of Our Army and would flank us before night if we did not stop them some way— Our Brigad was moved off towards the right of our line following the line of Breast works— until we came to the extreme right of the infantry, and found some dismounted cavalry deployed in the woods still further to the right. We find some Ark. troops on the end of our line, and we form on to their right making our line that much longer and it also puts us just where the scouts said the Yanks were going to try to flank our Army. Our position is in a heavy timbered section with chinquapin bushes as an undergrowth. From the end of the army, where the breastworks stop we followed a small trail or mill path and as soon as our Brigade got its whole length in this place the command is to halt! and at the same instant the cavalry skirmishers came running back to our lines, saying that we had better get away from there, for they were coming by the thousand. These cavalry men had been keeping up a very heavy fire until our arrival, when it got too hot for them. Col. Wilkes ordered me to deploy my men and go forward in the woods. I soon had them all in position and started to move forward, but found the enemy close up to our line on the right, so I advanced the left of the skirmish line by a right wheel until the skirmish line and our line of battle behind us were in the shape of the letter V with our right skirmisher nearly on the line of battle and the left skirmisher was 75 yards from the line. As soon as the skirmish line was put in position our men commenced firing at the enemy skirmishers who were not more than forty to fifty yards from us. One of my men Joe Harrison who never could stop on a line of that kind without seeing the Yanks ran forward through the brush, but came back as fast as he went, saying that they fired a broadside on him, but didn't hit him— He took his place on the skirmish line behind an Oak tree about 14 inches in diameter— The enemy kept advancing through the bushes from tree to tree until they were (some of them) in 30 or 40 feet of our line—nor would they give back. I had three as good men as ever fired a gun killed on this skirmish line—W J Maddox, T L Doran & T F Nolan. The two first named were shot thru the neck and killed instantly, the last one was shot in the bowels and died in about 15 hours after. When the sun was about an hour high in the evening we were ordered back to the line of battle. And it seems that the enemys line of battle was advancing when the order came for the skirmishers to fall back.

The frolick opened in fine style as soon as we got back into our places—instead of two skirmish lines—the two lines of battle open to their fullest extent. No artillery in this fight— nothing but small arms.

Our men have no protection, but they are lying flat on the ground, and shooting as fast as they can. This continues until dark when it gradually stops, until it is very dark, when every thing is very still, so still that the chirp of a cricket could be heard 100 feet away—all hands lying perfectly still, and the enemy not more than 40 feet in front of us.

About 9 O'Clock in the night the order from Genl Granbury is to "Charge in the woods at the sound of the bugle."

Col Wilkes sent his adjutant to me with an order to deploy my Company in front of Our Regt. and go in advance in the charge. While deploying my Company, by the right flank, commencing at the left of the Regt. and stop one man about every 8 or 10 ft. we took some prisoners who had crawled up to 8 or 10 feet of our line of battle. We were finally deployed about 10 ft. in front of the line of battle waiting for the bugle to sound the charge.

While waiting (all this time none had spoke above a whisper) we could hear the Yanks just in front of us moving among the dead leaves on the ground, like hogs rooting for acorns; but not speaking a word above a whisper. To make that charge in the dark, and go in front at that; and knowing that the enemy were just in front of us, was the most trying time I experienced during the whole war.

In about an hour from the time we rec'd Genl Granburys

order to charge, the bugle sounded the charge, and we raised a regular Texas Yell, or an Indian Yell or perhaps both together, and started forward through the brush, and so dark we could not see *anything at all.* We commenced to fire as soon as we started, and the Yanks turned loose, and the flash of their guns would light up the woods like a flash of lightning, and by it we could see a line of blue coats just there in front of us, but the noise we made with our mouths was too much for them. They broke, but not before we were among them with our skirmishers. We were so close that one Yank caught one of my men and told him to "fall in quick as Co. 'C' was gone already"—my man went about 20 steps with them and stoped beside a large tree untill we came up to him again, all of which did not occupy as much time as to write this history of it.

As soon as they broke to run we commenced to take prisoners. We were going down hill, still Yelling like all the devils from the lower regions had been turned loose, and occasionally a tree lying on the ground would have from 5 to 20 Yanks lying down behind the log. We kept finding them as we advanced. All they would say was, *"don't shoot" "don't shoot"*—finally we got down to the bottom of the hill to a little branch and under the banks were just lots of them— But just here at this little branch we lost trail of the enemy, and our men were badly mixed up.

After calling and some loud talking for a little time every man fell into his place when Col Wilkes ordered me to deploy my Company on the hill in front of us and hold the ground until day light, and said the Brigad would go back to where the fight began and make breastworks.

As soon as my Company was put in position I discovered that we were on the top of a ridge and the enemy if near could see us, where we could not see them. So I put my men back about 15 or 20 feet— So we could skylight to the top of the ridge. In the course of half an hour we could see the Yanks lighting their camp fires about a mile or more from us, but immediately in front of us. Their camp appeared to be on a hill side facing towards us. So we could see every fire in the whole camp—and there seemed to be a thousand of them. One of Our Batteries that had been put in position nearly in our rear on the line of the fight in the evening sent word to me that they were going to shell the enemys camp, over our heads—— Presently "BOOM" went a shell which burst right in their midst. The Artillery kept up the shelling, about an hour, at which time there was not a fire to be seen—no where— I walk from one end of my skirmish line to the other all night, and every man stands on his feet and holds his gun in his hands until day light— As soon as it gets light we see we have been standing among dead Yanks all night and did not know it.

I go out in front of the line and I find under a little pine bush a Yank knapsack with an Oil Cloth and blanket straped to it and in it is a plug of Tobacco needles thread, pins &c; all of which except the knapsack, I appropriate to my own use.

I also find scattered here and there tin cups tin plates— haversacks with knife & fork Bacon and crackers, coffee, *sure-nough coffee.* Oh I am rich; crackers bacon & coffee.

I also find guns, that seem to have been thrown away last night—several of them with Bayonets Cartridge Boxes with plenty of ammunition.

MAY 28th

About sun up this morning we were relieved and ordered back to the Brigade—and we have to pass over the dead Yanks of the battle field of yesterday; and here I beheld that which I cannot discribe; and which I hope never see again, dead men meet the eye in every direction, and in one place I stoped and counted 50 dead men in a circle of 30 ft. of me. Men lying in all sorts of shapes and [ ] just as they had fallen, and it seems like they have nearly all been shot in the head, and a great number of them have their skulls bursted open and their brains running out, quite a number that way. I have seen many dead men, and seen them wounded and crippled in various ways, have seen their limbs cut off, but I never saw anything before that made me sick, like looking at the brains of these men did. I do believe that if a soldier could be made to faint, that I would have fainted if I had not passed on and got out of that place as soon as I did— We learn thru Col Wilkes that we killed 703 dead on the ground, and captured near 350 prisoners.

Genl Joseph E Johnson, and Genl Hardee and Genl Cleburn and Genl Granbury all ride over the battle ground this morning and Genl Johnson compliments us very highly on the fight. They all say that the dead are strewn thicker on the ground than at any battle of the war; but it don't seem to be so funny now as it was when it was going on. I feel sick every time I think of those mens brains.

We were not permitted to sit down and reflect over it, but were ordered forw'd about an hour by sun, just our Reg't. We advanced cautiously for about a mile through the wood when we found them again, and open fire upon them and soon have them on the retreat— There is only a skirmish line of them but that is all we have shooting at them, so we drive them back about ½ mile to their breastworks, and here in these woods between their breastworks and where they went to fight us yesterday evening, we find three piles of Oil Clothes, piled up like, a big wagon load at each pile. Every man in our Regt. got one and had several to pick over so he could get a good one— A Lieutenant of Our Regt (from Yorktown Tex) was captured just here while walking about through the chinquapin bushes. He was shot in the leg, and carried into their lines— Late in the evening the 7th Texas relieves us and we go back to our battle ground again.

PROCLAIMING VICTORY: LOUISIANA, MAY 1864

Richard Taylor: General Orders No. 44

The son of President Zachary Taylor, Major General Richard Taylor commanded the Confederate forces opposing the Union advance up the Red River in the spring of 1864. After his victory at Mansfield, Louisiana, on April 8, Taylor pursued the retreating Union forces and attacked them at Pleasant Hill the following day. Although the battle of Pleasant Hill was tactically inconclusive, Major General Nathaniel P. Banks abandoned his offensive and withdrew to Alexandria, where shallow water in the Red River threatened to strand the gunboat flotilla that had accompanied the expedition. Union engineers eventually were able to build a series of dams that raised the water level and allowed the gunboats to escape. Banks abandoned Alexandria on May 13 and after a series of skirmishes retreated across the Atchafalaya Bayou on May 20. The Red River campaign cost the Union about 5,500 men killed, wounded, or missing, the Confederates about 4,300.

HEAD-QUARTERS DISTRICT WESTERN LOUISIANA,
IN THE FIELD, May 23, 1864.

General Orders No. 44.

Soldiers of the Army of Western Louisiana:

On the 12th of March the enemy, with an army of 30,000 men, accompanied by a fleet of iron-clads mounting 150 guns, moved forward for the conquest of Texas and Louisiana. After 70 days' continuous fighting you stand a band of conquering heroes on the banks of the Mississippi. Fifty pieces of cannon, 7,000 stand of small arms, three gun-boats, and eight transports captured or destroyed, 60 stands of colors, over 10,000 of the enemy killed, wounded or captured—those are the trophies which adorn your victorious banners. Along 300 miles of river you have fought his fleet, and over 200 miles of road you have driven his army. You have matched your bare breasts against his iron-clads, and proved victorious in the contest. You have driven his routed columns beyond the Mississippi, although fed by reinforcements of fresh troops, while many of your gallant comrades were withdrawn to other fields. The boasted fleet which late sailed triumphant over our waters has fled in dismay, after destroying guns and stripping off armor in its eagerness to escape you. Like recreant knights, the iron-clads have fled the field, leaving shield and sword behind.

The devotion and constancy you have displayed in this pursuit have never been surpassed in the annals of war, and you have removed from the Confederate soldier the reproach that he could win battles but could not improve victories.

Along 100 miles of his path, with more than average barbarity, the flying foe burned every house and village within his reach. You extinguished the burning ruins in his base blood, and were nerved afresh to vengeance by the cries of women and children left without shelter or food. Long will the accursed race remember the great river of Texas and Louisiana. The characteristic hue of his turbid waters has a darker tinge from the liberal admixture of Yankee blood. The cruel alligator and ravenous gar-fish wax fat on rich food, and our native vulture holds high revelry o'er many a festering corpse.

If the stern valor of our well-trained infantry was illustrated on the bloody fields of Mansfield and Pleasant Hill, this long pursuit has covered the cavalry with undying renown. Like generous hounds with the game in full view, you have known neither hunger nor fatigue, and the hoarse cannon and ringing rifle have replaced in this stern chase the sonorous horn and joyous halloo. Whether charging on foot, shoulder to shoulder with our noble infantry, or hurling your squadrons on the masses of the foe, or hanging on his flying columns with more than the tenacity of the Cossack, you have been admirable in all. Conquer your own vices, and you can conquer the world.

Our artillery has been the admiration of the army. Boldly advancing without cover against the heavy metal of the hostile fleet, unlimbering often without support, within range of musketry, or remaining last on the field to pour grape and canister into advancing columns, our batteries have been distinguished in exact proportion as opportunity was afforded.

Soldiers! These are great and noble deeds, and they will live in chronicle and in song as long as the Southern race exists to honor the earth. But much remains yet to do. The fairest city of the South languishes in the invader's grasp. Her exiled sons mourn her fate in every land. The cheeks of her fair daughters yet mantle with the blush raised by the tyrant's insult; not a Confederate soldier returns to his colors from this sad Venice of the South, but recounts with throbbing heart and tearful eye how, amidst danger and insult, these noble women—angels upon earth—cheered his confinement and relieved his wants. To view the smiles of these fair dames will be the soldier's proudest boast, the brightest leaf in his chaplet of laurels.

Soldiers! This army marches toward New-Orleans, and though it do not reach the goal, the hearts of her patriot women shall bound high with joy, responsive to the echoes of your guns.

R. TAYLOR, Major-General.

Official: F. R. LABBRET, Lieutenant-Colonel and Assistant Adjutant-General.

"I AM SCARED MOST TO DEATH": VIRGINIA, MAY 1864

Charles Harvey Brewster to Mary Brewster; to Martha Brewster; and to Mattie Brewster

The fighting in the "Mule Shoe" at Spotsylvania ended in the early hours of May 13 when the Confederates withdrew to a new defensive line across the base of the salient. Grant then tried to turn Lee's right flank on May 14, but called off his planned attack after heavy rain and mud delayed crucial troop movements. On May 18 Union forces assaulted the base of the Mule Shoe and were repulsed. The same day, Grant learned that his secondary offensives in the Shenandoah Valley and along the James River had met with defeat, thereby freeing up reinforcements for Lee's army. He decided to move the Army of the Potomac south to the North Anna River and end the fighting at Spotsylvania, which had cost the Union nearly 18,000 men killed, wounded, or missing, and the Confederates about 12,000. Union troops abandoned their positions at Spotsylvania on May 20–21 and began marching to the southeast. Lee left Spotsylvania at the same time and reached the North Anna before Grant, but was unable to prevent Union forces from crossing the river on May 23. Lieutenant Charles Henry Brewster of the 10th Massachusetts wrote to his mother and to his sisters as his regiment approached and then crossed the North Anna.

Head Quarters 10th Mass Vols Caroline Co VA May 23rd 1864

Dear Mary,

I had just sent my last letter to Mother when we received a mail from home and I got 4 letters and I cannot find words to express the joy it gave me and all the Regiment and you can little imagine the amount of happiness one such mail brings to even one Regt of this great Army. We had two large grain bags full, and I assorted it but alas there was terrible sorrow connected with it which was the many letters for our dead and wounded comrades. I think I found as many as a dozen letters for poor Lt Bartlett who was killed only the day before. We started from near Spottsylvania C H last Saturday night and marched all night long and all day yesterday arriving at this place about 8 o'clock last night. I don't know where we are except that we are some miles south west of Gurneys Station on the Richmond + F'ks'brg R R and in Caroline Co and not a great distance from Bowling Green. We were roused this morning at half past 3 o'clock with orders to get breakfast and be ready to resume the march at 5 o'clock but it is now 8 o'clock and we have not budged an inch.

there is every prospect of a heavy rain storm to day, which will of course add very much to our comfort. The men are entirely out of rations and we know of no chance to get any.

We are travelling through a beautiful country, with lots of splendid plantations but there is nothing growing but corn except an occassional field of wheat.

Just in front of where I am sitting in a sandy cornfield on a side hill is a small swamp full of magnolias in full bloom and thier perfume is very refreshing after the continual stench of the dead bodies of men and horses which we have endured for the last 19 days. One of Co C has just brought in a great boquet of the Magnolias and he has given me two and I will perhaps put one of them in this letter but when it gets to you its white waxen beauty will be all gone though perhaps it may retain some of its fragrance. We are in a country that the Yanks have never been in before and it is not so utterly devastated as the country north of the Rapidan + Rappahannock but it looks good enough here with most of its vast fields, bare and uncultivated, and its want of inhabitants hardly any white men are seen nothing but ragged negroes, and the women of the plantations though many of the latter abandoned everything at our approach and leave thier homes at our disposal. at others they set upon the Portico's and Piazzas of thier homes and stare at the long columns of Cavalry Infantry Artillery Wagons and Ambulances that cross thier fields and tear down thier fences and hedges, in stupid wonder and despair. A report has just come from Division Hd Quarters that the Rebs are all back across the North Anna River so I suppose then we shall have to repeat the desparate fighting of the Wilderness and Spottsylvania C H if so, by the time we get them out of thier strongholds there and on the South Anna we shall have very few men to take the works around Richmond.

We heard heavy firing yesterday which is said to have been Hancock thrashing Gen Ewells Corps at Bowling Green. The 2nd + 5th Corps are in advance of us I find our delay is occasioned by waiting for rations which are expected here every moment. This country is much more open than where we have been, and if it continues so and we come up with them they will get a taste of our Artillery in larger doses than they have had heretofore, as we have not been able to use it but very little as yet. it has succeeded however in killing and wounding of our own men as it is always in the rear and undertakes to throw shell over us and generally manage to burst them right in our own ranks.

There goes the Bugle so I must stop and finish some other time. our Regt leads the Brigade and our Brigade leads the Division, and our Division leads the Corps this morning.

Noon.

We started and our Regiment was immediately ordered out as advanced guard + skirmishers, at which we were greatly elated as it gives us the priviledge of the fields + c and relieves us from the march in the crowded column besides the Artillery + trains. to be sure there is always the prospect of coming upon the enemy or being met by a volley of thier bullets, but to counteract this is the coming first upon the houses before all the chickens are carried off + c. but this morning our hopes soon fell to the ground for after marching a little ways we came upon the rear of the 5th Corps so of course everything eatable was cleaned out from all the houses.

We continued the march to this place where our teams came up and we are now stopping to receive rations. they also brought a mail and in it a letter from Mattie for me dated the 16th by which it appears that you have not got any of my letters of which this makes the sixth I have sent since the campaign commenced. it is most discouraging and it almost seems no use to write. Tell Mattie our Division is the 2nd Division and our Brigade the 4th Brigade. our General was Getty but he was wounded and we are now commanded by Brig Gen Neil who is next thing to a fool if not the thing itself Oh, how hot it is I am seated by the roadside under a rail fence and covered with the dust of the Wagons + Artillery with the hot rays of the sun pressing upon me, and the sweat and dust rolling down my face hurrying to finish this to send back by the Wagons, you must excuse any mistakes Tell Mattie I will write to her as soon as possible meantime she must claim her share in your letters.

The inhabitants inform us that Lee was here yesterday morning 10,000 men and skeedadled out of this place in a hurry. I meant to have made this letter longer but have to seize every chance to send so good by. Love to all. Don't fail to write often, more so than if I recd them regularly for the mail comes through all sorts of channels and some of them will get here if all don't. I was much disappointed in not getting one from home to day. Matt says you have no boarders anything you want at the stores you can have chgd to me and I will pay for it when I come home. don't fail once of writing to

Your aff brother,
Charlie.

Head Quarters 10th Mass Vols South Bank North Anna River
May 24th 1864

Dear Mother,

I sent a letter yesterday while we were on the march to this place to Mary and as we are informed that we are to remain here to day I thought I would commence another although I do not know as the other one has gone any further than the wagon trains which are some where in our rear. I don't know where. You will know by the other letter that we were on the march. about 6 o'clock we began to hear heavy firing and they began to hurry us up and we came about 4 miles almost on a run arriving on the north bank of the river just after dark. We met the stream of wounded coming to the rear, and found that the 5th Corps which was in advance on this road were across the river.

we also met a large squad of Reb prisoners. the firing ceased and we went into line of battle on the other side of the river in the night the Rebels left our front and this morning there have been several hundred Rebel prisoners by us as we lie in line of battle. they are most all North Carolinians and they give themselves up one whole company came in Officers, Non-Commsd Officers and all. they acknowledged themselves whipped. we crossed the river early this morning. another squad of 15 Johnies had just gone by, and they look mighty glad to get in and I don't blame them. I expect they are even more tired and hungry than we are.

Gen Hancock with the 2nd Corps is engaged down the river on our left and it is reported he has not effected a crossing yet. we can hear the thundering of his Cannon and have all day long though it seems a little more distant this afternoon. it was reported by some of the prisoners that he had cut Ewells Corps all to pieces. poor Stewart Campbell I believe you said was in that Corps. I am afraid he may be killed or wounded for they have fared hard.

It is said that poor Munyan is going to die. he is in Fredericksburg. Major Parker has had his arm taken off Lieut Graves is very low also. I see the papers report his name as E. H. Sprague and Munyans as Munger. that is what Artemas Ward calls military glory getting killed and having your name spelled wrong in the newspapers.

We received another mail this morning and I got your letter of the 17th and am glad to hear you have finally received one of my letters. I began to think you never would. I also received Springfield Republicans as late as the 19th. You must not fail to write very often. I do not feel very well to day. I got poisoned in my face yesterday in coming through the woods and my eyes are almost shut up and they are all laughing at me.

There goes another Reb he looks about 7 feet high. he is almost as tall as the Cavalry man on horseback who is guarding him. And there goes some guns in our front so we may get a battle yet to day. Our time begins to look very short only 27 days. I wish we might be spared another battle, but I know we shall not be. the 2nd RI Regts time is out in 12 days and it is reported that they are going Saturday. Regts and parts of Regts are leaving every day now. the 7th Mass has 21 days more to serve. The Rebels are throwing an occasional shell at us but they do not reach the 2nd line where we are yet.

The prisoners who came in report that there are lots of others who want to come but our boys fire at them so they cannot. our men are much opposed to taking prisoners since the Fort Pillow affair, that has cost the Rebels many a life that would otherwise have been spared. I see that the papers are full of the terrible fighting that Burnsides negroes have done, but a few days ago they had not been into a fight at all and I don't believe they have now. I wish I could see them in a battle once, and know for certain whether they would fight or not.

May 25th, 5 o'clock AM.

We moved forward about a quarter of a mile last night and occupied some breast works which the 5th Corps had thrown up and the 5th moved farther to the right.

We had a report last night that the 2nd Corps had captured 15,000 prisoners but we do not know that there is any truth in it.

We heard thier firing all day and up to a late hour last night and it did not seem to move much. We are under marching orders and were ordered to be ready at 5 o'clock. it is now nearly half past but we do not move. I understand that our wagon trains are ordered to the white house. we cannot be far from the VA Central R R and Sextons Junction.

I have thought 50 times of what you spoke of in regard to the Mat Ta Po + the Ny, since we have been on those rivers. There was a house right on the battle line of the 5th Corps when they fought here night before last and the occupants went into the Rebel lines. next morning they came back 2 white women and about 20 Negro women. the soldiers had killed every chicken + pig about the premises and taken all the beds out of the house and slept in them and the chairs were scattered all along the line for the convenience of Uncle Sams nephews. They said when they came back that they thought that the Rebs were going to drive the Yanks all into the river. no doubt thier will was good enough but they found the Yanks a hard party to drive.

We hear no firing anywhere along the line this morning and I presume we shall take up our line of march southward pretty soon but I do not know.

Half past 2 o'clock PM

We finally marched about 8 o'clock this morning and after

marching about a mile we came upon the VA Central RR and the pioneers immediately commenced to tear up the track and burn the ties and bend the rails. we struck the RR at Niels Station according to the sign. we very soon came upon the Rebels and went into line of battle and have been expecting a fight every moment all day. there has been continual skirmishing all day. I suppose we are now near Little River. We have been gradually and carefully crawling along all day. We are protecting the flank to day. Our Corps received 7000 reenforcements yesterday.

Poor Munyan is dead. He died Saturday night he was occasionally out of his head and his brother says he would keep asking for me and inquiring if Adjutant was there. Poor fellow I did not know he was wounded until he was carried from the field and I never saw him afterwards. We have just heard that Capt Weatherells leg has been taken off above the knee. I sat down to finish this as the Q M 2nd RI has come up and offers to take back a mail, so this is right from a prospective battle field which may be one in five minutes from this time. Love to all write often to

Your aff son
Charlie

Hd Quarters 10th Mass Vols 4th Brig 2nd Division 6th Corps
Near Sextons Junction VA May 26th 1864
PS I shall have to stop writing letters pretty soon for want of paper + pencils. We have not seen our baggage wagon since we started.

Dear Mattie,

I received your welcome letter of the 15th and was very glad to get it for you cannot in the least imagine what a comfort letters from home are in these trying times. The mail takes rank even before rations with the soldiers, when our first mail came, it came on the same wagons with the supplies and although the men were all out of rations and hungry, and we might have to leave at any moment even before the rations could be issued, yet nobody would pay any attention to the rations until the mail was all distributed and there were two great grain bags full of it, but alas a large proportion of it could be claimed by no owners now with the Regt. as we did not get any mail until over 200 Officer + men were killed, wounded and missing our Lieut who was killed only the day before had as many as a dozen letters. it is very sad.

I sent a letter to Mother yesterday by the Quartermaster of the 2nd RI who took a mail back to the wagon trains.

We crossed the North Anna River day before yesterday morning and remained on the south bank all day and night. yesterday morning we started about 8 o'clock and crossed the VA Central RR and the pioneers immediately commenced tearing it up. they have utterly destroyed several miles of it. immediately after we came upon the pickets of the enemy, and pursued them to the Little River where the enemy were found in force and fortified on the south bank. we formed our lines and threw up breastworks which we have gradually extended nearer and nearer. the pickets are constantly firing at each other and as I write an occasional bullet goes hissing over my head. The enemy have got fourteen pieces of Artillery in front of us which can be seen, but our batteries have banged away at them at intervals ever since we arrived but do not succeed in getting any reply. We have been expecting to attack or be attacked every moment since we got here but have not as yet.

Word just came that the enemy were pressing Gen Griffins front, and we must hold ourselves ready to go to his assistance at a moments notice if required. Gen Griffin commands a Division of the 5th Corps who are on our left.

I have headed my letter so that you can see the number of our Brigade + Division + Corps. The lamented Sedgwick you know was our Corps Commander when we started, and the Corps is now commanded by Gen Wright.

Gen Getty was our Division Commander when we started but he was wounded in the Battle of the Wilderness and Gen Neil now commands the Div. Gen Wright formerly commanded the 1st Division of this Corps, and is an able commander and was much relied on by Gen Sedgwick. Gen Neil is the worst commander it was ever our misfortune to serve under, and I don't think he is fit to command a company. Gen Getty was a most able and gallant General. he had taken command of the Division but a short time before we left Brandy Station and I never saw him to know him. You will think this strange when I tell you that he was wounded not far from where our Regiment was at the time. I saw Gen Wadsworth not ten minutes before he was killed. we were right on the plank road and he told us to pull up the planks and make a breast work. he was an elderly gray headed man and rode his horse on up the road, while the enemy were making a furious attack and forcing our lines back. our Regt was almost the only one left in reserve, and it was just before Burnside came up. The enemies sharp shooters were firing down the road and his fate was certain. Capt Shurtleff was wounded on the same road, and several men.

Our Regt was also close to where Gen Sedgwick was killed and the same party of sharp shooters succeeded in wounding 5 of our men at a very long distance as we lay resting on the edge of a piece of woods. The men where he was cautioned him that there were sharp shooters who commanded that place but he laughed and said they could not hit an elephant at that distance and had hardly said so when he was hit and killed almost instantly.

In the Battle over the Rebel Breastworks (the one I wrote home about where the Rebels were piled up so) I was standing talking to a Capt Shaw of the 2nd RI. I stood partly turned towards him and my elbow just touching his, when a bullet came and struck square in the breast, tearing it open and making an awful sound, but one only too familiar to my ears. He turned round, fell on his face and was dead.

It is very sad to think of the happy party of Officers who spent the winter at Brandy Station. of 28 field line and staff Officers who were with our Regt 4 are dead and 13 wounded besides one (Capt Bishop) who was slightly wounded and returned to duty in 3 or 4 days. One of the others is very slightly wounded a bullet just scratched his face, Lt Cottrell of Pittsfield but he is not at all remarkable for courage and is making the most of it and staying round the Division Field Hospital in the rear. it is not the first time he has played sick to escape dangerous duties. his wound was not half as bad as Capt Bishops, or Geo Bigelows first wound in the throat, or my poisoned face. When we think that we have been on this campaign but 22 days and have got 25 men to stay and that considerably more than half our numbers are taken already, the prospect looks rather dark for the rest of us.

P W K is doing very well for him and keeps up tolerably well now he was in the Battle of the Wilderness, and part of the time at the next battle he disappeared for two or three days but has kept up since.

You are mistaken about thier being nothing cowardly about me. I am scared most to death every battle we have, but I don't think you need be afraid of my sneaking away unhurt. Capt Haydens leg was not shot away nor do I understand that it is taken off although it may have to be. I hear Mr Joel Hayden is in Fredericksburg also Joe + Sid Bridgeman. they say our wounded get but little care, there is but one surgeon for all the wounded Officers in the 6th Corps so you can judge what the enlisted mens chances are. it is a singular fact that two thirds of the killed and wounded in our Regt are Veteran Volunteers.

We get no intimation yet whether the Officers who recd the 35 five days furlough are to go home with the Regt or what is to be done with them. Our line of our breastworks here runs right through a farmers garden and close to his back door through peas in blossom and radishes + tomatoes + c + c I imagine how Mother and Mrs Clarke would look to have 100 blue jackets with musket + bayonette rush into thier gardens stack arms and seize the spade + shovel and go to throwing up a ridge of Earth five foot high. it makes ones prospect for garden sarse very poor indeed.

I have written this letter as it is reported that our Commissary is coming up to night and I may have a chance to send it. You must write often. Give my love to Thomas + Charles and to Mother + Mary, and respects to all

Your affectionate brother
Charlie.

ANDERSONVILLE PRISON: GEORGIA, MAY 1864

Eugene Forbes: Diary, May 24–27, 1864

Concerned about the difficulty of guarding and supplying the thousands of Union prisoners of war held in Richmond, the Confederate War Department decided in the late fall of 1863 to build a new prison camp at Andersonville in southwestern Georgia. Construction of a sixteen-acre stockade designed to hold up to 10,000 men began in January 1864, and the first two hundred prisoners arrived from Richmond on February 24. By the end of May the camp held more than 18,000 men, and nearly 1,500 prisoners had already died. A printer before the war, Sergeant Eugene Forbes had enlisted in the 4th New Jersey Infantry in 1861. Forbes, who was captured in the Wilderness on the evening of May 6 when the Confederates attacked the Union right flank north of the Orange Turnpike, recorded his arrival at Andersonville in a pocket diary.

Tuesday, May 24. Arrived at Macon about daylight; medium sized town, of good appearance; found I was in company with several men of my own regiment, Company H. Arrived at Andersonville, Ga., about noon, and after considerable delay, were turned into a large enclosure, where we found about 15,000 prisoners, many of whom had been prisoners for nine and ten months. Trafficing in tent-poles, salt, corn bread, &c., was soon going on extensively; some of the men are like skeletons, from chronic diarrhea, &c.; some are as black as charcoal men, and have evidently not washed for many days; they seem to have lost all ambition, and of the 15,000 now here, not one-half could march five miles; the camp is about six hundred yards long by four hundred wide, and surrounded by a high board fence, some twelve or fourteen feet high, with two gates on the west side; sentry boxes are placed at regular intervals along the wall. Drew rations of corn bread and bacon at dark.

Wednesday, May 25. Roll-call about 9 A.M.; a heavy shower last night; our squad is Detachment 57, Mess 1; washed ourselves and our clothes the first time since our capture. Gambling is carried on quite extensively; faro, sweat-cloths, dice, &c., are used, and $10 stakes are played for, as if money was as plenty as sand. Six men were carried out on the "dead line" last night from our (the south) side of the camp. A considerable marsh occupies the very center of the pen, which, if not drained, will be apt to create disease among us; the drinking water is very poor; wells are dug, and kept as private property, but the rebel surgeon says the running water is the most wholesome; we use the run water altogether; the well water appears impregnated with sulphur, or some mineral, looks blue, and induces diarrhea. A large squad of prisoners from the western army arrived this P.M.; they report that Gen. Joseph Johnston has been taken prisoner by Sherman. One of the old prisoners states that the deaths here in the last two months will reach 1,800. Trade is carried on with the guards on the outside of the wall, by talking through cracks, and throwing articles over the fence. Rigged up our tent anew, and commenced a regular "skirmish drill;" took no prisoners, but counted about a dozen dead on the field (my shirt). Several negroes are here, captured in Florida; a negro orderly sergeant has charge of a squad of whites and blacks; the negroes are treated in all respects like ourselves; several Indians are also here, so we make a motley crew. Drew rations towards night, corn bread, bacon, and boiled rice. Sentry fired a shot just after dark, but believe no one was hurt; some of our men came in with the squad which arrived this evening, and more are expected tomorrow; they report that only eighty men are left for duty in the regiment, and that Grant's headquarters are twenty-two miles from Richmond.

Thursday, May 26. "Skirmished," as usual. A party of negroes were set at work digging for tunnels, the existence of which is most probably only in the imaginations of the guards; the officer in charge says he will look no more, but give us a ration of grape and canister if an attempt to escape is made. Two men who were with me in the three months' service, came to see me last night (Louis and Kelly); they have been prisoners about four months, but look very well; Louis is now in the cavalry, and Kelly in the gunboat service. Reported that one man was killed and another wounded last night; various rumors afloat in regard to paroling, &c., but none of which the slightest reliance can be placed. Peddling still goes on; a "bunch" (two little onions,) for 25 cents; a 10 cent plug of tobacco, 50 cents and so on. Some of the dirtiest men were ducked and scrubbed today, and some of the "raiders" (thieves), bucked and gagged, and their heads shaved. The weather is warm, with frequent showers. Boxes and letters are received here by the prisoners. Drew pork and mush at dark, but no bread. A squad of prisoners arrived after dark, some of the 4th among them, who report the regiment reduced to eighty effective men.

Friday, May 27. A "raider" caught last night, and kept prisoner till daylight, when he was bucked and gagged, his head shaved, and afterwards marched around the camp; he took it very coolly. A fight occurred between a party of "raiders" and some of the "raidees", in which the latter got the worst of it; one man is said to be pretty badly hurt. Quite an excitement is apparent among the guards outside; the infantry are marching to various points, and horsemen carrying messages from one body to another. One tunnel was discovered yesterday, and the existence of others is probably suspected. Very hot, and the odor from the swamp and sinks by no means pleasant. Three tunnels discovered today, one said to extend sixty feet beyond the stockade. Drew bread, rice and meat about 8 P.M.; the ration appears to be getting smaller by degrees. Tore out the sleeve and back linings of my blouse, cut up our sugar and coffee bags, and cut off the flap of Hoffman's knapsack, sewed them together, and made an end for the tent. A prisoner who came in night before last reports Lieuts. Flannery and Heston captured on the 13th.

Charles Francis Adams Jr. to Charles Francis Adams

On May 24 advancing Union troops discovered that Lee's army was strongly entrenched near Hanover Junction just south of the North Anna River. Grant decided to again move to the southeast around Lee's right flank and sent his forces across the Pamunkey River on May 27–28. Captain Charles Francis Adams Jr. commanded a detached company of the 1st Massachusetts Cavalry that served on guard duty at Army of the Potomac headquarters. Adams assessed the ongoing campaign in a misdated letter to his father, the American minister to Great Britain, in which he exaggerated the degree of harmony that existed at the time between Grant and Meade. By the end of May Grant had grown frustrated with Meade's caution, while Meade resented Grant's increasing role in making tactical decisions.

H.Q. Army of Potomac.
Hanover Town Va. 29 April/64.

Hon. C. F. Adams
London.

My dear Father

I have a leisure day at last, & the means of writing I mean to pay off a little of my heavy arrears to all of you in London. I have no letters from London since I left Brandey Station I don't know what has become of them.—I suppose they were addressed to the regiment & went to it & may turn up; I sent you my present address in a letter to John, which he has probably forwarded. Two days ago I got two papers from Mamma,—please acknowledge them. I have only had two letters from John,—the latest of May 7th,—he speaks as though you were all well.

Meanwhile here we are.—South of the Pamunkey & only 16 miles from Richmond,—that Mecca & Jerusalem of this Army of the Potomac. As I look back over the campaign since the 4th of May, I don't know where to begin to write I feel vexed out of all bounds with myself for neglecting at the start to provide myself with the few writing conveniences which would have enabled me to send you day by day an account of what was saw, felt, & heard. It is lost now, but I think I might have made a contribution to history, besides relieving some of your anxiety. Now I can't tell you much, & that little won't be of much value. The campaign to us here gradually unfolds itself. Grant & Meade discuss & decide, but keep their own counsel & no one knows whether tomorrow the Army is to fight, to march, or to rest. Meanwhile marching now seems to be the order of the day, &, since day before yesterday Head Quarters have moved thirty odd miles,—turning all the exterior lines of Richmond & bringing us down to the interior line of the Chickahominy. Here we rest for to-day. Up to this time Gen. Grant seems to have looked on this campaign in Va as one necessarily to be made up of the hardest kind of fighting, combined with all the Generalship which he could command, &, as we were numerically the strongest, we might as well do the fighting first as last,—pounding & manoevering at the same time. If this was his idea, I think the wisdom of it is becoming apparent. I cannot believe that his operations have been or now are conducted on any fixed plan, he seems to have one end in view,—the capture of Richmond & destruction of Lee's army,—but I imagine his means to that end undergo daily changes & no man in this Army, but Meade perhaps, is even able to give grounds for a guess as to whether we are to approach Richmond from this side or from the other. Meanwhile, though Grant expected hard fighting, I have no idea that he expected anything like the fighting & the slaughter which took place in the Wilderness & at Spotsylvania,—he had never seen anything like it in the West, & the fierce, stubborn resistance we met far surpassed his expectation. Meade knew better what he had to expect, &, in fighting for him those battles, was I imagine of incalculable assistance to Grant. To-day, as near as I can see, results stand as follows,—these two great armies have pounded each other nearly to pieces for many days,—neither has achieved any real success over the other on the field of battle,—our loss has probably been greater than theirs, for ours has been the offensive,—but we have a decided balance of prisoners & captured artillery in our favor,—the enemy, I think, outfight us, but we outnumber them, &, finally, within the last three days one witnesses in this Army as it moves along, all the results of a victory when in fact it has done only barren fighting, for it has done the one thing needful before the enemy,—it has advanced. The result is wonderful,—hammered & pounded as this Army has been,—worked, marched, fought & reduced as it is,—it is in better spirits & better fighting trim to-day than it was on the first days fight in the Wilderness. Strange as it seems to me, it is, I believe, yet the fact, that this Army is now just on its second wind, & is more formidable than it ever was before,—this I see on every march & I attribute it to movement in advance after heavy, though barren, fighting. With the enemy it is otherwise. Heavier fighting, harder marching, & greater privations,—for with them deficiency in numbers was only to be made good by redoubled activity,—two men with them have done the work of three with us,—all these have led only to movements to the rear,—to the abandonment of line after line until now they find themselves with their backs against Richmond. Naturally this discourages troops,—particularly coming after as hard fighting as they know how to do,—& as a result we now get, as I am informed, from all sources but one story & that of discouragement & exhaustion,—the enemy is getting off his fight. What is to come next?—Will Lee try to revive the spirits of his men & the fortunes of his Army by taking the offensive?—Will he try to repeat the story of the Chickahominy & the six days fighting?—What does Grant mean next to do?—I have always noticed that when I try to divine the future of military operations, I am invariably wrong; & so I long ago gave up trying. Of a few things though I feel pretty sure,—Stonewall Jackson is dead,—Grant is not McClellan, nor is Meade McDowell,—Grant will not let his Army be idle, nor will he allow the initiative to be easily taken out of his hands & if Lee can outfight Meade he will do more than he was ever able to do yet when his troops were more numerous, in better heart & much fresher than they now are. Accordingly we find ourselves approaching the climax of the campaign,—under circumstances which certainly seem to me hopeful. The next few days will probably develop Grant's final move,—the line on which he means to approach Richmond & the point at which he means, unless Lee out-generals him, to have the final fight. I don't believe he will allow time to slip away or Lee to repair damages.—I do believe that while the Army is resting to-day, it is drawing breath for the great struggle & on the eve of great movements & decisive results.

Things meanwhile work in the Army charmingly. Grant is certainly a very extraordinary man; he does not look it & might pass well enough for a dumpy & slouchy little subaltern, very fond of smoking,—neither do I know that he shows it in his conversation, for he never spoke to me & doesn't seem to be a very talkative man anyhow;—they say his mouth shows character,—it may, but it is so covered with beard, that no one can vouch for it. The truth is, he is in appearance a very ordinary looking man,—one who would attract attention neither in the one way or the other,—not knowing who it is you would not pronounce him insignificant,—& knowing who it is, it would require some study to find in his appearance material for hero worship, though there is about his face no indication of weakness or lack of force. He has not nearly so strong a head & face as Humphreys for instance, who at once strikes you as a man of force. In figure Grant is comical,—he sits a horse well, but in walking he leans forward & toddles. Such being his appearance however I do not think that any intelligent person could watch him, even from such a distance as mine, without concluding that he is a remarkable man. He handles those around him so quietly & well,—he so evidently has the faculty of disposing of work & managing men,—he is cool & quiet, almost stolid & as if stupid,—in danger & in a crisis he is one against whom all around, whether few in number or a great army as here, would instinctively lean. He is a man of the most exquisite judgment & tact,—see how he has handled this Army,—he took command under the most unfavorable circumstances,—jealousy between East & West, the Army of the Potomac & the Army of the South West,—that general feeling that the officers from the West were going to swagger over those here & finally that universal envy which success creates & which is always ready to carp at it. The moment I came to Head Quarters I saw that; though nothing was said, yet the materials were all ready for an explosion at the first mistake Grant made. All this has passed away & now Grant has this Army as firmly as ever he had that of the S.W. He has effected this simply by the exercise of tact & good taste, he has humored us,—he has given some promotions,—he has made no parade of his authority,—he has given no orders except through Meade & Meade he treats with the utmost confidence & deference,—the result is that even from the most jealously disposed & most indiscreet of Meade's staff not a word is heard against Grant. The result is of inestimable importance,—the Army has a head & confidence in that head;—it has leaders & there is no discord among those leaders;—we seem to have gotten rid of jealousy & all now seem disposed to go in with a will to win.

At last we have gotten out of the Wilderness. That interminable outline of pines of all sizes which it seemed never would end has given way to a clearer & more cultivated country,—& now we come across the old Virginia plantation houses & can now & then see a regular clearing. The Wilderness was a most fearfully discouraging place,—an enemy always in front against whom the fiercest attack we could make made no impression, —incessant fighting day after day,—no progress forward,—& the hospitals cleared out only to be filled again, while the country was becoming peopled with graves. There the Army got very much discouraged & took blue views of life,—the straggling became terrible & you saw men the whole time & officers sometimes living in the woods or wandering round the country. At that time I take it Lee had accomplished his object & the Army of the Potomac was crippled,—it could not effectively have advanced. At that time however it experienced the great advantage of Grants presence & power for he at once re-enforced it by every available man round Washington thus at once restoring its efficiency, while but for his power & name the Administration would, as heretofore, doubtless have defended Washington at the cost of all the fruits of this Army's fighting. Thus Lee found himself again opposed by a fresh army, & every new man who came up from the rear served to revive the spirits of those who had been here before. Now the Army is in capital condition & I feel once more sanguine,—but the telegraphs of the steamer which brings this will tell the whole story.

Meanwhile I hear not a word of your negotiation. What has

become of it?—Is it not too late now?—or is it supposed that disaster or success will bring the rebels to your terms?—I do not even hear that that negotiation has as yet crept into the papers,—but after all, it is of less consequence now, for formerly it might have stopped bloodshed but now it can hardly be in time to do more than pave the way for conciliation,—since this month came in this war seems to have gone so far that now, in this last effort, either we must crush them or leave them so weak that little enough more blood will be left to shed. Pray keep me informed about this, & also do send me books & reading matter,—here at H. Q. I have time & even Shakespeare is getting read out.

As to myself I have little to say,—in this campaign I have been exposed hardly at all, in fact even less than I should wish, but casualties come very easily & no-one knows how or when he & bullets may be round together. Give my love to all, & in future I hope to write more frequently. Affy

C. F. Adams

May 29, 1864

ASSESSING BLACK TROOPS: MAY 1864

Lorenzo Thomas to Henry Wilson

Brigadier General Lorenzo Thomas, the adjutant general of the Union army, began recruiting and organizing black troops in the Mississippi Valley in the spring of 1863. He wrote about their achievements to Henry Wilson, the Massachusetts Republican who headed the Senate Committee on Military Affairs. When Garrett Davis of Kentucky proposed during a debate on June 6 that all black soldiers be disarmed and used as laborers, Wilson had Thomas's letter read into the Senate record.

Washington, May 30, 1864.

Dear Sir: On several occasions when on the Mississippi river I contemplated writing to you respecting the colored troops, and to suggest that as they have been fully tested as soldiers their pay should be raised to that of white troops, and I desire now to give my testimony in their behalf. You are aware that I have been engaged in the organization of freedmen for over a year, and have necessarily been thrown in constant contact with them.

The negro in a state of slavery is brought up by the master from early childhood to strict obedience, and to obey implicitly the dictates of the white man, and they are thus led to believe that they are an inferior race. Now, when organized into troops, they carry this habit of obedience with them; and their officers being entirely white men, the negro promptly obeys his orders. A regiment is thus rapidly brought into a state of discipline. They are a religious people, another high quality for making good soldiers. They are a musical people, and thus readily learn to march and accurately perform their maneuvers. They take pride in being elevated as soldiers, and keep themselves neat and clean, as well as their camp grounds. This I know from personal inspection, and from the reports of my special inspectors, two of my staff being constantly on inspecting duty.

They have proved a most important addition to our forces, enabling the generals in active operations to take a large force of white troops into the field; and now brigades of blacks are placed with the whites. The forts erected at the important points on the river are nearly all garrisoned by blacks—artillery regiments raised for the purpose—say at Paducah and Columbus, Kentucky; Memphis, Tennessee; Vicksburg and Natchez, Mississippi, and most of the works around New Orleans. Experience proves that they manage heavy guns very well. Their fighting qualities have also been fully tested a number of times, and I am yet to hear of the first case where they did not fully stand up to their work. I passed over the ground where the first Louisiana made the gallant charge at Port Hudson, by far the stronger part of the rebel works. The wonder is that so many made their escape. At Milliken's Bend, where I had three incomplete regiments, one without arms until the day previous to the attack; greatly superior numbers of rebels charged furiously up to the very breast-works. The negroes met the enemy on the ramparts, and both sides freely used the bayonet, a most rare occurrence in warfare, as one or other party gives way before coming in contact with the steel. The rebels were defeated with heavy loss. The bridge at Moscow, on the line of railroad from Memphis to Corinth, was defended by one small regiment of blacks. A cavalry attack of three times their number was made, the blacks defeating them in the three charges made by the rebels. They fought them hours, until our cavalry came up, when the defeat was made complete, many of the rebel dead being left on the field. A cavalry force of one hundred and fifty attacked three hundred rebel cavalry near the Big Black with signal success, a number of prisoners being taken and marched to Vicksburg. Forrest attacked Paducah with seven thousand five hundred. The garrison was between five and six hundred; nearly four hundred were colored troops, very recently raised. What troops could have done better? So, too, they fought well at Fort Pillow until overpowered by greatly superior numbers.

The above enumerated cases seem to me sufficient to demonstrate the value of the colored troops. I make no mention of the cases on the Atlantic coast with which you are perfectly familiar. I have the honor to be, Very respectfully, Your obedient servant,

L. Thomas

BEHIND THE UNION LINES: VIRGINIA, MAY–JUNE 1864

Cornelia Hancock to Her Sister

A Quaker woman from New Jersey, Cornelia Hancock began her service as a volunteer army nurse at Gettysburg in July 1863 and later worked at hospitals in Washington, D.C., and Brandy Station, Virginia. She arrived in Fredericksburg on May 12 to find scenes that "beggared all description" as rain "poured in through the bullet-riddled roofs of the churches until our wounded lay in pools of water made bloody by their seriously wounded condition." Hancock worked at Fredericksburg until the end of May, when her hospital was moved to the new Union supply base at White House on the Pamunkey River.

May 28th, 1864.

MY DEAR SISTER

IT is one of the most beautiful mornings that ever blew. We are just evacuating Fredericksburg, the wounded having been all sent to Washington. We had the pleasure of feeding the wounded who were kept prisoners in the Wilderness for nearly three weeks and almost starved. I met a surg. who asked me why the cavalry had not released them before and wanted to know what was going to be done with them. I told him they most of them had been sent back to the regt. in the front. He filled with tears and said they could not send *him* as he had but eleven men left in his Regt. I never felt more sorry for a man. The men, prepared for march, about 8,000, are all in line with shining bayonets. The cavalry, all mounted officers, riding up and down the line, flags waving, everything around is exhilarating. They go about one hundred yards, then halt. A courier who just brought in a dispatch from Gen. Grant is guarding our wagon. He is an intelligent German and goes out to the farm houses and gets us fresh milk and cakes. He is the most splendid rider I ever saw and is as brave as he can be. He had his horse shot under him yesterday but soon captured another, says he will try to get one for me before we arrive at Port

Royale. We have a battery at the front of the train and Cavalry on all sides, still they say the guerrillas have attacked the rear of the train and captured fourteen men and killed two. Poor soldiers. It is very hard on a march. They are constantly falling by the roadside. I have carried lots of their guns and knapsacks for them today. I felt many times like giving them my seat. I can enjoy myself in a march looking round. There is always something going on interesting and most of the time I can sleep in the most profound manner. They shoot the chickens, calves, pigs, and &c then lay them along the road and every man gets a stick and shoulders a piece. We stopped for dinner and have seen nothing of Grant's messenger since. I guess he has been gobbled by Guerrillas. Every few rods a man sings out: "There is Miss Hancock." Mrs. Lee is a very good singer. It is getting towards night and she is singing as we are wearily nearing Port Royale. In this town we cannot obtain any resting place except in the negro shanties but that does not concern my mind at all. We have a hoe cake for supper and no prospect for breakfast.

May 30th—we stayed in P. Royal all night in some negro quarters and this morning went to the Medical Director's office and heard from time to time that no passes were to be granted to any *ladies* except for them to *return* to *Washington*. I sat upon my trunk perfectly easy. There has always been a way provided and I always expect there will be, so never concern. At length a doctor comes up who volunteers us to go on the transport *without* a pass. That I often do. But I like going in the wagon train better and the Sanitary have offered to carry us thru, so now I am sitting in their wagon. We have plenty of provisions with us and I hope will get thru comfortably. They are making wounded all the time and our services will be needed by the time we get there. I hope you are doing well at home but I have had no tidings that you are as I have never received a letter except one from Ellen. Capt. Harris has just come, volunteers us to be as comfortable as possible.

Direct a letter to Miss Hancock
care of Sanitary Comm.
White House, V.

This morning this place is to be evacuated and the White House is to be the next base. Oh! what a sight. This place was one mass of tired, swearing soldiery, scrambling for a hard tack, killing chickens, pigs, calves &c. Seems like Bedlam let loose. I am always cared for tho'; before we had been in the town half an hour a guard was detailed over the house, so we slept in perfect security. I hope Grant is accomplishing something as he is making terrible suffering for the rear of his army. They never have been used to rapid evacuating and advancing into an enemy's country. The White House sounds nearer to Richmond. I shall always remember with pleasure some Secesh I met in Fredericksburg. I believe we are to have a Johnny cake for breakfast. I have always been well received where I am known and if I could be allowed to stay with them would be content to make few new acquaintances. I do not wish you to give a thought of uneasiness for me. I am always contented with my lot and if *you* will not concern I will promise you *I* will not. I would give lots to see our children especially Eddie. Yesterday during the shelling a child not 3 years old walked across the commons. If thee knows anything of Salem affairs write me. I expect Dr. Potter has lots of letters for me from mother; direct in his care 1st Div. 2nd Corps Hospital. I want a letter awfully, and if you have done your duty there will be some at the front. I have no fear but you have for when I am here I long since have been convinced I have the best sister and mother in the world. If Dr. Aiken returns send my things.

With much love,

I am thy sister—CORNELIA

May 31st, 1864—On March.

MY DEAR SISTER

WE left Port Royale on the Rappahannock 15 miles below Fredericksburg on the 30th of May, Mrs. Lee, Georgy Willets and I having come here from that place in an open wagon the day before. Now we are on our march for the White House—a distance of about 45 miles though the roads are very winding and it may be much farther. It is a very warm day and the guards suffer very much with the dust and heat. There is almost always an alarm along the line about Guerrillas, often just enough to make a pleasant excitement. I cannot feel afraid and strange as it may seem the soldiers want to have a brush with them. I almost worship our faithful soldiers who trudge on and never murmur or complain. I am in a Sanitary spring wagon and it is very comfortable—when I get tired I can lie down and sleep. Mrs. Lee is a very pleasant travelling companion. The army has not passed through this section and there appears to have been some attempt at cultivating the land, but we would not consider that there was anything worth harvesting. We are eating strawberries, peas, &c—Tonight we halted at a village called Newtown, went into a Secesh house, found a nice bed and room to sleep. They told us they have nothing to eat. We sent back to the train for rations and had the colored people to get us a good supper which we ate upon their table. The women are bitter Secessionists—one said her husband is a commisary in the Rebel army. We think he furnishes rations to the guerilla bands and I was not disposed to show them any favours but true to some people's idea of right they wanted to take Sanitary stuff and give those rebels to live on because they said they were starving. There was a splendid side saddle that I wanted to confiscate for I know that has been smuggled from the North. There was not a man in our crowd who had spunk enough to take it. I wish Dr. Dudley had been along, I would have had it then. Protecting Secesh property is entirely played out with me.

June 1st.

At 7 o'clock this morning we left our Secesh enemies and resumed the march which was extremely dusty. After we had gone about a mile on the road the guerrilas made a dash, but our cavalry immediately drove them back into the woods. I never saw anything more promptly accomplished, not a gun was fired, yet the woods have been searched and not a rebel can be found. Our train this morning is 15 miles long and more expected to catch up. Even the colored people are Secesh here and we cannot induce them to go along with us. A few stragglers have joined the teams this morning. In Fredericksburg I never found a disaffected colored person. No one need ever speak against Jersey, it is a paradise compared to Virginia. We rode on about a mile and found a house deserted, the owner of which was said to be a chief of Guerrillas, so the soldiers fired his house and it is now burning. Just beyond us, a line of our cavalry are chasing what appears to us a dozen mounted guerrillas. They have come in, however, finding only some colored people who say that there is a mounted guerrilla band 200 strong. Whether we will overtake them or not is a question. We have halted to water the train which is quite a job. If I ever get through this march safely I shall feel thankful. If not, I shall never regret having made the attempt for I am no better to suffer than the thousands who die. I think that the privates in the army who have nothing before them but hard marching, poor fare and terrible fighting are entitled to all the unemployed muscle of the North and they will get mine with a good will during this summer. Then if Grant does not take Richmond, I am afraid that I shall be discouraged. I can bear all I have witnessed in this campaign if we are only successful. We have, every day, evidences of the most distinguished gallantry of our troops and I know all they want is a leader and I hope that they will find him in Grant. The bridge over the Matapony is broken and we have to remain here about three hours. We hear the cannons dealing them deadly blows near Hanover Court House. I feel quite anxious to get out to the field but have started upon this Campaign possessing my mind with patience, and so I expect to try to continue. We have moved two or three hundred yards nearer the Matapony, over which the bridge is broken. If we cannot go on it is pleasant to rest. We make up our minds to anything that comes and so are not much disappointed. A few hours later finds us one and a half miles beyond the Matapony River around a poor white woman's house. She and her six children live in the most desolate wilderness. They have been plundered of all their eatables and she seemed forlorn indeed. Her husband died about a year ago. She is the nearest approach to a Union woman I have seen in Virginia. She is like the poor of our own neighborhood, only she wishes it settled in order that she may see better times. We left her plenty of supplies. She treated us the best she could and now we have bid her adieu and are just starting out on another day's tramp, expecting to reach Hanover town. There is continued firing both front and rear, but we have been preserved so far. I hope to reach our Division hospital to-day and see who is wounded. There are two young men belonging to the Sanitary Commission, Mr. Clarence Messer and Charles Wycoff, who try to make the trip agreeable. The latter is a brother-in-law to the gentleman who vacated the Chancellor's house and made his escape with his family to the North.

White House, June 3rd—I arrived at this place yesterday having joined a train of wounded coming from the battle field with Dr. Aiken. We got opposite the White House and found no bridge and were obliged to keep our wounded in ambulance 12 hours longer, making two days and nights they have been loaded and on the way. I have turned wound-dresser and cleaner generally. You can hardly imagine the appearance of our wounded men now brought in from the field, after having been under fire for 20 successive days. They hardly look like men but are extremely hopeful that Richmond will be taken. There are lots of women; but I seem to be still in favour in the 2nd Corps and certainly please the wounded men. Dr. Burmeister is in charge here. Dr. Aiken transports the wounded from the field. Dr. Dudley sends me letters but I do not see him. He is at a Division Hospital in the field. Such fighting never was recorded in any history. I hope the people are behaving in a becoming manner at the North for we are wearing sackcloth here, there is so much suffering. We hear the firing night and day, one continued belching forth of artillery. Miss Willets is here, very sick at present. I think it a cause of great thankfulness that I am preserved in health and strength. Mrs. Lee has a cooking shanty up and is therefore happy. I am not cooking, but have a ward and do everything else, which suits me better. I have no more knowledge whether you fare well or ill at home than if I was in my grave, but I hope that I shall receive letters now if they are directed White House, Virginia, care of the Sanitary Commission.

If any body feels an interest to send anything to me in care of the Sanitary Commission, it would be forwarded. I am certain that if the ladies of the North knew how important pads are to us they would send more than we now get. It is impossible to get beds and blankets sufficient and pads afford us great relief. Remember me to everybody. I am afraid I shall be old and gray by the time you see me again, but if I surrender my life it will not be as valuable as thousands of brave men who are falling hereabouts. Send all I write to Mother immediately with the request that she copy it in ink. I want my letters preserved as I keep no other diary. Give my love to the children. I have met with one loss; my photograph album was stolen or lost in the march and I regret the loss.

From thy sister
C. HANCOCK

BATTLE OF COLD HARBOR:
VIRGINIA, MAY–JUNE 1864

Frank Wilkeson: from Recollections of a Private Soldier in the Army of the Potomac

Lee responded to Grant's crossing of the Pamunkey on May 28 by withdrawing to the south and deploying his army along Totopotomoy Creek about ten miles north of Richmond. The two armies fought at Bethesda Church on May 30 as they extended their lines to the east. On May 31 Union troops captured the crossroads at Cold Harbor, about three miles south of Bethesda Church, and held it against a Confederate counterattack the next morning. An attack by two Union corps on the Confederate lines at Cold Harbor on the evening of June 1 was repulsed after heavy fighting. Both sides sent reinforcements, and by nightfall on June 2 Lee's army was strongly entrenched along a seven mile line extending from north of Bethesda Church to south of Cold Harbor. At 4:30 A.M. on June 3 the Army of the Potomac began a series of frontal assaults that failed to break through Lee's defenses and cost the Union about 7,000 men killed, wounded, or missing, and the Confederates about 1,500; most of the Union casualties were suffered in the first hour of fighting. Frank Wilkeson had run away from his family's Hudson Valley farm during the winter of 1863–64 and enlisted in the 11th New York Light Artillery Battery shortly before he turned sixteen. Wilkeson wrote about Cold Harbor, where his battery was assigned to the artillery brigade of the Second Corps, in an 1887 memoir.

ON the morning of May 28, 1864, the Second Corps crossed the Pamunkey River. Close by the bridge on which we crossed, and to the right of it, under a tree, stood Generals Grant, Meade, and Hancock, and a little back of them was a group of staff officers. Grant looked tired. He was sallow. He held a dead cigar firmly between his teeth. His face was as expressionless as a pine board. He gazed steadily at the enlisted men as they marched by, as though trying to read their thoughts, and they gazed intently at him. He had the power to send us to our deaths, and we were curious to see him. But the men did not evince the slightest enthusiasm. None cheered him, none saluted him. Grant stood silently looking at his troops and listening to Hancock, who was talking and gesticulating earnestly. Meade stood by Grant's side and thoughtfully stroked his own face. I stepped from the column and filled my canteens in the Pamunkey River, and looked my fill at the generals and their staffs, and then ran by the marching troops through a gantlet of chaff, as "Go it, artillery," "The artillery is advancing," "Hurry to your gun, my son, or the battle will be lost," and similar sarcastically good-natured remarks, which were calculated to stimulate my speed.

During the afternoon we heard considerable firing in front of us, and toward evening we marched over ground where dead cavalrymen were plentifully sprinkled. The blue and the gray lay side by side, and their arms by them. With the Confederates lay muzzle-loading carbines, the ramrods of which worked upward on a swivel hinge fastened near the muzzle of the weapon. It was an awkward arm and far inferior to the Spencer carbine with which our cavalry was armed. There were ancient and ferocious-looking horse-pistols, such as used to grace the Bowery stage, lying by the dead Confederates. The poverty of the South was plainly shown by the clothing and equipment of her dead. These dead men were hardly stiff when we saw them. All of their pockets had been turned inside out. That night, while searching for fresh, clean water, I found several dead cavalrymen in the woods, where they had probably crawled after being wounded. I struck a match so as to see one of these men plainly, and was greatly shocked to see large black beetles eating the corpse. I looked at no more dead men that night.

The next day the sound of battle arose again. At distant points it would break out furiously and then die down. In our immediate front heavy skirmishing was going on, and wounded men began to drift to the rear in search of hospitals. They said that there was a stream of water, swamps, and a line of earthworks, behind which lay the Confederate infantry, in our front, and that we could not get to the works. At no time did the fire rise to a battle's volume; it was simply heavy and continuous skirmishing, in which our men fought at great disadvantage, and were severely handled. Finding that these works were too strong to be taken by assault, Grant moved the army to the left. On June 1st we heard heavy fighting to our left, and that night we learned that a portion of the Sixth Corps, aided by ten thousand of Butler's men from Bermuda Hundreds, had forced the Chickahominy River at a loss of three thousand men, and that they held the ground they had taken. The news-gatherers said that the Confederates were strongly intrenched, and evidently had no intention of fighting in the open. We knew that a bloody battle was close at hand, and instead of being elated the enlisted men were depressed in spirits. That night the old soldiers told the story of the campaign under McClellan in 1862. They had fought over some of the ground we were then camped on. Some of the men were sad, some indifferent; some so tired of the strain on their nerves that they wished they were dead and their troubles over. The infantry knew that they were to be called upon to assault perfect earth-works, and though they had resolved to do their best, there was no eagerness for the fray, and the impression among the intelligent soldiers was that the task cut out for them was more than men could accomplish.

On June 2d the Second Corps moved from the right to the left. We saw many wounded men that day. We crossed a swamp or marched around a swamp, and the battery I belonged to parked in a ravine. There were some old houses on our line of march, but not a chicken or a sheep or a cow to be seen. The land was wretchedly poor. The night of June 2d was spent in getting into battle-line. There was considerable confusion as the infantry marched in the darkness. In our front we could see tongues of flames dart forth from Confederate rifles as their pickets fired in the direction of the noise they heard, and their bullets sang high above our heads. My battery went into position just back of a crest of a hill. Behind us was an alder swamp, where good drinking water gushed forth from many springs. Before we slept we talked with some of the Seventh New York Heavy Artillery, and found that they were sad of heart. They knew that they were to go into the fight early in the morning, and they dreaded the work. The whole army seemed to be greatly depressed the night before the battle of Cold Harbor.

Before daybreak of June 3d the light-artillery men were aroused. We ate our scanty breakfast and took our positions around the guns. All of us were loath to go into action. In front of us we could hear the murmurs of infantry, but it was not sufficiently light to see them. We stood leaning against the cool guns, or resting easily on the ponderous wheels, and gazed intently into the darkness in the direction of the Confederate earthworks. How slowly dawn came! Indistinctly we saw moving figures. Some on foot rearward bound, cowards hunting for safety; others on horseback riding to and fro near where we supposed the battle-lines to be; then orderlies and servants came in from out the darkness leading horses, and we knew that the regimental and brigade commanders were going into action on foot. The darkness faded slowly, one by one the stars went out, and then the Confederate pickets opened fire briskly; then we could see the Confederate earthworks, about six hundred yards ahead of us—could just see them and no more. They were apparently deserted, not a man was to be seen behind them; but it was still faint gray light. One of our gunners looked over his piece and said that he could see the sights, but that they blurred. We filled our sponge buckets with water and waited, the Confederate pickets firing briskly at us the while, but doing no damage. Suddenly the Confederate works were manned. We could see a line of slouch hats above the parapet. Smoke in great puffs burst forth from their line, and shell began to howl by us. Their gunners were getting the range. We sprung in and out from the three-inch guns and replied angrily. To our left, to our right, other batteries opened; and along the Confederate line cannon sent forth their balls searching for the range. Then their guns were silent. It was daylight. We, the light-artillery men, were heated with battle. The strain on our nerves was over. In our front were two lines of blue-coated infantry. One well in advance of the other, and both lying down. We were firing over them. The Confederate pickets sprang out of their rifle pits and ran back to their main line of works. Then they turned and warmed the battery with long-range rifle practice, knocking a man over here, killing another there, breaking the leg of a horse yonder, and generally behaving in an exasperating manner. The Confederate infantry was always much more effective than their artillery, and the battery that got under the fire of their cool infantry always suffered severely. The air began to grow hazy with powder smoke. We saw that the line of slouch-hatted heads had disappeared from the Confederate earthworks, leaving heads exposed only at long intervals. Out of the powder smoke came an officer from the battle-lines of infantry. He told us to stop firing, as the soldiers were about to charge. He disappeared to carry the message to other batteries. Our cannon became silent. The smoke drifted off of the field. I noticed that the sun was not yet up. Suddenly the foremost line of our troops, which were lying on the ground in front of us, sprang to their feet and dashed at the Confederate earthworks at a run. Instantly those works were manned. Cannon belched forth a torrent of canister, the works glowed brightly with musketry, a storm of lead and iron struck the blue line, cutting gaps in it. Still they pushed on, and on, and on. But, how many of them fell! They drew near the earthworks, firing as they went, and then, with a cheer, the first line of the Red Division of the Second Corps (Barlow's) swept over it. And there in our front lay, sat, and stood the second line, the supports; why did not they go forward and make good the victory? They did not. Intensely excited, I watched the portion of the Confederate line which our men had captured. I was faintly conscious of terrific firing to our right and of heavy and continuous cheering on that portion of our line which was held by the Fifth and Sixth Corps. For once the several corps had delivered a simultaneous assault, and I knew that it was to be now or never. The powder smoke curled lowly in thin clouds above the captured works. Then the firing became more and more thunderous. The tops of many battle-flags could be seen indistinctly, and then there was a heavy and fierce yell, and the thrilling battle-cry of the Confederate infantry floated to us. "Can our men withstand the charge?" I asked myself. Quickly I was answered. They came into sight clambering over the parapet of the captured works. All organization was lost. They fled wildly for the protection of their second line and the Union guns, and they were shot by scores as they ran. The Confederate infantry appeared behind their works and nimbly climbed over, as though intent on following up their success, and their fire was as the fury of hell. We manned the guns and drove them to cover by bursting shell. How they yelled! How they swung their hats! And how quickly their pickets ran forward to their rifle pits and sank out of sight! The swift, brave assault had been bravely met and most bloodily repulsed. Twenty minutes had not passed since the infantry had sprung to their feet, and ten-thousand of our men lay dead or wounded on the ground. The men of the Seventh New York Heavy Artillery came back without their colonel. The regiment lost heavily in enlisted men and line officers. Men from many commands sought shelter behind the crest of the hill we were behind. They seemed to be dazed and utterly discouraged. They told of the strength of the Confederate earthworks, and asserted that behind the line we could see was another and stronger line, and all the enlisted men insisted that they could not have taken the second line even if their supports had followed them. These battle-dazed visitors drifted off after a while and found their regiments, but some of them drifted to the rear and to coffee pots. We drew the guns back behind the crest of the hill, and lay down in the sand and waited. I noticed that the sun was now about a half an hour high. Soldiers came to the front from the rear, hunting for their regiments, which had been practically annihilated as offensive engines of war. Occasionally a man fell dead, struck by a stray ball from the picket line. By noon the stragglers were mostly gathered up and had rejoined their regiments, and columns of troops began to move to and fro in our rear in the little valley formed by the alder swamp. A column of infantry marching by fours passed to our right. I watched them, listlessly wondering if they were going to get something to eat, as I was hungry. I saw a puff of smoke between the marchers and myself, heard the report of a bursting shell, and twelve men of that column were knocked to the earth. Their officers shouted, "Close up! close up!" The uninjured men hurriedly closed the gap and marched on. The dead and wounded men lay on the ground, with their rifles scattered among them.

Soon some soldiers came out of the woods and carried the wounded men off, but left the dead where they fell. We buried them that night. Then, as the day wore away, and the troops were well in hand again, I saw staff officers ride along the lines, and then I saw the regimental commanders getting their men into line. About four o'clock in the afternoon I heard the charging commands given. With many an oath at the military stupidity which would again send good troops to useless slaughter, I sprang to my feet and watched the doomed infantry. Men, whom I knew well, stood rifle in hand not more than thirty feet from me, and I am happy to state that they continued to so stand. Not a man stirred from his place. The army to a man refused to obey the order, presumably from General Grant, to renew the assault. I heard the order given, and I saw it disobeyed. Many of the enlisted men had been up to and over the Confederate works. They had seen their strength, and they knew that they could not be taken by direct assault, and they refused to make a second attempt. That night we began to intrench.

By daylight we had our earthwork finished and were safe. The Seventh New York Heavy Artillery, armed as infantry, were intrenched about eighty yards in front of us. We were on the crest of a ridge; they were below us. Behind us, for supports, were two Delaware regiments, their combined strength being about one hundred and twenty men. Back of us was the alder swamp, where springs of cool water gushed forth. The men in front of us had to go to these springs for water. They would draw lots to see who should run across the dangerous, bullet-swept ground that intervened between our earthworks and theirs. This settled, the victim would hang fifteen or twenty canteens around him; then, crouching low in the rifle-pits, he would give a great jump, and when he struck the ground he was running at the top of his speed for our earthwork. Every Confederate sharpshooter within range fired at him. Some of these thirsty men were shot dead; but generally they ran into the earthwork with a laugh. After filling their canteens, they would sit by our guns and smoke and talk, nerving themselves for the dangerous return. Adjusting their burden of canteens, they would go around the end of our works on a run and rush back over the bullet-swept course, and again every Confederate sharpshooter who saw them would fire at them. Sometimes these water-carriers would come to us in pairs. One day two Albany men leaped into our battery. After filling their canteens, they sat with us and talked of the beautiful city on the Hudson, and finally started together for their rifle-pits. I watched through an embrasure, and saw one fall. Instantly he began to dig a little hollow with his hands in the sandy soil, and instantly the Confederate sharpshooters went to work at him. The dust flew up on one side of him, and then on the other. The wounded soldier kept scraping his little protective trench in the sand. We called to him. He answered that his leg was broken below the knee by a rifle ball. From the rifle-pits we heard his comrades call to him to take off his burden of canteens, to tie their strings together, and to set them to one side. He did so, and then the thirsty men in the pits drew lots to see who should risk his life for the water. I got keenly interested in this dicing with death, and watched intently. A soldier sprang out of the rifle-pits. Running obliquely, he stooped as he passed the canteens, grasped the strings, turned, and in a flash was safe. Looking through the embrasure, I saw the dust rise in many little puffs around the wounded man, who was still digging his little trench, and, with quickening breath, felt that his minutes were numbered. I noted a conspicuous man, who was marked with a goitre, in the rifle-pits, and recognized him as the comrade of the stricken soldier. He called to his disabled friend, saying that he was coming for him, and that he must rise when he came near and cling to him when he stopped. The hero left the rifle-pits on the run; the wounded man rose up and stood on one foot; the runner clasped him in his arms; the arms of the wounded man twined around his neck, and he was carried into our battery at full speed, and was hurried to the rear and to a hospital. To the honor of the Confederate sharpshooters, be it said, that when they understood what was being done they ceased to shoot.

One day during this protracted Cold Harbor fight, a battery of Cohorn mortars was placed in position in the ravine behind us. The captain of this battery was a tall, handsome, sweet-voiced man. He spent a large portion of his time in our earthworks, watching the fire of his mortars. He would jump on a gun and look over the works, or he would look out through the embrasures. Boy-like, I talked to him. I would have talked to a field-marshal if I had met one. He told me many things relative to mortar practice, and I, in turn, showed him how to get a fair look at the Confederate lines without exposing himself to the fire of the sharpshooters, most of whom we had "marked down." He playfully accused me of being afraid, and insisted that at six hundred yards a sharpshooter could not hit a man. But I had seen too many men killed in our battery to believe that. So he continued to jump on guns and to poke his head into embrasures. One day I went to the spring after water. While walking back I met four men carrying a body in a blanket. "Who is that?" I asked. "The captain of the mortars," was the reply. Stopping, they uncovered his head for me. I saw where the ball had struck him in the eye, and saw the great hole in the back of his head where it had passed out.

The killed and wounded of the first day's fight lay unburied and uncared for between the lines. The stench of the dead men became unbearable, and finally a flag of truce was sent out. There was a cessation of hostilities to bury the dead and to succor the wounded. I went out to the ground in front of our picket line to talk to the Confederate soldiers, and to trade sugar and coffee for tobacco. Every corpse I saw was as black as coal. It was not possible to remove them. They were buried where they fell. Our wounded—I mean those who had fallen on the first day on the ground that lay between the picket lines—were all dead. I saw no live man lying on this ground. The wounded must have suffered horribly before death relieved them, lying there exposed to the blazing southern sun o' days, and being eaten alive by beetles o' nights.

One day four men carrying a pale infantry-man stopped for an instant in my battery. The wounded man suffered intensely from a wound through the foot. My sympathy was excited for the young fellow, and as we at the moment were doing nothing, I asked for half an hour's leave. Getting it, I accompanied him back into the woods to one of the Second Corps' field hospitals. Here, groaning loudly, he awaited his turn, which soon came. We lifted him on the rude table. A surgeon held chloroform to his nostrils, and under its influence he lay as if in death. The boot was removed, then the stocking, and I saw a great ragged hole on the sole of the foot where the ball came out. Then I heard the coatless surgeon who was making the examination cry out, "The cowardly whelp!" So I edged around and looked over the shoulders of an assistant surgeon, and saw that the small wound on the top of the foot, where the ball entered, was blackened with powder! I, too, muttered "The coward" and was really pleased to see the knife and saw put to work and the craven's leg taken off below the knee. He was carried into the shade of a tree, and left there to wake up. I watched the skilful surgeons probe and carve other patients. The little pile of legs and arms grew steadily, while I waited for the object of my misplaced sympathy to recover his senses. With a long breath he opened his eyes. I was with him at once, and looked sharply at him. I will never forget the look of horror that fastened on his face when he found his leg was off. Utter hopelessness and fear that look expressed. I entered into conversation with him; and he, weakened and unnerved by the loss of the leg, and the chloroform, for once told the truth. Lying on his back, he aimed at his great toe, meaning to shoot it off; but being rudely joggled by a comrade at the critical instant, his rifle covered his foot just below the ankle, and an ounce ball went crashing through the bones and sinews. The wound, instead of being a furlough, was a discharge from the army, probably into eternity. Our guns at the front began to howl at the Confederates again, and I was forced to leave the hospital. So I hastened back to my guns. The utter contempt of the surgeons, their change from careful handling to almost brutality, when they discovered the wound was self-inflicted, was bracing to me. I liked it, and rammed home the ammunition in gun No. 1 with vim.

Constantly losing men in our earthwork, shot not in fair fight, but by sharpshooters, we all began to loathe the place. At last, one afternoon the captain ordered us to level the cornhills between the battery and the road, so that we could withdraw the guns without making a noise. At once understanding that a flank movement was at hand, we joyfully gathered up shovels and spades, and went at the obstructions with a will. No. 3 of No. 1 gun, an Albany man, was at my side. I was bent over shovelling. I straightened myself up. He leaned over to sink his shovel, pitched forward in a heap, dead, and an artilleryman beyond him clasped his stomach and howled a death howl. No. 3 was shot from temple to temple. The ball passed through his head and hit the other man in the stomach, fatally wounding him. They were the last men our battery lost at Cold Harbor.

That evening the horses were brought up, and all the guns but mine, No. 1, were taken off. We sat and watched them disappear in the darkness. Soon heavy columns of infantry could be indistinctly seen marching by the alder swamp in our rear. Then all was quiet, excepting the firing of the pickets. We sat and waited for the expected advance of the Confederates; but they did not come. Towards midnight an officer rode into the earthwork and asked lowly who was in command. The sergeant stepped forward and received his orders. Turning to us he whispered, "Limber to the rear." Silently the horses swung around. The gun was limbered, and, with the caisson in the lead, we pulled out of the earthwork, slowly drove across the cornfield, struck into a dusty road in the forest, and marched for the James River and the bloody disasters that awaited us beyond that beautiful stream.

"BORN ANEW IN BLOOD AND TEARS": NEW YORK, JUNE 1864

Maria Lydig Daly: Diary, June 8, 1864

The daughter of a wealthy New York family of Dutch-German ancestry, Maria Lydig Daly supported the war effort through her contributions to the Women's Central Association for Relief and other charitable activities. Her husband, Charles P. Daly, was an Irish-American Catholic active in Democratic politics who served as chief judge of the New York City Court of Common Pleas (the highest court in the city). She wrote about the news of Grant's campaign in Virginia.

June 8, 1864

I have so much to do and think of that I forget my diary, which, in such momentous times, is a *crime* against myself. Should I live to be an old lady, I shall deeply regret this.

Grant's success has been certain but slow; the enemy has been fighting every inch of the way. I had a letter from Badeau from the front, written in pencil, breathing the utmost confidence in the army, its leader, and the final success which, as he speaks from accurate knowledge, cannot but give us the greatest confidence. Both armies fight with the greatest bravery. Frank Barlow has again greatly distinguished himself, and Grant has recommended him to a major generalship. We have lost some of our best generals—Wadsworth, Sedgwick, Rice, and thousands of heroes whose names are known but to their sorrowing families. Our nationality will be born anew in blood and tears, but we trust it will rise purified and ennobled. On Saturday last, a meeting was called in Union Square in which the Judge took a prominent part to thank and encourage our soldiers and General-in-Chief. It was crowded and enthusiastic. The Judge wrote the resolutions and read them, making very judicious opening remarks, full of point and very practical, counseling moderation and good statesmanship.

I have been very busy lately in the Women's Patriotic League for Diminishing the Use of Imported Luxuries. I think it will succeed, although some of the ladies wish to push it forward much too fast. The manufacturers say they have not enough hands to fill the orders they already have, so we cannot now force people to buy what is not to be had, but must go to work gradually and systematically. I shall have some trouble to subdue the zeal of Miss Mary Hamilton and Miss Schuyler. I plainly see they have made me president but wish to rule themselves. I shall have to give my opinion officially, and I am afraid of Miss Mary. I must try and write out my views upon the subject.

Yesterday the Judge came home after being treated by some Irish gentlemen fresh from home who, it seems, were enthusiastic about him, telling him that no one in Ireland is so popular as himself. The poor Judge was almost abashed by their praises and compliments.

Maggie is at home. We are polite to each other and no more. She is sweet upon the Judge.

"THE WORK OF DEATH": GEORGIA, JUNE 1864

Robert Patrick to Alonzo Lewis

After the Union defeat at Pickett's Mill, Georgia, on May 27 Sherman abandoned his attempt to outflank Johnston at Dallas and began to maneuver his forces back toward the Chattanooga–Atlanta railroad. By June 6 most of Sherman's troops were resting around Acworth, four miles southeast of Allatoona, while Union engineers rebuilt the railroad bridge across the Etowah River and Confederate forces occupied the high ground to the north and west of Marietta. A bookkeeper before the war, Robert Patrick had enlisted in the 4th Louisiana Infantry in 1861, fought at Shiloh, and served under Johnston in the Vicksburg campaign before becoming a quartermaster's clerk in the brigade (later division) commanded by Brigadier General James Cantey. He wrote about the campaign in Georgia to a friend in Clinton, Louisiana.

In Camp near Atlanta, Georgia
June 9, 1864

Dear Friend,

I have frequently heard it said that there is a wide and beaten road leading to an inhospitable region, where fuel is furnished gratis and a man to stir up the chunks in the bargain, that is paved with the best quality of an article denominated "Good Intentions." My intentions to write have been good, but you know that if I do not turn into a road that is macadamized that I will never reach the place that we all desire to find, therefore, the highway of good intentions is here-by ignored and I leave this beaten track for one covered with rocks of "Practice" and "Execution."

I am now and have been ever since last winter, a clerk in the office of Major Woolfolk, Quartermaster in Cantey's Division. I have got along very well with him, though he is very inattentive to business and drinks to excess. This negligence of his and his dissipated habits will, unless he changes his mode of life, certainly lead to ruin.

I think I hear you exclaim—"He sees the beam in the eye of

another, but he does not discern the mote in his own!" But here you are wrong, for I see both, and of the two, the mote is the larger and is to me the most troublesome, and in the future, if I live, I shall use the utmost exertion to eradicate it, and if God is willing with due diligence and watchfullness, I will prevent its ever obstructing my morals ever again.

I have troubles and petty annoyances too numerous to mention with drunken, uncivil, ungentlemanly officers and ignorant, ill-bred and contentious men, who criticize and pass judgment upon matters of which they are totally ignorant and have not the capacity ever to learn. These are small matters, but you know it is the little things which constitute the sum of a man's exactness.

A soldier's life is that of a slave's, or worse, for he must act as the slave does while at the same time he is possessed of greater sensibility than the slave and his toils and sufferings are not confined to the physical man alone.

I hope this war will close soon, and I have made up my mind that this is the last year of the "Reign of Terror." So fully am I convinced of this, that I am even now making my arrangements for the future, as though it were a foregone conclusion. If I am right, it places me in a better position, and if I am wrong, there is no harm done. You will probably wish to know my reasons for being so sanguine.

Well, I do not know that I can give any really good reason for my opinion. Instead of drawing my conclusions as most persons do, by the slow process of deduction, I have discovered a shorter and easier method, to wit:

I *jump at it.* Taking for my stepping-stones, the precarious and critical condition of the financial affairs of the North, which, as sure as fate, will come down with a grand crash, and the aspect of political affairs which are very unsettled and are now being stirred up, as the Dutchman says, "mit a stick." I make a jump into the future, land in the middle of the month of January, 1865, and if at that time I do not have in my pocket a document showing that I have been mustered out of the Confederate Service, or that I shortly will be, then am I no prophet nor a son of a prophet.

I have been no nearer Dalton than Resaca, which is 16 miles south of that point. When the enemy first made his appearance at Resaca, there was only one brigade of Cantey's Division, consisting of three regiments and one battery there, though there were some guns placed in batteries on the heights overlooking the town. This force succeeded in checking the Yankees until reinforcements arrived, which by-the-way, did not come a moment too soon, for I verily believe that Johnston barely missed being caught in a bad box, and whatever may be said to the contrary, I shall always think that it was nothing more than sheer good luck and the lack of enterprise on the part of the Yankees that his communication was not cut off. I know that the wires were cut between Dalton and Resaca and all dispatches were sent by couriers.

On Saturday afternoon and Sunday, the hardest fighting occurred, after which we evacuated the place, burning the bridges after us. We lost some guns and a considerable quantity of stores, and some of the men were forced to swim the river (Oostanaula) to escape capture. The order was well made without a doubt, though I am no military man and not capable of criticizing military movements. I have ventured to give you my ideas of what occurred there.

The order has been well conducted through-out and I do not believe that any General except Johnston could have effected it without serious loss. Sherman's plan seems to be to flank us all the time; although Johnston has offered him battle time and again, he invariably declines it, and sets to work at his wire-pulling gun. The two armies are now confronting each other, each maneuvering for a pass. Sherman is massing his men on our right and has planted his troops on the Altoona Mountains. I presume his intention is to form a new base of operation at the Etowah River.

The citizens all along the line of our march had pulled up root and branch, and removed with all their personnel. Folks farther south say that there is not much falling into the hands of the enemy.

The armies are doing nothing now. I say doing nothing for unless there is a heavy fight, we always say there is nothing going on, but there are many killed and wounded every hour, for even if there is no heavy engagement the skirmish is kept up night and day, and the work of death goes on the while like the current of the flowing river, slow and even sometimes, and at others, as rapid as a catarack. There is not a day passes now that many victims are not offered up at the sacred shrine of Southern Liberty and every breeze brings the roar of the artillery.

The morale of the army was never better than it is now and the men are sanguine of success and their confidence in Johnston is undiminished. I will venture to say that if Bragg had conducted this order, that he would now have had a discontented and demoralized army. It has been remarked by everybody that there is less straggling than ever was known before, and every man is at the post assigned him.

I see that General Pemberton has been promoted down hill. He is now in the regiment, a Lieutenant Colonel of Artillery. If they would give the man that never won a battle (Bragg) the same rank and get him out of the way of better men, I think it very probable that our forces would be more prosperous. I did not know until the other day that the 4th Regiment was up here, my impression being that they were still at Mobile. They have been in a pretty heavy engagement and lost between 20 and 30 men.

General Quarles speaks in very high terms of the regiment and says it is the best in the service.

Give my compliments to Mrs. Lewis. When you write, address your letter to the care of Major Woolfolk, Quarter-Master Cantey Brigade, Polks Corps, Atlanta, Georgia.

Your friend,
s/Rob. D. P.

RUINED PLANTATIONS: VIRGINIA, JUNE 1864

Judith W. McGuire: Diary, June 11, 1864

Judith W. McGuire had fled her home in Alexandria, where her husband was the principal of the Episcopal High School of Virginia, in May 1861 when the town was occupied by Union troops. In February 1862 the McGuires settled in Richmond, where she later found work as a clerk in the Confederate commissary department. She wrote in her diary about the fate of Westwood, the estate of her brother, Dr. William S. R. Brockenbrough, and Summer Hill, the home of her nephew's widow, Mary Newton. Both plantations were located south of the Pamunkey River near Hanovertown, Virginia, and were occupied by Union cavalry on May 27.

11*th*.—Just heard from W. and S. H. Both places in ruins, except the dwelling-houses. Large portions of the Federal army were on them for eight days. S. H. was used as a hospital for the wounded brought from the battle-fields; this protected the house. At W. several generals had their head-quarters in the grounds near the house, which, of course, protected it. General Warren had his tent in the "shrubbery" for two days, General Burnside for a day or two, and those of lesser rank were there from time to time. General Grant was encamped at S. H. for a time. Dr. B. was at home, with several Confederate wounded from the battle of "Haw's Shop" in the house. Being absent a mile or two from home when they arrived, they so quickly threw out pickets, spread their tents over the surrounding fields and hills, that he could not return to his house, where his wife and only child were alone, until he had obtained a pass from a Yankee officer. As he approached the house, thousands and tens of thousands of horses and cattle were roaming over the fine wheat fields on his and the adjoining estate, (that of his niece, Mrs. N.,) which were now ripe for the sickle. The clover fields and fields of young corn were sharing the same fate. He found his front porch filled with officers. They asked him of his sentiments with regard to the war. He told them frankly that he was an original Secessionist, and ardently hoped to see the North and South separate and distinct nations now and forever. One of them replied that he "honoured his candour," and from that moment he was treated with great courtesy. After some difficulty he was allowed to keep his wounded Confederates, and in one or two instances the Federal surgeons assisted him in dressing their wounds. At S. H. the parlour was used for an amputating room, and Yankee blood streamed through that beautiful apartment and the adjoining passage. Poor M. had her stricken heart sorely lacerated in every way, particularly when her little son came running in and nestled up to her in alarm. A soldier had asked him, "Are you the son of Captain Newton, who was killed in Culpeper?" "Yes," replied the child. "Well, I belong to the Eighth Illinois, and was one of the soldiers that fired at him when he fell," was the barbarous reply.

On these highly cultivated plantations not a fence is left, except mutilated garden enclosures. The fields were as free from vegetation after a few days as the Arabian desert; the very roots seemed eradicated from the earth. A fortification stretched across W., in which were embedded the fence rails of that and the adjoining farms. Ten thousand cavalry were drawn up in line of battle for two days on the two plantations, expecting the approach of the Confederates; bands of music were constantly playing martial airs in all parts of the premises; and whiskey flowed freely. The poor servants could not resist these intoxicating influences, particularly as Abolition preachers were constantly collecting immense crowds, preaching to them the cruelty of the servitude which had been so long imposed upon them, and that Abraham Lincoln was the Moses sent by God to deliver them from the "land of Egypt and the house of bondage," and to lead them to the promised land. After the eight days were accomplished, the army moved off, leaving not a quadruped, except two pigs, which had ensconced themselves under the ruins of a servant's house, and perhaps a dog to one plantation; to the other, by some miraculous oversight, two cows and a few pigs were left. Not a wheeled vehicle of any kind was to be found; all the grain, flour, meat, and other supplies were swept off, except the few things hid in those wonderful places which could not be fathomed even by the "Grand Army." Scarcely a representative of the sons and daughters of

Africa remained in that whole section of country; they had all gone to Canaan, by way of York River, Chesapeake Bay, and the Potomac—not dry-shod, for the waters were not rolled back at the presence of these modern Israelites, but in vessels crowded to suffocation in this excessively warm weather. They have gone to homeless poverty, an unfriendly climate, and hard work; many of them to die without sympathy, for the invalid, the decrepit, and the infant of days have left their houses, beds, and many comforts, the homes of their birth, the masters and mistresses who regarded them not so much as property as humble friends and members of their families. Poor, deluded creatures! I am grieved not so much on account of the loss of their services, though that is excessively inconvenient and annoying, but for their grievous disappointment. Those who have trades, or who are brought up as lady's maids or house servants, may do well, but woe to the masses who have gone with the blissful hope of idleness and free supplies! We have lost several who were great comforts to us, and others who were sources of care, responsibility, and great expense. These particulars from W. and S. H. I have from our nephew, J. P., who is now a scout for General W. H. F. Lee. He called by to rest a few hours at his uncle's house, and says he would scarcely have known the barren wilderness. The Northern officers seemed disposed to be courteous to the ladies, in the little intercourse which they had with them. General Ferrara, who commanded the negro troops, was humane, in having a coffin made for a young Confederate officer who died in Dr B's house, and was kind in other respects. The surgeons, too, assisted in attending to the Confederate wounded. An officer one morning sent for Mrs. N. to ask her where he should place a box of French china for safety; he said that some soldiers had discovered it buried in her garden, dug it up and opened it, but he had come up at this crisis and had placed a guard over it, and desired to know where she wished it put. A place of safety of course was not on the premises, but she had it taken to her chamber. She thanked him for his kindness. He seemed moved, and said, "Mrs. N., I will do what I can for you, for I cannot be too thankful that my wife is not in an invaded country." She then asked him how he could, with his feelings, come to the South. He replied that he was in the regular army, and was obliged to come. Many little acts of kindness were done at both houses, which were received in the spirit in which they were extended. *Per contra:* On one occasion Miss D., a young relative of Mrs. N's, was in one of the tents set aside for the Confederate wounded, writing a letter from a dying soldier to his friends at home. She was interrupted by a young Yankee surgeon, to whom she was a perfect stranger, putting his head in and remarking pertly, "Ah, Miss D., are you writing? Have you friends in Richmond! I shall be there in a few days, and will with pleasure take your communications." She looked up calmly into his face, and replied, "Thank you; *I* have no friends in the Libby!" It was heard by his comrades on the outside of the tent, and shouts and peals of laughter resounded at the expense of the discomfited surgeon. The ladies frequently afterwards heard him bored with the question, "Doctor, when do you go to the Libby?"

“MISERABLE LONG DREARY DAYS”: VIRGINIA, JUNE 1864

Charles Harvey Brewster to Mattie Brewster

The opposing armies remained in close contact at Cold Harbor for more than a week after the failed Union assault on June 3, with skirmishing, sharpshooting, and artillery fire taking its toll of casualties on both sides. Lieutenant Brewster of the 10th Massachusetts Infantry wrote to his sister about the fieldworks built by Union troops and the strain caused by the continual fighting.

Head Quarters 10th Mass Vols In a Bomb Proof
June 11th 1864

Dear Mattie,

I received yesterday your welcome letter of June 7th and am very much obliged to you all for writing so frequently for these are miserable long dreary days for even the bullets now fail to furnish cause for attention or a remark as they go singing by our ears, or whack into the trees around us.

I wish I could furnish you a description that would convey to you any idea of the place where I am now sitting to you but I do not believe I can. it is on top of a ridge or hill and forms part of our line of battle. there is a square place dug out about a foot deep on the sloping side away from the enemy and on the edge of this is built up a double row of pine logs in this form. and the space between is filled with sand. the space between the logs is about 4 feet wide and it is about six feet high over this are placed poles covered with branches of trees to protect us from the sun. across the corner of this runs the rifle pit over the hills and through the ravines. the rifle pit is more properly the breastwork is built of logs laid one above the other to the height of about 4 feet and earth piled up against these upon the side towards the enemy in this lie the men all day and all night with equipments on and musket at hand ready to spring up at any moment and repel any attack of the enemy. in front of us is another breastwork running parallel to this and distant about 30 yards this is the front or first line of battle ours is the 2nd line in front of this about 20 or 30 yards are dug little holes in the ground with the earth thrown up towards the enemy and there lie the sharpshooters and skirmishers. they lie in these little holes, in the sun all day long and can only be relieved after dark and continually crack away at any head they can see across the open field in front at a distance varying from 50 to 200 yards. the enemy return these compliments continually and so we eat sleep and drink with the continual cracking of all sorts of fire-arms day and night. the bullets come singing whistling or humming some making more, some less noise, patting against the outside of our mimic fort, or whack into the pine and oak trees, and occasionally thug into the body limbs or head of some poor blue coat for the men cannot be kept lying still but get up and move about with a most supreme indifference to these messages of death. we know when one gets hit by an occasional Oh, or a groan. he is picked up and carried off to the hospitals in the rear by stretcher bearers perhaps to die perhaps to have his arm or leg cut off or perhaps to be fixed up and lie round a few days and come back and begin the same life over again.

Along the line is occasionally a heavy fort of earth provided with one two or more guns as its position or the circumstances warrant and in these lie the Cannoniers all day long watching enemys lines and occasionally he jumps up, says fire, and another Cannonier pulls a little string and bang goes the gun followed by the rush of the shot shell or cannister and the crashing through the trees and limbs in the woods on the enemys side and if it is a shell the dull report of its bursting to the damage of numerous grey backs as we fondly hope, but probably do very little damage to anyone. these higher compliments are also returned at intervals by the enemy, and so the work and war goes on. We came up here last night about half past one o'clock taking position considerably to the left of the one we have been holding for 8 or 9 days past, in consequence of the stretching out and thinning of our line. the 6th 18th + 9th Wrights Smiths and Burnsides Corps are now holding the line which has heretofore been held by them and the 2nd + 5th Corps the two latter have been withdrawn and have gone off on some mysterious expedition probably to our left of which you will probably hear sooner than I shall.

Meantime we possess our souls with what patience we can for 10 days longer. I wrote to Mother two or three days ago and told her it would probably be my last letter, I begin to fear that I may have to stay after the Regt goes home. I do not know what to do if I had anything to do when I came home I should try and see if I could not get away anyhow but I do not know as I can get any employment if I came home and I might have to enlist as a private soldier again for my daily bread, which I should dread to do worse than anything but *sawing wood*. But I am very much worried to hear that Mother is so ill both from you and Mary and am now sorry that I signified any willingness to reenter the service. besides if I staid I should have to give up my horse and I feel that I could not stand it a great while as a foot soldier. However, perhaps I shall not be called upon to stay at all I hope not. the 7th Mass Regt goes out in 3 days and I can judge better by what they do with thier Officers. it is impossible to get any information in advance and they keep all the Regiments on the line of battle until thier time is out to the last moment. You ask why they do not put the Negroes in the fights I imagine that they do not amount to any certain sum in a fight and in such tough battles as we have it will not do often times to put in troops which you cannot depend upon. another reason I presume is because the Rebels show them no mercy if captured and our government is too weak to protect them and compel fair usage for them, but if they do not save any lives of white men they add considerably to the strength of the army for they can do many of the duties in the rear which white soldiers once had to do. But though I have seen accounts of thier fighting in the Northern papers I do not believe they have been in any fight at all. still I may be mistaken as they are all in the Burnsides Corps and we see but little of them.

Tell Mary I received her letter at the same time I did yours and will answer it soon. I have written you quite a long letter as I had plenty of time nothing to do but lie around and dodge bullets. Give my love to Mother Mary Thomas and Charlie and my respects to all enquiring friends With much love

Your aff brother
Charlie.

COMPLETING "THE GREAT IDEA": LONDON, JUNE 1864

Charles Francis Adams to Charles Francis Adams Jr.

The grandson of John Adams and son of John Quincy Adams, Charles Francis Adams had served as U.S. minister to Great Britain since May 1861. He wrote about the historical significance of the war to his son, who was still serving with the cavalry guard at the headquarters of the Army of the Potomac.

Charles F Adams Jr.

London *17 June* 1864

My Dear Charles

As I write the date, my mind very naturally recurs to the time when, as a people, we were first subjected to the baptism of blood, under the necessity of maintaining a great idea. The sufferings of that period, terrible as they proved, were amply compensated for by the blessings enjoyed by the generation succeeding. One slight precaution only was neglected, or its importance undervalued. The consequences we now see and feel in the events that are passing in front of Richmond. As I read the sad accounts of the losses experienced by both sides in the strife, the warning words of Jefferson will ring in my ears— "I tremble for my country, when I reflect that God is just." The moral evil which we consented to tolerate for a season has become a terrific scourge, that brings the life blood at every instant of its application. How long this chastisement is to be continued, it is idle to attempt to predict. Only one thing is clear to me, and that is the paramount duty to future generations of not neglecting again to remove the source of that evil. It is this that completes the great idea for which the first struggle was endured. It is this, and this only that will compensate for the calamities that attend the second. There is not an event that takes place in the slaveholding states that does not confirm me in the conviction that the social system they have fostered has become a standing menace to the peace of America. The very ferocity and endurance with which they fight for their bad principle only contribute to prove the necessity of extirpating it in its very root. This is not simply for the good of America but likewise for that of the civilised world. The sympathy elicited in Europe with this rotten cause, among the aristocratic and privileged classes, is a sufficient proof of the support which wrongful power hopes to obtain from its success. For these reasons, painful as is the alternative, I am reconciled to the continuance of the fearful horror of this strife. Looking back on the progress made since we began, it is plain to my mind that the issue, if persevered in, can terminate only in one way. There is not a moment in which the mere force of gravitation does not incline one scale of the balance more and more at the expense of the other. In resistance to this neither labor nor skill will in the long run avail. The laws of nature are uniform—The question with the South is only of more or less of annihilation by delay. Yet I cannot conceal from myself the nature of the penalty which all of us are equally to pay for our offence before God. If the great trial have the effect of purifying and exalting us in futurity, we as a nation may yet be saved. The labor of extricating us from our perils will devolve upon the young men of the next generation who shall have passed in safety through this fiery furnace. I am now too far advanced to be able to hope to see the day of restoration, if it shall come. But it may be reserved for some of my children—indeed for you if it please God, you survive the dangers of the hour. Great will be the responsibility that devolves upon you! May you acquit yourselves of it with honor and success! The great anniversary has inspired me to write you in this strain. I feel that even at this moment events may be happening in America which will make the memory of it still more dear to the lovers of human liberty and free Institutions all over the world. I accept the omen. May it be verified!

In this old world to which I now turn there is less to stimulate the imagination or to rouse the hopes of the observer. The contention here is now not so much for principle as place. The Conservative-liberal wishes to obtain the office held by the Liberal-conservative. The juggle of names only signifies that neither is in earnest. The day is one of truce between ideas. "Jeshurun has waxed fat"—And the octogenarian leader who represents him, like old Maurepas in anterevolutionary France, thinks to settle every difference with a joke. Such men thrive in periods of transition. But the time is coming when all these frivolities will pass away, and the great national problem of privilege only to the select few will come up and demand a stern solution. Goodbye. God bless you

yr aff father
CFA.

FIGHTING THE ALABAMA:
THE ENGLISH CHANNEL, JUNE 1864

Charles B. Fisher: Diary, June 19–21, 1864

A bark-rigged sailing ship equipped with an auxiliary steam engine, the *Alabama* was built at the Laird shipyard in Liverpool. She left port on July 29, 1862, and was armed with eight guns off the Azores before being commissioned as a Confederate warship on August 24. Over the next twenty-two months the *Alabama* sank a Union gunboat off Texas and captured or burned sixty-four American whalers and merchant ships in the Atlantic, Gulf of Mexico, Indian Ocean, and the East Indies, becoming the most destructive commerce raider in the Confederate navy. On June 11, 1864, she sailed into Cherbourg, France, for much-needed repairs to her hull and engine. News of her arrival quickly reached the U.S.S. *Kearsarge*, a steam sloop armed with seven guns, at the Dutch port of Flushing, and the Union ship reached Cherbourg on June 14. Raphael Semmes, the captain of the *Alabama*, decided to risk battle in order to avoid being blockaded in port, and on June 19 sailed out to fight in international waters. Although the *Kearsarge* had been patrolling European waters and the North Atlantic for Confederate raiders since 1862, her battle with the *Alabama* would be the first time she saw action. Charles B. Fisher had signed onto the *Kearsarge* in February 1862 and served as a novice seaman, officer's cook, and steward. He was one of fifteen black sailors in a crew of about 160 men.

June 19th: 1864: Battle

Off the land twelve miles. The morning is thick and hazy. The shore is scarcely distinguishable. There is all the preparations being made for our Sabbath Day devotions. Inspection at quarters at ten oclock after which we are all waiting to hear the Church bell toll. At ten minutes after ten the fore top man at the mast head sang out—Steamer under the land! Standing out! That's the Alabama, said the quarter master. We all were anxious to catch a glimpse of her before going into battle. The bell sounded fire quarters and the boys were to be seen tumbling down the forecastle ladders—fore rigging Jacobs Ladders & c trying who could be first at their quarters. She was coming straight out for us and we were all ready for the conflict in just three minutes. Decks sanded down. Batteries cast loose and manned. Magazines opened & all reported ready. Go ahead fast, said the Captain. The Alabama was now about two miles distant and coming on fast. Lay down! Every man, said the Captain, and down we all lay flat on the deck. And now as I lay down not knowing how soon I might be killed or maimed for life I thought of home and how I had been neglected by those who should have been all in all to me. My thoughts were bitter, bitter scenes long since forgotten came back to my memory as vividly as if they were being enacted now. Friends and those who were dear to me came before me and I wondered if any of them could know my situation now. Would they feel my sorrow or think kindly of me after I was no more. These and many other thoughts went through my mind swift as lightning. I also thought of Bud and prayed that he might not get hurt in any way. But no time was now given for thoughts or feelings. The Alabama had now opened fire with her starboard battery. Distance one thousand yards. The shell were flying screaming through our rigging and bursting far astern of us. She fired seven times. We keeping head on to her and going full speed. At the seventh shot the 30 pound rifle parrott on our forecastle paid our compliments to her and down came her flag. The gaff was shot away—we still going ahead—she broadside too. She fired five more shot. None of her shot had as yet struck us. We were not quite near her and our helm was put hard a starboard and our noble ship came up beautifully and showed her an awful battery with no men but the Marines on the forecastle. "Ready." "Fire," and our two eleven inch three broadsides & rifle pivot sent death and destruction aboard her. We kept around in a circle and it seemed strange how cooly our men now faced her fire amidst the groans of the dying and cusses of the wounded. Around went the Kearsarge—the Alabama keeping up a hot fire upon us. We could see the shell and solid shot coming and some of them would pass so close that the hot wind from them would puff in our faces. Still nobody hurt aboard of us. One shot had now struck our rudder post and another went through our smoke stack. To those who have never heard the whistle of a shell there is something unearthly and terrible in the sound. One is led to imagine that all the devils in hell are let loose to play around ones ears. The conflict had now lasted half an hour and our boys had commenced to warm to their work. Everytime the Alabama fired a broadside we could see the shot and shell coming at us and everyone of us would drop flat on deck seeking the protection of the water ways. In this way a good many lives were saved from the passing balls. As soon as her shot passed our boys were up in a minute and had our guns loaded & fired before she could again bring her guns to bear. We were steaming fast around her in a circle all the time and they fired two shots to our one, but our boys were cool and took deliberate aim and then fired and we could see the shell pass clean through her and burst on the other side. Our second broadside. Every shell done its work—we could see the splinters and coal dust fly in every direction. The battle had now lasted three quarters of an hour and she commenced to set sail and try to escape to the French coast—seeing which our boys sent up cheer after cheer which made the ship fairly shake—and the battle raged fiercer than ever. One of her shell now struck our engine house and explodings wounded three men two severely and one not. The Chief Engineer Mr. Cushman also had a narrow escape at this time. The Captain also narrowly escaped but was pushed down by Clem Johnson who pushed him down out of the way. A shell from our forward pivot 11 inch now exploded right in her stern carrying away the stern—breaking her fan and killing the men at the wheel also wounding Capt. Semmes and a great number more. She now became perfectly unmanageable and we came around on her port side and pound in a murderous fire of shot and shell and the sight was awful and sublime. The execution was terrible. We came up again intending to rake her decks fore & aft which would have killed or wounded every soul on her. But she fired three *Sea Guns* and haul down her flag. The order passed *Cease Firing*. The battle had been fought and won in one hour and ten minutes. Her boat was not coming toward us but we noticed her settling down and made all haste to lower out boats to save the wounded and survivors. But before our boats could get to her she gave a wild leap forward, threw her bow high in air and went down stern first. It was painful to see her men as they jumped into the sea to meet a watery grave or threw their arms wildly above their heads to cry for help.

We who one moment before would have cut them down to a man, now strained every nerve and made every effort to save them. A perfect sea of heads could now be seen floating on the surface, some clinging to the pieces of wreck or such frail support as they could find. Our boats—that is two of them were picking them up as fast as they could, but numbers of the wounded were sinking fast. The English Yacht *Deerhound* now came up and assisted us in picking up the drowning men, but she did not pick up many. She got Semmes and steamed away to Southampton. We did not follow her but continued to pick up the men. Several French pilots now came up and saved eight men all together. The French iron clad "Corunne" did not lend any assistance. The sight was pitiful to see them dragged half drowned on board the ship with no clothing on and all with the "shivers" from being so long in the water. We gave them dry clothes and rubbed them in blankets to bring them too, and the wounded were carried below and received the same attention from our surgeon that our own did. Her surgeon was killed and her assistant was brought on board us and assisted our surgeon to care for the wounded. We picked up 42 not wounded and eleven wounded and three dead. One of the latter was the carpenter Robinson of New Orleans. Of her crew of one hundred and fifty—only eighty were saved all told. The rest went down with their ship. On our side John W. Dempsey, quarter gunner, lost his right arm. William Gowan, seaman, leg broken in two places. James Macbeth, seaman, wounded in the calf of his leg. None were killed on our ship and except a splitting head ache I was neither frightened nor hurt. We now broke our three flags at the mast heads in token of the great victory we had won. We commenced fighting at the same time people at home were going to church and ended as the minister completed his sermon. We are all too busy now to think of our success but we know the weight of the service we have now rendered our country and will impatiently await the news from home. At two oclock we stood away for the port of Cherbourg and left the Alabama down—down 200 fathoms in her watery home beneath the waves. We came to anchor in the harbor at 3½ oc and sent the wounded ashore to the French hospital. The Kearsarge was struck twenty eight times in her hull and rigging and received no damage but what can be repaired in a few hours. The shore is lined with anxious people and boats are coming off to see us. The French admiral has sent two launches to help convey the wounded men ashore and they are now alongside. The blood from the wounded Pirates covers our berth deck and their groans are awful to hear as they lay dying on our deck. Scarcely five hours have elapsed since they left this port in their noble cruiser hoping to capture the U.S. Sloop Kearsarge and murder her crew. As they said before going into action they would show us no quarter, but the Lord protected us and their fate was sealed.

June 20th: Cherbourg. After the Battle

Up this morning bright and early to remove the blood from our decks and put the ship to rights again. After Holy stones and sand and plenty of fresh water was freely used at 8 ock every vestage of the conflict was removed except the gap in our smoke stack and the dead on the quarter deck. We all feel the effect of the heavy fireing being very sore and stiff and head ache. While the battle waged fiercest our little dog *Mose* would run out from under the Forecastle and pick up the splinters in his mouth and run in again. It was evidently good fun for him. The other dogs run away and hid when the firing commenced. Another incident of the fight but more terrible was when our second shell busted aboard of her. It was just in the midst of her rifle guns crew and out of a crew of ten men it killed eight dead. A quick as a flash another rifle shell from us struck a man on her Knight head taking out all of his stomach. He run to the starboard gangway and there fell down on a pile of the wounded and died. The same shell cut two other men completely in two and exploded beyond her. They all say our firing was just as accurate as target practise and did terrible execution and that we may be glad we did not see her decks before she went down as the sight was sickening in the extreme. She was perfectly riddled fore and aft. One shot passed clean through her.

June 21st: After the Battle

Just after she went down Tom Holloway and myself pulled

one poor fellow out of the boat that was very nearly gone. We carried him down below and after rubbing him with towels & blankets brought him too. The first thing he said was. Oh! Boys you showed us no quarter. They told us you would not and you didn't. We did fire into five times after her flag was first struck, but they continued firing after the flag was struck—and as we had shot it away three times and it had been put up again, when the flag was hauled down we did not know it. One thing we knew if we had fell into their hands not one of us would have been left to tell the tale as they had sworn to show us no quarter and the hatred between us previous to the battle was very bitter. But now we have nothing against them and our kindness have quite won their esteem. While our boats were picking them up in our boats three or four jumped out and swam to the Deerhound. They were terror stricken and many would rather have drowned than come on board our ship—to me as they thought a worse fate. One little messenger boy came over the gangway crying bitterly and it was some time before the 1st Lieut. could pacify him. The other was saucy and defiant and didn't care whether he lived or died. Many other incidents occured during the fight.

BATTLE OF PETERSBURG: VIRGINIA, JUNE 1864

Wilbur Fisk to The Green Mountain Freeman

After the failed assault at Cold Harbor on June 3 Grant decided to cross the James River and attack Petersburg, twenty miles south of Richmond, where three of the four railroads used to supply Lee's army converged. The Army of the Potomac left its positions at Cold Harbor on June 12 and began crossing the James by boat and pontoon bridge two days later. Lee failed to detect the crossing and kept his army north of the river to protect Richmond, leaving the defense of Petersburg to a small garrison commanded by General Pierre G. T. Beauregard. On the evening of June 15 Union troops overran the outer line of defenses east of Petersburg but were unable to capture the city itself. A series of poorly coordinated Union attacks over the three days failed to break through the inner defenses, and on June 18 troops from Lee's army began to reinforce the outnumbered Petersburg garrison. Grant decided not to launch further assaults on the city, and on June 19 Union troops began to entrench around Petersburg. Between the crossing of the Rapidan on May 4 and the movement toward the James on June 12 the Army of the Potomac lost about 55,000 men killed, wounded, or missing, while casualties in the Army of Northern Virginia are estimated at about 33,000 men. Private Wilbur Fisk's regiment, the 2nd Vermont Infantry, lost two-thirds of its men in the Wilderness and at Spotsylvania before escaping the worst of the fighting at Cold Harbor. "I have sometimes hoped that if I must die while I am a soldier," Fisk observed after the battle for the Mule Shoe on May 12, "I should prefer to die on the battlefield, but after looking at such a scene, one cannot help turning away and saying, Any death but that." He wrote to the *Freeman* three days after his regiment crossed the James.

Near Petersburg, Va.
June 19, 1864

Another flank movement has been made by the army, and to-day we find ourselves within a mile of Petersburg with our old enemy in front. For three days there has been pretty severe fighting here, but this time our corps escaped the worst of it.

Our division reached the front night before last. The Second Regiment was sent at once on to the skirmish line, from which we were relieved last night after twenty-four hours hard duty.

We left Cold Harbor the night of the 12th. It was a bright moonlight night, just right for marching, except that the air everywhere was filled with choking dust, which the dampness of evening could not lay. We fell into line at the order, and the most of us guessed where we were going, but our calculations were a little puzzled, when instead of marching off to the left, we started out "right in front" and marched back on to the right flank. It soon became evident that we were sent there only as a rear guard, and after remaining behind good breastworks till midnight, we changed our course towards the Chickahominy. The interval we improved the best we could in catching a little sleep. It was short, and less satisfactory than sweet, scarcely better than none, for it makes a fellow feel more stupid than ever to call him up suddenly from a refreshing sleep just begun. At daylight we halted an hour for breakfast, then pushed on again through the dust and heat till night. We crossed the Chickahominy at Jones' bridge just before sundown, but continued our march a number of miles further before we came to a halt. I don't know exactly how far we marched, it is variously estimated at from twenty to twenty-five miles, but the choking dust and heat and the many crooked turns we made, made the march doubly difficult. We were completely exhausted before we bivouacked for the night. Those last miles were doled out in suffering by inches. If a man wants to know what it is to have every bone in his body ache with fatigue, every muscle sore and exhausted, and his whole body ready to sink to the ground, let him diet on a common soldier's fare till he has only the strength that imparts, and then let him shoulder his knapsack, haversack, gun and equipments, and make one of our forced marches, and I will warrant him to be satisfied that the duties of war are stern and severe, whether we march or face the enemy on the field of battle. A fellow feels very much like grumbling at such times as that, and when we march on and on, expecting every minute to halt but still hurrying forward, when every spark of energy seems about to be extinguished, and the last remnant of strength gone, tired, hungry, sick and sore, who blames a soldier if he finds it hard work to suppress thoughts of a quiet home he has left behind him, with its comforts and endearments, and if he sometime turns his thoughts to himself and wonders if he, as an individual, will ever be compensated for the sacrifice he is making. What if the rebels are whipped, and what if they are not? How does it matter to him? One blunder of General Grant's may make final victory forever impossible and all our lost toil go for nothing. I tell you some of our hard marches put one's patriotism severely to the test. It finds out a fellow's weak points if he has got any, and we don't claim to be without them.

About ten o'clock that night we were ready to lie down for our night's rest, and at four in the morning we were called onto our feet again. We advanced towards the James River, just before Harrison's Landing, where we had a camp two years ago. It would have been quite a treat to have visited that old camp again, but we did not have the opportunity. We crossed the James River the night of the 16th on a pontoon bridge and came directly to this place. The first and third division of this corps, more fortunate than ourselves, were carried to City Point on transports while we made the distance on foot. The whole movement was well planned to save time.

As we were coming on to the ground, we had positive assurance that Petersburg was taken, and of course felt highly elated at the cheering news, but we found when we got here that the news was not quite so good as reported, although we had captured their outer line of fortifications and were almost within musket range of the city. Burnside's negroes claim a large share of credit in taking these works. They made a splendid charge, capturing the whole line of works, thirteen guns, and some prisoners. The negroes were remarkably well pleased with their prowess on this occasion. It was a glorious day for them. They won great favor in the eyes of white soldiers by their courage and bravery. I am sure I never looked upon negroes with more respect than I did upon those soldiers, and I did not hear a word of disrespect towards them from any of the boys. Yesterday they made another charge here, and it was done in excellent style. The best military critic could hardly find fault with it. In a steady straight line they advanced right over the crest of the hill and right up to the enemy's works, under a terrible fire, but without wavering or faltering, compelling the enemy to leave his works in the hands of the blacks. The stream of wounded that came pouring back, some leaning on a comrade and some carried on stretchers, told of the bloody work they had done. Our picket reserve was in the road where they passed by. They captured some prisoners and brought them off. The proud Southerner might have felt a little humbled to be taken prisoner in open fight by a class of people that they refuse to recognize as men, and be conducted off the field in charge of a negro guard. But this they had to submit the best they could. One of the guard, a small, comical looking darkey, rolling up his large white eyes and looking at a tall rebel with a peculiar expression of triumph inquired, "Who rides a horseback now?" The rebel did not deign a reply. He bore the shout that followed with philosophical coolness. Sometimes the negroes treat their prisoners rather roughly in remembrance of Fort Pillow, and similar outrages. I have no doubt, if the truth were known, that many a rebel lost his life at their hands at the taking of the first line fortifications after they had fallen into our hands. Their wrath was especially directed against the officers. The rebels would plead with them, tell them they had no desire to harm them, but the negroes would say, How was it at Fort Pillow? and pay no attention to their entreaties. One of our officers who was a free mason, told of rescuing a rebel brother mason whom the negroes decided to kill. He drew his revolver and peremptorily ordered the negroes who had gathered around him to disperse and had the wounded rebel cared for, otherwise he would have counted as one to pay the terrible bill of retaliation that we have against the enemy. Such a kind of warfare is too horrible to contemplate, though we cannot blame the negroes under the present circumstances.

Notwithstanding the negroes fight so well and show so much bravery, they have hitherto been allowed but the bare pittance of seven dollars a month. Chaplain Hunter, of the 4th U.S. colored troops, a colored man of remarkable ability, denounces with just indignation this rank injustice. He says there are men in his regiment who have left families at home, and seven dollars a month in times like these, is not enough to keep them from actual suffering. In a conversation with a Major

General a short time since, he said he asked him in a case of a battle where all the commissioned officers were killed or wounded in a company or regiment, who would take the command. (Commissioned officers are white but the non-commissioned officers may be black, but a negro is never commissioned—miserable compromise to an unreasonable prejudice.) The General replied that it would devolve upon the ranking non-commissioned officer of course. Then said the chaplain, when the regiment comes to re-organize and new officers be chosen, what will you do with these men that, according to military custom, are entitled to the position they have filled, and who have proved that they are worthy of it. Well, said the General a little puzzled at the annoying question, Congress will have to settle that.

And Congress has wrangled over that question all winter trying to settle it. It seems strange that a question where justice and injustice, right and wrong, are so plainly apparent, should require any wrangling or debate at all. They seem to think that it is degrading to the white soldiers to pay the blacks equally as well. Do they think we are afraid of fair competition with blacks? If negroes can fight as well as we, can we not have magnanimity enough to acknowledge it. Certainly to propose especial legislation to keep our *status* ahead of the blacks is acknowledging them our superiors and in a most humiliating way. Whether it suits our tastes or not, it is doubtless true that the golden rule applies to colored as well as to white people, and Congress as well as everybody else will do well to bear this in mind and act accordingly.

"BUTCHERED TIME AND AGAIN": VIRGINIA, JUNE 1864

Stephen Minot Weld to Stephen Minot Weld Sr.

Stephen Minot Weld was commissioned as a Union officer in January 1862. He served in the Army of the Potomac as an aide to corps commanders Fitz John Porter, John Reynolds, and John Newton until August 1863, when he became the lieutenant colonel of the newly formed 56th Massachusetts Infantry. Assigned to the First Brigade, First Division of the Ninth Corps, the regiment crossed the Rapidan on May 5, 1864, with about 550 men in its ranks. Weld took command of the 56th Massachusetts the next day when its colonel was killed in the Wilderness, and then led the First Brigade for nearly a week at Spotsylvania after its commander became "sun-struck." The regiment crossed the James on June 15 and assaulted the Petersburg defenses two days later, capturing a line of rifle pits before being driven back by a Confederate counterattack after it ran out of ammunition. (In a memoir written in 1912, Weld blamed the lack of ammunition on his division commander, Brigadier General James H. Ledlie, "a coward" who "took the liquor to try and fortify himself for the fight," and described finding him in "a drunken sleep" after the June 17 attack.) Weld wrote to his father about the course of the Virginia campaign.

HEADQUARTERS 56TH MASS. VOLS., *June* 21, 1864.

DEAR FATHER,—We moved out to the front last evening, relieving General Barlow's division of the Second Corps. The idea is, I believe, to have the Second Corps moved to the left, to prevent a flank movement by the rebels.

There is one thing that I have noticed throughout this campaign. The newspapers have been giving a false and incorrect report of the state of the army and of our battles. They have claimed great victories, where we have been repulsed, and have not stated our losses correctly. It is perhaps necessary to have such reports go abroad in order to prevent our people from being discouraged, but I don't like to see them.

The only time that Grant has got ahead of Lee, was in

crossing the James River, and attacking Petersburg. He did outmanœuvre him there, most certainly, but did not follow up his advantage. The feeling here in the army is that we have been absolutely butchered, that our lives have been periled to no purpose, and wasted. In the Second Corps the feeling is so strong that the men say they will not charge any more works. The cause of the whole trouble, in my opinion, is owing to the carelessness of those high in command, such as corps commanders and higher officers still, who have time and again recklessly and wickedly placed us in slaughter-pens. I can tell you, Father, it is discouraging to see one's men and officers cut down and butchered time and again, and all for nothing.

I don't wish you to think from all this that I am croaking. I feel that we shall take Richmond in time, but hope that some consideration and some regard for life will be shown in doing so. We can't afford to make many more such bloody attacks as we have been doing. The enemy will outnumber us if we do so. We shall have to settle down to a siege of Petersburg and take the place in that way. We have our lines so near the city that it will not be a difficult matter to burn and shell the whole concern out, if necessary.

I have 180 men left for duty in my regiment, and this is a fair-sized regiment.

We are quite fortunate in our position here. We are in woods, with the enemy's line about 300 yards in our front. The woods screen us from them, so that we can walk around with comparative safety, but on our left the line is outside the woods, and woe betide any man who shows his head. The whistling of innumerable bullets around him warns him of the dangerous proximity of the enemy. The camp that we left yesterday was in the middle of a dusty field, where all the dead on both sides, killed during the charge of the 17th, were buried. The effluvia got to be unbearable finally, and we were all glad enough to change to any position, no matter where.

Can you do anything to help recruit this regiment? If you have a chance, I wish you would put some good men in it, as we need them very much.

My health has been remarkably good during the whole campaign. We have been remarkably fortunate in regard to weather, having had pleasant and dry weather almost all the time.

"A HORRID, HELLISH DREAM": VIRGINIA, JUNE 1864

George E. Chamberlin to Ephraim Chamberlin

The fighting at Petersburg from June 15 to June 18 cost the Union about 8,000 men killed, wounded, or missing, and the Confederates about 3,000, and gave the Union control of the Norfolk & Petersburg, one of the three main railroads that converged on the city. By June 19 the Army of the Potomac was deployed to the east of the Petersburg in an arc extending from the Appomattox River to the Jerusalem Plank Road. On June 21 Grant sent the Second and Sixth Corps west to cut the Weldon & Petersburg Railroad, which connected Richmond and Lee's army with North Carolina and the Deep South. The Confederates counterattacked on June 22, taking 1,800 prisoners from the Second Corps, and then capturing 400 prisoners from the Sixth Corps the next day. On June 24 Union troops retreated from the railroad and took up positions to the west of the Jerusalem Plank Road. George E. Chamberlin had been appointed major of the 11th Vermont Volunteers in the summer of 1862. The regiment was posted to the fortifications defending Washington, D.C., and in December 1862 was designated the 1st Vermont Heavy Artillery. After the battle of the Wilderness the 1st Vermont was one of several heavy artillery regiments sent from the capital to reinforce the Army of the Potomac. It reached Spotsylvania on May 15 and was assigned to the Second Brigade, Second Division of the Sixth Corps. The regiment came under fire for the first time on May 18, lost 119 men killed or wounded in the June 1 fighting at Cold Harbor, and arrived at Petersburg on June 18. A week later Chamberlin wrote to his father about the experience of "trench life."

HEADQUARTERS 1ST ART'Y, 11TH VT. VOLS.,
June 27, 1864.

MY DEAR FATHER:

How often, in the midst of all these dangers and privations, my mind turns back to that delightful *home* where I once lived so joyfully, so peacefully with my father, my mother, and brother and sisters. What blessed days, when the country was at peace; what awful days *these*, of blood, and carnage, and hate. The realities of war, you who have never been on the battlefield can never know or even imagine. To me, who have seen it, it seems more like a horrid, hellish dream, rather than a fact. There will be a fearful reckoning with those who are responsible for all this. Ours is the right side, but we have hard work before us. God will give us the victory sometime, and will surely put our wicked enemies to shame and confusion.

I wish I could write you oftener, but it has been impossible. To Delie I have written very frequently, but beyond this have done no writing, except what was required in my official capacity. I think I have written you only once before since leaving Washington. The campaign has been intensely active and laborious. The night work has been particularly severe, the greater part of the marching having been done by night. At dark, on the evening of June 12th, we left Cold Harbor, and marched all night and all the next day. At evening we rested on the right bank of the Chickahominy, and I was laying my blankets preparing for a good night's sleep, when an order came, detailing me as division officer of the day, and I was on picket line all night without sleep, and marched the greater part of next day. Fatigues, that at home would be thought terrible, entirely too much for flesh and blood to endure, are an every week's occurrence here, and we learn to bear them very naturally.

Delie has written you often, and through her you have been made acquainted with the items of news from time to time. I have been in command of the regiment for about two weeks. Lieutenant-Colonel Benton has resigned and gone home. Colonel Warner is at his home still.

On the 23d, the regiment met with a very great misfortune. We were in line of battle, facing the Garton Branch and Petersburg railroad. A report came in that a party of sharpshooters had pushed forward and taken the road, and wanted support. Two hundred men from our regiment were called for, and immediately sent under charge of Captain M., to be reported to Lieutenant-Colonel P., corps officer of the day. Soon after, I was called on for more men, and sent out Major F. with his battalion. Four hundred of our men were now out. In the afternoon the enemy moved two brigades rapidly down the railroad, formed as a skirmish line, and advanced on our skirmish line, which, not being properly supported, was finally driven back, and a portion of it captured. In that part of the line were our noble boys, and we have lost the greater part of them. Our total loss on that day was twenty-four killed and wounded, and two hundred and seventy-five prisoners. Of these, one officer was killed (Second-Lieutenant Sherman, a fine man and officer) and eighteen captured. My old company, A, is among the unfortunate. Captain M. and Lieutenant R. will know the beauties of a Southern prison. The batteries captured are F, L, K, H and A. A and K were my Totten companies, and L was with me at Lincoln. The greater part of the Fourth Vermont was taken at the same time. The fault was with the corps commander in not ordering proper supports. Our officers and men did their whole duty.

We have had a good deal of trench life during the campaign at Cold Harbor and at Petersburg. We dig up into the very teeth of the enemy, and then watch him. It is not safe to expose one's head above the embankment, as a few sharpshooters keep up their murderous work through little loopholes in the parapet; otherwise there is not much firing. Living under ground is very dirty work, as you can imagine. One night, I remember to have been awakened by something on my neck, which I discovered to be a medium sized toad. Bugs and worms crawl over us promiscuously. What a sad sight, in this enlightened age, to see the sections of this civilized nation fighting each other with such insatiable fury. How much more congenial to our tastes, and how much more consonant with all our christian feelings and impulses, is peace, harmony, brotherly love. God deliver the nation soon from the chastisement of fire and blood which He has seen fit to send upon us.

How soon Carrie will graduate—day after to-morrow. It is probably an occasion of as much interest to her as mine was to me, nearly four years ago. Do any of you go to Troy? Delie wrote that mother would not go. I hope some of you will be there to see her take her honors. I well remember my gratification at seeing you all at Hanover. Delie, I think, has decided to go to Vermont. This I am very glad of, and have advised it all the time. How she will enjoy a visit there! You must drive away her sadness. She is very anxious for me, and I fear it is wearing upon her severely. I hope the Green Mountain air, and the many dear friends she will find there, will cause her to rally, and be as cheerful and healthy as ever. A husband and wife who love each other as we do, have no business to be separated as we are. You will all take good, tender care of her, won't you? Cheer her up and comfort her by every means in your power. If you knew how kind, attentive and devoted she has always been to me, you could not help loving her for my sake. And you do know all about it, and you do love her for my sake, and for herself too. You have seen her, and you know that nobody has a better wife than I. How I wish I might be there with you. All will be there but the "boys." You will miss us. How happy we should be together around that home circle again. I should be happier than ever to be there with my new companion, and you would be happier to see me with her than alone, for I know you joy in my joy. God has blessed me with the kindest of friends always, and I pray for a life long enough to show them that I am grateful. We were very sorry you did not return *via* Washington with Mary. I have had an intimation that you would remove West this fall. Is it so? I want to hear all about it. By the way, why haven't I heard from any of you? I think I have not had a single letter since the campaign commenced. That isn't right. My address is 1st Artillery, 11th Vt. Vols., 2d Brig., 2d Division, 6th Corps, Washington. The weather is very hot. The army is comparatively quiet, and will remain so, probably, until after muster day, the 30th.

Much love to my dear mother and sisters, and also to Edward, when you write. How dear is each and every one to me! Let me hear soon.

Your affectionate son.

LIFE AT ANDERSONVILLE: GEORGIA, JUNE 1864

Eugene Forbes: Diary, June 13–30, 1864

By the end of June 1864 more than 26,000 Union prisoners were crowded into the sixteen-acre stockade at Andersonville. Sergeant Eugene Forbes recorded events and conditions in the camp, including the depredations of the "raiders" who preyed on their fellow prisoners.

Monday, June 13. Rainy all day. Wheat flour has declined to 50c. per pint; salt, to 25c. per five spoonfuls; rice, 25c. per pint, butter, $4.50 per lb. Rumored that Sherman has cut communications, thus putting us on short allowance. No roll call. No medicine for several days. There are quite a number of insane men in camp; one of them has been plundered of everything but his shirt, and while he was asleep, some scoundrel cut off the front tail of that garment, thus leaving him almost without anything to cover his nakedness. Today and yesterday have been so cold that an overcoat would be a comfort, and he must suffer extremely; he was refused admission to the hospital today. Several of the old Belle Island prisoners were vaccinated, before leaving that place, with impure or scrofulous matter; some of these men have since had their arms amputated, while others are walking around with their bones and muscles exposed, the flesh having dropped out piecemeal. Lame men, blind men, deaf men, one-armed men, all alike exposed to the inclemency of the storm, or the blistering rays of the sun; "As ye do unto others it shall be done unto you, and with what measure ye mete, it shall be measured to you again." Drew rice, salt and bacon P.M. Some of the squads drew rice and molasses, but no bacon. Rain continued all night. A few prisoners came in; no news.

Tuesday, June 14. Rain continues. A few prisoners came in. Drew meal, bacon, salt and boiled rice. At about 11 P.M. a terrible row seemed to be taking place about the center of the camp; cries of murder and the sound of blows were heard, alarming the rebs so much that the sentries cried the time every half hour, instead of every hour, as usual. No squads allowed out for wood, two men having escaped yesterday. Last night no response was heard from seven sentry boxes, commencing at No. 17; this morning it was ascertained that fourteen of our men had "tunneled out," and that seven guards had accompanied them, taking their arms and accoutrements. Active skirmishing.

Wednesday, June 15. Saw one man laid out, who died from cold and exposure last night. On the north side they are riding one of the raiders on a rail. A large squad of prisoners came in this A.M., among whom are several from the 4th Regiment; Cooper, of Co. B., is said to be among the number, and to have been captured on the 8th ult. They report that they could hear musketry as they left Libby Prison; they have heard nothing regarding parole or exchange. An individual who was getting a list of names of shoemakers who were willing to go outside and work for the benefit of the Southern Confederacy, was seized by some of the boys on the north side, bucked and gagged, his head shaved, his list taken away from him, and then turned loose, amid the hootings of the crowd. The Captain and Quartermaster told the Sergeant of 57-3 that paroles would be issued tomorrow up to the 20th Detachment. Bet he lies. Drew meal, salt, bacon and raw rice. No one allowed out for wood. Reported that Lincoln has been renominated by the Republicans, and McClellan by the Democrats. Cooper says Grant has 16,000 prisoners in rear of Fredericksburg; First Battalion Veteran Reserve Corps reported ordered to the field. Rainy A.M., but cleared up P.M.

Thursday, June 16. Cloudy all day, with some little rain. Two squads on the north side were deprived of their rations, on account of their connection with the shaving of the shoemaker's head yesterday. (I believe his name is Kearney some of the raiders appear acquainted with him.) Drew meal and bacon. A large squad of prisoners (some 300) came in P.M.; they are mostly from the Army of the Potomac; they report desperate fighting; that Grant moves his picket line every evening close to the rebs, during the night moves his line of battle up to the picket line, throws up earthworks and mounts artillery, in the morning charges, &c. Some of these men were taken at Gaines' Mill, the scene of the Fourth's Capture in 1862. Fifty-seven deaths reported in hospital last night. Letters came for many of the men today. Of course the captain lied yesterday about the parole. One of the sailors lent Atwood a History of America, and it helps to pass time very pleasantly. Used my last chew of tobacco. Rained very hard after dark.

Friday, June 17. Rainy all day. Gen. Winder reported here. Several men out on wood squads turned on the guard, took their guns, and made their escape. No more allowed out for wood. Drew meal and bacon P.M. Raiding is getting very extensively practiced. Six weeks prisoners today. Wood getting scarce.

Saturday, June 18. One man slept in the mush box last night; he was surrounded by five or six men during the night, and his pocket cut out; another, walking around with a blanket on his shoulders, was seized by four men, and his blanket taken away.

About 11 o'clock today a man was knocked down and robbed of his watch and $80. "Things is lovely." Rainy by spells. Atwood got tired of his job as commissary sergeant, and threw up the "sit." Some of the men who escaped yesterday were returned today; one of them was shot through the thigh, the other one's forehead was grazed. A squad of prisoners came in about noon, all from hospitals, wounded and sick. Atwood resigned, and Buckley accepted commissary sergeant. "Run." got some vinegar yesterday; it was the color of egg nog, and was made of some acid and water mixed. Potatoes $1.50 per dozen; about 16 fill a quart pot. More parole rumors, but without credibility. Went to see Mat. Hill; he lives near the "raiders." Showery all day, but with a promise of clearing.

Sunday, June 19. A rainbow this morning. A large black snake was seen by one of the men between the "dead line" and the stockade. He asked permission of the nearest guard to pass the line and kill it, which was given. A sentry on a distant post fired at the man killing the snake, missed him, but struck a tent, wounding two men, one in the head, and the other in the thigh. Some of the prisoners who came in yesterday were wounded as late as May 16th, and their arms, legs, &c. which have been amputated or otherwise acted upon, are perfectly raw. Last night a well, which had been dug very near some tents, caved in, burying three men, who slept in a tent near the edge of the well. Two of them were got out safely, but the third was injured so badly that he was dead by roll call. The camp was more quiet last night than any time since we have been in it. The rebel sergeant says that Gen. Winder is here. Atwood asserts that two of our men were to have been hung, by order of Capt. Wurtz, for over powering the guard, and that Gen. Winder gave orders that no such execution should take place. Some of the men who were in that party are now in camp, the General having forbidden the balls and chains to be put on them. They say that they wandered about that night, but there being no stars to guide their course, they become bewildered, and twice before daylight found themselves close to the stockade. So much for going without a map or compass. A large squad of prisoners came in on the north side this afternoon. Rainy all the afternoon. Our surplus meal has soured from the damp weather. Oak. traded a quart of it for a piece of tobacco. Drew meal, bacon and salt; got a bone for my ration, with more meat on it than on two ordinary rations. Rainy by spells all day. Drew wood.

Monday, June 20. Cloudy and drizzling A.M. No roll call this morning. Blackberries are selling at fifty cents a pint; green apples are in camp, but I did not price them. Washed my shirt, but did not get it dry. Traded two quarts of meal for a pint of beans, and tried to make some bean soup; rained all P.M. putting out our fire, and we had to eat our beans half cooked. Got the diarrhea very bad, may be raw beans will cure it. Had to sleep without my shirt.

Tuesday, June 21. Cleared up this morning. Find I will have to reduce my chirography to its fighting standard, as the book is getting pretty well filled up. Heavy rain P.M. Drew meal, salt and tainted bacon P.M. Went out to the Doctor in the morning, but did not get prescribed for. Saw a large number of men at the dead-house, so many that it would not hold them all, some fifteen or twenty being laid outside. Every one was searched on returning through the gate. Lost nothing. A man was shot on or near the dead-line this P.M. A raider caught stealing a frying pan near 12 P.M. Rumored that Sherman has been defeated, and that Grant has fallen back 14 miles; also, that Fort Darling has been captured for the 999th time. No room in the hospital for more sick, a large number lying outside now. A few prisoners came in. Considerable excitement among the rebs, by a report that Kilpatrick is near here. Rebs drawn up in line of battle all day and night. Hope he will come. No roll call today. Squads still working on the stockade.

Wednesday, June 22. Clear this morning. All quiet. Brown, of our detachment, has been shamefully treated by some of the men. He has the chronic diarrhea, and having met with an accident, washed his pants and drawers and hung them up to dry. Some scoundrel stole them, leaving him with nothing but a shirt. One of the men gave him a pair of drawers, and he now lies near the runlet, his feet awfully swollen and gradually sinking under disease. Our own men are worse to each other than the rebels are to us. A tunnel was discovered today, and the men ordered to dig it out and then fill it up. The man who was shot last night reported dead today. Saw two men carried out this morning from our side. Louis Traute is very bad with scurvy and diarrhea, and Jagers has the dysentery very bad. Gambling still goes on very extensively, and *hundreds of dollars* are changing hands daily. No roll call again this morning. Made a regular dinner today; soup, dumplings, bread and coffee, all made of Indian meal. Rumored that paroling is to commence between the 7th and 17th July. A few sprinkles of rain in the afternoon, just enough to maintain the reputation of the month. Drew meal, salt and bacon P.M. Cucumbers in market today. Heard a chase after a raider after we had turned in; don't think they caught him.

Thursday, June 23. Clear this morning, and very warm. Tent next to us had their meat stolen last night; a fight near the sinks, and another near the sailors' tent, early this A.M., but did not amount to much; no roll call; two more tunnels discovered, one on the north side, and the other on the south side, near us. Brown went to the hospital good bye Brown! One man came in from the hospital today, as convalescent. He had been wounded, and *is the first one who has returned from the hospital*; they generally go the other way. A squad of prisoners came in today, mostly from Grant's army; the 7th N.Y. Heavy Artillery seems to own most of the prisoners; they were taken at or near Petersburg; they report Petersburg as now in our possession, and that Richmond is cut off from all railroad communication with the South; that Grant has received reinforcements of 110,000 one hundred day men, and that he will not storm the city, but starve it out. We'll see. Drew meal at night, but nothing else; expect to draw salt and fresh beef in the morning. Not a drop of rain today, being the second day this month. Boys next door think one of their own chums went back on them. No wood today.

Friday, June 24. Clear and warm this morning. Drew salt and fresh beef about 10 A.M., the latter fly-blown; traded a ration of beef for an onion, boiled the rest, and made some soup, which we relished very highly. Atwood sold his tobacco-box for two onions. Took a walk on the north side; it reminds me of Chatham street, New York; it is quite as crowded, and the cries of the peddlers are incessantly heard; "Who wants the wood?" "Come up, now, gentlemen, and give us another bet here's your chance to double your money," &c., &c. Saw a dead man carried out. Seven weeks a prisoner today. Drew meal at night, but no salt or meat. Very warm all day, and no rain. The rumor of the day is, that prisoners who had money taken from them at Richmond are to apply at the gate and receive it back. Jagers is no better, and Mulvaney and Hoffman are both sick; my diarrhea is better. A few prisoners from Sherman came in.

Saturday, June 25. A crazy man is running around naked this morning, some scoundrel having stolen his clothing. Very hot, but a good breeze stirring; clear all day. Drew bacon and salt A.M., and meal, salt and fresh beef P.M.; also a small ration of liver. Fried our liver and some beef, made a gravy thickened with corn meal, scalded our meal and made some improved cakes, and had a "bully" supper. Some 50 prisoners came in from Sherman's army. The rumor that money was to be returned to the prisoners is beginning to take a tangible form; today the sergeants of squads were furnished with blank printed rolls, with columns for name, regiment, company, number of detachment and mess; this looks like business, and has given rise to all sorts of rumors regarding paroling, &c. The work on the new stockade has been discontinued, the men having refused to work. No roll call today. Took a "bully" wash at the spring last night and tonight; the water in the creek is so coated with grease from the cook house, that it is unfit to wash with, much less for drinking.

Sunday, June 26. Drew nothing today, as the drawing commenced on the north side. Saw a regular ring fight today, between two of the old prisoners, near the creek; they fought some fifteen minutes, when one got enough; both were somewhat scratched, but not much injured. No roll call. A party of raiders "cleaned out" Tarbell, McNeese and Nelson, of 57-1; they took boots, blankets, &c. Some few prisoners came in from Sherman, and report him near Atlanta, preparing to attack that place. The latest parole rumors are that 700 barrels of hard tack were unloaded at this depot today; that the rebs are fixing up cars to transport the sick, and that 20,000 reb prisoners are at Fortress Monroe, awaiting shipment. Fried beef for breakfast, and made beef soup for dinner; quite luxurious living for Yankee prisoners. Blackberries are selling at 60 cents a pint; wood is very scarce, as the squads do not get out half the time. Find that scalding our meal saves about one-half of it. We did not eat all our rations before, so now we will have plenty to trade off. Very hot all day. A "raider" was caught and his head shaved this morning; he sold his pint cup for $1.50, and then went at night and stole it back.

Monday, June 27. Two years ago today, I was first taken prisoner; have a mighty good sight of spending another 4th of July in captivity. A "raider" was chased early this morning, but I do not know if he was captured. Drew meal, salt and fresh beef this A.M., and made some beef tea for dinner; drew meal, salt and fresh beef P.M. A fine prospect of a general row this afternoon; the raiders were out in full force; an orderly sergeant was enticed into their tent, and robbed of $50; the raiders near the gate were contemplating an attack on this part of the camp last night; the sailors and raiders in this corner combined their forces, sent out skirmishing parties, and made arrangements to repel the attack, but the fight did not come off. Atwood sold a haversack of meal, and bought an onion and a piece of bacon, so we will live high tomorrow. A squad of prisoners came in today; I heard that a Jerseyman of the 15th regiment was with them, but I did not see him. Petersburg reported taken, also Beauregard and 10,000 prisoners. Clear and hot all day.

Tuesday, June 28. Two years ago I entered Richmond. The night passed without disturbance. Two shots fired last night, but don't know whether any one was hurt. A squad of prisoners came in this P.M., among whom were some from our regiment; Ackerson, of Co. D, reports Jack States as killed at Spottsylvania Court House, Col. Ewing as seriously wounded, and Capt. Gaul in command of the regiment; he says Oakley and myself are reported as taken prisoners; Kinney, Dougherty and Lovett, of Co. D, are wounded. Drew meal P.M. A row was imminent about 11 o'clock tonight, but did not amount to anything. A heavy shower this afternoon, and rainy most of the night. Very sick all night, with chill and fever, diarrhea, and terrible pain in the right breast and side. Grant is reported within 2½ miles of Richmond, and that he has thrown some shells into the city; his army is said to be all on the south side of the James river; Danville is said to be in our hands, and McClellan, with 250,000 one hundred day men, operating at various points. The new comers know nothing about exchange arrangements, and we have no hope of getting away from here before August or September; the veterans of the 1st regiment have been incorporated with the 4th regiment.

Wednesday, June 29. Drew salt and bacon A.M. Cleared up this morning. Feel better today, but still have a violent pain in the right side. The 1st, 2d and 3d regiments started for home on the 4th of June. Drew meal and bacon P.M. About two P.M. two men came along, trying to sell a watch; Dowd asked to look at it, and did so, after which they went away; in short time they returned with reinforcements, and attacked him as he sat in his tent, with clubs, brass knuckles, &c.; he defended himself bravely, and they again departed; he came out of his tent, and put on his pants, when they again attacked him, and finally got him down, took his watch, cut out his money, (which he had sewed in the waistband of his pants,) to the amount of $170; he was badly cut up, but finally got away and reached the gate, and reported to Capt. Wurtz, who came up with him and demanded that the robbers should be given up, under penalty of no rations for one week; in a short time a guard came in, and took eight men from a tent near the dead line on our side; very soon the camp was in an uproar, for the men came into the arrangement, and the raiders were hunted from one end of the camp to the other; by dark the tumult was nearly over, but the raiders are not all caught yet; about 50 were taken outside; the issuing of rations was stopped. Heavy showers P.M. Large quantities of clothing, blankets, &c., were found in some of the raiders' tents. Capt. Wurtz deserves great credit for his prompt action in the matter, and will probably be successful in checking the operations of these thieving scoundrels.

Thursday, June 30. Very warm today. The crusade against the raiders still continues, and several were taken today; three of those who robbed Dowd are reported to be among the number; the fourth and worse one has been caught since the above writing; they are now pretty well cleared out; the sergeants of messes (90) were called up at 9 A.M. and taken to Capt. Wurtz's headquarters, where 24 of them were selected, their names taken, and 12 drawn by lot as a jury for the trial of the principal raiders; this P.M. the trial is progressing; this course is pursued to prevent retaliation on the part of our Government, to whom the whole proceedings are to be sent; it is an act of justice on the part of the Confederate authorities which the men have not expected, they supposing that no notice would be taken of their complaints; but the reverse has been the case, and we can now feel secure from the attacks of daylight assassins or midnight murderers; the issuing of rations was promptly commenced as soon as the men known as ringleaders were captured. We expect to move to the new stockade either today or tomorrow. Oak. went out as a witness; towards night news came in that Sarsfield, one of the principals, who said he "would cut Dowd's heart out and throw it in his face," had been convicted and sentenced to be hung; the trial of the others is to come off tomorrow. Drew fresh meal and meat P.M. I forgot to mention in connection with the raiders, that large amounts of money were discovered in some of the tents today, as well as watches, jewelry, and articles of all descriptions. No rain. Dowd moved his things to the outside today, where he has liberty to the extent of one mile.

William T. Sherman to Ellen Ewing Sherman

Sherman resumed his advance in northern Georgia on June 10, moving his troops south from Acworth toward Johnston's positions on the high ground north and west of Marietta. After a week of fighting and maneuvering, on June 18 Johnston withdrew to a defensive line anchored on Kennesaw Mountain. Uncertain of his ability to outflank the position and believing that Johnston had overextended his army across an eight-mile front, Sherman ordered an assault against the Confederate center. On the morning of June 27 about 15,000 Union troops attacked the western end of Kennesaw Mountain and the high ground to the south. The assaults were repulsed with the loss of about 3,000 men killed, wounded, or missing, three times the Confederate casualties. Sherman wrote to his wife three days after the battle.

Head-Quarters, Military Division
of the Mississippi,
In the Field, near Marietta
June 30, 1864.

Dearest Ellen,

I got Mary Ewings letter, also that of Susan Stambaugh telling me of your serious illness after the birth of the new baby, but I had got Phil's dispatch saying you had been very sick but were much better and on the mend. I have no doubt your anxiety on many accounts has caused your illness but now having a new object of interest I hope your interest will revive & restore you rapidly to health. It is enough to make the whole world start at the awful amount of death & destruction that now stalks abroad. Daily for the past two months has the work progressed and I see no signs of a remission til one or both and all the armies are destroyed when I suppose the balance of the People will tear each other up, as Grant says reenacting the Story of the Kilkenny cats. I begin to regard the death & mangling of a couple thousand men as a small affair, a kind of morning dash—and it may be well that we become so hardened. Each day is killed or wounded some valuable officers and men, the bullets coming from a concealed foe. I suppose the people are impatient why I dont push or move rapidly to Atlanta but those who are here are satisfied with the progress. It is as much as our Railroad can do to Supply us bread meat & corn, and I cannot leave the Railroad to Swing on Johnstons flank or rear without giving him the Railroad which I cannot do without having a good supply on hand. I am moving heaven and earth to accomplish this, in which event I shall leave the Railroad & move to the Chattahoochee, threatening to cross which will I think force him to do that very thing when I will swing round on the road again. In that Event we may be all ready and attempt to hold both Road & river, but my opinion is he has not force enough to do both. In that Event you will be without news of us for ten days. I think we can whip his army in fair battle, but behind the hills and trunks our loss of life & limb on the first assault would reduce us too much, in other words at this distance from home we cannot afford the losses of such terrible assaults as Grant has made. I have only one source of supply, Grant had several in Succession. One of my chief objects was to prevent Joe Johnston from detaching against Grant till he got below Richmond & that I have done. I have no idea of besieging Atlanta, but may cross the Chattahoochee & circle round Atlanta breaking up its Roads. As you begin to get well I fear you will begin to fret again about changing your abode. If you are not comfortable at home try and rent some house, not the Small one of Martins you bespoke, but get Martin or Phil to find some other, & live as quietly & comfortably as possible. The worst of the war is not yet begun, the civil strife at the North has to come yet, and the tendency to Anarchy to be cured. Look at matters in Kentucky & Missouri and down the Mississipi & Arkansas where Shallow People have been taught to believe the war is over & you will see troubles enough to convince you I was right in my view of the case from the first. Stay as quietly as you can at Lancaster till Grant & I have our downfall, or are disposed of & then if we can do better, will be time enough to change. In such a quiet place as Lancaster you can hardly realize the truth that is so plain & palpable to me.

I hardly think Johnston will give us a chance to fight a decisive Battle, unless at such a disadvantage that I ought not to accept, and he is so situated that when threatened or pressed too hard he draws off leaving us a barren victory. He will thus act all summer unless he gives a great advantage in position or succeeds in breaking our Roads.

My love to all the children & folks and believe me always Yrs.

W. T. Sherman

AN APPEAL FOR NEGOTIATIONS:
NEW YORK CITY, JULY 1864

Horace Greeley to Abraham Lincoln

In January 1863 Horace Greeley, the influential founder and editor of the *New-York Daily Tribune*, had become involved with the Colorado mining promoter William Cornell Jewett in an unsuccessful attempt to gain support for European mediation of the war. On July 5, 1864, Jewett wrote to Greeley from Niagara Falls that "*two Ambassaders—of Davis & Co. are now in Canada—with full & complete powers for a peace*" and that the Confederate envoys wished to meet with Greeley and President Lincoln. The next day Jewett telegraphed to ask if Greeley would come to Niagara Falls. Greeley forwarded Jewett's messages to Lincoln on July 7 with an accompanying letter.

New York, July 7th, 1864.

My Dear Sir:

I venture to inclose you a letter and telegraphic dispatch that I received yesterday from our irrepressible friend, Colorado Jewett, at Niagara Falls. I think they deserve attention. Of course, I do not indorse Jewett's positive averment that his friends at the Falls have "full powers" from J. D., though I do not doubt that *he* thinks they have. I let that statement stand as simply evidencing the anxiety of the Confederates everywhere for peace. So much is beyond doubt.

And thereupon I venture to remind you that our bleeding, bankrupt, almost dying country also longs for peace—shudders at the prospect of fresh conscriptions, of further wholesale devastations, and of new rivers of human blood. And a wide-spread conviction that the Government and its prominent supporters are not anxious for Peace, and do not improve proffered opportunities to achieve it, is doing great harm now, and is morally certain, unless removed, to do far greater in the approaching Elections.

It is not enough that we anxiously *desire* a true and lasting peace; we ought to demonstrate and establish the truth beyond cavil. The fact that A. H. Stephens was not permitted, a year ago, to visit and confer with the authorities at Washington, has done harms, which the tone of the late National Convention at Baltimore is not calculated to counteract.

I entreat you, in your own time and manner, to submit overtures for pacification to the Southern insurgents which the impartial must pronounce frank and generous. If only with a view to the momentous Election soon to occur in North Carolina, and of the Draft to be enforced in the Free States, this should be done at once.

I would give the safe conduct required by the Rebel envoys at Niagara, upon their parole to avoid observation and to refrain from all communication with their sympathizers in the loyal States; but *you* may see reasons for declining it. But, whether through them or otherwise, do not, I entreat you, fail to make the Southern people comprehend that you and all of us are anxious for peace, and prepared to grant liberal terms. I venture to suggest the following

Plan of Adjustment.

1. The Union is restored and declared perpetual.
2. Slavery is utterly and forever abolished throughout the same.
3. A complete Amnesty for all political offenses, with a restoration of all the inhabitants of each State to all the privileges of citizens of the United States.
4. The Union to pay $400,000,000 in five per cent. U. S. Stock to the late Slave States, loyal and Secession alike, to be apportioned *pro rata* according to their Slave population respectively, by the Census of 1860, in compensation for the losses of their loyal citizens by the Abolition of Slavery. Each State to be entitled to its quota upon the ratification, by its Legislature, of this adjustment. The bonds to be at the absolute disposal of the Legislature aforesaid.
5. The said Slave States to be entitled henceforth to representation in the House on the basis of their *total* instead of their *Federal* population—the whole being now Free.
6. A National Convention, to be assembled so soon as may be, to ratify this adjustment and make such changes in the Constitution as shall be deemed advisable.

Mr. President, I fear you do not realize how intently the People desire any Peace consistent with the National integrity and honor, and how joyously they would hail its achievement and bless its authors. With U. S. Stocks worth but forty cents, in gold, per dollars, and drafting about to commence on the third million of Union soldiers, can this be wondered at?

I do not say that a just Peace is now attainable, though I believe it to be so. But I *do* say that a frank *offer* by you to the insurgents of terms which the impartial will say *ought* to be accepted, will, at the worst, prove an immense and sorely-needed advantage to the National cause: it *may* save us from a Northern insurrection.

Yours truly,
Horace Greeley

P. S. Even though it should be deemed unadvisable to *make* an offer of terms to the Rebels, I insist that, in any possible way it is desirable that any offer *they* may be disposed to make should be *received* and either accepted or rejected. I beg you to write those now at Niagara to exhibit their credentials and submit their ultimatum. H. G.

"AN INFINITY OF HILLS": GEORGIA, JULY 1864

John White Geary to Mary Geary

On July 2 Sherman succeeded in turning the southern end of Johnston's defensive line and forcing the evacuation of Kennesaw Mountain and Marietta. By July 5 Johnston had withdrawn to a fortified position extending for several miles along the west bank of the Chattahoochee River about six miles from Atlanta. A lawyer from Pennsylvania who had fought at Cedar Mountain, Chancellorsville, Gettysburg, and Chattanooga, Brigadier General John White Geary commanded the Second Division, Twentieth Corps, in the Army of the Cumberland. Geary wrote to his wife about the campaign in northern Georgia.

Hd. Qrs. 2nd Div. 20th Army Corps
Near Chattahoochie River, Ga. July 8th 1864

My Dearest Mary

I am the recipient of three letters from you bearing date at Germantown, and I assure you it afford me no ordinary pleasure to know that you have had the enjoyment of a congenial visit among friends and true hearted people. I sincerely trust that you will also enjoy your return home among the household jewels. I exceedingly regret that I have not yet been paid, (no paymaster having arrived) or I would have furnished sufficient funds for procuring furniture sufficient for the house. This was my intention had the P.M. done his duty. I am astonished to find there is nine hundred dollars to my credit in the Harrisburg Bank. Either Snodgrass or Mrs Brown has not collected the money due them and it still remains there on deposit, subject to my drafts which they hold. This is the only way in which I can account for that at present. If I could remit to you I would do so at once in sufficient amount to pay all our debts and furnish the house. I wish it was done.

We have had much hard fighting in Northern Georgia. The enemy has stubbornly contested every inch of ground. As fast as we drive him from one fortified position he simply falls back to another perhaps stronger, better, and more easy of defence aided by natural as well as artificial defences. The surface of the country is broken into an infinity of hills of the most irregular shapes and running in every possible direction. No two of them parallel. The valleys are deep ravines, and very marshy, being difficult to pass our artillery & waggons across them. It is almost universally covered with heavy timber with a dense undergrowth, and here and there *only* a field forms the exception. The country is well watered, and here in the vicinity of the river we find some cool springs which afford most delicious beverage. The inhabitants with but few exceptions have fled from before us as we have advanced in our victorious career. There is scarcely a man, woman, or child, or negro to be seen, not a horse (except the dead ones our cannon forced the enemy to leave behind) nor a cow, hog, or sheep is to be seen, even the very chickens, geese, and turkeys are driven before us as the enemy recedes, and not a living thing is left to tell the tale. Talking of turkeys reminds me of an incident a day or two ago. We were driving the enemy before us at a furious rate when near the head of my column a fine turkey mounted into the top of a hickory tree. It was very tempting, to think of the delicious meal it would make, so I drew my trusty revolver, and fired with deadly aim, down came the bird, and subsequently our agreeable anticipations were fully realized with a sumptuous repast.

The enemy are encamped partly on this side and partly on the south side. They are very strongly fortified and have an immense amount of artillery in position. They will undoubtedly make a stubborn resistance in this position. This Camp is about 1½ miles from the river, with the enemy between us and them. The only way to beat them here will be to outflank them as we have done heretofore.

The weather is excruciatingly warm, and it is almost impossible to perform more than half a day's labor in 24 hours. There is much remittant fever among the soldiers in consequence of the malarious influences arising from the decaying vegetable matter around us.

My own health, admist all my exposures, wettings, burnings, and dangers, is unusually good, and although death and sickness and every evil to which humanity is heir dwells around me, I am still by the mercy and goodness of Our Heavenly

Father, a spared monument of His mercy. Let us devoutly and sincerely thank and praise Him for His manifold mercy to us.

We are now in full view of Atlanta (8 miles). Like Moses, we can find a high toped Pisgah, and from it view the promised land. *Geographically* speaking it is only 8 miles from us, but *militarily* it may be much further.

Kenesaw Mountain and the city of Marietta were taken on the 3rd inst. and since then we have fought our way here.

I am pleased that the Philadelphia fair was so grand a success, and that you and Willie Geary had the satisfaction of visiting it. Such an occurrence may never happen again in a lifetime.

I long to see you and our dear ones at home once more. May God bless us and preserve us from every evil and soon restore our country to peace. Ever your true & loving husband

Jno W Geary

WASHINGTON, D.C., JULY 1864

Abraham Lincoln: Proclamation Concerning Reconstruction

In December 1863 President Lincoln used his annual message to Congress and an accompanying proclamation to outline a plan for restoring loyal governments in the insurrectionary states. Under his proposal, a new state government committed to the abolition of slavery could be established after 10 percent of the state's voters had sworn future allegiance to the Union. Although his plan was initially well received by most Republicans, it came under increasing criticism by Radicals for being too lenient and for failing to guarantee the rights of the freed people. On July 2 Congress passed a reconstruction bill, sponsored by Ohio senator Benjamin F. Wade and Maryland congressman Henry Winter Davis, that required a majority of a state's white male voters to swear allegiance before elections could be held for a new state constitutional convention. Suffrage in the new elections would be restricted to voters who took the "Ironclad Oath" swearing that they had never voluntarily supported or aided the Confederacy. The Wade-Davis bill also abolished slavery in all of the Confederate states. (It was passed after the Thirteenth Amendment failed, 93–65, to win passage in the House of Representatives on June 15.) Lincoln pocket vetoed the bill and then issued a proclamation on reconstruction.

July 8, 1864

By the President of the United States.
A Proclamation.

Whereas, at the late Session, Congress passed a Bill, "To guarantee to certain States, whose governments have been usurped or overthrown, a republican form of Government," a copy of which is hereunto annexed:

And whereas, the said Bill was presented to the President of the United States, for his approval, less than one hour before the *sine die* adjournment of said Session, and was not signed by him:

And whereas, the said Bill contains, among other things, a plan for restoring the States in rebellion to their proper practical relation in the Union, which plan expresses the sense of Congress upon that subject, and which plan it is now thought fit to lay before the people for their consideration:

Now, therefore, I, Abraham Lincoln, President of the United States, do proclaim, declare, and make known, that, while I am, (as I was in December last, when by proclamation I propounded a plan for restoration) unprepared, by a formal approval of this Bill, to be inflexibly committed to any single plan of restoration; and, while I am also unprepared to declare, that the free-state constitutions and governments, already adopted and installed in Arkansas and Louisiana, shall be set aside and held for nought, thereby repelling and discouraging the loyal citizens who have set up the same, as to further effort; or to declare a constitutional competency in Congress to abolish slavery in States, but am at the same time sincerely hoping and expecting that a constitutional amendment, abolishing slavery throughout the nation, may be adopted, nevertheless, I am fully satisfied with the system for restoration contained in the Bill, as one very proper plan for the loyal people of any State choosing to adopt it; and that I am, and at all times shall be, prepared to give the Executive aid and assistance to any such people, so soon as the military resistance to the United States shall have been suppressed in any such State, and the people thereof shall have sufficiently returned to their obedience to the Constitution and the laws of the United States,—in which cases, military Governors will be appointed, with directions to proceed according to the Bill.

In testimony whereof, I have hereunto set my hand and caused the Seal of the United States to be affixed.

Done at the City of Washington this eighth day of July, in the year of Our Lord, one thousand eight hundred and sixty-four, and of the Independence of the United States the eighty-ninth.

ABRAHAM LINCOLN.

By the President:

WILLIAM H. SEWARD, Secretary of State.

CONDITIONS FOR PEACE:
WASHINGTON, D.C., JULY 1864

Abraham Lincoln to Horace Greeley

President Lincoln replied on July 9 to Horace Greeley's letter concerning possible peace negotiations. Greeley responded the following day that "I have neither purpose nor desire to be made a confidant, far less an agent in such negotiations." He continued: "Meantime, I wish you would consider the propriety of *somehow* apprising the People of the South, especially those of North Carolina, that *no* overture or advance looking to Peace and Reunion has ever been repelled by you, but that such a one would at any time have been cordially received and favorably regarded—and would still be."

Hon. Horace Greely — Washington, D.C.
Dear Sir — July 9. 1864

Your letter of the 7th., with inclosures, received. If you can find, any person anywhere professing to have any proposition of Jefferson Davis in writing, for peace, embracing the restoration of the Union and abandonment of slavery, what ever else it embraces, say to him he may come to me with you, and that if he really brings such proposition, he shall, at the least, have safe conduct, with the paper (and without publicity, if he choose) to the point where you shall have met him. The same, if there be two or more persons. Yours truly

A LINCOLN

HANGING THE ANDERSONVILLE RAIDERS: GEORGIA, JULY 1864

Eugene Forbes: Diary, July 11, 1864

Six of the Andersonville "raiders" were tried and condemned by their fellow prisoners and publicly executed after their sentences were approved by the Confederate authorities in Richmond. Sergeant Eugene Forbes watched as they were hanged by the "regulators" who had banded together and defeated the raiders in late June. In September Forbes was transferred to the prison camp at Florence, South Carolina, where he would die on February 7, 1865.

Monday, July 11. Cloudy A.M. Atlanta reported in flames, and Johnston gone to reinforce Lee. A Charleston prisoner, captured yesterday week, told me Foster had been repulsed in an attack on Fort Johnston, on James Island. A slight shower came up about 4 P.M., cooling the air considerably. About 5 o'clock P.M. a rebel guard was seen marching toward the stockade, preceded by a drum corps, playing the "Dead March," and conducting six prisoners. They entered the gate at the southeast part of the stockade, when Capt. Wurtz (commanding the camp) delivered the prisoners over to a body of the Regulators, headed by "Limber Jim." A gallows had been previously erected in the street leading from the southwest gate. The prisoners names were given as follows: "Moseby," "Murray," "Terry," "Sarsfield," "Delainy," and "Curtis." They were all of Irish birth or extraction, except "Moseby," who was English. "Limber Jim," with his assistants, proceeded to bind the prisoners' hands, the Captain having withdrawn the guard to the outside, leaving the condemned to be disposed of by our men. When Curtis was about to be bound, he exclaimed, "This cannot be," and made a dash through the crowd and toward the creek; he succeeded in reaching the other side, but was arrested and brought back. Shortly after five o'clock, the whole six were swung off, but "Moseby's" rope broke, bringing him to the ground, but he was soon swung up again. After having hung about fifteen minutes they were cut down, when the crowd quietly dispersed. So endeth the raid on Dowd, three of his principal assailants being among those executed. And it is to be hoped that it will also end the system of organized robbery and ruffianism which has so long ruled this camp. "Limber Jim" and his assistants were taken out of the stockade after the execution, and it is supposed they will be employed outside. A squad (1700?) of prisoners came in today from Grant's Army; they bring a report that the Exchange Commissioners have agreed on terms for exchange and parole, to commence on the 16th inst. Drew pork, salt and meal P.M. Changed our sergeant, appointing Emmett in place of Buckley.

THREATENING WASHINGTON: MARYLAND, JULY 1864

Henry Robinson Berkeley: Diary, July 4–13, 1864

Major General Franz Sigel had advanced up the Shenandoah Valley with a force of 9,000 men in early May as part of Grant's plan for a coordinated Union offensive in Virginia. Sigel was defeated at New Market on May 15 by 5,000 Confederates under Major General John C. Breckinridge, and was replaced by Major General David Hunter. After reorganizing his forces, Hunter defeated Brigadier General William E. Jones at Piedmont on June 5, occupied Lexington, and then began advancing on Lynchburg, an important rail junction that linked Petersburg and Richmond with the Shenandoah Valley. On June 13 Lee sent his Second Corps, now commanded by Lieutenant General Jubal A. Early, to help defend Lynchburg. Early's troops began to arrive on June 17, and after two days of skirmishing Hunter abandoned his offensive and retreated into the mountains of West Virginia. His withdrawal allowed Early to march north through the Shenandoah Valley and launch a raid into Maryland intended to draw Union troops away from Petersburg. A veteran of Yorktown, Glendale, Fredericksburg, Gettysburg, the Wilderness, Spotsylvania, and Cold Harbor, Private Henry Robinson Berkeley served in an artillery battalion in the Confederate Second Corps.

July 4. Taking the right-hand road, we passed through Smithfield and Charlestown, Jefferson County, Virginia and encamped on the Harpers Ferry Pike four miles south of Harpers Ferry. Here we remained all night. The Yanks who were in Harpers Ferry have retired to the Maryland Heights, leaving a good deal of plunder in the Ferry. Some of our boys went into the town to plunder. They got quite a lot of sugar, coffee, hardtack, molasses, etc. John McCorkle went in on a mule and undertook to bring out a water bucket of molasses on his mule. The Yanks were amusing themselves by throwing among our plundering boys a lot of shell. They did no harm and no one was hurt; but a lamp post (i.e. a nine-inch shell) whizzing from the Maryland Heights, "busted" about three yards in rear of John's mule's tail, while John was on his way back to camp with his water bucket of molasses. This shell lighted up all the surroundings for a few seconds, and John's mule lighted out for camp; that mule made two-forty time to camp. John, however, clung bravely to his molasses, knowing full well that "lasses" was "lasses" in Dixie in those days, and finally arrived in camp covered completely with molasses, having about two quarts left in his bucket. He spent the rest of the night washing his clothes and his mule. Thus ended for us, The Glorious Fourth of July, 1864.

July 5. In the afternoon we marched over to Shepherdstown and encamped near the town for the night.

July 6. Left camp near Shepherdstown and, after crossing the Potomac River, which came a little above our waist, we encamped near Sharpsburg, Maryland. Had to examine my caisson boxes to see if the water had gotten into any of them, while crossing the Potomac. I found them O.K.

July 7. Remained in camp near Sharpsburg all day.

July 8. Marched to Frederick City, Maryland, and encamped near the town.

July 9. Passed through Frederick City and took the Washington, D. C., Pike and came upon the Yanks in line of battle on Washington side of the Monocacy River; the latter is a small stream flowing into the Potomac. We first took a position on the left of the Washington Pike and afterwards crossed over to right and put our battery on a hill fronting a still higher hill held by the Yanks. We got here about 1 P.M. We were ordered to open on the Yankees, as soon as we heard Gen. Gordon's Division open on our right. Gordon was flanking the Yanks on our right. About 3:45 P.M. we heard, on our right, some heavy fighting in a big field of big corn. We immediately opened on the Yanks in our front. I was acting as gunner, which position I had filled since R. B. Winston was wounded on June 3, 1864. We were hotly engaged only for about twenty minutes, the Yanks in our front giving away very soon; but, alas! We had three splendid men killed: viz., Gardner and Page were killed instantly by a shell and Lieut. George Hobson was killed by a sharpshooter after the enemy had been routed, and was retreating rapidly from the field. Hobson had had a wheel on his gun knocked to pieces by a cannon shot and could not go with us as we moved rapidly down the pike after the Yanks. While his men were putting a new wheel on his gun, he and J. H. Berkeley, being on their horses, rode to the brow of the hill in front of them (which hill overlooked the river), and halted their horses. Just at the moment they halted, two Minié balls whizzed over from beyond the river, one of which struck Lieut. Hobson on the right shoulder and, passing diagonally downward, stopped on his left hip. He sank from his horse and was caught by my brother and laid on the grass. He never spoke after being struck and breathed his last in about ten minutes. Just as he was shot, he was talking to my brother (J. H. Berkeley) of Gardner and Page, who had been killed a few moments before and whose bodies had been left unburied a short way behind us. And these were the last words on his lips, "Those poor boys must be buried and their graves marked, if I have to go back." As he reached the word, "back," the fatal ball struck him and he sank from his horse. Our chaplain, Mr. Gilmer, carried his body and those of Gardner and Page back to Frederick City and had them all three put into coffins, neatly buried and their graves marked. Lieut. Woodruff is missing tonight and has not been seen or heard of since one o'clock today. A cannon ball came very near taking my head off today. I think it was the same ball which killed Gardner and Page. I was leaning over aiming my cannon and it passed just over my head. If I had been standing up it would have struck me full in the face. We crossed the Monocacy River and after having followed the enemy for three miles we went into camp in a wheat field, which had just been cut. We found a wounded Yank in the fence corner near our campfire and carried him to our fire, gave him some water and after dressing his wound (he had been shot through the leg) and giving him some supper and a cup of coffee we fixed him a bed with some bundles of wheat and put him on it. He was very grateful and told us that he was a Marylander and was only about ten miles from his home. He said he was only eighteen. He looked very young. He said that he had been told that we were very cruel to our prisoners, and that when we first came to him, he thought we were going to kill him immediately.

July 10. The Yanks are falling back on Baltimore. We took

the Washington Pike, and after a long and hot day's march encamped for the night twenty miles from that city. We gave our wounded Yankee some breakfast this morning and fixed up his blanket on four stakes to keep off the sun. We left him to his friends. I have no doubt that by this time he is at home. Lieut. Woodruff still missing. He is supposed to have been killed or captured. He was last seen in Capt. Carpenter's Battery, asking for us and left there to find us. Some of our boys think he has deserted to the Yanks. I have very little confidence in him. I have just found, on going to bed, that it is Sunday. In times of marching and fighting, a soldier frequently forgets the days of the week, all being just alike.

July 11. We marched to within two miles of the corporate limits of Washington City and encamped at "Silver Spring," the home of Postmaster General Blair. We can see the dome of the capitol and a large part of the city. There has been some heavy picket fighting this evening. There is a rumor that we are to try and storm the fortifications at daybreak tomorrow.

July 12. Remained near Washington, D. C., all day on the farm of Francis P. Blair. It is called "Silver Spring." Is a beautiful place with a large lawn running down to a beautiful and cold spring fixed up with marble basins, etc. There was very heavy skirmishing this evening, but no attempt to take the strong fortifications in our front. We retreated after dark and marched all night towards Leesburg, Virginia.

July 13. Continued to march towards Leesburg, marching all night, only stopping at 4 P.M. long enough for the men to cook and eat and for our horses to be fed. We reached the Potomac River, at Edwards' Ferry about day.

THE CAPITAL UNDER ATTACK: WASHINGTON, D.C., JULY 1864

Lois Bryan Adams to the Detroit Advertiser and Tribune

Although Washington was surrounded in July 1864 by a ring of strongly built fortifications, most of the capital's garrison had been sent on Grant's orders to Virginia to reinforce the Army of the Potomac, leaving about 10,000 semi-invalid veterans and inexperienced militiamen to defend the city. Jubal Early crossed the Potomac into Maryland on July 5–6 and advanced with 14,000 men to the Monocacy River near Frederick, where he defeated 6,000 Union troops under Major General Lew Wallace on July 9. The battle of Monocacy delayed Early's arrival at Washington by one day, allowing time for reinforcements sent by Grant from Petersburg to reach the capital. Early sent skirmishers toward Fort Stevens north of the city on July 11 as troops from the Sixth Corps began arriving by boat along the Potomac. The next day President Lincoln came under fire as he watched the fighting from the fort's parapet. Convinced that he could not break through the strengthened Union defenses, Early withdrew on the night of July 12. Lois Bryan Adams wrote about the Confederate attack in letters that appeared in the *Detroit Advertiser and Tribune* on July 20 and July 21, 1864.

Washington During the Siege

EXPERIENCES OF A RESIDENT

From Our Own Correspondent

Washington, July 13, 1864

I write you today from the center of the besieged capital, not knowing how or when my letter may reach you. Communication with the rest of world by rail or telegraph, is, as Michigan doubtless knows before this date, entirely cut off. The Potomac, however, is still running, and, as far as we know, its connection with the Chesapeake and Atlantic coast is still unbroken. So there is hope that in the course of time the waves may wash this waif on its northward way.

After the adjournment of Congress and the "noise and confusion" consequent upon a proper observation of the Fourth were past, the old Federal city, having assured itself that between Christian and Sanitary Commissions and State Relief Associations its sick and wounded defenders would be decently cared for, quietly addressed itself to preparations for its usual summer siesta. Confident of Grant's ability to whittle, smoke, and burrow himself into Richmond, and devoutly believing that the rebels would kindly stay there to witness his *entree* and grace his triumph, Washington stretched itself beside its slimy canal in the shadow of its unfinished monument, and said, "Now for a 'little more slumber, a little more folding of the hands to sleep,'" and was dreamily dozing off when startled by Maryland's cry of alarm and the smoke and flame of her burning dwellings. Hardly yet awake, she sprang to her feet barely in time to turn the key of her own door against the invader who already had his hand upon the latch. His coming was sudden, but still not altogether unprepared for.

This is the third day of our isolation from the civilized world, yet but for the lack of outside news, the addition of more stir among the inside military, and the distant roll of drums and roar of cannon around the borders, there is little to remind us that we are not one with the rest of the world as ever. Business seems progressing about the same as before, with the exception perhaps of a little rise in the prices of wares and goods. The workmen at the north front of the Patent Office still keep up their steady, monotonous pecking at the great marble blocks; laborers are quietly relaying and repairing street pavements; shop and tradespeople are going on with their business as usual; the tinsmith over the alley makes more noise than ever with the inevitable clattering hammer of his, and the dozens of rattle-brained children on the pavement rattle on, happily oblivious of the change.

It seems strange to be sitting here so quietly listening to the measured tread of armies and the ceaseless roll of their heavy trains through our streets. We know that "the front" now is no mythical or distant place far down the Rapidan, the Rappahannock, or the James; but, for the present at least, a reality terribly near, a dark horizon shutting us in, flashing with fire and streaming with blood. The neighing of the war horse in on our very ears—"the thunder of Captains and the noise of the shouting."

Yesterday and the day before there was considerable cannonading along our northern boundaries, only three or four miles from the city. Today we have but little; as yet there has been only skirmishing, and the throwing of shot and shell from the forts to prevent the rebels from concentrating in favorable positions. Surmises, conjectures, and rumors of every sort are in circulation, as to the number and object of the enemy, and as many differences of opinions probably, in regard to the result of this dashing venture. It will all very likely end in a little more than a great scare, some loss of life, the devastation of Maryland, the abstraction of millions of valuable property, and final escape of the daring raiders with it to Dixie. Even while I write, a rumor comes that they are across the Potomac again with their booty. Whether they will be intercepted or not remains to be seen.

Quite an engagement took place last evening, and it is said that the rebels have left some three or four hundred wounded on the field. They made Postmaster General Blair's house their headquarters, and did not burn it as they did the residences of known Union men. This fact is considered significant. It is reported that Sheridan will meet these plunderers on their way back to Richmond. Union people here will be terribly exasperated if they are allowed to escape.

L.

Letter from Washington

THE SIEGE RAISED | DEVELOPMENTS BY THE LATE EXCITEMENT | WEEDS IN UNCLE SAM'S GARDEN | DISLOYALTY IN DEPARTMENTS | THE SPIRIT MANIFEST | BRIGHT TINTS | AN INCIDENT OF THE SEVENTH STREET BATTLE

From Our Own Correspondent

Washington, July 15, 1864

The two days' siege of the capital is raised, cars are again running on the road that never was torn up, the valorous government clerks after enduring the hardships of war for several hours, returned yesterday, covered with dust and glory, to do duty at their desks and ledgers once more; secessionists, who in the moment of government alarm had become jubilant at the prospect of the fall of the capitol, and were shut in prison for safe keeping, are released and restored to favor—in short Washington is itself again, with all the symptoms of summer noontide somnolence creeping over its heart and brain.

The recent stir and excitement have had the effect to develop to a fuller extent than has heretofore been shown, the strong pro-slavery and Southern sympathetic elements existing here. People in distant States and cities have no knowledge of the prevalence and strength of these elements, or what inevitable, and it would seem irremediable, clogs they are upon the energies of the government.

The truth is, Uncle Sam's house, garden, and, for that matter, some of his large fields, too, have become weedy and foul beyond description. He has hesitated about pulling up the tares lest he might root up the wheat also; and now not only tares in the fields at large, but rank pigweeds, purslane, couch-grass and nettles, in his very conservatory and dooryard, claim his protection, and get it too, as it were in spite of himself and his most vigilant gardeners. It is easy to say, "pull them up and throw them to the dogs," but the doing of it is another thing. Still it does seem to some of us who stand peeping through the fence, that better use might be made of the rich ground occupied by those pompous pigweeds, sneaking couch-grass and purslane, and vindictive nettles.

It is a fact shamefully notorious here that there is scarcely one, indeed, I think it may be said with certainty, not one, of the government departments where the pro-slavery sentiment and the enemies of the Administration are not strongly represented. The representatives of rebeldom have secured appointments through the favor and influence of Copperhead Congressmen, or have bought them of tinctured or temporizing officials, and hold them probably because Government has more important matters to attend to than ferreting out "little foxes." Yet they are the very ones that are spoiling the grapes in the heart of the vineyard.

A case is publicly known and talked of where a woman

employed in one of the departments, at a salary of $50 per month, had a brother in the Union army who was wounded and brought to one of the hospitals in the city, but whom she never visited or took the least notice of, though she went daily with a government pass to carry comforts and luxuries to a rebel uncle who was confined in prison in the Old Capitol. Many other instances of the same nature transpire everyday, and many of these lady employees of government have relatives and friends in the rebel army, with whom they are in constant correspondence, and to whom it is said portions of their salaries are often transmitted. Is not this a delicate and unselfish way of aiding and comforting traitors?

But the women are far from being alone in this business; indeed they would not be in it at all if men were what they ought to be; for if all heads of Departments and Bureaus were what they should be in times like these, no such traitoresses would find their way into them under such flimsy pretenses as they do, to plunder and betray. This last raid seemed for a while to promise certain success to the rebels; sympathizers here appeared confident of it, and were quite open and insolent in the avowal of their sentiments. In no way perhaps did they better manifest the true spirit of their principles than in their insolent behavior towards the colored population. Even little misses spread themselves across the pavement when one of that luckless race was seen coming, and signified that "nigger might take their place in the gutter again."

These things are humiliating to national pride, but they go to show that there is a great deal of human nature, with a strong cross of Southern blood in it, still to be found in this good city of Washington. What the President and his trusty advisers have to contend with in the manifestation of this mongrel nature among officials, civil and military, no pen need undertake to tell. Happy will it be for us if, in spite of all, the old ship of State is at last brought safely through the storm.

A woman living near the battleground north of the city, has a brother in the rebel army who took the opportunity of being near to make her a visit, hoping also to get much needed supplies of food and clothing; but she indignantly drove him from her house, and threatened to shoot him for a traitor, as he is, if he ever attempted to appeal to her or call her sister again.

Union soldiers, though strangers, she fed and gave drink to with blessings and God speed, but the brother who had betrayed his country and sought its ruin, she cast from her as a wretch worthy only of the traitor's doom—the scorn and detestation of all loyal hearts.

L.

PURSUING EARLY: VIRGINIA, JULY 1864

Ulysses S. Grant to Henry W. Halleck

Throughout the war the Shenandoah Valley had served as a crucial source of food, fodder, and livestock for the Confederate forces in Virginia. As Early withdrew from Maryland, Grant issued directions for the pursuit of the retreating Confederates and the devastation of the valley.

City Point, Va, July 14th *1864*

MAJ. GEN. H. W. HALLECK,
CHIEF OF STAFF OF THE ARMY,
GENERAL,

It would seem from dispatches just received from Mr. Dana, Asst. Sec. of War, that the enemy are leaving Maryland. If so Hunter should follow him as rapidly as the jaded condition of his men and horses will admit. The 6th & 19th Corps should be got here without any delay so that they may be used before the return of the troops sent into the valley by the enemy. Hunter moving up the valley will either hold a large force of the enemy or he will be enabled to reach Gordonsville & Charlottesville. The utter destruction of the road at, and between, these two points will be of immense value to us.

I do not intend this as an order to bring Wright back whilst he is in pursuit of the enemy with any prospect of punishing him, but to secure his return at the earliest possible moment after he ceases to be absolutely necessary where he is.

Col. Comstock who takes this can explain to you fully the situation here. The enemy have the Weldon road completed but are very cautious about bringing cars through on it. I shall endeavor to have it badly destroyed, and for a long distance, within a few days. I understand from a refugee that they have twenty-five miles of track yet to lay to complete the Danville road.

If the enemy has left Maryland, as I suppose he has, he should have upon his heels, veterans, Militiamen, men on horseback and everything that can be got to follow, to eat out Virginia clear and clean as far as they go, so that Crows flying over it for the balance of this season will have to carry their provender with them.

I am Gen. very respectfully
your obt. svt.
U. S. GRANT
Lt. Gen.

"THE DEEPEST SHAME": WASHINGTON, D.C., JULY 1864

Charles A. Dana to Ulysses S. Grant

Assistant Secretary of War Charles A. Dana wrote to Grant after it had become clear that Early, like Lee after Antietam in 1862 and Gettysburg in 1863, had escaped across the Potomac into Virginia. A former newspaper editor, Dana had become Grant's confidant during the Vicksburg campaign while serving at his headquarters as a special emissary of the War Department.

WASHINGTON, D. C., *July* 15, 1864—11.30 A.M.

Lieut. Gen. U. S. GRANT:

Our latest advices indicate that the head of the retreating rebel column has reached Ashby's Gap. Wright is not yet at Edwards Ferry. The enemy will doubtless escape with all his plunder and recruits, leaving us nothing but the deepest shame that has yet befallen us.

C. A. DANA.

"TO WHOM IT MAY CONCERN": WASHINGTON, D.C., JULY 1864

Abraham Lincoln: Offer of Safe Conduct for Peace Negotiators

On July 13 Horace Greeley assured Lincoln "that two persons, duly commissioned and empowered to negotiate for peace, are at this moment not far from Niagara Falls, in Canada." Lincoln responded two days later that "I was not expecting you to *send* me a letter, but to *bring* me a man, or men." In a separate letter sent the same day, the President told Greeley, "I not only intend a sincere effort for peace, but I intend that you shall be a personal witness that it is made." Greeley then went to Niagara Falls with a safe conduct pass, issued on Lincoln's orders, allowing four Confederate agents to travel to Washington. On July 18 Lincoln issued a proclamation calling for 500,000 volunteers and ordering a draft for September 5 to fill the quota for new troops. That day, Greeley telegraphed from Niagara Falls that while the Confederate envoys presently in Canada lacked the authority to negotiate, they or other representatives would be authorized to do so if Lincoln expressed interest. The President wrote a new offer of safe conduct, addressed "To Whom it may concern," and gave it to his secretary John Hay to take with him to Niagara Falls.

To Whom It May Concern

Executive Mansion,
Washington, July 18, 1864.

To Whom it may concern:

Any proposition which embraces the restoration of peace, the integrity of the whole Union, and the abandonment of slavery, and which comes by and with an authority that can control the armies now at war against the United States will be received and considered by the Executive government of the United States, and will be met by liberal terms on other substantial and collateral points; and the bearer, or bearers thereof shall have safe-conduct both ways.

ABRAHAM LINCOLN

Clement C. Clay and James P. Holcombe to Horace Greeley

John Hay crossed into Canada with Horace Greeley on July 20 and gave Lincoln's offer of safe conduct to James P. Holcombe, one of the Confederate agents who had been corresponding with Greeley. Instead of replying to Hay, Holcombe and his colleague Clement C. Clay addressed a letter to Greeley and released it on July 21 to the Associated Press. The letter was widely printed in the northern press the following day, along with earlier correspondence between Greeley and the Confederate agents that did not mention the conditions for peace Lincoln had set forth on July 9 (see p. 243 in this volume). Greeley asked the President on August 4 to publish their correspondence regarding the Niagara Falls episode. Lincoln agreed, but requested that Greeley suppress passages in his letters the President believed "give too gloomy an aspect to our cause, and those which present the carrying of elections as a motive of action." Greeley refused, and their correspondence remained unpublished. Clay, Holcombe, and their colleagues continued to meet with Peace Democrats in an effort to influence the platform and nomination of the Democratic national convention, which was scheduled to meet in Chicago on August 29.

NIAGARA FALLS, CLIFTON HOUSE, July 21.

To Hon. Horace Greeley:

SIR: The paper handed to Mr. HOLCOMBE on yesterday, in your presence, by Maj. HAY, A.A.G., as an answer to the application in our note of the 18th inst., is couched in the following terms:

EXECUTIVE MANSION, WASHINGTON, D.C.,
July 18, 1864.

To whom it may Concern:

Any proposition which embraces the restoration of peace, the integrity of the whole Union, and the abandonment of Slavery, and which comes by and with an authority that can control the armies now at war against the United States, will be received and considered by the Executive Government of the United States, and will be met by liberal terms, on other substantial and collateral points, and the bearer or bearers thereof shall have safe conduct both ways.

ABRAHAM LINCOLN.

The application to which we refer was elicited by your letter of the 17th instant, in which you inform Mr. JACOB THOMPSON and ourselves that you were authorized by the President of the United States to tender us his safe conduct on the hypothesis that we were "duly accredited from Richmond as bearers of propositions looking to the establishment of peace," and desired a visit to Washington in the fulfillment of this mission. This assertion, to which we then gave, and still do, entire credence, was accepted by us as the evidence of an unexpected but most gratifying change in the policy of the President, a change which we felt authorized to hope might terminate in the conclusion of a peace mutually just, honorable and advantageous to the North and to the South, exacting no condition but that we should be "duly accredited from Richmond as bearers of propositions looking to the establishment of peace." Thus proffering a basis for conference as comprehensive as we could desire, it seemed to us that the President opened a door which had previously been closed against the Confederate States for a full interchange of sentiments, free discussion of conflicting opinions and untrammeled effort to remove all causes of controversy by liberal negotiations. We, indeed, could not claim the benefit of a safe conduct which had been extended to us in a character we had no right to assume and had never affected to possess; but the uniform declarations of our Executive and Congress, and their thrice repeated, and as often repulsed, attempts to open negotiations, furnish a sufficient pledge to assure us that this conciliatory manifestation on the part of the President of the United States would be met by them in a temper of equal magnanimity. We had, therefore, no hesitation in declaring that if this correspondence was communicated to the President of the Confederate States, he would promptly embrace the opportunity presented for seeking a peaceful solution of this unhappy strife. We feel confident that you must share our profound regret that the spirit which dictated the first step toward peace had not continued to animate the counsels of your President. Had the representatives of the two Governments met to consider this question, the most momentous ever submitted to human statesmanship, in a temper of becoming moderation and equity, followed as their deliberations would have been by the prayers and benedictions of every patriot and Christian on the habitable globe, who is there so bold as to pronounce that the frightful waste of individual happiness and public prosperity which is daily saddening the universal heart, might not have been terminated; or if the desolation and carnage of war must still be endured through weary years of blood and suffering, that there might not at least have been infused into its conduct something more of the spirit which softens and partially redeems its brutalities. Instead of the safe conduct which we solicited, and which your first letter gave us every reason to suppose would be extended for the purpose of initiating a negotiation in which neither Government would compromise its rights or its dignity, a document has been presented which provokes as much indignation as surprise. It bears no feature of resemblance to that which was originally offered, and is unlike any paper which ever before emanated from the constitutional Executive of a free people. Addressed "to whom it may concern," it precludes negotiation, and prescribes in advance the terms and conditions of peace. It returns to the original policy of "No bargaining, no negotiations, no truces with rebels except to bury their dead, until every man shall have laid down his arms, submitted to the Government, and sued for mercy." What may be the explanation of this sudden and entire change in the views of the President, of this rude withdrawal of a courteous overture for negotiation at the moment it was likely to be accepted, of this emphatic recall of words of peace just uttered, and fresh blasts of war to the bitter end, we leave for the speculation of those who have the means or inclination to penetrate the mysteries of his Cabinet, or fathom the caprice of his imperial will. It is enough for us to say that we have no use whatever for the paper which has been placed in our hands. We could not transmit it to the President of the Confederate States without offering him an indignity, dishonoring ourselves and incurring the well-merited scorn of our countrymen.

Whilst an ardent desire for peace pervades the people of the

Confederate States, we rejoice to believe that there are few, if any among them, who would purchase it at the expense of liberty, honor and self-respect. If it can be secured only by their submission to terms of conquest, the generation is yet unborn which will witness its restitution. If there be any military autocrat in the North who is entitled to proffer the conditions of this manifesto, there is none in the South authorized to entertain them. Those who control our armies are the servants of the people, not their masters; and they have no more inclination, than they have right, to subvert the social institutions of the sovereign States, to overthrow their established Constitutions, and to barter away their priceless heritage of self-government. This correspondence will not, however, we trust, prove wholly barren of good results.

If there is any citizen of the Confederate States who has clung to a hope that peace was possible with this Administration of the Federal Government, it will strip from his eyes the last film of such a delusion. Or, if there be any whose hearts have grown faint under the suffering and agony of this bloody struggle, it will inspire them with fresh energy to endure and brave whatever may yet be requisite to preserve to themselves and their children all that gives dignity and value to life or hope and consolation to death. And if there be any patriots or Christians in your land, who shrink appalled from the illimitable virtue of private misery and public calamity which stretches before them, we pray that in their bosoms a resolution may be quickened to recall the abused authority and vindicate the outraged civilization of their country. For the solicitude you have manifested to inaugurate a movement which contemplates results the most noble and humane, we return our sincere thanks; and are, most respectfully and truly, your obedient servants,

C. C. CLAY, Jr.
JAMES P. HOLCOMBE.

James R. Gilmore to the Boston Evening Transcript

July 22, 1864

In early July President Lincoln gave Colonel James F. Jaquess, a Methodist minister on leave from the 73rd Illinois Infantry, and James R. Gilmore, an author of books and sketches under the pen name Edmund Kirke, permission to travel to Richmond and hold unofficial talks on peace terms with Confederate leaders. Jaquess and Gilmore crossed into Confederate-held territory on July 16 and met with Jefferson Davis the following day. They returned to the Union lines on July 18, having obtained, as Lincoln hoped, an unyielding statement from Davis regarding the Confederacy's war aims. Gilmore published a letter about his trip with Jaquess in the *Boston Evening Transcipt* on July 22 that was reprinted in *The New York Times* and other northern newspapers. He wrote a longer account of his mission, "Our Trip to Richmond," which appeared in the *Atlantic Monthly* in September 1864 (see pp. 338–357 in this volume).

A CARD FROM EDMUND KIRKE

Editor of the Transcript: As the small amount of printer's ink which you used upon me in last evening's Transcript somewhat affects my friend Col. Jaquess—for whom you charge me with having "a weakness"—you will, I know, allow me a small space in reply.

I confess to a "weakness" for Colonel Jaquess, and I hope the day may never come when I have not a weakness for him, and for all men like him. I consider him a brave, true, patriotic, Christian gentleman. He is widely known and esteemed at the West. Before the war he was for fourteen years President of Quincy College, Illinois, and at the breaking out of the rebellion was selected by Gov. Yates to raise a three years' regiment.

He did so, and with that regiment was in the front of the assault at Fort Donelson; did effective service at Pittsburg Landing; saved our left wing at Perryville; "fought as *I* never saw man fight before" (those were General Rosecrans's exact words to me) at Stone river; stood his ground till three horses were shot under him, and three fourths of his men lay dead or wounded about him, at Chickamauga, and was the *first* man to enter the rebel intrenchments on the heights of Mission Ridge. Such a record, I think, should justify any weakness I have for him.

With his supposed "mission," I have nothing to do. I went with him—or rather he went with me, for my pass directed General Grant to "allow J. R. Gilmore and *friend* to pass our lines and go South,"—to Richmond, on Saturday last, and I can say, unequivocally, that the President knew nothing of his accompanying me.

Mr. Lincoln, though an old-time friend and acquaintance of Col. Jaquess, has not even *seen* him for now nearly three years.

How the newspaper statements in reference to our visit to Mr. Davis, originated, I do not know. Until twelve o'clock last night—when I returned to my home in this city—I had communicated to no human being, except Generals Butler and Grant and the President, the fact of having been in the rebel capital at all.

So much for your paragraph. Now, allow me a few words in reference to a telegram in this morning's Advertiser, which charges me with being an *attache* of the New York Tribune, and with having some connection with the Sanders-Greeley negotiation that is said to be going on at Niagara Falls.

I am *not*, and *never have been*, connected with the New York Tribune. At the urgent solicitation of Mr. Sidney Howard Gay, the managing editor of that journal (who is a very dear and intimate friend of mine,) I *did* consent, nearly two years ago, to the *Tribune Association* publishing a cheap edition of my books, (but that arrangement was long since discontinued,) and I did, in July last, write half a dozen sketches for that paper.

I have not, however, exchanged a word with Mr. Greeley, or even seen him, for fully three months, and I have no connection with, in fact I know nothing of, his "negotiations."

This much, however, in reference to that much-talked-of matter, being a Yankee, I can *guess. It will result in nothing.* Jefferson Davis said to me last Sunday (and with all his faults I believe him a man of truth) "This war must go on till the last of this generation falls in his tracks, and his children seize his musket and fight our battle, *unless you acknowledge our right to self government.* We are not fighting for slavery. We are fighting for INDEPENDENCE, and that, or extermination, we *will* have."

If Messrs. Sanders, Holcomb, Thompson & Co. have "pulled the wool" over the eyes of Mr. Greeley, they have not pulled it over the eyes of Mr. Lincoln. He, I know, fully understands and appreciates their overtures, and you can safely assure your readers that the interests and honor of the country are safe in his hands. If every man, woman and child in this nation knew him as I do, they would believe this, and would say, as I do, GOD BLESS HIM.

I have returned from the South much prostrated by disease contracted there, but if my strength allows, I shall tell you, and your readers, "how and why I went to Richmond," in the next (September) number of the Atlantic Monthly. You have alluded to me as "Edmund Kirke," and the reading public know me by that cognomen, but as I desire to be considered "personally responsible" for the statements herein, I subscribe my true name hereto.

JAMES R. GILMORE,
37 West Cedar street, Boston.

Friday Morning.

FIGHTING IN THE SHENANDOAH:
VIRGINIA, JULY 1864

Henry Robinson Berkeley: Diary, July 14–24, 1864

Jubal Early crossed the Potomac on July 14 and returned to the northern Shenandoah Valley two days later. After fighting with Union forces near Berryville on July 18, he began retreating south toward Strasburg the next day. Convinced that Early was about to rejoin Lee's army, Major General Horatio G. Wright, the commander of the pursuing Union forces, ordered most of his troops to return to the Petersburg front by way of Washington. Instead, Early marched north with 14,000 men and attacked 9,000 Union troops under Brigadier General George R. Crook at Kernstown on July 24. Confederate artilleryman Henry Robinson Berkeley wrote about the fighting at Kernstown and the earlier battle of Rutherford's Farm (or Stephenson's Depot), fought near Winchester on July 20.

July 14. Crossed the Potomac about 7 A.M. and encamped at the Big Spring two miles north of Leesburg. The march from Washington to this place has been the most severe I have ever experienced. We marched two nights and two days consecutively and during that time only halted our march the second afternoon long enough for men and horses to get something to eat. This heavy marching was made necessary because three Yankee armies were after us, any one of which was as large as our army under Gen. Early. These Yankee armies were Canby's at Washington, D. C., Gen. Wallace's at Baltimore and Gen. Hunter's now at Frederick City, Maryland. We marched out from between their converging lines. We got to the Big Spring about 9 A.M. I never had been so sleepy and tired before in all my life. I threw off my knapsack and blanket, crawled under an Osage orange hedge and in two minutes was fast asleep. We slept until 5 P.M. and then woke up and cooked and ate a hearty supper, feeling much refreshed after a bath.

July 15. Remained near Big Spring and washed our clothes.

July 16. We pulled out this morning and taking the Winchester Pike marched to Snickersville and encamped for the night. The Yankee cavalry made a dash on our wagon train about 3 P.M. and burnt a few wagons. We fired a few rounds at them. Two Yankees were killed and a few captured.

July 17. Sunday. We crossed the mountains by Snicker's Gap and continued our march towards Winchester and encamped near Berryville.

July 18. Remained near Berryville. Received six letters from home. Some of these letters had been following us ever since we left Richmond.

July 20. Moved last night from Berryville and marched three miles north of Winchester and there halted to get breakfast for men and horses. We remained in this place until 4 P.M. when we were ordered to follow Ramseur's Division down the pike towards Martinsburg. The Yanks in the meanwhile had driven back our cavalry. After going about a mile down the pike, Ramseur ran into an ambush the Yanks had set for us. Just as we reached the farther edge of a piece of woods, and while our men were still in line of march; the Yanks opened on us from behind a stone fence at close quarters before our line of battle could be formed, or our men load their guns which were empty. Our men gave way and, the Yanks charging when they saw our confusion, the whole thing soon became a panic. We lost our entire battery, bringing out only one limber and a caisson. We had twenty-five horses killed and four men killed in our battery. The following men were wounded, viz., Lieut. Basye, lost right foot, Lieut. Latham, believed to be mortally wounded, left at his aunt's in Winchester, Bolling Hewitt, John Hawkins, Frank Miller, Billy Good. The last two were left on the battle field and fell into the hands of the Yankees. Several other men were slightly hurt. Lieut. Basye's foot was cut off late tonight after we got back to Newtown, where we encamped for the night. Today's loss takes from our battery all four of our lieutenants, who started from winter quarters the first of April. Our sergeants are acting as lieutenants, and privates as corporals and sergeants.

July 21. We marched three miles towards Strasburg and then stopped and cooked, and fed the few horses we had left. We then went on to Strasburg and encamped there for the night.

July 22. Marched just beyond Strasburg and took the right-hand road; went out towards North Mountain for a mile and encamped there for the night.

July 23. Saturday. Remained here all day and washed our clothes.

July 24. We moved back towards Winchester early this morning and came on the Yanks at Kernstown. It is Sunday and I am riding Frank Kinckle's horse, Frank being sick and riding in our ambulance. Having lost our guns, and not having gotten others, we (I and my company) had the pleasure of looking on at this hot and successful little fight without taking part in it. After a short and hot fight our men drove the Yankees from all parts of the field, killing and capturing a good many. The Yankee cavalry at one time during the battle, charged the 61st and 2nd Virginia Regiments in an apple orchard. It was a very daring charge, and they did it to save their wagon train, but their loss was very heavy. It seemed to me, looking on from a distant hill, that every man was killed or captured and few horses went back, but most were without riders. I went to the spot when the fight was over. The wounded had been removed, but dead Yankees lay thick. Oh! How horrid is war. We ran the Yanks through Winchester and followed them, until night stopped us near Bunker Hill. We found in Winchester this evening Lieut. Latham, and Frank Miller. William Good had died of his wounds and been buried by the good people of Winchester. I visited the place where we lost our battery and am fully convinced if Gen. Ramseur had not interfered with us, we would never have lost our guns or the battle. We had taken position on the right and were ready to fire, when Gen. Ramseur ordered us to limber up and come over on the left of the pike. We did limber up and started over and it was while we were crossing the pike that the Yankees charged us and our infantry gave way. We could have fired at least a dozen rounds of canister into the crowded ranks of the Yanks while we were limbering up and I believe the canister would have saved the day, because I have never seen them fail to run when you went for them with canister at close quarters. It is sad to think of that mistake which cost us at least a hundred men killed and two hundred wounded. I would not like to be a general having men killed by my errors and mistakes.

Frank Miller's right leg has been amputated above the knee; this puts an end to his soldier life. He joined our company in March. He is only sixteen years old. He behaved in the fight like an old soldier. No doubt his mother will be glad to have her boy back home minus his leg. Alas! How many boys we have buried since we left our winter quarters in Orange. Who will be the next to fall?

FIGHTING FOR ATLANTA: GEORGIA, JULY 1864

Samuel T. Foster: Diary, July 18–23, 1864

On July 8 Sherman began sending troops across the Chattahoochee River to the north of the fortified position Johnston had retreated into after evacuating Kennesaw Mountain. Johnston withdrew from the west bank of the Chattahoochee on the night of July 9 and deployed his army of 60,000 men along Peachtree Creek, about three miles north of Atlanta. During the week that followed Sherman moved most of his 90,000 men across the Chattahoochee while sending cavalry to attack the railroad connecting Atlanta with Montgomery, Alabama. On July 17 Jefferson Davis relieved Johnston and replaced him with Lieutenant General John B. Hood, a corps commander in the Army of Tennessee who had previously led a division in the Army of Northern Virginia and been seriously wounded at Gettysburg and Chickamauga. Hood saw an opportunity to seize the initiative on July 19 when Sherman divided his forces, sending the Army of the Cumberland south across Peachtree Creek while the Army of the Tennessee occupied Decatur, six miles east of Atlanta. The next day, Hood attacked the Army of the Cumberland without success in fighting that cost the Confederates 2,500 men killed, wounded, or missing, and the Union 1,900. Captain Samuel T. Foster, a company commander in the dismounted 24th Texas Cavalry, served in Cleburne's Division in the corps commanded by Lieutenant General William J. Hardee. After being held in reserve during the battle on July 20, Cleburne's Division was posted to the east of Atlanta. On July 22 Hood launched another counterattack, sending Hardee's corps around the southern flank of the Army of the Tennessee. The resulting battle cost the Confederates 5,500 men killed, wounded, or missing, and the Union 3,700.

JULY 18

No move today— A circular from Genl Johnson announces that he has been removed from the command of this Army, and that Gen Hood succeeds him.

In less than an hour after this fact becomes known, groups of three, five, seven, ten or fifteen men could be seen all over camp discussing the situation— Gen. Johnson has so endeared himself to his soldiers, that no man can take his place. We have never made a fight under him that we did not get the best of it. And the whole army had become so attached to him, and to put such implicit faith in him, that whenever he said for us to fight at any particular place, we went in feeling like Gen Johnson knew all about it and we were certain to whip.

He never deceived us once. It is true we have had hard fighting and hard marching, but we always had something to eat, and in bad weather, or after an extra hard march we would have a little whiskey issued.

He was always looking after our comfort and safety. He would investigate our breastworks in person, make suggestions as to any little addition or improvement that would make them safer or more comfortable.

Gen Johnson could not have issued an order that these men would not have undertaken to accomplish—

For the first time, we hear men openly talk about going home, by tens (10) and by fifties (50). They refuse to stand guard, or do any other camp duty, and talk open rebellion against all Military authority— All over camp, (not only among Texas troops) can be seen this demoralization—and at all hours in the afternoon can be heard Hurrah for Joe Johnson and God D——n Jeff Davis.

JULY 19th

The noise and confusion was kept up all night. Genl Johnson was serenaded, and if Jeff Davis had made his appearance in this army during the excitement he would not have lived an hour.

This morning, in order (I suppose) to quiet the men, It is reported that Hood refuses to take command, and that Johnson will remain in command until after the fight at Atlanta.

In the afternoon we are put in position, build breastworks, and by night we are ready for the Yanks.

JULY 20

I am Brigade-officer-of-the-day today. And as it has been my luck heretofore to have trouble with the Yanks every time I am officer of the day—I suppose we will have a Muss of some sort. The Yanks have crossed the river above us and are coming, in fact they are shooting away to our right now, and have been since yesterday—

They are extending their line around Atlanta to the east, and now reaches from the river north of the rail road to the Augusta R.R. and cut us off from that direction—and they are still extending their lines in that direction. About 3 O'Clock PM Cheathams Div. in front of our Div. advanced through the woods until we found the Yanks, behind breastworks— We opened a tremendous fire with artillery and small arms, which is kept up until it is dark—*very dark.*

This was a little east of north from Atlanta— As soon as it gets dark our Brigade is withdrawn very quietly and marched to the city. Thence down the Augusta RR until we reach our line of breastworks running south.

We take along the breastwork to the south for about 1½ miles when we find the end of them. We then turn more to the west and stop and commence to build works—connecting with the main line.

JULY 21st

Made breastworks of logs, and by nine Oclock A.M. the Yanks artillery open on us from our left, their shell enfalading our lines. They have heard us chopping down trees and building our works and have our range—and the woods are so thick we can't see them. Their artillery are killing our men very fast— One company just to my left after finishing their works sat down to rest in a little ditch they had dug, when a shell came and took them at one end and killed and crippled every man in the ditch. Knocked one man in a hundred pieces—one hand and arm went over the works and his cartridge box was ten feet up in a tree.

My Company had completed their works when as I was lying down resting on my elbow—and another man in about the same position with our heads about two feet apart and our feet in opposite directions, a shell (schrapnell) exploded just between us—blowing me one way and him the other hurting neither one of us but killing three men about 10 ft. from us eating their breakfast.

About the middle of the day the small arms open on us in

front of us and as soon as our pickets came in a general fire opens along our line.

There are some dismounted cavalry to our right making our line longer and when the Yanks make the charge the cavalry shoot their guns off as fast as possible, while our pickets are getting in front of them. The pickets could do nothing but lie down and be captured by the Yanks—I lost three thus. As soon as the cavalry discharge their guns they all break and run like good fellows which leaves our right exposed and the Yanks following the cavalry pass by the right end of our line while those in front of us are held back by us.

Our Regt. which is on the right are taken out of the works and form a line at a double quick behind our works and perpendicular to it, which puts the left of the regt at the works—while the right is the length of the regt. off— We go forward quick time and drive the Yanks out in short order, and swing around and occupy our line again—then we are put in single file so as to cover the ground that had been occupied by the cavalry.

Here is where Lt Boerner of Capt Flys Co and Bud Martin same company were killed—both shot in the head, and while we were driving the Yanks out from our rear, one man (Joe Harrison) of my Co. ran up to a Yank, that was cursing a wounded Confed, put the muzzle of his gun to his back and blew him up.

I lost today out of my Company Sergt [ ] Chas Pepper and John Sutton killed— Thos Fisher wounded; and three captured on the picket line.

I am put in charge of the Picket line today to bring off the Pickets tonight— Our whole corps (Hardees) will move tonight some where, and the Yanks are so close to us in front that it is a dangerous maneuver—and requires considerable skill.

JULY 22nd

Last night about midnight the command moved off and left me out with the Pickets. I soon had all the pickets to move cautiously back to the breastworks and had them so scattered that they occupied the whole line, built little fires, and would knock with sticks on the log breastworks and talk pretty loud.

Kept this up until nearly day light when I had them all assemble about the centre and move off in a pretty fast walk.

We followed the command, passing through Atlanta again, turning south. Kept turning to the left. Caught up with the command about 12 O'clock M. and by 2 PM we are opposite to where we left this morning, in the rear of the Yanks. Hardees whole Corpse is here and form line-of-battle facing towards Atlanta with the Yanks in front of us with their backs to us. A skirmish line is put out to cover the whole front—and by 2½ PM we go forward. I and my whole Company are on the skirmish line. The enemy are about 2½ miles from us—as we go forward we go through fields, woods, briars &c with order for the skirmishers to go to the enemys line without firing a gun.

About 2 miles we see a Yank in front of us, when two or three men fire at him and kill him dead on the spot.

A little further on we find QuarterMasters wagons and tents, find a table set ready for dinner for 4 men—two wagons loaded with spades and picks &c a battery of artillery—but the skirmish line pass right on—woods very thick consisting of Oak Chestnut poplar and undergrowth— A Yankee General was back here and a man in my Co. (Cowan) shot at him and wounded him very badly—but did not know who it was only that he was an officer.

Cowan ran back from the skirmish line to get the litter bearers, so they could carry him back into our lines; but before he got back he had been taken in to *their* lines— The skirmishers push on until we find their works which they are preparing to leave.

The skirmishers stop in about 150 yards of the Yanks line-of-battle, to wait our own line to come up with us.

It appears that Genl Walker of a Georgia Brigade got killed about this time and the enemys line being crooked some parts of our line struck them before other parts.

All these or something else broke our line behind us, so they never came to us, but were fighting to our right and left.

I remained here for half an hour or more during which time the Yanks had discovered that there was only a skirmish line of us, they began to get over their scare and get together again, and began to shoot at us— They also turned their Artillery on us and began shelling the woods.

Soon they began sending out bodies of men into the woods where we are, and Occasionally, there is a terrible shooting to our right or left, and sometimes nearly behind us, but the woods are so thick that we can't see but a short distance.

After taking in the situation I assemble my own Company, and start back to find the line-of-battle that should have been close in our rear. Just here we capture three teamsters in the bushes. We start back through the wood, but had not got more than fifty yards before a Yank appeared before us. I ordered him to throw his gun down. Instead of doing so he cocked his gun, and aimed it at me not more than 20 feet away, and in an instant would have fired, but one of my men (Jake Eastman) was too quick for him and shot him down, the ball passing in the lower part of his bowels and out at the small of his back, which droped him in his tracks. Eastman then went up to the Yank, gave him some water and they made friends, the Yank forgiving him saying, that he done wrong, in not throwing his gun down when I told him to.

While they were talking, I with the rest of the Company and prisoners moved on and was soon out of sight of them.

While they were still there (only a few moments) a squad of Yanks came close to them, when the wounded Yank told my man to squat down by the tree, or they would see him, and take him prisoner. He did so, but they saw him and came and captured him surenough.

They took his gun from him, and put him in charge of one man to take him back to their lines— All this time I was getting further from him at every step, not dreaming of his trouble—

These two men (the Yank and his prisoner) soon got lost and my man kept telling him to go a little further this way else he would come into our line, until he saw there was no chance to get Mr Yank to come voluntarily into our line, when he concluded he would try to take the Yanks gun from him. So he picked a favorable spot and sprang upon him and caught the gun. Then they had it there all alone in the woods, each one wanting that gun but neither could get it. They soon began to get wearied out when Eastmans eye happened to catch sight of the Yanks bayonett still in his scabbard.

He grabbed it and put the point of it to the Yanks breast, when the Yank let loose the gun and surrendered.

Eastman of course brought him in to our lines. We soon found the command, reforming, and soon went in where I had just come out.

The fight is kept up all the evening. Jr. Harrison is severely wounded also Sam Fisher Alf Neil and Ogle Love— Three killed one wounded and three captured yesterday. Today four wounded is cutting the Company down very fast. We look loansome.

The fighting is kept up til night, very heavy. We charged in the woods then fall back—repeated it several times until night puts an end to the conflict.

JULY 23

All quiet this morning, after a terrible day yesterday all along the lines.

Our men are getting boots hats &c watches knives &c off of the dead Yanks near us in the woods—lots of them.

Alf Neil and Ogle Love come back this morning, having been over heated yesterday, and retired. Our dead have all been buried, and the Yanks will be as soon as they can do so.

We cook and eat, talk and laugh with the enemys dead lying all about us as though they were so many logs.

"TAKE MY CHILDREN FROM THOSE MEN": MASSACHUSETTS, JULY 1864

John Q. A. Dennis to Edwin M. Stanton

In July 1863 Colonel William Birney, son of the abolitionist leader James G. Birney, began recruiting black soldiers in eastern Maryland. Although his instructions limited his recruiting to free blacks and the slaves of disloyal owners, Birney used his position to free slaves regardless of the loyalty of their masters. It is likely that John Q. A. Dennis was freed by an expedition Birney ("Cornel borne") sent in the fall of 1863 to Worcester County. No record has been found in the War Department archives of a response to the appeal Dennis made to Secretary of War Stanton for help in freeing his family. On October 12–13, 1864, Maryland voters approved, 30,174–29,799, a new constitution that abolished slavery in the state on November 1.

Boston July 26th 1864

Dear Sir I am Glad that I have the Honour to Write you afew line I have been in troble for about four yars my Dear wife was taken from me Nov 19th 1859 and left me with three Children and I being a Slave At the time Could Not do Anny thing for the poor little Children for my master it was took me Carry me some forty mile from them So I Could Not do for them and the man that they live with half feed them and half Cloth them & beat them like dogs & when I was admited to go to see them it use to brake my heart & Now I say agian I am Glad to have the honour to write to you to see if you Can Do Anny thing for me or for my poor little Children I was keap in Slavy untell last Novr 1863. then the Good lord sent the Cornel borne Down their in Marland in worsester Co So as I have been recently freed I have but letle to live on but I am Striveing Dear Sir but what I went too know of you Sir is is it possible for me to go & take my Children from those men that keep them in Savery if it is possible will you pleas give me a permit from your hand then I think they would let them go I Do Not know what better to Do but I am sure that you know what is best for me to Do my two son I left with Mr Josep Ennese & my litle daughter I left with Mr Iven Spence in worsister Co [ ] of Snow hill

Hon sir will you please excuse my Miserable writeing & answer me as soon as you can I want get the little Children out of Slavery, I being Criple would like to know of you also if I Cant be permited to rase a Shool Down there & on what turm I Could be admited to Do so No more At present Dear Hon Sir

John Q A Dennis

Hon Sir will you please direct your letter to No 4½ Milton St Boston mass

Benjamin F. McIntyre: Diary, July 29, 1864

A Union expeditionary force of 6,000 men landed on Brazos Island at the mouth of the Rio Grande on November 2, 1863, and occupied Brownsville, Texas, four days later in an attempt to block Confederate trade with Europe through Mexican ports. Although the garrison at Brownsville was able to control the lower Rio Grande valley, the Confederates continued to export cotton and import supplies across the river west of the town. In the summer of 1864 the Union troops along the Rio Grande, now numbering 2,700, came under attack by a force of 1,300 irregular Confederate cavalry. After a series of skirmishes the Union forces evacuated Brownsville on July 29 and withdrew to the coast, where a small garrison would continue to hold Brazos Island. Second Lieutenant Benjamin F. McIntyre of the 19th Iowa Infantry had fought at Prairie Grove, in the siege of Vicksburg, and at Stirling's Plantation before being sent to Brownsville.

White House Ranch July 29th 1864

The Illinois 94th boys were favored with a ride from here on the Mustang, while the 91st Ill., 38th 20th & 19th Iowa under the command of Col Day of the 91st took up the line of march and by the judicious management in marching of Col Day we made this point at an early hour.

I Know not from what this place derives its name—if however a little white house the size of a hen coop is a white house and patches of cactus and chapperal on a barren sandy plain is a ranch this place must be rightly named. The 91st Ill. 20th Wis. have gone on to Brazos. I noticed on the steamer this morning the wives of Maj Pettybone, Capt Drake, & Lieut Yorke who has been on a visit to their husbands at Brownsville for several weeks past. At present we seem to form an Iowa Brigade our Colonel Com'dg.

In review of the past two days march of our troops It was as pleasant as could have been expected under circumstance. The Rio Grande was high and the country was flooded to a great extent and very many places the troops were compelled to pass through water two and three feet deep. The roads were very muddy and the days excessively hot with occasional rain and in passing through the closely matted chapperal upon either side excluding every breath of air and yet not sufficient in height to afford a shade.

A provost guard, left at Brownsville after our departure to watch unobserved a few Strong Union men left behind, captured some half dozen who as soon as we had left raised the Confederate flag & took formal possession of the place in the name of Godly "Jeff"—they were brought along as the guards did not think Brownsville a healthy place for them.

A melancholy accident happened this morning. The 20th Wis. & 94th Ill. were in camp with the Division last night at Union Ranch and for which two steamers were sent up last evening on which they were to embark. The boats were lying side by side in the stream. The two regiments were ordered upon them at an early hour—it was very dark and no lights were placed on the boats so that the troops could desern their way distinctly over piles of freight of every variety. The 20th Wis. Reg. were to take the outside boat—necessitating them of course to pass over the inside one. The river was full banks, the current very swift. Each man had his Knapsack strapped to his back and of course had also a full set of equipments beside his cartridge box containing forty rounds. One of the soldiers of the 20th thus equipped in passing over boxes, coils of rope, barrels, wood, tents &c made a misstep and fell into the river. As I Stated the river was high & swift and it was very dark. The unfortunate man Sustained himself upon the water for some time and had floated quite a half a mile. A yawl was put after him which in the confusion took minits to unloosen and got to within a few feet of the drowning man when he sank.

It would be folly in me to say anything regarding this matter—it is but a reiteration of many similar cases and was occasioned merely by officers not properly attending to their duties and not attending to the care of their men—a single lantern upon the bow of the Steamer would have Spared this meloncholy accident. He will soon be forgotten and the incidents attending his death be lost amoung the things of the past so far as his regiment is concerned, and the country will forget such a man ever existed—Yet far distant in the Badger

State near a little glassy lake are hearts who will preserve his memory green. It was a happy home and joy and happiness has lingered in the little domicil with its shades of vine—Sorrow henceforth will be its companion and that little glassy lake will mirror back the pale tearful faces of that once happy household desolated by the lack of care by the officer who was over him who today would be amoung us had ordinary precaution been taken and usual care exercised. The two days march has been a hot one—the 2d day while under the command of Col Day was rendered comfortable as far as marching is concerned for he understands how to march men—which not one out of a dozen of our Commanders do understand.

Gen Herron complimented his men on the dispatch with which they accomplished this march. Compliments are very good but when a man has been compelled to do his utmost & can do no more, compliments—even from a Major General—proves no balm—rather let our Generals use discretion and a little sense and his men will prove hereafter of benefit to him. Under the circumstances his compliments are in bad grace.

Gen Herron and his immortal Staff left this evening by steamer for Brazos. Two steamers—the James Hale and Mustang—remain here.

Col Bruce will receive orders from the General tomorrow probably regarding our future.

Col Dye is at the Island where his wife lies dangerously ill—it is a happiness for the husband to meet with his family after a long absence, yet here to some it has brought a great sorrow—the Surgeon of the 20th Wis. buried his wife at Brownsville—Lieut Yorke a staff officer left an interesting little child. Others were quite sick and came near their end and now they are left in a strangers land—a land soon to which no Union man holds any claim—but amid the chapperal and cactus they will rest—the mockingbird will carroll for them his morning anthem while gentle breezes will waft over them its orange ladened breeze. O how oft will the Kindred heart of loved ones yearn for this sacred Spot and wish their dead could repose in their own native soil. Over them sad memories might call up pleasing recollections and in their sorrow find a melancholy joy which is now forever denied them.

PREPARING FOR BATTLE:
GULF OF MEXICO, JULY 1864

David G. Farragut: General Orders Nos. 10 and 11

A veteran of the War of 1812 and the U.S.-Mexican War, Rear Admiral David G. Farragut had led the Union squadron that forced a passage between Forts Jackson and St. Philip on the lower Mississippi in April 1862 and captured New Orleans. In July 1864 Farragut issued tactical instructions to his ship captains as his squadron prepared to fight its way past Forts Gaines and Morgan at the entrance to Mobile Bay. The texts of General Orders Nos. 10 and 11 printed here are taken from the *Official Records of the Union and Confederate Navies in the War of the Rebellion* (1894–1922). In *The Life of David Glasgow Farragut, First Admiral of the United States Navy, Embodying His Journal and Letters* (1879), Loyall Farragut, the admiral's son, published a somewhat different version of General Orders No. 11 that is probably based on a manuscript draft; the substantive differences between the two texts are presented in the endnotes to this volume.

U. S. FLAGSHIP HARTFORD,
Off Mobile Bay, July 12, 1864.

GENERAL ORDERS,
No. 10.

Strip your vessels and prepare for the conflict. Send down all your superfluous spars and rigging. Trice up or remove the whiskers. Put up the splinter nets on the starboard side, and barricade the wheel and steersmen with sails and hammocks. Lay chains or sand bags on the deck over the machinery, to resist a plunging fire. Hang the sheet chains over the side, or make any other arrangement for security that your ingenuity may suggest. Land your starboard boats or lower and tow them on the port side, and lower the port boats down to the water's edge. Place a leadsman and the pilot in the port quarter boat, or the one most convenient to the commander.

The vessels will run past the forts in couples, lashed side by side, as hereinafter designated. The flagship will lead and steer from Sand Island N. by E. by compass, until abreast of Fort Morgan; then N. W. half N. until past the Middle Ground; then N. by W., and the others, as designated in the drawing, will follow in due order until ordered to anchor; but the bow and quarter line must be preserved to give the chase guns a fair range, and each vessel must be kept astern of the broadside of the next ahead; each vessel will keep a very little on the starboard quarter of his next ahead, and when abreast of the fort, will keep directly astern, and as we pass the fort will take the same distance on the port quarter of the next ahead, to enable the stern guns to fire clear of the next vessel astern.

It will be the object of the admiral to get as close to the fort as possible before opening fire. The ships, however, will open fire the moment the enemy opens upon us, with their chase and other guns, as fast as they can be brought to bear. Use short fuzes for the shell and shrapnel, and as soon as within 300 or 400 yards give them grape. It is understood that heretofore we have fired too high, but with grapeshot it is necessary to elevate a little above the object, as grape will dribble from the muzzle of the gun.

If one or more of the vessels be disabled, their partners must carry them through, if possible; but if they can not then the next astern must render the required assistance; but as the admiral contemplates moving with the flood tide, it will only require sufficient power to keep the crippled vessels in the channel.

Vessels that can must place guns upon the poop and topgallant forecastle and in the tops on the starboard side. Should the enemy fire grape, they will remove the men from the topgallant forecastle and poop to the guns below until out of grape range.

The howitzers must keep up a constant fire from the time they can reach with shrapnel until out of its range.

D. G. FARRAGUT,
Rear-Admiral, Commanding West Gulf Blockading Squadron.

FLAGSHIP HARTFORD,
Mobile Bay, July 29, 1864.

GENERAL ORDERS,
No. 11.

Should any vessel be disabled to such a degree that her consort is unable to keep her in her station, she will drop out of line to the westward and not embarrass the vessels next astern by attempting to regain her station. Should she repair damages, so as to be able to reenter the line of battle, she will take her station in the rear as close to the last vessel as possible.

So soon as the vessels have passed the fort and kept away N. W., they can cast off the gunboats at the discretion of the senior officer of the two vessels, and allow them to proceed up the bay to cut off the enemy's gunboats that may be attempting to escape up to Mobile. There are certain black buoys placed by the enemy from the piles on the west side of the channel across it toward Fort Morgan. It being understood that there are torpedoes and other obstructions between the buoys, the vessels will take care to pass to the eastward of the easternmost buoy, which is clear of all obstructions.

So soon as the vessels arrive opposite the end of the piles, it will be best to stop the propeller of the ship and let her drift the distance past by her headway and the tide, and those having side-wheel gunboats will continue on by the aid of their paddle wheels, which are not likely to foul with the enemy's drag ropes.

D. G. FARRAGUT,
Rear-Admiral.

THE BATTLE OF THE CRATER:
VIRGINIA, JULY 1864

Stephen Minot Weld: Diary, July 30, 1864, and Memoir from 1912

Lieutenant Colonel Henry Pleasants, the commander of the 48th Pennsylvania Infantry outside of Petersburg, was a mining engineer, and many of his men were coal miners. With the approval of Major General Ambrose Burnside, the commander of the Ninth Corps, Pleasants and his men began digging a tunnel on June 25 that eventually extended more than 500 feet and ended beneath a strongpoint overlooking the Union siege lines. When completed, the mine would be loaded with gunpowder and exploded, creating a breach in the center of the Confederate defenses that the Ninth Corps would attack through. Of the four divisions in the corps, three were badly understrength after suffering heavy losses in the spring campaign, while the Fourth Division, made up of nine regiments of the U.S. Colored Troops, had previously been used only to guard bridges and wagon trains. Impressed by the morale of his black troops, Burnside chose them to lead the assault, and had the division practice the maneuvers that would be needed to advance around the crater formed by the blast. On July 28 Meade ordered Burnside to place the Fourth Division in reserve, citing its inexperience in battle, and to use white troops in the initial assault. His decision was supported by Grant, who feared the political repercussions if it appeared that black troops had been deliberately sacrificed in a costly attack. Burnside had his three other division commanders draw lots to determine who would lead the assault. The task fell to the First Division, while the two other white divisions would protect its flanks. At 4:45 A.M. on July 30 the battle began as a lit fuse detonated 8,000 pounds of gunpowder. Lieutenant Colonel Stephen Minot Weld of the 56th Massachusetts Infantry advanced with the First Brigade of the First Division. He wrote about the battle in his diary and in reminiscences published in *War Diary and Letters of Stephen Minot Weld, 1861–1865* (1912).

Saturday, July 30.—We were formed in column of brigade wings, the 2d Brigade leading, under Colonel Marshall. General Bartlett commanded our brigade, Colonel Gould having the right wing, and I the left, consisting of the 21st Massachusetts on the right, the 56th Massachusetts in the centre, and the 100th Pennsylvania on the left. We were in position about three quarters of an hour before the mine was blown up, and while waiting my feelings were anything but pleasant. The officers and men were disappointed and discouraged at having to lead, as we had heard all along that the negroes were to do this, and we had no confidence in Ledlie. He had failed us on several occasions, notably on June 17. At 4.30 A.M. the mine was blown up. It was just early dawn, light enough to distinguish a person a few yards off. The explosion was the grandest spectacle I ever saw. The first I knew of it, was feeling the earth shaking. I looked up and saw a huge mass of earth and flame rising some 50 or 60 feet in the air, almost slowly and majestically, as if a volcano had just opened, followed by an immense volume of smoke rolling out in every direction. The noise was very slight indeed, considering that there were nine tons of powder exploded. The men of the division were stampeded at first, but were soon rallied. We charged, having to go by the flank, as we could only get over in one or two places, and entered the enemy's pits under a moderately heavy fire. We found an immense hole here, formed by the explosion, some 30 feet deep by 100 long and 40 wide. We were ordered to go to the right of the crater, and here I endeavored to re-form my regiments. The scene inside was horrible. Men were found half buried; some dead, some alive, some with their legs kicking in the air, some with the arms only exposed, and some with every bone in their bodies apparently broken. We held the enemy's line about three or four hours, capturing some 500 prisoners. When we had been there about four hours, the negro troops charged over, filling our pits and crowding us so that our men could not use their muskets. They made a charge on the enemy in our front, which was repulsed and followed by a countercharge, driving the negroes head over heels on to us, trampling down every one, and adding still more to the confusion. Several negroes were shot down close by me. I was taken prisoner and sent to the rear, where I found several of my men, together with Captain Fay. While on the way, I had to climb a breastwork exposed to our men's fire. I saw the rebs run up and shoot negro prisoners in front of me. One was shot four times.

We were taken to a place about half a mile from Petersburg, and kept there until evening. General Bartlett, Colonel Marshall and Captain Amory arrived about 4 P.M., in a squad that was captured later. We were moved still nearer the city, and camped in an open lot there. Charlie Amory had his boots stolen from under his head while asleep. He was using them as a pillow.

[These notes are written fifty years after the event, but it seems to me as if the whole matter was as vivid and clear as if it had happened yesterday. We started down late that evening and got into the covered way, which was a zigzag trench leading up to our rifle-pits. The rifle-pits had strong abattis trenches and wires and everything else, including chevaux-de-frise, to impede any of the enemy who were charging us. Orders had been given that the trenches were to be filled up with sandbags, and the abattis removed for a space of 200 yards, so that a regiment could march forward practically in line of battle. This was not done, for when we charged we had to go by the flank, not more than four men at a time, a space only about eight or ten feet having been filled up, and none of the abattis removed. This delayed the advance very much and undoubtedly had a great deal to do with losing us the battle this day. The mine was planned to be blown up at half-past four, but the fuse went out and they had to send men in to unpack the stuff which had been put around the fuse to prevent the force of the powder blowing out the tunnel, which took some time, so that it finally blew up at about half-past six or seven. The minute the mine exploded, a hundred and forty of our guns opened fire from the lines in the rear, shelling the Confederate lines all around on both sides of us. It was a magnificent sight and one never to be forgotten. I never shall forget my mortification while waiting for this mine to blow up. The troops were all standing in line, ready to charge, and bullets fired by sharpshooters and pickets kept zipping over us all the time and the men kept ducking. They were not to blame for this, as the orders were, when we were in the rifle-pits, invariably to duck if they saw a puff of smoke from the other side. This was absolutely necessary, as we lost men every day from their curiosity in peeking up to see what was going on. The minute a cap appeared it was the target for a dozen sharpshooters. Of course we were all nervous, standing there waiting for a charge which we were very uncomfortable about, owing to reasons which I have explained later on, and the men kept ducking as a bullet passed by. I said, "Steady, men, that bullet has gone by you by the time you hear it." Just then a bullet, which I am convinced was specially meant for me, went whizzing by me and I at once ducked. Every one laughed and I did not blame them, but a more mortified man than I was never lived.

When the mine did go up, it looked as if this immense cloud of timber, dirt and stones and everything was going to fall right down on us and we involuntarily shrank back. We at once got over this and started to make the charge. When we got to the pits, as I have said, there was no getting over except by a flank. Instead of going over about in line of battle, we moved by the flank through this narrow space, and before I could get over, the firing had become very hot and the dust was knocked up all around my feet all the time as I went over. The neglect to fix the works in our front also had another very bad effect. It broke the regiments all up. The men went over by the flank, scattered along as they could get through, and with almost no organization. As soon as we got into the crater, I did all I could to get my men together, and in some sort of shape for a fight. By that time it was almost impossible to do anything. We were as badly off then as we were in our own pits. There was no head. Our division commander was off on the other side and did not come over with us. General Bartlett was a cripple and had his wooden leg broken, and it was almost impossible to get anything done. I came near having my head knocked off by grape-shot two or three times. Finally the rebels charged on both our flanks. I was packed in there in the midst of the negroes. It was a perfect pandemonium. The negroes charged into the mine, and we were packed in there like sardines in a box. I literally could not raise my arms from my side. Finally, when the Confederates charged, those of the men nearest the rifle-pits next our line got over the line and got away. Luckily most of my men I had formed there, so that they were able to get away and protect our colors.

I got cut off and took refuge in a bomb-proof, as I could not run away, being surrounded on all sides. Pretty soon the rebels yelled, "Come out of there, you Yanks." I walked out, and the negro who had gone in there with me, and Captain Fay came out also. The negro was touching my side. The rebels were about eight feet from me. They yelled out, "Shoot the nigger, but don't kill the white man"; and the negro was promptly shot down by my side. They then grabbed my sword and my hat. "Come out of that hat, you Yank!" they yelled; and one of them cried, "What do you 'uns come down here and fight we 'uns for?" Then they told me to get over our embankment in their rear, which formed their second line, and I scrambled up, the bullets from our own men striking the dirt on all sides of me. I got over the embankment all right, and was walking to the rear, when I saw a negro soldier ahead of me. Three rebels rushed up to him in succession and shot him through the body. He dropped dead finally at the third shot. It was altogether the most miserable and meanest experience I ever had in my life. You could not fight, you could not give an order, you could not get anything done. Out of the nine regiments in my brigade I was the only regimental commander left alive. The others were all killed outright or mortally wounded. We were sent back about a mile to the rear and camped on a hill that night.

My diary for the year 1864, during the Wilderness Campaign, was carried in my boot-leg and so escaped seizure when I was captured at the mine.]

"MURDER THEM IN COLD BLOOD": VIRGINIA, JULY 1864

William Pegram to Virginia Johnson Pegram

In the assault following the mine explosion many men from the First Division became trapped when they took shelter inside the crater instead of moving around it. As the attack became increasingly disorganized, the black troops of the Fourth Division were sent forward. They succeeded in capturing a Confederate defense line beyond the crater before being driven back by a counterattack launched around 9 A.M. Fighting continued into the afternoon as the Confederates eventually regained the ground they had lost in the morning. Union losses totaled about 3,800 men killed, wounded, or missing, including 1,300 from the Fourth Division, while the Confederates lost about 1,500 men. Brigadier General James H. Ledlie, who had spent much of the battle drinking liquor in a bombproof shelter, was relieved of command of the First Division, while Burnside was sent home on leave for the remainder of the war. Lieutenant Colonel William Pegram, a veteran artillery officer in the Army of Northern Virginia, wrote to his sister about the battle and the killing of black prisoners by Confederate troops.

Petersburg, Aug: 1*st* 1864.

My dear Jenny

I believe that you owe me a letter, but of this I am not certain; and even if I was, it would not prevent my writing to you, as I wish to set you a good example as a correspondent.

I supose you all have gotten, before this, a correct account of the affair on Saturday. It was an exceedingly brilliant one for us.

The enemy avoided our mine, & ran theirs under Cousin Dick's Batty. They blew it up about daylight, & taking advantage of the temporary confusion & demoralization of our troops at that point, rushed a large body of whites & blacks into the breach. This turned out much worse for them in the end. The ever ready Mahone was carried down to retake the line with his fine troops, which he did, with comparatively small loss to himself, & great loss to the enemy. I never saw such a sight as I saw on that portion of the line—for a good distance in the trenches, the Yankees, white & black, principally the latter, were piled two or three or four deep. A few of our men were wounded by the negroes, which exasperated them very much. There were hardly less than six hundred dead—four hundred of whom were negroes. As soon as we got upon them, they threw down their arms to surrender, but were not allowed to do so. Every bomb proof I saw, had one or two dead negroes in it, who had skulked out the fight, & been found & killed by our men. This was perfectly right, as a matter of policy. I think over two hundred negroes got into our lines, by surrendering & running in, along with the whites, while the fighting was going on. I don't believe that much over half of these ever reached the rear. You could see them lying dead all along the route to the rear. While there was a temporary lull in the fighting, after we had recaptured the first portion of the line, & before we recaptured the second, I was down there, & saw a fight between a negro & one of our men in the trench. I suppose that the Confederate told the negro he was going to kill him, after he had surrendered. This made the negro desperate, & he grabbed up a musket, & they fought quite desperately for a little while with bayonets, until a bystander shot the negro dead.

It seems cruel to murder them in cold blood, but I think the men who did it had very good cause for doing so. Gen. Mahone told me of one man who had a bayonet run through his cheek, which instead of making him throw down his musket & run to the rear, as men usually do when they are wounded, exasperated him so much that he killed the negro, although in that condition. I have always said that I wished the enemy would bring some negroes against this army. I am convinced, since Saturday's fight, that it has a splendid effect on our men.

I did not fire any guns on Saturday, but got some in position, where they were exposed to some shelling & musketry. My hat was struck by a Minie ball just over the place I was wounded at Sharpsburg, which was quite a singular coincidence. I saw Cousin Dick Pegram after the fight. Fortunately, he had been relieved, & was not in the trenches when the mine was sprung.

On the whole, Saturday was, through the merciful kindness

of an all & ever-merciful God, a very brilliant day to us. The enemy's loss was, at the lowest figures, three to our one—but the moral effect to our arms was very great. For it shews that he cannot blow us out of our works; or, at least, that he cannot hold a breach after making it. Saturday's fight shewed also the superiority of veterans to new troops—i.e. of Lee's to Beauregard's troops. They had to take Mahone's Division from this portion of the line, to that point, near the centre, to retake & reestablish the line, because those troops failed, although, as I was told by one of Beauregard's staff, they had a very fine opportunity for doing so immediately after the explosion.

Uncle William will probably go over with his family about the middle of the week. In case they do, I will write to Mother by them. Uncle William is now laid up with the gout, & it is somewhat doubtful.

Uncle Duke told me that he saw all at home, but yourself—that you had gone out.

I suppose you are all grieving today at Brother's proposed departure tomorrow. I wish very much that I could be with him & you all, but this is impossible. God has been so merciful to us, that I trust implicitly that we will be reunited again on this earth. If not, then certainly in a far better home. Have Uncle Robert & Jimmy determined yet about going abroad? Tell Jimmy to remember that he owes me a letter, which I hope to receive soon.

Tell Mother & Sister, with much love, that they had better go with you to the country somewhere, as you will all be benefitted by the change. How are Aunt Lelia & Mattie? Tell Aunt Lelia that I was at Aunt Martha's yesterday, & all were well. Aunt Martha told me that Aunt Lelia had written over, with an invitation from Mother for Nannie to come over to Richmond. I was glad to hear this. She is a very sweet child, & will be a very pretty woman; but lacks grace.

Is there any news from Atlanta? I am looking daily for its fall. If Maj Bradford is still with you, give him my love—& Ask him why he does not run over. Excuse haste. Your devoted brother

W. J. Pegram

Col. McIntosh was slightly wounded on Saturday—not sufficiently however to go off duty.

"THIS ABOMINABLE DESPOTISM": NEW YORK, AUGUST 1864

C. Chauncey Burr: from The Old Guard

August 1864

A friend of Edgar Allan Poe, Charles Chauncey Burr had edited an anti-slavery reform magazine in the late 1840s, but later became a pro-Southern Democrat. In 1862 Burr founded *The Old Guard*, a monthly magazine published in New York City "devoted to the principles of 1776 and 1787." Burr used its pages to defend slavery and secession, relentlessly attack President Lincoln, and support Peace Democrats who advocated negotiating an armistice with the Confederacy. He began his August 1864 "Editor's Table" by criticizing Grant's campaign in Virginia.

EDITOR'S TABLE.

—We are informed by a member of Congress (not a Democrat) that for the first three weeks of Gen. Grant's campaign against Richmond, Mr. Lincoln and the Cabinet had no idea that all was not progressing well. But, at the end of that period, they came to comprehend the fact, which had all the time been perfectly understood by all who are not demented by passion, that every one of Grant's so-called flank movements was a most ruinous and mortifying defeat of the Abolition army. Now, all who are not willing to lie outright, confess that Gen. Grant has not obtained a single victory in battle since he crossed the Rapidan. But this failure in battle is really the least of Grant's misfortunes. He has destroyed the best part of his veteran army, and has fearfully demoralized what is remaining of it. An army as badly shattered as Gen. Grant's has been in these conflicts with Lee, must be necessarily, to a greater or lesser extent, demoralized. But the soldiers under Grant believe that their comrades in arms have been recklessly and foolishly slaughtered. A gallant officer, wounded in one of the last of Grant's disastrous defeats, in speaking of the useless and horrible waste of life, said in our hearing, "If this is generalship, I have misunderstood the meaning of the word." The feeling shown by this officer pervades Gen. Grant's army to-day. It pervades the country. Of all the unfortunate commanders who have fallen in the public estimation since we began this war, Gen. Grant is the most unfortunate and the most to be pitied. Curses will follow his head to his grave. Of the seven Generals who have commanded the Army of the Potomac, only two, McClellan and Mead, have escaped public contempt; but poor Grant, from the highest, has fallen to the lowest niche of fame. McDowell will be pitied, Pope laughed at, Burnside and Hooker jeered, but Grant will be despised. With better means than all the rest put together, he has wasted all in such a manner as to plunge the most sanguine hope into despair. Never more can he go into a town or village in the whole North where his name will not excite horror in the breasts of numberless widows and orphans. He is the death's head of a whole people. Thus lies prostrate the seventh and last idol of the Potomac. Where is the next victim?

—Are we not tired of hearing so much about "supporting the government," "resisting the government," "destroying the government," and a great deal of like nonsense? Who resists the government? Before we can answer that question, it is important to settle the matter as to who is the government. Mr. Lincoln is not the government. Congress is not the government. The Supreme Court is not the government. All these united do not form the governing power of our country. Under our system *The People* is the government; and the President, the Congress, and the Supreme Court, are only official agents to execute the will of the *sovereign* people, or to administer their laws under carefully guarded Constitutional limitations. All of Mr. Lincoln's usurpations are assaults upon the government. He is the guilty party, who is opposing and seeking to *destroy the government!* In England, the governing power, instead of being the *people*, is the *aristocracy*. Suppress the aristocracy in England, and there is no political organization left—the government of that country would be overthrown, just as Lincoln is seeking to overthrow the government of this country by suppressing the rights and powers of the *people*. Said Napoleon: "If religion had been taken away from Rome, nothing would have been left." The reason was that the government of Rome was the priesthood. If we take *sovereignty* from the people of America, there is nothing left of our government. It would be as effectually destroyed as the government of Great Britain would be by the overthrow of the *aristocracy*, or as the government of Austria would be by ignoring the crown. So if it be true, as these noisy imbeciles declare, that those who are opposing, and trying to destroy our government, ought to be hanged, Mr. Lincoln's neck is the one to which they must fit their halter. He is the *traitor* who is opposing the government established by the *people* of the United States.

—A foolish editor, the organ of Mr. Lincoln's abominations, says: "The greatest mistake we have made is that we did not crush out the last vital spot of Copperhead Democracy at the start." No, poor fool, the greatest mistake you made was to compel the people of the South to fight for their liberty, which also compelled all good people in the North to denounce your despotism. The greatest good of a people is their liberty. Liberty is to the collective body what health is to the individual. Without health no pleasure can be tasted by man. Without liberty no happiness can be enjoyed by society. The obligation, therefore, to defend liberty is greater than all others; and he is a traitor to a free country who will not gladly devote his life to preserve its freedom. Mr. Lincoln has forced upon Gen. Lee the honor, which we should gladly have withheld from him, of fighting the battle of defensive liberty on this continent, while Lincoln and his party carry on a war of offensive despotism. Lincoln's war is not upon the South alone; it is upon the North also. It is a war against a great principle—the principle of liberty and self-government. It is a war against Democracy—against the party that made the Constitution, and conducted the country through every step of its progressive glory, up to the hour when it fell by falling into the hands of a clan of despots and desperadoes. It is possible that we have only entered the field of blood—that the terrible struggle is but just commenced. If, as is more than intimated by the leading Republican papers, the despotism inaugurated over the North is to be continued, then, indeed, the sword is as yet but just started from its scabbard. If we have not a right to our thoughts, our sympathies, our hopes and faith, then shall the battle rage until we have vindicated our liberties and our manhood. We are coming to a point where the fight must be with those who are attempting to rob us of our freedom. The delusion of fighting for the skeleton of a Union, after we have ourselves crushed the soul out of it, is nearly over. For one, we do not hesitate to declare that we a thousand times prefer death in an honorable conflict to preserve our liberties, than a life of servitude and submission to the bloated despotism which hourly threatens us. If we are not free, let us make ourselves so! We know what we say. We hear, but we despise the threats! We may individually fall, but we know that we leave those behind us who are sworn to execute our last will and testament, which is that of death to the assassins. We are weary of hearing and reading the threats of Mr. Lincoln's satraps. If they stop where they are, all is well—all that is demanded is peace, liberty, and justice; but this we will have, or, failing, we will take our foes along with us, to be tried at that high court from which there is no appeal. Shall we longer walk the street to be threatened with "arrest," or "hanging," every time we exercise the freeman's sacred right of thinking and speaking the honest thought that is in us? Shall we longer owe our peace or safety to the whim or passion of slavering ignorance, or brutal prejudice and fanaticism? In God's name, *no!* For instance, if we believe that Jeff. Davis is a wise man, and that Abraham Lincoln is a fool, we shall take the liberty to say so, just whenever and wherever we please. If we have not the same right to respect the intellect of Jefferson Davis that another has to admire the ignorance and the trifling obscenity of Abraham Lincoln, let us set ourselves to work to regain that right. If we have not the right to prefer the Government and the Union that were formed by our fathers to this abominable despotism which Lincoln and his party are attempting to fasten upon us, let us strike for that right, and strike as our fathers did! This, then, is what we have to say to the besotted wretches who talk of "*crushing out Democrats.*"

Better stop where you are, and learn to carry a civil tongue, or you will be convinced that you are nearer the judgment day than your delusion has permitted you to imagine!

—The "Rebel Invasion" turns out to have been only a raid of the larger dimensions, to retaliate for our numerous plundering and burning expeditions in the South. Never before has Lee allowed his army to wantonly destroy private property; and, to his credit be it spoken, that he did not permit the late devastating raid as a means of civilized warfare, but placed it upon the ground of retaliation for barbarisms the Abolition soldiery have inflicted upon his people. For three years he has protested against the unsoldierly and uncivilized fashion of Lincoln's warfare. So has all Europe done the same; but nothing has been able to check the thieving and burning proclivities of the Abolitionists. In this instance Gen. Lee has resorted to the painful expedient of visiting upon the Abolitionists a taste of their own style of war; but he did not, like Lincoln, allow his soldiers to burn and plunder all private houses indiscriminately, for it seems that an individual, perfectly acquainted with the locality, accompanied his army to point out the dwellings of the Abolition leaders, who are considered the authors of the war. If the war continues as long as Lincoln lays out for it, there will, no doubt, be plenty more of opportunities for the invasion of the North; and if we would save ourselves from a repetition of this terrible raid, we have only to stop plundering and burning private property in the South. The Maryland victims may thank Lincoln and his generals for all they have suffered. The raiders, it is said, took away six millions of property, besides what they destroyed. And Gen. Lee could safely spare the large force to do this, even while Grant's army was making all the thunder in its power at the gates of Richmond. This looks very much like treating Grant with contempt. Gen. Lee himself says that he considers that Grant's campaign was virtually ended at the battle of Spottsylvania. And it is true that there has been no general engagement of all the forces of the two armies since that battle. From that spot Lee swung him round into McClellan's old shoes in the deadly swamp, where he, too, is practicing the sublime art of digging, so much despised by the Abolitionists. From a blazing *King of Diamonds*,

Grant has fallen down into a sombre *Jack of Spades.* All in six weeks! Where will he be at the end of the next six weeks?

—The Newburyport *Herald*, (Mass.,) an influential Republican paper, says:

> "We never did knowingly, and never intend to infringe upon the Constitution, and trample down the laws and usages, and compromises upon which the nation stands, for the emancipation of slaves in the southern States. Holding to State rights—the right of each community to legislate upon and control its local affairs, which idea is at the bottom of American freedom—the very keel of our ship of state, we do now and have always repudiated all interference with local matters in States to which we do not belong. It was never necessary or justifiable. We have no slavery in Massachusetts, and we would resist to the death its imposition upon us; but if we had slavery here, established by the free will of the people, as just, right and expedient for us, though we might differ from the majority, we would resent and resist any interference on the part of Maine or Vermont, or any other community or government under heaven, to forcibly or unlawfully abolish that slavery.
>
> "When even slavery is abolished by violence, at the expense of the Constitution and Union, it will not make the negroes free, but it certainly will destroy the liberties of thirty millions of whites. There can be no other result."

This is, indeed, light in the darkness. It is a voice of reason and truth from Massachusetts! Let not the world despair. What is to become of Mr. Lincoln and his war, when Republican newspapers begin to talk in that fashion?

—A lady writing in the Macon *Telegraph*, of Georgia, makes this noble appeal:

> "A word or two to my own sex. How many of you have passed through this terrible war unscathed? Oh, God, how many of us have lost our all, homes, comforts, and friends! Yet where is the southern woman who would be willing to yield to Yankee despotism? If such there be, let me say to you, death were preferable. I have felt their power; I know their meanness. They have deprived me of every worldly possession. Heart strings have been severed. Yet I would say to those loved ones still baring their breasts—Conquer or die. Many of us may go

> through life with crushed and bleeding hearts; but liberty has ever been purchased at a costly sacrifice."

We envy not the wretch whose heart kindles not with a glow of admiration at these thrilling words from the pen of a woman. We pity the soldier who would not rather himself die than wage barbarous war to deprive such a people of their liberty.

—A Republican contemporary complains of the language we apply to Mr. Lincoln. It is not our fault. No other language would suit the occasion. Shall we speak of a blackguard as a gentleman? Of an ignoramus as a scholar? Of an obscene joker and clown as a well-bred man of refinement and taste? All this would be out of character, and in bad taste. *Oderint dum metuant*, came properly out of the mouth of a tyrant; but Euripides would never have put that execrable sentence into the mouth of Minos or Æacus, any more than we would put decent language into the mouth of Abraham Lincoln. To say that we shall not speak of Lincoln *coarsely* is to forbid us to mention his name.

—We present the patrons of THE OLD GUARD this month with an excellent likeness of the Hon. Gideon J. Tucker, of whom it can be truly said, but rarely said, that he has never been known to be politically wrong in his life. Among all the divisions and subdivisions and factions that have so often demoralized the Democratic party of this city and State, Mr. Tucker is one of the few men who have faithfully followed one line of principle. He has often found himself in small minorities, but has, we believe, never yielded to the pressure of that *policy* which would immolate *principle* upon the selfish altars of personal ambition or mere party success. We know of no man who has a more consistent or a more honorable political record.

When Mr. Tucker was elected Surrogate two years ago, it was demanded that he, and the officers under him, should take the oath of allegiance which Elijah F. Purdy, a so-called Democrat, had caused to be adopted by the Board of Supervisors. This extra Lincoln oath, imposed upon all the county officials, Mr. Tucker refused to take, nor would he allow it to be administered to any officer in his department, notwithstanding the Supervisors had ordered that no county officers refusing to take the Lincoln oath should receive their salaries. This act of defiance of the unconstitutional orders of a corrupt and foolish Board of Supervisors, was characteristic of Mr. Tucker's whole political life. When this war was commenced by Mr. Lincoln, he was one of the very first to denounce it as alike unconstitutional, impolitic and unjust. He was one of the very few public men who had the integrity and courage to denounce the damning usurpation and despotism in the terms they deserved. He never shrunk from the extreme peace ground for a moment. As an unflinching advocate of peace, he went before the voters of this city a candidate for the very honorable and responsible office of Surrogate, and was elected by a far larger majority than any other official in that canvass. The "War Democrats" were pained at the "indiscretion" of Mr. Tucker in so boldly proclaiming his peace principles, and yet he was elected by nearly double the majority received by any "War Democrat" in that election.

Mr. Tucker is a man of ability, and is considered one of the best political writers in the United States. In 1857 he was Secretary of the State of New York, an office in which he acquitted himself so ably and faithfully as to command the respect of even his political opponents.

—It is often asked what the Democrats mean to do. They mean, as a first step, to fill the executive chair with patriotism, and to banish faction and despotism from the administration of the Federal Government. What next they will do depends upon what they can do to restore peace and prosperity to our country. They are in the condition of a skillful surgeon who is called to a man who fell into the hands of assassins. If his wounds are not mortal he will restore him. If Abolition has not killed the Union, the Democrats will restore it. But, at any rate, they will save liberty from going entirely down in the whirlpool of blood.

—The New York *World*, in trying to comfort the poor, says, there are five hundred dollars of bounty money between every poor man and extreme poverty. That is, he can go into the army and throw away his life for negroes. That is a remedy, indeed! The $500 bounty is really only about $200. It would serve his family, possibly, two months, when they would become paupers, and he, probably, dead, or mutilated, crippled and helpless for life. The *World* gives the poor strange advice—such advice as ought not to come from a human heart or brain. The poor man, of all others, should not go into the army; he owes it to his family not to expose his life to such deadly peril. It is advising him to throw away his life for two months' subsistence, and to leave his wife and children paupers.

"RETRIBUTION AT LAST": VIRGINIA, AUGUST 1864

Edgeworth Bird to Sallie Bird

A cotton planter from Hancock County, Edgeworth Bird served as a company commander in the 15th Georgia Infantry until he was wounded at Second Manassas. In the spring of 1863 he returned to duty with the Army of Northern Virginia as quartermaster of Benning's Brigade in Hood's (later Field's) Division. Bird wrote home to his wife shortly after a raid on Macon, Georgia, by 2,000 Union cavalry ended on July 31 with the capture of Major General George Stoneman and 700 of his men.

Near Richmond Va
Aug 4th 1864

Yesterday's mail brought me Sallie's letter and your "leaves from the blank book"—written whilst you all were in such excitement & dread of a raiding visit from our hated foes—My own best loved darling, whilst I read I was fully aware that you had escaped the danger, that their route was not immediately in our neighbourhood, and that elsewhere they had been routed and dispersed—but yet my innermost heart was moved, and my very soul troubled to learn of the deep anxiety and distress you had been subjected to—I sorrow for all our people, darling, that such times have come upon us—that the merciless din of war has reached our very homesteads that we thought so remote from its cruel ravages—but that my dear, dear children and more than loved wife should be so near the reach of these accursed vandals is a trial not to be quietly borne, and a ceaseless pain to my soul—Revolution in all its horrors is indeed upon us, and there is but one trust, one arm on which to lean—that *can save* us—and to its unfailing support I commit you & my dear ones at home—Your brave hopefullness & self reliance fill me with pleasure, and are a double assurance of your improving health—God grant that all our Ladies may be alike calm & resolute—a firm front always goes far to intimidate a cowardly foe—but dearest darling, if possible I never wish you to be in their power—At this distance I cannot advise what course of action would be wisest under circumstances transpiring at so great a distance—under sudden emergencies the advice of friends is best—Should they come on our little town suddenly be with some tried friends—I do not think they would harm a few resolute Ladies who stood by each other—Should they overrun our immediate country, I don't know where you'd go unless to your Cousin Mrs. Springs—Augusta will be a prominent point of interest to them—So much for the gloomy side—but, precious darling, I don't believe they will reach Hancock—They have already made their outer circle—Hood's army is strengthening every week—our people are arming & organizing—the defence of Macon has taught them these itinerant horse thieves can be checked and beaten—and Iverson has shown how they may be torn to pieces—Lieut Genl S. D. Lee now commands our Cavalry and he has acquired a *habit* of victory—So cheer up, dearest, all will yet go well—Hood is an able man, and his industry and perseverance are endless—tho much inferior to Johnston I have great faith in him—and he is so ably supported—then the Govt will give *him* every support—the enemies Cavalry were never dashing around the Army after this style while Johnston commanded—But I earnestly and truly believe we have seen the worst—S. D. Lee brought reinforcements to Hood—others *must* be coming—the *fable* that Forrest is to be turned loose on Sherman's rear, must one day become a fact—And, darling, there seems a general, accepted idea that the rout of that Army would ensure peace—the North seems almost ripe for it—it's a growing sentiment there—we are nowhere unsuccessful except in Georgia—Here Grant is at a deadlock—his last well planned and desperate move of blowing up a way into Petersburg is a total and to him disastrous failure—he will be foiled in every effort—his gunboats and position on the river is all that has saved him so far—Early's main force has not crossed the Potomac yet—but his Cavalry has taken a little turn—Pennsylvania has burning homesteads and desolate wives—The beautiful town of Chambersburg is a black, charred mass—there is retribution at last—We all recall the defiant & scornful faces of its ladies as we marched through a year ago—I then and still respect them for their spirit—but their scorn has been turned into wailing—Each month's continuance of this war will witness an increased ferocity—but the very violence of the contest will sooner bring peace—Precious old fellow—how troubled you must have been—you and daughter alone—and all those terrible rumours coming in on you thick & fast—you do right to supply any demand that may be made upon you under such circumstances—and do so promptly & cheerfully—bless your cheerful, brave heart—It strengthens me away off here to read your letters—May you never be subjected to such another trial—tho our loved state is welcome to the last horse we have in her sore need, I must confess I was glad our men took the cars, and Lucille and Blandy came back—cars ride better than horses and go faster—What do our black people think of the hubbub and near approach of the Yankees—when they come, if ever, such as wish to go with them are welcome—those of the men who do not should take to the woods—for they will seize every one of them and enroll them in their army to meet such fates as the poor creatures at Ft Pillow and the other day at Petersburg—They force every negro man they get hold of into their Army. The negro women I do not think they'll interfere with—It is not worth while for your Mother to persist in staying in Athens in case of a Raid there—she could do no good and seems to me you should all be together to mutually sustain each other—I wish Mrs Waddell would come to you—I feel quite sure the Col will bring her down before he returns—he'll be dogmean not to do so, that he may tell me how you are—I readily understand how dreadfully anxious you were about your dear Mother when you thought they were coming towards Athens—I feel with you through it all, my darling, fully and truly—would to God I could take the burden from you—and that I could be there to assist in defending our own homes—Bud would be a comfort to you now—but I suppose it best for him to be with his Grandma—Alone as she is she surely needs him—but I wish both were with you—I know now that the enemy did not go to Athens and that all there is safe—including that very necessary factory—Twould indeed be a blow to us to lose that—But Twould take a pretty strong raiding party to take Athens if they are fortifying it—Sallie's expresses undying confidence in Cook's batallion, and there is considerable local force—Ah, dearest, could we only be near each other in such times—but it has not been given us—Dr Jervey Robinson paid me a visit a day or so since—he is on duty with 1st S. Carolina—McGowan's Brigade—has been a prisoner since we saw him—he desired very particular remembrances to you—he is not very far off and I promised to ride by and see him—says he wrote you as soon as he heard I was wounded—did you get the letter—I couldn't remember to have heard you speak of it—He sought out my company to learn the extent of the wound—very kind wasn't it—Doc Pierce has a letter from home telling of the excitement there—he is quite well as is also Sammie, Pete & Dud A—Ben A—has been quite sick with dyspepsia—is now about well—Everything here quiet just now—Field's division, and several other Brigades are on North side of James—our troops here are having a comparative time of rest after their severe hardships in Trenches around Petersburg—Dearest, I'm afraid you've lost ground this time—do make it up by extra care—tell me how your contrabands all behaved—neither you or Sallie speak of having had a rain yet—I am so profoundly thankful the hateful Yankees have not fed upon our cribs or polluted our grounds with their presence—Darling present my congratulations to Mrs Lucy upon her contribution of strength to the Confederacy—I am very glad for her & Edgar—and I hope Mrs Terrell is in health again—Thank dear Sallie for her letter only I don't look for half sheets from a young & healthy damsel—Will her school be interrupted—Love to Father—How does he bear our adversity—Bob is well and sends love to all our people—Says he wishes he was at home about these times of trouble there—Remembrances to all our negroes—

My own darling—May God bless and care for you in these days of trial—look to him for strength & guidance—Let me hear often—A thousand loves and kisses to dear daughter and yourself from your own loving—

Edge.

Benjamin F. Wade and Henry Winter Davis: To the Supporters of the Government

August 5, 1864

Ohio senator Benjamin F. Wade and Maryland congressman Henry Winter Davis published their response to President Lincoln's pocket veto of their reconstruction bill in the *New-York Daily Tribune* on August 5. Their radical denunciation of the President's policies, drafted by Davis, was described by the Democratic *New York World* as "an impeachment" and by the Republican *New York Times* as "by far the most effective Copperhead campaign document thus far issued." Lincoln did not publicly respond to the Wade-Davis manifesto, telling Gideon Welles that he "could himself take no part in such a controversy as they seemed to wish to provoke." In a memoir published in 1895, the journalist Noah Brooks would recall Lincoln saying: "To be wounded in the house of one's friends is perhaps the most grievous affliction that can befall a man."

TO THE SUPPORTERS OF THE GOVERNMENT.

We have read without surprise, but not without indignation, the Proclamation of the President of the 8th of July, 1864.

The supporters of the Administration are responsible to the country for its conduct: and it is their right and duty to check the encroachments of the Executive on the authority of Congress, and to require it to confine itself to its proper sphere.

It is impossible to pass in silence this Proclamation without neglecting that duty; and, having taken as much responsibility as any others in supporting the Administration, we are not disposed to fail in the other duty of asserting the rights of Congress.

The President did not sign the bill "to guarantee to certain States whose Governments have been usurped, a Republican form of Government"—passed by the supporters of his Administration in both Houses of Congress after mature deliberation.

The bill did not therefore become *a law*: and it is therefore *nothing*.

The Proclamation is neither an approval nor a veto of the bill; it is therefore a document unknown to the laws and Constitution of the United States.

So far as it contains an apology for not signing the bill, it is a political manifesto against the friends of the Government.

So far as it proposes to execute the bill which is not a law, it is a grave Executive usurpation.

It is fitting that the facts necessary to enable the friends of the Administration to appreciate the apology and the usurpation be spread before them.

The Proclamation says:

> "And whereas the said bill was presented to the President of the United States for his approval less than one hour before the *sine die* adjournment of said session, and was not signed by him—"

If that be accurate, still this bill was presented with other bills which were signed.

Within that hour, the time for the sine die adjournment was three times postponed by the votes of both Houses; and the least intimation of a desire for more time by the President to consider this bill would have secured a further postponement.

Yet the Committee sent to ascertain if the President had any further communication for the House of Representatives reported that he had none; and the friends of the bill, who had anxiously waited on him to ascertain its fate, had already been informed that the President had resolved not to sign it.

The time of presentation, therefore, had nothing to do with his failure to approve it.

The bill had been discussed and considered for more than a month in the House of Representatives, which it passed on the 4th of May; it was reported to the Senate on the 27th of May without material amendment, and passed the Senate absolutely as it came from the House on the 2d of July.

Ignorance of its contents is out of the question.

Indeed, at his request, a draft of a bill substantially the same in all material points, and identical in the points objected to by the Proclamation, had been laid before him for his consideration in the Winter of 1862–1863.

There is, therefore, no reason to suppose the provisions of the bill took the President by surprise.

On the contrary, we have reason to believe them to have been so well known that this method of preventing the bill from becoming a law without the constitutional responsibility of a veto, had been resolved on long before the bill passed the Senate.

We are informed by a gentleman entitled to entire confidence, that before the 22d of June in New-Orleans it was stated by a member of Gen. Banks's staff, in the presence of other gentlemen in official position, that Senator Doolittle had written a letter to the department that the House Reconstruction bill would be staved off in the Senate to a period too late in the session to require the President to veto it in order to defeat it, and that Mr. Lincoln would retain the bill, if necessary, and thereby defeat it.

The experience of Senator Wade, in his various efforts to get the bill considered in the Senate, was quite in accordance with that plan; and the fate of the bill was accurately predicted by letters received from New-Orleans before it had passed the Senate.

Had the Proclamation stopped there, it would have been only one other defeat of the will of the people by an Executive perversion of the Constitution.

But it goes further. The President says:

> "And whereas the said bill contains, among other things, a plan for restoring the States in rebellion to their proper practical relation in the Union, which plan expresses the sense of Congress upon that subject, and which plan it is now thought fit to lay before the people for their consideration—"

By what authority of the Constitution? In what forms? The result to be declared by whom? With what effect when ascertained?

Is it to be a law by the approval of the people without the approval of Congress at the will of the President?

Will the President, on his opinion of the popular approval, execute it as law?

Or is this merely a device to avoid the serious responsibility of defeating a law on which so many loyal hearts reposed for security?

But the reasons now assigned for not approving the bill are full of ominous significance.

The President proceeds:

> "Now, therefore, I, ABRAHAM LINCOLN, President of the United States, do proclaim, declare and make known, that, while I am (as I was in December last, when by proclamation I propounded a plan for restoration) unprepared, by a formal approval of this bill, to be inflexibly committed to any single plan of restoration—"

That is to say, the President is resolved that the people shall not *by law* take any securities from the Rebel States against a renewal of the Rebellion, before restoring their power to govern us.

His wisdom and prudence are to be our sufficient guarantees!

He further says:

> "And, while I am also unprepared to declare that the Free-State Constitutions and Governments already adopted and installed in Arkansas and Louisiana shall be set aside and held for naught, thereby repelling and discouraging the loyal citizens who have set up the same as to further effort—"

That is to say, the President persists in recognizing those shadows of Governments in Arkansas and Louisiana, which Congress formally declared should not be recognized—whose Representatives and Senators were repelled by formal votes of both Houses of Congress—which it was declared formally should have no electoral vote for President and Vice-President.

They are mere creatures of his will. They cannot live a day without his support. They are mere oligarchies, imposed on the people by military orders under the forms of election, at which generals, provost-marshals, soldiers and camp-followers were the chief actors, assisted by a handful of resident citizens, and urged on to premature action by private letters from the President.

In neither Louisiana nor Arkansas, before Banks's defeat, did the United States control half the territory or half the population. In Louisiana, Gen. Banks's proclamation candidly declared: "*The fundamental law of the State is martial law.*"

On that foundation of freedom, he erected what the President calls "the free Constitution and Government of Louisiana."

But of this State, whose fundamental law was martial law, only sixteen parishes out of forty-eight parishes were held by the United States; and in five of the sixteen we held only our camps.

The eleven parishes we substantially held had 233,185 inhabitants; the residue of the State not held by us, 575,617.

At the farce called an election, the officers of Gen. Banks returned that 11,346 ballots were cast; but whether any or by whom the people of the United States have no legal assurance; but it is probable that 4,000 were cast by soldiers or employees of the United States military or municipal, but none according to any law, State or National, and 7,000 ballots represent the State of Louisiana.

Such is the free Constitution and Government of Louisiana; and like it is that of Arkansas. Nothing but the failure of a military expedition deprived us of a like one in the swamps of Florida; and before the Presidential election, like ones may be organized in every Rebel State where the United States have a camp.

The President, by preventing this bill from becoming a law, holds the electoral votes of the Rebel States at the dictation of his personal ambition.

If these votes turn the balance in his favor, is it to be supposed that his competitor, defeated by such means, will acquiesce?

If the Rebel majority assert their supremacy in those States, and send votes which elect an enemy of the Government, will we not repel his claims?

And is not that civil war for the Presidency, inaugurated by the votes of Rebel States?

Seriously impressed with these dangers, Congress, "*the proper constitutional authority*," formally declared that there are no State Governments in the Rebel States, and provided for their erection at a proper time; and both the Senate and the House of Representatives rejected the Senators and Representatives chosen under the authority of what the President calls the free Constitution and Government of Arkansas.

The President's Proclamation "*holds for naught*" this judgment, and discards the authority of the Supreme Court, and strides headlong toward the anarchy his Proclamation of the 8th of December inaugurated.

If electors for President be allowed to be chosen in either of those States, a sinister light will be cast on the motives which induced the President to "hold for naught" the will of Congress rather than his Government in Louisiana and Arkansas.

That judgment of Congress which the President defies was the exercise of an authority exclusively vested in Congress by the Constitution to determine what is the established Government in a State, and in its own nature and by the highest judicial authority binding on all other departments of the Government.

The Supreme Court has formally declared that under the 4th section of the IVth article of the Constitution, requiring the United States to guarantee to every State a republican form of government, "*it rests with Congress to decide what Government is the established one in a State;*" and "*when Senators and Representatives of a State are admitted into* the councils of the Union, the *authority* of the *Government under which they are appointed*, as well as its republican character, *is recognized by the proper constitutional authority, and its decision is binding on every other department of the Government*, and could not be questioned in a judicial tribunal. It is true that the contest in this case did not last long enough to bring the matter to this issue; and, as no Senators or Representatives were elected under the authority of the Government of which Mr. Dorr was the head, Congress was not called upon to decide the controversy. Yet the right to decide is placed *there*."

Even the President's proclamation of the 8th of December, formally declares that "Whether members sent to Congress from any State shall be admitted to seats, constitutionally rests exclusively with the respective Houses, and not to any extent with the Executive."

And that is not the less true because wholly inconsistent with the President's assumption in that proclamation of a right to institute and recognize State Governments in the Rebel States, nor because the President is unable to perceive that his recognition is a nullity if it be not conclusive on Congress.

Under the Constitution, the right to Senators and Representatives is inseparable from a State Government.

If there be a State Government, the right is absolute.

If there be no State Government, there can be no Senators or Representatives chosen.

The two Houses of Congress are expressly declared to be the sole judges of their own members.

When, therefore, Senators and Representatives are admitted, the State Government, under whose authority they were chosen, is conclusively established; when they are rejected, its existence is as conclusively rejected and denied; and to this judgment the President is bound to submit.

The President proceeds to express his unwillingness "to declare a constitutional competency in Congress to abolish Slavery in States" as another reason for not signing the bill.

But the bill nowhere proposes to abolish Slavery in States.

The bill did provide that all *slaves* in the Rebel States should be *manumitted.*

But as the President had already signed three bills manumitting several classes of slaves in States, it is not conceived possible that he entertained any scruples touching *that* provision of the bill respecting which he is silent.

He had already himself assumed a right by proclamation to free much the larger number of slaves in the Rebel States, under the authority given him by Congress to use military power to suppress the Rebellion; and it is quite inconceivable that the President should think Congress could vest in him a discretion it could not exercise itself.

It is the more unintelligible from the fact that, except in respect to a small part of Virginia and Louisiana, the bill covered only what the Proclamation covered—added a Congressional title and judicial remedies by law to the disputed title under the Proclamation, and perfected the work the President professed to be so anxious to accomplish.

Slavery as an institution can be abolished only by a change of the Constitution of the United States or of the law of the State; and this is the principle of the bill.

It required the new Constitution of the State to provide for that prohibition; and the President, in the face of his own proclamation, does not venture to object to insisting on *that* condition. Nor will the country tolerate its abandonment—yet he defeated the only provision imposing it!!

But when he describes himself, in spite of this great blow at emancipation, as "sincerely hoping and expecting that a constitutional amendment abolishing Slavery throughout the nation may be adopted," we curiously inquire on what his expectation rests, after the vote of the House of Representatives at the recent session, and in the face of the political complexion of more than enough of the States to prevent the possibility of its adoption within any reasonable time; and why he did not indulge his sincere hopes with so large an installment of the blessing as his approval of the bill would have secured.

After this assignment of his reasons for preventing the bill from becoming a law, the President proceeds to declare his purpose *to execute it as a law by his plenary dictatorial power.*

He says:

> "Nevertheless, I am fully satisfied with the system for restoration contained in the bill as one very proper plan for the loyal people of any State choosing to adopt it; and that I am, and at all times shall be, prepared to give the Executive aid and assistance to any such people so soon as the military resistance to the United States shall have been suppressed in any such State, and the people thereof shall have sufficiently returned to their obedience to the Constitution and the laws of the United States; in which cases Military Governors will be appointed, with directions to proceed according to the bill."

A more studied outrage on the legislative authority of the people has never been perpetrated.

Congress passed a bill; the President refused to approve it, and then by proclamation puts as much of it in force as he sees fit, and proposes to execute those parts by officers unknown to the laws of the United States and not subject to the confirmation of the Senate!

The bill directed the appointment of Provisional Governors by and with the advice and consent of the Senate.

The President, after defeating the law, proposes to appoint without law, and without the advice and consent of the Senate, *Military* Governors for the Rebel States!

He has already exercised this dictatorial usurpation in Louisiana, and he defeated the bill to prevent its limitation.

Henceforth we must regard the following precedent as the Presidential law of the Rebel States:

"EXECUTIVE MANSION,
"WASHINGTON, March 15, 1864.

"*His Excellency* MICHAEL HAHN, *Governor of Louisiana*,

"Until further orders, you are hereby invested with the powers exercised hitherto by the Military Governor of Louisiana.

Yours, "ABRAHAM LINCOLN."

This Michael Hahn is no officer of the United States; the President, without law, without the advice and consent of the Senate, by a private note not even countersigned by the Secretary of State, makes him Dictator of Louisiana!

The bill provided for the civil administration of the laws of the State—till it should be in a fit temper to govern itself—repealing all laws recognizing Slavery, and making all men equal before the law.

These beneficent provisions the President has annulled. People will die, and marry and transfer property, and buy and sell: and to these acts of civil life courts and officers of the law are necessary. Congress legislated for these necessary things, and the President deprives them of the protection of the law!

The President's purpose to instruct his Military Governors "to proceed according to the bill"—a makeshift to calm the disappointment its defeat has occasioned—is not merely a grave usurpation but a transparent delusion.

He cannot "proceed according to the bill" after preventing it from becoming a law.

Whatever is done will be at his will and pleasure, by persons responsible to no law, and more interested to secure the interests and execute the will of the President than of the people; and the will of Congress is to be "*held for naught*," "unless the loyal people of the Rebel States choose to adopt it."

If they should graciously prefer the stringent bill to the easy proclamation, still the registration will be made under no legal sanction; it will give no assurance that a majority of the people of the States have taken the oath; if administered, it will be without legal authority, and void; no indictment will lie for false swearing at the election, or for admitting bad or rejecting good votes; it will be the farce of Louisiana and Arkansas acted over again, under the forms of this bill, but not by authority of *law*.

But when we come to the guarantees of future peace which Congress meant to exact, the forms, as well as the substance of the bill, must yield to the President's will that *none* should be *imposed*.

It was the solemn resolve of Congress to protect the loyal men of the nation against three great dangers, (1) the return to power of the guilty leaders of the Rebellion, (2) the continuance of Slavery, and (3) the burden of the Rebel debt.

Congress *required* assent to those provisions by the Convention of the State; and if refused, it was to be dissolved.

The President "holds for naught" that resolve of Congress, because he is unwilling "to be inflexibly committed to any one plan of restoration," and the people of the United States are not to be allowed to protect themselves unless their enemies agree to it.

The order to proceed according to the bill is therefore merely at the will of the Rebel States; and they have the option to reject it, accept the proclamation of the 8th of December, and demand the President's recognition!

Mark the contrast! The bill requires a majority, the proclamation is satisfied with one-tenth; the bill requires one oath, the proclamation another; the bill ascertains voters by registering; the proclamation by guess; the bill exacts adherence to existing territorial limits, the proclamation admits of others; the bill governs the Rebel States *by law*, equalizing all before it, the proclamation commits them to the lawless discretion of military Governors and Provost-Marshals; the bill forbids electors for President, the proclamation and defeat of the bill threaten us with civil war for the admission or exclusion of such votes; the bill exacted exclusion of dangerous enemies from power and the relief of the nation from the Rebel debt, and the prohibition of Slavery forever, so that the suppression of the Rebellion will double our resources to bear or pay the national debt, free the masses from the old domination of the Rebel leaders, and eradicate the cause of the war; the proclamation secures neither of these guaranties.

It is silent respecting the Rebel debt and the political exclusion of Rebel leaders; leaving *Slavery* exactly where it was by law at the outbreak of the rebellion, and adds no guaranty even of the freedom of the slaves he undertook to manumit.

It is summed up in an illegal oath, without a sanction, and therefore void.

The oath is to support all proclamations of the President, during the Rebellion having reference to slaves.

Any Government is to be accepted at the hands of one-tenth of the people not contravening *that oath.*

Now that oath neither secures the abolition of Slavery, nor adds any security to the freedom of the slaves the President declared free.

It does not secure the abolition of Slavery; for the proclamation of freedom merely professed to free certain slaves while it recognized the institution.

Every Constitution of the Rebel States at the outbreak of the Rebellion may be adopted without the change of a letter; for none of them contravene that Proclamation; none of them establish Slavery.

It adds no security to the freedom of the slaves.

For their title is the Proclamation of Freedom.

If it be unconstitutional, an oath to support it is void. Whether constitutional or not, the oath is without authority of law, and therefore void.

If it be valid and observed, it exacts no enactment by the State, either in law or Constitution, to add a State guaranty to the proclamation title; and the right of a slave to freedom is an open question before the State courts on the relative authority of the State law and the Proclamation.

If the oath binds the one-tenth who take it, it is not exacted of the other nine-tenths who succeed to the control of the State Government; so that it is annulled instantly by the act of recognition.

What the State courts would say of the Proclamation, who can doubt?

But the master would not go into court—he would seize his slave.

What the Supreme Court would say, who can tell?

When and how is the question to get there?

No habeas corpus lies for him in a United States Court; and

the President defeated with this bill its extension of that writ to this case.

Such are the fruits of this rash and fatal act of the President—a blow at the friends of his Administration, at the rights of humanity, and at the principles of republican government.

The President has greatly presumed on the forbearance which the supporters of his Administration have so long practiced, in view of the arduous conflict in which we are engaged, and the reckless ferocity of our political opponents.

But he must understand that our support is of a cause and not of a man; that the authority of Congress is paramount and must be respected; that the whole body of the Union men of Congress will not submit to be impeached by him of rash and unconstitutional legislation; and if he wishes our support, he must confine himself to his executive duties—to obey and execute, not make the laws—to suppress by arms armed Rebellion, and leave political reorganization to Congress.

If the supporters of the Government fail to insist on this, they become responsible for the usurpations which they fail to rebuke, and are justly liable to the indignation of the people whose rights and security, committed to their keeping, they sacrifice.

Let them consider the remedy for these usurpations, and, having found it, fearlessly execute it.

B. F. WADE, Chairman Senate Committee.
H. WINTER DAVIS, Chairman Committee
House of Representatives on the Rebellious States.

Robert Garlick Hill Kean: Diary, August 7, 1864

A lawyer from Lynchburg, Virginia, Robert Garlick Hill Kean had served since April 1862 as head of the Bureau of War, an administrative division of the Confederate War Department. Kean wrote in his diary about the war's increasing harshness.

Aug. 7. From the 16th to the 21st ult. I was sick and on the 22nd left Richmond for a fortnight in Albemarle to recruit, returned on the 4th inst. Mr. G. A. Trenholm was appointed secretary of the treasury, when he came to Richmond as indicated in last entry, which was the end of that imbroglio. Bragg has been absent nearly a month in the South; hence no further trouble with him. Hood has held his own at Atlanta pretty well and has delivered some good blows.

On the 5th inst. the Yankee fleet passed the forts at the entrance of Mobile Bay, 14 ships and 3 ironclads getting in Fort Morgan; sank one monitor. Our fleet was then destroyed, the *Tennessee* captured, the *Selma* sunk, the *Gaines* run aground. The *Morgan* alone escaped.

Yesterday a week ago Grant sprang his great mine at Petersburg and Meade his grand assault, which was prognosticated with much flourishing of trumpets by the Yankee press. The disastrous defeat he met with in the assault has manifestly struck a chill to the Northern heart, as is indicated by their newspapers. The *World* declaims his whole campaign a disastrous failure and declares the opinion that Richmond and Petersburg cannot be taken. The Democratic and anti-administration papers suggest that their army had better be moved to a position in which it will protect 'loyal' territory from invasion. The *Times* (N.Y.) argues at great length that the failure at Petersburg should not produce such excessive discouragement, that Sebastopol was ineffectually assaulted several times, etc. Recent Northern papers intimate that there is to be a change in the command of the army below Petersburg and indicated Hooker as Meade's successor. Meade being as near a gentleman as a Yankee comes, he's probably become distasteful to the Washington concern.

The war is taking on features of exaggerated harshness. Hunter when he re-entered the Valley caused a number of private residences of the finest character to be burned, e. g. Mr. Andrew Hunter's, McCaig's, etc. Early has burned Chambersburg to enforce a refractory town into paying a requisition. The Yankees have had the unutterable meanness to make an expedition up the Rappahannock for the purpose of burning the house of Mrs. May Seddon, the widow of Major John Seddon, the brother of the Secretary. Her condition was perfectly well known to them, and the fact of her connection with the Secretary of War was avowed as the reason!! Somebody over the border will smoke for this outrage. I am satisfied that this thing which they have been doing now for three years in Florida (Jacksonville), Mississippi (Jackson), South Carolina on the Combahee, and all through Virginia on the northern border, can be stopped by deliberate and stern retaliation. They are in more of our territory but their people live so much more in towns that one expedition can burn more houses than they can destroy in a campaign. That they are amenable to the influences of retaliation is plain for the well known fact that when they have to deal with a man who they know will be as good as his word they are awed.

The whole Yankee army harks to Jack Mosby. He caught a fellow who had burned a home near or in New Market, Shenandoah County, and shot him. The officer in command swore he would burn the village; Mosby sent him word if he did he would execute prisoners of whom he held a number. A party was sent to burn the village but receiving the message in time did nothing, and New Market is yet safe.

Captain Brooke of Fauquier, delegate in the Virginia Legislature, told me (he has a son in Mosby's command) that one of Mosby's men, a captive, was murdered in Upperville by a Yankee. Mosby sent a citizen to investigate the facts, and sent the commanding officer word that unless the case was satisfactorily explained or the murderer punished he would take ample vengeance. The message produced great consternation, the case was inquired into, no explanation could be made—it was a brutal murder—and he promised that the offender should be punished. He failed to keep faith, which Mosby discovered, and he executed *ten*. Of the substantial truth of this I have no doubt.

It is a curious fact that precisely coincident with his tendency to aggravation in the character of the war, a great development of a disposition towards peace is making in public sentiment in the North. With their conscription in September and their election in November, this sentiment may be fairly expected to increase to a head that will be influential, though it will probably not suffice to defeat Lincoln. It may get control of the next U. S. Congress. Gold 252.

Mathella Page Harrison: Diary, August 17, 1864

The Union defeat at Kernstown, Virginia, on July 24 and the burning of Chambersburg, Pennsylvania, by Jubal Early's cavalry on July 30 led Lincoln and Grant to reorganize the forces opposing Early in the Shenandoah Valley. Major General Philip H. Sheridan, the commander of the Army of the Potomac's Cavalry Corps, took command of the new Army of the Shenandoah on August 7 and began advancing south from Harpers Ferry three days later. When his cavalry encountered infantry reinforcements from Lee's army near Front Royal on August 16, Sheridan decided to withdraw to the north and guard the Potomac River crossings. From her farm in Millwood, Mathella Page Harrison watched as Union soldiers carried out Grant's orders to confiscate or destroy the Valley's provisions, forage, and livestock.

Wednesday, August 17th—Night has closed at last on this day of horrors. Years almost seem to have rolled since I opened my eyes this morning. The first sound that greeted my ears was the rumbling of Yankee waggons passing onward with their troops to swell the hosts of those who passed last week and who were assembled in and around Winchester waiting for Early's return. At nine o'clock Yankee pickets were stationed in every hill. Fires of barns, stockyards etc. soon burst forth and by eleven, from a high elevation, fifty could be seen blazing forth. The whole country was enveloped with smoke and flame. The sky was lurid and but for the green trees one might have decided the shades of Hades had descended suddenly. The shouts, ribald jokes, awful oaths, demoniacal laughter of the fiends added to the horrors of the day. They demanded feed when they had just applied the torch to the provisions of the year, and indeed years, for now the seed which would have been sown has been destroyed. In almost every instance every head of stock was driven off. Those young animals that refused to go were shot down. Near a farm where eight fires were blazing, Custer and his staff sat exulting over the ruin they had wrought. Large families of children were left without one cow. In many of the barns were stowed in and around carriages, all kinds of farming implements, waggons, plows etc., and in no instance did they allow anything to be saved. The loss is inestimable and unpardonable in these times, situated as we are, communications with our lines so difficult, and no trade with the enemy even if we wished it. Hay, oats and straw were burnt with the wheat. I cannot imagine what the poor cattle are to live on this winter. Owing to the great drought the field grass burnt like tinder. About half of the county was in flames. Some of the dwellings were sacked, clothing, provisions, male and female taken indiscriminately. Remember Chambersburg was their watch word. Thoroughly did they enjoy their days work. When one fire was at its hottest, the dwelling in peril of being added to the number, one turned to the other, "Haven't we had a nice day?" Retaliation may be glorious for the interior of Dixie but to those in this poor debatable land its fires are almost beyond endurance.

WASHINGTON, D.C., AUGUST 1864

Abraham Lincoln: Memorandum on Probable Failure of Reelection

Lincoln became the first president since 1840 to be nominated for a second term when he received the nearly unanimous vote of the National Union convention, a coalition of Republicans and War Democrats on June 8. By August the President feared that he would lose the election to George B. McClellan, his likely Democratic opponent. His pessimism was shared by many Republican leaders. On August 22 Thurlow Weed wrote to Secretary of State William H. Seward, his close political ally, that Lincoln's reelection was an impossibility because the "People are wild for Peace." The same day Henry J. Raymond, the editor of *The New York Times* and chairman of the National Union executive committee, wrote to Lincoln that he would probably lose Illinois, Pennsylvania, and New York. Raymond attributed "this great reaction in public sentiment" to "the want of military successes, and the impression in some minds, the fear and suspicion in others, that we are not to have peace *in any event* under this Administration until Slavery is abandoned. In some way or other the suspicion is widely diffused that we *can* have peace with Union if we would." Lincoln wrote his memorandum on a sheet of paper, folded it, and then had the members of his cabinet sign the paper without reading its contents.

Executive Mansion
Washington, Aug. 23, 1864.

This morning, as for some days past, it seems exceedingly probable that this Administration will not be re-elected. Then it will be my duty to so co-operate with the President elect, as to save the Union between the election and the inauguration; as he will have secured his election on such ground that he can not possibly save it afterwards. A. LINCOLN

EXCHANGING PRISONERS: VIRGINIA, AUGUST 1864

Benjamin F. Butler to Robert Ould

By the summer of 1864 both the Union and the Confederacy held tens of thousands of prisoners in overcrowded camps as a result of the breakdown of the exchange cartel during the previous year. Colonel Robert Ould, the Confederate commissioner of exchange, signaled on August 10 his government's willingness to resume general exchanges using a formula previously proposed by the Union authorities. Grant advised against resuming exchanges in a letter to Major General Benjamin F. Butler, the Union exchange commissioner. "It is hard on our men held in Southern prisons not to exchange them but it is humanity to those left in the ranks to fight our battles," he wrote on August 18. "Every man released, on parole or otherwise, becomes an active soldier against us at once either directly or indirectly. If we commence a system of exchanges which liberates all prisoners taken we will have to fight on until the whole South is exterminated." Butler responded to Ould by restating the Union position that black and white prisoners be treated equally in exchanges. Ould did not respond to Butler's letter, which was published in the northern press on September 6.

HDQRS. DEPT. OF VIRGINIA AND NORTH CAROLINA,
In the Field, August 27, 1864.

HON. ROBERT OULD, *Commissioner for Exchange:*

SIR: Your note to Major Mulford, assistant agent of exchange, under date of 10th of August, has been referred to me.

You therein state that Major Mulford has several times proposed to exchange prisoners respectively held by the two belligerents, officer for officer, and man for man, and that "the offer has also been made by other officials having charge of matters connected with the exchange of prisoners," and that "this proposal has been heretofore declined by the Confederate authorities;" that you now consent to the above proposition, and agree to deliver to you (Major Mulford) the prisoners held in captivity by the Confederate authorities, provided you agree to deliver an equal number of officers and men. As equal numbers are delivered from time to time they will be declared exchanged. This proposal is made with the understanding that the officers and men on both sides who have been longest in captivity will be first delivered, where it is practicable.

From a slight ambiguity in your phraseology, but more, perhaps, from the antecedent action of your authorities, and because of your acceptance of it, I am in doubt whether you have stated the proposition with entire accuracy.

It is true, a proposition was made both by Major Mulford and myself, as agent of exchange, to exchange all prisoners of war taken by either belligerent party, man for man, officer for officer, of equal rank, or their equivalents. It was made by me as early as the first of the winter of 1863–64, and has not been accepted. In May last I forwarded to you a note desiring to know whether the Confederate authorities intended to treat colored soldiers of the U. S. Army as prisoners of war. To that inquiry no answer has yet been made. To avoid all possible misapprehension or mistake hereafter as to your offer now, will you say now whether you mean by "prisoners held in captivity" colored men, duly enrolled and mustered into the service of the United States, who have been captured by the Confederate forces, and if your authorities are willing to exchange all soldiers so mustered into the U. S. Army, whether colored or otherwise, and the officers commanding them, man for man, officer for officer?

At an interview which was held between yourself and the agent of exchange on the part of the United States, at Fort Monroe, in March last, you will do me the favor to remember the principal discussion turned upon this very point, you, on behalf of the Confederate Government, claiming the right to hold all negroes who had heretofore been slaves and not emancipated by their masters, enrolled and mustered into the service of the United States, when captured by your forces, not as prisoners of war, but, upon capture, to be turned over to their supposed masters or claimants, whoever they might be, to be held by them as slaves.

By the advertisements in your newspapers, calling upon masters to come forward and claim these men so captured, I suppose that your authorities still adhere to that claim; that is to say, that whenever a colored soldier of the United States is captured by you, upon whom any claim can be made by any person residing within the States now in insurrection, such soldier is not to be treated as a prisoner of war, but is to be turned over to his supposed owner or claimant, and put at such labor or service as that owner or claimant may choose; and the officers in command of such soldiers, in the language of a supposed act of the Confederate States, are to be turned over to the Governors of States, upon requisitions, for the purpose of being punished by the laws of such States for acts done in war in the armies of the United States.

You must be aware that there is still a proclamation by Jefferson Davis, claiming to be Chief Executive of the Confederate States, declaring in substance that all officers of colored troops mustered into the service of the United States were not to be treated as prisoners of war, but were to be turned over for punishment to the Governors of States.

I am reciting these public acts from memory, and will be pardoned for not giving the exact words, although I believe I do not vary the substance and effect. These declarations on the part of those whom you represent yet remain unrepealed, unannulled, unrevoked, and must therefore be still supposed to be authoritative. By your acceptance of our proposition, is the Government of the United States to understand that these several claims, enactments, and proclaimed declarations are to be given up, set aside, revoked, and held for naught by the Confederate authorities, and that you are ready and willing to exchange, man for man, those colored soldiers of the United States, duly mustered and enrolled as such, who have heretofore been claimed as slaves by the Confederate States, as well as white soldiers?

If this be so, and you are so willing to exchange these colored men claimed as slaves, and you will so officially inform the Government of the United States, then, as I am instructed, a principal difficulty in effecting exchanges will be removed.

As I informed you personally, in my judgment, it is neither consistent with the policy, dignity, nor honor of the United States, upon any consideration, to allow those who, by our laws solemnly enacted, are made soldiers of the Union, and who have been duly enlisted, enrolled, and mustered as such soldiers—who have borne arms in behalf of this country, and who have been captured while fighting in vindication of the rights of that country—not to be treated as prisoners of war, and remain unexchanged and in the service of those who claim them as masters; and I cannot believe that the Government of the United States will ever be found to consent to so gross a wrong.

Pardon me if I misunderstood you in supposing that your acceptance of our proposition does not in good faith mean to include all the soldiers of the Union, and that you still intend, if your acceptance is agreed to, to hold the colored soldiers of the Union unexchanged, and at labor or service, because I am informed that very lately, almost cotemporaneously with this offer on your part to exchange prisoners, and which seems to include all prisoners of war, the Confederate authorities have made a declaration that the negroes heretofore held to service by owners in the States of Delaware, Maryland, and Missouri, are to be treated as prisoners of war when captured in arms in the service of the United States. Such declaration, that a part of the colored soldiers of the United States were to be prisoners of war, would seem most strongly to imply that others were not to be so treated; or, in other words, that colored men from the insurrectionary States are to be held to labor and returned to their masters, if captured by the Confederate forces while duly enrolled and mustered into and actually in the armies of the United States.

In the view which the Government of the United States takes of the claim made by you to the persons and services of these negroes, it is not to be supported upon any principle of national or municipal law.

Looking upon these men only as property, upon your theory of property in them, we do not see how this claim can be made; certainly not how it can be yielded. It is believed to be a well-settled rule of public international law, and a custom and part of the laws of war, that the capture of movable property vests the title to that property in the captor, and therefore, when one belligerent gets into full possession of property belonging to the subjects or citizens of the other belligerent, the owner of that property is at once divested of his title, which rests in the belligerent government capturing and holding such possession. Upon this rule of international law all civilized nations have acted, and by it both belligerents have dealt with all property, save slaves, taken from each other during the present war.

If the Confederate forces capture a number of horses from the United States, the animals are immediately claimed to be, and, as we understand it, become the property of the Confederate authorities.

If the United States capture any movable property in the rebellion, by our regulations and laws, in conformity with the international law and the laws of war; such property is turned over to our Government as its property. Therefore, if we obtain possession of that species of property known to the laws of the insurrectionary States as slaves, why should there be any doubt that that property, like any other, vests in the United States?

If the property in the slave does so vest, the *jus disponendi*, the right of disposing of that property, rests in the United States.

Now, the United States have disposed of the property which they have acquired by capture in slaves taken by them, by giving that right of property to the man himself, to the slave—*i. e.*, by emancipating him and declaring him free forever; so that if we have not mistaken the principles of international law and the laws of war, we have no slaves in the armies of the United States. All are free men, being made so in such manner as we have chosen to dispose of our property in them which we acquire by capture.

Slaves being captured by us, and the right of property in them thereby vested in us, that right of property has been disposed of by us by manumitting them, as has always been the acknowledged right of the owner to do to his slave. The manner in which we dispose of our property while it is in our possession certainly cannot be questioned by you.

Nor is the case altered if the property is not actually captured in battle, but comes either voluntarily or involuntarily from the belligerent owner into the possession of the other belligerent.

I take it no one would doubt the right of the United States to a drove of Confederate mules, or a herd of Confederate cattle, which should wander or rush across the Confederate lines into the lines of the U.S. Army. So it seems to me, treating the negro as property merely, if that piece of property passes the Confederate lines and comes into the lines of the United States, that property is as much lost to its owner in the Confederate States as would be the mule or ox, the property of the resident of the Confederate States, which should fall into our hands.

If, therefore, the principles of international law and the laws of war used in this discussion are correctly stated, then it would seem that the deduction logically flows therefrom, in natural sequence, that the Confederate States can have no claim upon the negro soldiers captured by them from the armies of the United States, because of the former ownership of them by their citizens or subjects, and only claim such as result, under the laws of war, from their capture merely.

Do the Confederate authorities claim the right to reduce to a state of slavery freemen, prisoners of war, captured by them? This claim our fathers fought against under Bainbridge and Decatur when set up by the Barbary powers on the northern shore of Africa, about the year 1800, and in 1864 their children will hardly yield it upon their own soil.

This point I will not pursue further, because I understand you to repudiate the idea that you will reduce freemen to slaves because of capture in war, and that you base the claim of the Confederate authorities to re-enslave our negro soldiers when captured by you upon the *jus postlimini*, or that principle of the law of nations which rehabilitates the former owner with his property taken by an enemy when such property is recovered by the forces of his own country. Or, in other words, you claim that, by the laws of nations and of war, when property of the subjects of one belligerent power captured by the forces of the other belligerent is recaptured by the armies of the former owner, then such property is to be restored to its prior possessor, as if it had never been captured; and therefore under this principle your authorities propose to restore to their masters the slaves which heretofore belonged to them which you may capture from us.

But this postliminary right under which you claim to act, as understood and defined by all writers of national law, is applicable simply to immovable property, and that, too, only after the complete subjugation of that portion of the country in which the property is situated upon which this right fastens itself. By the laws and customs of war this right has never been applied to movable property.

True it is, I believe, that the Romans attempted to apply it in the case of slaves, but for 2,000 years no other nation has attempted to set up this right as ground for treating slaves differently from other property.

But the Romans even refused to re-enslave men captured from opposing belligerents in a civil war, such as ours unhappily is.

Consistently, then, with any principle of the law of nations, treating slaves as property merely, it would seem impossible for the Government of the United States to permit the negroes in their ranks to be re-enslaved when captured, or treated otherwise than as prisoners of war.

I have forborne, sir, in this discussion to argue the question upon any other or different grounds of right than those adopted by your authorities in claiming the negro as property, because I understand that your fabric of opposition to the Government of the United States has the right of property in man as its corner stone. Of course it would not be profitable in settling a question of exchange of prisoners of war to attempt to argue the question of abandonment of the very corner stone of their attempted political edifice. Therefore I have omitted all the considerations which should apply to the negro soldier as a man, and dealt with him upon the Confederate theory of property only.

I unite with you most cordially, sir, in desiring a speedy settlement of all these questions, in view of the great suffering endured by our prisoners in the hands of your authorities, of which you so feelingly speak. Let me ask, in view of that suffering, why you have delayed eight months to answer a proposition which, by now accepting, you admit to be right, just, and humane, allowing that suffering to continue so long? One cannot help thinking, even at the risk of being deemed uncharitable, that the benevolent sympathies of the Confederate authorities have been lately stirred by the depleted condition of their armies, and a desire to get into the field, to affect the present campaign, the hale, hearty, and well-fed prisoners held by the United States, in exchange for the half-starved, sick, emaciated, and unserviceable soldiers of the United States now languishing in your prisons. The events of this war, if we did not know it before, have taught us that it is not the Northern portion of the American people alone who know how to drive sharp bargains.

The wrongs, indignities, and privations suffered by our soldiers would move me to consent to anything to procure their exchange, except to barter away the honor and faith of the Government of the United States, which has been so solemnly pledged to the colored soldiers in its ranks.

Consistently with national faith and justice we cannot relinquish this position. With your authorities it is a question of property merely. It seems to address itself to you in this form: Will you suffer your soldier, captured in fighting your battles, to be in confinement for months rather than release him by giving for him that which you call a piece of property, and which we are willing to accept as a man?

You certainly appear to place less value upon your soldier than you do upon your negro. I assure you, much as we of the North are accused of loving property, our citizens would have no difficulty in yielding up any piece of property they have in exchange for one of their brothers or sons languishing in your prisons. Certainly there could be no doubt that they would do so were that piece of property less in value than $5,000 in Confederate money, which is believed to be the price of an able-bodied negro in the insurrectionary States.

Trusting that I may receive such a reply to the questions propounded in this note as will lead to a speedy resumption of the negotiations for a full exchange of all prisoners and a delivery of them to their respective authorities,

I have the honor to be, very respectfully,
your obedient servant,
BENJ. F. BUTLER,
Major-General and Commissioner for Exchange.

DEFENDING ATLANTA: GEORGIA, AUGUST 1864

Robert Toombs to Alexander H. Stephens

After the battle of July 22 the opposing armies at Atlanta entrenched along three sides of the city. While Union artillery shelled Atlanta, Sherman launched a series of cavalry raids that failed to cut the two railroads that supplied the city from the south. On August 25 Sherman withdrew his troops from their trenches east and north of Atlanta and began moving his forces south of the city. Robert Toombs was a former U.S. senator from Georgia who had briefly served as the Confederate secretary of state in 1861 and commanded a brigade in the Army of Northern Virginia in 1862. He wrote about the situation at Atlanta to his fellow Georgian, Confederate vice president Alexander H. Stephens.

ATLANTA, GEO., *30th Aug., 1864.*

DEAR STEPHENS, I wrote you some fortnight ago but hearing thro' a letter from Linton to Genl. Smith that he had heard nothing from either of us and my letter to him being of same date I think it probable from not hearing from you that yours also miscarried. I have been very closely engaged here since the enemy began shelling the city. He hauled off a few days ago and the army seemed as much elated as tho' we had gained a great victory, whereas it was simply changing his mode of attack. Our works were formidable; he felt of them half a dozen times; his men could not be got to charge them. He then wisely fell back, massed himself 6 or 7 miles west so. west of the town on the West Point R. Road, entrenched, and is gradually moving, entrenching as he goes, until he straddles the Macon road, cuts off our supplies, and compels us to fight him in his works or evacuate the place as soon as our rations are out. In the mean time he places a corps on the Chattahoochee defending his line from Vining's Station to Sand Town in his rear and thus protecting his line of communications. In fact, allowing for the topography of the country, it is precisely the Vicksburg movement acted over again, except we can get out when we want to and Pemberton could not. But we shall be equally unable to hold the place. The enemy care nothing for Wheeler and his seven thousand cavalry in the rear. They did not obstruct his trains more than four days, if that; and Wheeler avoided all depots where there were as much as armed sutlers. He has been gone for three weeks. I cannot say he has done no good, for he has relieved the poor people of this part of the country temporarily from his plundering marauding bands of cowardly robbers. It is said he is in Tennessee. I hope to God he will never get back into Georgia. We have a question of famine upon us. His band consumes more than the whole army besides and will accelerate the evil day. This army of Tennessee is in a deplorable condition. Hood is getting ridd of Bragg's worthless pets as fast as he can, but Davis supports a great number of them, and many other incompts. are sent from other places to take their commands. Hood I think the very best of the generals of his school; but like all the rest of them he knows no more of business than a ten year old boy, and don't know who does know anything about it. The longer the war lasts the more and more important it becomes to husband the resources of the country; but ours are wasted with a wild recklessness that would disgrace the Choctaw Indians. One third of the white population in Georgia are in the enemy's lines or so close to them as to make them or their industry unavailable to us. About a fourth of the residue is devastated by our armies and the villains around posts. Behold the prospect! This army has less than thirty thousand musketts present for duty, leaving out the militia who have under four thousand. Sherman I do not think has over 45 thousand musketts, and the possession of empire depends on this small force. Kirby Smith and Dick Taylor have over thirty thousand musketts in La. They have not fired a gun or perhaps marched ten miles since Banks left Alexandria last spring. I have a strong opinion that this force was promised to Hood. I saw Gov. Lubbock of Texas last night, who came direct thro' Dick Taylor's camp and therefore spoke on his personal knowledge of these important events. Therefore upon the whole our affairs here are gloomy enough. A good victory would change them much for the better.

I have been interrupted more than a dozen times in writing this letter and have not written you one tenth part that I want to. I will write you again tomorrow or next. Hood has sent me a request to send out people to collect and send him bacon in waggons to Social Circle en route for this place and a whole crowd of them are now in my tent waiting orders.

I hope if Linton gets well he will come back. Urge him to do so if his health will allow. There are many reasons for it.

“FOUR YEARS OF FAILURE”:
ILLINOIS, AUGUST 1864

Platform of the Democratic National Convention

August 30, 1864

Originally scheduled to meet in Chicago on July 4, the Democratic national convention was postponed until August 29 due to the uncertain military situation. The plank in the platform calling for “a cessation of hostilities” was drafted by former Ohio congressman Clement L. Vallandigham, who had been left undisturbed by the Lincoln administration after returning from his exile in Canada in June 1864.

RESOLUTIONS:

Resolved, That in the future, as in the past, we will adhere with unswerving fidelity to the Union under the Constitution as the only solid foundation of our strength, security and happiness as a people, and as a framework of government equally conducive to the welfare and prosperity of all the States, both northern and southern.

Resolved, That this convention does explicitly declare, as the sense of the American people, that after four years of failure to restore the Union by the experiment of war, during which, under the pretence of a military necessity, or war power higher than the Constitution, the Constitution itself has been disregarded in every part, and public liberty and private right alike trodden down and the material prosperity of the country essentially impaired,—justice, humanity, liberty and the public welfare demand that immediate efforts be made for a cessation of hostilities, with a view to an ultimate convention of the States, or other peaceable means, to the end that at the earliest practicable moment peace may be restored on the basis of the Federal Union of the States.

Resolved, That the direct interference of the military authorities of the United States in the recent elections held in

Kentucky, Maryland, Missouri, and Delaware, was a shameful violation of the Constitution; and a repetition of such acts in the approaching election, will be held as revolutionary, and resisted with all the means and power under our control.

Resolved, That the aim and object of the Democratic party is to preserve the Federal Union and the rights of the States unimpaired; and they hereby declare that they consider that the administrative usurpation of extraordinary and dangerous powers not granted by the constitution; the subversion of the civil by military law in States not in insurrection; the arbitrary military arrest, imprisonment, trial and sentence of American citizens in States where civil law exists in full force; the suppression of freedom of speech and of the press; the denial of the right of asylum; the open and avowed disregard of State rights; the employment of unusual test oaths; and the interference with and denial of the right of the people to bear arms in their defence, is calculated to prevent a restoration of the Union and the perpetuation of a government deriving its just powers from the consent of the governed.

Resolved, That the shameful disregard of the administration to its duty in respect to our fellow citizens who now are, and long have been, prisoners of war in a suffering condition, deserves the severest reprobation on the score alike of public policy and common humanity.

Resolved, That the sympathy of the Democratic party is heartily and earnestly extended to the soldiery of our army and sailors of our navy, who are, and have been in the field and on the sea, under the flag of their country; and in the event of its attaining power, they will receive all the care, protection and regard that the brave soldiers and sailors of the Republic have so nobly earned.

James R. Gilmore: Our Visit to Richmond

September 1864

Gilmore published this account of the trip he had made to Richmond in July with James F. Jaquess in *The Atlantic Monthly* under his pen name Edmund Kirke.

WHY WE WENT THERE.

WHY my companion, the Rev. Dr. Jaquess, Colonel of the Seventy-Third Regiment of Illinois Volunteers, recently went to Richmond, and the circumstances attending his previous visit within the Rebel lines,—when he wore his uniform, and mixed openly with scores of leading Confederates,—I shall shortly make known to the public in a volume called "Down in Tennessee." It may now, however, be asked why I, a "civil" individual, and not in the pay of Government, became his travelling-companion, and, at a time when all the world was rushing North to the mountains and the watering-places, journeyed South for a conference with the arch-Rebel, in the hot and dangerous latitude of Virginia.

Did it never occur to you, reader, when you have undertaken to account for some of the simplest of your own actions, how many good reasons have arisen in your mind, every one of which has justified you in concluding that you were of "sound and disposing understanding"? So, now, in looking inward for the why and the wherefore which I know will be demanded of me at the threshold of this article, I find half a dozen reasons for my visit to Richmond, any one of which ought to prove that I am a sensible man, altogether too sensible to go on so long a journey, in the heat of midsummer, for the mere pleasure of the thing. Some of these reasons I will enumerate.

First: Very many honest people at the North sincerely believe that the revolted States will return to the Union, if assured of protection to their peculiar institution. The Government having declared that no State shall be readmitted which has not first abolished Slavery, these people hold it responsible for the continuance of the war. It is, therefore, important to know whether the Rebel States will or will not return, if allowed to retain Slavery. Mr. Jefferson Davis could, undoubtedly, answer that question; and that may have been a reason why I went to see him.

Second: On the second of July last, C. C. Clay, of Alabama, J. P. Holcombe, of Virginia, and G. N. Sanders, of nowhere in particular, appeared at Niagara Falls, and publicly announced that they were there to confer with the Democratic leaders in reference to the Chicago nomination. Very soon thereafter, a few friends of the Administration received intimations from those gentlemen that they were Commissioners from the Rebel Government, with authority to negotiate preliminaries of peace on something like the following basis, namely: A restoration of the Union as it was; all negroes actually freed by the war to be declared free, and all negroes not actually freed by the war to be declared slaves.

These overtures were not considered sincere. They seemed concocted to embarrass the Government, to throw upon it the odium of continuing the war, and thus to secure the triumph of the peace-traitors at the November election. The scheme, if well managed, threatened to be dangerous, by uniting the Peace-men, the Copperheads, and such of the Republicans as love peace better than principle, in one opposition, willing to make a peace that would be inconsistent with the safety and dignity of the country. It was, therefore, important to discover—what was then in doubt—whether the Rebel envoys really had, or had not, any official authority.

Within fifteen days of the appearance of these "Peace Commissioners," Jefferson Davis had said to an eminent Secession divine, who, late in June, came through the Union lines by the Maryland back-door, that he would make peace on no other terms than a recognition of Southern Independence. (He might, however, agree to two governments, bound together by a league offensive and defensive,—for all external purposes *one*, for all internal purposes *two*; but he would agree to nothing better.)

There was reason to consider this information trustworthy, and to believe Mr Davis (who was supposed to be a clear-minded man) altogether ignorant of the doings of his Niagara satellites. If this were true, and were proven to be true,—if the *great* Rebel should reiterate this declaration in the presence of a trustworthy witness, at the very time when the *small* Rebels were opening their Quaker guns on the country,—would not the Niagara negotiators be stripped of their false colors, and their low schemes be exposed to the scorn of all honest men, North and South?

I may have thought so; and that may have been another reason why I went to Richmond.

Third: I had been acquainted with Colonel Jaquess's peace-movements from their inception. Early in June last he wrote me from a battle-field in Georgia, announcing his intention of again visiting the Rebels, and asking an interview with me at a designated place. We met, and went to Washington together. Arriving there, I became aware that obstacles were in the way of his further progress. Those obstacles could be removed by my accompanying him; and that, to those who know the man and his "mission," which is to preach peace on earth and good-will among men, would seem a very good reason why I went to Richmond.

Fourth,—and this to very many may appear as potent as any of the preceding reasons,—I had in my boyhood a strange fancy for church-belfries and liberty-poles. This fancy led me, in school-vacations, to perch my small self for hours on the cross-beams in the old belfry, and to climb to the very top of the tall pole which still surmounts the little village-green. In my youth, this feeling was simply a spirit of adventure; but as I grew older it deepened into a reverence for what those old bells said, and a love for the principle of which that old liberty-pole is now only a crumbling symbol.

Had not events shown that Jeff. Davis had never seen that old liberty-pole, and never heard the chimes which still ring out from that old belfry? Who knew, in these days when every wood-sawyer has a "mission," but *I* had a "mission," and it was to tell the Rebel President that Northern liberty-poles still stand for Freedom, and that Northern church-bells still peal out, "Liberty throughout the land, to *all* the inhabitants thereof"?

If that *was* my mission, will anybody blame me for fanning Mr. Davis with a "blast" of cool Northern "wind" in this hot weather?

But enough of mystification. The straightforward reader wants a straightforward reason, and he shall have it.

We went to Richmond because we hoped to pave the way for negotiations that would result in peace.

If we should succeed, the consciousness of having served the country would, we thought, pay our expenses. If we should fail, but return safely, we might still serve the country by making public the cause of our failure. If we should fail, and *not* return safely, but be shot or hanged as spies,—as we might be, for we could have no protection from our Government, and no safe-conduct from the Rebels,—two lives would be added to the thousands already sacrificed to this Rebellion, but they would as effectually serve the country as if lost on the battle-field.

These are the reasons, and the only reasons, why we went to Richmond.

HOW WE WENT THERE.

WE went there in an ambulance, and we went together,—the Colonel and I; and though two men were never more unlike, we worked together like two brothers, or like two halves of a pair of shears. That we got *in* was owing, perhaps, to me; that we got *out* was due altogether to him; and a man more cool, more brave, more self-reliant, and more self-devoted than that quiet "Western parson" it never was my fortune to encounter.

When the far-away Boston bells were sounding nine, on the morning of Saturday, the sixteenth of July, we took our glorious Massachusetts General by the hand, and said to him,—

"Good bye. If you do not see us within ten days, you will know we have 'gone up.'"

"If I do not see you within that time," he replied, "I'll demand you; and if they don't produce you, body and soul, I'll take two for one,—better men than you are,—and hang them higher than Haman. My hand on that. Good bye."

At three o'clock on the afternoon of the same day, mounted on two raw-boned relics of Sheridan's great raid, and armed with a letter to Jeff. Davis, a white cambric handkerchief tied to a short stick, and an honest face,—this last was the Colonel's,—we rode up to the Rebel lines. A ragged, yellow-faced boy, with a carbine in one hand, and another white handkerchief tied to another short stick in the other, came out to meet us.

"Can you tell us, my man, where to find Judge Ould, the Exchange Commissioner?"

"Yas. Him and t' other 'Change officers is over ter the plantation beyont Miss Grover's. Ye 'll know it by its hevin' nary door nur winder [the mansion, he meant]. They 's all busted in. Foller the bridle-path through the timber, and keep your rag a-flyin', fur our boys is thicker 'n huckelberries in them woods, and they mought pop ye, ef they did n't seed it."

Thanking him, we turned our horses into the "timber," and, galloping rapidly on, soon came in sight of the deserted plantation. Lolling on the grass, in the shade of the windowless mansion, we found the Confederate officials. They rose as we approached; and one of us said to the Judge,—a courteous, middle-aged gentleman, in a Panama hat, and a suit of spotless white drillings,—

"We are late, but it 's your fault. Your people fired at us down the river, and we had to turn back and come overland."

"You don't suppose they saw your flag?"

"No. It was hidden by the trees; but a shot came uncomfortably near us. It struck the water, and ricochetted not three yards off. A little nearer, and it would have shortened me by a head, and the Colonel by two feet."

"That would have been a sad thing for you; but a miss, you know, is as good as a mile," said the Judge, evidently enjoying the "joke."

"We hear Grant was in the boat that followed yours, and was struck while at dinner," remarked Captain Hatch, the Judge's Adjutant,—a gentleman, and about the best-looking man in the Confederacy.

"Indeed! Do you believe it?"

"I don't know, of course"; and his looks asked for an answer. We gave none, for all such information is contraband. We might have told him that Grant, Butler, and Foster examined their position from Mrs. Grover's house,—about four hundred yards distant,—two hours after the Rebel cannon-ball danced a break-down on the Lieutenant-General's dinner-table.

We were then introduced to the other officials,—Major

Henniken of the War Department, a young man formerly of New York, but now scorning the imputation of being a Yankee, and Mr. Charles Javins, of the Provost-Guard of Richmond. This latter individual was our shadow in Dixie. He was of medium height, stoutly built, with a short, thick neck, and arms and shoulders denoting great strength. He looked a natural-born jailer, and much such a character as a timid man would not care to encounter, except at long range of a rifle warranted to fire twenty shots a minute, and to hit every time.

To give us a *moonlight view* of the Richmond fortifications, the Judge proposed to start after sundown; and as it wanted some hours of that time, we seated ourselves on the ground, and entered into conversation. The treatment of our prisoners, the *status* of black troops, and non-combatants, and all the questions which have led to the suspension of exchanges, had been good-naturedly discussed, when the Captain, looking up from one of the Northern papers we had brought him, said,—

"Do you know, it mortifies me that you don't hate us as we hate you? You kill us as Agassiz kills a fly,—because you love us."

"Of course we do. The North is being crucified for love of the South."

"If you love us so, why don't you let us go?" asked the Judge, rather curtly.

"For that very reason,—because we love you. If we let you go, with slavery, and your notions of 'empire,' you 'd run straight to barbarism and the Devil."

"We 'd take the risk of that. But let me tell you, if you are going to Mr. Davis with any such ideas, you might as well turn back at once. He can make peace on no other basis than Independence. Recognition must be the beginning, middle, and ending of all negotiations. Our people will accept peace on no other terms."

"I think you are wrong there," said the Colonel. "When I was here a year ago, I met many of your leading men, and they all assured me they wanted peace and reunion, even at the sacrifice of slavery. Within a week, a man you venerate and love has met me at Baltimore, and besought me to come here, and offer Mr. Davis peace on such conditions."

"That may be. Some of our old men, who are weak in the knees, may want peace on any terms; but the Southern people will not have it without Independence. Mr. Davis knows them, and you will find he will insist upon that. Concede that, and we 'll not quarrel about minor matters."

"We 'll not quarrel at all. But it 's sundown, and time we were 'on to Richmond.'"

"That 's the 'Tribune' cry," said the Captain, rising; "and I hurrah for the 'Tribune,' for it 's honest, and—I want my supper."

We all laughed, and the Judge ordered the horses. As we were about to start, I said to him,—

"You 've forgotten our parole."

"Oh, never mind that. We 'll attend to that at Richmond."

Stepping into his carriage, and unfurling the flag of truce, he then led the way, by a "short cut," across the corn-field which divided the mansion from the high-road. We followed in an ambulance drawn by a pair of mules, our shadow—Mr. Javins—sitting between us and the twilight, and Jack, a "likely darky," almost the sole survivor of his master's twelve hundred slaves, ("De ress all stole, Massa,—stole by you Yankees,") occupying the front-seat, and with a stout whip "working our passage" to Richmond.

Much that was amusing and interesting occurred during our three-hours' journey, but regard for our word forbids my relating it. Suffice it to say, we saw the "frowning fortifications," we "flanked" the "invincible army," and, at ten o'clock that night, planted our flag (against a lamp-post) in the very heart of the hostile city. As we alighted at the doorway of the Spotswood Hotel, the Judge said to the Colonel,—

"Button your outside-coat up closely. Your uniform must not be seen here."

The Colonel did as he was bidden; and, without stopping to register our names at the office, we followed the Judge and the Captain up to No. 60. It was a large, square room in the fourth story, with an unswept, ragged carpet, and bare, white walls, smeared with soot and tobacco-juice. Several chairs, a marble-top table, and a pine wash-stand and clothes-press straggled about the floor, and in the corners were three beds, garnished with tattered pillow-cases, and covered with white counterpanes, grown gray with longing for soapsuds and a wash-tub. The plainer and humbler of these beds was designed for the burly Mr. Javins; the others had been made ready for the extraordinary envoys (not envoys extraordinary) who, in defiance of all precedent and the "law of nations," had just then "taken Richmond."

A single gas-jet was burning over the mantel-piece, and above it I saw a "writing on the wall" which implied that Jane Jackson had run up a washing-score of fifty dollars!

I was congratulating myself on not having to pay that woman's laundry-bills, when the Judge said,—

"You want supper. What shall we order?"

"A slice of hot corn-bread would make *me* the happiest man in Richmond."

The Captain thereupon left the room, and shortly returning, remarked,—

"The landlord swears you 're from Georgia. He says none but a Georgian would call for corn-bread at this time of night."

On that hint we acted, and when our sooty attendant came in with the supper-things, we discussed Georgia mines, Georgia banks, and Georgia mosquitoes, in a way that showed we had been bitten by all of them. In half an hour it was noised all about the hotel that the two gentlemen the Confederacy was taking such excellent care of were from Georgia.

The meal ended, and a quiet smoke over, our entertainers rose to go. As the Judge bade us good-night, he said to us,—

"In the morning you had better address a note to Mr. Benjamin, asking the interview with the President. I will call at ten o'clock, and take it to him."

"Very well. But will Mr. Davis see us on Sunday?"

"Oh, that will make no difference."

WHAT WE DID THERE.

THE next morning, after breakfast, which we took in our room with Mr. Javins, we indited a note—of which the following is a copy—to the Confederate Secretary of State.

"Spotswood House, Richmond, Va.
"July 17th, 1864.

"Hon. J. P. Benjamin,
"Secretary of State, etc.

"DEAR SIR,—The undersigned respectfully solicit an interview with President Davis.

"They visit Richmond only as private citizens, and have no official character or authority; but they are acquainted with the views of the United States Government, and with the sentiments of the Northern people relative to an adjustment of the differences existing between the North and the South, and earnestly hope that a free interchange of views between President Davis and themselves may open the way to such *official* negotiations as will result in restoring PEACE to the two sections of our distracted country.

"They, therefore, ask an interview with the President, and awaiting your reply, are

"Truly and respectfully yours."

This was signed by both of us; and when the Judge called, as he had appointed, we sent it—together with a commendatory letter I had received, on setting out, from a near relative of Mr. Davis—to the Rebel Secretary. In half an hour Judge Ould returned, saying,—"Mr. Benjamin sends you his compliments, and will be happy to see you at the State Department."

We found the Secretary—a short, plump, oily little man in black, with a keen black eye, a Jew face, a yellow skin, curly black hair, closely trimmed black whiskers, and a ponderous gold watch-chain—in the northwest room of the "United States" Custom-House. Over the door of this room were the words, "State Department," and round its walls were hung a few maps and battle-plans. In one corner was a tier of shelves filled with books,—among which I noticed Headley's "History," Lossing's "Pictorial," Parton's "Butler," Greeley's "American Conflict," a complete set of the "Rebellion Record," and a dozen numbers and several bound volumes of the "Atlantic Monthly,"—and in the centre of the apartment was a black-walnut table, covered with green cloth, and filled with a multitude of "state-papers." At this table sat the Secretary. He rose as we entered, and, as Judge Ould introduced us, took our hands, and said,—

"I am glad, very glad, to meet you, Gentlemen. I have read your note, and"—bowing to me—"the open letter you bring from ———. Your errand commands my respect and sympathy. Pray be seated."

As we took the proffered seats, the Colonel, drawing off his "duster," and displaying his uniform, said,—

"We thank you for this cordial reception, Mr. Benjamin. We trust you will be as glad to hear us as you are to see us."

"No doubt I shall be, for you come to talk of peace. Peace is what we all want."

"It is, indeed; and for that reason we are here to see Mr. Davis. Can we see him, Sir?"

"Do you bring any overtures to him from your Government?"

"No, Sir. We bring no overtures and have no authority from our Government. We state that in our note. We would be glad, however, to know what terms will be acceptable to Mr. Davis. If they at all harmonize with Mr. Lincoln's views, we will report them to him, and so open the door for official negotiations."

"Are you acquainted with Mr. Lincoln's views?"

"One of us is, fully."

"Did Mr. Lincoln, *in any way*, authorize you to come here?"

"No, Sir. We came with his pass, but not by his request. We say, distinctly, we have no official, or unofficial, authority. We come as men and Christians, not as diplomatists, hoping, in a frank talk with Mr. Davis, to discover some way by which this war may be stopped."

"Well, Gentlemen, I will repeat what you say to the President, and if he follows my advice,—and I think he will,—he will meet you. He will be at church this afternoon; so, suppose you call here at nine this evening. If anything should occur in the mean time to prevent his seeing you, I will let you know through Judge Ould."

Throughout this interview the manner of the Secretary was cordial; but with this cordiality was a strange constraint and diffidence, almost amounting to timidity, which struck both my companion and myself. Contrasting his manner with the quiet dignity of the Colonel, I almost fancied our positions reversed,—that, instead of our being in his power, the Secretary was in ours, and momently expecting to hear some unwelcome sentence from our lips. There is something, after all, in moral power. Mr. Benjamin does not possess it, nor is he a great man. He has a keen, shrewd, ready intellect, but not the *stamina* to originate, or even to execute, any great good or great wickedness.

After a day spent in our room, conversing with the Judge, or watching the passers-by in the street,—I should like to tell who they were and how they looked, but such information is just now contraband,—we called again, at nine o'clock, at the State Department.

Mr. Benjamin occupied his previous seat at the table, and at his right sat a spare, thin-featured man, with iron-gray hair and beard, and a clear, gray eye full of life and vigor. He had a broad, massive forehead, and a mouth and chin denoting great energy and strength of will. His face was emaciated, and much wrinkled, but his features were good, especially his eyes,—though one of them bore a scar, apparently made by some sharp instrument. He wore a suit of grayish-brown, evidently of foreign manufacture, and, as he rose, I saw that he was about five feet ten inches high, with a slight stoop in the shoulders. His manners were simple, easy, and quite fascinating; and he threw an indescribable charm into his voice, as he extended his hand, and said to us,—

"I am glad to see you, Gentlemen. You are very welcome to Richmond."

And this was the man who was President of the United States under Franklin Pierce, and who is now the heart, soul, and brains of the Southern Confederacy!

His manner put me entirely at my ease,—the Colonel would be at his, if he stood before Cæsar,—and I replied,—

"We thank you, Mr. Davis. It is not often you meet men of our clothes, and our principles, in Richmond."

"Not often,—not so often as I could wish; and I trust your coming may lead to a more frequent and a more friendly intercourse between the North and the South."

"We sincerely hope it may."

"Mr. Benjamin tells me you have asked to see me, to"——

And he paused, as if desiring we should finish the sentence. The Colonel replied,—

"Yes, Sir. We have asked this interview in the hope that you may suggest some way by which this war can be stopped. Our people want peace,—your people do, and your Congress has recently said that *you* do. We have come to ask how it can be brought about."

"In a very simple way. Withdraw your armies from our territory, and peace will come of itself. We do not seek to subjugate you. We are not waging an offensive war, except so far as it is offensive-defensive,—that is, so far as we are forced to invade you to prevent your invading us. Let us alone, and peace will come at once."

"But we cannot let you alone so long as you repudiate the Union. That is the one thing the Northern people will not surrender."

"I know. You would deny to us what you exact for yourselves,—the right of self-government."

"No, Sir," I remarked. "We would deny you no natural right. But we think Union essential to peace; and, Mr. Davis, *could* two people, with the same language, separated by only an imaginary line, live at peace with each other? Would not disputes constantly arise, and cause almost constant war between them?"

"Undoubtedly,—with this generation. You have sown such bitterness at the South, you have put such an ocean of blood between the two sections, that I despair of seeing any harmony in my time. Our children may forget this war, but *we* cannot."

"I think the bitterness you speak of, Sir," said the Colonel, "does not really exist. *We* meet and talk here as friends; our soldiers meet and fraternize with each other; and I feel sure, that, if the Union were restored, a more friendly feeling would arise between us than has ever existed. The war has made us know and respect each other better than before. This is the view of very many Southern men; I have had it from many of them,—your leading citizens."

"They are mistaken," replied Mr. Davis. "They do not understand Southern sentiment. How can we feel anything but bitterness towards men who deny us our rights? If you enter my house and drive me out of it, am I not your natural enemy?"

"You put the case too strongly. But we cannot fight forever; the war must end at some time; we must finally agree upon something; can we not agree now, and stop this frightful carnage? We are both Christian men, Mr. Davis. Can *you*, as a Christian man, leave untried any means that may lead to peace?"

"No, I cannot. I desire peace as much as you do. I deplore bloodshed as much as you do; but I feel that not one drop of the blood shed in this war is on *my* hands,—I can look up to my God and say this. I tried all in my power to avert this war.

I saw it coming, and for twelve years I worked night and day to prevent it, but I could not. The North was mad and blind; it would not let us govern ourselves; and so the war came, and now it must go on till the last man of this generation falls in his tracks, and his children seize his musket and fight his battle, *unless you acknowledge our right to self-government.* We are not fighting for slavery. We are fighting for Independence,—and that, or extermination, we *will* have."

"And there are, at least, four and a half millions of us left; so you see you have a work before you," said Mr. Benjamin, with a decided sneer.

"We have no wish to exterminate you," answered the Colonel. "I believe what I have said,—that there is no bitterness between the Northern and Southern *people.* The North, I know, loves the South. When peace comes, it will pour money and means into your hands to repair the waste caused by the war; and it would now welcome you back, and forgive you all the loss and bloodshed you have caused. But we *must* crush your armies, and exterminate your Government. And is not that already nearly done? You are wholly without money, and at the end of your resources. Grant has shut you up in Richmond. Sherman is before Atlanta. Had you not, then, better accept honorable terms while you can retain your prestige, and save the pride of the Southern people?"

Mr. Davis smiled.

"I respect your earnestness, Colonel, but you do not seem to understand the situation. We are not exactly shut up in Richmond. If your papers tell the truth, it is your capital that is in danger, not ours. Some weeks ago, Grant crossed the Rapidan to whip Lee, and take Richmond. Lee drove him in the first battle, and then Grant executed what your people call a 'brilliant flank-movement,' and fought Lee again. Lee drove him a second time, and then Grant made another 'flank-movement'; and so they kept on,—Lee whipping, and Grant flanking,—until Grant got where he is now. And what is the net result? Grant has lost seventy-five or eighty thousand men,—*more than Lee had at the outset,*—and is no nearer taking Richmond than at first; and Lee, whose front has never been broken, holds him completely in check, and has men enough to spare to invade Maryland, and threaten Washington! Sherman, to be sure, *is* before Atlanta; but suppose he is, and suppose he takes it? You know, that, the farther he goes from his base of supplies, the weaker he grows, and the more disastrous defeat will be to him. And defeat *may* come. So, in a military view, I should certainly say our position was better than yours.

"As to money: we are richer than you are. You smile; but admit that our paper is worth nothing,—it answers as a circulating-medium; and we hold it all ourselves. If every dollar of it were lost, we should, as we have no foreign debt, be none the poorer. But it *is* worth something; it has the solid basis of a large cotton-crop, while yours rests on nothing, and you owe all the world. As to resources: we do not lack for arms or ammunition, and we have still a wide territory from which to gather supplies. So, you see, we are not in extremities. But if we were,—if we were without money, without food, without weapons,—if our whole country were devastated, and our armies crushed and disbanded,—could we, without giving up our manhood, give up our right to govern ourselves? Would *you* not rather die, and feel yourself a man, than live, and be subject to a foreign power?"

"From your stand-point there is force in what you say," replied the Colonel. "But we did not come here to argue with you, Mr. Davis. We came, hoping to find some honorable way to peace; and I am grieved to hear you say what you do. When I have seen your young men dying on the battle-field, and your old men, women, and children starving in their homes, I have felt I could risk my life to save them. For that reason I am here; and I am grieved, grieved, that there is no hope."

"I know your motives, Colonel Jaquess, and I honor you for them; but what can I do more than I am doing? I would give my poor life, gladly, if it would bring peace and good-will to the two countries; but it would not. It is with your own people you should labor. It is they who desolate our homes, burn our wheat-fields, break the wheels of wagons carrying away our women and children, and destroy supplies meant for our sick and wounded. At your door lies all the misery and the crime of this war,—and it is a fearful, fearful account."

"Not all of it, Mr. Davis. I admit a fearful account, but it is not *all* at our door. The passions of both sides are aroused.

Unarmed men are hanged, prisoners are shot down in cold blood, by yourselves. Elements of barbarism are entering the war on both sides, that should make us—you and me, as Christian men—shudder to think of. In God's name, then, let us stop it. Let us do something, concede something, to bring about peace. You cannot expect, with only four and a half millions, as Mr. Benjamin says you have, to hold out forever against twenty millions."

Again Mr. Davis smiled.

"Do you suppose there are twenty millions at the North determined to crush us?"

"I do,—to crush your *government*. A small number of our people, a very small number, are your friends,—Secessionists. The rest differ about measures and candidates, but are united in the determination to sustain the Union. Whoever is elected in November, he *must be* committed to a vigorous prosecution of the war."

Mr. Davis still looking incredulous, I remarked,—

"It is so, Sir. Whoever tells you otherwise deceives you. I think I know Northern sentiment, and I assure you it is so. You know we have a system of lyceum-lecturing in our large towns. At the close of these lectures, it is the custom of the people to come upon the platform and talk with the lecturer. This gives him an excellent opportunity of learning public sentiment. Last winter I lectured before nearly a hundred of such associations, all over the North,—from Dubuque to Bangor,—and I took pains to ascertain the feeling of the people. I found a unanimous determination to crush the Rebellion and save the Union at every sacrifice. The majority are in favor of Mr. Lincoln, and nearly all of those opposed to him are opposed to him because they think he does not fight you with enough vigor. The radical Republicans, who go for slave-suffrage and thorough confiscation, are those who will defeat him, if he is defeated. But if he is defeated before the people, the House will elect a worse man,—I mean, worse for you. It is more radical than he is,—you can see that from Mr. Ashley's Reconstruction Bill,—and the people are more radical than the House. Mr. Lincoln, I know, is about to call out five hundred thousand more men, and I can't see how you *can* resist much longer; but if you do, you will only deepen the radical feeling of the Northern people. They will now give you fair, honorable, *generous* terms; but let them suffer much more, let there be a dead man in every house, as there is now in every village, and they will give you *no* terms,—they will insist on hanging every Rebel south of—— Pardon my terms. I mean no offence."

"You give no offence," he replied, smiling very pleasantly. "I would n't have you pick your words. This is a frank, free talk, and I like you the better for saying what you think. Go on."

"I was merely going to say, that, let the Northern people once really feel the war,—they do not feel it yet,—and they will insist on hanging every one of your leaders."

"Well, admitting all you say, I can't see how it affects our position. There are some things worse than hanging or extermination. We reckon giving up the right of self-government one of those things."

"By self-government you mean disunion,—Southern Independence?"

"Yes."

"And slavery, you say, is no longer an element in the contest."

"No, it is not, it never was an *essential* element. It was only a means of bringing other conflicting elements to an earlier culmination. It fired the musket which was already capped and loaded. There are essential differences between the North and the South that will, however this war may end, make them two nations."

"You ask me to say what I think. Will you allow me to say that I know the South pretty well, and never observed those differences?"

"Then you have not used your eyes. My sight is poorer than yours, but I have seen them for years."

The laugh was upon me, and Mr. Benjamin enjoyed it.

"Well, Sir, be that as it may, if I understand you, the dispute between your government and ours is narrowed down to this: Union or Disunion."

"Yes; or to put it in other words: Independence or Subjugation."

"Then the two governments are irreconcilably apart. They have no alternative but to fight it out. But it is not so with the people. They are tired of fighting, and want peace; and as they bear all the burden and suffering of the war, is it not right they should have peace, and have it on such terms as they like?"

"I don't understand you. Be a little more explicit."

"Well, suppose the two governments should agree to something like this: To go to the people with two propositions: say, Peace, with Disunion and Southern Independence, as your proposition,—and Peace, with Union, Emancipation, No Confiscation, and Universal Amnesty, as ours. Let the citizens of all the United States (as they existed before the war) vote 'Yes,' or 'No,' on these two propositions, at a special election within sixty days. If a majority votes Disunion, our government to be bound by it, and to let you go in peace. If a majority votes Union, yours to be bound by it, and to stay in peace. The two governments can contract in this way, and the people, though constitutionally unable to decide on peace or war, can elect which of the two propositions shall govern their rulers. Let Lee and Grant, meanwhile, agree to an armistice. This would sheathe the sword; and if once sheathed, it would never again be drawn by this generation."

"The plan is altogether impracticable. If the South were only one State, it might work; but as it is, if one Southern State objected to emancipation, it would nullify the whole thing; for you are aware the people of Virginia cannot vote slavery out of South Carolina, nor the people of South Carolina vote it out of Virginia."

"But three-fourths of the States can amend the Constitution. Let it be done in that way,—in any way, so that it be done by the people. I am not a statesman or a politician, and I do not know just how such a plan could be carried out; but you get the idea,—that the PEOPLE shall decide the question."

"That the *majority* shall decide it, you mean. We seceded to rid ourselves of the rule of the majority, and this would subject us to it again."

"But the majority must rule finally, either with bullets or ballots."

"I am not so sure of that. Neither current events nor history shows that the majority rules, or ever did rule. The contrary, I think, is true. Why, Sir, the man who should go before the Southern people with such a proposition, with *any* proposition which implied that the North was to have a voice in determining the domestic relations of the South, could not live here a day. He would be hanged to the first tree, without judge or jury."

"Allow me to doubt that. I think it more likely he would be hanged, if he let the Southern people know the majority could n't rule," I replied, smiling.

"I have no fear of that," rejoined Mr. Davis, also smiling most good-humoredly. "I give you leave to proclaim it from every house-top in the South."

"But, seriously, Sir, you let the majority rule in a single State; why not let it rule in the whole country?"

"Because the States are independent and sovereign. The country is not. It is only a confederation of States; or rather it *was*: it is now *two* confederations."

"Then we are not a *people*,—we are only a political partnership?"

"That is all."

"Your very name, Sir, '*United* States,' implies that," said Mr. Benjamin. "But, tell me, are the terms you have named—Emancipation, No Confiscation, and Universal Amnesty—the terms which Mr. Lincoln authorized you to offer us?"

"No, Sir, Mr. Lincoln did not authorize me to offer you any terms. But I *think* both he and the Northern people, for the sake of peace, would assent to some such conditions."

"They are *very* generous," replied Mr. Davis, for the first time during the interview showing some angry feeling. "But Amnesty, Sir, applies to criminals. We have committed no crime. Confiscation is of no account, unless you can enforce it. And Emancipation! You have already emancipated nearly two millions of our slaves,—and if you will take care of them, you may emancipate the rest. I had a few when the war began. I was of some use to them; they never were of any to me. Against their will you 'emancipated' them; and you may 'emancipate' every negro in the Confederacy, but *we will be free*! We will govern ourselves. We *will* do it, if we have to see every Southern plantation sacked, and every Southern city in flames."

"I see, Mr. Davis, it is useless to continue this conversation," I replied; "and you will pardon us, if we have seemed to press our views with too much pertinacity. We love the old flag, and that must be our apology for intruding upon you at all."

"You have not intruded upon me," he replied, resuming his usual manner. "I am glad to have met you, both. I once loved the old flag as well as you do; I would have died for it; but now it is to me only the emblem of oppression."

"I hope the day may never come, Mr. Davis, when *I* say that," said the Colonel.

A half-hour's conversation on other topics—not of public interest—ensued, and then we rose to go. As we did so, the Rebel President gave me his hand, and, bidding me a kindly good-bye, expressed the hope of seeing me again in Richmond in happier times,—when peace should have returned; but with the Colonel his parting was particularly cordial. Taking his hand in both of his, he said to him,—

"Colonel, I respect your character and your motives, and I wish you well,—I wish you every good I can wish you consistently with the interests of the Confederacy."

The quiet, straightforward bearing and magnificent moral courage of our "fighting parson" had evidently impressed Mr. Davis very favorably.

As we were leaving the room, he added,—

"Say to Mr. Lincoln from me, that I shall at any time be pleased to receive proposals for peace on the basis of our Independence. It will be useless to approach me with any other."

When we went out, Mr. Benjamin called Judge Ould, who had been waiting during the whole interview—two hours—at the other end of the hall, and we passed down the stairway together. As I put my arm within that of the Judge, he said to me,—

"Well, what is the result?"

"Nothing but war,—war to the knife."

"Ephraim is joined to his idols,—let him alone," added the Colonel, solemnly.

I should like to relate the incidents of the next day, when we visited Castle Thunder, Libby Prison, and the hospitals occupied by our wounded; but the limits of a magazine-article will not permit. I can only say that at sundown we passed out of the Rebel lines, and at ten o'clock that night stretched our tired limbs on the "downy" cots in General Butler's tent, thankful, devoutly thankful, that we were once again under the folds of the old flag.

Thus ended our visit to Richmond. I have endeavored to sketch it faithfully. The conversation with Mr. Davis I took down shortly after entering the Union lines, and I have tried to report his exact language, extenuating nothing, and coloring nothing that he said. Some of his sentences, as I read them over, appear stilted and high-flown, but they did not sound so when uttered. As listened to, they seemed the simple, natural language of his thought. He spoke deliberately, apparently weighing every word, and knowing well that all he said would be given to the public.

He is a man of peculiar ability. Our interview with him explained to me why, with no money and no commerce, with nearly every one of their important cities in our hands, and with an army greatly inferior in numbers and equipment to ours, the Rebels have held out so long. It is because of the sagacity, energy, and indomitable will of Jefferson Davis. Without him the Rebellion would crumble to pieces in a day; with him it may continue to be, even in disaster, a power that will tax the whole energy and resources of the nation.

The Southern masses want peace. Many of the Southern leaders want it,—both my companion and I, by correspondence and intercourse with them, know this; but there can be no peace so long as Mr. Davis controls the South. Ignoring slavery, he himself states the issue,—the only issue with him,—Union, or Disunion. That is it. We must conquer, or be conquered. We can negotiate only with the bayonet. We can have peace and union only by putting forth all our strength, crushing the Southern armies, and overthrowing the Southern government.

REQUESTING REINFORCEMENTS: VIRGINIA, SEPTEMBER 1864

Robert E. Lee to Jefferson Davis

Grant began his second attempt to cut the Weldon & Petersburg Railroad on August 14 by attacking north of the James River at Deep Bottom, ten miles southeast of Richmond. In fighting that continued until August 20 the Union forces failed to gain ground, but succeeded in drawing Confederate troops away from the Petersburg front. Union troops were then able to cut the Weldon Railroad six miles south of Petersburg in the battle of Globe Tavern, August 18–21. A subsequent Union expedition sent to destroy the railroad to a point twenty miles south of Petersburg ended in defeat at Reams Station on August 25. Together, the three battles cost the Union about 10,000 men killed, wounded, or missing, and the Confederates about 4,000. The defeat at Globe Tavern forced the Confederates to stop trains on the Weldon Railroad sixteen miles south of Petersburg and then transport supplies by wagon over thirty miles of road. Lee wrote to Davis a week after the offensive ended.

Headquarters, Army of Northern Virginia
September 2, 1864

Mr. President:

I beg leave to call your attention to the importance of immediate and vigorous measures to increase the strength of our armies, and to some suggestions as to the mode of doing it. The necessity is now great, and will soon be augmented by the results of the coming draft in the United States. As matters now stand, we have no troops disposable to meet movements of the enemy or strike where opportunity presents, without taking them from the trenches and exposing some important point. The enemy's position enables him to move his troops to the right or left without our knowledge, until he has reached the point at which he aims, and we are then compelled to hurry our men to meet him, incurring the risk of being too late to check his progress and the additional risk of the advantage he may derive from their absence. This was fully illustrated in the late demonstration north of James River, which called troops from our lines here, who if present might have prevented the occupation of the Weldon Railroad. These rapid and distant movements also fatigue and exhaust our men, greatly impairing their efficiency in battle. It is not necessary, however, to enumerate all the reasons for recruiting our ranks. The necessity is as well known to Your Excellency as to myself and as much the object of your solicitude. The means of obtaining men for field duty, as far as I can see, are only three.

A considerable number could be placed in the ranks by relieving all able bodied white men employed as teamsters, cooks, mechanics, and laborers, and supplying their places with negroes. I think measures should be taken at once to substitute negroes for whites in every place in the army, or connected with it, where the former can be used. It seems to me that we must choose between employing negroes ourselves, and having them employed against us.

A thorough and vigorous inspection of the rolls of exempted and detailed men is in my opinion of immediate importance. I think you will agree with me that no man should be excused from service for any reason not deemed sufficient to entitle one already in service to his discharge.

I do not think that the decision of such questions can be made so well by any as by those whose experience with troops has made them acquainted with those urgent claims to relief, which are constantly brought to the attention of commanding officers, but which they are forced to deny. For this reason I would recommend that the rolls of exempts and details in each State be inspected by officers of character and influence who have had experience in the field and have had nothing to do with the exemptions and details. If all that I have heard be true, I think it will be found that very different rules of action have been pursued towards men in service and those liable to it in the matter of exemptions and details, and I respectfully recommend that Your Excellency cause reports to be made by the Enrolling Bureau of the number of men enrolled in each State, the number sent to the field, and the number exempted or detailed. I regard this matter as of the utmost moment. Our ranks are constantly diminishing by battle and disease, and few recruits are received. The consequences are inevitable, and I feel confident that the time has come when no man capable of bearing arms should be excused, unless it be for some controlling reason of public necessity. The safety of the country requires this in my judgment, and hardship to individuals must be disregarded in view of the calamity that would follow to the whole people if our armies meet with disaster. No detail of an arms bearing man should be continued or granted, except for the performance of duty that is indispensable to the army, and that cannot be performed by one not liable to or fit for service. Agricultural details take numbers from the army without any corresponding advantage. I think that the interest of land owners and cultivators may be relied upon to induce them to provide means for saving their crops, if they be sent to the field. If they remain at home their produce will only benefit the enemy, as our armies will be insufficient to defend them. If the officers and men detailed in the Conscript Bureau have performed their duties faithfully, they must have already brought out the chief part of those liable to duty, and have nothing to do now except to get such as from time to time reach military age. If this be true many of these officers and men can now be spared for the army. If not, they have been derelict, and should be sent back to the ranks, & their places supplied by others who will be more active. Such a policy will stimulate the energy of this class of men. The last resource is the reserve force. Men of this class can render great service in connection with regular troops, by taking their places in trenches, forts, &c., and leaving them free for active operations.

I think no time should be lost in bringing out the entire strength of this class, particularly in Virginia & North Carolina. If I had the reserves of Virginia to hold the trenches here, or even enough to man those below Richmond on the north side of the river, they would render greater service than they can in any other way. They would give me a force to act with on the defensive or offensive, as might be necessary, without weakening any part of our lines. Their mere presence in the works below Richmond would prevent the enemy from making feints in that quarter to draw troops from here, except in such force as to endanger his own lines around Petersburg. But I feel confident that with vigorous effort, and an understanding on the part of the people of the necessity of the case, we could get more of this class than enough for the purpose last indicated. We could make our regular troops here available in the field.

The same remarks are applicable to the reserves of North Carolina, who could render similar services at Wilmington, and allow the regular troops to take the field against any force that might land there. I need not remind Your Excellency that the reserves are of great value in connection with our regular troops to prevent disaster, but would be of little avail to retrieve it. For this reason they should be put in service before the numerical superiority of the enemy enables him to inflict a damaging blow upon the regular forces opposed to him. In my opinion the necessity for them will never be more urgent, or their services of greater value than now. And I entertain the same views as to the importance of immediately bringing into the regular service every man liable to military duty. It will be too late to do so after our armies meet with disaster, should such unfortunately be the case.

I trust Your Excellency will excuse the length and earnestness of this letter, in view of the vital importance of its subject, and am confident that you will do all in your power to accomplish the objects I have in view.

With great respect, your obt servt

R. E. Lee

Genl

"MY CHILDREN IS MY OWN":
MISSOURI, SEPTEMBER 1864

Spottswood Rice to His Children and to Kitty Diggs

Spottswood Rice escaped from a Missouri tobacco plantation and enlisted in the 67th U.S. Colored Infantry in February 1864. He wrote to his children and to Kitty Diggs, the owner of his daughter Mary, from Benton Barracks in St. Louis. F. W. Diggs, Kitty Diggs's brother and the owner of Rice's daughter Cora, sent both of his letters to Major General William S. Rosecrans, the Union commander in Missouri, on September 10. In an accompanying note Diggs professed his loyalty to the Union and wrote that "to be thus insulted by such a black scoundrel is more than I can stand." Rice was eventually reunited with his daughters.

My Children I take my pen in hand to rite you A few lines to let you know that I have not forgot you and that I want to see you as bad as ever now my Dear Children I want you to be contented with whatever may be your lots be assured that I will have you if it cost me my life on the 28th of the mounth. 8 hundred White and 8 hundred blacke solders expects to start up the rivore to Glasgow and above there thats to be jeneraled by a jeneral that will give me both of you when they Come I expect to be with, them and expect to get you both in return. Dont be uneasy my children I expect to have you. If Diggs dont give you up this Government will and I feel confident that I will get you Your Miss Kaitty said that I tried to steal you But I'll let her know that god never intended for man to steal his own flesh and blood. If I had no cofidence in God I could have confidence in her But as it is If I ever had any Confidence in her I have none now and never expect to have And I want her to remember if she meets me with ten thousand soldiers she will meet her enemy I once thought that I had some respect for them but now my respects is worn out and have no sympathy for Slaveholders. And as for her cristianantty I expect the Devil has Such in hell You tell her from me that She is the frist Christian that I ever hard say that aman could Steal his own child especially out of human bondage

You can tell her that She can hold to you as long as she can I never would expect to ask her again to let you come to me because I know that the devil has got her hot set againsts that that is write now my Dear children I am a going to close my letter to you Give my love to all enquiring friends tell them all that we are well and want to see them very much and Corra and Mary receive the greater part of it you sefves and dont think hard of us not sending you any thing I you father have a plenty for you when I see you Spott & Noah sends their love to both of you Oh! My Dear children how I do want to see you

September 3, 1864

I received a leteter from Cariline telling me that you say I tried to steal to plunder my child away from you now I want you to understand that mary is my Child and she is a God given rite of my own and you may hold on to hear as long as you can but I want you to remembor this one thing that the longor you keep my Child from me the longor you will have to burn in hell and the qwicer youll get their for we are now makeing up a bout one thoughsand blacke troops to Come up tharough and wont to come through Glasgow and when we come wo be to Copperhood rabbels and to the Slaveholding rebbels for we dont expect to leave them there root neor branch but we thinke how ever that we that have Children in the hands of you devels we will trie your vertues the day that we enter Glasgow I want you to understand kittey diggs that where ever you and I meets we are enmays to each orthere I offered once to pay you forty dollers for my own Child but I am glad now that you did not accept it Just hold on now as long as you can and the worse it will be for you you never in you life befor I came down hear did you give Children any thing not eny thing whatever not even a dollers worth of expencs now you call my children your property not so with me my Children is my own and I expect to get them and when I get ready to come after mary I will have bout a powrer and autherity to bring hear away and to exacute vengencens on them that holds my Child   you will then know how to talke to me   I will assure that and you will know how to talk rite too   I want you now to just hold on to hear if you want to   iff your conchosence tells thats the road go that road and what it will brig you to kittey diggs   I have no fears about geting mary out of your hands   this whole Government gives chear to me and you cannot help your self

Spottswood Rice

September 3, 1864

PRESERVING "OUR OWN RACE": KENTUCKY, SEPTEMBER 1864

Thomas Bramlette to Abraham Lincoln

Thomas Bramlette commanded a Union regiment and served as U.S. district attorney for Kentucky before being nominated for governor by the Union Democrats in the spring of 1863. In August he overwhelmingly defeated Charles A. Wickliffe, a Peace Democrat, in an election marked by Union military interference. As governor, Bramlette supported the war but strongly opposed the recruitment of black troops in Kentucky. The continued guerrilla warfare in Kentucky caused Lincoln to issue a proclamation on July 5, 1864, suspending the writ of habeas corpus and declaring martial law in the state. Lincoln did not reply to the governor's letter.

Frankfort Sept 3rd 1864

Sir: Kentucky is and ever has been loyal as a State and people. Her people have triumphantly passed through the severest ordeal, and borne without yielding the severest tests ever applied to the loyalty of any people. Yet we are dealt with as though Kentucky was a rebellious and conquered province, instead of being as they are a brave and loyal people.—

Without any occasion for such measures the State has by special Executive edict been declared under Martial law; and this just preceding the elections.

Without rebuke the Military Commandant issued an order directly interfering with the most important election then depending; and in open Conflict with the Constitution and laws of the State, and in dereliction of the most sacred rights of a free and loyal people.

The ordinary and necessary trade of the State is now by Military trade regulations subjected to restrictions, which harrass the citizen without any compensating public good; and which wear more the phase of subjecting the citizens to odious political tests, than looking to the public good. I send herewith a copy of a permit, with the test questions as appended, the original I retain as a specimen and memorial of the military follies and harrassments to which Kentuckians are subjected.

The citizens of Western Kentucky have for a long while been the subjects of insult, oppression, and plunder by officers who have been placed to defend and protect them.

Having on yesterday stated the conduct of Genl Payne & his accomplices & heretofore Communicated in reference to Cunningham who is now overshadowed by Genl Payne, I will not again state it.—

The Military Authorities throughout the State assume at pleasure to make assessments upon the citizens and enforce the payment of heavy fines without a hearing. And yet the laws of Kentucky are ample and the Courts open for redress of every just grievance, without any such military judgements.

I send herewith a copy of one of those orders assessing a citizen—merely as a specimen of what is of daily occurrence.

That these measures with others of kindred nature have been urged by the Counsels of a class of men who represent the *evil genius* of loyalty, I am well assured.

No one who has a love for our Country and a desire to preserve our Government, if possessed of ordinary intellect and a common inteligence with a knowledge of our people, would advise such measures. My hope is that in the multifarious affairs of State, your attention has not been caught to these matters, and that by my drawing your attention to them your sense of justice and what is due to a loyal people will prompt you to order a revocation of those orders and a correction of these evils. The course pursued by many of those entrusted with Federal authority in Kentucky, has made to your Administration and re-election, thousands of bitter and irreconcileable opponents, where a wise and just policy and action would more easily have made friends.

Extreme measures by which they sought to break the just pride and subdue the free spirit of the people; and which would only have fitted them for enslavement, have aroused the determined opposition to your re-election of at least three fourths of the people of Kentucky; when a different and just policy might have made them friends. You will pardon me for speaking thus plainly, for I assure you it is done in the kindest spirit;

although I am opposed to your re-election, and regard a change of policy as essential to the salvation of our Country.

In common with the loyal masses of Kentucky *my Unionism is unconditional.* We are for preserving the rights and liberties of our own race—and upholding the character and dignity of our position. We are not willing to sacrifice a single life, or imperil the smallest right of free white men for the sake of the negro. We repudiate the Counsels of those who say the Government must be restored *with Slavery*, or that it must be restored *without Slavery, as a condition of their Unionism.* We are for the restoration of our Government throughout our entire limits regardless of what may happen to the negro. We reject as spurious, the Unionism of all who make the Status of the negro a sine qua non to peace and unity. We are not willing to imperil the life liberty and happiness of our own race and people for the freedom or enslavement of the negro. To permit the question of the freedom or slavery of the negro, to obstruct the restoration of National authority and unity is a blood stained sin. Those whose sons are involved in this strife demand, as they have the right to do, *that the negro be ignored in all questions of settlement, and not make his condition*—whether it shall be free or slave, *an obstacle to the restoration of national unity & peace.* Such are the sentiments of the loyal masses of Kentucky. Why therefore are unequal burdens laid upon the people of Kentucky? Is it not unwise, not to say unjust that this is done. Surely the appealing blood of her sons, which crimsons the battlefields, sufficiently attests the loyalty of Kentucky and her people, to entitle the State to be freed from those Military manacles, which fetter her noble limbs, and chafe the free spirit of her loyal people.

It cannot surely be the purpose of any to ascertain by actual experiment how much a brave and manly people will bear rather than revolt against their Government.

And yet some of the measures adopted wear much the aspect of such an experiment.

May the God of our Fathers speedily give to us deliverance, by a restoration of our Government in unity and peace

Respectfully

Thos E Bramlette

"SHOUTING FOR McCLELLAN":
WASHINGTON, D.C., SEPTEMBER 1864

Gideon Welles: Diary, September 3, 1864

On August 31 the Democratic national convention nominated Major General George B. McClellan for president and Ohio congressman George H. Pendleton, a leading Peace Democrat, for vice president. Secretary of the Navy Gideon Welles wrote about McClellan's nomination and reports that Sherman had taken Atlanta.

September 3, *Saturday.* New York City is shouting for McClellan, and there is a forced effort elsewhere to get a favorable response to the proceeding at Chicago. As usual some timid men are alarmed, and there are some like Raymond, Chairman of the National Committee who have no fixed and reliable principles that are without confidence and another set, like Greeley, who have a lingering hope that they can yet have an opportunity to make a new candidate. But this will soon be over. The issue is made up. It is whether a war shall be made against Lincoln to get peace with Jeff Davis. Those who met at Chicago prefer hostility to Lincoln rather than to Davis. Such is extreme partisanism.

We have to-day word that Atlanta is in our possession, but we have yet no particulars. It has been a long hard struggle, continued through weary months. This intelligence will not be gratifying to the zealous partisans who have just sent out a peace platform. But it is a melancholy and sorrowful reflection that there are among us so many who do not rejoice in the success of the Union arms. They feel a conscious guilt, and affect not to be dejected, but discomfort is in their countenances, deportment and tone. While the true Unionists are cheerful and hilarious, greeting all whom they meet, the Rebel sympathizers shun company and are dolorous. This is the demon of party,—the days of its worst form,—a terrible spirit, which in its excess leads men to rejoice in the calamities of their country and to mourn its triumphs. Strange, and wayward, and unaccountable are men. While the facts are as I have stated, I cannot think these men are destitute of love of country; but they permit party prejudices and party antagonisms to absorb their better natures. The leaders want power. All men crave it. Few, comparatively, expect to attain high position, but each hopes to be benefited within a certain circle which limits perhaps his present ambition. There is fatuity in nominating a general and warrior on a peace platform.

POLITICAL ADVICE: OHIO, SEPTEMBER 1864

Clement L. Vallandigham to George B. McClellan

Vallandigham wrote to McClellan while the general was still drafting a letter accepting the nomination. The "Eastern friends" Vallandigham refers to included the banker August Belmont, chairman of the Democratic national committee, and Samuel L. M. Barlow, an attorney and railroad executive active in Democratic politics. As Vallandigham anticipated, both men advised McClellan to reject the peace plank in the Democratic platform.

Dayton, Ohio
Sept. 4, 1864

Strictly Private
Maj. Gen. Geo. B. McClellan, Orange, N.J.

My Dear Sir:—Pardon the liberty I take, but for Heaven's Sake, hear the words of one who has now nothing so much at heart as your success. Do not listen to any of your Eastern friends who in an evil hour, may advise you to *insinuate* even, a little war into your letter of acceptance. We have difficulty in preventing trouble now, tho all will come right; but if any thing implying war is presented, two hundred thousand men in the West will withold their support, & many go further still. Accept the word, on this subject of one who knows, & whose heart's desire is that nothing may be done to take away his power to aid you with his whole might in this campaign.

Very truly
C. L. Vallandigham

P.S. I shall be in Trenton on the 14th or 15th of this month.

"THE WRATH TO COME": LOUISIANA, SEPTEMBER 1864

Kate Stone: Diary, September 5, 1864

Kate Stone and her family had fled their cotton plantation near the Mississippi in Madison Parish, Louisiana, in March 1863 to escape Union foraging parties. After spending a year in eastern Texas, Stone returned to northeastern Louisiana in the summer of 1864 to stay with family friends near Oak Ridge in Morehouse Parish. She wrote about reports of a Union retaliatory raid in the area.

Sept. 5: Intense excitement in the neighborhood. Yankees reported advancing in large force—destroying, burning, and murdering as they come!! Capt. Lea with his small band of guerrillas contesting every mile of the way but being steadily forced back by superior numbers! Praying Col. Parsons, who has the only troops near, for reinforcements, but who refuses to send them as he is under stringent orders and making forced marches! Blank consternation among the citizens who hear that the Federals have vowed vengeance against this section on account of Capt. Lea and his guerrillas. Everyone is preparing to flee the wrath to come.

Such were the startling reports brought to Col. Templeton by terrified Mr. Philips this morning, frightening us nearly to death, for great is our horror of the vandal hordes since their ruthless destruction of Floyd and Pin Hook and their outrageous conduct at those doomed places. Mrs. Templeton soon had everything arranged for our rapid flight through the swamp across the Ouachita to the safe haven of Col. Wadley's home, should the reports prove true, leaving Mrs. Templeton and Mrs. Savage here to brave the storm, Col. Templeton going with us. We were on the *qui vive* all day looking for a mounted messenger galloping up through the wooded lawn shouting, "Flee, Flee." But about sunset the tension relaxed. We heard that the Yankees came out only as far as Floyd on a reconnaisance and are retiring to the river, and so we breathe freely once more.

The Yankee raids are no joke, though we laugh at each other for being frightened. Last week 200 of the Corps D'Afrique, officered by six big white men (wretches they are), came out and laid the two little villages of Floyd and Pin Hook in ashes, not allowing the people to remove any of their possessions from their houses and thus leaving them utterly destitute. They were very rough and insulting in their language to the ladies, tore the pockets from their dresses and the rings from their fingers, cursing and swearing, and frightening the helpless folks nearly into fits. This was done in revenge for a guerrilla raid a few days before, in which a good many government stores were destroyed and eighty or ninety Negroes brought out. The Yankees know they make it ten times worse for us by sending Negroes to commit these atrocities. The Paternal Government at Washington has done all in its power to incite a general insurrection throughout the South, in the hopes of thus getting rid of the women and children in one grand holocaust. We would be practically helpless should the Negroes rise, since there are so few men left at home. It is only because the Negroes do not want to kill us that we are still alive. The Negroes have behaved well, far better than anyone anticipated. They have not shown themselves revengeful, have been most biddable, and in many cases have been the only mainstay of their owners.

Five or six citizens, unarmed, were murdered by the Yankees in that Floyd raid. How thankful I am we left home when we did. To lose everything is bad, but constant terror and insult are worse.

The guerrillas report that the cotton crop on the river is a complete failure, entirely eaten up by the worms. The fields are swept of every vestige of green and there is hardly a matured boll to a stalk. This news rejoices our very hearts. Those are true "Confederate worms," working for the good of the Cause.

Emmie and I are practising singing. Neither of us is gifted with the voice of a siren, but enough to amuse the noncritical. Am making a calico dress which promises to be a love, if I can only get it long enough.

"AUDACIOUS INFAMY": NEW YORK, SEPTEMBER 1864

George Templeton Strong: Diary, September 5–8, 1864

A successful New York lawyer, George Templeton Strong served as treasurer of the U.S. Sanitary Commission and was a founder of the Union League Club. In his diary he reflected on the fall of Atlanta and the Democratic convention.

September 5. Two days of cold easterly storm. Thank God the fall of Atlanta is fully confirmed. We hardly dared believe it till today. Its importance, both moral and military, is immense. Hardee is said to be killed, and two less notorious rebel generals. He is no great loss to Secessia. Hood seems to have destroyed much rolling stock and stores, which he could not carry off. We have news that the rebel privateer, *Georgia*, has been bagged by the *Niagara* (her name makes the event a coincidence, for I suppose Sherman's success gives us mastery of nearly all that state) and there is some reason to fear a complication with England, as the *Georgia* was sailing under British colors.

Dined with Agnew after a busy day. He is overworked and may be in danger of breaking down, which would be a grave misfortune.

The general howl against the base policy offered for our endorsement at Chicago is refreshing. Bitter opponents of Lincoln join in it heartily, and denounce the proposition that the country should take its hands off the throat of half-strangled treason, go down on its knees before its prostrate but insolent enemy, and beg it to do a little friendly negotiating. The audacious infamy of the Chicago traitors seems likely to produce a reaction and make the Administration party vigorous and united once more. Friends of the government have been somewhat languid and disheartened for a couple of months, always on the defensive, and apologetic in the tone of their talk. Chicago has put new life into them.

> Is all our travail turned to this effect?
> After the slaughter of so many peers,
> So many captains, gentlemen, and soldiers,
> That in this quarrel have been overthrown,
> And sold their bodies for their country's benefit,
> Shall we at last conclude effeminate peace?

Lord help us and save us from ourselves, our own deadliest enemy!

September 6. . . . Belmont tells Charley, who returned from Newport this morning, that McClellan's letter of acceptance will be most satisfactory even to the most resolute "War Democrats," and will secure his election. He may succeed in mystifying people with plausible generalities and commonplaces. If he take his stand on the Chicago platform, without some attempt at a protest, my faith in his honesty and loyalty will be shattered. Major Halpine (Miles O'Reilly) tells —— that he and Jem Brady and others are urging "little Mac" to say in substance: "I accept the nomination, and I adopt the platform. I want negotiation, armistice, and peace as badly as anybody. My policy will be to expedite them by a very vigorous prosecution of the war, which must soon put us in a position to negotiate with advantage for settlement, reconstruction, and pacification." Halpine is a very shrewd fellow, and on the fence till McClellan shall distinctly define his ground. He wants to support him, which he can do most efficiently—provided McClellan set himself right and repudiate the Vallandigham wing of his party. He thinks the defeat of Lincoln would give the rebels "a canoe to come ashore in"; that we cannot hope they will consent to scuttle their own ship and founder at sea, even after many calamities like the loss of Atlanta; that they are tired of war and will come back if we do something that looks like compromise. Perhaps. It would be a most hazardous experiment.

A new danger looms up, larger and darker every day. It is nothing less than civil war in the Northwest States! They are honeycombed by secret societies, working in aid of the rebellion, and controlled by reckless, desperate traitors for whom the gallows is far too good. The navigation of the Mississippi is still closed to ordinary trade, and that fact enables these "Knights of the Golden Circle" (more properly caitiffs of the Hempen Circle) to spread disaffection among western farmers and tradesmen. Both parties seem to be arming.

The great experiment of democracy may be destined to fail a century sooner than I expected in disastrous explosion and general chaos, and this our grand republic over which we have bragged so offensively may be cast down as a great milestone into the sea and perish utterly—and all this within sixty days from the date of these presents. So much for traitors, demagogues, and lunatics! All the South and half the North are absolutely demented. Neither Lincoln nor McClellan is strong enough to manage so large and populous an asylum. Who is? Satan seems superintendent *de facto* just now. Old Fuller wrote two hundred years ago, when civil war was ravaging English homes: "Our sins were ripe. God could no longer be just if we were prosperous."

September 8. Political indications furnished by our Quogue family are encouraging. A fortnight ago Blake and Charley Lawrence expected to stump the state for McClellan. But the Chicago platform has changed their views. They cannot support McClellan, no matter what he says in his letter of acceptance. If he accept the nomination, he is bound by the resolutions that define the policy he is nominated to represent; and how can his co-nominee for the Vice-Presidency (George H. Pendleton, an avowed peacemonger), and members of Congress and governors of states nominated by the same party convention or by affiliated conventions, be disposed of? Must they each and all write letters denouncing their own party principles, or explaining them away? Blake insists that Lincoln possesses neither ability nor honesty, but he cannot oppose him *now*. He undervalues Lincoln, but no matter. Lincoln is an honest man, of considerable ability (far below the first grade), but made odious by the vagaries and the arbitrary temper of Mr. Secretary Stanton. As for McClellan, approved by Vallandigham and the London *Times* and the asylum-burning rioters, who hurrahed for him in July, 1863, *noscitur a sociis qui non noscitur ab ipso.* His name generates what old Fuller calls (in his *Worthies of England*) a most "valiant and offensive" stench. But there are men among us base enough to support him and to

> Sue for bondage, yielding to demands
> As impious as they're insolent and base.

ACCEPTING THE NOMINATION:
NEW JERSEY, SEPTEMBER 1864

George B. McClellan to the Democratic Nomination Committee

McClellan had been instructed to await "further orders" after Lincoln relieved him as commander of the Army of the Potomac in November 1862. Despite his hopes for reinstatement McClellan received no further command assignments, although he retained his commission as a major general in the regular army. In October 1863 he had endorsed George W. Woodward, the unsuccessful Democratic candidate for governor of Pennsylvania, and began to make his willingness to accept the 1864 presidential nomination known to influential party leaders. McClellan wrote six drafts of his letter of acceptance and completed the final version with the help of his friend Samuel L. M. Barlow. In a private message to the financier William H. Aspinwall, McClellan wrote that "my letter will be acceptable to all true patriots, & will only drive off the real adherents of Jeff Davis this side of the line."

Gentlemen Orange New Jersey Sept 8 1864

I have the honor to acknowledge the receipt of your letter informing me of my nomination by the Democratic National Convention, recently assembled at Chicago, as their candidate, at the next election, for President of the United States.

It is unnecessary for me to say to you that this nomination comes to me unsought. I am happy to know that when the nomination was made the record of my public life was kept in view. The effect of long and varied service in the Army, during war and peace, has been to strengthen and make indelible in my mind and heart the love and reverence for the Union, Constitution, Laws and Flag of our country impressed upon me in early youth.

These feelings have thus far guided the course of my life, and must continue to do so to its end.

The existence of more than one Government over the region which once owned our flag is incompatible with the peace, the power, and the happiness of the people.

The preservation of our Union was the sole avowed object for which the war was commenced.

It should have been conducted for that object only, and in accordance with those principles which I took occasion to declare when in active service. Thus conducted, the work of reconciliation would have been easy, and we might have reaped the benefits of our many victories on land and sea.

The Union was originally formed by the exercise of a spirit of conciliation and compromise.

To restore and preserve it the same spirit must prevail in our Councils, and in the hearts of the people. The reestablishment of the Union in all its integrity is, and must continue to be, the indispensable condition in any settlement. So soon as it is clear, or even possible, that our present adversaries are ready for peace upon the basis of the Union, we should exhaust all the resources of statesmanship practiced by civilized nations, and taught by the traditions of the American people, consistent with the honor and interests of the country, to secure such peace, reestablish the Union, and guarantee for the future the Constitutional rights of every State. The Union is the one condition of peace. We ask no more.

Let me add what I doubt not was, although unexpressed, the sentiment of the Convention, as it is of the people they represent, that when any one State is willing to return to the Union, it should be received at once, with a full guarantee of all its Constitutional rights.

But if a frank, earnest and persistent effort to achieve these objects should fail, the responsibility for ulterior consequences will fall upon those who remain in arms against the Union. But the Union must be preserved at all hazards. I could not look in the face of my gallant comrades of the Army and Navy, who have survived so many bloody battles, and tell them that their labors, and the sacrifice of so many of our slain and wounded brethren had been in vain—that we had abandoned that Union for which we have so often perilled our lives.

A vast majority of our people, whether in the Army and Navy or at home, would, as I would, hail with unbounded joy the permanent restoration of peace, on the basis of the Union under the Constitution, without the effusion of another drop of blood. But no peace can be permanent without Union.

As to the other subjects presented in the resolutions of the Convention, I need only say that I should seek in the Constitution of the United States, and the laws framed in accordance therewith, the rule of my duty and the limitations of executive power,—endeavor to restore economy in public expenditure, reestablish the supremacy of law, & by the assertion of a more vigorous nationality reserve our commanding position among the nations of the Earth. The condition of our finances, the depreciation of the paper currency, and the burdens thus imposed on labor & capital show the necessity of a return to a sound financial system; while the rights of citizens and the rights of States, and the binding authority of law over President, Army and people are subjects of not less vital importance in war than in peace. Believing that the views here expressed are those of the Convention and the people you represent, I accept the nomination.

I realize the weight of the responsibility to be borne should the people ratify your choice.

Conscious of my own weakness, I can only seek fervently the guidance of the Ruler of the Universe, and, relying on His all-powerful aid, do my best to restore Union and Peace to a suffering people, and to establish and guard their liberties and rights.

I am, Gentlemen very respectfully your obedient servant

Geo B McClellan

Hon Horatio Seymour
and others, Committee etc.

JONESBORO AND ATLANTA:
GEORGIA, SEPTEMBER 1864

James A. Connolly to Mary Dunn Connolly

Sherman's turning movement south of Atlanta achieved its objective on August 31 when Union troops reached the Macon & Western Railroad near Rough and Ready. The same day, entrenched Union troops repulsed a Confederate counterattack farther south at Jonesboro. With his main supply line cut, Hood ordered the evacuation of Atlanta on September 1, and Union forces entered the city the following day. The four-month-long Atlanta campaign cost the Union about 37,000 men killed, wounded, or missing, and the Confederates about 32,000. Major James A. Connolly served in the Army of the Cumberland as an aide to Brigadier General Absalom Baird, the commander of the Third Division, Fourteenth Corps. He wrote to his wife about the second day of fighting at Jonesboro.

Atlanta, Sunday, September 11, 1864.

Dear wife:

It is a pleasant, breezy afternoon in September, and as I sit here in my tent, on a beautiful grassy hill in the suburbs of the fallen city, and watch our National colors floating gaily from its spires, I feel profoundly thankful that God has permitted me to pass safely through all the stern struggles of this long campaign, and that mine eyes are permitted to see the old flag floating over still another stronghold of the enemy. I knew we would triumph; in the darkest hours of this campaign my faith in our ultimate success was strong; I did not expect the city would fall into our hands without terrible fighting, but I knew we could do the fighting, and had no fears of the result. Our Corps had the honor of giving the grand finishing stroke to the campaign, on the first day of this month, at Jonesboro, on the Macon railroad, about 20 miles south of Atlanta, where we met the enemy, charged his works and carried them with the bayonet, capturing 8 pieces of artillery, instead of 4 as I wrote you before, several stands of colors, over 1,000 prisoners, instead of 500, among them Brig. Gen. Govan, and utterly routing and scattering the rest of the army confronting us. Oh, it was a glorious battle! But this Division suffered terribly. There was no chance for flinching there. Generals, Colonels, Majors, Captains and privates, all had to go forward together over that open field, facing and drawing nearer to death at every step we took, our horses crazy, frantic with the howling of shells, the rattling of canister and the whistling of bullets, ourselves delirious with the wild excitement of the moment, and thinking only of getting over those breast works—great volleys of canister shot sweeping through our lines making huge gaps, but the blue coated boys filled the gaps and still rushed forward right into the jaws of death—we left hundreds of bleeding comrades behind us at every step, but not one instant did that line hesitate—it moved steadily forward to the enemy's works—over the works with a shout—over the cannon —over the rebels, and then commenced stern work with the bayonet, but the despairing cries of surrender soon stopped it, the firing ceased, and 1,000 rebels were hurried to the rear as prisoners of war. The General rode forward with the front line despite our protests and had two horses shot under him during the charge, my tent mate, Capt. A——— was shot in the right arm, why the other five of us escaped is one of the strange things found in a battle, when we were all similarly exposed to the fire. When the cheer of victory went up I recollect finding myself in a tangled lot of soldiers, on my horse, just against the enemy's log breast-works, my hat off, and tears streaming from my eyes, but as happy as a mortal is ever permitted to be. I could have lain down on that blood stained grass, amid the dying and the dead and wept with excess of joy. I have no language to express the rapture one feels in the moment of victory, but I do know that at such a moment one feels as if the joy were worth risking a hundred lives to attain it. Men at home will read of that battle and be glad of our success, but they can never feel as we felt, standing there quivering with excitement, amid the smoke and blood, and fresh horrors and grand trophies of that battle field. That night, as we lay on the ground without blankets or tents, we were aroused by sound of distant explosions away off to the North, in the direction of Atlanta, and many were the conjectures as to the cause, but the afternoon brought us the intelligence that the enemy had "evacuated Atlanta last night, blowing up 86 car loads of ammunition, and destroying large amounts of public stores." Then went up more lusty cheers than were ever heard in that part of Georgia before. Atlanta was ours; the object of our campaign was accomplished, and *of course*, we were happy. I expect the newspaper correspondents will tell you all about the various movements by which Hood was deceived, his army divided, and Atlanta won; it would take me too long to do it here, and besides I want to reserve it until I get home, and then I'll tell you all about it, and puzzle your head over military maps, plans, diagrams, &c., until I make quite a soldier of you. Now I suppose you want to know something about the great "Golden Apple," Atlanta, for the possession of which these two armies have been struggling so long. It is situated on high rolling land; two or three small streams run through the city in irregular courses, breaking the continuity of streets, and giving those parts of the city a very ragged appearance; the population is variously estimated at from 15,000 to 70,000; a good many citizens remain in the city, but the majority of them have gone to other Southern cities to escape from "the vandals." I have noticed some fine residences in the city, but the business buildings, so far as I have observed, are of mediocre quality, not comparable with business buildings in a Northern city of similar size. Atlanta looks more like a new, thriving Western city than any place I have seen in the South.

It has none of that built-up, finished, moss grown, venerable, aristocratic air, so noticeable in Southern cities; and in days of peace, I have no doubt Atlanta throbbed with the pulsations of that kind of enterprise that is converting our Western prairies into gardens, and dotting them with cities that rise up with the magic and suddenness of the coral isles. I notice that many of the buildings in the region of the depot have been struck by our shells, but I have only been in the city once since we returned from Jonesboro, and have only seen a small part of it, so that I do not know the full extent of damage our artillery did. As soon as I can get time I shall explore it thoroughly, and can give you a full report when I get home. I presume everybody at home is so deeply immersed in politics as to scarcely give a thought to the armies in the field. One party seems to want peace. That suits us here. We want peace too, *honorable* peace, won in the full light of day, at the cannon's mouth and the bayonet's point, with our grand old flag flying over us as we negotiate it, instead of cowardly peace purchased at the price of national dishonor. I received your letter of August 30th today. xxxx

I don't know how it will be about leaves of absence from here now, but will soon know, and if there is an opportunity I will get a leave, but I think our stay here will be brief, Hood has *some* army left, and we must destroy it, and I want to be "in at the death." You have not yet told me about that poetical quotation I wrote you about. Please don't forget it.

Your husband.

"WAR IS CRUELTY": GEORGIA, SEPTEMBER 1864

William T. Sherman to James M. Calhoun and Others

On September 7 Sherman ordered the expulsion of the remaining civilian population of Atlanta. His decision was protested by the mayor and city council, who warned that it would cause "consequences appalling and heartrending." Sherman's response was widely printed in the northern press, along with a heated exchange of letters between Sherman and Hood regarding the expulsion order and the laws of war. About 1,600 Atlanta residents were sent south across the Confederate lines, while perhaps an equal number chose to go north.

Headquarters, Military Division of the Mississippi,
In the Field, Atlanta Sept. 12 1864.

James M. Calhoun, Mayor, E. E. Rawson, and S. C. Wells, representing City Council of Atlanta.

Gentlemen,

I have your letter of the 11th in the nature of a Petition to revoke my orders removing all the inhabitants from Atlanta. I have read it carefully and give full credit to your statements of the distress that will be occasioned by it, and yet shall not revoke my orders, simply because my orders are not designed to meet the humanities of the case, but to prepare for the future struggles in which millions yea hundreds of millions of Good People outside of Atlanta have a deep interest. We must have *Peace*, not only at Atlanta, but in All America. To secure this we must stop the war that now desolates our once Happy and Favored country. To stop war we must defeat the Rebel Armies, that are arrayed against the Laws and Constitution which all must respect and obey. To defeat those armies we must prepare the way to reach them in their recesses provided with the arms and instruments which enable us to accomplish our purpose. Now, I know the vindictive nature of our enemy, and that we may have many years of military operations from this Quarter, and therefore deem it wise and prudent to prepare in time.

The use of Atlanta for warlike purposes is inconsistent with its character as a home for families. There will be no manufactures, commerce, or agriculture here for the maintenance of families and Sooner or later want will compel the Inhabitants to go. Why not go *now*, when all the arrangements are completed for the transfer instead of waiting till the plunging shot of contending armies will renew the scenes of the past month? Of course I do not apprehend any such thing at this moment, but you do not suppose this army will be here till the war is over. I cannot discuss this subject with you fairly, because I cannot impart to you what I propose to do, but I assert that my military plans make it necessary for the Inhabitants to go away, and I can only renew my offer of services to make their exodus in any direction as easy and comfortable as possible. You cannot qualify war in harsher terms than I will. War is cruelty, and you cannot refine it: and those who brought war into our Country deserve all the curses and maledictions a people can pour out. I know I had no hand in making this war, and I know I will make more sacrifices today than any of you to Secure Peace. But you cannot have Peace and a Division of our Country. If the United States submits to a Division now it will not stop, but will go on till we reap the Fate of Mexico, which is Eternal War. The United States does and must assert its authority wherever it once had power, if it relaxes one bit to pressure it is gone, and I know that Such is the National Feeling. This Feeling assumes various shapes, but always comes back to that of *Union*. Once admit the Union, once more acknowledge the Authority of the National Government, and instead of devoting your houses, and Streets and Roads to the dread uses of War. I & this army become at once your protectors & supporters, shielding you from danger let it come from what quarter it may. I know that a few individuals cannot resist a torrent of error and passion such as swept the South into rebellion, but you can part out, so that we may know those who desire a Government, and those who insist on war & its desolation.

You might as well appeal against the thunder storm as against these terrible hardships of war. They are inevitable and the only way the People of Atlanta can hope once more to live in peace & quiet at home is to Stop the war, which can alone be done by admitting that it began in Error and is perpetuated in pride. We don't want your negros or your horses, or your houses or your Lands, or any thing you have, but we do want and will have a just obedience to the Laws of the United States. That we will have and if it involves the destruction of your improvements we cannot help it. You have heretofore read public sentiment in your newspapers that live by falsehood & excitement and the quicker you seek for truth in other quarters the better for you.

I repeat then that by the original compact of Government the United States had certain Rights in Georgia which have never been relinquished, and never will be: that the South began the war by seizing Forts, Arsenals Mints Custom Houses &c. &c. long before Mr. Lincoln was installed, & before the South had one jot or tittle of provocation. I myself have seen in Missouri, Kentucky Tennessee and Mississipi hundreds and thousands of women & children fleeing from your armies & desperadoes, hungry and with bleeding feet. In Memphis Vicksburg and Mississipi we fed thousands upon thousands of the families of Rebel Soldiers left on our hands and whom we could not see starve. Now that war comes home to you you feel very different. You deprecate its horrors, but did not feel them when you sent car-loads of soldiers and ammunition, moulded shells & shot to carry on war into Kentucky & Tennessee, & desolate the homes of hundreds & thousands of good People who only asked to live in Peace at their old homes, and under the Government of their inheritance. But these comparisons are idle. I want peace, and believe it can now only be reached through union and war, and I will ever conduct war partly with a view to perfect & early success.

But my dear sirs when that Peace do come you may call on me for anything—Then will I share with you the last cracker, and watch with you to shield your homes & families against danger from every quarter.

Now you must go, & take with you the old & feeble, feed & nurse them, & build for them in more quiet places proper habitations, to shield them against the weather till the mad passions of men cool down, and allow the Union and peace once more settle over your old homes at Atlanta. Yrs., in haste,

W. T. Sherman

EQUAL PAY FOR BLACK SOLDIERS:
OHIO, SEPTEMBER 1864

Rachel Ann Wicker to John A. Andrew

The men who enlisted in the 54th and 55th Massachusetts Regiments in the winter and spring of 1863 were promised equal pay with white soldiers. However, in June 1863 the War Department ruled that black soldiers would receive the pay authorized by the Militia Act of July 17, 1862, which had envisioned that blacks would serve mainly as military laborers. Privates and noncommissioned officers would both be paid $10 a month minus a $3 clothing allowance, at a time when white privates received $13 (later $16) a month plus $3.50 for clothing. The men of the 54th and 55th Massachusetts refused to accept unequal pay, and rejected as well the attempt by the Massachusetts legislature to make up the difference using state funds. In June 1864, Congress equalized pay and authorized back pay for all black soldiers to January 1, 1864, and to their date of enlistment for soldiers who swore an oath that they had been free men on April 19, 1861. John A. Andrew, the Republican governor of Massachusetts, forwarded Rachel Ann Wicker's letter to the War Department, which was in the process of implementing the new legislation. The 55th Massachusetts would be paid in full on October 7, 1864, and in March 1865, Congress authorized back pay for freed slaves who had enlisted early in the war.

Piqua Miama Co ohio Sep 12 1864

Sir i write to you to know the reason why our husbands and sons who enlisted in the 55 Massichusette regiment have not Bin paid off i speak for my self and Mother and i know of a great many others as well as ourselve are suffering for the want of money to live on when provision and Clotheing wer Cheap we might have got a long But Every thing now is thribbl and over what it was some thre year Back But it matters not if Every thing was at the old Price i think it a Piece of injustice to have those soldiers there 15 months with out a cent of Money for my part i Cannot see why they have not th same rite to their 16 dollars per month as th Whites or Even th Coulord Soldiers that went from ohio i think if Massichusette had left off Comeing to other States for Soldiers th Soldirs would have bin Better off and Massichusette saved her Credit i wish you if you pleas to Answer this Letter and tell me Why it is that you Still insist upon them takeing 7 dollars a month when you give the Poorest White Regiment that has went out 16 dollars Answer this if you Pleas and oblige Your humble Servant

Rachel Ann Wicker

A REPORT FROM MOBILE BAY: ALABAMA, SEPTEMBER 1864

Alexander McKinley to Samuel Francis Du Pont

Alexander McKinley served on the staff of Rear Admiral David Farragut as his secretary and on August 5 had witnessed the battle of Mobile Bay from the Union flagship *Hartford*. McKinley had previously been secretary to Rear Admiral Samuel Francis Du Pont, the former commander of the South Atlantic Blockading Squadron, and wrote to him about the battle.

Hartford, Mobile Bay, 18 Sept. 1864

Dear Admiral,

Your letter mailed on the 10th of August was a long time on its passage, as I never received it until the 14th of this month, just four days ago. Where it has been delayed I cannot imagine. However I was very glad to receive it. Until Captain Drayton heard from you I was uncertain whether my letter had ever reached you, fearing that it might have gone down in the *Locust Point* or fallen into rebel hands. The pirates seem to be more active of late, despite of Fox's fast *Eutaw* class of vessels. Corbin paid us a visit with the *Augusta* as a convoy to the ill-fated *Tecumseh* but did not get nearer us than Pensacola. Fearing that such would probably be the case, I got leave of absence for a few days and ran over to Pensacola and remained as his guest for that time. Old times were discussed with mutual pleasure—it did my heart good to meet with an old South Atlantic Blockading Squadron officer and particularly one who may be said to have been on your staff. He has however gone away disgusted with sundry grievances against our squadron, which doubtless he has mentioned to you, and I am afraid that Admiral Farragut has not found favor in his eyes. His criticisms in connection with the fight of August 5th, so far as the Admiral is concerned, are I think unjust, based probably upon one-sided statements, and I have very plainly told him so in a few lines I wrote to him a few days ago, but I will refer to this matter again in another part of my letter. Captain Jenkins has fallen particularly under his displeasure for taking from his ship his executive officer and bringing him over to Mobile to join in the attack on the forts, thus, as he says, preventing him from being present himself. The *Augusta* needed repairs and after a month's detention at Pensacola sailed on the 3d of this month for the North Atlantic Blockading Squadron. Corbin's description of the character of the blockade off Wilmington would be amusing, were it not so disgraceful to the government. We are almost openly defied by the blockade runners, who run in and out at all hours of the day and night and laugh at the Department's fast cruisers. Of course I know full well the difficulties of blockading any port, but I should think much more could be done in checking the evil at Wilmington than has been done heretofore. The Charleston and Mobile blockades were frequently broken by the rebels but in no instance that I am aware of in broad daylight. However there may be some excuses unknown to me.

Long ere this you have read full accounts of the engagement of the 5 of August last, and I am not sure that I could give you any additional information. Of course many of the reports are ridiculous, as always will be the case when attempts are made to glorify particular individuals or particular ships. The Admiral's brief report, written hurriedly on the evening of the attack, contained however all the material facts, though inadvertently it was not stated that the ram *Tennessee* attacked the fleet instead of the fleet attacking the ram. The Admiral's detailed report, mailed on the 12th instant, corrected this oversight and gave an accurate and clear account of the whole engagement. I do not know whether this has been published, though I have seen extracts from it in the *Army and Navy Journal.* The best report, up to a certain point, which has yet been published is contained in the New York *Herald* of the 27th of August. The description of the topography of the bay, the description of the channels and the advance of the fleet until they had passed the fort, is not only graphic but truthful. Here however the value of the report ceases—the account of the *second* fight, viz., with the ram, is full of error and absurdities. The ironclads had been ordered to take up their position on the starboard side of the fleet or between the advanced wooden vessels and Fort Morgan, for the double purpose of keeping down the enemy's fire from their *water battery* and to interpose between them and the rebel ironclads after we had passed the fort. I say *fort* because "Gaines" never did and never could have molested us, the distance being too great for any effective fire from her guns. These monitors, as you are aware, are not very easily handled and on the morning of the 5th could not get into their proper position very readily—so that when the advance of our wooden line of vessels was well up with Fort Morgan, one of them, the *Manhattan*, I believe, was in the way of the *Brooklyn* and our progress was stopped. The *Brooklyn*, which was the leading vessel, actually ceased going ahead and was in fact backing. At this critical moment the *Tecumseh*, which was in advance of all and heading directly for the rebel ram *Tennessee*, was blown up by a torpedo and sunk in less than a minute. Our line was getting crowded and very soon we should all have been huddled together, a splendid mark for the enemy's guns. The Admiral immediately gave the word to go ahead with the *Hartford* and pass the *Brooklyn*. We sheered to port, passing the *Brooklyn* on our starboard side and, as we cleared her bows, fired shell and shrapnel into the water battery like hail. We passed directly over the line of torpedoes planted by the enemy, and we could hear the snapping of the submerged devilish contrivances as our hull drove through the water—but it was neck or nothing and that risk must be taken. All the other vessels followed in our wake and providentially all escaped. Why more of the torpedoes did not explode is a mystery, for though doubtless many of them by long submersion may have been rendered harmless, yet we have learned since, to our cost, that some at least retained their vitality. The only part of the channel free from obstructions was immediately adjacent to the fort and directly under all its guns. The *Tecumseh* was just on the edge of this channel, and had she passed fifty feet further to the eastward she would have escaped. After passing the fort the *Hartford* steamed up the bay, where she was attacked by the whole rebel fleet, consisting of the ram, the gunboats *Selma*, *Morgan*, and *Gaines*. The first named, however, did not continue long in chase of us but turned to attack the rest of the vessels as they emerged from under the fire of the forts.

The other gunboats devoted themselves almost exclusively to us. The *Selma* got into a raking position directly ahead of us where none of our guns could bear upon her—one heavy shell came on our forecastle, disabled the gun carriage of one of our two 100-pounders and killed over one half of the gun's crew. To get rid of him the *Metacomet* was cast off and sent in pursuit when she hauled off and tried to escape. Our broadside guns had in the meantime done effective execution on the *Gaines*, compelling her to turn back and seek shelter under the guns of Fort Morgan, and the *Morgan* followed her example. We continued on our course, followed by the other ships, until we had passed perhaps three miles beyond Fort Morgan, when the vessels were told to anchor. The *Tennessee* was observed in our rear not far from the fort where it was supposed she would remain, but to our astonishment it was soon observed that she was heading directly for the flagship with the evident determination of fighting the whole of us, and considering that *we* had three monitors (though two only carried 11-inch guns), it really was one of the most daring and gallant attacks that any officer of any navy ever attempted before. Orders were at once given to all the larger ships to weigh anchor and attack the foe, not only with their guns but by ramming her at full speed—then began one of the most exciting contests mortal eye ever witnessed. Unfortunately, for some reason which I cannot explain, our monitors were not in their right place, and the wooden vessels were compelled to do the work. The *Monongahela* was the first that struck her as she was making for our flagship, but after the collision and an exchange of shots the ram steadily continued her course. The *Lackawanna* then dashed at full speed against her side, but she still kept on, and then at each other the two flagships went. It so happened that in weighing anchor the last time we could not get our anchor up; it therefore hung dangling over our port bow, and as the two ships came together the ram's bow struck against the anchor, forcing her off from the ship's side so that we struck her only a slanting blow and the two vessels ground against each other as we rushed in opposite directions. Just before or at the time of striking us, however, she sent one of her 7-inch rifled shells into our berth deck which did fearful execution, and as she was passing us we could hear the priming of another gun snap just as she was abreast of our boilers—if this gun had gone off we might have been disabled. Our port battery was fired scarcely ten feet from her casemate, but we might as well have thrown loaves of bread at her. As soon as we cleared each other, orders were given to turn again and ram her. We had succeeded in this and was once more bearing down upon her when the *Lackawanna*, bound on the same errand, unfortunately struck us just forward of the mizzenmast, crashing in the bulwarks, capsizing one of our 11-inch guns and, as we then thought, cutting us down to the water's edge. In a moment however it was discovered that we had two feet to spare above the water line, and orders were given to dash on. But before we reached the enemy the contest was over, the white flag was flying from the *Tennessee*, and the fight was closed. Her smokestack had been shot away and her steering gear jammed and one of the Mississippi monitors had gotten a position under her stern and poured in shot after shot against that part of her casemate, jamming the port shutters, wounding Admiral Buchanan, and bidding fair in a short time to dash in her armor and rake the ship. Our old friend Captain Le Roy in the *Ossipee* was just about trying the virtue of his vessel against the ram's iron ribs when she surrendered, but his heading was such that though he backed his engine and sheered off he could not avoid giving her a glancing blow.

You have doubtless read the report of the board of survey ordered to examine the *Tennessee*'s hull, etc., after the fight, and to that I must refer you to show what actual damage was done to her. What might have been the result, had she not lost her smokestack and had her steering gear injured, it is difficult to say. She might have run the gantlet and got back to Fort Morgan, for certainly she was, until these misfortunes happened, much more manageable and much quicker in her movements than our monitors. I believe myself that Admiral Buchanan made a great mistake in rushing into the combat as he did. Had he waited until night he might have come upon us and done us terrible injury, for as it was even difficult for us in broad daylight to keep out of each other's way in attacking her, at night the danger of running into each other would have been increased tenfold. However, as he has since said, so much reproach had been cast upon the navy (rebel) that he was determined to remove it if possible from his shoulders. I am also of the opinion that if Admiral Buchanan had not been placed hors de combat, the *Tennessee* would have been fought for some time longer. Commander Johnston is not, I think, remarkable for pluck and certainly has none of the "die in the last ditch valor." Prudence suggested, "Surrender," and he listened to her warning voice when other men would have said, "Get thee behind me, Satan." The Marine officer of the *Hartford*, Captain Heywood, was on the *Cumberland* when Buchanan in the *Merrimack* rammed her, and it so happened that Heywood was ordered with some of his guard on board the *Tennessee* to take charge and look after the police of the ship. He had a conversation with the Admiral and, on some allusion being made to the *Cumberland*, Buchanan said, "Well it must be confessed, to give the devil his due, you never surrendered." "No," replied Heywood, "we had no thought of surrendering."

But I am afraid that you are already tired of reading this long epistle, and as the mail will shortly leave I will only add a few lines more. On the afternoon of the 5th the *Chickasaw* was sent towards Fort Powell, the fort which from the outside of the bay had defied all our attacks. This monitor, only drawing between six and seven feet, was able to approach within a few hundred yards and throw her 11-inch shell, grape, canister, and everything else without fear of response. The result was that when night came on the fort was abandoned, the garrison escaping to the mainland by wading—previously, however, blowing up the magazine. On the afternoon of the next day this same vessel approached Fort Gaines and tried the same experiment. The colonel commanding (Anderson) soon perceived that between the Navy on one side and the Army on the other the case was hopeless. The next morning he sent off a boat to our ship with a proposal to surrender to the fleet, but Admiral Farragut would not thus ignore the Army. He therefore sent for General Granger, and the surrender was made to the Army and Navy. When the ceremony of giving up swords took place, the officers (having previously asked whether *they* had any option to surrender their side arms to Army or Navy and having been told such choice was theirs) with only one exception surrendered to the Navy! The surrender took place in the morning, and by the dawn of the next day the Army's force were in the rear of *Morgan*. General Page shortly after fired all his outlying buildings and retired to the fort. The result is well known and has been generally truthfully told. On the day our batteries opened fire, the rebels never *answered once*. In truth made only a passive resistance which did not continue over twenty-four hours. There was no *pluck* shown by either Page or his officers. Very little has been done since. General Canby has withdrawn all his forces except such as are necessary to garrison the forts elsewhere, but whether he can spare them again is yet uncertain. Of course without an army Mobile cannot be taken. *Water* will not admit the approach of our vessels. The enemy still have the *Nashville*, which is a side-wheel ironclad and said to be very formidable, but she is watched by the two Mississippi monitors. The *Brooklyn* has gone North; whether any other vessel will follow is not yet determined on.

I regret to hear that you have had a renewal of your old complaint, but I trust that you have entirely recovered. Please give my best regards to Mrs. Du Pont and all my friends in your family. Captain Drayton desires to be remembered to you and Mrs. Du Pont.

I wish Duvall and Stimers had their deserts but hope in this case is, I fear, hopeless.

The ram *Tennessee* has been appraised at $883,000. The *Selma* has not yet been appraised. I could write much more but I am afraid of wearing your patience out. Yours most truly,

A. McKinley

BATTLE OF WINCHESTER: VIRGINIA, SEPTEMBER 1864

Henry Robinson Berkeley: Diary, September 19, 1864

By the middle of September Sheridan had concentrated about 35,000 Union troops around Berryville in the northern Shenandoah Valley, while Early held Winchester ten miles to the west with 12,500 men. Early then divided his forces, sending two of his four infantry divisions north to disrupt the Baltimore & Ohio Railroad at Martinsburg while the other two divisions remained near Winchester. On the morning of September 19 Sheridan attacked toward Winchester as Early moved to reunite his troops. Although a Confederate counterattack in the late morning almost succeeded in breaking the Union line, Sheridan was able to turn Early's left flank in the afternoon and force the Confederates to flee south toward Strasburg. The battle cost the Union about 5,000 men killed, wounded, or missing, and the Confederates about 3,600. Private Berkeley recorded his experiences after the fighting ended.

September 19. Monday. This has been one the longest and hardest day's fighting that I have done since this awful war began. The Yankees attacked us before sunrise this morning on the Berryville Pike. Our battery has been engaged all day. We had, it seemed to me, not less than five or six to one against us. We kept them back the entire day, until about 5 P.M. when their cavalry, breaking into our wagon train, caused our left, composed of Vaughan's cavalry, to give way, and our army was compelled to fall back. We came back in good order, even stopping to water our horses, and retreated towards Strasburg and going into camp for the night near Kernstown. We had some ten or twelve men wounded in my company. Capt. Massie, of our battalion, had four or five men killed and some ten or twelve wounded. Capt. Milledge, of our battalion, lost two men killed and some eight or ten wounded. This was a great artillery fight, and the artillery covered itself with honor and glory; but its loss has been very heavy. My battery was engaged from sunrise until 9 P.M. with short intervals of cessation between fierce engagements at close quarters. The Yanks would come at us frequently, with three heavy lines of infantry. When we would concentrate on the first a very heavy artillery fire, which never failed to break it, and this falling back on their second line made that line give way, and the two routed lines going back on their third line made that line also give way. The Yankee loss must have been very heavy in killed. Bluecoats, our infantry say, never laid thicker than they did today in front of Rodes's Division; but, alas, Gen. Rodes was killed. We, in our company, fired about sixteen hundred rounds of ammunition, about four times as much as we have ever used in a fight before. All our wounded were left in Winchester and consequently are in Yankee hands. Little George Ware acted bravely and gallantly today. He is our ambulance driver and he carried his ambulance frequently between the lines of battle, and under heavy fire, to bring out our wounded as bravely and as gallantly as anyone could possibly do, although he is a boy of only sixteen. I acted today as gunner, sergeant and lieutenant. Col. Nelson acted as chief of artillery, and our Capt. Kirkpatrick was commanding our battalion. This left us with only one commissioned officer, Bill Harris, recently acting as lieutenant. This shows our heavy loss since leaving winter quarters. We started out with four lieutenants; three of these have been killed and the fourth has not been seen or heard of for two months. At one time today there came a Yankee shell, which struck the middle horse of my limber right between its eyes, and bursting, took off the middle horse's head, cut off the hind legs of the saddle horse in front of him and the front legs of the horse just behind him, cut the pole of the limber in two pieces, passed through the limber box, which fortunately was nearly empty, and knocked Bill McDaniel down, who was standing just behind the limber box. Bill was acting as Number 6. None of the drivers were hurt and Bill soon picked himself up, being more frightened than hurt. I don't see how Charley Taliaferro, who was the driver of the horse that had its head carried away, could possibly have escaped, but he did most wonderfully. He was holding his horse close up near the bit, when the shell struck it, and, after the bursting of the shell, Charley was left unhurt, holding the reins and bit in his right hand, but covered from his face to his knees with the brains and blood of the horse. I could not help being amused at his appearance, yet it was an awful gruesome place to be amused. But Charles quietly went to the limber, gathered up a handful of cotton, dipped it into the sponge bucket and proceeded to wipe his face and clothes off. Soldiers are never made cooler, or braver, than Charles Taliaferro. It is sad to think that such men are falling around us every day. When will this cruel war be over? It happened on another part of the field today that at my gun, three men, one after the other, were shot down at my right hand: viz., Jim Pleasants, John Graves and James Monroe. Jim Pleasants lost his right foot, by a musket ball burying itself in his ankle; John Graves was knocked over, but the strap on his belt saved his life. Jim Monroe was wounded in the fleshy part of his right leg and will get well. These three men, with several others at our other guns, were wounded by Yankee shooters who had gotten up into trees and whom we could not bring our guns to bear on. I thought my time would certainly come next. A sharpshooter's ball went through my gaiter and scraped my ankle. Gen. Ramseur came up about this time, and I told him that if he kept us there much longer that every one of my men would be picked off by the Yankee sharpshooters. He then ordered me to retire to the hill just behind where we then were, and which we did very handsomely and without loss of men or horses.

GEORGIA, SEPTEMBER 1864

Jefferson Davis: Speech at Macon

September 23, 1864

On September 20 Jefferson Davis left Richmond to meet with Hood and try to rally support for his administration. Georgia was home to some of his most outspoken critics, including Robert Toombs, Governor Joseph E. Brown, and the Confederate vice president, Alexander H. Stephens. Although all three men supported the war, they strongly opposed conscription and the suspension of habeas corpus and questioned Davis's competence and character. Davis arrived in Macon on September 23 and spoke at a public meeting held to raise funds for Atlanta refugees. His speech was printed in the *Macon Telegraph* the next day and widely reported in both the southern and northern press. Davis went on to Palmetto, twenty-four miles southwest of Atlanta, where he conferred with Hood and his corps commanders for two days.

LADIES AND GENTLEMEN, FRIENDS AND FELLOW-CITIZENS:—

It would have gladdened my heart to have met you in prosperity instead of adversity—But friends are drawn together in adversity. The son of a Georgian, who fought through the first Revolution, I would be untrue to myself if I should forget the State in her day of peril.

What, though misfortune has befallen our arms from Decatur to Jonesboro', our cause is not lost. Sherman cannot keep up his long line of communication, and retreat sooner or later, he must. And when that day comes, the fate that befel the army of the French Empire and its retreat from Moscow will be reacted. Our cavalry and our people will harrass and destroy his army as did the Cossacks that of Napoleon, and the Yankee General, like him will escape with only a body guard.

How can this be the most speedily effected? By the absentees of Hood's army returning to their posts And will they not? Can they see the banished exiles, can they hear the wail of their suffering country-women and children, and not come. By what influences they are made to stay away, it is not necessary to speak. If there is one who will stay away at this hour, he is unworthy of the name of a Georgian. To the women no appeal is necessary. They are like the Spartan mothers of old. I know of one who had lost all her sons, except one of eight years. She wrote me that she wanted me to reserve a place for him in the ranks. The venerable Gen. Polk, to whom I read the letter, knew that woman well, and said that it was characteristic of her. But I will not weary you by turning aside to relate the various incidents of giving up the last son to the cause of our country known to me. Wherever we go we find the heart and hands of our noble women enlisted. They are seen wherever the eye may fall, or step turn. They have one duty to perform—to buoy up the hearts of our people.

I know the deep disgrace felt by Georgia at our army falling back from Dalton to the interior of the State, but I was not of those who considered Atlanta lost when our army crossed the Chattahoochee. I resolved that it should not, and I then put a man in command who I knew would strike an honest and manly blow for the city, and many a Yankee's blood was made to nourish the soil before the prize was won.

It does not become us to revert to disaster. "Let the dead bury the dead." Let us with one arm and one effort endeavor to crush Sherman. I am going to the army to confer with our Generals. The end must be the defeat of our enemy. It has been said that I had abandoned Georgia to her fate. Shame upon such a falsehood. Where could the author have been when Walker, when Polk, and when Gen. Stephen D. Lee was sent to her assistance. Miserable man. The man who uttered this was a scoundrel. He was not a man to save our country.

If I knew that a General did not possess the right qualities to command, would I not be wrong if he was not removed? Why, when our army was falling back from Northern Georgia, I even heard that I had sent Bragg with pontoons to cross into Cuba. But we must be charitable.

The man who can speculate ought to be made to take up his musket When the war is over and our independence won, (*and we will establish our independence*,) who will be our aristocracy? I hope the limping soldier. To the young ladies I would say when choosing between an empty sleeve and the man who had remained at home and grown rich, always take the empty sleeve. Let the old men remain at home and make bread. But should they know of any young men keeping away from the service who cannot be made to go any other way, let them write to the Executive. I read all letters sent me from the people, but have not the time to reply to them.

You have not many men between 18 and 45 left. The boys—God bless the boys—are as rapidly as they become old enough going to the field. The city of Macon is filled with stores, sick and wounded. It must not be abandoned, when threatened, but when the enemy come, instead of calling upon Hood's army for defence, the old men must fight, and when the enemy is driven beyond Chattanooga, they too can join in the general rejoicing.

Your prisoners are kept as a sort of Yankee capital. I have heard that one of their Generals said that their exchange would defeat Sherman. I have tried every means, conceded everything to effect an exchange to no purpose. Butler the Beast, with whom no Commissioner of Exchange, would hold intercourse, had published in the newspapers that: that if we would consent to the exchange of negroes, all difficulties might be removed. This is reported as an effort of his to get himself whitewashed by holding intercourse with gentlemen. If an exchange could be effected, I dont know but that I might be induced to recognise Butler. But in the future every effort will be given as far as possible to effect the end. We want our soldiers in the field, and we want the sick and wounded to return home.

It is not proper for me to speak of the number of men in the field. But this I will say, that two-thirds of our men are absent—some sick, some wounded, but most of them absent without leave. The man who repents and goes back to his commander voluntarily, at once appeals strongly to executive clemency. But suppose he stays away until the war is over and his comrades return home, when every man's history will be told, where will he shield himself? It is upon these reflections that I rely to make men return to their duty, but after conferring with our Generals at headquarters, if there be any other remedy it shall be applied.

I love my friends and I forgive my enemies. I have been asked to send reinforcements from Virginia to Georgia. In

Virginia the disparity in numbers is just as great as it is in Georgia. Then I have been asked why the army sent to the Shenandoah Valley was not sent here? It was because an army of the enemy had penetrated that Valley to the very gates of Lynchburg, and Gen. Early was sent to drive them back. This he not only successfully did, but, crossing the Potomac, came well-nigh capturing Washington itself, and forced Grant to send two corps of his army to protect it. This the enemy denominated a raid. If so, Sherman's march into Georgia is a raid. What would prevent them now, if Early was withdrawn, penetrating down the valley and putting a complete cordon of men around Richmond? I counselled with that great and grave soldier, Gen. Lee, upon all these points. My mind roamed over the whole field.

With this we can succeed. If one-half the men now absent without leave will return to duty, we can defeat the enemy. With that hope I am going to the front. I may not realize this hope, but I know there are men there who have looked death in the face too often to despond now. Let no one despond. Let no one distrust, and remember that if genius is the beau ideal, hope is the reality.

The President then alluded to the objects for which the meeting had assembled, and expressed the hope that the refugees and exiles would be well provided for.

A CABINET RESIGNATION:
MARYLAND, SEPTEMBER 1864

Elizabeth Blair Lee to Samuel Phillips Lee

A coalition of abolitionists, radical German Americans, and War Democrats had gathered in Cleveland on May 31 and nominated Major General John C. Frémont for president. Although the Frémont candidacy failed to attract significant Republican support, Lincoln worried that it might draw enough votes to swing key states to the Democrats. At the same time, many Radical Republicans sought the removal from the cabinet of the conservative postmaster general Montgomery Blair, whose father, Francis Preston Blair, served as an adviser to Lincoln. On September 22 Frémont announced his withdrawal from the race. Elizabeth Blair Lee, Montgomery Blair's sister, wrote about political developments to her husband, the commander of the North Atlantic Blockading Squadron. She enclosed a copy of a letter from her father to her brother Frank Blair, a former Missouri congressman who now commanded a corps in the Army of the Tennessee.

Silver Spring September 24

Dear Phil Brother resigned his place in the Cabinet yesterday & last night when Father was going to bed he handed me the following addressed to Frank who is on leave of 30 days at St Louis now— saying you will please copy that for Phil & send it to him from me— He may want to know my views of *the position* "My Dear Frank

Your brother resigned today and in consequence of a conversation I had with the President when your Brother was at Portsmouth— I called one night on the P. at the Soldiers Home to talk with him about the election— things looking then very gloomy and he had been very much depressed I told him that he might rely on my sons to do all they could for him & suggested that he ought recall you from the army to heal party divisions in Missouri & Stump the States that Montgomery would go the rounds also— and would very willingly be a martyr to the Radical phrenzy or jealousy, that would feed on the Blairs, if that would help He said nobody but enemies wanted Montgy out of the Cabinet with one exception & this man was your friend in the Frémont controversy & was also Montgomerys friend. He told me that he replied to this gentleman that he did not think it good policy to sacrifice a true friend to a false one or an avowed enemy— though he remarked "Montgomery had himself told him that he would cheerfully resign to conciliate the class of men who had made their war on the Blairs because they were his friends— and sought to injure him among the ignorant partizans of those seeking to supplant him

When Montg returned some weeks ago, he broached the conversation I had reported to him again to the President & made the same suggestion, & in some conversations & I believe letters to some of Frémonts associates intimated that he would quit the Cabinet in case Frémont would retire from the Canvass— Some of those who thought this a good suggestion & were glad to get rid of Montgy pressed this matter, I have no doubt on Frémont & got him to resign on this condition & urged the President to avail himself of Montgomerys overture— & he is out—

In my opinion it is all for the best— In the first place if it tends to give a greater certainty of the defeat of McClellan, which I look upon as the salvation of the Republic, it is well The Blairs prefer a restoration of the Union to all their earthly personal interests— Again you know my greatest solicitude for M's advancement is in the line of his profession in which I would have his old age crowned with its highest honor— I know he would wear it with greatest advantage to his Country— This is my ambition for him— Lincoln I know entertains unbounded confidence in his probity, patriotism & judicial capacities— And this act of self sacrifice to him will secure his gratitude & he will be glad to shew it, especially as it will mortify those common enemies of himself & myself who worked this martyrdom—

I hope you will concur with the views I have taken The true interests of the Country require the reelection of Lincoln— McClellan whose depths I sounded lately as I wrote you in my last letter will, if elected by the Copperheads, will close with the enemy on something short of the integrity of the Union— Whatever compromise they may hatch up will end in the dissolution of the great nation of the Western Hemisphere— If Lincoln triumphs the vile Harpies that surround him will be killed off by public opinion If they remain with him to the end it will result in building up a new party of reform & the war which delivers us from Negro slavery, will be followed by a new political era which will establish a popular power in our commonalty— which will preserve our white laboring class from the fangs of a corrupt aristocracy The Shoddy Aristocracy of the War will perish with the slave aristocracy— All well— Your affectionate father FPB

There you have the whole as it looks to us— I think I am more hurt than anybody else Betty laughs at my "bruised feelings sticking out" but I confess to a proclivity for Mr. Lincolns first view— of the poor policy of sacrificing his friends to his enemies— but I can feel— rather— *think*— it is for the best & *feel*— uncomfortable at the same time Brother went to Frederick today to make a speech— he shows a fine manly bearing & I believe it hurts only his wife & me—

Blair still suffers from a severe cold— but it would be a small matter save that it keeps me haunted with fear of croup— I received a letter from Horace & one from Sara— both urging me to go to Aunt Becky who is still feeble— My duties are all here now— Sarah says William Preston & his family are now in Montreal & she sees a great deal of them Susan Preston a widow the second time was also with them— They are debating about staying there or going to New York to stay Kentucky is too much in the strife for them to live there comfortably We were robbed of about 300 bushels of perserving peaches this week & this morning there is scarce one left to eat— & one of our neighbors sold his off of 60 trees for $300— so our hundred trees were a great loss— but we are a helpless set of people as you ever saw & yet I see no way of helping to a better condition— Ever your own Lizzie

SOUTH CAROLINA, OCTOBER 1864

Jefferson Davis: Speech at Columbia

Davis left Hood's headquarters at Palmetto on September 27. During his return to Richmond he spoke in Montgomery, Columbus, and Augusta before arriving in Columbia, South Carolina, where he addressed a large crowd from the home of James and Mary Chesnut. His speech was printed in the *South Carolinian* on October 6.

October 4, 1864

LADIES AND GENTLEMEN OF THE METROPOLIS OF SOUTH CAROLINA:

Your Mayor has welcomed me to your home. I receive his greeting with that gratitude which one only feels when he hears expressed the language of commendation from those whose silence would have made him realize that his conduct had been bad indeed. If in this great struggle for the rights of the States and the liberties of the people, to secure the possession of which and to transmit which to us, our fathers of the revolution shed their blood, South Carolina, who has stood for thirty years in the vanguard, should give him who asserted those rights, no word of well done, he might turn convinced that he had failed as a public servant to perform his mission, and as a man had proven unable to cope with the responsibilities of his position. Therefore it is, Mr. Mayor, and fellow-citizens of Columbia, that I feel heartily grateful for the welcome received at your hands.

South Carolina has struggled nobly in the war and suffered many sacrifices. There is, indeed, no portion of our land where the pall of mourning has not been spread; but I thank the Giver of all Good that our people still remain firm there, above all other places. I am told there have been none to waver and none to doubt. It often happens that at a distance from a scene of action, men, who if present would easily measure it, magnify danger, until at last those become despondent whose hearts, if actually stirred by perils, would no sooner think of shrinking from the prompt performance of duty, than the gallant sons of Carolina, whose blood has so generously flowed on the many battle-fields of this war. But if there be any who feel that our cause is in danger; that final success may not crown our efforts; that we are not stronger to-day than when we began this struggle; that we are not able to continue the supplies to our armies and to our people, let all such read a contradiction in the smiling face of our land, and the teaming evidences of plenty which every where greet the eye; let them go to those places where brave men are standing in front of the foe, and there receive the assurance that we *shall* have final success, and that every man who does not live to see his country free, will see a freeman's grave. (Applause.)

There are those who, like the Israelites of old, are longing to turn back to the flesh pots they have left; who have thought there may still be some feasible mode of reconciliation, and would even be willing to rush into a reconstruction of the Union. Such, I am glad to know, do not flourish on the soil of South Carolina. Such cannot be the sentiment of any man in the Confederate States, if he will only recollect that from the beginning down to the present hour, your Government has made every effort within its power, to avoid a collision of arms in the first instance, and since then to obtain every possible means of settlement honorable to ourselves, based on a recognition of our independence. First, we sent commissioners to ask on what terms the quarrel could be adjusted, and since that time we have proclaimed in every public paper our desire for peace. Insolently, our every effort has been met. The Vice-President of the Confederate States was refused a passport to the North, when his object was negotiation—that means by which all wars must be terminated. The door was rudely shut in our faces. Intervention and recognition by foreign States, so long anticipated, has proved an *ignis fatuus.* There is, then, but one means by which you can hope to gain independence and an honorable peace, and that is by uniting with harmony, energy and determination in fighting those great battles and achieving those great victories, which will teach the world that we can defend our rights, and the Yankee nation that it is death to invade them. (Applause.)

With every Confederate victory, our stocks rise in the

foreign market—that touch stone of European sentiment. With every noble achievement that influences the public mind abroad, you are taking one step forward, and bringing foreign nations one step nearer your aid in recognizing and lending you friendly intervention, whenever they are satisfied that, intervention or no intervention, the Confederacy can sustain itself.

Does any one believe that Yankees are to be conciliated by terms of concession? Does any man imagine that we can conquer the Yankees by retreating before them, or do you not all know that the only way to make spaniels civil is to whip them? And you *can* whip them, if all the men capable of bearing arms will do their duty by taking their places under the standard of their country, before the veteran troops of the North receive the fresh increment which is being gathered in the Northern States. Now is the good and accepted time for every man to rally to the standard of his country and crush the invader upon her soil; and this, I believe, is in your power. If every man fit to bear arms will place himself in the ranks with those who are already there, we shall not battle in vain, and our achievement will be grand, final and complete. Is this a time to ask what the law demands of you—to inquire whether or not you are exempt under the law, or to ask if the magistrate will take you out of the enrolling office by a writ of *habeas corpus*? Rather is it not the time for every man capable of bearing arms to say: "My country needs my services, and my country shall have them!" When your heroic fathers, the Whigs of the Revolution, fought in that war which secured your birth-right, their armies were not gathered by asking who can be forced into the field? but "who are able to fight?" No man was too old and no boy too young, if he had the physical capacity to enter the ranks of the army. In the days of the Revolution, the boy left his paternal roof only to return to its blackened ruins. He grew to manhood among its struggles; and may not your country claim similar services from the youth of the present day? Like them, you must emulate the glory of your sires. Say not that you are unequal to the task, for I believe that our people are even better than were our honored ancestors. They have fought more and bloodier battles, and there are fewer who are luke-warm in the cause now, than existed in the days of the Revolution. What a glorious reflection it is, that wherever the tide of war has rolled its devastating wave over the land, just then do you find every heart beating true to the Confederacy, strengthened, as it were, by vicissitudes, and every woman ready to share her last loaf with the soldier who is fighting for our rights.

A plan of negociation has been offered for consideration—a plan of negociation by States. Well, it is easy to see on what terms the States can negotiate. In the first place, they have no constitutional power to do so. In the second place, Mr. Lincoln has said that he will not negotiate with them unless they can control the army, and they can only obtain the power to control the army by traitorously attempting to enter into a treaty contrary to the Government they have instituted. But suppose this were possible, what are the terms offered? If you will acknowledge your crime, lay down your arms, emancipate your slaves and turn over your leaders—as they call your humble servant—to be punished, then you will have permission to vote together with your negroes upon the terms under which Mr. Lincoln will be graciously pleased to allow you to live as a part of the nation over which he presides. If there be a man within the sound of my voice who contemplates such a proposition, I pity him from the bottom of my heart. My only wish is that he was North of the dividing line. His is not the spirit that animated our fathers, and he is not fit to exist among the men who are now periling their lives in the cause in which we are engaged, for he who is so slavish cannot be trusted with the sacred guardianship of the widows and orphans of the soldiers who have died in battle.

I have just returned from that army from which we have had the saddest accounts—the army of Tennessee; and I am able to bear to you words of good cheer. That army has increased in strength since the fall of Atlanta. It has risen in tone; its march is onward; its face looking to the front. So far as I am able to judge, General Hood's strategy has been good and his conduct has been gallant. His eye is now fixed upon a point far beyond that where he was assailed by the enemy. He hopes soon to have his hand upon Sherman's line of communications, and to fix it where he can hold it. And if but a half, nay, one-fourth, of the men to whom the service has a right, will give him their strength, I see no chance for Sherman to escape from a defeat or a disgraceful retreat. I therefore hope, in view of all the contingencies of war, with all the confidence which I found in the army, that within thirty days that army, which has so boastfully taken up its winter quarters in the heart of the Confederacy, will be in search of a crossing on the Tennessee River.

That our army retreated far, was but a natural precursor of that despondency which spread itself over the country; but as I approached the region occupied by our troops the hope increased, until at last I found in the army the *acme* of confidence itself. Gen. Beauregard, so well known to you all, is going there with a general command, which will enable him to concentrate all the troops that can be made available for the public defence. I therefore say, be of good cheer, for I hope that brighter intelligence will soon reach you. (Applause.)

But, my friends, if it be otherwise—if we suffer reverses, it is what is to be expected from the fortunes of war. It is the fate of all human designs. In that event, we shall have reason to anticipate from all brave men a conduct becoming the occasion, and shall look to you to redress your misfortunes, to rise in the face of disaster, and resolve to succeed, determined that you will live or die free. (Applause.)

Your brave sons are battling for the cause of the country everywhere; your Fort Sumter, where was first given to the breeze the flag of the Confederacy, still stands. The honor of the State has not been dimmed in the struggle, and her soldiers will be sustained by the thought that when they are no more, South Carolina will still retain that honor with which she commenced the war, and have accumulated that greatness and glory which will make her an exemplar of all that is chivalric and manly in a nation struggling for existence. You who have so long been the advocates of State Rights have never raised a clamor against the laws which seem to invade them, and I think, for obvious reasons, you are not like those new-born lights who, perhaps, are just beginning to appreciate the great principles of that creed. You saw laws passed which were necessary to make those States which are in co-operation effective for the good of the whole. You understood the nature of the compact entered into by the sovereign States, and you have not been fearful that the agent created by yourselves was likely to turn against that Government for which he and you had been so long struggling. Understanding the means of preserving your State Governments, you have not been frightened by the clamor of those who do not breathe the pure air of State sovereignty. Then you have had no difficulty in the organization of the three forces incident to military service. You are in that condition in which your defence must depend upon what does not belong to the active force of the country. Your battles are fought on other fields. You have on the coast some necessity for what is termed an active army, and should it be incumbent upon you to furnish troops from your reserves, you have no constitutional scruples, like Gov. Strong, of Massachusetts, against marching your militia from the borders of the State, to fight the battles of the cause in which you are engaged. I honor you for it. It is needless for me to argue questions here which have been discussed elsewhere, for here I am among the disciples of him from whom I learned my lessons of State Rights—the great, the immortal John C. Calhoun.

Among those to whom we are indebted in South Carolina, I have not yet alluded to that peculiar claim of gratitude which is due to the fair countrywomen of the Palmetto State—they who have gone to the hospital to watch by the side of the sick—those who throng your way-side homes—who have nursed as if nursing was a profession—who have used their needle with the industry of sewing women—who have borne privation without a murmur and who have given up fathers, sons and husbands with more than Spartan virtue, because they called no one to witness and record the deed. Silently, with all the dignity and grandeur of patriotism, they have made their sacrifices—sacrifices which, if written, would be surpassed by nothing in history. If all the acts of heroism and virtue of the women of the South could be transmitted to the future, it would present such a record as the world has never seen. All honor, then, I say, to the ladies of the Palmetto State. Their gallantry is only different from that of her sons in this, that they deem it unfeminine to strike; and yet such is the heroism they have displayed—such the noble demeanor they have exhibited—that at the last moment, when trampled upon and it became a necessity, they would not hesitate to strike the invader a corpse at their feet. (Applause.)

It is scarcely necessary for me, at a time like this, to argue grave questions, respecting policy past, present or prospective.

I only ask you to have faith and confidence, and to believe that every faculty of my head and my heart is devoted to your cause, and to that I shall, if necessary, give my life. Let every one in his own sphere and according to his own capacity, devote himself to the single purpose of filling up and sustaining our armies in the field. If required to stay at home, let him devote himself, not to the acquisition of wealth, but to the advancement of the common cause. If there is to be any aristocracy in the land after this war, I hope that it will be an aristocracy of those men who have become poor while bleeding to secure our liberty. (Applause.) If there are to be any peculiarly favored by public opinion hereafter, I trust it will be those men who have longest borne a musket and oftenest bled upon the battle fields. If there is to be any man shunned by the young ladies when he seeks their favor, I trust it will be the man who has grown rich by skulking.

And with all sincerity, I say to my young friends here, if you want the right man for a husband, take him whose armless sleeve and noble heart betokens the duties that he has rendered to his country, rather than he who has never shared the toils, or borne the dangers of the field. If there still be left any of those military critics who have never spoken of our generals but to show how much better things could have been managed, or of our Government, but to find fault with it, because it never took their advice—in mercy's name, let these wise men go to the front and aid us in achieving our independence. With their wisdom and strength swelling our armies, I should have some hopes that I will not be a corpse before our cause is secured, and that our flag would never trail in dishonor, but would wave victoriously above the roar and smoke of battle.

I believe it is in the power of the men of the Confederacy to plant our banners on the banks of the Ohio, where we may say to the Yankee, "be quiet, or we shall teach you another lesson." Within the next thirty days much is to be done, for upon our success much depends. Within the next thirty days, therefore, let all who are absentees, or who ought to be in the army, go promptly to their ranks. Let fresh victories crown our arms, and the peace party, if there be such at the North, can elect its candidate. But whether a peace candidate is elected or not,

Yankee instinct will teach him that it is better to end the war and leave us to the enjoyment of our own rights.

Prayerful for your welfare, confiding in the army of the Confederate States to do that which soft words can never achieve, and in the hope that God will preserve the little ones of all brave men who are in the field, or who are going to it, and trusting that in the future, under brighter auspices, it may be my fortune to meet the good people of Columbia, I wish you all for the present farewell. (Applause.)

A CALL FOR POLITICAL EQUALITY:
NEW YORK, OCTOBER 1864

Address of the Colored National Convention

October 6, 1864

Frederick Douglass, William Wells Brown, Henry Highland Garnet, and John Mercer Langston were among the 145 delegates from eighteen states who attended the National Convention of Colored Men held in Syracuse, New York, from October 4 to October 7. The convention established the National Equal Rights League and adopted an address to the public written by Douglass.

ADDRESS
OF THE
COLORED NATIONAL CONVENTION
TO THE
PEOPLE OF THE UNITED STATES.

FELLOW-CITIZENS,—

The members of the Colored National Convention, assembled in Syracuse, State of New York, October the 4th, 1864, to confer with each other as to the complete emancipation, enfranchisement, and elevation of our race, in essaying to address you on these subjects, warmly embrace the occasion to congratulate you upon the success of your arms, and upon the prospect of the speedy suppression of the slaveholders' rebellion. Baptized in the best blood of your noblest sons, torn and rent by a strife full of horrors,—a strife undertaken and prosecuted for aims and objects the guiltiest that can enter the wicked hearts of men long in the practice of crime,—we ardently hope with you that our country will come out of this tremendous conflict, purer, stronger, nobler, and happier than ever before. Having shared with you, in some measure, the hardships, perils, and sacrifices of this war for the maintenance of the Union and Government, we rejoice with you also in every sign which gives promise of its approaching termination, and of the return of our common country again to those peaceful, progressive, and humanizing activities of true national life, from which she has been so wantonly diverted by the insurrection of slaveholders.

In view of the general cheerfulness of the national situation, growing brighter every day; the rapid dispersement of the heavy clouds of dismal terror, which only a few weeks ago mantled our land with the gloomiest forebodings of national disaster and ruin,—we venture to hope that the present is a favorable moment to commend to your consideration the subject of our wrongs, and to obtain your earnest and hearty co-operation in all wise and just measures for their full redress.

When great and terrible calamities are abroad in the land, men are said to learn righteousness. It would be a mark of unspeakable national depravity, if neither the horrors of this war, nor the dawning prospect of peace, should soften the heart, and dispose the American people to renounce and forsake their evil policy towards the colored race. Assuming the contrary, we deem this a happily chosen hour for calling your attention to our cause. We know that the human mind is so constituted, that all postponement of duty, all refusal to go forward when the right path is once made plain, is dangerous.

After such neglect of, and disobedience to, the voice of reason and conscience, a nation becomes harder and less alive than before to high moral considerations. If won to the path of rectitude at all, thereafter, it must be by means of a purer light than that which first brought right convictions and inclinations to the national mind and heart. We speak, then, fellow-citizens, at an auspicious moment. Conviction has already seized the public mind. Little argument is needed. We shall appeal rather than argue; and we may well implore an attentive hearing for our appeal. The nation is still in tears. The warm blood of your brave and patriotic sons is still fresh upon the green fields of the Shenandoah. Mourning mingles everywhere with the national shout of victory; and though the smoke and noise of battle are rolling away behind the southern horizon, our brave armies are still confronted in Georgia and Virginia by a stern foe, whose haughtiness and cruelty have sprung naturally from his long and undisputed mastery over men. The point attained in the progress of this war is one from which you can if you will view to advantage the calamities which inevitably follow upon long and persistent violation of manifest duty; and on the other hand, the signs of final triumph enable you to anticipate the happy results which must always flow from just and honorable conduct. The fear of continued war, and the hope of speedy peace, alike mark this as the time for America to choose her destiny. Another such opportunity as is now furnished in the state of the country, and in the state of the national heart, may not come again in a century. Come, then, and let us reason together.

We shall speak, it is true, for our race,—a race long oppressed, enslaved, ignored, despised, slandered, and degraded; but we speak not the less for our country, whose welfare and permanent peace can only result from the adoption of wise and just measures towards our whole race, North and South.

Considering the number and the grievous character of the wrongs and disabilities endured by our race in this country, you will bear witness that we have borne with patience our lot, and have seldom troubled the national ear with the burden of complaint. It is true that individuals among us have constantly testified their abhorrence of this injustice; but as a people, we have seldom uttered, as we do this day, our protest and remonstrance against the manifold and needless injustice with which we are upon all sides afflicted. We have suffered in silence, trusting that, though long delayed, and perhaps through terrible commotions, the hour would come when justice, honor, and magnanimity would assert their power over the mind and heart of the American people, and restore us to the full exercise and enjoyment of the rights inseparable from human nature. Never having despaired of this consummation so devoutly wished, even in the darkest hours of our history, we are farther than ever from despairing now. Nowhere in the annals of mankind is there recorded an instance of an oppressed people rising more rapidly than ourselves in the favorable estimation of their oppressors. The change is great, and increasing, and is viewed with astonishment and dread by all those who had hoped to stand forever with their heels upon our necks.

Nevertheless, while joyfully recognizing the vast advances made by our people in popular consideration, and the apparent tendency of events in our favor, we cannot conceal from ourselves, and would not conceal from you, the fact that there are many and powerful influences, constantly operating, intended and calculated to defeat our just hopes, prolong the existence of the source of all our ills,—the system of slavery,—strengthen the slave power, darken the conscience of the North, intensify popular prejudice against color, multiply unequal and discriminating laws, augment the burdens long borne by our race, consign to oblivion the deeds of heroism which have distinguished the colored soldier, deny and despise his claims to the gratitude of his country, scout his pretensions to American citizenship, establish the selfish idea that this is exclusively the white man's country, pass unheeded all the lessons taught by these four years of fire and sword, undo all that has been done towards our freedom and elevation, take the musket from the shoulders of our brave black soldiers, deny them the constitutional right to keep and bear arms, exclude them from the ballot-box where they now possess that right, prohibit the extension of it to those who do not possess it, overawe free speech in and out of Congress, obstruct the right of peaceably assembling, re-enact the Fugitive-slave Bill, revive the internal slave-trade, break up all diplomatic relations with Hayti and Liberia, reopen our broad territories to the introduction of slavery, reverse the entire order and tendency of the events of the last three years, and postpone indefinitely that glorious deliverance from bondage, which for our sake, and for the sake of the future unity, permanent peace, and highest welfare of all concerned, we had fondly hoped and believed was even now at the door.

In surveying our possible future, so full of interest at this moment, since it may bring to us all the blessings of equal liberty, or all the woes of slavery and continued social degradation, you will not blame us if we manifest anxiety in regard to the position of our recognized friends, as well as that of our open and declared enemies; for our cause may suffer even more from the injudicious concessions and weakness of our friends, than from the machinations and power of our enemies. The weakness of our friends is strength to our foes. When the "Anti-slavery Standard," representing the American Anti-slavery Society, denies that that society asks for the enfranchisement of colored men, and the "Liberator" apologizes for excluding the colored men of Louisiana from the ballot-box, they injure us more vitally than all the ribald jests of the whole proslavery press.

Again: had, for instance, the present Administration, at the beginning of the war, boldly planted itself upon the doctrine of human equality as taught in the Declaration of Independence; proclaimed liberty to all the slaves in all the Slave States; armed every colored man, previously a slave or a freeman, who would or could fight under the loyal flag; recognized black men as soldiers of the Republic; avenged the first act of violence upon colored prisoners, in contravention of the laws of war; sided with the radical emancipation party in Maryland and Missouri; stood by its antislavery generals, instead of casting them aside,—history would never have had to record the scandalous platform adopted at Chicago, nor the immeasurable horrors of Fort Pillow. The weakness and hesitation of our friends, where promptness and vigor were required, have invited the contempt and rigor of our enemies. Seeing that, while perilling every thing for the protection and security of our country, our country did not think itself bound to protect and secure us, the rebels felt a license to treat us as outlaws. Seeing that our Government did not treat us as men, they did not feel bound to treat us as soldiers. It is, therefore, not the malignity of enemies alone we have to fear, but the deflection from the straight line of principle by those who are known throughout the world as our special friends. We may survive the arrows of the known negro-haters of our country; but woe to the colored race when their champions fail to demand, from any reason, equal liberty in every respect!

We have spoken of the existence of powerful re-actionary forces arrayed against us, and of the objects to which they tend. What are these mighty forces? and through what agencies do they operate and reach us? They are many; but we shall detain by no tedious enumeration. The first and most powerful is slavery; and the second, which may be said to be the shadow of slavery, is prejudice against men on account of their color. The one controls the South, and the other controls the North. Both are original sources of power, and generate peculiar sentiments, ideas, and laws concerning us. The agents of these two evil influences are various: but the chief are, first, the Democratic party; and, second, the Republican party. The Democratic party belongs to slavery; and the Republican party is largely under the power of prejudice against color. While gratefully recognizing a vast difference in our favor in the character and composition of the Republican party, and regarding the accession to power of the Democratic party as the heaviest calamity that could befall us in the present juncture of affairs, it cannot be disguised, that, while that party is our bitterest enemy, and is positively and actively re-actionary, the Republican party is negatively and passively so in its tendency. What we have to fear from these two parties,—looking to the future, and especially to the settlement of our present national troubles,—is, alas! only too obvious. The intentions, principles, and policy of both organizations, through their platforms, and the antecedents and the recorded utterances of the men who stand upon their respective platforms, teach us what to expect at their hands, and what kind of a future they are carving out for us, and for the country which they propose to govern. Without using the word "*slavery*," or "*slaves*," or "*slaveholders*," the Democratic party has none the less declared, in its platform, its purpose to be the endless perpetuation of slavery. Under the apparently harmless verbiage, "*private rights*," "*basis of the Federal Union*," and under the language employed in denouncing the Federal Administration for "*disregarding the Constitution in every part*," "*pretence of military necessity*," we see the purpose of the Democratic party to restore slavery to all its ancient power, and to make this Government just what it was before the rebellion,—simply an instrument of the slave-power. "The basis of the Federal Union" only means the alleged compromises and stipulations, as interpreted by Judge Taney, by which black men are supposed to have no rights which white men are bound to respect; and by which the whole Northern people are bound to protect the cruel masters against the justly deserved violence of the slave, and to do the fiendish work of hell-hounds when slaves make their escape from thraldom. The candidates of that party take their stand upon its platform; and will, if elected,—which Heaven forbid!—carry it out to the letter. From this party we must look only for fierce, malignant, and unmitigated hostility. Our continued oppression and degradation is the law of its life, and its sure passport to power. In the ranks of the Democratic party, all the worst elements of American society fraternize; and we need not expect a single voice from that quarter for justice, mercy, or even decency. To it we are nothing; the slave-holders every thing. We have but to consult its press to know that it would willingly enslave the free colored people in the South; and also that it would gladly stir up against us mob-violence at the North,—re-enacting the sanguinary scenes of one year ago in New York and other large cities. We therefore pray, that whatever wrath, curse, or calamity, the future may have in store for us, the accession of the Democratic party to the reins of power may not be one of them; for this to us would comprise the sum of all social woes.

How stands the case with the great Republican party in question? We have already alluded to it as being largely under the influence of the prevailing contempt for the character and rights of the colored race. This is seen by the slowness of our Government to employ the strong arm of the black man in the work of putting down the rebellion: and in its unwillingness, after thus employing him, to invest him with the same incitements to deeds of daring, as white soldiers; neither giving him the same pay, rations, and protection, nor any hope of rising in the service by meritorious conduct. It is also seen in the fact, that in neither of the plans emanating from this party for reconstructing the institutions of the Southern States, are colored men, not even those who had *fought* for the country, recognized as having any political existence or rights whatever.

Even in the matter of the abolition of slavery,—to which, by its platform, the Republican party is strongly committed, as well by President Lincoln's celebrated Proclamation of the first of January, 1863, and by his recent letter "To whom it may concern,"—there is still room for painful doubt and apprehension. It is very evident, that the Republican party, though a party composed of the best men of the country, is not prepared to make the abolition of slavery, in all the Rebel States, a consideration precedent to the re-establishment of the Union. However antislavery in sentiment the President may be, and however disposed he may be to continue the war till slavery is abolished, it is plain that in this he would not be sustained by his party. A single reverse to our arms, in such a war, would raise the hands of the party in opposition to their chief. The hope of the speedy and complete abolition of slavery, hangs, therefore, not upon the disposition of the Republican party, not upon the disposition of President Lincoln; but upon the slender thread of Rebel power, pride, and persistence. In returning to the Union, slavery has a fair chance to live; out of the Union, it has a still better chance to live: but, fighting against the Union, it has no chance for any thing but destruction. Thus the freedom of our race and the welfare of our country tremble together in the balance of events.

This somewhat gloomy view of the condition of affairs—which to the enthusiastic, who have already convinced themselves that slavery is dead, may not only seem gloomy, but untruthful—is nevertheless amply supported, not only by the well-known sentiment of the country, the controlling pressure of which is seriously felt by the Administration; but it is sustained by the many attempts lately made by the Republican press to explain away the natural import of the President's recent address "To whom it may concern," in which he makes the abolition of Slavery a primary condition to the restoration of the Union; and especially is this gloomy view supported by the remarkable speech delivered only a few weeks ago at Auburn, by Hon. William H. Seward, Secretary of State. Standing next to the President in the administration of the government, and fully in the confidence of the Chief Magistrate, no member of the National Cabinet is better qualified than Mr. Seward to utter the mind and policy of the Administration upon this momentous subject, when it shall come up at the close of the war. Just what it will do in the matter of slavery, Mr. Seward says,—

"When the insurgents shall have disbanded their armies, and laid down their arms, the war will instantly cease; and all the war measures then existing, including those which affect slavery, will cease also; and all the moral, economical, and political questions, as well affecting slavery as others, which shall then be existing between individuals and States and the Federal Government, whether they arose before the civil war began, or whether they grew out of it, will, by force of the Constitution, pass over to the arbitrament of courts of law, and the counsels of legislation."

These, fellow-citizens, are studied words, full of solemn and fearful import. They mean that our Republican Administration is not only ready to make peace with the Rebels, but to make peace with slavery also; that all executive and legislative action launched against the slave-system, whether of proclamation or confiscation, will cease the instant the Rebels shall disband their armies; and lay down their arms. The hope that the war will put an end to slavery, has, according to this exposition, only one foundation; and that is, that the courts and Congress will so decree. But what ground have we here? Congress has already spoken, and has refused to alter the Constitution so as to abolish Slavery. The Supreme Court has yet to speak; but what it will say, if this question shall come before it, is very easily divined. We will not assert positively what it will say; but indications of its judgment are clearly against us. What then have we? Only this, as our surest and best ground of hope; namely, that the Rebels, in their madness, will continue to make war upon the Government, until they shall not only become destitute of men, money, and the munitions of war, but utterly divested of their slaves also.

But, fellow-citizens, the object of this Address is not merely to state facts, and point out sources of danger. We would distinctly place our whole cause before you, and earnestly appeal to you to make that cause practically your cause; as we believe it is the cause of justice and of our whole country. We come before you altogether in new relations. Hitherto we have addressed you in the generic character of a common humanity; only as men: but to-day, owing to the events of the last three years, we bring with us an additional claim to consideration. By the qualities displayed, by the hardships endured, and by the services rendered the country, during these years of war and peril, we can now speak with the confidence of men who have deserved well of their country. While conscious of your power and of our comparative weakness, we may still claim for our race those rights which are not less ours by our services to the country than by the laws of human nature. All, therefore, that justice can demand, and honor grant, we can now ask, without presumption and without arrogance, of the American people.

Do you, then, ask us to state, in plain terms, just what we

want of you, and just what we think we ought to receive at your hands? We answer: First of all, the complete abolition of the slavery of our race in the United States. We shall not stop to argue. We feel the terrible sting of this stupendous wrong, and that we cannot be free while our brothers are slaves. The enslavement of a vast majority of our people extends its baleful influence over every member of our race; and makes freedom, even to the free, a mockery and a delusion: we therefore, in our own name, and in the name of the whipped and branded millions, whose silent suffering has pleaded to the humane sentiment of mankind, but in vain, during more than two hundred years for deliverance, we implore you to abolish slavery. In the name of your country, torn, distracted, bleeding, and while you are weeping over the bloody graves of more than two hundred thousand of your noblest sons, many of whom have been cut down, in the midst of youthful vigor and beauty, we implore you to abolish slavery. In the name of peace, which experience has shown cannot be other than false and delusive while the rebellious spirit of Slavery has an existence in the land, we implore you to abolish slavery. In the name of universal justice, to whose laws great States not less than individuals are bound to conform, and the terrible consequences of whose violation are as fixed and certain as the universe itself, we implore you to abolish slavery; and thus place your peace and national welfare upon immutable and everlasting foundations.

Why would you let slavery continue? What good thing has it done, what evil thing has it left undone, that you should allow it to survive this dreadful war, the natural fruit of its existence? Can you want a second war from the same cause? Are you so rich in men, money, and material, that you must provide for future depletion? Or do you hope to escape the consequences of wrong-doing? Can you expect any better results from compromises in the future, than from compromises with slavery in the past? If the South fights desperately and savagely to-day for the possession of four millions of slaves, will she fight less savagely and desperately when the prize for which she fights shall become eight instead of four millions? and when her ability to war upon freedom and free institutions shall have increased twofold?

Do you answer, that you have no longer any thing to fear? that slavery has already received its death-blow? that it can only have a transient existence, even if permitted to live after the termination of the war? We answer, So thought your Revolutionary fathers when they framed the Federal Constitution; and to-day, the bloody fruits of their mistake are all around us. Shall we avoid or shall we repeat their stupendous error? Be not deceived. Slavery is still the vital and animating breath of Southern society. The men who have fought for it on the battle-field will not love it less for having shed their blood in its defence. Once let them get Slavery safely under the protection of the Federal Government, and ally themselves, as they will be sure to do, to the Democratic party of the North; let Jefferson Davis and his Confederate associates, either in person or by their representatives, return once more to their seats in the halls of Congress,—and you will then see your dead slavery the most living and powerful thing in the country. To make peace, therefore, on such a basis as shall admit slavery back again into the Union, would only be sowing the seeds of war; sure to bring at last a bitter harvest of blood! The sun in the heavens at noonday is not more manifest, than the fact that slavery is the prolific source of war and division among you; and that its abolition is essential to your national peace and unity. Once more, then, we entreat you—for you have the power—to put away this monstrous abomination. You have repeatedly during this wanton slaveholding and wicked Rebellion, in the darkest hours of the struggle, appealed to the Supreme Ruler of the universe to smile upon your armies, and give them victory: surely you will not now stain your souls with the crime of ingratitude by making a wicked compact and a deceitful peace with your enemies. You have called mankind to witness that the struggle on your part was not for empire merely; that the charge that it was such was a gross slander: will you now make a peace which will justify what you have repeatedly denounced as a calumny? Your antislavery professions have drawn to you the sympathy of liberal and generous minded men throughout the world, and have restrained all Europe from recognizing the Southern Confederacy, and breaking up your blockade of Southern ports. Will you now proclaim your own baseness and hypocrisy by making a peace which shall give the lie to all such professions? You have over and over again, and very justly, branded slavery as the inciting cause of this Rebellion; denounced it as the fruitful source of pride and selfishness and mad ambition; you have blushed before all Europe for its existence among you; and have shielded yourselves from the execrations of mankind, by denying your constitutional ability to interfere with it. Will you now, when the evil in question has placed itself within your constitutional grasp, and invited its own destruction by its persistent attempts to destroy the Government, relax your grasp, release your hold, and to the disappointment of the slaves deceived by your proclamations, to the sacrifice of the Union white men of the South who have sided with you in this contest with slavery, and to the dishonor of yourselves and the amazement of mankind, give new and stronger lease of life to slavery? We will not and cannot believe it.

There is still one other subject, fellow-citizens,—one other want,—looking to the peace and welfare of our common country, as well as to the interests of our race; and that is, political equality. We want the elective franchise in all the States now in the Union, and the same in all such States as may come into the Union hereafter. We believe that the highest welfare of this great country will be found in erasing from its statute-books all enactments discriminating in favor or against any class of its people, and by establishing one law for the white and colored people alike. Whatever prejudice and taste may be innocently allowed to do or to dictate in social and domestic relations, it is plain, that in the matter of government, the object of which is the protection and security of human rights, prejudice should be allowed no voice whatever. In this department of human relations, no notice should be taken of the color of men; but justice, wisdom, and humanity should weigh alone, and be all-controlling.

Formerly our petitions for the elective franchise were met and denied upon the ground, that, while colored men were protected in person and property, they were not required to perform military duty. Of course this was only a plausible excuse; for we were subject to any call the Government was pleased to make upon us, and we could not properly be made to suffer because the Government did not see fit to impose military duty upon us. The fault was with the Government, not with us.

But now even this frivolous though somewhat decent apology for excluding us from the ballot-box is entirely swept away. Two hundred thousand colored men, according to a recent statement of President Lincoln, are now in the service, upon field and flood, in the army and the navy of the United States; and every day adds to their number. They are there as volunteers, coming forward with other patriotic men at the call of their imperilled country; they are there also as substitutes filling up the quotas which would otherwise have to be filled up by white men who now remain at home; they are also there as drafted men, by a certain law of Congress, which, for once, makes no difference on account of color: and whether they are there as volunteers, as substitutes, or as drafted men, neither ourselves, our cause, nor our country, need be ashamed of their appearance or their action upon the battle-field. Friends and enemies, rebels and loyal men,—each, after their kind,—have borne conscious and unconscious testimony to the gallantry and other noble qualities of the colored troops.

Your fathers laid down the principle, long ago, that universal suffrage is the best foundation of Government. We believe as your fathers believed, and as they practised; for, in eleven States out of the original thirteen, colored men exercised the right to vote at the time of the adoption of the Federal Constitution. The Divine-right Governments of Europe, with their aristocratic and privileged classes of *priests* and *nobles*, are little better than cunningly devised conspiracies against the natural rights of the people to govern themselves.

Whether the right to vote is a natural right or not, we are not here to determine. Natural or conventional, in either case we are amply supported in our appeal for its extension to us. If it is, as all the teachings of your Declaration of Independence imply, a *natural right*, to deny to us its exercise is a wrong done to our human nature. If, on the other hand, the right to vote is simply a conventional right, having no other foundation or significance than a mere conventional arrangement, which may be extended or contracted, given or taken away, upon reasonable grounds, we insist, that, even basing the right upon this uncertain foundation, we may reasonably claim a right to a voice in the election of the men who are to have at their command our time, our services, our property, our persons, and our lives. This command of our persons and lives is no longer theory, but now the positive practice of our Government. We say, therefore, that having required, demanded, and in some instances compelled, us to serve with our time, our property, and our lives, coupling us in all the obligations and duties imposed upon the more highly favored of our fellow-citizens in this war to protect and defend your country from threatened destruction, and having fully established the precedent by which, in all similar and dissimilar cases of need, we may be compelled to respond to a like requisition,—we claim to have fully earned the elective franchise; and that you, the American people, have virtually contracted an obligation to grant it, which has all the sanctions of justice, honor, and magnanimity, in favor of its prompt fulfilment. Are we good enough to use bullets, and not good enough to use ballots? May we defend rights in time of war, and yet be denied the exercise of those rights in time of peace? Are we citizens when the nation is in peril, and aliens when the nation is in safety? May we shed our blood under the star-spangled banner on the battle-field, and yet be debarred from marching under it to the ballot-box? Will the brave white soldiers, bronzed by the hardships and exposures of repeated campaigns, men who have fought by the side of black men, be ashamed to cast their ballots by the side of their companions-in-arms? May we give our lives, but not our votes, for the good of the republic? Shall we toil with you to win the prize of free government, while you alone shall monopolize all its valued privileges? Against such a conclusion, every sentiment of honor and manly fraternity utters an indignant protest.

It is quite true, that some part of the American people may, with a show of plausibility, evade the force of this appeal and deny this claim. There are men in all countries who can evade any duty or obligation which is not enforced by the strong arm of the law. Our country is no exception to the rule. They can say in this case, "Colored men, we have done you no wrong. We have purchased nothing at your hands, and owe you nothing. From first to last, we have objected to the measure of employing you to help put down this rebellion; foreseeing the very claim you now set up. Were we to-day invested with the power and authority of this Government, we would instantly disband every colored regiment now in front of Richmond, and everywhere else in the Southern States. We do not believe in making soldiers of black men." To all that, we reply, There need be no doubt whatever. No doubt they would disband the black troops if they had the power; and equally plain is it that they would disband the white troops also if they had the power.

They do not believe in making black men soldiers; but they equally do not believe in making white men soldiers to fight slaveholding rebels. But we do not address ourselves here to particular parties and classes of our country-men: we would appeal directly to the moral sense, honor, and magnanimity of the whole nation; and, with a cause so good, cannot believe that we shall appeal in vain. Parties and classes rise and fall, combine and dissolve: but the national conscience remains forever; and it is that to which our cause is addressed. It may, however, be said that the colored people enlisted in the service of the country without any promise or stipulation that they would be rewarded with political equality at the end of the war; but all the more, on this very account, do we hold the American people bound in honor thus to reward them. By the measure of confidence reposed in the national honor and generosity, we have the right to measure the obligation of fulfilment. The fact, that, when called into the service of the country, we went forward without exacting terms or conditions, to the mind of the generous man enhances our claims.

But, again, why are we so urgent for the possession of this particular right? We are asked, even by some Abolitionists, why we cannot be satisfied, for the present at least, with personal freedom; the right to testify in courts of law; the right to own, buy, and sell real estate; the right to sue and be sued. We answer, Because in a republican country, where general suffrage is the rule, personal liberty, the right to testify in courts of law, the right to hold, buy, and sell property, and all other rights, become mere privileges, held at the option of others, where we are excepted from the general political liberty. What gives to the newly arrived emigrants, fresh from lands governed by kingcraft and priestcraft, special consequence in the eyes of the American people? It is not their virtue, for they are often depraved; it is not their knowledge, for they are often ignorant; it is not their wealth, for they are often very poor: why, then, are they courted by the leaders of all parties? The answer is, that our institutions clothe them with the elective franchise, and they have a voice in making the laws of the country. Give the colored men of this country the elective franchise, and you will see no violent mobs driving the black laborer from the wharves of large cities, and from the toil elsewhere by which he honestly gains his bread. You will see no influential priest, like the late Bishop Hughes, addressing mobocrats and murderers as "gentlemen;" and no influential politician, like Governor Seymour, addressing the "misguided" rowdies of New York as his "friends." The possession of that right is the keystone to the arch of human liberty: and, without that, the whole may at any moment fall to the ground; while, with it, that liberty may stand forever,—a blessing to us, and no possible injury to you. If you still ask why we want to vote, we answer, Because we don't want to be mobbed from our work, or insulted with impunity at every corner. We are men, and want to be as free in our native country as other men.

Fellow-citizens, let us entreat you, have faith in your own principles. If freedom is good for any, it is good for all. If you need the elective franchise, we need it even more. You are strong, we are weak; you are many, we are few; you are protected, we are exposed. Clothe us with this safeguard of our liberty, and give us an interest in the country to which, in common with you, we have given our lives and poured out our best blood. You cannot need special protection. Our degradation is not essential to your elevation, nor our peril essential to your safety. You are not likely to be outstripped in the race of improvement by persons of African descent; and hence you have no need of superior advantages, nor to burden them with disabilities of any kind. Let your Government be what all governments should be,—a copy of the eternal laws of the universe; before which all men stand equal as to rewards and punishments, life and death, without regard to country, kindred, tongue, or people.

But what we have now said, in appeal for the elective franchise, applies to our people generally. A special reason may be urged in favor of granting colored men the right in all the rebellious States.

Whatever may be the case with monarchical governments;

however they may despise the crowd, and rely upon their *prestige*, armaments, and standing armies, to support them,—a republican government like ours depends largely upon the friendship of the people over whom it is established, for its harmonious and happy operation. This kind of government must have its foundation in the affections of the people: otherwise the people will hinder, circumvent, and destroy it. Up to a few years of the rebellion, our government lived in the friendship of the masses of the Southern people. Its enemies were, however, numerous and active; and these at last prevailed, poisoned the minds of the masses, broke up the government, brought on the war. Now, whoever lives to see this rebellion suppressed at the South, as we believe we all shall, will also see the South characterized by a sullen hatred towards the National Government. It will be transmitted from father to son, and will be held by them "as sacred animosity." The treason, mowed down by the armies of Grant and Sherman, will be followed by a strong undergrowth of treason which will go far to disturb the peaceful operation of the hated Government.

Every United-States mail-carrier, every custom-house officer, every Northern man, and every representive of the United-States Government, in the Southern States, will be held in abhorrence; and for a long time that country is to be governed with difficulty. We may conquer Southern armies by the sword; but it is another thing to conquer Southern hate. Now what is the natural counterpoise against this Southern malign hostility? This it is: give the elective franchise to every colored man of the South who is of sane mind, and has arrived at the age of twenty-one years, and you have at once four millions of friends who will guard with their vigilance, and, if need be, defend with their arms, the ark of Federal Liberty from the treason and pollution of her enemies. You are sure of the enmity of the masters,—make sure of the friendship of the slaves; for, depend upon it, your Government cannot afford to encounter the enmity of both.

If the arguments addressed to your sense of honor, in these pages, in favor of extending the elective franchise to the colored people of the whole country, be strong, that which we are prepared to present to you in behalf of the colored people of rebellious States can be made tenfold stronger. By calling them to take part with you in the war to subdue their rebellious masters, and the fact that thousands of them have done so, and thousands more would gladly do so, you have exposed them to special resentment and wrath; which, without the elective franchise, will descend upon them in unmitigated fury. To break with your friends, and make peace with your enemies; to weaken your friends, and strengthen your enemies; to abase your friends, and exalt your enemies; to disarm your friends, and arm your enemies; to disfranchise your loyal friends, and enfranchise your disloyal enemies,—is not the policy of honor, but of infamy.

But we will not weary you. Our cause is in some measure before you. The power to redress our wrongs, and to grant us our just rights, is in your hands. You can determine our destiny,—blast us by continued degradation, or bless us with the means of gradual elevation. We are among you, and must remain among you; and it is for you to say, whether our presence shall conduce to the general peace and welfare of the country, or be a constant cause of discussion and of irritation,—troubles in the State, troubles in the Church, troubles everywhere.

To avert these troubles, and to place your great country in safety from them, only one word from you, the American people, is needed, and that is JUSTICE: let that magic word once be sounded, and become all-controlling in all your courts of law, subordinate and supreme; let the halls of legislation, state and national, spurn all statesmanship as mischievous and ruinous that has not justice for its foundation; let justice without compromise, without curtailment, and without partiality, be observed with respect to all men, no class of men claiming for themselves any right which they will not grant to another,—then strife and discord will cease; peace will be placed upon enduring foundations; and the American people, now divided and hostile, will dwell together in power and unity.

"MAKE GEORGIA HOWL": GEORGIA, OCTOBER 1864

William T. Sherman to Ulysses S. Grant

During his visit to Georgia, Jefferson Davis had approved Hood's plan to force Sherman to retreat from Atlanta by cutting his railroad supply line. Hood crossed the Chattahoochee River southwest of Atlanta, September 28–29, and began advancing toward the Chattanooga–Atlanta railroad. Leaving one corps to guard the city, Sherman set off in pursuit of Hood with the remainder of his troops on October 3. After destroying eight miles of track between Big Shanty and Acworth, Confederate forces were repulsed when they tried to capture the Union supply depot at Allatoona on October 5. When Sherman telegraphed Grant from Allatoona on October 9, Hood was twenty miles to the southwest preparing to advance on Resaca. Sherman previously proposed a march on Savannah in a telegram sent to Grant on October 1.

Allatoona 7.30 P.M.
Oct. 9th 1864

Lt. Gen. Grant
City Point

It will be a physical impossibility to protect this road now that Hood, Forrest, Wheeler and the whole batch of Devils are turned loose without home or habitation. I think Hoods movements indicate a direction to the end of the Selma and Talladega road to Blue Mountain about sixty miles south west of Rome from which he will threaten Kingston, Bridgeport and Decatur and I propose we break up the road from Chattanooga and strike out with wagons for Milledgeville Millen and Savannah.

Until we can repopulate Georgia it is useless to occupy it, but the utter destruction of its roads, houses, and people will cripple their military resources. By attempting to hold the roads we will lose a thousand men monthly and will gain no result. I can make the march and make Georgia howl. We have over 8000 cattle and 3,000,000 pounds of bread but no corn, but we can forage in the interior of the state.

W. T. Sherman
M. Genl.

Stephen Dodson Ramseur to Ellen Richmond Ramseur

Following his victory at Winchester, Sheridan pursued Early's retreating army and defeated it at Fisher's Hill near Strasburg on September 22. Sheridan then advanced as far south as Staunton before withdrawing to the north. As they fell back, Union troops carried out Grant's instructions to turn the Shenandoah Valley into "a barren waste." An 1860 graduate of West Point, Major General Stephen Dodson Ramseur led a division in Early's army at the age of twenty-seven. He wrote to his wife nine days before he was fatally wounded during the Confederate defeat at Cedar Creek on October 19.

Camp near New Market Va.
Oct. 10th 1864

My Own Darling Wife

Yesterday my Courier handed me a letter from Mr. S, one from Charley and *three* from your dear Self. Yours were dated respectively 23rd 26th Sept. and 30th ditto.

Do you know how much better I feel after getting these letters from you. I have been questioning Mr. Harding too, and he tells me you are perfectly well and "sweet accordin." Oh me! how I want to be with you. Every day I think more and more about you. I cant help feeling the most intense anxiety and solicitude on your behalf. Since our disasters over here in the Valley, my prospects for a furlough are greatly diminished. I think my duty is plain. I ought not to leave *now* even if I could do so.

So my Beloved Darling you must be brave and cheerful without me for a while, a short while I hope. I do earnestly pray that your life may not be endangered. That you may be soon restored to health. And that both of our hearts may be gladdened and our natures improved by the issue of your confinement. Oh! My beautiful Darling Wife! I can not begin to write what I feel now that you need so much my presence and sympathy. I do so long to be with you! 'Tis the greatest trial of my life to be separated from you *now*! But these trials do us good, even as gold is refined by the fire. When in God's good Providence we are permitted again to meet and live together in Peace, we can look back to these dark days as the time when we were tried and not found wanting. I hope and pray that we may be benefited spiritually as well as mentally by the trials to which we are now subjected.

Mr. S. writes me that all are well at home, that Father tho' much discouraged by the late disasters to our army, is still hopeful as to the final result. I agree with you in your remarks about the Croakers. I must confess, I would be willing to take a musket and fight to the bitter end, rather than submit to these miserable Yankees. I think they have placed themselves outside of the pale of civilization by the course they have pursued in this Campaign. This beautiful and fertile Valley has been totally destroyed. Sheridan has had *some* houses, *all* the mills & barns, every straw & wheat stack burned. This Valley is one great desert. I do not see how these poor people are to live. We have to haul our supplies from away up the Valley. It is rumoured that the Yankees are rebuilding the Manassa Gap Rail Road. If this is so, Sheridan will not give up his hold upon the Valley and we will probably remain here for the Winter, unless Gen'l. Lee becomes so hard pressed that we will have to go to him. It is (or rather was, before our disasters) more pleasant campaigning in the Valley than in those terrible trenches before Richmond.

My hope now is from Hood. I do hope he may be enabled to overwhelm Sherman and send reinforcements to our great Gen'l. Lee. When Providence smiled on us here, one always had bad news from the West. May we not hope now for cheer and support from that Quarter?

The last private advices I had from Georgia were very encouraging. Time is an important element. I believe Hood will whip Sherman. I hope he'll do it quickly.

I rec'd. a long, kind letter from Col. Frank Huger a few days ago. He is full of hope and sprightliness. Says his sister Mrs. Preston has the finest boy (so she says) in the Confederacy. May be we will have something to say about that some of these days. Nous verrons!

I have not been writing to you so often recently My Darling Wife, because I have been either so constantly occupied or (I must acknowledge it) so much mortified at the recent disasters to our Army of the Valley that I could not write with any pleasure. There is something now to write about. Dr. David has just come in & sends love to you. He is very well and is doing well. Caleb sends love & will write soon. Mr. H was with me sometime today. He is very homesick, talks about his babies all the time. Do give my love to all! Write as often as you can. Telegraph anything that happens to you. If you need me I'll try to get home. Telegraph to Maj Gen'l. R. army of the Valley. Near Harrisonburg. Give my very best love to dear Mama. I know she will take the very best care of you. Accept my heart full of love my Beloved Wife. God bless you and keep you and may He in Mercy speedily grant us peace. Yr devoted Husband

DESERTION AND "DESPOTISM": VIRGINIA, OCTOBER 1864

John B. Jones: Diary, October 10–13, 1864

On September 29, Union troops attacked north of the James River and succeeded in capturing New Market Heights and Fort Harrison but were unable to break through the inner defensive line protecting Richmond. The next day a Confederate attempt to retake the fort was repulsed. With Confederate reserves committed north of the James, Grant again attacked south of Petersburg with the goal of cutting the Southside Railroad. In three days of fighting around Peebles Farm, September 30–October 2, Union forces failed to reach the railroad but were able to extend their trench line closer to the Boydton Plank Road, which was used to supply Petersburg by wagon train. On October 7 a Confederate attempt to turn the Union right flank north of the James was defeated in fighting along the Darbytown and New Market roads. The three engagements cost the Union about 6,700 men killed, wounded, or missing, and the Confederates about 4,300. During the battle for Fort Harrison, John B. Jones had watched white smoke from artillery fire "floating along the horizon over the woods and down the river" from the Confederate War Department, where he worked as a clerk. He wrote about the measures taken to reinforce the ranks of Richmond's defenders.

OCTOBER 10TH.—*A white frost*; first frost of the season. All quiet below.

Gen. W. M. Gardner (in Gen. Winder's place) reports that of the exempts and citizens taken from the streets to the front, last week, *a majority have deserted* This proves that even a despotic military act cannot be committed with impunity.

Gen. Beauregard telegraphs from Opeleka, Ala., that he has arranged matters satisfactorily between Gov. Brown of Georgia and Gen. Cobb, regarding exempts and State militia.

The President directs the Secretary to ascertain if this has been done in accordance with law and the interests of the service.

Gen. R. Taylor telegraphs that Gen. E. K. Smith has proclaimed pardon to deserters, from trans-Mississippi Department, after he had arrested most of them and sent them to their regiments, and now he recommends that no more troops be brought over the river or they will be sure to desert. The President directs the Secretary to correspond with Gen. Smith on the subject. Gen. Taylor is the President's kinsman—by his first marriage.

Gen. Beauregard left Opeleka on the 7th inst. for Hood's army, so in a few days we may expect a battle.

OCTOBER 11TH.—Bright and pleasant. All is quiet below.

From Georgia we have many rumors. It is reported that a battle has been fought (second time) at Altoona, which we captured, with 4000 prisoners; that Rome has been taken, with 3000 negro prisoners; and, finally, that we have Atlanta again. I have seen no such dispatches. But the gentleman who assured me it was all true, has a son a clerk at the President's office, and a relative in the telegraph office. Dispatches may have come to the President; and, if so, it may be our policy to forbid their publication for the present, as the enemy would derive the first intelligence of their disaster from our newspapers.

Well, Gen. Gardner reports, officially, that of the number of exempts, and of the mixed class of citizens arrested in the streets, and summarily marched to the "front," "a majority have deserted!" Men, with exemptions in their pockets, going to or returning from market, have been seized by the Adjutant-General's orders, and despotically hurried off without being permitted even to send a message to their families. Thousands were entrapped, by being directed to call at Gen. Barton's headquarters, an immense warehouse, and receive passes; but no Gen. Barton was there—or if there, not visible; and all the anxious seekers found themselves in prison, only to be liberated as they were incorporated into companies, and marched "to the front." From the age of fifteen to fifty-five, all were seized by that order—no matter what papers they bore, or what the condition of their families—and hurried to the field, where there was no battle. No wonder there are many deserters—no wonder men become indifferent as to which side shall prevail, nor that the administration is falling into disrepute at the capital.

OCTOBER 12TH.—Bright and beautiful. All quiet below, save an occasional booming from the fleet.

Nothing from Georgia in the papers, save the conjectures of the Northern press. No doubt we have gained advantages there, which it is good policy to conceal as long as possible from the enemy.

Squads of able-bodied *detailed* men are arriving *at last*, from the interior. Lee's army, in this way, will get efficient reinforcements.

The Secretary of the Treasury sends a note over to the Secretary of War to-day, saying the Commissary-General, in his estimates, allows but $31,000,000 for tax in kind—whereas the tax collectors show an actual amount, credited to farmers and planters, of $145,000,000. He says this will no doubt attract the notice of Congress.

Mr. Peck, our agent to purchase supplies in North Carolina, has delivered no wheat yet. He bought supplies for his family; 400 bushels of wheat for 200 clerks, and 100 for Assistant Secretary of War, Judge Campbell, and Mr. Kean, the young Chief of the Bureau. This he says he bought with private funds; but he brought it at the government's expense. The clerks are resolved not to submit to his action.

I hear of more desertions. Mr. Seddon and Mr. Stanton at Washington are engaged in a singular game of chance. The harsh orders of both cause mutual abandonments, and now we have the spectacle of men deserting our regiments, and quite as many coming over from the enemy's regiments near the city.

Meantime Gen. Bragg is striving to get the able-bodied men out of the bureaus and to place them in the field.

The despotic order, arresting every man in the streets, and hurrying them to "the front," without delay, and regardless of the condition of their families—some were taken off when getting medicine for their sick wives—is still the theme of execration, even among men who have been the most ultra and uncompromising secessionists. The terror caused many to hide themselves, and doubtless turned them against the government. They say now such a despotism is quite as bad as a Stanton despotism, and there is not a toss-up between the rule of the United States and the Confederate States. Such are some of the effects of bad measures in such critical times as these. Mr. Seddon has no physique to sustain him. He has intellect, and has read much; but, nevertheless, such great men are sometimes more likely to imitate some predecessor at a critical moment, or to adopt some bold yet inefficient suggestion from another, than to originate an adequate one themselves. He is a scholar, an invalid, refined and philosophical—but effeminate.

OCTOBER 13TH.—Rained all night; clear and cool this morning.

The government publishes nothing from Georgia yet; but it is supposed there is intelligence of an important character in the city, which it would be impolitic to communicate to the enemy.

All still remains quiet below the city. But the curtain is expected to rise on the next act of the tragedy every moment. Gen. Grant probably furloughed many of his men to vote in Pennsylvania and Ohio, on Tuesday last—elections preliminary to the Presidential election—and they have had time to return to their regiments.

If this pause should continue a week or two longer, Gen. Lee would be much strengthened. Every day the farmers, whose details have been revoked, are coming in from the counties; and many of these were in the war in '61 and '62—being experienced veterans. Whereas Grant's recruits, though greater in number, are raw and unskilled.

The Medical Boards have been instructed to put in all men that come before them, capable of bearing arms *ten days*. One died in the trenches, on the eleventh day, of consumption!

There is a rumor of a fight on our extreme left. It is said Field's division (C. S.) repulsed three assaults of the enemy. If the battle be still continued (4 P.M.—the wind from the west prevents us from hearing guns), no doubt it is the beginning of a general engagement—decisive, perhaps, of the fate of Richmond.

We have many accounts of evasions of military service, occasioned by the alleged bad faith of the government, and the despotic orders from the Adjutant-General's office.

And yet Gov. Smith's certificates for exemption of rich young Justices of the Peace, Commissioners of the (county) Revenue, Deputy Sheriffs, clerks, constables, officers and clerks of banks, still come in daily; and they are "allowed" by the Assistant Secretary of War. Will the poor and friendless fight their battles, and win their independence for them? It may be so; but let not rulers in future wars follow the example! Nothing but the conviction that they are fighting for their families, their sacred altars, and their little property induces thousands of brave Southerners to remain in arms against such fearful odds as are now arrayed against them.

Mr. Kean, the young Chief of the Bureau of War, has come in from "the front," with a boil on his thigh. He missed the sport of the battle to-day.

Mr. Peck, the agent to purchase supplies for his starving fellow-clerks, confesses that he bought 10 barrels of flour and 400 pounds of bacon for himself; 4 barrels of flour for Judge Campbell, Assistant Secretary of War; 4 barrels for Mr. Kean, 1 for Mr. Cohen, and 1 for Mr. Shepherd. This has produced great indignation among the 200 clerks who sent him, and who got but 73½ pounds each, and they got 13 pounds of bacon each; while Mr. P. bought for himself 400 pounds.

ENGLAND AND THE CIVIL WAR: DELAWARE, OCTOBER 1864

Samuel Francis Du Pont to William King Hall

A career naval officer, Samuel Francis Du Pont had commanded the South Atlantic Blockading Squadron at the capture of Port Royal Sound, South Carolina, in November 1861 and was promoted to rear admiral the following year. In April 1863 Du Pont led an unsuccessful attack on the fortifications guarding Charleston Harbor and was relieved of command of the South Atlantic squadron three months later. He wrote about the war to his friend Sir William King Hall, a captain in the Royal Navy he met while serving in China in 1858.

Near Wilmington, 13 Oct. 1864

My dear Hall,

I received a few days since your most kind letter of the 13th ultimo from Dover. You put coals of fire on my head by this second evidence of friendly remembrance, and the coals burned none the less that you had the delicacy not to allude to my delinquency.

Your letter after my return from the Southern coast was directed to Washington and was a long time reaching me. It found me much absorbed in my own affairs, and the reaction from two and a half years of intense war work, where the *pen* labor as you know is more than the sword, gave me a repugnance to taking up the former and threw me into procrastination, thus letting the accepted time go by. I sent you an especial message by Goodenough—it was a great pleasure to me to meet him; we talked over China affairs and you occupied a conspicuous place in our reminiscences.

Our friend Foote had scarcely passed away when his wife followed him; fortunately his children will be well cared for. He was a great loss to his country and to his profession. To myself he was a true friend to the last as you saw. For these reasons I greatly regretted him, but I had also an additional one, perhaps a selfish one. It would have been greatly to my professional interest had I been relieved in my command by him as first intended—things could not have gone differently at Charleston even with his skill, pluck, and prestige, and the question would have been more *quickly* settled with a small portion of our public and press. Time however has done this most effectually. I am proud to say the Navy never doubted. How could it? When did an admiral ever come out of an unsuccessful engagement with each and all of his commanding officers in *perfect accord* with *every* act from the beginning to end of the affair? These officers too had been selected with especial care for their professional cleverness, tried men under fire, and in all emergencies—yet differing much from each other. Never committed by me to any opinion, never consulted, and perfectly free to dissent and catch a popular breath. You saw a sample of them in Rodgers, and they were eleven in number—all have clung to me with hooks of steel. Unworthy ambition or an ugly temper among them might have entailed a controversy for life upon me, such as your service and ours have many examples. The controversy here has been kept up by ironmongers and their sympathizers, and I have not deigned to notice them. Strange as it may seem I have been simply the victim of *menials* in office, and I have been too proud to appeal to their superiors, who are too absorbed in this terrible rebellion to look themselves into individual cases. But, my dear Hall, I did not intend to go so much into my personal affairs, and you must ascribe my doing so to the kind remarks and inquiries in your two much prized letters.

You refer to our terrible civil war. I wish so much we could talk it over together—the subject is too vast to attempt even to allude to it in the brief space of a letter. We feel here how little the subject is understood in Europe, because our political institutions have never been comprehended there. One sentiment across the water seems quite pervasive and I perceive you share in it, viz., that we cannot be a united people again. Why should we be an exception to the world's history and to your own history in this respect? Is there bad blood between England and Scotland now? Is not Ireland united with you? How is it across the Channel? Has Louis Napoleon more devoted adherents than in Brittany? Your historians tell us there was a dead body or wounded man in every hamlet in La Vendée during the civil war in that desolated country—where the forests were burned in order to extinguish the last haunts of the opposition, smoked and burnt out, after the manner of Pélissier in Algeria.

All right-minded Christian men must be shocked at the atrocities of civil war—it entails countless woes, and its ramifications of evil are infinite—and ours is a gigantic one, having no parallel in history. But who made it and who fired the first gun? The patience and forbearance of the North only brought on arrogance and insult to add to the injury done—those silly duelists and bowie-knife knights thought the North would not fight. But what has caused me most surprise has been the course pursued by England in these our troubles. During previous years when slavery, the whole and sole cause of our rebellion, began to excite our land, England aided and abetted in every way the extremists in the North on this vexed question. Enthusiasts, including members of Parliament, traveled over the land exhorting and reproaching us for having an institution so repugnant to our political organization. Dukes and duchesses threw open their gilded mansions to the authoress of a clever antislavery novel—she was feted throughout the kingdom. Lord Brougham insulted our minister in London, Mr. Dallas, by the tone, manner, and occasion on which he called the latter's attention to the presence of a Negro admitted as a member of a society where the nobility and gentry of the land were assembled. In short all that brought upon us the taunts of England for the last quarter of a century were of Southern origin and growth—slavery, repudiation, filibustering, lynch law! What then was the surprise of the nation to find that England not only immediately recognized the Southern Confederacy as belligerents but gave her sympathy to their cause, backed by material aid. As if aware of the inconsistency involved, the British press represented that it was a tariff quarrel—it had nothing to do with slavery, etc. Why! Jefferson Davis has recently stated that they have lost two millions of the four millions of slaves, doubtless a great exaggeration to suit the purpose in hand. Still we have already 100,000 of them in the ranks of the Army, and as the latter march South those not "run off" are practically liberated, amounting now I should think to about one million. Be the process what it may, slavery was sure to fall with the first gun.

To the general *sore* produced by the withdrawal of all sympathy with the North have been added special acts calculated to irritate a nation—such as the destruction of our commerce by privateers, built, equipped, and manned in the United Kingdom; rejoicing at our defeats; making that poor creature Semmes a hero, and British naval officers of high rank and position getting up subscriptions to replace his sword. When Buchanan surrendered in the *Tennessee* after the most wonderful of naval combats and was lying wounded, he *sent* his sword to Farragut by his aide. All these matters to my deep regret have reopened the wounds of the wars of the Revolution and of 1812–15. These had become healed and forgotten, and replaced by most cordial sentiments of regard and admiration—even the Fourth of July orations were less and less vaunting on the olden times, and the country looked upon England as the great bulwark of liberty and Protestantism in the old world, as we hoped to be in the new.

The war has lasted longer than most persons believed. We have blundered dreadfully, as all free people and popular governments do at the first. The pervading radical error has been to permit the contest to become an equal one—this equilibrium has lasted now three and a half years but is fortunately disappearing; our superior numbers are telling everywhere as they should have done in the beginning. When those foolish Carolinians fired the first gun on Sumter, which sounded the death knell of slavery, the North rose *en masse* and we could have had a half million of men in a week as we had 75,000 in a day—and in that case the rebellion would have been crushed out in a year.

In June last we had raised 1,800,000 men (official records), for our people never flinched. In September 300,000 more were called for and are all enlisted at this date, volunteers mostly. These great masses have been better paid, fed, clothed, and armed, the wounded more cared for, and the system of sanitary appliances more complete than ever known before in the history of armies. Among the causes of delay in closing up this ugly work, I ought to have mentioned that when the rebellion broke out, it had four full months the start of us. The government was in the hands of Southern sympathizers, to use a mild expression. The Secretary of War, the Secretary of the Treasury, and of the Interior were all three traitors, the two first now in arms. Our small Army had been sent to Texas and to Utah among the Mormons—and our Southern forts, arsenals, and depots were purposely left without garrisons and fell without a show of resistance. Our few ships in commission had also been scattered and were kept away. We soon had 3,500 miles of coast to blockade. Four squadrons were organized—in my section of the coast I had sixty-odd vessels; Farragut has now ninety. Very great efforts were made to create this immense navy, for we always apprehended intervention—not on the part of England, for I always believe the word of a British minister, but that Gallic gentleman is a very freaky personage.

I have not spoken of the blockade running—that must be charged to the cupidity of man and is irrespective of country; our injuries from it were greatly aggravated by having your colonies, the Bermudas and Bahamas, on our flanks for depots and entrepots, and the Havana as the fitting-out place for the Gulf coast. The last port now run into to any extent will soon be effectually closed. Have you ever reflected how steam has changed, indeed inverted almost, the old system of blockades—the advantages are nine tenths in favor of the *runner*. In olden times of sailing ships, a frigate and her boats were sufficient to cover almost any one port. I wrote a paper on this subject while on the coast to satisfy our people—if I could put my hands on it I would send it to you. Notwithstanding the difficulties, the captures have amounted to twenty-six millions of dollars—one half goes to the officers and men.

But, my dear Hall, I must bring this letter to a close. I doubt if you ever ask me again to write you a long one. I have been compelled to scribble in haste for I leave my home today to be absent some weeks, to attend to my church matters, for I am president and member of various societies which meet in Boston this year. You of course hear of and see occasionally your former chief, Sir Michael Seymour—if he has not forgotten me, will you make my best regards; I have always spoken of him as a model admiral and gentleman.

Also whenever you may meet any of my old China friends please mention me—Sir Robert McClure, Shadwell, Hand,

Osborn, Dew, Saumarez, Hoskins, etc. I saw much of Captain Hancock of the *Immortalité* and fancied him prodigiously. He brought Barnard of the *Nile* to see me while I was in New York last year—their ships were in magnificent order, and I think I have never seen even in former days so fine a crew as the *Nile*'s. You do wonders in keeping up your sailors in spite of steam and iron pots. I missed Sir Alexander Milne but had a kind note from him, from Halifax.

You asked me about our spirit ration. It worked well with me for some ten months, until I left—the sailors were perfectly satisfied; drunken mechanics who ship as landsmen complain the most. Congress have no intention of repealing the law.

Until I can find the report of my monitor captains which you ask for, I enclose a letter of mine which covers most of my affairs—and which may afford you some interest.

I also enclose a "carte de visite" which perhaps Mrs. Hall will do me the honor to accept. Mrs. Du Pont bids me ask for yours if you have one. Mine, my relations and friends pronounce the only good one that has been taken of me.

I sent your message to Mr. Reed and I suppose he got Goodenough to give you one in return—he requested me to do so at the time, saying he had frequently inquired after you.

When this war closes I hope to go to Europe with Mrs. DP—it may not be a great while, though everyone has stopped predicting except the newspapers. The rebels now seem sorely pressed, if we take their own *accounts*, more than ever before; they admit a want of men and their armies are greatly thinned by desertions.

I hope your children are quite recovered and that Mrs. Hall is now well—please present me respectfully and cordially to her, and believe me, my dear Hall, Yours most sincerely,

S. F. Du Pont

Catherine Edmondston: Diary, October 18, 1864

Catherine Edmondston followed news of the war and the northern elections from her plantation in North Carolina. The congressional elections held in Indiana, Ohio, and Pennsylvania on October 11 had resulted in Republican gains in all three states.

OCTOBER 18, 1864

On Sunday the 16th Father & Mama left us for their own home, the early frost having rendered such a step safe a full month earlier than usual. I all day yesterday with Mr E at the plantation; his molasses mills being out of order he was kept busy all day. Have just gathered my tea nuts, nearly a peck of them & clipped my Tea plants a second time. How I wish we had plants enough to supply us; we would laugh at Yankee Blockaders.

The war news is good. We repulsed a heavy attack on the North side of the James on the Darby town road on Tuesday the 11th. Our loss small; that of the enemy heavy. In the Valley our cavalry have met with a repulse from pressing too far ahead of their infantry supports annoying Sheridan's rear. We lost five guns & many prisoners, but Early coming up, Sheridan continued to fall back. Grant has issued an order which, for barbarity, equals anything yet done in this most barbarous of all wars. He directs the Valley of Va to be laid entirely waste, everything which can support life to be destroyed and all the stock of all kind to be driven off or killed. His Lieutenants are carrying it out to the letter! In one day Sheridan reports he burned [ ] Mills, [ ] Barns filled to the roof with wheat, oats, & corn enough to maintain Early for three months, all the farming implements, the seed wheat, has fed 3000 sheep to his army & driven off stock & horses in such quantity that there has been as yet no account taken of them! Grant tells him "to leave the Valley such a waste that next year a crow flying across will have to carry his own rations with him." What a monster! Fit associate for Butler & Sherman! He is a disgrace to humanity! His cheif engineer was killed by a band of guerrillas & as retaliation he ordered every dwelling within an area of five miles to be burnt! I preserve Grants order & Sheridans report, both official, & such conduct is tolerated by a nation who *calls itself Christian*!

From Georgia we get but little news, the War Depart surpressing all details for fear of giving information to the enemy. Hood is well in Sherman's rear & has possession of the RR. We beleive we were victorious at Alatoona & that we captured 3000 Yankees altho Stanton reports officially that we were beaten with heavy loss. Rome is in our hands, but Stanton publishes a dispatch from that point. Atlanta we beleive to be evacuated but of that have no confirmation, mere rumours. One thing is certain, Stanton & Lincoln are terribly alarmed & lie more than ever to hide their fears & to prevent their reverses having an unfavourable effect on the coming election. By their falsities they have influenced in their favor the Penn & Ohio State Elections & if they can continue keep the public mind in the dark until the 8th of next month, it may be well for them. Grant us overwhelming victories at all points ere then! But why should I wish to disappoint them? Lincolns election, if there is a choice, is better for us than McClellan's, because he is the greater fool. I honestly beleive McClellan will be a better President for the Yankees & a more formidable antagonist to us than Lincoln; so therefore, Hurrah for Lincoln, the greatest and most corrupt fool of the age! He has attempted to buy off McClellan from the Presidential contest by an offer of the command of the army, flattering him with the assurance that a man of his patriotism will, he is sure, choose that post in which he can render the greatest service to his country & that his (McClellan's) military are greater than his diplomatic talents, but little Mac is "too old a bird to be caught by such chaff."

UNITY AND CIVIL FREEDOM:
NEW YORK, OCTOBER 1864

Francis Lieber: Lincoln or McClellan

October 1864

A German immigrant who taught history and political science at Columbia College, Francis Lieber had drafted General Orders No. 100, an influential code of the laws of war issued by the Union army in April 1863. Lieber also served as the president of the Loyal Publication Society, which published dozens of pamphlets and broadsides supporting the Union cause. In September 1864 Lieber wrote *Lincoln oder McClellan? Aufruf an die Deutschen in Amerika* for circulation among German-American voters. The Loyal Publication Society published an English translation of the pamphlet in October, as well as a Dutch version. Before receiving his professorship at Columbia, Lieber had taught at South Carolina College for twenty years. His eldest son had joined the Confederate army and been mortally wounded in 1862, while his other two sons served as Union officers and would survive the war.

LINCOLN OR McCLELLAN.
APPEAL TO THE GERMANS IN AMERICA.

TRANSLATED FROM THE GERMAN BY T. C.*

COUNTRYMEN AND FELLOW-CITIZENS:

The presidential election is rapidly approaching, and it is time for every citizen to reflect and decide conscientiously for whom he shall give his ballot. At an election of such impor-

* This appeal was written several weeks before the letter of Alexander H. Stephens to some friends in Georgia, and the report of Judge Advocate Holt, on the conspiracy in this country, for the subversion of its government in favor of the rebels, were published. These two documents, the first speaking of "the ultimate and absolute sovereignty of the states," the other showing many prominent men of the Chicago Convention loaded with crimes of the deepest dye—these documents would have furnished the writer of the appeal with many sad illustrations.—*Translator.*

tance, when everything dear to us, as citizens, is staked on the issue, it is unworthy—it is cowardly—to throw away the right of voting. No patriot will choose political impotency at this crisis. The entire political existence of this country, of which we became citizens by the choice of our mature years, and not by the accident of birth, rests upon the free ballot; and he who has the right, has also the duty to vote. If sensible and honest voters stay away from the polls, they may be sure that those whose votes have been bought, and those who have no right to vote at all, will be ready there to appear in their stead.

The great majority of those who come from Germany to America are Democrats in the true sense, and when they find in this country a large party, which for years has been called the Democratic party, many allow themselves to be deceived by the mere name. The assemblage which gathered at Chicago, and nominated General McClellan for the Presidency, also calls itself the Democratic party—and of what sort of people was this mixed-up convention composed? In the first place, a great proportion consisted of old "Know-nothings." They openly proclaimed themselves such. Can you, Germans, vote on the same side with these men, whose only principle has been to shut in your faces the gates of this wide continent, to which their own fathers came from Europe, or else, as you are here already, to take from you the right of citizenship? Will you vote with those who, like their friends, the rebels, would load you with infamy, and who speak of you as the offscouring of the earth? The Know-nothings plot in secret. They have their lodges, and form a secret society. Is that, in a free country, democratic? Freedom, above all, rests on publicity.

Another portion of the Chicago convention consisted of those who set State-Rights, as they call it, above everything else; who openly say that Americans have not a country! and that the sovereignty of the single state stands high above everything else—is absolute; that each state has the right to tear itself away, and be a separate dominion; that there is therefore no right anywhere to compel such a state to remain in the Union. They utter untruths, and they know it! What would these same people have done if Ohio or Massachusetts had suddenly broken away and declared itself a monarchy? What do the rulers in Richmond at this very instant say of those men in North Carolina, who desire to withdraw their own state from the so-called confederacy? They call them rebels. How comes it that, up to this very day, there are men sitting in the congress at Richmond, as delegates from Missouri and Kentucky? Have these states seceded? Why have the rebels all along claimed Maryland as belonging to them? The delegates from Kentucky and Missouri sit in their congress; Maryland troops fight in their ranks, because Kentucky, Missouri, and Maryland are, or were, slaveholding states. With these enemies of the Union, therefore, slavery is the principle of cohesion of a new country, and state-sovereignty is not the basis of the right of secession. Why did these gentlemen all support General Jackson, when the old hero told South Carolina she should be compelled, by force of arms, to stay in the Union? And is the doctrine of state-sovereignty democratic? I feel almost ashamed to ask such a question of a German. The Democracy has always, and everywhere, been for the unity of the country; it will have but one country, worthy of a great nation. All Pumpernickel sovereignties, all the "Algerine states," as in Germany they are now called, have always been objects of loathing and execration to the Democracy.

Unquestionably each state in the United States has its rights, and ought to have them. But so, too, each man has his rights, and the rights of the individual which belong to every person in a free country are far more valuable, and are more important, taken on the whole, than the rights of states are. But the individual man is not for this reason a sovereign. Do you know that the word "sovereignty" does not once occur in that great instrument, the Constitution of the United States? The word "sovereignty" was smuggled into our political dictionary when this Constitution had already been adopted. Who then is sovereign in America if the states are not? Nobody! No man, no corporation, no congress, no president, no officer, no body of men, is sovereign in a free country. The United States are sovereign in respect to all other sovereign nations. We are sovereign when we treat with France and England, or when we engage in war; but within the country itself no one is sovereign.

This is no new theory, nor is it any theory at all. It is a fact.

Two hundred years ago, when the famous Bill of Rights was under consideration in the English Parliament, the greatest lawyer in England declared that the word "sovereign" was not known to English law. He said this because the dynasty which had just then been expelled had constantly talked of the king's sovereign power.

But can it be necessary to argue with Germans against a hankering after petty state domination and provincial pomposity. State sovereignty, indeed! Have we not had enough of that sort of thing in the land from which we came? If a German wants to have a stew of states, he never need come for it to America. Has he not got enough of sovereign states, big, little, and minute, at home?

What are the ideas which most animate the German in Germany? They are the unity of Germany and civil freedom. And shall he here give his vote for those who would see the country torn asunder in fragments while the cause of human slavery should triumph?

German working men! why did you leave home, family, the friends of your youth, and seek this distant America? It was because you had heard that in the United States you would find a country wherein you and your children would enjoy all the rights of the free citizen; where skill and industry would surely find their reward, and where your children would never find themselves debarred from any merited attainment by the privileges of others. If then you would not have, in place of this Union, a land where the working man should be delivered over to a grinding tyranny far worse than any endured in the oppressed countries of Europe, do not lend your aid to the party which would give up the Union to the dominion of the Southern landholders.

For do you know what this slave-owning, would-be oligarchy pretends to aim at? Perhaps you suppose they struggle only to retain possession of their negro slaves. The Southern slaveholders are fighting for that which was for so long a time the prerogative of the owners of the soil, the privilege of using the working man, whether white or black, as the instrument of their power, their pleasure, and their arrogance. The working man is to bear all the burdens of the state, but he is to have no rights in it. It is for him to obey, and for the rich man alone to rule. Hear what the secession leaders have said:

> "No state can endure in which the laboring class has political rights. Those alone who own the soil and the capital must govern and be the masters of those who labor."

And they say this, remember it well:

> "Capital has an inherent right to own labor."

If you would have masters set up over you, on this principle, vote for McClellan. Would you retain your equal rights as the citizens of a free country, vote for Lincoln, who has been an honest working man like yourselves.

Another part of the Chicago Convention consisted of those who seem to believe that all can be made right if people will only keep on shouting "the Constitution, the Constitution," as loud as they can.

We think we understand the Constitution quite as well as these gentlemen, and respect it more. For it should be noticed that the so-called Democratic party has of late years always set the Constitution aside whenever it seemed to be for their advantage. Was Nullification constitutional? Was it constitutional when Mr. Douglas, shortly before the last Presidential election, promised the South to advocate a law subjecting to heavy punishment the mere discussion of the slavery question? Was it constitutional, when, for twenty years, and probably longer, the letterbags in the South were opened to see whether they contained abolition documents? Was it constitutional to deny the right of petition? Is Secession constitutional? Is it consistent with the Constitution to say with those Chicago people that it is the President's right and duty to release any State that may desire to leave the Union? Is it constitutional to speak of secession as "one of the reserved rights of the State"? Is it constitutional to declare that our whole political State-structure exists only to benefit a single class of men—a class known by the complexion of the skin? Even the ancient heathen had a higher view of the State and of the objects of civil government. Is it constitutional to represent one whole government as a mere Confederation or League—that poorest of all governments for a modern and free people? Was it in the spirit of the Constitution when Mr. Calhoun and all his followers proclaimed that the Senate should always be equally divided between slave states and free states, thus making for the first time in our history slavery an immutable institution? Was the precious Ostend proclamation conceived in a constitutional spirit?

We too honor the Constitution, but the Constitution is not a deity. We love our country, the nation, freedom; and these things are superior even to the Constitution; and it should never be forgotten that by this Southern Rebellion a state of things is brought upon us for which the Constitution never was, and never could be calculated. Shall we fold our hands, as did Mr. Buchanan, and declare that nothing can be done on our part to save the country because the Constitution does not prescribe what we are to do in such a case? Such was the opinion which his Attorney-General of the United States gave to Mr. Buchanan. God forbid! We are one nation; we mean to remain one people, and our country must not be suffered to perish. The life of the patient must be saved whether the case is mentioned in the recipe book or not. The Constitution did not make the people, for the people made the Constitution. But has the Constitution been violated at all? We have not space for an examination of the question. But, my countrymen, admitting that some things may have occurred which could not be justified by existing laws, I am, as I think I may safely say, as well acquainted with the history of the past as any of these Chicago gentlemen, and I can advisedly affirm that never yet has there been any civil war, nor even any ordinary war in which the government has tolerated the thousandth part of that liberty which the enemies of the Government and the friends of those enemies enjoy among us—infinitely more, than the latter would allow us in a reversed case.

It is the so-called Democratic party which has brought this civil war upon us, and now they say that they only can end it. Why so? Does a man in America acquire some mysterious power or wisdom as soon as he calls himself a Democrat? They want to make up a peace, to give still greater guarantees to the South—everything to the rebels; in short, they belong to those in the North who have always been the obsequious servants of the

South, and who seem to think themselves honored by fulfilling the behests of an arrogant slaveholder. Is that Democracy?

My friends, let us vote for Lincoln. Many of you doubtless say that he has done some things which you do not like, or that sometimes he has not acted with sufficient promptitude. But the simple question before the people now is, shall Lincoln or McClellan be the next President? No other man can be elected; and now is there a German who can hesitate, or one who can be so indifferent as not to vote for either. The one candidate is *national*, the other is not. The one is for freedom and for the removal of that which is the disgrace of this century—he is opposed to slavery, which has brought upon us the demon of civil war. The other would preserve slavery. The one is out-spoken and candid; is the other so? The one is for all the citizens of this great country, whether they were born here or not; the other owes his nomination in a great degree to the Know-Nothings. The one is truly a Democrat—he is a man of the people; the other is no real Democrat—at least those who have set him up before the people are anything but democratic in feeling. The one, though surrounded by unparalleled difficulties, has at least so guided the ship of state that we are now in sight of the desired haven; the other, when he was at the head of one of the grandest armies that had been seen in a century, did little more than hesitate, when he might, as the enemy now admits, have put an end to the war.

It is easy to understand why some very rich and some very poor Germans, who want to get into office, exert themselves for McClellan. But of every German who has no such views, who simply gives his vote for the honor, the unity, and the freedom of his adopted country, and who does not allow himself to be deluded by the mere name of "Democrat," we may naturally expect that when he has calmly reflected on the vast importance of the occasion, and the character of the candidates, he will vote for Lincoln.

Every citizen ought to exert himself to the utmost in this remarkable election, when a great nation is called upon at the very crisis of a gigantic civil war, to elect a ruler by the popular and untrammelled ballot. It is not sufficient to carry the election of Mr. Lincoln by a bare overplus of numbers. A sweeping national majority is required to prove to Europe, to the South, and to its friends here in the midst of us, that this people is resolved to maintain this country in its integrity, a great and unimpaired commonwealth. The result of this election should be like a great national harvest, garnering its full sheaves from every portion of the land.

George Templeton Strong: Diary, November 9, 1864

Sherman's capture of Atlanta, Sheridan's victories in the Shenandoah Valley, and McClellan's rejection of the peace plank in the Democratic platform brought about a reversal in Lincoln's political fortunes. On November 8 he became the first president to be reelected since Andrew Jackson in 1832, winning 55 percent of the popular vote and 212 of 233 electoral votes. George Templeton Strong followed the results in New York City.

VICTORIA! Te Deum laudamus. Te Dominum confitemur.

November 9. *Laus Deo!* The crisis has been past, and the most momentous popular election ever held since ballots were invented has decided against treason and disunion. My contempt for democracy and extended suffrage is mitigated. The American people can be trusted to take care of the national honor. Lincoln is reëlected by an overwhelming vote. The only states that seem to have McClellanized are Missouri, Kentucky, Delaware, and New Jersey. New York, about which we have been uneasy all day, is reported safe at the Club tonight. The Copperheads are routed—*Subversi sunt quasi plumbum in aequis vehementibus.* Poor "little Mac" will never be heard of any more, I think. No man of his moderate calibre ever had such an opportunity of becoming illustrious and threw it away so rapidly. Notwithstanding a certain lukewarmness in the national cause, his instincts and impulses were, on the whole, right and loyal. Had he acted on them honestly and manfully, he would have been elected. But his friends insisted on his being *politic*, and he had not the strength to resist them. He allowed Belmont and Barlow to strike out of his letter of acceptance a vigorous sentence declaring an armistice with armed rebels out of the question, and to append to it its unmeaning finale (which imposed on no man) stating that he assumed the views he had expressed to be what the Chicago

Convention really meant to say in its treasonous resolutions. *Fuit* McClellan, Napoleoniculus. Five years hence people will wonder how such a fuss ever came to be made about him.

A very wet, warm day. Copperheads talk meekly and well. "It's a terrible mistake, but we have got to make the best of it and support the government." The serene impudence of this morning's *World* can hardly be matched. It says the mission of the Democratic Party for the next four years will be to keep A. Lincoln from making a dishonorable disunion peace with the South. So a gentleman who has just received a sentence of four years in the State Prison might (if cheeky enough) inform the court and jury that their unjust decision would oblige him to be especially careful during his term that law and order were maintained throughout the state and that no crime failed to meet prompt punishment. The *World* is, moreover, uncommonly proud of the "Democratic masses" (Governor Seymour's "friends," the liquor dealers, roughs, and brutal Irishry of the city) because they committed no disorders yesterday, *though* so easily tempted to make a general row by the offensive and insulting presence of General Butler with sundry regiments to back him. . . .

George Anthon dined here, and we proceeded to the Union League Club, where was much folk. Discoursed with General Banks among others. It would seem that William E. Dodge is defeated by James Brooks, that most coprophagous of Copperheads, in this congressional district. A great pity, but Dodge's election was hardly hoped for. Would we were quite sure that Seymour is beaten! John Astor says he thinks Seymour's election would be more mischievous than McClellan's, and he may be right. Seymour and McClellan are weak men, but the latter means well. Seymour's instincts are all evil. He is quite as bad as Fernando Wood.

READING A SEALED PAPER:
WASHINGTON, D.C., NOVEMBER 1864

John Hay: Diary, November 11, 1864

Lincoln's secretary John Hay was present when the President read to his cabinet the memorandum he had written eleven weeks before the election.

---

11 NOVEMBER 1864, FRIDAY

This morning Nicolay sent a dispatch from Illinois giving us 25000 majority and 10 Congressmen which we take to mean Wentworth Farnsworth Washburne Cook Ingersoll Harding Cullom Bromwell Kuykendall, and Moulton at Large, leaving the Copperheads Thornton Morrison Ross and Marshall.

At the meeting of the Cabinet today, the President took out a paper from his desk and said, "Gentlemen do you remember last summer I asked you all to sign your names to the back of a paper of which I did not show you the inside? This is it. Now, Mr Hay, see if you can get this open without tearing it!" He had pasted it up in so singular style that it required some cutting to get it open. He then read as follows:

Executive Mansion
Washington
Aug. 23, 1864.

This morning, as for some days past, it seems exceedingly probable that this Administration will not be re-elected. Then it will be my duty to so cooperate with the President elect, as to save the Union between the election and the inauguration; as he will have secured his election on such ground that he cannot possibly save it afterwards.

A Lincoln.

This was indorsed:

William H. Seward
W. P. Fessenden
Edwin M Stanton
Gideon Welles

Edw. Bates
M Blair
JP Usher
August 23, 1864

The President said "you will remember that this was written at a time (6 days before the Chicago nominating convention) when as yet we had no adversary, and seemed to have no friends. I then solemnly resolved on the course of action indicated above. I resolved, in case of the election of General McClellan being certain that he would be the Candidate, that I would see him and talk matters over with him. I would say, 'General, the election has demonstrated that you are stronger, have more influence with the American people than I. Now let us together, you with your influence and I with all the executive power of the Government, try to save the country. You raise as many troops as you possibly can for this final trial, and I will devote all my energies to assisting and finishing the war.'"

Seward said, "And the General would answer you '*Yes, Yes*'; and the next day when you saw him again & pressed these views upon him he would say 'Yes—yes' & so on forever and would have done nothing at all."

"At least" added Lincoln "I should have done my duty and have stood clear before my own conscience."

Seward was abusing Forney today for a report of his (S's) remarks last night at the serenade, which appeared horribly butchered in the Chronicle, in which S.s Biblical lore is sadly out at the elbows.

The speech of the President at the two last Serenades are very highly spoken of. The first I wrote after the fact, to prevent the "loyal Pennsylvanians" getting a swing at it themselves. The second one, last night, the President himself wrote late in the evening and read it from the window. "Not very graceful" he said "but I am growing old enough not to care much for the manner of doing things."

Today I got a letter from Raymond breathing fire and vengeance against the Custom House which came so near destroying him in his District. I read it to the President. He answered that it was the spirit of such letters as that that created the faction and malignity of which Raymond complained.

It seems utterly impossible for the President to conceive of the possibility of any good resulting from a rigorous and exemplary course of punishing political dereliction. His favorite expression is "I am in favor of short statutes of limitations in politics."

RETALIATORY EXECUTIONS: VIRGINIA, NOVEMBER 1864

John S. Mosby to Philip H. Sheridan

A lawyer from southwest Virginia, John S. Mosby had served in the 1st Virginia Cavalry and as a scout for Major General J.E.B. Stuart before being given command of a small detachment of partisan rangers in northern Virginia in January 1863. Using guerrilla tactics, Mosby raided Union outposts and supply wagons in Fairfax, Prince William, Fauquier, and Loudoun counties, sometimes striking within fifteen miles of Washington. By the summer of 1864 Mosby commanded about 300 men in the 43rd Battalion Virginia Cavalry, and in August he began attacking Sheridan's supply lines in the Shenandoah Valley. While the Confederate authorities considered members of the 43rd Battalion to be lawful combatants, most Union soldiers believed them to be no different from civilian guerrillas. On September 23 six of his men were captured near Front Royal during a skirmish in which a Union cavalry officer was mortally wounded while allegedly trying to surrender. Major General Alfred Torbert, Sheridan's cavalry commander, had two of the prisoners hanged, while the other four were shot by Union soldiers. Another one of Mosby's men was hanged on October 14 by Colonel William H. Powell in response to the killing of a Union soldier by two Confederate civilians. After receiving approval from Robert E. Lee, Mosby had seven Union prisoners selected on November 6 for retaliatory execution. The next day three of the prisoners were hanged, two were shot but survived after being left for dead, and two escaped unharmed. No further executions were authorized by either Sheridan or Mosby, but in late November Sheridan sent a cavalry division into Fauquier and Loudoun counties with orders to seize or destroy all food, forage, and livestock.

NOVEMBER 11, 1864.

Maj. Gen. P. H. SHERIDAN,

Commanding U. S. Forces in the Valley:

GENERAL: Some time in the month of September, during my absence from my command, six of my men who had been captured by your forces were hung and shot in the streets of Front Royal, by the order and in the immediate presence of

Brigadier-General Custer. Since then another, captured by a Colonel Powell on a plundering expedition into Rappahannock, was also hung. A label affixed to the coat of one of the murdered men declared that "this would be the fate of Mosby and all his men." Since the murder of my men not less than 700 prisoners, including many officers of high rank, captured from your army by this command, have been forwarded to Richmond, but the execution of my purpose of retaliation was deferred in order, as far as possible, to confine its operation to the men of Custer and Powell. Accordingly on the 6th instant seven of your men were, by my order, executed on the Valley pike, your highway of travel. Hereafter any prisoners falling into my hands will be treated with the kindness due to their condition, unless some new act of barbarity shall compel me reluctantly to adopt a course of policy repulsive to humanity.

Very respectfully, your obedient servant,

JNO. S. MOSBY,
Lieutenant-Colonel.

A SLAVEOWNER'S DECEPTION:
MARYLAND, NOVEMBER 1864

Jane Kamper: Statement Regarding Her Emancipation

The constitutional convention that met in Annapolis, Maryland, on April 27, 1864, voted in favor of the immediate abolition of slavery and rejected proposals to compensate slaveowners and to apprentice the minor children of freed slaves to their masters. After being approved by the voters in October, the new constitution went into effect on November 1, 1864. Two weeks later, a newly freed woman from the eastern shore of Maryland told the military authorities in Baltimore how her former master had tried to deceive her regarding the legal status of her children.

Balto. Novr 14"/64

Statement of Jane Kamper

Slave of Wm Townsend of Talbot County Md.

I was the slave of Wm Townsend of Talbot county & told Mr. Townsend of my having become free & desired my master to give my children & my bedclothes he told me that I was free but that my Children Should be bound to him. he locked my Children up so that I could not find them I afterwards got my children by stealth & brought them to Baltimore. I desire to regain possession of my bed clothes & furniture.

My Master pursued me to the Boat to get possession of my children but I hid them on the boat

her
Jane X Kamper (fn)
mark

"VOX POPULI, VOX DEI": NEW YORK, NOVEMBER 1864

Maria Lydig Daly: Diary, November 15, 1864

In the November 8 election Lincoln lost New York City to McClellan by about 37,000 votes, but managed to carry the state by a margin of 6,749. Maria Lydig Daly reflected on the election results.

November 15, 1864

The election has taken place. Lincoln has been reelected. *Vox Populi, vox Dei.* So it must be for the best. All now left us is to put the shoulder to the wheel and do our best to draw the governmental machine out of the slough. There was some ill feeling about General Butler's being sent here to overawe the election. However, there seems to be little ill feeling on either side—a hopeful sign for the country. It is well that Lincoln has so large a majority, as now there will be no one to lay the blame upon.

I wish our political parsons could be done away with together with slavery. What autocrats they are! Beecher, a few Sundays since, before he began to preach, announced: "I am going to preach a political sermon, and if anyone does not like it, he can leave the church." A man rose up and gave three cheers for McClellan.

Poor McClellan! What a lesson he has had of the instability of popular favor and of fair-weather friends. None of his old companions-in-arms, hardly, have voted for him, and the reason is clear—it would not be the way to promotion. A lady said to me a few days since, "What, your husband votes for McClellan and you have a brother in the army?"

Yesterday, Mr. Theodore Fay from Bremen, our former minister to Prussia, came in. He is for Lincoln and quoted what he called "Mr. Lincoln's very appropriate though homely saying that a countryman in crossing a dangerous stream or ford would not willingly change horses." I answered very mildly that Mr. Lincoln was very happy in these little sayings, that like in Scripture, you could always find a story or text to suit the occasion. Now those who, like my husband, voted for McClellan, could quote another of his aphorisms as their excuse. When removing some General (Rosecrans, I believe), he said, "They that made the mess are not exactly the ones to finish it." Mr. Fay, however, is a perfectly sincere and conscientious man.

Butler has been serenaded and feted as though he had saved the country, whereas he did nothing. It was the policy of the Democrats to keep the peace, as they wanted to poll as many votes as possible, whereas the policy of the others was to institute, if possible, martial law. The Judge was asked to meet him on Saturday, but he did not go. Beecher, at the Loyal League Club, proposed him as the next President. In Butler's speech, he adopts McClellan's ideas and thinks everything should now be done to make peace.

Darley and his wife spent the evening with us. The Judge got out his theatrical portraits, I brought forward some doppelkümmel and cake, and we had quite a pleasant time around the blazing woodfire until twelve o'clock. Sunday likewise we had company: Mr. Hackett, Mr. Young, and Mr. Dykes. Tonight I am alone. The Judge has gone out with a great friend of his, a bookworm like himself, to see another of their species, and I shall write up all my letters. His "Chancellor Kent," I think, will be a great success. He has been much complimented on the opening chapters.

I have been writing an article explaining the reasons that we cannot find American goods and exposing the tricks of the manufacturers and shopkeepers, which Mr. Field has promised to publish.

Mrs. Dana came in to bid me good-by, and very kindly invited us to come and stay with her in Washington. Her husband is Assistant Secretary of War. I thought it very kind of her but declined. If I go at all, it will be only as the guest of Baron Gerolt. The dear old gentleman has just left us after a stay of a fortnight. I like him every day more and more. He is so good a Christian, so wise and observing, and so amiable and generous.

James A. Connolly: Diary, November 17–23, 1864

Hood continued his offensive against the Chattanooga–Atlanta railroad on October 13, capturing the Union garrison at Dalton and destroying twenty-five miles of track between Resaca and Tunnel Hill. He then moved his army into northern Alabama and advanced along the south bank of the Tennessee River until he reached Tuscumbia on October 31. Sherman pursued Hood as far as Gaylesville, Alabama, before returning to northwest Georgia. While Hood gathered supplies and prepared to invade Middle Tennessee, Sherman received Grant's approval on November 2 for his proposed march on Savannah. After sending 25,000 of his men north to help George H. Thomas defend Tennessee against Hood, Sherman burned much of Atlanta and began his march to the sea on November 15 with 62,000 troops. Major Connolly recorded the progress of the Union forces, which were opposed by about 13,000 Confederates, many of them Georgia militia.

Thursday, Nov. 17th.

Division marched at daylight. Passed through Lithonia, on the R. R., at 9 A.M., where I noticed Gen. Sherman standing on the R. R. track giving directions as to how he wanted the track torn up and destroyed. Several buildings were burning as we passed through. We arrived at Conyers at noon, and as our Division had four miles of R. R. to destroy before moving any further, Capt. Acheson, who plays the piano finely, and myself started out to walk around through the town and find a piano, so that we could have some music while our soldiers were destroying the track. Meeting a little girl on the street who told us where there was a piano, we went to the house and on knocking at the door a grey headed, meek, ministerial looking old rebel opened the door and asked what we wanted. I had agreed to do the talking so I told him "we wanted" to destroy the R. R. first, and asked him what he thought of it. The old gent looked wise and said nothing; I then asked him if he had a piano in the house; the old man looked worried and replied that his daughter had one. All right, said I, that's just what we want, we want some music; the old man said he didn't think his daughter could play, and looked incredulous when we pushed by him into the room, and the Captain sat down at the piano; but the Captain's fingers soon made the keys dance to the air of the Star Spangled Banner, and the old man sat there astonished at the thought that a rough, vulgar, brutal Yankee should be able to play so skillfully. Then the Captain played "Dixie" in excellent style; this made the old man talkative, brought in the daughter and some other young ladies, and we soon had them playing for us, while the Captain and I sat back and quietly enjoyed the discomfiture of the old man, and laughed at the efforts of the rebel damsels to appear composed. Finally, to cap the climax, we induced these Southern ladies to sing us the "Confederate Toast", which they told us was their favorite song, and one verse of it I remember, viz:

"Here's to old Butler and his crew,
Drink it down!
Here's to old Butler and his crew,
Drink it down!
Here's to old Butler and his crew,
May the devil get his due,
Drink it down! Drink it down! Drink it down!"

We left them, though, notwithstanding their elegant and patriotic songs—they, no doubt, hoping we might be shot before night. Our troops having finished their work on the R. R. we moved forward 4 miles, and encamped on Mr. Zachry's plantation having marched 15 miles today, and utterly destroyed 4 miles of R. R. Old Zachry has a son who is a Colonel in the rebel army in Virginia, and the negroes, i. e. his own negroes tell us tonight that the old sinner has a federal flag hid away in his house which his son captured and sent home from Virginia a year ago. We have searched the house all over for it, but can't find it yet, and the old man and old woman deny having it, but one of their house servants told me most positively tonight that it *is* in the house, and that they know where it is. If we don't get it before we leave tomorrow morning the old fellow's house will surely be burnt, for the soldiers have all heard of it. They *did* burn the old fellow's cotton gin, filled with cotton, tonight. Passed through fine country today. Conyers is a village of about 500 inhabitants, and Lithonia about 300, both stations on the R. R.; a good many negroes came into camp with us tonight; they are of all shades and sizes; and are apparently happy if they can be permitted to go along with us.

Friday, Nov. 18th.

After striking tents this morning I took old Zachry out one side, and with an air of great concern, and in the greatest confidence told him that unless he produced that flag, the soldiers were determined to burn his house as soon as General Baird got out of sight. The old sinner was alarmed and asked me to leave him a guard until the soldiers all passed, at the same time protesting that he knew nothing about the flag. I, of course, told him that we never left guards, and parted from him, expressing deep sympathy, for I assured him that the soldiers would in all probability burn his house. In less than ten minutes the old rascal brought the flag out and delivered it up. I don't know whether his house was burned or not. I know he owns about 40 niggers less tonight than he did last night. We crossed "Yellow River" about noon, and commenced destroying R. R. just after crossing. We destroyed about 4 miles. Yellow River, where we crossed, is quite a deep clear stream, about 6 rods wide and with high bluff banks. I stopped at a dwelling on the east side of the river, which the occupants (Merriwether's) dignified with the name of "Airy Mount." Had quite a discussion here with a strong minded elderly woman, on Abolition and Amalgamation; the old lady forced it on me, and as there were three or four very light colored mulatto children running around the house, they furnished me an admirable weapon to use against the old lady's remark that the Northern people were Amalgamationists. She didn't explain to my entire satisfaction how her slaves came to be so much whiter than African Slaves are usually supposed to be. Marched on through Covington and encamped a short distance east of it. Covington is a place of some pretension, and on the whole is rather a pretty place. The houses are very neat, built in modern Southern style, and painted white. The good people of Covington only heard of our advance yesterday so they are all at home, not having had time to run away. The "leading citizens" were affable when we entered the place, and everybody invited officers to stay all night at their house. I was in the Court Room and Masonic Lodge, the door of which was open.

Saturday, Nov. 19th.

Division moved at daybreak and crossed the Ulcofauhatchee River. This stream is not very deep, rapid, without any well defined banks, the water spreading out and making a swamp on either side of the stream for a considerable distance. The name of this stream is pronounced by the inhabitants "Alcovy." Land in its vicinity looks very poor; the ears of corn only grow about 6 inches long, and the stalks are very light. An old man told us today that some of his land averaged 6 bushels of corn to the acre and some of it "don't average anything." There are no wealthy planters in the immediate vicinity of the "Ulcofauhatchee" along our line of march. The farms are all in hundred acre lots, but their owners call them "Plantations"; the citizens look at our troops as they pass, with the utmost astonishment; they have no idea where we are going, and the negroes stare at us with open eyes and mouths, but generally, before the whole column has passed they pack up their bundles and march along, going, they know not whither, but apparently satisfied they are going somewhere toward freedom; but these wretched creatures, or a majority of them, don't know what freedom is. Ask them where they are going as they trudge along with their bundles on their heads, and the almost invariable reply is: "Don't know Massa; gwine along wid you all." Our men are foraging on the country with the greatest liberality. Foraging parties start out in the morning; they go where they please, seize wagons, mules, horses, and harness; make the negroes of the plantation hitch up, load the wagons with sweet potatoes, flour, meal, hogs, sheep, chickens, turkeys, barrels of molasses, and in fact everything good to eat, and sometimes considerable that's good to drink. Our men are living as well as they could at home and are in excellent health. Rain falling all the forenoon, roads heavy and marching difficult. Passed through Sand Town today about 2 o'clock. It is a little weather beaten village of about 250 or 300 inhabitants. The citizens were not much expecting us, but they heard of our approach day before yesterday and have spent the time since in carrying off and hiding in the swamp their valuables, but the negroes told the soldiers of these hiding places and most of these hidden valuables found their way into our camp tonight. Went into camp at dark. We have neither seen nor heard of any armed rebels yet, and we march along with as much unconcern as if we were marching through Ohio. We are beginning to talk about Milledgeville, and speculate on the probabilities of a battle there. There can't be much of a battle there though, for we have troops enough to eat up all the army Georgia's capital can muster.

Sunday, Nov. 20th.

Division moved at daylight, and at 9 A.M. passed through "Shady Dale." I have known for the past 3 days that our line of march led through "Shady Dale", and judging from the name I had fancied to myself that Shady Dale was probably a nice, clean, quiet, aristocratic country town, situated in some romantic, shaded valley, and as we started this morning I retouched my mental picture of "Shady Dale", so that I might have it entirely finished to my taste before seeing the place itself, and then have the satisfaction of determining whether "there's anything in a name" by comparing my ideal "Shady Dale" with the real "Shady Dale." I am now satisfied that "there is something in a name", but it was proven to me this morning in a manner that totally surprised me. As we rode along we came to a beautiful plantation, and by the roadside was a cluster of about 50 whitewashed negro houses, and in the midst of them an old fashioned frame house with porch all around it and dormor windows. The negro houses were filled with nice cleanly looking negroes of all ages and sizes, and as the head of our column came up with band playing, such a nest of negroes I never saw before; they poured out of those cabins to the road side in such numbers as to lead me to suppose they had been packed away inside like mackerel in a barrel. The music of the band started the young niggers at dancing, and they capered around like little imps; the old ones stood with uncovered heads, hands raised, mouths open and eyes turned up; the young negresses stood bowing and curtseying, trying to bow to every soldier that passed; while each negro in his or her own style kept uttering ejaculations of wonder such as "Lawd, jest look at em"; "whar'd dey cum from"; "looks like de whole wuld was comin" &c, &c. Each one expressing his wonder in some original and quaint style. I sat on my horse and listened to and watched them, while I laughed at their comicalities until tears rolled down my cheeks. There is as much difference between the negroes we see in the North and the plantation negroes of the South, as there is between a cultivated gentleman and a clown in the circus ring.

Presently I asked a venerable old African patriarch where "Shady Dale" was, and he told me: "Dis is it massa"; why, said I, is it called "Shady Dale"? "Cos" said he grinning, "deres so many of us black uns here." Whereupon I laughed too, and rode on, satisfied that there *is* something in a name, when a plantation can figure on the maps as "Shady Dale", on account of the number of "Shades" living there. This plantation is owned by a man named "Whitfield", and it is the finest one I ever saw, but by the time our column has all passed Mr. Whitfield won't have a sweet potato, a pig, chicken, turkey, horse, mule, cow, and scarcely a nigger left. The negroes on all these plantations tell us their masters have given them no meat to eat during the past two years, and as a consequence the negroes have been in the habit of prowling about the country at night, foraging, as they call it; that is stealing chickens, hogs, &c, and killing them in the swamps. They raise turnips extensively through Georgia so far as we have been, and every turnip patch we pass is thoroughly stripped by the soldiers and negroes, who, by the way, make excellent foragers. Our stock of negroes is increasing rapidly; many of them travel on horseback now; they furnish their own, i. e., their masters, horses, saddles and bridles, so they are no expense to Uncle Sam; a great many of our privates are getting negro servants for themselves; the negro walks along beside the soldier, with his knapsack and cooking utensils strapped upon his back, thus relieving the soldier of his load, and helping him along. What soldier *wouldn't* be an abolitionist under such circumstances. We have marched through beautiful country today. Halted one hour for dinner. We made 18 miles today, and encamped 6 miles from Eatonton, and 27 from Milledgeville.

Monday, Novr. 21st.

Division moved at daylight. Crossed "Murder Creek" at noon, and went into camp 4 miles beyond, having marched only 9 miles today, and being, tonight within 18 miles of Milledgeville. Rain falling heavily all day. Roads in a horrible condition. Things have not looked promising today. What would become of us if this weather should continue two weeks? We couldn't march; would be compelled to halt here in the midst of a hostile country, and thus let the enemy have time to recover from his surprise and concentrate against us. Well, let the worst come, will get to the capital of Georgia anyhow, and my long desire to see it will at length be gratified. We are all wet through and covered with mud, and our horses jaded, but our supper of coffee, fried chickens, sweet potatoes, &c, and a good sleep will bring us out all right in the morning, and if our horses give out, the stable of some wealthy Georgian must furnish us a remount. Citizens everywhere look paralyzed and as if stricken dumb as we pass them. Columns of smoke by day, and "pillars of fire" by night, for miles and miles on our right and left indicate to us daily and nightly the route and location of the other columns of our army. Every "Gin House" we pass is burned; every stack of fodder we can't carry along is burned; every barn filled with grain is destroyed; in fact everything that can be of any use to the rebels is either carried off by our foragers or set on fire and burned.

Tuesday, Nov. 22d.

Division moved at daylight, crossing Cedar Creek at 9 A.M., passing through the camp of Morgan's Division, and taking the advance for Milledgeville. Rather cold today. I spent most of the day in advance of the column searching for roads to the capital and picking up such items of information as I could get from negroes and white citizens in regard to the enemy, but I have not been able to ascertain that there are any rebel soldiers in the city. The negroes and others say that all the soldiers that were in Milledgeville have gone to Macon, under command of General Howell Cobb. We are encamped tonight on a plantation belonging to "General Cobb," and the 23d Missouri has received permission to burn all the rails and buildings on the plantation tonight. General Sherman has his tents pitched in the dooryard of the overseer's house on this plantation tonight. About 3 P.M. while the column was halted I rode ahead in the direction of Milledgeville, in company with General Baird, Colonel Poe, chief topographical engineer on General Sherman's staff, and Captain Buttrick of our staff. After we had ridden about a mile ahead of the column, admiring the beautiful country and speculating on the probability of taking Milledgeville without fighting, we suddenly discovered a mounted man in the middle of the road coming toward us. He was then about one-half mile from us and just on the crest of a little hill in the road. He discovered us at the same time we did him and we halted at the same time. Glasses were out in a minute and we discovered that his uniform was gray. Ah, ha! This, then, is the outer picket watching our approach to the capital. This settles the question; we'll have to fight for Milledgeville. The solitary horseman in rebel uniform turned his horse toward the city and disappeared behind the crest of the hill. There were some negro houses by the roadside about half way between where we were and where the gray clad horseman appeared. The negroes were out in the road looking at us. We were very anxious to get as far down the road as the negro houses, but didn't think it safe. In a few moments two gray clad horsemen appeared on the hill. They looked at us—were counting us evidently; they turned their horses around uneasily. Presently another horseman appeared, then another and another, until at least twenty were in sight on the crest of the hill. They were evidently too strong for us, even if we had been well armed, which we were not. But they were at least half a mile from us and our column was only about a mile from us—the road behind us was good, we were well mounted and we felt that if they *did* make a dash at us we could run the mile back to our troops before they could overtake us. But what if one of our horses should stumble and fall in the chase? Oh, well! Let the rider jump over a fence and run as fast as he can somewhere, anywhere, to gain a few minutes time. But look! The gray clad horsemen are starting forward and now they are waving a white handkerchief. It must be a deputation of citizens coming out to surrender the capital to us. So the General thought; so we all thought. The General directed Colonel Poe to go forward and meet the party and see what they wanted and who they were. Forward dashed Poe, and there we sat watching the scene with intense anxiety. Can it be possible that we are to meet with such good fortune as to receive the formal surrender of Georgia's capital? Poe meets the horsemen, they halt a few moments, then Poe turns, and they all come on to where the General, Captain Buttrick and myself are waiting in the road. We ask each other what this means. Can there be treachery here? Do they mean to deceive us with a white flag and capture us all? They approach within 200 yards and we plainly see their rebel uniforms. Shall we run or stand? Moments are precious. They come steadily on. The General looks pale. I *feel* pale and nervous, but the General stands, and therefore I *must*. They reach us, rein up their horses and the gray clad officer riding at the head of the party salutes the General and announces himself and party as Kilpatrick's scouts just from Milledgeville; they say there is not a rebel soldier there. Hurrah! Milledgeville is ours, and our sensations are now quite different from what they were ten minutes ago. The scouts go on to report to General Sherman and we ride on to the negro houses ahead, which the negroes tell us belong to "Ginral Cobb." In the dooryard of the overseer's house stand three large new iron kettles for boiling sorghum. Poe picked up an axe and with a few blows shivered one of them into atoms. Buttrick took the axe and shivered the second one. I then took the axe and paid my respects to "Ginral Cobb" by shattering the third one. The General sent back and ordered the troops forward and placed them in camp on the arch rebel's plantation. General Sherman coming up in about an hour, placed his headquarters in the yard where we broke the sorghum kettles. About dark this evening, it is said, the old negro who is the commissary of the plantation told some of General Sherman's staff officers that he wanted to see the great General, just to see how he looked. He was taken to the door of Sherman's tent, and the old man took off his hat, looked at the General a few moments, then bowing respectfully turned and walked off, saying to himself as he walked off shaking his head: "He's got the Linkum head, the Linkum head, he's got the Linkum head." We are only ten miles from Milledgeville tonight.

Wednesday, Nov. 23d.

Division moved at daylight. A bright, beautiful day; roads excellent and surrounding country magnificent. We reached the capital at about 9 A.M., but our troops didn't get up until noon on account of the 20th Corps, which came in from Eatonton, entering the city on the same road with us and in advance of us, as they struck the road first. Our troops encamped just outside the city limits on the west side. Our headquarters in the city in a dwelling house of some runaway citizen. General Davis' headquarters in the city near the Governor's mansion. General Sherman's in the mansion and General Slocum's at the Milledgeville Hotel, opposite the capitol square. Here I am, finally, at Milledgeville. My boyish desire is gratified, and I find that my boyish fancy in regard to the appearance of the city was quite correct. The dwellings are scattered and surrounded by large and tastefully decorated grounds. As one rides along its sandy streets, even at this season of the year, the faint perfume from every variety of tree and shrub, bud, blossom and flower fills the air with delicious fragrance. The exterior of the residences bespeak refinement within, and everything about the city serves to impress one with the idea that he is in an old, aristocratic city, where the worth of a man is computed in dollars and cents. The streets are regularly laid out and the capitol stands on a slight elevation rather east of the center of the city and overlooking the Oconee River. It is built of reddish looking sandstone and is a large square building, with rather a superabundance of fancy cornice outside. It has entrances on the north, south, east and west, each having a broad flight of stone steps. The offices and State library are on the first floor, the legislative halls on the second floor, and also the committee rooms. Each chamber has life size oil paintings of the prominent old men of Georgia hung around its walls in plain gilt frames. I should have thought "Oglethorpe" would have appeared in this State picture gallery, but he does not. General Jackson does, though, tricked out in a line officer's coat with a general's epaulettes on his shoulders, a line officer's sash around his waist, and a sort of cross between a Turkish scimeter and an artillery sabre by his side. Our soldiers and even some officers have been plundering the State library today and carrying off law and miscellaneous works in armfuls. It is a downright shame. Public libraries should be sacredly respected by all belligerents, and I am sure General Sherman will, some day, regret that he permitted this library to be destroyed and plundered. I could get a thousand dollars worth of valuable law books there if I would just go and take them, but I wouldn't touch them. I should feel ashamed of myself every time I saw one of them in my book case at home. I don't object to stealing horses, mules, niggers and all such *little things*, but I will not engage in plundering and destroying public libraries. Let them alone, to enlarge and increase for the benefit of the loyal generations that are to people this country long after we shall have fought our last battle and gone into our eternal camp. The State penitentiary was burned last night. There are but few business buildings here, and the population never could have been more than ten thousand. I shall devote myself to looking around town tomorrow, as I understand we will not march in the morning.

John Wilkes Booth: "To whom it may concern"

In August 1864 the actor John Wilkes Booth, a fervent Confederate sympathizer, began recruiting potential co-conspirators in a plot to abduct President Lincoln, take him to Richmond, and use him as a hostage in order to force the resumption of prisoner exchanges. Booth visited his sister, Asia, in Philadelphia in the latter part of November while on his way to New York, where he would appear with his brothers Edwin and Junius in a benefit performance of *Julius Caesar* on November 25. During this visit Booth gave his sister a packet for safekeeping that contained two letters. One was addressed to Booth's mother, while the other was probably intended for Asia's husband, John Sleeper Clarke, a successful comic actor and theater manager whom Booth had quarreled with over politics. Addressed "To whom it may concern," it would be published in the *Philadelphia Inquirer* on April 19, 1865, the day after Clarke turned it over to the U.S. marshal in Philadelphia.

1864

My Dear Sir

You may use this, as you think best, but as some, may wish to know and, and as I know not, *how*, to direct, I give it. (In the words of your Master)

"To whom it may concern"

Right, or wrong, God, judge me, not man. For be my motive good or bad, of one thing I am sure, the lasting condemnation of the north.

I love peace more than life. Have loved the Union beyond expression. For four years have I waited, hoped and prayed, for the dark clouds to break, And for a restoration of our former sunshine, to wait longer would be a crime. All hope for peace is dead, my prayers have proved as idle as my hopes. God's will be done. I go to see, and share the bitter end.

I have ever held the South were right. The very nomination of Abraham Lincoln four years ago, spoke plainly—war, war upon Southern rights and institutions. His election proved it. "Await an overt act." Yes till you are bound and plundered. What folly, the South were wise. Who thinks of argument or patience when the finger of his enemy presses on the trigger. In a *foreign war*, I too could say "Country right or wrong," but in a struggle *such as ours* (where the brother tries to pierce the brothers heart) for God's sake choose the right. When a country like this spurns *justice* from her side, She forfeits the allegiance of every honest freeman, and should leave him untrammeled by any fealty soever, to act, as his conscience may approve.

People of the north, to hate tyranny to love liberty and justice, to strike at wrong and oppression, was the teaching of our fathers. The study of our early history will not let *me* forget it, And may it never.

This country was formed for the *white* not for the black man. And looking upon *African slavery* from the same standpoint, held by those noble framers of our Constitution. I for one, have ever considered *it*, one of the greatest blessings (both for themselves and us,) that God even bestowed upon a favored nation. Witness heretofore our wealth and power. Witness their elevation in happiness and enlightment above their race, elsewhere. I have lived among it most of my life and have seen *less* harsh treatment from Master to Man than I have beheld in the north from father to son. Yet Heaven knows *no one* would be willing to do, *more* for the negro race than I. Could I but see a way to still better their condition, But Lincoln's policy is only preparing the way for their total annihilation. The South *are not, nor have they been fighting* for the continuance of slavery, the first battle of Bull-run did away with that idea. Their causes *since* for *war* have been as *noble*, and *greater far than those that* urged our *fathers on. Even* should we allow, they were *wrong* at the beginning of this contest, *cruelty and injustice*, have made the wrong become the *right*. And they stand *now*, (before the wonder and admiration of the *world*) as a noble band of patriotic heroes. Hereafter, reading of *their deeds*, Thermopylae will be forgotten.

When I aided in the capture and execution of John Brown, (Who was a murderer on our Western Border, and who was fairly *tried* and *convicted*,—before an impartial judge & jury—of treason,—And who by the way has since been made a

God—I was proud of my little share in the transaction, for I deemed it my duty And that I was helping our common country to perform an act of justice. But what was a crime in poor John Brown is now considered (by themselves) as the greatest and only virtue, of the whole Republican party. Strange transmigration, *vice* to become a *virtue*. Simply because *more* indulge in it. I thought then, *as now*, that the abolitionists, *were the only traitors* in the land, And that the entire party, deserved the fate of poor old Brown. Not because they wish to abolish slavery, but on account of the means they have even endeavored to use, to effect that abolition. If Brown were living, I doubt if he *himself*, would set slavery, against the Union. Most, or many, in the North do, And openly curse the Union, if the South are to return and retain a *single right* guaranteed them by every tie which we once *revered as sacred*. The south can make no choice. It is either extermination or slavery for *themselves* (worse than death) to draw from. I would know *my* choice.

I have, also, studied hard to discover upon what grounds, the rights of a state to Secede have been denied, when our very name (United States) and our Declaration of Independence, *both* provide for secession. But there is no time for words. I write in haste. I know how foolish I shall be deemed, for undertaking such a step, as this, Where on the one side, I have many friends, and everything to make me happy. Where my profession *alone* has gained me an income of *more than* Twenty thousand dollars a year. And where my great personal ambition in my profession has such a great field for labor. On the other hand—the south have never bestowed upon me one kind word. A place now, where I have no friends, except beneath the sod. A place where I must either become a private soldier or a beggar. To give up all of the *former* for the *latter*, besides my mother and sisters whom I love so dearly, (although they so widely differ with me in opinion) seems insane, But God is my judge I love *justice*, more than I do a country, that disowns it. More than fame and wealth. More (Heaven pardon me if wrong) more than a happy home. I have never been upon a battlefield, but, O my countrymen, could you all but see the *reality* or effects of this horrid war, as I have seen them (in *every State*, save Virginia) I know you would think like me.

And would pray the Almighty to create in the northern mind a sense of *right* and *justice* (even should it possess no seasoning of mercy.) and that he would dry up this Sea of blood between us,—which is daily growing wider. Alas, poor Country, Is she to meet her threatened doom. Four years ago, I would have given a thousand lives, to see her remain (as I had always known her) powerful and unbroken. And even now I would hold my life as naught, to see her what she was. O my friends, if the fearful scenes of the past four years had never been enacted, and if what has been had been but a frightful dream, from which we could now awake, with what overflowing hearts could we bless our God And pray for his continued favor. How I have loved the *old flag* can never, now, be known. A few years since and the entire world could boast of *none* so pure and spotless. But I have of late been seeing and hearing of the *bloody deeds* of which She has *been made, the emblem*. And would shudder to think how changed she had grown. O How I have longed to see her break from the mist of blood and death that circles round her folds, spoiling her beauty and tarnishing her honor. But no, day by day has she been draged deeper and deeper into cruelty and oppression, till now (in my eyes) her once bright red stripes look like *bloody gashes* on the face of Heaven. I look now upon my early admiration of her glories as a dream. My love (as things stand today) is for the South alone. Nor, do I deem it a dishonor in attempting to make for her a prisoner of this man, to whom she owes so much of misery. If success attends me, I go penniless to her side. They say she has found *that* "last ditch" which the north have so long derided, and been endeavoring to force her in, forgetting they are our brothers, and that its impolitic to goad an enemy to madness. Should I reach her in safety and find it true, I will proudly beg permission to triumph or die in that same "ditch" by her side,

A Confederate, doing duty *upon his own responsibility.*

J Wilkes Booth

November 1864

LINCOLN'S REELECTION:
LONDON, NOVEMBER 1864

Henry Adams to Charles Francis Adams Jr.

Henry Adams had accompanied his father, Charles Francis Adams, to London in 1861 and served as his confidential secretary. He wrote about the recent American election to his brother, who in July had been appointed lieutenant colonel of the 5th Massachusetts Cavalry, a black regiment.

No. 29. London. 25 Nov. 1864.

My dear Colonel:

Our last advices announce your arrival at home. I hope you will not return to camp until you have got wholly rid of your dysentery.

The election is over then, and after all that excitement, worry and danger, behold all goes on as before! It was one of those cases in which life and death seemed to hang on the issue, and the result is so decisive as to answer all our wishes and hopes. It is a curious commentary upon theoretical reasoning as to forms of Government, that this election which ought by all rights to be a defect in the system, and which is universally considered by the admirers of "strong Governments" to be a proof of the advantage of their own model, should yet turn out in practice a great and positive gain and a fruitful source of national strength. After all, systems of Government are secondary matters, if you've only got your people behind them. I never yet have felt so proud as now of the great qualities of our race, or so confident of the capacity of men to develop their faculties in the mass. I believe that a new era of the movement of the world will date from that day, which will drag nations up still another step, and carry us out of a quantity of old fogs. Europe has a long way to go yet to catch us up.

Anything that produces a great effect in our favor on this side, usually produces a sort of general silence as the first proof of its force. So this election has been met on this side by a species of blindness. People remark the fact with wonder and anger, but they have only just such a vague idea of what are to be its consequences, as shuts their mouths without changing their opinions. Only the most clear-headed see indistinctly what bearing it is likely to have on English politics, and I expect that it will be years yet before its full action gets into play. Meanwhile the Government is now stronger than ever and our only weak point is the financial one. May our name not have to stand guard on that!

You can imagine with what enthusiasm we received the news, and drank to the success of the new Administration. For the time, all interest has centered in the election, and even the incomprehensible state of things in Georgia has been overlooked. How many more campaigns we shall have to make, seems very doubtful, but thus far our rate of progression has been regular, and if continued, ought to bring us to Augusta at the next round. We can afford to be patient however, now, for all we have to fear is pecuniary ruin, and that is tolerably certain.

I don't know that I've anything to tell you that's new or original on this side. Loo Brooks came through this week on her way home after five weeks of most harrassing contact with her mamma-in-law, who appears to have been superbly herself. Poor Loo was happy to escape, and we cheered her and little Fanny amazingly by a few hours at Ealing. I sent by her a cargo of books to the young 'uns, our nephews which ought to keep them in literature till they're old men. By the way, should you go to Washington, try and have a talk with Seward about our affairs. The Chief, by this steamer, sends *privately* a request to be relieved. You can intimate to S. that if compelled to stay, he means at any rate to send his family home and break up the establishment, remaining himself as a temporary occupant till a successor is appointed. He even talks of doing so at once, and sending the women to Italy in January preparatory to their going home in June. Seward must see that a change, if necessary at all, had best be made quickly for the public good. Don't quote me however. On no account let what I say, come back. You will probably get at first hand all the information you want. Best say nothing at all, yet, of the idea of retirement except to S. if you see him. Let me know what he says.

You see we are in a "transition state." But I do not see a chance of release before March—unless for worse chains.

“MY BOY WAS DEAD”: KENTUCKY, NOVEMBER 1864

Joseph Miller: Statement Regarding His Family

Located twenty miles south of Lexington, Kentucky, the Union supply depot at Camp Nelson became a major recruitment center for the U.S. Colored Troops in June 1864, and almost 4,000 black soldiers had enlisted there by the end of October. Some of the soldiers were accompanied to the camp by their families, who were either fleeing slavery or had been driven from their homes by whites bitterly opposed to black enlistment. In an effort to conciliate slaveholding Kentucky unionists who objected to the military giving refuge to slaves, Adjutant-General Lorenzo Thomas issued orders in July barring the families of black soldiers from Camp Nelson. Despite his instructions, families continued to live in the camp. On November 22 Brigadier General Speed S. Fry, the Kentucky unionist who commanded Camp Nelson, ordered the expulsion in freezing weather of some 400 women and children and the destruction of their huts and cabins. Captain Theron E. Hall, a quartermaster who had served at the camp, protested Fry's action to Brigadier General Stephen G. Burbridge, the Union commander in Kentucky. Writing as "Humanitas," Hall published an account of the expulsions in the *New-York Daily Tribune* that was accompanied by Joseph Miller's affidavit. Burbridge countermanded Fry's order, and on November 29 gave Hall authority over the refugees. Hall and the Reverend John G. Fee established a refugee home at Camp Nelson in January 1865, but were unable to save many of those who had been driven out in November. On February 21, 1865, Fee wrote that of the 400 expelled, about 250 had returned to the camp, and that 102 of those who returned had died "in consequence of being exposed to cold & then herded together in Barracks" where "noise, disease & death rage." Among the dead were the Miller family. Joseph Miller's sons, Joseph Jr. and Calvin; his daughter, Maria; and his wife, Isabella, all died at Camp Nelson between December 17, 1864, and January 2, 1865. They were followed on January 6 by Joseph Miller himself.

Camp Nelson Ky November 26, 1864

Personally appered before me E. B W Restieaux Capt. and

Asst. Quartermaster Joseph Miller a man of color who being duly sworn upon oath says

I was a slave of George Miller of Lincoln County Ky. I have always resided in Kentucky and am now a Soldier in the service of the United States. I belong to Company I 124 U.S.C. Inft now Stationed at Camp Nelson Ky. When I came to Camp for the purpose of enlisting about the middle of October 1864 my wife and children came with me because my master said that if I enlisted he would not maintain them and I knew they would be abused by him when I left. I had then four children ages respectively ten nine seven and four years. On my presenting myself as a recruit I was told by the Lieut. in command to take my family into a tent within the limits of the Camp. My wife and family occupied this tent by the express permission of the aforementioned Officer and never received any notice to leave until Tuesday November 22" when a mounted guard gave my wife notice that she and her children must leave Camp before early morning. This was about six O'clock at night. My little boy about seven years of age had been very sick and was slowly recovering My wife had no place to go and so remained until morning. About eight Oclock Wednesday morning November 23" a mounted guard came to my tent and ordered my wife and children out of Camp The morning was bitter cold. It was freezing hard. I was certain that it would kill my sick child to take him out in the cold. I told the man in charge of the guard that it would be the death of my boy I told him that my wife and children had no place to go and I told him that I was a soldier of the United States. He told me that it did not make any difference. he had orders to take all out of Camp. He told my wife and family that if they did not get up into the wagon which he had he would shoot the last one of them. On being thus threatened my wife and children went into the wagon My wife carried her sick child in her arms. When they left the tent the wind was blowing hard and cold and having had to leave much of our clothing when we left our master, my wife with her little one was poorly clad. I followed them as far as the lines. I had no Knowledge where they were taking them. At night I went in search of my family. I found them at Nicholasville about six miles from Camp. They were in an old meeting house belonging to the colored people. The building was very cold having only one fire. My wife and children could not get near the fire, because of the number of colored people huddled together by the soldiers. I found my wife and children shivering with cold and famished with hunger They had not recieved a morsel of food during the whole day. My boy was dead. He died directly after getting down from the wagon. I Know he was Killed by exposure to the inclement weather I had to return to camp that night so I left my family in the meeting house and walked back. I had walked there. I travelled in all twelve miles Next morning I walked to Nicholasville. I dug a grave myself and buried my own child. I left my family in the Meeting house—where they still remain And further this deponent saith not

his
(Signed) Joseph Miller
mark

BATTLE OF FRANKLIN: TENNESSEE,
NOVEMBER–DECEMBER 1864

Samuel T. Foster: Diary, November 30–December 1, 1864

John B. Hood began his invasion of Middle Tennessee on November 21, advancing from Florence, Alabama, with 38,000 men. The Union troops opposing Hood's offensive were divided between Pulaski, Tennessee, where John M. Schofield commanded 30,000 men, and Nashville, seventy miles to the north, where George H. Thomas had assembled a force of 25,000 men. As Hood attempted to maneuver between the two Union armies, Schofield withdrew north to Columbia on the Duck River. On November 29 Hood succeeded in turning Schofield's flank by crossing the Duck, but was unable to overcome Union resistance near Spring Hill and block the Columbia–Franklin turnpike before dusk. During the night Schofield retreated past Hood's army and reached Franklin. Angered by the Union escape and determined to prevent Schofield from joining Thomas at Nashville, Hood ordered a series of frontal assaults on the entrenchments outside Franklin late in the afternoon of November 30. (In his postwar memoir *Advance and Retreat*, Hood would partially blame his failure at Spring Hill on the unwillingness of his army "to accept battle unless under the protection of breastworks," a reluctance he attributed to the "ruinous" and "timid" defensive policy followed by his predecessor Joseph E. Johnston during the Confederate retreat from Dalton to Atlanta.) Captain Foster of the dismounted 24th Texas Cavalry wrote about the battle, which cost the Confederates 6,200 men killed, wounded, or missing, and the Union 2,300. After the fighting ended, Schofield withdrew across the Harpeth River and joined Thomas at Nashville.

Nov 30th

Our Corpse were sent across Duck river yesterday above the town with orders to go around and strike the Pike at Spring Hill. The Yanks seem to have found out that we were flanking them and they left in the night last night and went to Franklin.

This morning I leave Columbia at 9½ O'Clock AM and reach Spring Hill at 12.

I overtake the command three (3) miles from Franklin.

The line of battle is formed, with our Brigade near the centre and just on the right of the Turn Pike. Our regiment being on the left of the Brigd. put our Regt. next the Pike, and my Company being on the left of the regiment—it puts us on the Pike— A skirmish line is put out two or three hundred yards in advance of the main line. Here we have something new in the way of fighting. At the command forward the Bands begin to play and we march off to the music, in a few minutes our skirmishers commenced firing.

We soon came up to the skirmishers fighting the Yanks in line of battle behind breastworks. We make no halt, but keep strait on without firing a gun, and they fire a few shots and break to run, and as soon as they break to run our men break after them. They have nearly ½ mile to run to get back to their next line—so here we go right after them and yelling like fury and shooting at them at the same time. Kill some of them before they reach their works, and those that are in the second line of works are not able to shoot us because their own men are in front of us—and between us and them. So here we go, Yanks runing for life and we for the fun of it, but the difference in the objects are so great that they out run us, but loose quite a number of their men before they get there.

By the time they get to their 2nd line of works the men that were in them are out and on the run, and they all run back to the 3rd line of breastworks, while we stop at the 2nd line. The 3rd line was not over 40 yds from us— We take position out side of their works, and they come out and charge us in return.

They come up and meet us at this 2nd line and stop on one side and we on the other—with a bank of dirt between us. By this time it was getting dark and the firing was stoping gradually.

We are just in the edge of the town, and the dead and wounded are all around us, and Yank and Confed. lie dead near each other— The firing by an hour after night has nearly ceased, except when one man will hold his gun up as high as he can and shoot over the bank of dirt.

They throw clods of dirt over and sticks or anything they can get hold of.

We hear that Gen Pat Cleburn, and Gen Granbury are both dead. We hear that Hood has ordered all of our artillery (112 pieces) to be put in position to open on the town at daylight.

About 1 O'Clock in the night we find that the Yanks have all left, actually sliped off and we did not know it. As soon as Hood hears of it he ordered all the Artillery to shell the road on the other side of the river. This was about 2 O'Clock in the morning.

When every thing is still (in the night) and one hundred and twelve pieces of artilery all open at once, it makes no little noise, but it did not last long. They were all gone, out of reach towards Nashville— Now we strike a light and make fires and begin to look around, and count noses.

I find that eight of my men are wounded—two killed and two missing, supposed to be captured.

DEC 1st At Daylight this morning we can see the terrible results of the fight on yesterday and last night— The dead of both armies are lying together all over the ground—sometimes they are together.

There is great destruction of human life here— I have seen places where the blood run off in a stream, and also to stand in pools in places— Eighteen men dead on the ground out of our Regt.

Col. Young killed Maj Taylor captured and our Brigade is left without a field officer. Hickox of my Co. that was captured last night made his escape and came to us this morning. He is wounded also.

All the army follow the Yanks this morning on to Nashville. Our Brigd and the Ark. Brigd are so badly cut up that we can't move. Some officers have no men, and some companies have no officers— So we have to reorganize and consolidate, a Captain has to command the Brigade.

Gen. Hood has betrayed us (The Army of Tenn). This is not the kind of fighting he promised us at Tuscumbia and Florence Ala. when we started into Tenn.

This was not a "fight with equal numbers and choice of the ground" by no means.

And the wails and cries of widows and orphans made at Franklin Tenn Nov 30th 1864 will heat up the fires of the bottomless pit to burn the soul of Gen J B Hood for Murdering their husbands and fathers at that place that day. It can't be called anything else but cold blooded Murder.

He sacrificed those men to make the name of Hood famous; when if the History of it is ever written it will make him *infamous.*

He had near 10,000 men murdered around Atlanta trying to prove to the world that he was a greater man than Genl Johnson— Because Johnson said that Atlanta was untenable, and could not be held with the men he had against the men that Sherman had. And how small he must have felt when he had to leave there in the night to keep from being captured.

And now in order to recover from the merited disgrace of that transaction he brings this Army here into middle Tenn. and by making them false promises and false statements get these men killed— Put them into a fight where the Yanks have three lines of breastworks; the second or middle line being lined with artillery.

The men have a right to believe he told the truth and go forward to certain and sure destructions; but "Vengeance is mine Sayeth the Lord" and it will surely overtake him.

WASHINGTON, D.C., DECEMBER 1864

Abraham Lincoln: Annual Message to Congress

President Lincoln sent his annual message to Congress four weeks after his reelection. The voting figures for the 1864 presidential election that accompanied it were supplied by the governors of the Union states after Lincoln sent telegrams requesting them on November 15 and November 29. His prediction that the 39th Congress, which was scheduled to meet in December 1865, would "almost certainly" pass a constitutional amendment abolishing slavery was based on the Republican gain of forty-three House seats in the 1864 elections.

December 6, 1864

Fellow-citizens of the Senate and House of Representatives:

Again the blessings of health and abundant harvests claim our profoundest gratitude to Almighty God.

The condition of our foreign affairs is reasonably satisfactory.

Mexico continues to be a theatre of civil war. While our political relations with that country have undergone no change, we have, at the same time, strictly maintained neutrality between the belligerents.

At the request of the states of Costa Rica and Nicaragua, a competent engineer has been authorized to make a survey of the river San Juan and the port of San Juan. It is a source of much satisfaction that the difficulties which for a moment excited some political apprehensions, and caused a closing of the inter-oceanic transit route, have been amicably adjusted, and that there is a good prospect that the route will soon be reopened with an increase of capacity and adaptation. We could not exaggerate either the commercial or the political importance of that great improvement.

It would be doing injustice to an important South American state not to acknowledge the directness, frankness, and cordiality with which the United States of Colombia have entered into intimate relations with this government. A claims convention has been constituted to complete the unfinished work of the one which closed its session in 1861.

The new liberal constitution of Venezuela having gone into effect with the universal acquiescence of the people, the government under it has been recognized, and diplomatic intercourse with it has opened in a cordial and friendly spirit. The long-deferred Aves Island claim has been satisfactorily paid and discharged.

Mutual payments have been made of the claims awarded by the late joint commission for the settlement of claims between the United States and Peru. An earnest and cordial friendship continues to exist between the two countries, and such efforts as were in my power have been used to remove misunderstanding and avert a threatened war between Peru and Spain.

Our relations are of the most friendly nature with Chile, the Argentine Republic, Bolivia, Costa Rica, Paraguay, San Salvador, and Hayti.

During the past year no differences of any kind have arisen with any of those republics, and, on the other hand, their sympathies with the United States are constantly expressed with cordiality and earnestness.

The claim arising from the seizure of the cargo of the brig Macedonian in 1821 has been paid in full by the government of Chile.

Civil war continues in the Spanish part of San Domingo, apparently without prospect of an early close.

Official correspondence has been freely opened with Liberia, and it gives us a pleasing view of social and political progress in that Republic. It may be expected to derive new vigor from American influence, improved by the rapid disappearance of slavery in the United States.

I solicit your authority to furnish to the republic a gunboat at moderate cost, to be reimbursed to the United States by instalments. Such a vessel is needed for the safety of that state against the native African races; and in Liberian hands it would be more effective in arresting the African slave trade than a squadron in our own hands. The possession of the least organized naval force would stimulate a generous ambition in the republic, and the confidence which we should manifest by furnishing it would win forbearance and favor towards the colony from all civilized nations.

The proposed overland telegraph between America and Europe, by the way of Behring's Straits and Asiatic Russia, which was sanctioned by Congress at the last session, has been undertaken, under very favorable circumstances, by an association of American citizens, with the cordial good-will and support as well of this government as of those of Great Britain and Russia. Assurances have been received from most of the South American States of their high appreciation of the enterprise, and their readiness to co-operate in constructing lines tributary to that world-encircling communication. I learn, with much satisfaction, that the noble design of a telegraphic communication between the eastern coast of America and Great Britain has been renewed with full expectation of its early accomplishment.

Thus it is hoped that with the return of domestic peace the country will be able to resume with energy and advantage its former high career of commerce and civilization.

Our very popular and estimable representative in Egypt died in April last. An unpleasant altercation which arose between the temporary incumbent of the office and the government of the Pacha resulted in a suspension of intercourse. The evil was promptly corrected on the arrival of the successor in the consulate, and our relations with Egypt, as well as our relations with the Barbary powers, are entirely satisfactory.

The rebellion which has so long been flagrant in China, has at last been suppressed, with the co-operating good offices of this government, and of the other western commercial states. The judicial consular establishment there has become very difficult and onerous, and it will need legislative revision to adapt it to the extension of our commerce, and to the more intimate intercourse which has been instituted with the government and people of that vast empire. China seems to be accepting with hearty good-will the conventional laws which regulate commercial and social intercourse among the western nations.

Owing to the peculiar situation of Japan, and the anomalous form of its government, the action of that empire in performing treaty stipulations is inconstant and capricious. Nevertheless, good progress has been effected by the western powers, moving with enlightened concert. Our own pecuniary claims have been allowed, or put in course of settlement, and the inland sea has been reopened to commerce. There is reason also to believe that these proceedings have increased rather than diminished the friendship of Japan towards the United States.

The ports of Norfolk, Fernandina, and Pensacola have been opened by proclamation. It is hoped that foreign merchants will now consider whether it is not safer and more profitable to themselves, as well as just to the United States, to resort to these and other open ports, than it is to pursue, through many hazards, and at vast cost, a contraband trade with other ports which are closed, if not by actual military occupation, at least by a lawful and effective blockade.

For myself, I have no doubt of the power and duty of the Executive, under the law of nations, to exclude enemies of the human race from an asylum in the United States. If Congress should think that proceedings in such cases lack the authority of law, or ought to be further regulated by it, I recommend that provision be made for effectually preventing foreign slave traders from acquiring domicile and facilities for their criminal occupation in our country.

It is possible that, if it were a new and open question, the maritime powers, with the lights they now enjoy, would not concede the privileges of a naval belligerent to the insurgents of the United States, destitute, as they are, and always have been, equally of ships-of-war and of ports and harbors. Disloyal emissaries have been neither less assiduous nor more successful during the last year than they were before that time in their efforts, under favor of that privilege, to embroil our country in foreign wars. The desire and determination of the governments of the maritime states to defeat that design are believed to be as sincere as, and cannot be more earnest than our own. Nevertheless, unforeseen political difficulties have arisen, especially in Brazilian and British ports, and on the northern boundary of the United States, which have required, and are likely to continue to require, the practice of constant vigilance, and a just and conciliatory spirit on the part of the United States as well as of the nations concerned and their governments.

Commissioners have been appointed under the treaty with

Great Britain on the adjustment of the claims of the Hudson's Bay and Puget's Sound Agricultural Companies, in Oregon, and are now proceeding to the execution of the trust assigned to them.

In view of the insecurity of life and property in the region adjacent to the Canadian border, by reason of recent assaults and depredations committed by inimical and desperate persons, who are harbored there, it has been thought proper to give notice that after the expiration of six months, the period conditionally stipulated in the existing arrangement with Great Britain, the United States must hold themselves at liberty to increase their naval armament upon the lakes, if they shall find that proceeding necessary. The condition of the border will necessarily come into consideration in connection with the question of continuing or modifying the rights of transit from Canada through the United States, as well as the regulation of imposts, which were temporarily established by the reciprocity treaty of the 5th of June, 1854.

I desire, however, to be understood, while making this statement, that the Colonial authorities of Canada are not deemed to be intentionally unjust or unfriendly towards the United States; but, on the contrary, there is every reason to expect that, with the approval of the imperial government, they will take the necessary measures to prevent new incursions across the border.

The act passed at the last session for the encouragement of emigration has, so far as was possible, been put into operation. It seems to need amendment which will enable the officers of the government to prevent the practice of frauds against the immigrants while on their way and on their arrival in the ports, so as to secure them here a free choice of avocations and places of settlement. A liberal disposition towards this great national policy is manifested by most of the European States, and ought to be reciprocated on our part by giving the immigrants effective national protection. I regard our emigrants as one of the principal replenishing streams which are appointed by Providence to repair the ravages of internal war, and its wastes of national strength and health. All that is necessary is to secure the flow of that stream in its present fullness, and to that end the government must, in every way, make it manifest that it neither needs nor designs to impose involuntary military service upon those who come from other lands to cast their lot in our country.

The financial affairs of the government have been successfully administered during the last year. The legislation of the last session of Congress has beneficially affected the revenues, although sufficient time has not yet elapsed to experience the full effect of several of the provisions of the acts of Congress imposing increased taxation.

The receipts during the year, from all sources, upon the basis of warrants signed by the Secretary of the Treasury, including loans and the balance in the treasury on the first day of July, 1863, were $1,394,796,007 62; and the aggregate disbursements, upon the same basis, were $1,298,056,101 89, leaving a balance in the treasury, as shown by warrants, of $96,739,905 73.

Deduct from these amounts the amount of the principal of the public debt redeemed, and the amount of issues in substitution therefor, and the actual cash operations of the treasury were: receipts, $884,076,646 57; disbursements $865,234,087 86; which leaves a cash balance in the treasury of $18,842,558 71.

Of the receipts, there were derived from customs, $102,316,152 99; from lands, $588,333 29; from direct taxes, $475,648 96; from internal revenue, $109,741,134 10; from miscellaneous sources, $47,511,448 10; and from loans applied to actual expenditures, including former balance, $623,443,929 13.

There were disbursed, for the civil service, $27,505,599 46; for pensions and Indians, $7,517,930 97; for the War Department $690,791,842 97; for the Navy Department $85,733,292 77; for interest of the public debt $53,685,421 69;—making an aggregate of $865,234,087.86, and leaving a balance in the treasury of $18,842,558.71, as before stated.

For the actual receipts and disbursements for the first quarter, and the estimated receipts and disbursements for the three remaining quarters of the current fiscal year, and the general operations of the treasury in detail, I refer you to the report of the Secretary of the Treasury. I concur with him in the opinion that the proportion of moneys required to meet the expenses consequent upon the war derived from taxation should be still further increased; and I earnestly invite your attention to this subject, to the end that there may be such additional legislation as shall be required to meet the just expectations of the Secretary.

The public debt on the first day of July last, as appears by the books of the treasury, amounted to $1,740,690,489 49. Probably, should the war continue for another year, that amount may be increased by not far from five hundred millions. Held as it is, for the most part, by our own people, it has become a substantial branch of national, though private, property. For obvious reasons, the more nearly this property can be distributed among all the people the better. To favor such general distribution, greater inducements to become owners might, perhaps, with good effect, and without injury, be presented to persons of limited means. With this view, I suggest whether it might not be both competent and expedient for Congress to provide that a limited amount of some future issue of public securities might be held by any bona fide purchaser exempt from taxation, and from seizure for debt, under such restrictions and limitations as might be necessary to guard against abuse of so important a privilege. This would enable every prudent person to set aside a small annuity against a possible day of want.

Privileges like these would render the possession of such securities, to the amount limited, most desirable to every person of small means who might be able to save enough for the purpose. The great advantage of citizens being creditors as well as debtors, with relation to the public debt, is obvious. Men readily perceive that they cannot be much oppressed by a debt which they owe to themselves.

The public debt on the first day of July last, although somewhat exceeding the estimate of the Secretary of the Treasury made to Congress at the commencement of the last session, falls short of the estimate of that officer made in the preceding December, as to its probable amount at the beginning of this year, by the sum of $3,995,097 31. This fact exhibits a satisfactory condition and conduct of the operations of the Treasury.

The national banking system is proving to be acceptable to capitalists and to the people. On the twenty-fifth day of November five hundred and eighty-four national banks had been organized, a considerable number of which were conversions from State banks. Changes from State systems to the national system are rapidly taking place, and it is hoped that, very soon, there will be in the United States, no banks of issue not authorized by Congress, and no bank-note circulation not secured by the government. That the government and the people will derive great benefit from this change in the banking systems of the country can hardly be questioned. The national system will create a reliable and permanent influence in support of the national credit, and protect the people against losses in the use of paper money. Whether or not any further legislation is advisable for the suppression of State bank issues, it will be for Congress to determine. It seems quite clear that the treasury cannot be satisfactorily conducted unless the government can exercise a restraining power over the bank-note circulation of the country.

The report of the Secretary of War and the accompanying documents will detail the campaigns of the armies in the field since the date of the last annual message, and also the operations of the several administrative bureaus of the War Department during the last year. It will also specify the measures deemed essential for the national defence, and to keep up and supply the requisite military force.

The report of the Secretary of the Navy presents a comprehensive and satisfactory exhibit of the affairs of that Department and of the naval service. It is a subject of congratulation and laudable pride to our countrymen that a navy of such vast proportions has been organized in so brief a period, and conducted with so much efficiency and success.

The general exhibit of the navy, including vessels under construction on the 1st. of December, 1864, shows a total of 671 vessels, carrying 4,610 guns, and of 510,396 tons, being an actual increase during the year, over and above all losses by shipwreck or in battle, of 83 vessels, 167 guns, and 42,427 tons.

The total number of men at this time in the naval service, including officers, is about 51,000.

There have been captured by the navy during the year 324 vessels, and the whole number of naval captures since hostilities commenced is 1,379, of which 267 are steamers.

The gross proceeds arising from the sale of condemned

prize property, thus far reported, amount to $14,396,250 51. A large amount of such proceeds is still under adjudication and yet to be reported.

The total expenditures of the Navy Department of every description, including the cost of the immense squadrons that have been called into existence from the 4th of March, 1861, to the 1st. of November, 1864, are $238,647,262 35.

Your favorable consideration is invited to the various recommendations of the Secretary of the Navy, especially in regard to a navy yard and suitable establishment for the construction and repair of iron vessels, and the machinery and armature for our ships, to which reference was made in my last annual message.

Your attention is also invited to the views expressed in the report in relation to the legislation of Congress at its last session in respect to prize on our inland waters.

I cordially concur in the recommendation of the Secretary as to the propriety of creating the new rank of vice-admiral in our naval service.

Your attention is invited to the report of the Postmaster General for a detailed account of the operations and financial condition of the Post Office Department.

The postal revenues for the year ending June 30, 1864, amounted to $12,438,253.78 and the expenditures to $12,644,786.20; the excess of expenditures over receipts being $206,652.42.

The views presented by the Postmaster General on the subject of special grants by the government in aid of the establishment of new lines of ocean mail steamships and the policy he recommends for the development of increased commercial intercourse with adjacent and neighboring countries, should receive the careful consideration of Congress.

It is of noteworthy interest that the steady expansion of population, improvement and governmental institutions over the new and unoccupied portions of our country have scarcely been checked, much less impeded or destroyed, by our great civil war, which at first glance would seem to have absorbed almost the entire energies of the nation.

The organization and admission of the State of Nevada has been completed in conformity with law, and thus our excellent system is firmly established in the mountains, which once seemed a barren and uninhabitable waste between the Atlantic States and those which have grown up on the coast of the Pacific ocean.

The territories of the Union are generally in a condition of prosperity and rapid growth. Idaho and Montana, by reason of their great distance and the interruption of communication with them by Indian hostilities, have been only partially organized; but it is understood that these difficulties are about to disappear, which will permit their governments, like those of the others, to go into speedy and full operation.

As intimately connected with, and promotive of, this material growth of the nation, I ask the attention of Congress to the valuable information and important recommendations relating to the public lands, Indian affairs, the Pacific railroad, and mineral discoveries contained in the report of the Secretary of the Interior, which is herewith transmitted, and which report also embraces the subjects of patents, pensions and other topics of public interest pertaining to his department.

The quantity of public land disposed of during the five quarters ending on the 30th of September last was 4,221,342 acres, of which 1,538,614 acres were entered under the homestead law. The remainder was located with military land warrants, agricultural scrip certified to States for railroads, and sold for cash. The cash received from sales and location fees was $1,019,446.

The income from sales during the fiscal year, ending June 30, 1864, was $678,007,21, against $136,077,95 received during the preceding year. The aggregate number of acres surveyed during the year has been equal to the quantity disposed of; and there is open to settlement about 133,000,000 acres of surveyed land.

The great enterprise of connecting the Atlantic with the Pacific States by railways and telegraph lines has been entered upon with a vigor that gives assurance of success, notwithstanding the embarrassments arising from the prevailing high prices of materials and labor. The route of the main line of the road has been definitely located for one hundred miles westward from the initial point at Omaha City, Nebraska, and a preliminary location of the Pacific railroad of California has been made from Sacramento eastward to the great bend of the Truckee river in Nevada.

Numerous discoveries of gold, silver and cinnabar mines have been added to the many heretofore known and the country occupied by the Sierra Nevada and Rocky mountains, and the subordinate ranges, now teems with enterprising labor, which is richly remunerative. It is believed that the product of the mines of precious metals in that region has, during the year, reached, if not exceeded, one hundred millions in value.

It was recommended in my last annual message that our Indian system be remodelled. Congress, at its last session, acting upon the recommendation, did provide for reorganizing the system in California, and it is believed that under the present organization the management of the Indians there will be attended with reasonable success. Much yet remains to be done to provide for the proper government of the Indians in other parts of the country to render it secure for the advancing settler, and to provide for the welfare of the Indian. The Secretary reiterates his recommendations, and to them the attention of Congress is invited.

The liberal provisions made by Congress for paying pensions to invalid soldiers and sailors of the republic, and to the widows, orphans, and dependent mothers of those who have fallen in battle, or died of disease contracted, or of wounds received in the service of their country, have been diligently administered. There have been added to the pension rolls, during the year ending the 30th day of June last, the names of 16,770 invalid soldiers, and of 271 disabled seamen, making the present number of army invalid pensioners 22,767, and of navy invalid pensioners 712.

Of widows, orphans and mothers, 22 198 have been placed on the army pension rolls, and 248 on the navy rolls. The present number of army pensioners of this class is 25,433, and of navy pensioners 793. At the beginning of the year the number of revolutionary pensioners was 1,430; only twelve of them were soldiers, of whom seven have since died. The remainder are those who, under the law, receive pensions because of relationship to revolutionary soldiers. During the year ending the

30th of June, 1864, $4,504,616.92 have been paid to pensioners of all classes.

I cheerfully commend to your continued patronage the benevolent institutions of the District of Columbia which have hitherto been established or fostered by Congress, and respectfully refer, for information concerning them, and in relation to the Washington aqueduct, the Capitol and other matters of local interest, to the report of the Secretary.

The Agricultural Department, under the supervision of its present energetic and faithful head, is rapidly commending itself to the great and vital interest it was created to advance. It is peculiarly the people's department, in which they feel more directly concerned than in any other. I commend it to the continued attention and fostering care of Congress.

The war continues. Since the last annual message all the important lines and positions then occupied by our forces have been maintained, and our arms have steadily advanced; thus liberating the regions left in rear, so that Missouri, Kentucky, Tennessee and parts of other States have again produced reasonably fair crops.

The most remarkable feature in the military operations of the year is General Sherman's attempted march of three hundred miles directly through the insurgent region. It tends to show a great increase of our relative strength that our General-in-Chief should feel able to confront and hold in check every active force of the enemy, and yet to detach a well-appointed large army to move on such an expedition. The result not yet being known, conjecture in regard to it is not here indulged.

Important movements have also occurred during the year to the effect of moulding society for durability in the Union. Although short of complete success, it is much in the right direction, that twelve thousand citizens in each of the States of Arkansas and Louisiana have organized loyal State governments with free constitutions, and are earnestly struggling to maintain and administer them. The movements in the same direction, more extensive, though less definite in Missouri, Kentucky and Tennessee, should not be overlooked. But Maryland presents the example of complete success. Maryland is secure to Liberty and Union for all the future. The genius of rebellion will no more claim Maryland. Like another foul spirit, being driven out, it may seek to tear her, but it will woo her no more.

At the last session of Congress a proposed amendment of the Constitution abolishing slavery throughout the United States, passed the Senate, but failed for lack of the requisite two-thirds vote in the House of Representatives. Although the present is the same Congress, and nearly the same members, and without questioning the wisdom or patriotism of those who stood in opposition, I venture to recommend the reconsideration and passage of the measure at the present session. Of course the abstract question is not changed; but an intervening election shows, almost certainly, that the next Congress will pass the measure if this does not. Hence there is only a question of *time* as to when the proposed amendment will go to the States for their action. And as it is to so go, at all events, may we not agree that the sooner the better? It is not claimed that the election has imposed a duty on members to change their views or their votes, any further than, as an additional element to be considered, their judgment may be affected by it. It is the voice of the people now, for the first time, heard upon the question. In a great national crisis, like ours, unanimity of action among those seeking a common end is very desirable—almost indispensable. And yet no approach to such unanimity is attainable, unless some deference shall be paid to the will of the majority, simply because it is the will of the majority. In this case the common end is the maintenance of the Union; and, among the means to secure that end, such will, through the election, is most clearly declared in favor of such constitutional amendment.

The most reliable indication of public purpose in this country is derived through our popular elections. Judging by the recent canvass and its result, the purpose of the people, within the loyal States, to maintain the integrity of the Union, was never more firm, nor more nearly unanimous, than now. The extraordinary calmness and good order with which the millions of voters met and mingled at the polls, give strong assurance of this. Not only all those who supported the Union ticket, so called, but a great majority of the opposing party also, may be fairly claimed to entertain, and to be actuated by, the same purpose. It is an unanswerable argument to this effect, that no candidate for any office whatever, high or low, has ventured to seek votes on the avowal that he was for giving up the Union. There have been much impugning of motives, and much heated controversy as to the proper means and best mode of advancing the Union cause; but on the distinct issue of Union or no Union, the politicians have shown their instinctive knowledge that there is no diversity among the people. In affording the people the fair opportunity of showing, one to another and to the world, this firmness and unanimity of purpose, the election has been of vast value to the national cause.

The election has exhibited another fact not less valuable to be known—the fact that we do not approach exhaustion in the most important branch of national resources—that of living men. While it is melancholy to reflect that the war has filled so many graves, and carried mourning to so many hearts, it is some relief to know that, compared with the surviving, the fallen have been so few. While corps, and divisions, and brigades, and regiments have formed, and fought, and dwindled, and gone out of existence, a great majority of the men who composed them are still living. The same is true of the naval service. The election returns prove this. So many voters could not else be found. The States regularly holding elections, both now and four years ago, to wit, California, Connecticut, Delaware, Illinois, Indiana, Iowa, Kentucky, Maine, Maryland, Massachusetts, Michigan, Minnesota, Missouri, New Hampshire, New Jersey, New York, Ohio, Oregon, Pennsylvania, Rhode Island, Vermont, West Virginia, and Wisconsin cast 3.982.011 votes now, against 3.870.222 cast then, showing an aggregate now of 3.982.011. To this is to be added 33.762 cast now in the new States of Kansas and Nevada, which States did not vote in 1860, thus swelling the aggregate to 4.015.773 and the net increase during the three years and a half of war to 145.551. A table is appended showing particulars. To this again should be added the number of all soldiers in the field from Massachusetts, Rhode Island, New Jersey, Delaware, Indiana, Illinois, and California, who, by the laws of those States, could not vote away from their homes, and which number cannot be less than 90.000. Nor yet is this all. The number in organized Territories is triple now what it was four years ago, while thousands, white and black, join us as the national arms press back the insurgent lines. So much is shown, affirmatively and negatively, by the election. It is not material to inquire *how* the increase has been produced, or to show that it would have been *greater* but for the war, which is probably true. The important fact remains demonstrated, that we have *more* men *now* than we had when the war *began*; that we are not exhausted, nor in process of exhaustion; that we are *gaining* strength, and may, if need be, maintain the contest indefinitely. This as to men. Material resources are now more complete and abundant than ever.

The national resources, then, are unexhausted, and, as we believe, inexhaustible. The public purpose to re-establish and maintain the national authority is unchanged, and, as we believe, unchangeable. The manner of continuing the effort remains to choose. On careful consideration of all the evidence accessible it seems to me that no attempt at negotiation with the insurgent leader could result in any good. He would accept nothing short of severance of the Union—precisely what we will not and cannot give. His declarations to this effect are explicit and oft-repeated. He does not attempt to deceive us. He affords us no excuse to deceive ourselves. He cannot voluntarily reaccept the Union; we cannot voluntarily yield it. Between him and us the issue is distinct, simple, and inflexible. It is an issue which can only be tried by war, and decided by victory. If we yield, we are beaten; if the Southern people fail him, he is beaten. Either way, it would be the victory and defeat following war. What is true, however, of him who heads the insurgent cause, is not necessarily true of those who follow. Although he cannot reaccept the Union, they can. Some of them, we know, already desire peace and reunion. The number of such may increase. They can, at any moment, have peace simply by laying down their arms and submitting to the national authority under the Constitution. After so much, the government could not, if it would, maintain war against them. The loyal people would not sustain or allow it. If questions should remain, we would adjust them by the peaceful means of legislation, conference, courts, and votes, operating only in constitutional and lawful channels. Some certain, and other possible, questions are, and would be, beyond the Executive power to adjust; as, for instance, the admission of members into Congress, and whatever might require the appropriation of money. The Executive power itself would be greatly diminished by the cessation of actual war. Pardons and remissions of forfeitures, however, would still be within Executive control. In what spirit and temper this control would be exercised can be fairly judged of by the past.

A year ago general pardon and amnesty, upon specified terms, were offered to all, except certain designated classes; and, it was, at the same time, made known that the excepted classes were still within contemplation of special clemency. During the year many availed themselves of the general provision, and many more would, only that the signs of bad faith in some led to such precautionary measures as rendered the practical process less easy and certain. During the same time also special pardons have been granted to individuals of the excepted classes, and no voluntary application has been denied. Thus, practically, the door has been, for a full year, open to all, except such as were not in condition to make free choice—that is, such as were in custody or under constraint. It is still so open to all. But the time may come—probably will come—when public duty shall demand that it be closed; and that, in lieu, more rigorous measures than heretofore shall be adopted.

In presenting the abandonment of armed resistance to the national authority on the part of the insurgents, as the only indispensable condition to ending the war on the part of the government, I retract nothing heretofore said as to slavery. I repeat the declaration made a year ago, that "while I remain in my present position I shall not attempt to retract or modify the emancipation proclamation, nor shall I return to slavery any person who is free by the terms of that proclamation, or by any of the Acts of Congress." If the people should, by whatever mode or means, make it an Executive duty to re-enslave such persons, another, and not I, must be their instrument to perform it.

In stating a single condition of peace, I mean simply to say that the war will cease on the part of the government, whenever it shall have ceased on the part of those who began it.

December 6. 1864. ABRAHAM LINCOLN

Table showing the aggregate votes in the States named, at the presidential election respectively in 1860 and 1864.

	1860.	1864.
California	118,840	*110,000
Connecticut	77,246	86,616
Delaware	16,039	16,924
Illinois	339,693	348,235
Indiana	272,143	280,645
Iowa	128,331	143,331
Kentucky	146,216	*91,300
Maine	97,918	115,141
Maryland	92,502	72,703
Massachusetts	169,533	175,487
Michigan	154,747	162,413
Minnesota	34,799	42,534
Missouri	165,538	*90,000
New Hampshire	65,953	69,111
New Jersey	121,125	128,680
New York	675,156	730,664
Ohio	442,441	470,745
Oregon	14,410	†14,410
Pennsylvania	476,442	572,697
Rhode Island	19,931	22,187
Vermont	42,844	55,811
West Virginia	46,195	33,874
Wisconsin	152,180	148,513
	3,870,222	3,982,011
Kansas		17,234
Nevada		16,528
		33,762
		3,982,011
Total		4,015,773
		3,870,222
Net increase		145,551

*Nearly †Estimated.

REPORTS OF A SLAVE INSURRECTION: NORTH CAROLINA, DECEMBER 1864

Henry Nutt to Zebulon B. Vance

Henry Nutt, a prominent Wilmington merchant, wrote to Governor Zebulon B. Vance about reports of a planned slave insurrection in southeastern North Carolina and the measures taken to suppress it. By 1864 the shortage of white men available to enforce slavery had become a widespread problem for the Confederacy, where in some counties as many as 90 percent of white males of military age had been taken into the army. With so few white men at home, it became increasingly difficult to sustain the patrols that had helped maintain slavery in the antebellum South by monitoring roads and capturing runaways. Authorities in North Carolina and elsewhere were further alarmed by cases in which escaped slaves joined bands of Confederate deserters. The number of persons who were executed for their involvement with the slave rebellion allegedly planned in North Carolina in December 1864 is not known. Captain Lewis H. Webb, an artillery officer from Richmond County serving near Weldon, would write in his diary on December 22 that "numerous arrests of slaves have been made & several hung by the incensed citizens" after the discovery of an insurrection planned for Christmas night. In what may have been a reference to the same incident, David P. Conyngham of the *New York Herald* reported in a dispatch sent from Fayetteville on March 12, 1865, that Confederate authorities had discovered a plot by slaves from nearby Laurinburg to "force their way" toward Sherman's army as it marched through the Carolinas, and that "after a kind of a mock trial, twenty-five were hung."

Prospect Hall P.O. Bladen Cty. N.C.
12th Decr 1864

To his Excellency
Z. B. Vance Governor N.C.
Raleigh N.C.

Governor

I presume, on this, you have heard all the particulars, from parties on the spot, but as it is possible you may not have been so informed, I feel it my duty to avail myself of this, the earliest opportunity to inform you of the discovery of a well planned, formidable, & most diabolical scheme of Insurrection among the negroes of this section of the state, extending from Troy, in Montgomery County to Society Hill in So Carolina, how far it extends on either side of the line between these points is not known. Their courier was arrested on his way into Robeson County, his confessions led to the arrest of some forty or fifty others on the above line, a list of one hundred & ten names were found. The country is aroused & every one on the alert & parties are now out in search of as many of the culprits as can be found, but the country is very deficient in men to arrest & convey them to a safe prison. The negroes all tell the same story. That there are some white men (deserters) concerned. That they were regularly organized, by the election of a Chief, Captains, Lieutenants, couriers &c. rules & regulations were adopted for their government & action, one of their rules was that all negroes who refused to participate were to be murdered, & about Christmas the general massacre was to commence of all white persons, regardless of age, sex or condition, except such as they might choose & select for wives or concubines. One of the negroes was hung in Richmond County on friday last & some four or five others were to be hung to day, some forty others would be sent to prison for safety & trial, but their is no jail in Robeson, or this county & there are no spare men to send them by, it is considered unsafe to keep or to send them away. Consequently I think it is more than probable the whole of them will be hung by the enraged populace without the form or sanction of the civil Law.

Under such circumstances, I submit, whether it would not be well to call the attention of the Legislature now in session to the subject of local defence & protection against such enemies, & if there is no existing law for summary punishment and execution, whether it would not be well for them to enquire into the practicability of authorizing three or more Magistrates to try & adjudge under proper restrictions all such, & similar cases, & to dispose of them summarily, without the delays, risk of escapes, expence, & demoralizing effects of a long course of law through the courts, for such offences as Insurrection, Rape, Murder, Rebellion &c by negroes upon whites. Summary punishment is required, & such punishment, is & will be sustained by public opinion, with or without the sanction of the Civil Law, & if public opinion sanctions the violation of one Law, the precedent is laid for other violations, & where the Civil Law is set aside, where will you look for the limit of excesses, & what protection will remain to the people for life, liberty or property.

While at Lumberton to day, I was told of a most aggravated case of rape by a negro upon the person of a young Lady daughter of a most respectable & wealthy farmer, the negro had been sent off to be sold, the agrieved party followed him to Lumberton, & would have shot him down on sight.

Our Country (this region particularly) is so thoroughly drained of white males from 13 years old upwards, that it is impossible to sustain a patrol, or any police regulations whatever, there is hardly any government of negroes at all, the few old men & women who own negroes tell them what to do & that is all, they have no power whatever, to enforce any order, & you know what the result of such a state of things must lead to, & you know further, enough of the negro character to know, "*that he will exist in no community, in any other Capacity, than as Slave or Master.*" In connection with this subject I beg leave to suggest, most respectfully to your Excellency, the propriety of instituting, or organizing some systematic plan of preserving, under practicable restrictions & limitations, a sufficient number of men, uniformly scattered over the country, to help make provisions for the people & for the families of those who are in the army, & to serve in some degree as a protection to their homes & families, if it is not done, I fear that it will be difficult to keep our soldiers in the field, & desertions in the army will increase. The scenes being enacted around us at this time, is calculated to increase them. To give you some idea of the condition of the families of soldiers in this county. The court last year appropriated $40,000 to buy bread for them, it was found insufficient, & at last November term $100,000 was appropriated for that purpose, which is now thought to be inadequate. There is, in this whole district (Hollow District) (a large one too) but four white males slave holders that I know of, above the age of 50. & exempt from military service, so thoroughly has been the drain for the army.

And I may here add, that in addition to all the other grievances men calling themselves 'Impressing officers' are travelling through the country stripping farmers of (in some cases) all their work animals Horses & mules, & in no case as I learn, has a sufficient number been left to cultivate the farm. Cattle have been impressed as I learn, at the rate of one eighth, counting work oxen, cows, calves, yearlings & all.

What is to be done, are the people to be stripped of not only their own support, but of the means of supporting the government & the war? And then, the assessing & collecting of taxes & impressing of property is so unequal & unjust in its operation, & from which no appeal can be taken, the agents have it in their power, & not unfrequently exercise it, of punishing private enemies, & rewarding friends, thus taxpayers are entirely at the mercy of collectors, who interpret the law as it pleases them, owing to the ambiguity of the law, & the law itself makes them the judges of it & from which there is no appeal. No body complains of the amount of taxes, the people would pay with cheerfulness five times the amt. if the wants of the Government required it, but its ambiguity, which makes it unequal & unjust in its operations, is what makes it onerous & I may say even odious.

I trust Governor you will pardon this long & perhaps uninteresting communication, & hope you will not consider it impertinent. You are the father of us all, living away yonder in Raleigh & it is not presumed you can know the wants & grievances of all your people, unless they tell you of them, hence this liberty

I am Governor
Very Respectfully & truly
Your friend & Obt Servt
H. Nutt

MEETING SHERMAN: GEORGIA, DECEMBER 1864

John Chipman Gray to John C. Ropes

Before Sherman's army left Atlanta it destroyed the railroad and telegraph lines connecting the city with the North. As the Union forces marched across Georgia to the coast, few people outside the region knew much about their progress beyond what they read in the often contradictory reports printed in the southern press. President Lincoln noted in his annual message to Congress that the result of Sherman's venture "not yet being known, conjecture in regard to it is not here indulged," and told a crowd of well-wishers on December 6: "We all know where he went in at, but I can't tell where he will come out at." Sherman's troops reached the outer defenses of Savannah on December 10 and captured Fort McAllister south of the city three days later, opening a supply line down the Ogeechee River to Union ships in Ossabaw Sound. Major John Chipman Gray joined the Union army in 1862 and had served as an aide to George H. Gordon, a division commander in several theaters, before becoming judge advocate general of the Department of the South, commanded by Major General John G. Foster, in the fall of 1864. He wrote about meeting Sherman to his friend John C. Ropes, a Boston lawyer.

STR. NEMALA, *December* 14, 1864

DEAR JOHN,—I have just passed a whole morning in the company of the greatest military genius of the country in the height of his success. If I were to write a dozen pages I could not tell you a tenth part of what he said, for he talked incessantly and more rapidly than any man I ever saw. A despatch boat goes North immediately on our arrival at Hilton Head with the glorious news of Sherman's success, but I will try to scribble a word or two as we go along in this shaky boat.

A line first about preliminary movements; about the 25th of November General Foster received orders to make demonstrations against the Charleston and Savannah Road and cut it, if possible, with the view of helping General Sherman, and on the 27th I started with General Foster on board the steamer *Nemala*, together with 5000 troops, who after they were landed were to be under the command of General Hatch. General Foster's wound makes him unable either to walk or ride so that he remained on the steamer, and directed operations therefrom. We first attempted to reach the Railroad near Grahamville, but met a battery which barred our progress and we retired after considerable loss. Other demonstrations were made in different directions, and finally a force was landed at Tallifinny Creek and pushing forward after a sharp skirmish gained a position about three-fourths of a mile from the R.R. which we still occupy and from which with our artillery we can prevent the passage of trains at least in the day time. When this force landed I accompanied General Potter who was in command, and the fight which ensued was the first time I was ever under musketry fire or indeed any fire of consequence. It is singular that I should have been two years an aide-de-camp on the staff of a fighting brigadier without hearing a bullet whistle, and within two months after becoming the legal adviser of a supposed sleeping department, I should be in the midst of a hot fire, for it was brisk work and looked badly for a few minutes. I suppose you may by this time have seen Colonel Hartwell who was slightly wounded in the fight at Grahamville while landing his regiment in a most gallant manner. All this, which I would like to dwell on, must give place to the great news. I had a long talk with General Foster about Fort Sumter, but this also I must reserve for a future time. On the morning of the 11th news came that a scout of General Howard's had come through and reported all well and last night after General Foster had once attempted in vain to open communication with General Sherman, he again started on the *Nemala* for Ossabaw Sound, and throwing all business aside, I was bound to go with him. We started about half past seven P.M., and reached Ossabaw Sound at two A.M., where we were boarded by a signal officer who informed us that Fort McAllister had been captured by General Hazen's division in an assault at five o'clock the night before, and that he (the signal officer) had seen General Sherman. We steamed up the Ogeechee as near to Fort McAllister as the obstructions and supposed torpedoes would allow us, and sending a boat on shore General Sherman with a captain of his staff came off, arriving about half past seven o'clock and remaining till half past one.

First about Fort McAllister, the 'all important capture' of which as General S. terms it, secures an excellent base for such supplies as may be needed. The Fort is very strong mounting twenty-one guns, some of which are field pieces, and many months ago beat off three heavy ironclads, inflicting considerable damage; the assault was made by three columns each of three regiments, and twenty-five minutes by the watch, as General Sherman says, after the first order was given the fort was in our possession. The garrison fought desperately, and several refusing to surrender were killed inside of the Fort. Our loss was about eighty, of whom half were killed and wounded by the explosion of torpedoes buried in the ground which were exploded by our men walking over the works after they were captured. General Sherman set the prisoners to work digging them up and informed the commander of the fort that he had it in consideration to shut him up with a number of his men equal to the number of our men who were killed by torpedoes and blow them up by gunpowder.

General Sherman is the most American looking man I ever saw, tall and lank, not very erect, with hair like thatch, which he rubs up with his hands, a rusty beard trimmed close, a wrinkled face, sharp, prominent red nose, small, bright eyes, coarse red hands; black felt hat slouched over the eyes (he says when he wears anything else the soldiers cry out, as he rides along, 'Hallo, the old man has got a new hat'), dirty dickey with the points wilted down, black, old-fashioned stock, brown field officer's coat with high collar and no shoulder straps, muddy trowsers and one spur. He carries his hands in his pocket, is very awkward in his gait and motions, talks continually and with immense rapidity, and might sit to *Punch* for the portrait of an ideal Yankee. He was of course in the highest spirits and talked with an openness which was too natural not to be something more than apparent. In striving to recall his talk, I find it impossible to recall his language or indeed what he talked about, indeed it would be easier to say what he did not talk about than what he did. I never passed a more amusing or instructive day, but at his departure I felt it a relief and experienced almost an exhaustion after the excitement of his vigorous presence.

He has Savannah securely invested, his left rests securely on the Savannah River, his right at Fort McAllister, his line is within the three mile post from the city, he intends to throw a division across the Savannah to prevent the escape of Hardie from the city, and says he shall take his own time about reducing the city, unless he is hurried by despatches from General Grant, he has 60,000 men with him and only wishes there were more men in Savannah; he says the city is his sure game and stretches out his arm and claws his bony fingers in the air to illustrate how he has his grip on it. There is a 'whip the creation' and an almost boastful confidence in himself which in an untried man would be very disgusting, but in him is intensely comic. I wish you could see him, he is a man after your own heart. Like Grant he smokes constantly, and producing six cigars from his pocket said they were his daily allowance, but judging at the rate at which he travelled through them while he was on our boat, he must often exceed it. He scouted the idea of his going on ships and said he would rather march to Richmond than go there by water, he said he expected to turn north toward the latter end of December, at the same time the sun did, and that if he went through South Carolina, as he in all probability should, that his march through that state would be one of the most horrible things in the history of the world, that the devil himself could not restrain his men in that state, and I do not think that he (that is Sherman, not the devil) would try to restrain them much; he evidently purposes to make the South feel the horrors of war as much as he legitimately can, and if the men trespass beyond the strict limits of his orders he does not inquire into their cases too curiously. He told with evident delight how on his march he could look forty miles in each direction and see the smoke rolling up as from one great bonfire.

His army has been and is in perfect health and spirits, with everything they want, in much better condition than if they had remained at Atlanta, they are all ready to march anywhere with the 'old man' in five minutes. The army has not been on diminished rations a day since they left Chattanooga, and since they started on this last march General Sherman says that they have had turkeys every morning for breakfast, and won't condescend to eat hogs. His better disciplined regiments have now in their knapsacks seven of eight days' bread with which they started and the army brought in great droves of cattle, mules and negroes, the latter of whom he wants to turn over to General Saxton, and evidently does not believe in the African as a soldier; he says he has destroyed $50,000,000.00 worth of property and saved the Government $3,000,000.00 for the expenses of his army.

The steamer is going and I have to close without beginning to say what I wish; General Sherman says the opposition to him was puerile and his infantry was never attacked.

Please show this to my father, and let him take it home, or better take it yourself.

J. C. Gray, Jr.

BESIEGING SAVANNAH: GEORGIA, DECEMBER 1864

John White Geary to Mary Geary

Brigadier General John White Geary commanded the Second Division in the Twentieth Corps, which formed part of the left wing of Sherman's army as it marched through Georgia. Geary wrote to his wife after Lieutenant General William J. Hardee, who held Savannah with 10,000 men, refused Sherman's demand for the surrender of the city.

Near Savannah Ga. Dec 1864

My Dearest Mary

Yesterday was a day racy and rare, and under all the circumstances long to be remembered. We had been thirty-one days cut off from the world and "the rest of mankind," during which period we had not received a single word concerning the affairs of the North, except occasionally through the unreliable and lying *sheets* of the South, but yesterday we had a carnival of letters and newspapers. From you I acknowledge favors of Nov 10th, 13th, 15th & 17th. Also two from Willie G. and one from Mary Lee. Of course I proceed to write to you first, and at a more convenient season I will reply to theirs. The news of the presidential election was all fresh to us, although we had learned, through rebel sources, of Mr. Lincoln's election. I hope the friends of "little Mac" are satisfied now. They certainly understand by this time that they are making a very large sized error and that their dogmas are not in keeping with the progress of the age, in which our lots have been cast, away up in the noon of the nineteenth century. They seem to be antiquated fossils, and like the Jews in the Christian era, cannot discern the signs of the times. It is now certain that the United States must be all *free* or all *slave*, and the momentous question has been decided in favor of freedom by the edict of the people in November. The rebellion is certainly much crippled by the result, and as Mr. Lincoln has had so great a triumph, he can afford to make *peace* by the offer of most generous terms.

This last campaign of Sherman's has almost disembowelled the rebellion. The state of Georgia is about as badly destroyed as some of the tribes of the land of Canaan were by the Israelitish army, according to Biblical record. One hundred millions of dollars would not restore it to its former condition. But I will come at once to our present condition. We are in sight of the "promised land," after a pilgrimage of three hundred miles, and we are also once more beseiging a city of huge proportions, and a huge and defiant army, with whom we have to contend for its possession by force of arms, which seems to be the only arbitrament left, as they have just refused Sherman's demand for the surrender of the city. The place is a great prize, and like all things of great value, very difficult to obtain.

There will therefore be some hard fighting, but I think it must yield. My troops are now engaged throwing up immense batteries from which we expect to commence the bombardment of the city on next Tuesday. Being in good shelling range we will soon knock it to pieces. As I intend to write you frequently, I will not anticipate results, but will wait to chronicle each in its turn as it occurs. The climate is very warm here now, and every insect is creeping about. Butter flies are dallying in the sunshine, and even snakes of every kind are creeping about. Shad are most abundant in the rivers, but the luxury of fish or oysters has not yet been tasted by us, as the fishing waters are covered by the enemy's cannon. Almost every breeze bears the hostile blast of the trumpet, and the thunder of the enemy's guns answers loudly to the thunder of our own. But I think our success is certain.

Although our "Cracker Line" is open, still through the laziness of some party our fresh supplies have not yet reached us. Though we look for the first installment almost hourly. We are now on very short allowance.

I do not recollect whether I told you, in my last, about the death of my famous black horse, "Charly." He died near the city of Milledgeville, *full of honor*. He was a noble *charger* and carried me safely through a score of battles. I miss the old fellow very much, and I hope ere long to find one as good, but probably never will find one with so much nobleness of character.

John Brooks (my servant) while out foraging was captured a few days ago. He was in company with a Captain Geary of one of my batteries who was also captured.

Give my love to all the children. Remember me most kindly to Captain Lee and Mrs Church and Comfort, and be particular not to forget my good friend Eberly.

Hoping that God will stand by me during this struggle and preserve me from wound and death, and restore me again in health to my family to enjoy repose in its loved society. I am as ever

Your loving husband
J. W. Geary

December 17, 1864

Mary S. Mallard: Journal, December 15–21, 1864

A week before his army left Atlanta, Sherman issued orders directing his troops to "forage liberally on the country" during their march through Georgia. His orders prohibited foraging parties from entering dwellings and placed restrictions on the destruction of property. During the march Sherman's infantry moved in four large columns roughly twenty miles apart, while his cavalry maneuvered along the front and flanks of the advance. As a result, Georgia residents were sometimes visited by different parties of Union "bummers" (foragers), as well as by groups of stragglers and Confederate deserters. At the end of the march Sherman estimated that his troops had consumed or destroyed resources worth $100 million, of which $20 million was used by the army, while the rest was "simple waste and destruction." Union troops engaged in very few acts of physical violence against white civilians, while violence against African Americans was more common. In December 1864 Mary S. Mallard was staying with her widowed mother Mary Jones at Montevideo, a rice and cotton plantation on the North Newport River in Liberty County south of Savannah. She wrote about her encounters with Union soldiers.

Thursday, December 15th. About ten o'clock Mother walked out upon the lawn, leaving me in the dining room. In a few moments Elsie came running in to say the Yankees were coming. I went to the front door and saw three dismounting at the stable, where they found Mother and rudely demanded of her: "Where are your horses and mules? Bring them out!"—at the same instant rushing by her as she stood in the door. I debated whether to go to her or remain in the house. The question was soon settled, for in a moment a stalwart Kentucky Irishman stood before me, having come through the pantry door. I scarcely knew what to do. His salutation was: "Have you any whiskey in the house?"

I replied: "None that I know of."

"You ought to know," he said in a very rough voice.

I replied: "This is not my house, so I do not know what is in it."

Said he: "I mean to search this house for arms, but I'll not hurt you." He then commenced shaking and pushing the folding door and calling for the key.

Said I: "If you will turn the handle and slide the door you will find it open."

The following interrogatories took place:

"What's in that box?"

"Books."

"What's in that room beyond?"

"Search for yourself."

"What's in that press?"

"I do not know."

"Why don't you know?"

"Because this is my mother's house, and I have recently come here."

"What's in that box?"

"Books and pictures."

"What's that, and where's the key?"

"My sewing machine. I'll get the key."

He then opened the side door and discovered the door leading into the old parlor. "I want to get into that room."

"If you will come around, I will get the key for you."

As we passed through the parlor into the entry he ran upstairs and commenced searching my bedroom. "Where have you hid your arms?"

"There are none in the house. You can search for yourself."

He ordered me to get the keys immediately to all my trunks and bureaus. I did so, and he put his hands into everything, even a little trunk containing needle books, boxes of hair, and other small things. All this was under cover of searching for arms and ammunition. He called loudly for *all* the keys; I told him my mother would soon be in the house and she would get her keys for him.

While he was searching my bureau he turned to me and asked: "Where is your watch?"

I told him my husband had worn my watch, and he had been captured the day before at Walthourville.

Shaking his fist at me, he said: "Don't you lie to me! You have got a watch!"

I felt he could have struck me to the floor; but looking steadily at him, I replied: "I have a watch and chain, and my husband has them with him."

"Well, were they taken from him when he was captured?"

"That I do not know, for I was not present."

Just at this moment I heard another Yankee coming up the stair steps and saw a young Tennessean going into Mother's room, where he commenced his search. Mother came in soon after and got her keys; and there we were, following these two men around the house, handing them keys (as they would order us to do in the most insolent manner), and seeing almost everything opened and searched and tumbled about.

The Tennessean found an old workbox, and hearing something rattling in it, he thought it was coin and would have broken it open. But Dick, the Kentuckian, prevented him until Mother got the key, and his longing eyes beheld a bunch of keys.

In looking through the bureaus, to Mother's surprise, Dick pulled out a sword that had belonged to her deceased brother and had been in her possession for thirty-one years. Finding it so rusty, they could scarcely draw it from the scabbard, and concluded it would not kill many men in this war and did not take it away.

The Tennessean found a large spyglass which had belonged to Mr. Mallard's father, and brought it out as quite a prize.

I said to him: "You won't take that!"

"No," said he, "I only want to look through it. It's of no use to me."

Dick went into the attic, but did not call for the keys to the two locked rooms. He took up the spyglass, and winking at me said: "I mean to take this to Colonel Jones." (Susan had told him Mary Ruth was Colonel Jones's child.)

Mother said to him: "Is your commanding officer named Jones?"

He laughed and said he meant to take the glass to Colonel Jones.

I said: "You won't take that, for I value it very much, as it belonged to my father."

Said he: "It's of no use to you."

"No, none whatever beyond the association, and you have much finer in your army."

He did not take it, though we thought he would have done so if we had not been present. He turned to Mother and said: "Old lady, haven't you got some whiskey?"

She replied: "I don't know that I have."

"Well," said he, "I don't know who ought to know if you don't!"

Mother asked him if he would like to see his mother and wife treated in this way—their house invaded and searched.

"Oh," said he, "none of us have wives!"

Whilst Mother walked from the stable with one of the Yankees from Kentucky he had a great deal to say about the South bringing on the war. On more than one occasion they were anxious to argue political questions with her. Knowing it was perfectly useless, she would reply: "This is neither the time nor place for these subjects. My countrymen have decided that it was just and right to withdraw from the Union. We wished to do it peaceably; you would not allow it. We have now appealed to arms; and I have nothing more to say with you upon the subject."

Mother asked him if he would like to see his mother and sisters treated as they were doing us.

"No," said he, "I would not. And I never do enter houses, and shall not enter yours."

And he remained without while the other two men searched. They took none of the horses or mules, as they were too old.

A little before dinner we were again alarmed by the presence of five Yankees dressed as marines. One came into the house—a very mild sort of a man. We told him the house had already been searched. He asked if the soldiers had torn up anything. One of the marines (as they called themselves) came into the pantry and asked if they could get anything to eat. Mother told them she had only what was prepared for our own dinner, and if they chose they could take it where it was—in the kitchen. They said they preferred to take it there, and going to the kitchen, they cursed the servants awfully, ordered milk, potatoes, and other things. They called for knives and forks, and having no others Mother sent out those we used; but they ordered Milton to take them immediately back and to tell his mistress to put them away in a safe place, as "a parcel of damned Yankees" would soon be along, and they would take every one from her.

We hoped they would not intrude upon the dwelling; but as soon as they finished eating, the four came in, and one commenced a thorough search, ordering us to get him all the keys. He found some difficulty in fitting the keys, and I told him I would show them to him if he would hand me the bunch.

He replied: "I will give them to you when I am ready to leave the house."

He went into the attic and instituted a thorough search into every hole and corner. He opened a large trunk containing the private papers of my dear father, and finding a tin canister, he tried to open it. Mother could not immediately find the key, and as he spoke insolently to her about getting the key, she told him he had better break it, but she could assure him it contained only the private papers of her husband, who was a minister of the gospel.

"Damn it," he said, "if you don't get the key I will break it. I don't care!"

In looking through the trunk he found a beautiful silver goblet which had been given to Mother by her dear little granddaughter Julia, and which she had valued as a keepsake. His eyes sparkled as he held it up and called out: "Here's something pretty, boys!"

Mother looked at him scornfully and said: "And would you take it?"

He said no, and put it quickly down, although we believe only our presence kept him from pocketing it.

One of the party came in with a secession rosette which Brother Charlie had worn at the great meeting in Savannah when he was mayor of the city. Mother had given it to Jack with a few letters to put away. As they were riding up he took it from Jack, and we were quite amused to see him come in with it pinned on the lapel of his jacket. This one was quite inclined to argue about the origin of the struggle.

One of them had an old cap—the helmet-shaped cap with horsehair plume belonging to the Liberty Independent Troop, and the jacket also, as we afterwards understood were those formerly used by the troop. Being blue with bell buttons, they could very well pass for sailors' jackets. They had rigged themselves from some house they had searched before coming here.

After spending a long time in the search, they prepared to leave with all the horses. Mother told them they were over seventeen years old and would do them no service. They took away one mule, but in a short time we saw it at the gate: they had turned it back.

After they left I found that my writing desk had been most thoroughly searched and everything scattered, and all my little articles of jewelry, pencils, etc., scattered. A gold pen was taken from my workbox.

Mother felt so anxious about Kate King that she sent Charles and Niger in the afternoon to urge her coming over to us, and told them if she was too unwell to walk or ride, they must take her up in their arms and let someone help to bring the little children. But they did not reach South Hampton, as they met a Yankee picket which turned Niger back and took Charles with them to assist in carrying horses to Midway, promising to let him return.

Friday, December 16th. Much to our relief, Prophet came over this morning with a note from Kate to know if we thought she could come to us. Mother wrote her to come immediately, which she did in great fear and trembling, not knowing but that she would meet the enemy on the road. We all felt truly grateful she had been preserved by the way.

About four in the afternoon we heard the clash of arms and noise of horsemen, and by the time Mother and I could get downstairs we saw forty or fifty men in the pantry, flying hither and thither, ripping open the safe with their swords and breaking open the crockery cupboards. Fearing we might not have a chance to cook, Mother had some chickens and ducks roasted and put in the safe for our family. These the men seized whole, tearing them to pieces with their teeth like ravenous beasts. They were clamorous for whiskey, and ordered us to get our keys. One came to Mother to know where her meal and flour were, insisted upon opening her locked pantry, and took every particle. They threw the sacks across their horses. Mother remonstrated and pointed to her helpless family; their only reply was: "We'll take it!"

They flew around the house, tearing open boxes and everything that was closed. They broke open Mother's little worktable with an andiron, hoping to find money or jewelry; it contained principally little mementos that were valuable only to herself. Failing to find treasure, they took the sweet little locks of golden hair that her mother had cut from the heads of her angel children near a half century ago, and scattering them upon the floor trampled them under their feet. A number of them rifled the sideboard, taking away knives, spoons, forks, tin cups, coffeepots, and everything they wished. They broke open Grandfather's old liquor case and carried off two of the large square gallon bottles, and drank up all the blackberry wine and vinegar which was in the case. It was vain to utter a word, for we were completely paralyzed by the fury of these ruffians.

A number of them went into the attic into a little storeroom and carried off twelve bushels of meal Mother had stored there for our necessities. She told them they were taking all she had to support herself and daughter, a friend, and five little children. Scarcely one regarded even the sound of her voice; those who did laughed and said they would leave one sack to keep us from starving. But they only left some rice which they did not want, and poured out a quart or so of meal upon the floor. At other times they said they meant to starve us to death. They searched trunks and bureaus and wardrobes, calling for shirts and men's clothes.

We asked for their officer, hoping to make some appeal to him; they said they were all officers and would do as they pleased. We finally found one man who seemed to make a little show of authority, which was indicated by a whip which he carried. Mother appealed to him, and he came up and ordered the men out. They instantly commenced cursing him, and we thought they would fight one another. They brought a wagon and took another from the place to carry off their plunder.

It is impossible to imagine the horrible uproar and stampede through the house, every room of which was occupied by them, all yelling, cursing, quarreling, and running from one room to another in wild confusion. Such was their blasphemous language, their horrible countenances and appearance, that we realized what must be the association of the lost in the world of eternal woe. Their throats were open sepulchres, their mouths filled with cursing and bitterness and lies. These men belonged to Kilpatrick's cavalry. We look back upon their conduct in the house as a horrible nightmare, too terrible to be true.

When leaving they ordered all the oxen to be gotten up early next morning.

Montevideo, *Saturday*, December 17th, 1864

As soon as it was light Kate discovered an officer near the house, which was a great relief to our feelings. Mother and I went down immediately, when she said to him: "Sir, I see that you are an officer; and I come to entreat your protection for my family, and that you will not allow your soldiers to enter my dwelling, as it has been already three times searched and every particle of food and whatever they wanted taken." He replied it was contrary to orders for the men to be found in houses, and the penalty was death; and so far as his authority extended with his own men, none of them should enter the house. He said he and his squad (there were many others present) had come on a foraging expedition, and intended to take only provisions.

Upon Mother's inviting him to see some of the work of the previous evening he came in and sat awhile in the parlor. Before leaving he discovered a portable desk on a table and walked up and opened it. She said: "That is my private property; it is here for my own use, and has only a little paper in it." He closed it immediately. (It had previously escaped observation and removal.)

The Yankees made the Negroes bring up the oxen and carts, and took off all the chickens and turkeys they could find. They carried off all the syrup from the smokehouse. We had one small pig, which was all the meat we had left; they took the whole of it. Mother saw everything like food stripped from her premises, without the power of uttering one word. Finally they rolled out the carriage and took that to carry off a load of chickens. They took everything they possibly could.

The soldier who acted as our volunteer guard was from Ohio, and older than anyone we had seen; for generally they were young men and so active that Mother called them "fiery flying serpents." As he was going Mother went out of the house and said to him: "I cannot allow you to leave without thanking you for your kindness to myself and family; and if I had anything to offer I would gladly make you some return."

He replied: "I could not receive anything, and only wish I was here to guard you always."

It was not enough that they should insult us by converting our carriage into a chicken-cart and take it away drawn by our own carriage horses; but they sent in to tell Mother if she wanted her carriage to send for it, and when they were done with it she might have it. We afterwards learned it was broken to pieces and left beyond Midway Church.

They took off today June, Martin, George, Ebenezer, Little Pulaski, our house servant Jack, and Carpenter Pulaski. Seeing the two last-named going away, Mother called to the soldier who had them in charge: "Why are you taking my young men away?"

He said: "They need not go if they do not want to."

She then asked: "Boys, do you wish to go or stay?"

They immediately replied: "We wish to stay."

She then said: "Do you hear that? Now, by what right do you force them away?"

They had Pulaski laden down with our turkeys, and wanted Jack to drive one of the carts. So they were all carried off—carriages, wagons, carts, horses and mules and servants, with food and provisions of every kind—and, so far as they were concerned, leaving us to starvation.

A little while after this party started, Mother walked to the smokehouse and found an officer taking sugar that had been put to drip. He was filling a bag with all that was dry. He seemed a little ashamed of being caught in the act, but did not return the sugar, but carried it off on his horse. He was mounted on Mr. Audley King's pet horse, a splendid animal which he had just stolen, and as he rode off said: "How the man who *owns* this horse will curse the Yankee who took him when he goes home and finds him gone!" He had Mr. King's servant mounted on another of his horses, and no doubt knew Mrs. King was with us and would hear the remark.

Immediately we went to work moving some salt and the little remaining sugar into the house; and while we were doing it a Missourian came up and advised us to get everything into the house as quickly as possible, and he would protect us while doing so. He offered to show Mother how to hide her things. She said: "We need instruction from Yankees, for we have never been accustomed to any such mean business." He said he had enlisted to fight for the *Constitution*; but since then the war had been turned into another thing, and he did not approve this abolitionism, for his wife's people all owned slaves. He told us what afterwards proved false—that ten thousand infantry would soon pass through Riceboro on their way to Thomasville.

Soon after this some twenty rode up and caught me having a barrel rolled toward the house. They were gentlemanly. A few only dismounted; said they were from various of our Confederate States. They said the war would soon be over, for they would have Savannah in a few days.

I replied: "Savannah is not the Confederacy."

They spoke of the number of places they had taken.

I said: "Yes, and do you hold them?"

One of them replied: "Well, I do admire your spunk."

They inquired for all the large plantations.

Squads came all day until near dark. We had no time to eat a mouthful. The remaining ox-wagons were taken to the cornhouse and filled with corn.

Sabbath, December 18th. We passed this day with many fears, but no Yankees came to the lot; though many went to Carlawter and were engaged carrying off corn, the key of the cornhouse having been taken from Cato the day before and the door ordered to be left open. A day comparatively free from interruptions was very grateful to us, though the constant state of apprehension in which we were was distressing.

In the afternoon, while we were engaged in religious services, reading and seeking protection of our Heavenly Father, Captain Winn's Isaiah came bringing a note from Mr. Mallard to me and one from Mr. John Stevens to Mother, sending my watch. This was our first intelligence from Mr. Mallard, and oh, how welcome to us all; though the note brought no hope of his release, as the charge against him was taking up arms against the U.S. Captain Winn had been captured but released. We were all in such distress that Mother wrote begging Mr.

Stevens to come to us. We felt so utterly alone that it would be a comfort to have him with us.

Monday, December 19th. Squads of Yankees came all day, so that the servants scarcely had a moment to do anything for us out of the house. The women, finding it entirely unsafe for them to be out of the house at all, would run in and conceal themselves in our dwelling. The few remaining chickens and some sheep were killed. These men were so outrageous at the Negro houses that the Negro men were obliged to stay at their houses for the protection of their wives; and in some instances they rescued them from the hands of these infamous creatures.

Tuesday, December 20th. A squad of Yankees came soon after breakfast. Hearing there was one yoke of oxen left, they rode into the pasture and drove them up, and went into the woods and brought out the horse-wagon, to which they attached the oxen. Needing a chain for the purpose, they went to the well and took it from the well bucket. Mother went out and entreated them not to take it from the well, as it was our means of getting water. They replied: "You have no right to have even wood or water," and immediately took it away.

Wednesday, December 21st. 10 A.M. Six of Kilpatrick's cavalry rode up, one of them mounted on Mr. Mallard's valuable gray named Jim. They looked into the dairy and empty smokehouse, every lock having been broken and doors wide open day and night. They searched the servants' houses; then they thundered at the door of the dwelling. Mother opened it, when one of them presented a pistol to her breast and demanded why she dared to keep her house closed, and that "he be damned if he would not come into it."

She replied: "I prefer to keep my house closed because we are a helpless and defenseless family of women and little children. And one of your officers informed me that the men were not to enter private dwellings. And it is also contrary to the published orders of your general."

He replied: "I'll be damned if I don't come in and take just what I want. Some of the men got wine here, and we must have some."

She told them her house had been four times searched in every part, and everything taken from it. And recognizing one who had been of the party that had robbed us, she said: "You know my meal and everything has been taken."

He said: "We left you a sack of meal and that rice."

Mother said: "You left us some rice; but out of twelve bushels of meal you poured out a quart or so upon the floor—as you said, to keep us from starving."

She then entreated them, on account of the health of her daughter, not to enter the house. With horrible oaths they rode off, shooting two ducks in the yard.

About half an hour after, three came. One knocked in the piazza and asked if Mother always kept her doors locked. She said she had recently done so by the advice of an officer; and Kate King said: "We have been compelled to do so since the house has been so repeatedly ransacked."

He said: "Well, I never do that and did not come for that." Asked if we knew Mrs. S—— of Dorchester, for he had turned some men out of her house who were ransacking it. He demeaned himself with respect, and did not insist upon coming in.

Upon one occasion one of the men as he sat on the bench in the piazza had his coat buttoned top and bottom, and inside we could plainly see a long row of stolen breast pins and jewelry—gallant trophies, won from defenseless women and children at the South to adorn the persons of their mothers, wives, sisters, and friends in Yankeeland!

One hour after, five came. Mother and Kate trembled from head to feet. It appeared as if this day's trials were more than they could bear. They knelt and asked strength from God; went down and found that three had already entered the pantry with false keys brought for the purpose. They immediately proceeded to cut open the wires of the safe and took all they wanted, amongst other things a tin kettle of eggs we had managed to get.

Mother said to them: "Why, you have entered my house with false keys!"

With demoniacal leer they said: "We want none of your keys," and tried to put in one of those they brought into the pantry door.

She told them: "Your soldiers have already broken the key in that lock, and it cannot be opened; but everything has already been taken." When they insultingly insisted the door should be opened, Mother told them: "Very well, break it open just as soon as you please."

She remonstrated against their coming over the house, and told them of the order of the officers. They replied none of their officers prohibited them from coming in, and they would be damned if they would mind any such orders, would be damned if they did not go where they pleased, and would be damned if they did not take what they pleased. Mother remonstrated, and in her earnest entreaty placed her hand upon the shoulder of one of them, saying: "You must not go over my house." Strange to say, they did not go beyond the pantry, and appeared restrained, as we afterwards believed, by the hand of God. They said they wanted pots and buckets, for they were in camp and had nothing to cook in. One asked for whiskey. To our amusement the man who stole the eggs stumbled and fell as he went down the steps and broke them all—but carried off the bucket. (Psalm 27:2—"When the wicked, even mine enemies and my foes, came upon me to eat up my flesh, they stumbled and fell.")

At dinner time twelve more came—six or seven to the door asking for flour and meal. Mother told them she was a defenseless widow with an only daughter on the eve of again becoming a mother, a young friend, and five little children dependent on her for food and protection. They laughed and said: "Oh, we have heard just such tales before!" They wanted to know why the house was kept locked; said it would only make it worse for us. (This had proven false, for when the doors were open it was impossible to keep them out.) Kate observed a large cravat upon the neck of one made of a black silk dress of hers which had been taken by one of them a few days before. Every species of men's clothing in our trunks and bureaus and portmanteaus was taken, but none of our personal apparel, for we generally stood by when they were searching our wardrobes. They took every piece of jewelry they could find. Twelve sheep were found shot and left in the pasture—an act of wanton wickedness.

Late in the afternoon more came and carried off the few remaining ducks. Going to the Negro houses, they called Cato, the driver, and told him they knew he was feeding "that damned old heifer in the house," and they would "blow out his damned brains" if he gave her another morsel to eat, for they meant to starve her to death. Pointing to the chapel, they asked what house that was. Cato answered: "A church which my master had built for the colored people on the place to hold prayers in the week and preach in on Sunday." They said: "Yes, there he told all his damned lies and called it preaching." And with dreadful oaths they cursed him. To Patience, when they were taking good and valuable books from his library (as they said, to send their old fathers at home), they said, when she spoke with honor of her master and his labors for the good of the colored people: "He was a damned infernal villain, and we only wish he was now alive; we would blow his brains out." To Sue they said, when she spoke of his goodness to the people: "We wish he was now here; we would cut his throat." They stole two blankets from July, and attempted to steal his hat. They took a piggin of boiled potatoes from Sue, and threw the piggin in the marsh when they had eaten them.

After all the day's trials, late at night came Kate's servant Prophet bringing her some clothing and chickens. We were rejoiced to see anyone. He reported South Hampton had been visited by a hundred and fifty men, who had taken all the corn given to the Negroes (three months' allowance), killed forty or fifty hogs and taken seven beef cattle, stolen all the syrup and sugar from the Negroes, and taken their clothing, crawling under their houses and beds searching for buried articles.

"THE TORTURE OF LOYAL MEN":
NEW YORK, JANUARY 1865

Harper's Weekly: *Retaliation*

January 7, 1865

In May 1864 the congressional Joint Committee on the Conduct of the War published testimony from recently paroled Union soldiers recounting their suffering from cold and hunger in the Belle Isle prison camp in Richmond, along with lithographic images of several emaciated former prisoners. As reports of the horrific conditions at Andersonville and other southern prison camps reached the North in the summer and fall of 1864, there were increasing calls for retaliation. *Harper's Weekly*, an illustrated journal with a circulation of more than 100,000 copies, addressed the question early in the New Year. Retaliation was an accepted practice under the laws of war, but one that the Lincoln administration was reluctant to engage in, as shown by its response to the Fort Pillow massacre (see pp. 57–59 in this volume). Beginning on January 16, 1865, the Senate would debate a resolution calling for captured Confederate officers to be given the same food, clothing, and shelter as Union prisoners, and on January 31 adopt an amended version that "directed" the executive to retaliate on Confederate prisoners in an "effective" manner. The resolution was never considered by the House of Representatives. On January 24 Robert Ould, the Confederate commissioner for exchange, would write to Grant offering to exchange "all" Union prisoners. His letter was understood to signal a willingness to treat black and white prisoners equally, and general exchanges would resume in February 1865. During the war at least 30,000 Union and 26,000 Confederate soldiers died while being held as prisoners.

IF we were at war with cannibals who ate alive the prisoners whom they took from our armies, we could not retaliate in kind. If we were fighting Indians who burned their captives at the stake, we could not retaliate in kind. We are at war with men whom the long habit of enslaving other men has imbruted and barbarized, and who starve and freeze to death the prisoners who fall into their hands. Of the fact there can be no reasonable doubt. The testimony is conclusive. Nor is there any reason why men who do not hesitate in time of peace to force other men to work for them without wages, that they may live in idleness and call themselves "gentlemen," should be reluctant to expose their prisoners to starvation. It is not so barbarous to starve a prisoner who has been fighting against you as it is to whip a man to death because he will not work for you for nothing.

What ought to be done? It is a question which is constantly asked and is not easy to answer. It is estimated that we have some sixty thousand rebel prisoners, and that the rebels have about forty-five thousand loyal men in their hands. If we exchange them man for man we give the staggering rebellion a fresh army. That is one of the purposes of the rebel starvation of our men. Yet how can we relieve their unhappy condition if they are not exchanged?

Retaliation is a policy authorized by the customs of all nations. It has its limits of course. With us the object of retaliation would be to put an end to the torture of loyal men. But it could not use torture as a means. Northern men would not tolerate it. They are not used to seeing women whipped for so loving their children as to try to save them from being sold at the shambles, and they could not starve helpless men to death.

But if retaliation does not admit torture it does allow death. Retaliation need not necessarily be in kind. If it be wise to resort to it at all in the present instance—and of that there must always be a question—then for the Union prisoners put to death by the slow agony of starvation and exposure, certain designated rebel prisoners should be shot to death. When two Union officers were to be hung in Richmond the prompt order of the Government that two rebel officers in our hands should suffer the same fate saved our men. So when the rebel officers were placed in the trenches before Charleston, it procured the release of Union officers who had been put under fire. And when retaliation on either side has been carried to extremity it has not occasioned a general massacre, as some unwise persons predicted.

The question at best is very difficult. No Government ought to be severely censured either for refusing to reinforce its enemy's army, or for declining to destroy prisoners of war. To justify retaliation in the abstract is very easy: to advise it in a specific instance is to assume a very solemn responsibility.

"THE MOST PERNICIOUS IDEA": GEORGIA, JANUARY 1865

Howell Cobb to James A. Seddon

In January 1864 Major General Patrick R. Cleburne presented a memorandum to the senior commanders of the Army of Tennessee proposing that the Confederacy emancipate slaves and enlist them as soldiers. A copy was sent to Jefferson Davis, who ordered the suppression of the memorandum and of discussion about it. By the autumn of 1864 the Confederate need for manpower had forced Davis to revisit the question. In his message to the Confederate Congress on November 7, Davis called for enlisting 40,000 slaves as military laborers and emancipating them once their service was completed. While rejecting the arming of slaves at the present time, he wrote that "should the alternative ever be presented of subjugation or of the employment of the slave as a soldier, there seems no reason to doubt what should then be our decision." At about the same time, Robert E. Lee endorsed using slaves as soldiers in a private letter to Confederate congressman William Porcher Miles. As the use of black soldiers was debated in the Confederate Congress and the southern press, Howell Cobb, a prominent Georgia politician who now commanded the state's local defense troops, wrote to the Confederate secretary of war.

HDQRS. GEORGIA RESERVES AND MIL. DIST. OF GEORGIA,
Macon, Ga., January 8, 1865.

Hon. JAMES A. SEDDON,
Secretary of War, Richmond, Va.:

SIR: Your letter of the 30th of December received by yesterday's mail. I beg to assure you that I have spared no efforts or pains to prosecute vigorously the recruiting of our Army through the conscript camp. It is true, as you say, there are many liable to conscription who have not been reached, and for reasons I have heretofore given I fear never will be reached. Rest assured, however, that I will not cease my efforts in that regard. In response to your inquiries, how our Army is to be recruited, I refer with strength and confidence to the policy of opening the door for volunteers. I have so long and so urgently pressed this matter that I feel reluctant even to allude to it, and yet I should not be true to my strong convictions of duty if I permitted any opportunity to pass without urging and pressing it upon the proper authorities. It is in my opinion not only the best but the only mode of saving the Army, and every day it is postponed weakens its strength and diminishes the number that could be had by it. The freest, broadest, and most unrestricted system of volunteering is the true policy, and cannot be too soon resorted to. I think that the proposition to make soldiers of our slaves is the most pernicious idea that has been suggested since the war began. It is to me a source of deep mortification and regret to see the name of that good and great man and soldier, General R. E. Lee, given as authority for such a policy. My first hour of despondency will be the one in which that policy shall be adopted. You cannot make soldiers of slaves, nor slaves of soldiers. The moment you resort to negro soldiers your white soldiers will be lost to you; and one secret of the favor with which the proposition is received in portions of the Army is the hope that when negroes go into the Army they will be permitted to retire. It is simply a proposition to fight the balance of the war with negro troops. You can't keep white and black troops together, and you can't trust negroes by themselves. It is difficult to get negroes enough for the purpose indicated in the President's message, much less enough for an Army. Use all the negroes you can get, for all the purposes for which you need them, but don't arm them. The day you make soldiers of them is the beginning of the end of the revolution. If slaves will make good soldiers our whole theory of slavery is wrong—but they won't make soldiers. As a class they are wanting in every qualification of a soldier. Better by far to yield to the demands of England and France and abolish slavery, and thereby purchase their aid, than to resort to this policy, which leads as certainly to ruin and subjugation as it is adopted; you want more soldiers, and hence the proposition to take negroes into the Army. Before resorting to it, at least try every reasonable mode of getting white soldiers. I do not entertain a doubt that you can by the volunteering policy get more men into the service than you can arm. I have more fears about arms than about men. For heaven's sake try it before you fill with gloom and despondency the hearts of many of our truest and most devoted men by resorting to the suicidal policy of arming our slaves.

Having answered the inquiries of your letter, let me volunteer in a few words a suggestion. Popularize your administration by some just concessions to the strong convictions of public opinion. Mark you, I do not say yield to popular clamor, but concede something to the earnest convictions of an overwhelming, and, I will say, an enlightened public opinion. First, yield your opposition to volunteering in the form and manner which I have heretofore urged; second, restore General Johnston to the command of the Army of Tennessee, and return General Beauregard to South Carolina.

With Lee in Virginia, Johnston here, and Beauregard in South Carolina you restore confidence and at once revive the hopes of the people. At present I regret to say that gloom and despondency rule the hour, and bitter opposition to the Administration, mingled with disaffection and disloyalty, is manifesting itself. With a dash of the pen the President can revolutionize this state of things, and I earnestly beseech him to do it.

Sincerely, yours,

HOWELL COBB,
Major-General.

"THE BIRTHRIGHT OF THE SOUTH": NORTH CAROLINA, JANUARY 1865

Catherine Edmondston: Diary, January 9, 1865

From her home in Halifax County, North Carolina, Catherine Edmondston followed the debate over arming slaves while drawing encouragement from the repulse of the Union expedition that attempted to capture Fort Fisher on December 24–25, 1864. The fort guarded the entrance to Wilmington, North Carolina, the last major port still in Confederate hands.

JANUARY 9, 1865

"Out of the abundance of the heart the mouth speaketh," but the hand writeth not. Never were we more absorbed in outward matters, never have we looked on them so anxiously as now, & yet it is days since I have written aught of them. This negro question, this vexed negro question, will if much longer discussed do us more injury than the loss of a battle. Gen Lee advises the Conscription & ultimate Emancipation of 200,000 Slaves to be used as soldiers. One or two rabid partizan papers, Democratic, I might almost say Agrarian to the core, seize on the proposal, hold it up to the people, to the army, in the most attractive lights. They promise the white soldier that if the negro is put in the army, for every negro soldier fifteen white ones will be allowed to return home. They use it as an engine to inflame the passions of one class against another, tell the poor man that the War is but for his rich neighbor's slaves, that his blood is poured out to secure additional riches to the rich, etc., etc., nay one paper, to its shame be it said, the Richmond Enquirer, openly advocates a general Emancipation! as the price for fancied benefits to be obtained by an alliance with England & France. Actually it offers to sell the birthright of the South, not for a mess of pottage, but only for the hope of obtaining one. The Traitor, recreant to principle, lost to every sense of national honour, & blind to what constitutes a true national prosperity—the wonder is that he finds anyone either to read or think seriously of his monstrous proposition. But so it is. Coming as it does on the evacuation of Savannah when we are almost ready to sink under the accumulation of Yankee lies & Yankee bragg, over their boasted Victory over Hood, our money depreciated & depreciating daily more & more, deafened on one side by loud mouthed politicians who advocate "Reconstruction to save Annihilation," "Reconstruction as a choice of Evils," & on the other by the opponents of the Government who expatiate with alass too much truth upon the mismanagement, the waste, the oppression which, cast our eyes which way we will we see around us, threatened again with a new suspension of Habeas Corpus, the Constitution daily trampled under foot by Impressment Laws & Government Schedules, what wonder that many unthinking people catch at this straw as at hope of salvation & delivery from present misery without pausing to ask themselves what will be their condition when they have accepted it. But sounder & better councils will prevail. This beaten and crushed Abolitionist, the Enquirer, will find that the body of the people are against him, that the foxes who have lost their tails are too few in number to govern those who still retain theirs. Slaveholders on principle, & those who hope one day to become slaveholders in their time, will not tacitly yeild their property & their hopes & allow a degraded race to be placed at one stroke on a level with them. But these discussions & these thoughts have occupied us for the past fortnight & such a deluge of gloomy forebodings have been penned out upon us that I almost hailed the frequent mail failures as a blessing.

The tide now seems turning. God has blessed us with a signal victory over the Yankee fleet. God's blessing & God's hand alone it is, for we had but little to do with it. Yankee accounts of the doings of their great Armada have reached us, which make our hearts rise in gratitude to Him who exalteth & who casteth down. In the first place there was no cooperation between the land & naval forces. Then came the gale which drove them out to sea, then the bombardment of Ft Fisher, when the bursting of six six-hundred-pound Parrot Guns on six different Vessels destroyed the confidence of the men who saw their comrades torn, mangled, & bleeding amongst the ruins of their own offensive engines. Then a barge with two hundred & *fifteen tons* of Powder was floated to within a short distance of Ft Fisher & exploded without the slightest result. "The Rebels were not even paralized by it," but why continue the tale of their disaster? Suffice it that God's hand is apparent in it all & the fleet has returned to Hampton Roads discomforted, defeated, dejected, & out of repair & quarrelling miserably amongst themselves. To God alone be the Glory.

Better news but still not authentic reaches us from Tenn. We hear that in a second battle we regained some of the prestige lost before Nashville, of which however we have still only Yankee accounts, but I will refrain all but passing mention of them until they are confirmed. Still they influence our spirits wonderfully. What cheers our very hearts is an intimation that Mr Davis has reinstated Gen Joe Johnston in command. The whole nation hails it with acclamation. Gen D H Hill too is ordered to report to Gen Beauregard, so our old dogs of War are unleashed again.

Sherman is reposing himself in Savannah after his leisurely saunter through Geo & bloodless conquest of that city. He makes a magnificent Christmas gift to Mr Lincoln of the City of Savannah with arms, munitions of war, cotton, Rice, seige guns, etc., too tedious for me to enumerate. He even includes the 25,000 inhabitants in his munificent donation; so, as other autocrats do, he has now only to enslave & deport them. God help them! The evacuation took them entirely by surprise we hear. Few of them escaped & they with the loss of all their effects. Sherman has a right to his self glorification. Let him indulge it whilst we cherish the hope that Beauregard will yet pluck the Laurel crown from his brow & trample it in the dust. His programme, as announced, is the capture of Branchville and advance along the lines of R R into Va. Nous verrons! No news from Petersburg or Richmond for days. All quiet since the defeat of the demonstration on Gordonsville.

As for ourselves, since the negroes holiday at Christmas, for Christmas shone no holiday to any but them, we have been engaged with our year's supply of meat. Frying up Lard, squeezing out cracklins, & all the, to me, disagreeable et ceteras of "a hog killing" are I beleive a perfect happiness to Cuffee! The excitement & interest over the weight of their favorites, the feasting on chitterlings & haslets, the dabbling in grease, seems to constitute a negro paradise, whilst the possession of a "bladder to blow" or better still a hog tail is all a negro child needs of earth's enjoyments. Well we "killed Hogs" here, then we went to Hascosea & did the same thing there.

As usual we were weatherbound & detained 24 hours longer than we intended to remain. Mr E ordered a large box of books, principally farming periodicals (which we had bound the winter before the commencement of the war & which came home whilst we were in great excitement about Ft Sumter & which we have since refrained from opening on account of our unsettled state & the determination we from time to time take to pack up all our books) to be opened, & we passed the time most pleasantly & profitable, rubbing up our old knoledge, forming new plans, agricultural, horticultural, & domestic which this spring & summer we hope to put in execution. I lent an especial eye to the Poultry yard—am armed with several infalible receipts to cure & to prevent "the gapes," all of which I shall try on my spring chickens. In Vinegar receipts too I have come home quite learned & I now sigh for a peice of genuine Vinegar plant! I have some very fine Vinegar made from the skimmings of last year's Sorghhum, but alas, it is too little for my many uses. I used to be famous for Pickles, but my cunning has departed, as the price of whisky and Apple Brandy has risen, for on them did I rely to give my Vinegar body. I am now making yeast by the pailful and even contemplate malting some corn to supply the deficiency. This war is teaching us many things. Dying, spinning, and weaving are no longer unknown mysteries to me. I think of making a compilation of all my practical knoledge on the subject and I intend for the future Peace or war to let *homespun* be my ordinary dress. The object of my ambition is to have a black watered silk trimmed with black thread lace. Think of it! How shall I feel when I pull off my russet yarn spun & woven on the Plantation & bedeck myself in that style! It seems so long since I wore a silk dress that I begin to doubt if I ever owned one.

I have been reading Motley's "United Netherlands" & have derived great comfort from it. We are not so divided, lean not so much on foreign aid, & are not reduced near so low as they were, & yet by perseverance they triumphed. Their advantage lay in a command of the Sea, however, an ability to export and import as they liked, an assistance we too would have did foreign nations uphold their own international Law on the subject of Blockades! International Law, a humbug & a sham, designed only by the strong as a police code to keep order amongst themselves but ignored & forgotten when a weak power suffers from its infringement. This it is which has changed our once strong love to England into Gall! this & the manner in which her boasted *Neutrality* is maintained. Her *Neutrality*, heaven save the mark, is only another word for *deceit*, for mean low petty trickery, for cringing to the U S, saying to us "Am I not in Peace my brother" & stabbing as Joab-like under the fifth rib. Neutrality, faugh! I am reading, too, Ld Bacon's Essays regularly through, one every day, & what a mine of thought they are! The foundation, nay the superstructure, of almost all modern moral Essays is found in them. It is sorrowful in the extreme to see how the human mind but reproduces itself, how the same gem appears generation after generation, modified only in the setting. Sometimes I come on a thought or an idea that I fancied I had thought out of myself, which I had hugged to my heart as my own, when hey presto! I recognize it again stamped by the hand of a master in a form at once so terse, so complete, so chisled, & so chaste that tho two hundred years old, it stands forth as clear, sharp, & distinct as tho just from the mint; & with a sigh I relinquish my proprietorship and take refuge with Solomon in the declaration that "there is nothing new under the sun."

THE RIGHT TO VOTE: TENNESSEE, JANUARY 1865

Petition of the Colored Citizens of Nashville to the Union Convention of Tennessee

After the battle of Franklin, John B. Hood followed the retreating Union army north and reached the outskirts of Nashville on December 2, 1864. Unable to assault the strongly defended city, Hood chose to entrench his army a few miles to the south and await a Union offensive. On December 15–16 George H. Thomas launched a series of attacks that routed Hood's army and forced it to retreat to northern Mississippi. Thomas's decisive victory sealed the fate of the Confederacy in Tennessee and allowed a "Liberty and Union" convention to meet in Nashville on January 9, 1865. Under the leadership of Andrew Johnson, a conservative War Democrat who had served as the military governor of Tennessee since 1862, the convention established a loyal civilian government and proposed amendments to the state constitution. Although the convention adopted an amendment abolishing slavery, it did nothing to extend civil or political rights to black Tennesseans. On February 22, 1865, the abolition amendment would be approved 25,293–48 in a referendum in which only white unionists were permitted to vote. The Tennessee legislature would pass legislation in 1866 allowing blacks to testify against whites and would extend the franchise to black men in 1867.

Nashville, January 9th, 1865:

PETITION OF THE COLORED CITIZENS OF NASHVILLE.

We the undersigned petitioners, American citizens of African descent, natives and residents of Tennessee, and devoted friends of the great National cause, do most respectfully ask a patient hearing of your honorable body in regard to matters deeply affecting the future condition of our unfortunate and long suffering race.

First of all, however, we would say that words are too weak to tell how profoundly grateful we are to the Federal Government for the good work of freedom which it is gradually carrying forward; and for the Emancipation Proclamation which has set free all the slaves in some of the rebellious States, as well as many of the slaves in Tennessee.

After two hundred years of bondage and suffering a returning sense of justice has awakened the great body of the American people to make amends for the unprovoked wrongs committed against us for over two hundred years.

Your petitioners would ask you to complete the work begun by the nation at large, and abolish the last vestige of slavery by the express words of your organic law.

Many masters in Tennessee whose slaves have left them, will certainly make every effort to bring them back to bondage after the reorganization of the State government, unless slavery be expressly abolished by the Constitution.

We hold that freedom is the natural right of all men, which they themselves have no more right to give or barter away, than they have to sell their honor, their wives, or their children.

We claim to be men belonging to the great human family, descended from one great God, who is the common Father of all, and who bestowed on all races and tribes the priceless right of freedom. Of this right, for no offence of ours, we have long been cruelly deprived, and the common voice of the wise and good of all countries, has remonstrated against our enslavement, as one of the greatest crimes in all history.

We claim freedom, as our natural right, and ask that in harmony and co-operation with the nation at large, you should cut up by the roots the system of slavery, which is not only a wrong to us, but the source of all the evil which at present afflicts the State. For slavery, corrupt itself, corrupted nearly all, also, around it, so that it has influenced nearly all the slave States to rebel against the Federal Government, in order to set up a government of pirates under which slavery might be perpetrated.

In the contest between the nation and slavery, our unfortunate people have sided, by instinct, with the former. We have little fortune to devote to the national cause, for a hard fate has hitherto forced us to live in poverty, but we do devote to its success, our hopes, our toils, our whole heart, our sacred honor, and our lives. We will work, pray, live, and, if need be, die for the Union, as cheerfully as ever a white patriot died for his country. The color of our skin does not lesson in the least degree, our love either for God or for the land of our birth.

We are proud to point your honorable body to the fact, that so far as our knowledge extends, not a negro traitor has made his appearance since the begining of this wicked rebellion.

Whether freeman or slaves the colored race in this country have always looked upon the United States as the Promised Land of Universal freedom, and no earthly temptation has been strong enough to induce us to rebel against it. We love the Union by an instinct which is stronger than any argument or appeal which can be used against it. It is the attachment of a child to its parrent.

Devoted as we are to the principles of justice, of love to all men, and of equal rights on which our Government is based, and which make it the hope of the world. We know the burdens of citizenship, and are ready to bear them. We know the duties of the good citizen, and are ready to perform them cheerfully, and would ask to be put in a position in which we can discharge them more effectually. We do not ask for the privilege of citizenship, wishing to shun the obligations imposed by it.

Near 200,000 of our brethren are to-day performing military duty in the ranks of the Union army. Thousands of them have already died in battle, or perished by a cruel martyrdom for the sake of the Union, and we are ready and willing to sacrifice more. But what higher order of citizen is there than the soldier? or who has a greater trust confided to his hands? If we are called on to do military duty against the rebel armies in the field, why should we be denied the privilege of voting against rebel citizens at the ballot-box? The latter is as necessary to save the Government as the former.

The colored man will vote by instinct with the Union party, just as uniformly as he fights with the Union army.

This is not a new question in Tennessee. From 1796 to 1835, a period of thirty-nine years, free colored men voted at all her elections without question. Her leading politicians and statesmen asked for and obtained the suffrages of colored voters, and were not ashamed of it. Such men as *Andrew Jackson*, President of the United States, Hon. *Felix Grundy*, John Bell, Hon. *Hugh L. White*, *Cave Johnson*, and *Ephraim H. Fos-*

ter, members of the United States Senate and of the Cabinet, *Gen. William Carroll, Samuel Houston*, Aaron V. Brown, and, in fact, all the politicians and candidates of all parties in Tennessee solicited colored free men for their votes at every election.

Nor was Tennessee alone in this respect, for the same privileges was granted to colored free men in North Carolina, today the most loyal of all the rebellious States, without ever producing any evil consequences.

If colored men have been faithful and true to the Government of the United States in spite of the Fugitive Slave Law, and the cruel policy often pursued toward them, will they not be more devoted to it now than ever, since it has granted them that liberty which they desired above all things? Surely, if colored men voted without harm to the State, while their brethren were in bondage, they will be much more devoted and watchful over her interests when elevated to the rank of freemen and voters. If they are good law-abiding citizens, praying for its prosperity, rejoicing in its progress, paying its taxes, fighting its battles, making its farms, mines, work-shops and commerce more productive, why deny them the right to have a voice in the election of its rulers?

This is a democracy—a government of the people. It should aim to make every man, without regard to the color of his skin, the amount of his wealth, or the character of his religious faith, feel personally interested in its welfare. Every man who lives under the Government should feel that it is his property, his treasure, the bulwark and defence of himself and his family, his pearl of great price, which he must preserve, protect, and defend faithfully at all times, on all occasions, in every possible manner.

This is not a Democratic Government if a numerous, law-abiding, industrious, and useful class of citizens, born and bred on the soil, are to be treated as aliens and enemies, as an inferior degraded class, who must have no voice in the Government which they support, protect and defend, with all their heart, soul, mind, and body, both in peace and war.

This Government is based on the teachings of the Bible, which prescribes the same rules of action for all members of the human family, whether their complexion be white, yellow, red or black. God no where in his revealed word, makes an invidious and degrading distinction against his children, because of their color. And happy is that nation which makes the Bible its rule of action, and obeys principle, not prejudice.

Let no man oppose this doctrine because it is opposed to his old prejudices. The nation is fighting for its life, and cannot afford to be controlled by prejudice. Had prejudice prevailed instead of principle, not a single colored soldier would have been in the Union army to-day. But principle and justice triumphed, and now near 200,000 colored patriots stand under the folds of the national flag, and brave their breasts to the bullets of the rebels. As we are in the battlefield, so we swear before heaven, by all that is dear to men, to be at the ballot-box faithful and true to the Union.

The possibility that the negro suffrage proposition may shock popular prejudice at first sight, is not a conclusive argument against its wisdom and policy. No proposition ever met with more furious or general opposition than the one to enlist colored soldiers in the United States army. The opponents of the measure exclaimed on all hands that the negro was a coward; that he would not fight; that one white man, with a whip in his hand could put to flight a regiment of them; that the experiment would end in the utter rout and ruin of the Federal army. Yet the colored man has fought so well, on almost every occasion, that the rebel government is prevented, only by its fears and distrust of being able to force him to fight for slavery as well as he fights against it, from putting half a million of negroes into its ranks.

The Government has asked the colored man to fight for its preservation and gladly has he done it. It can afford to trust him with a vote as safely as it trusted him with a bayonet.

How boundless would be the love of the colored citizen, how intense and passionate his zeal and devotion to the government, how enthusiastic and how lasting would be his gratitude, if his white brethren were to take him by the hand and say, "You have been ever loyal to our government; henceforward be voters." Again, the granting of this privilege would stimulate the colored man to greater exertion to make himself an intelligent, respected, useful citizen. His pride of character would be appealed to this way most successfully; he would send his children to school, that they might become educated and intelligent members of society. It used to be thought that ignorant negroes were the most valuable, but this belief probably originated from the fact that it is almost impossible to retain an educated, intelligent man in bondage. Certainly, if the free colored man be educated, and his morals enlightened and improved, he will be a far better member of society, and less liable to transgress its laws. It is the brutal, degraded, ignorant man who is usually the criminal.

One other matter we would urge on your honorable body. At present we can have only partial protection from the courts. The testimony of twenty of the most intelligent, honorable, colored loyalists cannot convict a white traitor of a treasonable action. A white rebel might sell powder and lead to a rebel soldier in the presence of twenty colored soldiers, and yet their evidence would be worthless so far as the courts are concerned, and the rebel would escape. A colored man may have served for years faithfully in the army, and yet his testimony in court would be rejected, while that of a white man who had served in the rebel army would be received.

If this order of things continue, our people are destined to a malignant persecution at the hands of rebels and their former rebellious masters, whose hatred they may have incurred, without precedent even in the South. Every rebel soldier or citizen whose arrest in the perpetration of crime they may have effected, every white traitor whom they may have brought to justice, will torment and persecute them and set justice at defiance, because the courts will not receive negro testimony, which will generally be the only possible testimony in such cases. A rebel may murder his former slave and defy justice, because he committed the deed in the presence of half a dozen respectable colored citizens. He may have the dwelling of his former slave burned over his head, and turn his wife and children out of doors, and defy the law, for no colored man can appear against him. Is this the fruit of freeedom, and the reward of our services in the field? Was it for this that colored soldiers fell by hundreds before Nashville, fighting under the flag of the Union? Is it for this that we have guided Union officers and soldiers, when escaping from the cruel and deadly prisons of the South through forests and swamps, at the risk of our own lives, for we knew that to us detection would be death? Is it for this that we have concealed multitudes of Union refugees in caves and cane-brakes, when flying from the conscription officers and tracked by bloodhounds, and divided with them our last morsal of food? Will you declare in your revised constitution that a pardoned traitor may appear in court and his testimony be heard, but that no colored loyalist shall be believed even upon oath? If this should be so, then will our last state be worse than our first, and we can look for no relief on this side of the grave? Has not the colored man fought, bled and died for the Union, under a thousand great disadvantages and discouragements? Has his fidelity ever had a shadow of suspicion cast upon it, in any matter of responsibility confided to his hands?

There have been white traitors in multitudes in Tennessee, but where, we ask, is the black traitor? Can you forget how the colored man has fought at Fort Morgan, at Milliken's Bend, at Fort Pillow, before Petersburg, and your own city of Nashville?

When has the colored citizen, in this rebellion been tried and found wanting?

In conclusion, we would point to the fact that the States where the largest measure of justice and civil rights has been granted to the colored man, both as to suffrage and his oath in court, are among the most rich, intelligent, enlightened and prosperous. Massachusetts, illustrious for her statesmen and her commercial and manufacturing enterprises and thrift, whose noble liberality has relieved so many loyal refugees and other sufferers of Tennessee, allows her colored citizens to vote, and is ever jealous of their rights. She has never had reason to repent the day when she gave them the right of voting.

Had the southern states followed her example the present rebellion never would have desolated their borders.

Several other Northern States permit negro suffrage, nor have bad effects ever resulted from it. It may be safely affirmed that Tennessee was quite as safe and prosperous during the 39 years while she allowed negro suffrage, as she has been since she abolished it.

In this great and fearful struggle of the nation with a wicked rebellion, we are anxious to perform the full measure of our duty both as citizens and soldiers to the Union cause we consecrate ourselves, and our families, with all that we have on earth. Our souls burn with love for the great government of freedom and equal rights. Our white brethren have no cause for distrust as regards our fidelity, for neither death nor life, nor angels, nor principalities, nor powers, nor things present, nor things to come, nor height, nor depth, nor any other creature, shall be able to separate us from the love of the Union.

Praying that the great God, who is the common Father of us all, by whose help the land must be delivered from present evil, and before whom we must all stand at last to be judged by the rule of eternal justice, and not by passion and prejudice, may enlighten your minds and enable you to act with wisdom, justice, and magnanimity, we remain your faithful friends in all the perils and dangers which threaten our beloved country.

ENLISTING SLAVES "WITHOUT DELAY": VIRGINIA, JANUARY 1865

Robert E. Lee to Andrew Hunter, January 11, 1865

Lee expressed his opinion on arming slaves in response to a letter soliciting his views from Andrew Hunter, a Virginia state senator whose house in Charlestown had been burned by the Union army in July 1864. While Lee's letter was not published until after the war, his recommendation that the Confederacy should enlist slaves was reported in the Richmond press. At the urging of Judah P. Benjamin, the Confederate secretary of state, Lee would write a letter intended for publication to Confederate congressman Ethelbert Barksdale on February 18. In his letter to Barksdale, Lee argued that arming slaves was "not only expedient but necessary" and that "those who are employed should be freed."

HEADQUARTERS ARMY OF NORTHERN VIRGINIA,
January 11, 1865.

HON. ANDREW HUNTER,
Richmond, Va.:

DEAR SIR: I have received your letter of the 7th instant, and without confining myself to the order of your interrogatories, will endeavor to answer them by a statement of my views on the subject. I shall be most happy if I can contribute to the solution of a question in which I feel an interest commensurate with my desire for the welfare and happiness of our people.

Considering the relation of master and slave, controlled by humane laws and influenced by Christianity and an enlightened public sentiment, as the best that can exist between the white and black races while intermingled as at present in this country, I would deprecate any sudden disturbance of that relation unless it be necessary to avert a greater calamity to both. I should therefore prefer to rely upon our white population to preserve the ratio between our forces and those of the enemy, which experience has shown to be safe. But in view of the preparations of our enemies, it is our duty to provide for continued war and not for a battle or a campaign, and I fear that we cannot accomplish this without overtaxing the capacity of our white population.

Should the war continue under existing circumstances, the enemy may in course of time penetrate our country and get access to a large part of our negro population. It is his avowed policy to convert the able-bodied men among them into soldiers, and to emancipate all. The success of the Federal arms in the South was followed by a proclamation of President Lincoln for 280,000 men, the effect of which will be to stimulate the Northern States to procure as substitutes for their own people the negroes thus brought within their reach. Many have already been obtained in Virginia, and should the fortune of war expose more of her territory, the enemy would gain a large accession to his strength. His progress will thus add to his numbers, and at the same time destroy slavery in a manner most pernicious to the welfare of our people. Their negroes will be used to hold them in subjection, leaving the remaining force of the enemy free to extend his conquest. Whatever may be the effect of our employing negro troops, it cannot be as mischievous as this. If it end in subverting slavery it will be accomplished by ourselves, and we can devise the means of alleviating the evil consequences to both races. I think, therefore, we must decide whether slavery shall be extinguished by our enemies and the slaves be used against us, or use them ourselves at the risk of the effects which may be produced upon our social institutions. My own opinion is that we should employ them without delay. I believe that with proper regulations they can be made efficient soldiers. They possess the physical qualifications in an eminent degree. Long habits of obedience and subordination, coupled with the moral influence which in our country the white man possesses over the black, furnish an excellent foundation for that discipline which is the best guaranty of military efficiency. Our chief aim should be to secure their fidelity.

There have been formidable armies composed of men having no interest in the cause for which they fought beyond their pay or the hope of plunder. But it is certain that the surest foundation upon which the fidelity of an army can rest, especially in a service which imposes peculiar hardships and privations, is the personal interest of the soldier in the issue of the contest. Such an interest we can give our negroes by giving immediate freedom to all who enlist, and freedom at the end of the war to the families of those who discharge their duties faithfully (whether they survive or not), together with the privilege of residing at the South. To this might be added a bounty for faithful service.

We should not expect slaves to fight for prospective freedom when they can secure it at once by going to the enemy, in whose service they will incur no greater risk than in ours. The reasons that induce me to recommend the employment of negro troops at all render the effect of the measures I have suggested upon slavery immaterial, and in my opinion the best means of securing the efficiency and fidelity of this auxiliary force would be to accompany the measure with a well-digested plan of gradual and general emancipation. As that will be the result of the continuance of the war, and will certainly occur if the enemy succeed, it seems to me most advisable to adopt it at once, and thereby obtain all the benefits that will accrue to our cause.

The employment of negro troops under regulations similar in principle to those above indicated would, in my opinion, greatly increase our military strength and enable us to relieve our white population to some extent. I think we could dispense with the reserve forces except in cases of necessity.

It would disappoint the hopes which our enemies base upon our exhaustion, deprive them in a great measure of the aid they now derive from black troops, and thus throw the burden of the war upon their own people. In addition to the great political advantages that would result to our cause from the adoption of a system of emancipation, it would exercise a salutary influence upon our whole negro population, by rendering more secure the fidelity of those who become soldiers, and diminishing the inducements to the rest to abscond.

I can only say in conclusion that whatever measures are to be adopted should be adopted at once. Every day's delay increases the difficulty. Much time will be required to organize and discipline the men, and action may be deferred until it is too late.

Very respectfully, your obedient servant,

R. E. LEE,
General.

“TO HAVE LAND”: GEORGIA, JANUARY 1865

Meeting of Colored Ministers with Edwin M. Stanton and William T. Sherman

When Sherman’s army reached Savannah it was accompanied by as many as 20,000 freed people who had liberated themselves by following the Union forces as they marched through Georgia. Although Sherman understood the debilitating effect the loss of slave labor had on the ability of the Confederacy to wage war, once he reached the coast he planned to “clear the army of surplus negros.” On January 11 Secretary of War Stanton arrived in Savannah to confer with Sherman and to investigate allegations that his army had treated black refugees cruelly. Reports had reached the North that an unknown number of freed people had drowned in early December while trying to escape Confederate cavalry after Union Brigadier General Jefferson C. Davis ordered his troops to remove a pontoon bridge across Ebenezer Creek, a decision Sherman defended as militarily necessary. At Stanton’s urging, Sherman then convened a meeting with local black leaders to solicit their views on emancipation. The minutes of their conference were published in the *New-York Daily Tribune* on February 13, 1865.

MINUTES OF AN INTERVIEW BETWEEN THE COLORED MINISTERS AND CHURCH OFFICERS AT SAVANNAH WITH THE SECRETARY OF WAR AND MAJOR-GEN. SHERMAN.

HEADQUARTERS OF MAJ.-GEN. SHERMAN,
CITY OF SAVANNAH, GA., Jan. 12, 1865—8 P.M.

On the evening of Thursday, the 12th day of January, 1865, the following persons of African descent met by appointment to hold an interview with Edwin M. Stanton, Secretary of War, and Major-Gen. Sherman, to have a conference upon matters relating to the freedmen of the State of Georgia, to-wit:

One: William J. Campbell, aged 51 years, born in Savannah, slave until 1849, and then liberated by will of his mistress, Mrs. May Maxwell. For ten years pastor of the 1st Baptist Church of Savannah, numbering about 1,800 members. Average congregation, 1,900. The church property belonging to the congregation. Trustees white. Worth $18,000.

Two: John Cox, aged fifty-eight years, born in Savannah; slave until 1849, when he bought his freedom for $1,100. Pastor of the 2d African Baptist Church. In the ministry fifteen years. Congregation 1,222 persons. Church property worth $10,000, belonging to the congregation.

Three: Ulysses L. Houston, aged forty-one years, born in Grahamsville, S.C.; slave until the Union army entered Savannah. Owned by Moses Henderson, Savannah, and pastor of Third African Baptist Church. Congregation numbering 400. Church property worth $5,000; belongs to congregation. In the ministry about eight years.

Four: William Bentley, aged 72 years, born in Savannah, slave until 25 years of age, when his master, John Waters, emancipated him by will. Pastor of Andrew's Chapel, Methodist Episcopal Church—only one of that denomination in Savannah; congregation numbering 360 members; church property worth about $20,000, and is owned by the congregation; been in the ministry about twenty years; a member of Georgia Conference.

Five: Charles Bradwell, aged 40 years, born in Liberty County, Ga.; slave until 1851; emancipated by will of his master, J. L. Bradwell. Local preacher in charge of the Methodist Episcopal congregation (Andrew's Chapel) in the absence of the minister; in the ministry 10 years.

Six: William Gaines, aged 41 years; born in Wills Co., Ga. Slave until the Union forces freed me. Owned by Robert Toombs, formerly United States Senator, and his brother, Gabriel Toombs, local preacher of the M.E. Church (Andrew's Chapel.) In the ministry 16 years.

Seven: James Hill, aged 52 years; born in Bryan Co., Ga. Slave up to the time the Union army came in. Owned by H. F. Willings, of Savannah. In the ministry 16 years.

Eight: Glasgon Taylor, aged 72 years, born in Wilkes County, Ga. Slave until the Union army came; owned by A. P. Wetter. Is a local preacher of the M.E. Church (Andrew's Chapel.) In the ministry 35 years.

Nine: Garrison Frazier, aged 67 years, born in Granville

County, N.C. Slave until eight years ago, when he bought himself and wife, paying $1,000 in gold and silver. Is an ordained minister in the Baptist Church, but, his health failing, has now charge of no congregation. Has been in the ministry 35 years.

Ten: James Mills, aged 56 years, born in Savannah; free-born, and is a licensed preacher of the first Baptist Church. Has been eight years in the ministry.

Eleven: Abraham Burke, aged 48 years, born in Bryan County, Ga. Slave until 20 years ago, when he bought himself for $800. Has been in the ministry about 10 years.

Twelve: Arthur Wardell, aged 44 years, born in Liberty County, Ga. Slave until freed by the Union army. Owned by A. A. Solomons, Savannah, and is a licensed minister in the Baptist Church. Has been in the ministry 6 years.

Thirteen: Alexander Harris, aged 47 years, born in Savannah; free born. Licensed minister of Third African Baptist Church. Licensed about one month ago.

Fourteen: Andrew Neal, aged 61 years, born in Savannah, slave until the Union army liberated him. Owned by Mr. Wm. Gibbons, and has been deacon in the Third Baptist Church for 10 years.

Fifteen: Jas. Porter, aged 39 years, born in Charleston, South Carolina; free-born, his mother having purchased her freedom. Is lay-reader and president of the board of wardens and vestry of St. Stephen's Protestant Episcopal Colored Church in Savannah. Has been in communion 9 years. The congregation numbers about 200 persons. The church property is worth about $10,000, and is owned by the congregation.

Sixteen: Adolphus Delmotte, aged 28 years, born in Savannah; free born. Is a licensed minister of the Missionary Baptist Church of Milledgeville. Congregation numbering about 300 or 400 persons. Has been in the ministry about two years.

Seventeen: Jacob Godfrey, aged 57 years, born in Marion, S.C. Slave until the Union army freed me; owned by James E. Godfrey—Methodist preacher now in the Rebel army. Is a class-leader and steward of Andrew's Chapel since 1836.

Eighteen: John Johnson, aged 51 years, born in Bryan County, Georgia. Slave up to the time the Union army came here; owned by W. W. Lincoln of Savannah. Is class-leader and treasurer of Andrew's Chapel for sixteen years.

Nineteen: Robt. N. Taylor, aged 51 years, born in Wilkes Co., Ga. Slave to the time the Union army came. Was owned by Augustus P. Welter, Savannah, and is class-leader in Andrew's Chapel for nine years.

Twenty: Jas. Lynch, aged 26 years, born in Baltimore, Md.; free-born. Is presiding elder of the M.E. Church and missionary to the department of the South. Has been seven years in the ministry and two years in the South.

Garrison Frazier being chosen by the persons present to express their common sentiments upon the matters of inquiry, makes answers to inquiries as follows:

First: State what your understanding is in regard to the acts of Congress and President Lincoln's proclamation, touching the condition of the colored people in the Rebel States.

Answer—So far as I understand President Lincoln's proclamation to the Rebellious States, it is, that if they would lay down their arms and submit to the laws of the United States before the first of January, 1863, all should be well; but if they did not, then all the slaves in the Rebel States should be free henceforth and forever. That is what I understood.

Second—State what you understand by Slavery and the freedom that was to be given by the President's proclamation.

Answer—Slavery is, receiving by *irresistible power* the work of another man, and not by his *consent*. The freedom, as I understand it, promised by the proclamation, is taking us from under the yoke of bondage, and placing us where we could reap the fruit of our own labor, take care of ourselves and assist the Government in maintaining our freedom.

Third: State in what manner you think you can take care of yourselves, and how can you best assist the Government in maintaining your freedom.

Answer: The way we can best take care of ourselves is to have land, and turn it and till it by our own labor—that is, by the labor of the women and children and old men; and we can soon maintain ourselves and have something to spare. And to assist the Government, the young men should enlist in the service of the Government, and serve in such manner as they may be wanted. (The Rebels told us that they piled them up and made batteries of them, and sold them to Cuba; but we don't believe that.) We want to be placed on land until we are able to buy it and make it our own.

Fourth: State in what manner you would rather live—whether scattered among the whites or in colonies by yourselves.

Answer: I would prefer to live by ourselves, for there is a prejudice against us in the South that will take years to get over; but I do not know that I can answer for my brethren. (Mr. Lynch says he thinks they should not be separated, but live together. All the other persons present, being questioned one by one, answer that they agree with Brother Frazier.)

Fifth: Do you think that there is intelligence enough among the slaves of the South to maintain themselves under the Government of the United States and the equal protection of its laws, and maintain good and peaceable relations among yourselves and with your neighbors?

Answer—I think there is sufficient intelligence among us to do so.

Sixth—State what is the feeling of the black population of the South toward the Government of the United States; what is the understanding in respect to the present war—its causes and object, and their disposition to aid either side. State fully your views.

Answer—I think you will find there are thousands that are willing to make any sacrifice to assist the Government of the United States, while there are also many that are not willing to take up arms. I do not suppose there are a dozen men that are opposed to the Government. I understand, as to the war, that the South is the aggressor. President Lincoln was elected President by a majority of the United States, which guaranteed him the right of holding the office and exercising that right over the whole United States. The South, without knowing what he would do, rebelled. The war was commenced by the Rebels before he came into office. The object of the war was not at first to give the slaves their freedom, but the sole object of the war was at first to bring the rebellious States back into the Union and their loyalty to the laws of the United States. Afterward, knowing the value set on the slaves by the Rebels, the President thought that his proclamation would stimulate them to lay down their arms, reduce them to obedience, and help to bring back the Rebel States; and their not doing so has now made the freedom of the slaves a part of the war. It is my opinion that there is not a man in this city that could be started to help the Rebels one inch, for that would be suicide. There were two black men left with the Rebels because they had taken an active part for the Rebels, and thought something might befall them if they stayed behind; but there is not another man. If the prayers that have gone up for the Union army could be read out, you would not get through them these two weeks.

Seventh: State whether the sentiments you now express are those only of the colored people in the city; or do they extend to the colored population through the country? and what are your means of knowing the sentiments of those living in the country?

Answer: I think the sentiments are the same among the colored people of the State. My opinion is formed by personal communication in the course of my ministry, and also from the thousands that followed the Union army, leaving their homes and undergoing suffering. I did not think there would be so many; the number surpassed my expectation.

Eighth: If the Rebel leaders were to arm the slaves, what would be its effect?

Answer: I think they would fight as long as they were before the bayonet, and just as soon as they could get away, they would desert, in my opinion.

Ninth: What, in your opinion, is the feeling of the colored people about enlisting and serving as soldiers of the United States? and what kind of military service do they prefer?

Answer: A large number have gone as soldiers to Port Royal to be drilled and put in the service; and I think there are thousands of the young men that would enlist. There is something about them that perhaps is wrong. They have suffered so long from the Rebels that they want to shoulder the musket. Others want to go into the Quartermaster's or Commissary's service.

Tenth: Do you understand the mode of enlistments of colored persons in the Rebel States by State agents under the Act of Congress? If yea, state what your understanding is.

Answer: My understanding is, that colored persons enlisted by State agents are enlisted as substitutes, and give credit to the States, and do not swell the army, because every black man enlisted by a State agent leaves a white man at home; and, also, that larger bounties are given or promised by State agents than are given by the States. The great object should be to push through this Rebellion the shortest way, and there seems to be something wanting in the enlistment by State agents, for it don't strengthen the army, but takes one away for every colored man enlisted.

Eleventh: State what, in your opinion, is the best way to enlist colored men for soldiers.

Answer: I think, sir, that all compulsory operations should be put a stop to. The ministers would talk to them, and the young men would enlist. It is my opinion that it would be far better for the State agents to stay at home, and the enlistments to be made for the United States under the direction of Gen. Sherman.

In the absence of Gen. Sherman, the following question was asked:

Twelfth: State what is the feeling of the colored people in regard to Gen. Sherman; and how far do they regard his sentiments and actions as friendly to their rights and interests, or otherwise?

Answer: We looked upon Gen. Sherman prior to his arrival as a man in the Providence of God specially set apart to accomplish this work, and we unanimously feel inexpressible gratitude to him, looking upon him as a man that should be honored for the faithful performance of his duty. Some of us called upon him immediately upon his arrival, and it is probable he would not meet the Secretary with more courtesy than he met us. His conduct and deportment toward us characterized him as a friend and a gentleman. We have confidence in Gen. Sherman, and think that what concerns us could not be under better hands. This is our opinion now from the short acquaintance and interest we have had. (Mr. Lynch states that with his limited acquaintance with Gen. Sherman, he is unwilling to express an opinion. All others present declare their agreement with Mr. Frazier about Gen. Sherman.)

Some conversation upon general subjects relating to Gen. Sherman's march then ensued, of which no note was taken.

WAR DEPT. ADJT. GEN.'S OFFICE
WASHINGTON, Feb. 1, 1865.

I do hereby certify that the foregoing is a true and faithful report of the questions and answers made by the colored ministers and church members of Savannah in my presence and hearing, at the chambers of Major-Gen. Sherman, on the evening of Thursday, Jan. 12, 1865. The questions of Gen. Sherman and the Secretary of War were reduced to writing and read to the persons present. The answers were made by the Rev. Garrison Frazier, who was selected by the other ministers and church members to answer for them. The answers were written down in his exact words, and read over to the others, who one by one expressed his concurrence or dissent as above set forth.

E. D. TOWNSEND, Asst.-Adjt.-Gen.

William T. Sherman: Special Field Orders No. 15

Following their meeting with Garrison Frazier and other black leaders in Savannah, Sherman and Stanton collaborated in drafting Special Field Orders No. 15, possibly in consultation with Brigadier General Rufus Saxton, the Union commander in the South Carolina Sea Islands. Special Field Orders No. 15 sought to provide land both for the refugees who had followed Sherman's army through Georgia and for the freed people who lived in the coastal region of South Carolina and Georgia. Before the war the cultivation of extra-long staple cotton had made the Sea Islands one of the wealthiest regions of the United States. Beginning with Union capture of Port Royal in November 1861, the plantation owners of the Sea Islands had fled inland. Some of the abandoned plantations in the islands were seized during the war by the U.S. treasury department and sold to northern investors, who experimented with raising cotton using paid labor. Their efforts were resisted by many of the freed people, who preferred to own their own land and grow food crops. By the summer of 1865 about 40,000 former slaves were living on the 400,000 acres of land set apart by Sherman's order. (Some of the settlers worked their forty-acre plots with surplus mules provided by the Union army, possibly giving rise to the phrase "forty acres and a mule.") In August 1865 President Andrew Johnson revoked Special Field Orders No. 15 by directing that abandoned southern lands be returned to owners who were willing to swear allegiance to the Union.

IN THE FIELD, SAVANNAH, GA., January 16th, 1865.

SPECIAL FIELD ORDERS,
No. 15.

I. The islands from Charleston, south, the abandoned rice fields along the rivers for thirty miles back from the sea, and the country bordering the St. Johns river, Florida, are reserved and set apart for the settlement of the negroes now made free by the acts of war and the proclamation of the President of the United States.

II. At Beaufort, Hilton Head, Savannah, Fernandina, St. Augustine and Jacksonville, the blacks may remain in their chosen or accustomed vocations—but on the islands, and in the settlements hereafter to be established, no white person whatever, unless military officers and soldiers detailed for duty, will be permitted to reside; and the sole and exclusive management of affairs will be left to the freed people themselves, subject only to the United States military authority and the acts of Congress. By the laws of war, and orders of the President of the United States, the negro is free and must be dealt with as such. He cannot be subjected to conscription or forced military service, save by the written orders of the highest military authority of the Department, under such regulations as the President or Congress may prescribe. Domestic servants, blacksmiths, carpenters and other mechanics, will be free to select their own work and residence, but the young and able-bodied negroes must be encouraged to enlist as soldiers in the service of the United States, to contribute their share towards maintaining their own freedom, and securing their rights as citizens of the United States.

Negroes so enlisted will be organized into companies, battalions and regiments, under the orders of the United States military authorities, and will be paid, fed and clothed according to law. The bounties paid on enlistment may, with the consent of the recruit, go to assist his family and settlement in procuring agricultural implements, seed, tools, boots, clothing, and other articles necessary for their livelihood.

III. Whenever three respectable negroes, heads of families, shall desire to settle on land, and shall have selected for that purpose an island or a locality clearly defined, within the limits above designated, the Inspector of Settlements and Plantations will himself, or by such subordinate officer as he may appoint, give them a license to settle such island or district, and afford them such assistance as he can to enable them to establish a peaceable agricultural settlement. The three parties named will subdivide the land, under the supervision of the Inspector, among themselves and such others as may choose to settle near them, so that each family shall have a plot of not more than (40) forty acres of tillable ground, and when it borders on some water channel, with not more than 800 feet water front, in the possession of which land the military authorities will afford them protection, until such time as they can protect themselves, or until Congress shall regulate their title. The Quartermaster may, on the requisition of the Inspector of Settlements and Plantations, place at the disposal of the Inspector, one or more of the captured steamers, to ply between the settlements and one or more of the commercial points heretofore named in orders, to afford the settlers the opportunity to supply their necessary wants, and to sell the products of their land and labor.

IV. Whenever a negro has enlisted in the military service of the United States, he may locate his family in any one of the settlements at pleasure, and acquire a homestead, and all other rights and privileges of a settler, as though present in person. In like manner, negroes may settle their families and engage on board the gunboats, or in fishing, or in the navigation of the inland waters, without losing any claim to land or other advantages derived from this system. But no one, unless an actual settler as above defined, or unless absent on Government service, will be entitled to claim any right to land or property in any settlement by virtue of these orders.

V. In order to carry out this system of settlement, a general officer will be detailed as Inspector of Settlements and Plantations, whose duty it shall be to visit the settlements, to regulate their police and general management, and who will furnish personally to each head of a family, subject to the approval of the President of the United States, a possessory title in writing, giving as near as possible the description of boundaries; and who shall adjust all claims or conflicts that may arise under the same, subject to the like approval, treating such titles altogether as possessory. The same general officer will also be charged with the enlistment and organization of the negro recruits, and protecting their interests while absent from their settlements; and will be governed by the rules and regulations prescribed by the War Department for such purposes.

VI. Brigadier General R. SAXTON is hereby appointed Inspector of Settlements and Plantations, and will at once enter on the performance of his duties. No change is intended or desired in the settlement now on Beaufort Island, nor will any rights to property heretofore acquired be affected thereby.

BY ORDER OF MAJOR GENERAL W. T. SHERMAN

WASHINGTON, D.C., JANUARY 1865

Thirteenth Amendment to the Constitution of the United States

Drafted in its final form by Senator Lyman Trumbull, an Illinois Republican, the Thirteenth Amendment was approved by the Senate, 38–6, on April 8, 1864. In a 93–65 vote in the House of Representatives on June 15, opposition from Democrats and conservative border state unionists prevented the amendment from winning the two-thirds majority necessary for passage. President Lincoln used his annual message in December to urge the 38th Congress to adopt the amendment in its final session, and, along with Secretary of State Seward, began to lobby vigorously for its passage. (Lincoln had previously hoped that slavery would be legally abolished in the border states and in the reconstructed South by amending the various state constitutions.) On January 31, 1865, the House of Representatives approved the amendment, 119–56, and it was submitted to the states for ratification. The following evening Lincoln told a crowd that the amendment was "a King's cure for all the evils" left unaddressed by the Emancipation Proclamation. Although Delaware, Kentucky, New Jersey, and Mississippi would vote against ratification, the Thirteenth Amendment would be approved by twenty-seven states, including eight former members of the Confederacy, by December 6, and on December 18, 1865, Seward declared that its ratification had been completed.

Article XIII.

SECTION 1. Neither slavery nor involuntary servitude, except as a punishment for crime whereof the party shall have been duly convicted, shall exist within the United States, or any place subject to their jurisdiction.

SECTION 2. Congress shall have power to enforce this article by appropriate legislation.

January 31, 1865

"THE GREATEST EVENT": WASHINGTON, D.C., FEBRUARY 1865

George W. Julian: Journal, February 1, 1865

An active abolitionist since the 1840s, George W. Julian was a Radical Republican congressman from Indiana whose commitment to racial equality was unusual for an officeholder from the antebellum Midwest. In 1831 Indiana had followed the example of Ohio and Illinois by adopting legislation forbidding black people from moving into the state without first posting a bond for good behavior, and in 1851 the state constitution was amended to include an outright prohibition on black migration into Indiana. (The constitutional prohibition would be overturned in 1866 by the Indiana supreme court in a decision based in part on the enforcement clause of the Thirteenth Amendment.) Speaking in support of the Second Confiscation Act in May 1862, Julian told Congress that slavery was ultimately responsible for "all the unutterable agonies of our many battle-fields, all the terrible sorrows which rend so many thousands of loving hearts, all the ravages and desolation of this stupendous conflict." Nearly three years later, he wrote in his journal about the passage of the Thirteenth Amendment.

WEDNESDAY NIGHT, February 1.

Just returned from Mr. Chase's reception, where I went with Mrs. Cheesman. Mrs. Sprague appeared grandly and so did the Chief Justice.

The greatest event of this century occurred yesterday in the passage of the Constitutional Amendment in the House. The spectacle during the vote was the most solemn and impressive I ever witnessed. The result for a good while remained in doubt, and the suspense produced perfect stillness. When it was certainly known that the measure had carried, the cheering in the hall and densely packed galleries exceeded anything I ever before saw and beggared description. Members joined in the shouting, and kept it up for some minutes. Some embraced one another, others wept like children. I never before felt as I then did, and thanked God for the blessed opportunity of recording my name where it will be as honored as those of the signers of the Declaration of Independence. What a grand jubilee for the old battle-scarred Abolitionists. Glorious fruit of the war. I have felt, ever since the vote, as if I were in a new country. I seem to breathe better, and feel comforted and refreshed.

Another event, following close after this, was the admission of Doctor Rock, of Boston, a colored lawyer and scholar, to practice in the Supreme Court. No objection was made, even by the old Dred Scott judges.

Have my bill ready to offer.

Robert Garlick Hill Kean: Diary, February 5, 1865

In January 1865, Francis Preston Blair, a former adviser to Andrew Jackson who served as an unofficial counselor to President Lincoln, traveled to Richmond twice to meet with Jefferson Davis. Blair proposed to Davis that the Union and Confederate armies should jointly expel the French from Mexico as a prelude to national reunion. Neither Davis nor Lincoln believed in Blair's proposal, but they were both willing to use him as an intermediary. On January 12 Davis asked Blair to tell Lincoln that he was willing to "enter into conference with a view to secure peace to the two countries." Lincoln responded on January 18 that he would accept an emissary "with the view of securing peace to the people of our one common country." Despite Lincoln's refusal to acknowledge Confederate independence, Davis appointed as commissioners Confederate vice president Alexander H. Stephens, Confederate senator Robert M. T. Hunter, and John A. Campbell, the Confederate assistant secretary of war. The three men met with Lincoln and Secretary of State Seward on February 3 onboard the Union steamboat *River Queen* at Hampton Roads, Virginia. No notes were taken during the meeting, but the various accounts written afterward by the participants agree that Lincoln insisted on a complete cessation of hostilities and the full restoration of the union while refusing to retreat from his emancipation policies. Robert Garlick Hill Kean, an administrator in the Confederate War Department who worked closely with Campbell, wrote about the Hampton Roads conference in his diary on February 5. The next day Davis attributed the meeting's failure in a message to the Confederate Congress to northern insistence on "unconditional submission."

Feb. 5. Last night at about 8 o'clock, Messrs. Stephens, Hunter and Campbell got back. After they were admitted into Grant's lines, they were carried down to City Point where they were taken in hand by Major Eckert, the censor of the telegraph, who was the person to have charge of their going forward. Some notes passed on the subject of the character and objects of their mission, and delay was produced by which they were kept at City Point till Thursday morning from Monday night. Judge Campbell thinks this was in order to give time for the announcement of the vote in the Yankee House of Representatives on the emancipation amendment to the Constitution and the action of the Eastern states legislatures on it—all of which Seward, who was all the while at Old Point, was waiting for, and brought out in the conference. Finally on Thursday they were taken down on Grant's steamboat, getting into the Roads. Lincoln arrived from Washington that evening and sent them word that he was tired with travel, but would see them the next day. So next morning they were taken on board the steamer where Lincoln and Seward were, and had a conference of about three hours, in which a great deal was talked over.

Mr. Stephens reminded Lincoln of their intimacy in the time when they served on the secret committee together, which engineered the election of General Taylor. Lincoln remembered the acquaintance but appeared oblivious of the 'sleeping together' after the manner of Botts and Tyler. Mr. Stephens then went into a long discussion of the 'Monroe Doctrine' in its relations to this quarrel. After he had proceeded for some time (this cue having been taken from Blair) Lincoln appeared to have become impatient and interrupted with the remark that there was but one ground on which propositions could be made or received, and that was the restoration of the national authority over all places in the states. This diverted the discussion, but Mr. Seward said he desired to hear Mr. Stephens out; his view was one in which he was interested.

Mr. Stephens cited historical instances of nations at war laying aside their quarrel to take up other matters of mutual interest to both. Mr. Lincoln replied that he knew nothing about history, 'You must talk history to Seward.' It having become distinctly understood that no terms short of reconstruction were to be considered, Judge Campbell took up the discussion and inquired searchingly into their ideas of the manner of it. It was brought out distinctly that submission was contemplated pure and simple, though they called our envoys to witness that they never used the word 'submission.' Their phrase was 'restoration of the national authority.' The terms of Lincoln's message in December last were all they had to offer.

On the subject of their penal legislation, Lincoln said that we must accept all the consequences of the application of the law, that he would be disposed to use liberally the power confided to him for the remission of pains and penalties. In this connection Judge Campbell remarked that he had never regarded his neck as in danger. Lincoln replied that there were a good many oak trees about the place where he lived, the limbs of which afforded many convenient points from which he might have dangled. This was said with temper, and was the only exhibition of it at all. They said there could be no convention on this subject with us either as a national government or as states, as to make such a convention would be a 'recognition.' Mr. Hunter replied that this did not follow; there were frequent instances of such conventions, as between Charles I and the parliament. Lincoln answered, 'And Charles I lost his head; that's all I know about that; you must talk history to Seward.' Judge Campbell stated the difference between the law of conquest and a pacification by convention. They left no opening for any convention. Everything was to be settled by the laws of Congress and the decisions of the courts.

The slavery question was mentioned. That, Lincoln said, would be decided by the courts. Some said his proclamations had no effect whatever; others, that they operated only in particular places; others, that they were of general operation. He supposed this would be tested by some one taking a negro, and the question of his freedom being brought before the courts.

(In this connection and in reply to Mr. Hunter's suggestion as to negro women and children in exposed places, like Eastern Virginia where productive labor had all absconded, Lincoln told his *story* of the pigs.)

In this connection Seward produced the vote in the House of Representatives on the amendment to the Constitution. He said this country was in a revolutionary condition, and as always was the case, the most extreme party succeeds. He cited Maryland. The first proposition was to get rid of slavery in 50 years. This would have been satisfactory, but a more extreme party arose for emancipation in seven years, then a more violent one for immediate emancipation, and this one succeeded. So in New York, the *Tribune* which a few years ago was the *only* abolition political paper supported by the country, was now the most conservative of the Northern press while the *Herald* leads the abolition party.

The conditions of a truce were also discussed, equally unsatisfactory. The only governments which could be recognized in states where there are two would be the bogus Yankee government. Judge Campbell also asked if Virginia went back whether it would be with her ancient limits. The reply was that it would be a question for the courts. West Virginia would be regarded as a state. The gentlemen prepared their answer to the President this morning, which I presume will be published. This ends this peace *fiasco* which must satisfy the most sceptical that we have nothing whatever to hope or expect short of the exaction of all the rights of conquest, whether we are overrun by force, or submit.

"WE MUST EMANCIPATE": VIRGINIA, FEBRUARY 1865

John H. Stringfellow to Jefferson Davis

Born in Virginia, John H. Stringfellow studied medicine in Philadelphia before moving to Missouri. In 1854 he helped found the town of Atchison, Kansas, and became a leader of the proslavery settlers in the territory. The speaker of the first territorial house of representatives, Stringfellow coedited the *Squatter Sovereign*, a weekly newspaper that urged its readers to "scourge the country of abolitionism, free soilism, and every other damnable ism that exists." Discouraged by the prospects of making Kansas a slave state, he returned to Virginia in 1858 and during the war served as a surgeon in Confederate army hospitals. Stringfellow wrote to Davis from his home outside Richmond as the Confederate Congress debated whether to arm slaves. On February 20 the Confederate house of representatives would approve, 40–37, a bill that authorized the Confederate army to enlist slaves with the permission of their masters, but without providing for their emancipation. The bill would pass the Confederate senate 9–8 on March 8 and was signed by Davis five days later. General Orders No. 14, issued by the Confederate adjutant general on March 23, would require that masters free their slaves before enlistment. The Confederate army would recruit only a few hundred black soldiers before the end of the war.

Glenn Allen Henrico Feby 8th 1865

My dear Sir Impelled by the perils of our country, and the thousand conflicting theories as to the cause, and cure; to continually have these things before me; I have been amazed to see, that no one thus far has concieved, or if concieved, had the boldness to present in my judgment, the only solution of all these perils and difficulties. I address you because you have already taken a long stride in the right direction & because I believe your mind has already reached the true solution, but owing to peculiar circumstances has hesitated to enunciate it. The history of this war demonstrates the wonderfull fact, that the Confederate states mainly subsists both of the immense armies engaged in the conflict, and actually after furnishing *all* the soldiers to our army, contributes about one half of those making the army of its enemies, and should the war continue for annother year, the south will probably furnish *two thirds* of the army of her foes. These facts which cannot be controverted show certainly any thing but *weakness, or inferiority* on the part of the south; but it does show that a change of policy in relation to the conduct of the war, and that a radical one must be adopted, or we shall be destroyed. Let us look at a few facts. The Yankees have now in their service 200 000 of our ex-slaves, and under their next draft, will probably have half as many more. We have not *one* soldier from that source in our ranks. It is held by us that *slaves* will not make soldiers, therefore we refuse to put them in the service & I think are correct in so doing. But while we thus think, and thus act, our enemies are creating, in addition to their *white force which we have found to our cost in the last year, to be quite as large as we could manage*, an auxiliary army of our own escaped slaves, of three or four hundred thousand men. Now however we may decry the negro as a soldier every one knows that if the white troops of the yankees are numerous enough to hold all ours in check, then this negro army can, at will, ravage and destroy our whole country, and we will be absolutely conquered by our own slaves. We allege that *slaves* will not fight in our armies, escaped slaves fight & fight bravely for our enemies, therefore a freed Slave will fight. If at the begining of this war, all our negroes had been free, does any one believe the Yankees would have been able to recruit an army amongst them, does any one know of a solitary free negro escaping to them and joining their army. If our slaves were *now* to be freed would the Yankees be able to raise another recruit amongst them? If freedom and amnesty were declared in favour of those already in the Yankee lines, would they not almost to a man desert to their old homes? Would not our *freed* negroes make us as good soldiers as they make for our enemies? Again suppose we free a portion of our slaves & put them in the army, we leave *all the rest* as a recruiting field for the enemy, from which we cannot get a single soldier and thus we see one half of our *entire* population of no avail to us, but on the contrary ready at every oportunity to join the ranks of our enemies. Now sir Southern soldiers are the best that ever drew a blade in the cause of liberty, but there are some things which *they* cannot do; they cannot fight our battles against overwhelming numbers, and raise the necessary supplies for the army and the women and children at home, and yet sir this is what they will be called upon to do if this war is protracted for two years longer. I ask sir then in view of these *facts* if the prompt abolition of slavery, will not prove a remedy sufficient to arrest this tide of disaster? The Yankee army will be diminished by it, our own army can be increased by it & our labour retained by it. Without it, if the war continues, we shall in the end be subjugated, our negroes emancipated, our lands parcelled out amongst them, and if any of it be left to us, only an equal portion with our own negroes, and ourselves given only equal (if any) social and political rights and privileges. If we emancipate, our independence is secured, the white man only will have any, and all political rights, retain all his real and personal property, exclusive of his property in his slave, make the laws to controll the freed negro, who having no land, must labor for the land owner; and being an adequate *supply of labor*, must work for the land owner on terms about as economical as tho owned by him.

We cannot consent to reconstruction even if they repeal all their laws, and withdraw all their proclamations in regard to us, our Lands & our Negroes, because they now have, or at any session of their congress can make the necessary number of states, to alter the Constitution, in a constitutional manner, and thus abolish slavery, and interfere in any other way they think proper. But even if the present administration should pledge any thing we may ask, it binds no one but themselves, during their own term of service, which you of course understand better than I do and suppose they should even promise and stand by their promise to pay us for our negroes, lost or to be emancipated, how will they pay us. They cannot by direct taxation, but only in levying an export duty on our products, Cotton, Tobacco & Naval stores: and this war has shown them & the world, if not us, how much they will bear, Cotton commanding one dollar pr pound, Tobacco three dollars, Tar two hundred dollars pr Barrel &c &c. To pay their war debt & for our negroes would make a debt of six (thousand) millions or probably eight the interest of which at five pr ct, would take four hundred millions of revenue to pay, and to raise something additional to extinguish the principal, would require an additional hundred million, thus you see an export duty to this extent would be levied & could easily be raised upon our own products; twenty cents upon cotton which would make the price about 32 or 33 cts, the world would pay, because they must have it & have bought it for much more, would bring an annual income of about four hundred million without countg the duty on Tobacco & Naval Stores but even with this most favorable view of the case we should loose the whole of our own war debt which is or will be say two thousand million of course this would be repudiated & justly by our enemies if we consent to reconstruction Whereas if *we* emancipate we save the two thousand million, & we can pay for the negroes four thousand million more, and the export duty on cotton alone (which we should have levied if we go back into the Union) will pay the interest upon this at 5 pr ct and leave a hundred million as a sinking fund to extinguish the principal in some 30 or 40 years & the slave owner have all his labour on his farm that he had before; (for having no home & no property to buy one with, he must live with & work for his old owner for such wages as said owner may choose to give, to be regulated by law hereafter as may suit the change of relation) And this six thousand million is not a debt we tax ourselves to pay, but the world pays it. The speculator who buys the cotton & pays the duty, makes the manufacturer pay him his ten or fifteen pr ct nett profit on his gross outlay, the manufacturer makes the merchant pay him his ten or fifteen pr ct on his gross outlay, the merchant charges the retail dealer his ten or fifteen pr ct on his gross outlay, and so on till the *shirt* is made *and he who wears it out pays the duty & all the diferent pr centages upon it.* Thus *we* will pay to the extent of our consumption of the exported article when manufactured & returned to us, a mere nothing when compared to the immense gratuity, six thousand million which the World makes to us, & which they so justly should be made to hand over to us, for the cold blooded, heartless indifferance with which thay have contemplated the bloody, inhuman, barbarous, and apparently hopeless contest in which we have been engaged, and which they at any moment could have arrested by a word.

By emancipation I think we would not only render our triumph secure as I have attempted to prove, in & of itself but in all future time the negro in place of being useless in time of war as a soldier, & really dangerous as we have seen to our cost, continues to be an element of strength. And I think we may *reasonably* hope that the nations of the earth would no longer be unwilling to recognise us, for surely no people ever before strugled so long, and under so many dificulties, and endured so many privations so uncomplainingly as we have without finding some friendly hand outstretched to encourage or to help; and there can be no other reason than that we are exclusively & peculiarly a nation of slaveholders. I think that even amongst our enemies numbers would be added to those who are already willing to let us go in peace, for we should thus give the lie at once & forever to the charge that we are waging a war only for negro slavery, and the heart of ever honest lover of human liberty throughout the world would sumpathise with the men who for their cherished rights as freemen, would wage such an unequal contest as we have waged & besides sacrefising all their earnest convictions as to the humanity & righteousness of slavery were willing to sacrefice their property interest of four thousand millions to secure their independence, which might all be saved so far as the *promises* of our enemies are concerned, by reconstruction. In my judgement, the only question for us to decide, is whether we shall gain our independence by freeing the negro, we retaining all the power to regulate them by law when so freed, or permit our enemies through our own slaves to compell us to submit to Emancipation with equal or superior political rights for our negroes and partial or complete confiscation of our property for the use & benefit of the negro And sir if the war continues as it is now waged, and we are forced, by the overwhelming odds of the Yankees and our own slaves in arms against us, into submission it would be but an act of simple justice for the Yankee Govt to see to it that their negro allies are at least as *well* provided for in the way of homes, as those who have been arrayed in arms against them.

I have always believed & still believe that slavery is an institution sanctioned if not established by the Almighty and the most humane & beneficial relation that can exist between Labor & Capital, still I think that this contest has proven that

in a military sense it is an element of weakness & the teachings of providence as exhibited in this war dictates conclusively & imperitively that *to secure & perpetuate our independence we must emancipate the negro.*
P.S. We should then get rid of the only impediment in the way of an exchange of prisoners thus getting 30 or 40 thousand more men in the field

I have given you what I conceive to be the only solution to our dificulties. How to effect this is a serious difficulty. Men are reluctant, in fact it might be imprudent, to discuss this thing publickly; but we know that in great crises men think & act rapidly, or at least should do so. If congress could be convinced of the correctness of this course they could in Convention with the Governors of the States devise some method, by which conventions of the states could be held and the necessary measures adopted; first by law of Congress if necessary provide for paying the owners for them I have not found a single slave holder with whom I have conversed but is willing to submit to the measure if deemed necessary by the proper Authorities Indeed I have no doubt of the power of Congress as a military necessity, to impress all of the able bodied male negroes & pay for them giving them their freedom & providing for paying for the rest upon the condition of manumission, but the other course would be least objectionable We burn an individuals cotton, corn or meat to keep it from the enemy so we can take his negro man & set him free to keep him from recruiting the enemys army.

I have written you this much, hoping it may aid you in some way. I have shown what I have written to no one, nor communicated my intentions to any one. If you think what I have written worth anything, make what use of it you chose, if not just stick it between the bars of your grate. What I have written is with an honest endeavour to aid you in guiding our ship through the perils & darkness which surround her & from no feeling of dissatisfaction or distrust as to yourself, for you have all my sympathies & all of my trust & confidence With diffidence & the warmest admiration & Respect I remain Your friend

J H Stringfellow

Written very hurriedly & with no effort at arrangement but only as "food for thought" JHS

I opened the envelope to say that my communication was written before I heard of the return of our commissioners, & that I am more than sustained by their report, and the action of the Yankee Congress on the slavery question, & now we have only to decide on or between *Emancipation for our independence*, or Subjugation & Emancipation coupled with negro equality or superiority, as our enemies may elect JHS

"LET SLAVERY DIE":
WASHINGTON, D.C., FEBRUARY 1865

Henry Highland Garnet: A Memorial Discourse

February 12, 1865

Born into slavery in Maryland, Henry Highland Garnet escaped with his parents and settled in New York, where Garnet became a Presbyterian minister and a prominent abolitionist. During the war he helped recruit black troops and aided victims of the New York City draft riots. At the invitation of William Henry Channing, the chaplain of the House of Representatives, Garnet preached a sermon in the House chamber on Sunday, February 12, becoming the first African American to speak before Congress.

> MATTHEW XXIII. 4: "For they bind heavy burdens, and grievous to be borne, and lay them on men's shoulders, but they themselves will not move them with one of their fingers."

IN this chapter, of which my text is a sentence, the Lord Jesus addressed his disciples, and the multitude that hung spell-bound upon the words that fell from his lips. He admonished them to beware of the religion of the Scribes and Pharisees, which was distinguished for great professions, while it succeeded in urging them to do but a little, or nothing that accorded with the law of righteousness.

In theory they were right; but their practices were inconsistent and wrong. They were learned in the law of Moses, and in the traditions of their fathers, but the principles of righteousness failed to affect their hearts. They knew their duty, but did it not. The demands which they made upon others proved that they themselves knew what things men ought to do. In condemning others they pronounced themselves guilty. They demanded that others should be just, merciful, pure, peaceable, and righteous. But they were unjust, impure, unmerciful—they hated and wronged a portion of their fellow-men, and waged continual war against the government of God.

On other men's shoulders they bound heavy and grievous burdens of duties and obligations. The people groaned beneath the loads which were imposed upon them, and in bitterness of spirit cried out, and filled the land with lamentations. But, with their eyes closed, and their hearts hardened, they heeded not, neither did they care. They regarded it to be but little less than intolerable insult to be asked to bear a small portion of the burdens which they were swift to bind on the shoulders of their fellow-men. With loud voice, and proud and defiant mien, they said these burdens are for them, and not for us. Behold how patiently they bear them. Their shoulders are broad, and adapted to the condition to which we have doomed them. But as for us, it is irksome, even to adjust their burdens, though we see them stagger beneath them.

Such was their conduct in the Church and in the State. We have modern Scribes and Pharisees, who are faithful to their prototypes of ancient times.

With sincere respect and reverence for the instruction, and the warning given by our Lord, and in humble dependence upon him for his assistance, I shall speak this morning of the Scribes and Pharisees of our times who rule the State. In discharging this duty, I shall keep my eyes upon the picture which is painted so faithfully and life-like by the hand of the Saviour.

Allow me to describe them. They are intelligent and well-informed, and can never say, either before an earthly tribunal or at the bar of God, "*We knew not of ourselves what was right.*" They are acquainted with the principles of the law of nations. They are proficient in the knowledge of Constitutional law. They are teachers of common law, and frame and execute statute law. They acknowledge that there is a just and impartial God, and are not altogether unacquainted with the law of Christian love and kindness. They claim for themselves the broadest freedom. Boastfully they tell us that they have received from the court of heaven the MAGNA CHARTA of human rights that was handed down through the clouds, and amid the lightnings of Sinai, and given again by the Son of God on the Mount of Beatitudes, while the glory of the Father shone around him. They tell us that from the Declaration of Independence and the Constitution they have obtained a guaranty of their political freedom, and from the Bible they derive their claim to all the blessings of religious liberty. With just pride they tell us that they are descended from the Pilgrims, who threw themselves upon the bosom of the treacherous sea, and braved storms and tempests, that they might find in a strange land, and among savages, free homes, where they might build their altars that should blaze with acceptable sacrifice unto God. Yes! they boast that their fathers heroically turned away from the precious light of Eastern civilization, and taking their lamps with oil in their vessels, joyfully went forth to illuminate this land, that then dwelt in the darkness of the valley of the shadow of death. With hearts strengthened by faith they spread out their standard to the winds of heaven, near Plymouth rock; and whether it was stiffened in the sleet and frosts of winter, or floated on the breeze of summer, it ever bore the motto, "*Freedom to worship God.*"

But others, their fellow-men, equal before the Almighty, and made by him of the same blood, and glowing with immortality, they doom to life-long servitude and chains. Yes, they stand in the most sacred places on earth, and beneath the gaze of the piercing eye of Jehovah, the universal Father of all men, and declare, "*that the best possible condition of the negro is slavery.*"*

"Thus man devotes his brother and destroys;
And more than all, and most to be deplored,
As human nature's broadest, foulest blot,
Chains him, and tasks him, and exacts his sweat
With stripes, that Mercy with bleeding heart,
Weeps to see inflicted on a beast."

In the name of the TRIUNE GOD I denounce the sentiment as unrighteous beyond measure, and the holy and the just of the whole earth say in regard to it, Anathema-maranatha.

What is slavery? Too well do I know what it is. I will present to you a bird's-eye view of it; and it shall be no fancy picture, but one that is sketched by painful experience. I was born among the cherished institutions of slavery. My earliest recollections of parents, friends, and the home of my childhood are clouded with its wrongs. The first sight that met my eyes was a

*Speech of FERNANDO WOOD, of New York, in Congress, 1864.

Christian mother enslaved by professed Christians, but, thank God, now a saint in heaven. The first sounds that startled my ear, and sent a shudder through my soul, were the cracking of the whip, and the clanking of chains. These sad memories mar the beauties of my native shores, and darken all the slave-land, which, but for the reign of despotism, had been a paradise. But those shores are fairer now. The mists have left my native valleys, and the clouds have rolled away from the hills, and Maryland, the unhonored grave of my fathers, is now the free home of their liberated and happier children.

Let us view this demon, which the people have worshiped as a God. Come forth, thou grim monster, that thou mayest be critically examined! There he stands. Behold him, one and all. Its work is to chattleize man; to hold property in human beings. Great God! I would as soon attempt to enslave GABRIEL or MICHAEL as to enslave a man made in the image of God, and for whom Christ died. Slavery is snatching man from the high place to which he was lifted by the hand of God, and dragging him down to the level of the brute creation, where he is made to be the companion of the horse and the fellow of the ox.

It tears the crown of glory from his head, and as far as possible obliterates the image of God that is in him. Slavery preys upon man, and man only. A brute cannot be made a slave. Why? Because a brute has not reason, faith, nor an undying spirit, nor conscience. It does not look forward to the future with joy or fear, nor reflect upon the past with satisfaction or regret. But who in this vast assembly, who in all this broad land, will say that the poorest and most unhappy brother in chains and servitude has not every one of these high endowments? Who denies it? Is there one? If so, let him speak. There is not one; no, not one.

But slavery attempts to make a man a brute. It treats him as a beast. Its terrible work is not finished until the ruined victim of its lusts, and pride, and avarice, and hatred, is reduced so low that with tearful eyes and feeble voice he faintly cries, "*I am happy and contented—I love this condition.*"

> "Proud Nimrod first the bloody chase began,
> A mighty hunter he; his prey was man."

The caged lion may cease to roar, and try no longer the

strength of the bars of his prison, and lie with his head between his mighty paws and snuff the polluted air as though he heeded not. But is he contented? Does he not instinctively long for the freedom of the forest and the plain? Yes, he is a lion still. Our poor and forlorn brother whom thou hast labelled "*slave*," is also a man. He may be unfortunate, weak, helpless, and despised, and hated, nevertheless he is a man. His God and thine has stamped on his forehead his title to his inalienable rights in characters that can be read by every intelligent being. Pitiless storms of outrage may have beaten upon his defenceless head, and he may have descended through ages of oppression, yet he is a man. God made him such, and his brother cannot unmake him. Woe, woe to him who attempts to commit the accursed crime.

Slavery commenced its dreadful work in kidnapping unoffending men in a foreign and distant land, and in piracy on the seas. The plunderers were not the followers of Mahomet, nor the devotees of Hindooism, nor benighted pagans, nor idolaters, but people called Christians, and thus the ruthless traders in the souls and bodies of men fastened upon Christianity a crime and stain at the sight of which it shudders and shrieks.

It is guilty of the most heinous iniquities ever perpetrated upon helpless women and innocent children. Go to the shores of the land of my forefathers, poor bleeding Africa, which, although she has been bereaved, and robbed for centuries, is nevertheless beloved by all her worthy descendants wherever dispersed. Behold a single scene that there meets your eyes. Turn not away neither from shame, pity, nor indifference, but look and see the beginning of this cherished and petted institution. Behold a hundred youthful mothers seated on the ground, dropping their tears upon the hot sands, and filling the air with their lamentations.

Why do they weep? Ah, Lord God, thou knowest! Their babes have been torn from their bosoms and cast upon the plains to die of hunger, or to be devoured by hyenas or jackals. The little innocents would die on the "Middle Passage," or suffocate between the decks of the floating slave-pen, freighted and packed with unparalleled human woe, and the slavers in mercy have cast them out to perish on their native shores. Such is the beginning, and no less wicked is the end of that system which the Scribes and Pharisees in the Church and the State pronounce to be just, humane, benevolent and Christian. If such are the deeds of mercy wrought by angels, then tell me what works of iniquity there remain for devils to do?

This commerce in human beings has been carried on until three hundred thousand have been dragged from their native land in a single year. While this foreign trade has been pursued, who can calculate the enormities and extent of the domestic traffic which has flourished in every slave State, while the whole country has been open to the hunters of men.

It is the highly concentrated essence of all conceivable wickedness. Theft, robbery, pollution, unbridled passion, incest, cruelty, cold-blooded murder, blasphemy, and defiance of the laws of God. It teaches children to disregard parental authority. It tears down the marriage altar, and tramples its sacred ashes under its feet. It creates and nourishes polygamy. It feeds and pampers its hateful handmaid, prejudice.

It has divided our national councils. It has engendered deadly strife between brethren. It has wasted the treasure of the Commonwealth, and the lives of thousands of brave men, and driven troops of helpless women and children into yawning tombs. It has caused the bloodiest civil war recorded in the book of time. It has shorn this nation of its locks of strength that was rising as a young lion in the Western world. It has offered us as a sacrifice to the jealousy and cupidity of tyrants, despots, and adventurers of foreign countries. It has opened a door through which a usurper, a perjured, but a powerful prince, might stealthily enter and build an empire on the golden borders of our southwestern frontier, and which is but a stepping-stone to further and unlimited conquests on this continent. It has desolated the fairest portions of our land, "until the wolf long since driven back by the march of civilization returns after the lapse of a hundred years and howls amidst its ruins."

It seals up the Bible, and mutilates its sacred truths, and flies into the face of the Almighty, and impiously asks, "*Who art thou that I should obey thee*?" Such are the outlines of this fearful national sin; and yet the condition to which it reduces man, it is affirmed, is the best that can possibly be devised for him.

When inconsistencies similar in character, and no more

glaring, passed beneath the eye of the Son of God, no wonder he broke forth in language of vehement denunciation. Ye Scribes, Pharisees, and hypocrites! Ye blind guides! Ye compass sea and land to make one proselyte, and when he is made ye make him twofold more the child of hell than yourselves. Ye are like unto whited sepulchres, which indeed appear beautiful without, but within are full of dead men's bones, and all uncleanness!

Let us here take up the golden rule, and adopt the self-application mode of reasoning to those who hold these erroneous views. Come, gird up thy loins and answer like a man, if thou canst. Is slavery, as it is seen in its origin, continuance, and end the best possible condition for thee? Oh, no! Wilt thou bear that burden on thy shoulders, which thou wouldest lay upon thy fellow-man? No. Wilt thou bear a part of it, or remove a little of its weight with one of thy fingers? The sharp and indignant answer is no, no! Then how, and when, and where, shall we apply to thee the golden rule, which says, "*Therefore all things that ye would that others should do to you, do ye even so unto them, for this is the law and the prophets.*"

Let us have the testimony of the wise and great of ancient and modern times:

"Sages who wrote and warriors who bled."

PLATO declared that "Slavery is a system of complete injustice."

SOCRATES wrote that "Slavery is a system of outrage and robbery."

CYRUS said, "To fight in order not to be a slave is noble."

If Cyrus had lived in our land a few years ago he would have been arrested for using incendiary language, and for inciting servile insurrection, and the royal fanatic would have been hanged on a gallows higher than Haman. But every man is fanatical when his soul is warmed by the generous fires of liberty. Is it then truly noble to fight in order not to be a slave? The Chief Magistrate of the nation, and our rulers, and all truly patriotic men think so; and so think legions of black men, who for a season were scorned and rejected, but who came quickly and cheerfully when they were at last invited, bearing a heavy burden of proscriptions upon their shoulders, and having faith in God, and in their generous fellow-countrymen, they went forth to fight a double battle. The foes of their country were before them, while the enemies of freedom and of their race surrounded them.

AUGUSTINE, CONSTANTINE, IGNATIUS, POLYCARP, MAXIMUS, and the most illustrious lights of the ancient church denounced the sin of slave-holding.

THOMAS JEFFERSON said at a period of his life, when his judgment was matured, and his experience was ripe, "There is preparing, I hope, under the auspices of heaven, a way for a total emancipation."

The sainted WASHINGTON said, near the close of his mortal career, and when the light of eternity was beaming upon him, "It is among my first wishes to see some plan adopted by which slavery in this country shall be abolished by law. I know of but one way by which this can be done, and that is by legislative action, and so far as my vote can go, it shall not be wanting."

The other day, when the light of Liberty streamed through this marble pile, and the hearts of the noble band of patriotic statesmen leaped for joy, and this our national capital shook from foundation to dome with the shouts of a ransomed people, then methinks the spirits of Washington, Jefferson, the Jays, the Adamses, and Franklin, and Lafayette, and Giddings, and Lovejoy, and those of all the mighty, and glorious dead, remembered by history, because they were faithful to truth, justice, and liberty, were hovering over the august assembly. Though unseen by mortal eyes, doubtless they joined the angelic choir, and said, Amen.

POPE LEO X. testifies, "That not only does the Christian religion, but nature herself, cry out against a state of slavery."

PATRICK HENRY said, "We should transmit to posterity our abhorrence of slavery." So also thought the Thirty-Eighth Congress.

LAFAYETTE proclaimed these words: "Slavery is a dark spot on the face of the nation." God be praised, that stain will soon be wiped out.

JONATHAN EDWARDS declared "that to hold a man in slavery is to be every day guilty of robbery, or of man stealing."

Rev. Dr. WILLIAM ELLERY CHANNING, in a *Letter on the Annexation of Texas in* 1837, writes as follows:

"The evil of slavery speaks for itself. To state is to condemn the institution. The choice which every freeman makes of death for his child and for every thing he loves in preference to slavery, shows what it is. The single consideration that by slavery one human being is placed powerless and defenceless in the hands of another to be driven to whatever labor that other may impose, to suffer whatever punishment he may inflict, to live as his tool, the instrument of his pleasure, this is all that is needed to satisfy such as know the human heart and its unfitness for irresponsible power, that of all conditions slavery is the most hostile to the dignity, self-respect, improvement, rights, and happiness of human beings. * * * Every principle of our government and religion condemns slavery. The spirit of our age condemns it. The decree of the civilized world has gone out against it. * * * Is there an age in which a free and Christian people shall deliberately resolve to extend and perpetuate the evil? In so doing we cut ourselves off from the communion of nations; we sink below the civilization of our age; we invite the scorn, indignation, and abhorrence of the world."

MOSES, the greatest of all lawgivers and legislators, said, while his face was yet radiant with the light of Sinai: "Whoso stealeth a man, and selleth him, or if he be found in his hand, he shall surely be put to death." The destroying angel has gone forth through this land to execute the fearful penalties of God's broken law.

The Representatives of the nation have bowed with reverence to the Divine edict, and laid the axe at the root of the tree, and thus saved succeeding generations from the guilt of oppression, and from the wrath of God.

Statesmen, Jurists, and Philosophers, most renowned for learning, and most profound in every department of science and literature, have testified against slavery. While oratory has brought its costliest, golden treasures, and laid them on the altar of God and of freedom, it has aimed its fiercest lightning and loudest thunder at the strongholds of tyranny, injustice, and despotism.

From the days of Balak to those of Isaiah and Jeremiah, up to the times of Paul, and through every age of the Christian Church, the sons of thunder have denounced the abominable thing. The heroes who stood in the shining ranks of the hosts of the friends of human progress, from Cicero to Chatham, and Burke, Sharp, Wilberforce, and Thomas Clarkson, and Curran, assaulted the citadel of despotism. The orators and statesmen of our own land, whether they belong to the past, or to the present age, will live and shine in the annals of history, in proportion as they have dedicated their genius and talents to the defence of Justice and man's God-given rights.

All the poets who live in sacred and profane history have charmed the world with their most enchanting strains, when they have tuned their lyres to the praise of Liberty. When the Muses can no longer decorate her altars with their garlands, then they hang their harps upon the willows and weep.

From Moses to Terence and Homer, from thence to Milton and Cowper, Thomson and Thomas Campbell, and on to the days of our own bards, our Bryants, Longfellows, Whittiers, Morrises, and Bokers, all have presented their best gifts to the interests and rights of man.

Every good principle, and every great and noble power, have been made the subjects of the inspired verse, and the songs of poets. But who of them has attempted to immortalize slavery? You will search in vain the annals of the world to find an instance. Should any attempt the sacrilegious work, his genius would fall to the earth as if smitten by the lightning of heaven. Should he lift his hand to write a line in its praise, or defence, the ink would freeze on the point of his pen.

Could we array in one line, representatives of all the families of men, beginning with those lowest in the scale of being, and should we put to them the question, Is it right and desirable that you should be reduced to the condition of slaves, to be registered with chattels, to have your persons, and your lives, and the products of your labor, subjected to the will and the interests of others? Is it right and just that the persons of your wives and children should be at the disposal of others, and be yielded to them for the purpose of pampering their lusts and greed of gain? Is it right to lay heavy burdens on other men's shoulders which you would not remove with one of your fingers? From the rude savage and barbarian the negative response would come, increasing in power and significance as it rolled up the line. And when those should reply, whose minds and hearts are illuminated with the highest civilization and with the spirit of Christianity, the answer deep-toned and prolonged would thunder forth, no, no!

With all the moral attributes of God on our side, cheered as we are by the voices of universal human nature,—in view of the best interests of the present and future generations—animated with the noble desire to furnish the nations of the earth with a worthy example, let the verdict of death which has been brought in against slavery, by the THIRTY-EIGHTH CONGRESS, be affirmed and executed by the people. Let the gigantic monster perish. Yes, perish now, and perish forever!

> "Down let the shrine of Moloch sink,
> And leave no traces where it stood;
> No longer let its idol drink,
> His daily cup of human blood.
> But rear another altar there,
> To truth, and love, and mercy given,
> And freedom's gift and freedom's prayer,
> Shall call an answer down from heaven."

It is often asked when and where will the demands of the reformers of this and coming ages end? It is a fair question, and I will answer.

When all unjust and heavy burdens shall be removed from every man in the land. When all invidious and proscriptive distinctions shall be blotted out from our laws, whether they be constitutional, statute, or municipal laws. When emancipation shall be followed by enfranchisement, and all men holding allegiance to the government shall enjoy every right of American citizenship. When our brave and gallant soldiers shall have justice done unto them. When the men who endure the sufferings and perils of the battle-field in the defence of their country, and in order to keep our rulers in their places, shall enjoy the well-earned privilege of voting for them. When in the army and navy, and in every legitimate and honorable occupation, promotion shall smile upon merit without the slightest regard to the complexion of a man's face. When there shall be no more class-legislation, and no more trouble concerning the black man and his rights, than there is in regard to other American citizens. When, in every respect, he shall be equal before the law, and shall be left to make his own way in the social walks of life.

We ask, and only ask, that when our poor frail barks are launched on life's ocean—

> "Bound on a voyage of awful length
> And dangers little known,"

that, in common with others, we may be furnished with rudder, helm, and sails, and charts, and compass. Give us good pilots to conduct us to the open seas; lift no false lights along the dangerous coasts, and if it shall please God to send us propitious winds, or fearful gales, we shall survive or perish as our energies or neglect shall determine. We ask no special favors, but we plead for justice. While we scorn unmanly dependence; in the name of God, the universal Father, we demand the right to live, and labor, and to enjoy the fruits of our toil. The good work which God has assigned for the ages to come, will be finished, when our national literature shall be so purified as to reflect a faithful and a just light upon the character and social habits of our race, and the brush, and pencil, and chisel, and Lyre of Art, shall refuse to lend their aid to scoff at the afflictions of the poor, or to caricature, or ridicule a long-suffering people. When caste and prejudice in Christian churches shall be utterly destroyed, and shall be regarded as totally unworthy of Christians, and at variance with the principles of the gospel. When the blessings of the Christian religion, and of sound, religious education, shall be freely offered to all, then, and not till then, shall the effectual labors of God's people and God's instruments cease.

If slavery has been destroyed merely from *necessity*, let every class be enfranchised at the dictation of *justice*. Then we shall have a Constitution that shall be reverenced by all: rulers who shall be honored, and revered, and a Union that shall be sincerely loved by a brave and patriotic people, and which can never be severed.

Great sacrifices have been made by the people; yet, greater still are demanded ere atonement can be made for our national sins. Eternal justice holds heavy mortgages against us, and will require the payment of the last farthing. We have involved ourselves in the sin of unrighteous gain, stimulated by luxury, and pride, and the love of power and oppression; and prosperity and peace can be purchased only by blood, and with tears of repentance. We have paid some of the fearful installments, but there are other heavy obligations to be met.

The great day of the nation's judgment has come, and who shall be able to stand? Even we, whose ancestors have suffered the afflictions which are inseparable from a condition of slavery, for the period of two centuries and a half, now pity our land and weep with those who weep.

Upon the total and complete destruction of this accursed sin depends the safety and perpetuity of our Republic and its excellent institutions.

Let slavery die. It has had a long and fair trial. God himself has pleaded against it. The enlightened nations of the earth have condemned it. Its death warrant is signed by God and man. Do not commute its sentence. Give it no respite, but let it be ignominiously executed.

Honorable Senators and Representatives! illustrious rulers of this great nation! I cannot refrain this day from invoking upon you, in God's name, the blessings of millions who were ready to perish, but to whom a new and better life has been opened by your humanity, justice, and patriotism. You have said, "Let the Constitution of the country be so amended that slavery and involuntary servitude shall no longer exist in the United States, except in punishment for crime." Surely, an act so sublime could not escape Divine notice; and doubtless the deed has been recorded in the archives of heaven. Volumes may be appropriated to your praise and renown in the history of the world. Genius and art may perpetuate the glorious act on canvass and in marble, but certain and more lasting monuments in commemoration of your decision are already erected in the hearts and memories of a grateful people.

The nation has begun its exodus from worse than Egyptian bondage; and I beseech you that you say to the people, "*that they go forward*." With the assurance of God's favor in all things done in obedience to his righteous will, and guided by day and by night by the pillars of cloud and fire, let us not pause until we have reached the other and safe side of the stormy and crimson sea. Let freemen and patriots mete out complete and equal justice to all men, and thus prove to mankind the superiority of our Democratic, Republican Government.

Favored men, and honored of God as his instruments,

speedily finish the work which he has given you to do. *Emancipate, Enfranchise, Educate, and give the blessings of the gospel to every American citizen.*

"Hear ye not how, from all high points of Time,—
From peak to peak adown the mighty chain
That links the ages—echoing sublime
A Voice Almighty—leaps one grand refrain,
Wakening the generations with a shout,
And trumpet-call of thunder—Come ye out!

"Out from old forms and dead idolatries;
From fading myths and superstitious dreams:
From Pharisaic rituals and lies,
And all the bondage of the life that seems!
Out—on the pilgrim path, of heroes trod,
Over earth's wastes, to reach forth after God!

"The Lord hath bowed his heaven, and come down!
Now, in this latter century of time,
Once more his tent is pitched on Sinai's crown!
Once more in clouds must Faith to meet him climb!
Once more his thunder crashes on our doubt
And fear and sin—'My people! come ye out!'

"From false ambitions and base luxuries;
From puny aims and indolent self-ends;
From cant of faith, and shams of liberties,
And mist of ill that Truth's pure day-beam bends:
Out, from all darkness of the Egypt-land,
Into my sun-blaze on the desert sand!

* * * * * *

"Show us our Aaron, with his rod in flower!
Our Miriam, with her timbrel-soul in tune!
And call some Joshua, in the Spirit's power,
To poise our sun of strength at point of noon!
God of our fathers! over sand and sea,
Still keep our struggling footsteps close to thee!"*

Then before us a path of prosperity will open, and upon us will descend the mercies and favors of God. Then shall the

*Atlantic Monthly, 1862.

people of other countries, who are standing tip-toe on the shores of every ocean, earnestly looking to see the end of this amazing conflict, behold a Republic that is sufficiently strong to outlive the ruin and desolations of civil war, having the magnanimity to do justice to the poorest and weakest of her citizens. Thus shall we give to the world the form of a model Republic, founded on the principles of justice, and humanity, and Christianity, in which the burdens of war and the blessings of peace are equally borne and enjoyed by all.

THE BURNING OF COLUMBIA: SOUTH CAROLINA, FEBRUARY 1865

Emma LeConte: Diary, February 17–18, 1865

After learning of Hood's defeat at Nashville, Grant approved on January 2, 1865, Sherman's proposal to march his army north from Savannah through the Carolinas and, if needed, join in a campaign against Lee. "The truth is the whole army is burning with an insatiable desire to wreak vengeance upon South Carolina," Sherman wrote about the state northerners most blamed for starting the war. "I almost tremble at her fate, but feel that she deserves all that seems in store for her." On February 1 Sherman began his advance, feinting toward Charleston and Augusta in order to conceal his intention to move on Columbia. Many Confederates hoped in vain that heavy winter rain and flooded rivers would slow the Union advance through the swampy South Carolina low country. General Joseph E. Johnston would later recall that "when I learned that Sherman's army was marching through the Salkehatchie swamps, making its own corduroy road at the rate of a dozen miles a day or more, and bringing its artillery and wagons with it, I made up my mind that there had been no such army in existence since the days of Julius Cæsar." On February 16 General Pierre G. T. Beauregard decided to evacuate his badly outnumbered forces from Columbia. Union troops entered the city the following morning as residents looted stores and warehouses and fires began among the bales of cotton stockpiled in the streets. Some Union soldiers fought the fires, while others lit new ones. Spread by high winds, the flames eventually burned almost half the city. When a woman seeking a guard for her house denounced the Union for waging war on women and children, Lieutenant Colonel Jeremiah W. Jenkins, the commander of the 31st Iowa Infantry, told her: "The women of the South kept the war alive—and it is only by making them suffer that we can subdue the men." Seventeen-year-old Emma LeConte was the daughter of Joseph LeConte, a professor of chemistry and geology at South Carolina College who had operated a laboratory on campus for the Confederate Niter and Mining Bureau.

Friday 17th Feb. How long is this distress of mind to continue! It is now about 11 o'clock and the longest morning I ever lived through. I threw myself on the bed late last night or rather early this morning without undressing, feeling if I did not take some rest I would be sick. I lay awake a long time, in spite of heavy eyelids listening to the occasional cannon reports, wondering if the shelling would be renewed and thinking of the tumult there was reigning up town. At last I fell into a heavy sleep. At about six o'clock while it was still quite dark and all in the room were buried in profound slumber, we were suddenly awakened by a terrific explosion,—The house shook, broken window panes clattered down and we all sat up in bed, for a few seconds mute with terror. My first impression on waking was that a shell had struck the house, but as soon as I could collect my senses I knew that no shell could make such a noise. We lit the candle and mother sent Jane to enquire of Henry the cause. Of course he did not know. I went out of doors—the day was beginning to break murkily and the air was still heavy with smoke. All continuing quiet we concluded that the authorities had blown up some stores before evacuating. Whatever the cause, the effect was to scare us very effectually and to drive away all thought of sleep. We got up an hour later, almost fainting, for we had eaten almost nothing the preceding day. I forced myself to eat a little and to drink a half a cup of coffee. After breakfast the cannon opened again and so near that every report shook the house. I think it must have been a cannonade to cover our retreat. It did not continue very long. The negroes all went up town to see what they could get in the general pillage, for all the shops had been opened and provisions were scattered in all directions. Henry says in some parts of Main St corn and flour and sugar cover the ground. An hour or two ago they came running back declaring the Yankees were in town and that our troops were fighting them in the streets. This was not true, for at that time every soldier nearly had left town but we did not know it then. I had been feeling wretchedly faint, and nauseated with every mouthful of food I swallowed. And now I trembled all over and thought I should faint. I knew this would not do. So I lay down awhile and by dint of a little determination got quiet again. Mother is down right sick. She had been quite collected and calm until this news but now she suddenly lost all self control and exhibited the most lively terror—indeed I thought she would grow hysterical. As for Sallie her fright may be more easily imagined than described. This condition of affairs only lasted about half an hour but it was dreadful while it did last. As soon as I could I put on my pockets and nerved my self to meet them, but by and by the firing ceased and all was quiet again. It was denied that the Yankees had yet crossed the river or even completed their pontoon bridge and most of the servants returned up town. They have brought back a considerable quantity of provisions—The negroes are very kind and faithful—they have supplied us with meat and Jane brought mother some rice and crushed sugar for Carrie knowing that she had none. How times change! Those whom we have so long fed and cared for now help us + + We are intensely eager for every item of news, but of course can only hear through the negroes. A gentleman told us just now that the mayor had gone forward to surrender the town.

1 o'clock P.M. Well they are here! I was sitting in the back parlour, when I heard the shouting of the troops. I was at the front door in a moment. Jane came running and crying, "O Miss Emma, they've come at last!" She said they were then marching down Main Street, before them flying a panic stricken crowd of women and children, who seemed crazy. As she came along by Aunt Josie's, Miss Mary was at the gate about to run out. "For God's sake Miss Mary" she cried "stay where you are!" I suppose she (Miss M.) thought of running to the convent. I ran up stairs to my bed room window, just in time to see the U.S. flag run up over the State House. O what a horrid sight! what a degradation—to see it over the capital of South Carolina. After four long bitter years of bloodshed and hatred—now to float there at last—that hateful symbol of despotism! I do not think I could possibly describe my feelings. I know I could not look at it. I left the window and went back downstairs to mother. In a little while a guard arrived to protect the hospital. They have already fixed a shelter of boards against the wall near the gate. Sentinels are stationed and they are cooking their dinner. The wind is very high today and blows their hats around. This is the first sight we have had of these fiends except as prisoners—the sight does not stir up very pleasant feelings in our hearts—we cannot look at them with any thing but horror and hatred—loathing and disgust.

The troops now in town is a brigade commanded by Col Stone. Everything is quiet and orderly. Guards have been placed to protect houses and Sherman has promised not to disturb private property. How relieved and thankful we feel after all our anxiety & distress! *Later*—Gen Sherman has *assured* the mayor "that he and all the citizens may sleep as securely and quietly tonight as if under *Confederate rule.* Private property shall be carefully respected. Some public buildings have to be destroyed, but he will wait until tomorrow, when the wind shall have entirely subsided." It is said that one or two stragglers from Wheeler's command fired on the flag as it was borne down Main St on the carriage containing the Mayor Col Stone and other officers.

Saturday Afternoon, 18th. What a night of horror misery and agony! It is so useless to try to put on paper any idea of it. The recollection of it is so fearful—yet any attempt to describe it seems so useless—it even makes one sick to think of writing down such scenes. And yet as I have written thus far, I ought, while it is still fresh, try even imperfectly to give some account of last night. Every incident is now so vividly before me and yet it does not seem real—rather like a fearful dream, or nightmare that still oppresses.

Until dinner time we saw little of the Yankees, except the guard about the Campus and the officers and men galloping up and down the street. It is true, as I have since learned, that as soon as the bulk of the army entered, the work of pillage began. But we are so far off and so secluded from the rest of the town that we were happily ignorant of it all. I do not know exactly when Sherman entered, but I should judge about two or between one & two P.M. We could hear their shouts as they surged down Main St and through the State House but were too far off to see much of the tumult nor did we dream what a scene of pillage and terror was being enacted. I hear they found a picture of President Davis in the Capitol, which was set up as a target and shot at amid the jeers of the soldiery. From three o'clock till seven their Army was passing down the street by the Campus, to encamp back of us in the woods. Two Corps entered town—Howards and Logans. One, the diabolical 15th which Sherman has hitherto never permitted to enter a city on account of their vile and desperate character. Slocum's Corps remained over the river and I suppose Davis' also. The devils as they marched by looked strong, and well clad in dark dirty-looking blue. The wagon trains were immense.

Night drew on—Of course we did not expect to sleep but we looked forward to a tolerably tranquil night. Strange as it may seem we were actually idiotic enough to believe Sherman would keep his word!—A *Yankee*—and *Sherman*! It does seem incredible, such credulity—but I suppose we were so anxious to believe him—The lying fiend! I hope retributive justice will find him out one day. At about 7 o'clock I was standing on the back piazza in the third story. Before me the whole southern horizon was lit up by camp-fires which dotted the woods. On one side the sky was illuminated by the burning of Gen Hampton's residence a few miles off in the country, on the other by some blazing buildings near the river. I had scarcely gone down stairs again when Henry told us there was a fire on Main Street. Sumter Street was brightly lighted by a burning house so near our piazza that we could feel the heat. By the red glare, we could watch the wretches walking—generally staggering—back and forth from the camp to the town. Shouting hurrahing cursing South Carolina swearing blaspheming, singing ribald songs and using such obscene language that we were forced to go indoors. The fire on Main Street was now raging and we anxiously watched its progress from the upper front windows. In a little while however the flames broke forth in every direction. The Drunken devils roamed about setting fire to every house the flames seemed likely to spare. They were fully equipped for the noble work they had in hand—each soldier was furnished with combustibles compactly put up—they would enter houses and in the presence of helpless women and children pour turpentine on the beds and set them on fire. Guards were rarely of any assistance—most generally they assisted in the pillaging and firing. The wretched people rushing from their burning homes were not allowed to keep even the few necessaries they gathered up in their flight—even blankets and food were taken from them and destroyed. The Firemen attempted to use their engines but the hose were cut to pieces and their lives threatened. The wind blew a fearful gale wafting the flames from house to house with frightful rapidity. By midnight the whole town (except the outskirts) was wrapt in one huge blaze. Still the flames had not approached sufficiently near us to threaten our immediate safety and for some reason not a single Yankee soldier had entered our house. And now the fire instead of approaching us seemed to recede. Henry said the danger was over and sick of the dreadful scene worn out with fatigue and excitement we went down stairs to our room and tried to rest. I fell into a heavy kind of stupor from which I was presently aroused by the bustle about me. Our neighbour Mrs. Caldwell and her two younger sisters stood before the fire wrapped in blankets and weeping—their home was on fire and the great sea of flame had again swept down our way to the very campus walls. I felt a kind of sickening despair and did not even stir to go and look out. After awhile Jane came in to say that Aunt Josies house was in flames—then we all went up to the front door—My God! what a scene! It was about four o'clock and the State House was one grand conflagration. Imagine night turned to noonday only with a blazing, scorching glare that was horrible—a copper coloured sky across which swept columns of black rolling smoke glittering with sparks and flying embers, while all around us were falling thickly showers of burning flakes. Everywhere the palpitating blaze walling the streets with solid masses of flame as far as the eye could reach—filling the air with its horrible roar—on every side the crackling and devouring fire while every instant came the crashing of timbers and the thunder of the falling buildings. A quivering molten ocean seemed to fill the air and sky. The library building opposite us seemed framed by the gushing flames & smoke while through the windows gleamed the liquid fire. This we thought must be Aunt Josie's house. It was the next one for although hers caught frequently it was saved. The college buildings caught all along that side, and had the incendiary work continued one half hour longer than it did they must have gone. All the physicians and nurses were on the roof trying to save the buildings and the poor inmates left to themselves such as could crawled out while those who could not move waited to be burned to death. The Common opposite the gate was crowded with homeless women & children—a few wrapped in blankets and many shivering in the night air. Such a scene as this with the drunken fiendish soldiery in their dark uniforms, infuriated cursing, screaming, exulting in their work, came nearer realizing the material ideal of hell than any thing I ever expect to see again. They call themselves Sherman's "hell hounds."

Mother collected together some bedding, clothing and food which Henry carried to the back of the garden and covered them with a hastily ripped up carpet to protect them from the sparks and flakes of fire. He worked so hard, so faithfully and tried to comfort mother as best he could while she was sobbing and crying at the thought of being left shelterless with a delicate baby. While this was going on I stood with Mary Ann at the kitchen door. She tried to speak hopefully—I could not cry—it was all too horrible—Yet I felt the house must burn. By what miracle it was saved I cannot think. No effort could be made—no one was on the roof which was old and dry and all the while the sparks and burning timbers were flying over it like rain. When the few things she tried to save were moved, mother took up little Carrie who was sleeping unconsciously, and wrapping ourselves in shawls and blankets we went to the front door and waited for the house to catch. There we stood watching and listening to the roaring and crashing. It seemed inevitable—they said they would not leave a house—and what would become of us! I suppose we owe our final escape to the presence of the Yankee wounded in the hospital. When all seemed in vain Dr Thomson went to an officer and asked if he would see his own soldiers burnt alive. He said he would save the hospital and he and his men came to Dr T's assistance. Then too about this time even the Yankees seemed to have grown weary of their horrible work. The signal for the cessation of the fire—a blast on the bugle was given—and in fifteen minutes the flames ceased to spread. By seven o'clock the last flame had expired. About six o'clock a crowd of drunken soldiers assaulted the campus gate and threatened to overpower the guard—swearing the buildings should not be spared. By great exertions Dr Thomson found Sherman and secured a strong guard in time to rescue the hospital.

Mrs C. who had been to see after her house now returned and sitting down sobbed convulsively as she told us of the insults she had received from the soldiery engaged in pillaging her home. An officer riding by ordered the men to stop. So broken down and humbled by the terrible experience of the night was she that she cried out—"O, sir! please make them stop—You do'n't know what I suffered this night!" "I don't care a damn for your sufferings" he replied, "but my men have no right to pillage against orders." Fortunately—oh, so fortunately for us the hospital is so strictly guarded that we are unmolested within the walls.

O that long twelve hours! Never surely again will I live through such a night of horrors—the memory of it will haunt me as long as I shall live! It seemed as if the day would never come. The sun rose at last, dim and red through the thick murky atmosphere. It set last night on a beautiful town full of women and children—it shone dully down this morning on smoking ruins and abject misery. I do not know how the others felt after the strain of the fearful excitement but I seemed to sink into a dull apathy. We none seemed to have the energy to talk. After awhile breakfast came in—a sort of mockery for no one could eat. After taking a cup of coffee and bathing my face begrimed with smoke I felt better and the memory of the night seemed like a frightful dream. I have scarcely slept for three nights yet my eyes are not heavy.

During the forenoon Aunt Josie and Aunt Jane came over to see how we had fared. We met as after a long separation and for some seconds no one could speak—then we exchanged experiences. They were nearer the flames than we, but they had Dr Carter with them—Some one to look to and to help them. Aunt Josie says the northern side of their house became so heated that no one could remain on that side. The house caught fire three times. Being outside the hospital buildings they were more exposed than we. Once a number of Yankees rushed in saying the roof was on fire. Andrew the negro boy, followed them up, saw them tear up the tin roofing and place lighted combustibles and after they went down he succeeded in extinguishing them. A tolerably faithful guard was some protection to them. The view from their attic windows commands the whole town and Aunt Jane said it was like one surging ocean of flame. She thought with us that it was more like the mediæval pictures of hell than any thing she had ever imagined. We do not know the extent of the destruction but we are told that the greater portion of the town is in ashes—perhaps the lovliest town in all our Southern country. This is civilized warfare! This is the way in which the "cultured" Yankee nation wars upon women and children. Failing with our men in the field *this* is the way they must conquer! I suppose there was scarcely an able bodied man except the hospital physicians in the whole 20000 people. It is so easy to burn the homes over the heads of the helpless women and children and turn them with insults & sneers into the streets. One expects these people to lie and steal but it does seem such an outrage even upon degraded humanity that those who practise such wanton and useless cruelty should call themselves men. It seems to us even a contamination to look at these devils. Think of the degradation of being conquered and ruled by such a people! It seems to me now as if we would choose extermination first. I have only had to speak once to one of the blue coated fiends. I went to the front door to bid Francena & Nellie C. goodbye early this morning when a soldier came up the steps and asked me who was the Mayor. "Dr Goodwyn," I answered shortly and turned away. "Do you know his initials?" "No" and I shut the door quickly behind me.

The State House of course is burned and they talk of blowing up the new uncompleted granite one, but I do not know if it can be done in its unfinished unroofed condition. We dread tonight. Mother asked Dr Thomson (who has been very kind about coming in and in keeping us posted) for a guard but he says it is unnecessary as double guards will be placed throughout the city. Dr T. says some of the officers feel very much ashamed of last night's work. Their compunctions must have visited them since daylight. The men openly acknowledge that they received orders to burn & plunder before they crossed the river. The drunken scoundrels who tried to force their way into the Campus this morning have been under guard at the gate. Several hundred of them—fighting and quarrelling among themselves for two or three hours.

Poor father! What will be his state of mind when he hears of all this—the first reports that reach him will be even exaggerated. It is some comfort to us in our uncertainty & anxiety to hope that he may be safe. The explosion last night was the accidental blowing up of the Charleston freight depot. There had been powder stored there and it was scattered thickly over the floor. The poor people and negroes went in with torches to search for provisions.

When will these Yankees go that we may breathe freely again! The past three days are more like three weeks. And yet when they are gone we may be worse off with the whole country laid waste—the railroads out in every direction, starvation seems to stare us in the face. Our two families have between them a few bushels of corn and a little musty flour. We have no meat but the negroes give us a little bacon every day.

8 P.M. There has been no firing as yet. All is comparatively quiet. These buildings are surrounded by a heavy guard and we are told they are distributed throughout the city. All day the devils have been completing their work of plunder but in the hospital here we have been exempt from this. When I remember how blest we have been I cannot be too thankful. We have the promise of a quiet night but I dare not trust our hopes—there is no telling what diabolical intentions they may have. O if they were only gone—even to the last straggler. What a load would be lifted from our hearts. We are anxious to learn the fate of our friends but the little we can gather (except from Aunt Josie and Mrs. Green) is through the negroes, and ours scarcely dare venture up town. The Yankees plunder the negroes as well as the whites and I think they are becoming somewhat disgusted with their *friends.* Although the servants seem quite willing, it is difficult to get any work out of them on account of the wild excitement. Ah, the dreadful excitement. I seem to stand it very well, but it seems to me we must all be ill when it is over. Anxiety, distress, want of rest and food must tell upon us. Mrs Wilson (Mr Shand's daughter) with a babe one week old, was moved last night from her father's burning house. The Burroughs escaped with only the clothing they wore. Many many fared similarly. Some tried to save a little food—even this was torn from their hands. I have heard a number of distressing incidents but have not time to write them down. O the sorrow and misery of this unhappy town!

From what I hear their chief aim while taunting helpless women has been to "humble their pride"—"Southern pride." "Where now" they would hiss "is all your pride" "See what we have brought you to!" "This is what you get for setting yourselves up as better than other folks." The women acted with quiet dignity and refused to lower themselves by any retort. Some one told me the following: Some soldiers were pillaging the house of a lady. One asked her if they had not humbled her pride *now*. "No indeed" she said "nor can you ever." "You *fear* us anyway"—"No" she said. "By G— but you *shall* fear me." And he cocked his pistol and put it to her head. "Are you afraid now?" She folded her arms and looking him steadily in the eye, said contemptuously: "No." He dropped his pistol and with an exclamation of admiration left her.

Luther Rice Mills to John Mills

On October 27–28, 1864, Grant had launched another offensive against Lee's flanks, attacking without success southwest of Petersburg at Hatcher's Run and east of Richmond at the Darbytown Road and Fair Oaks. Both armies went into winter quarters in November as bad weather brought a halt to major operations. A second Union offensive at Hatcher's Run, February 5–7, failed to cut the Boydton Plank Road but succeeded in further stretching the overextended Confederate lines. During the winter inadequate food, clothing, and shelter; cancelled leaves; and letters from home telling of increased privation and insecurity increasingly undermined morale in the Army of Northern Virginia and caused thousands of men to leave its ranks. On February 28 Lee reported to the Confederate War Department that nearly 1,100 men had deserted from his army in a single ten-day period (February 15–25), and that some of them had left in armed groups. "I regret to say that the greatest number of these desertions have occurred among the North Carolina troops," he wrote, "who have fought as gallantly as any soldiers in the army." Lieutenant Luther Rice Mills, a company commander in the 26th Virginia Infantry, wrote to his brother about the situation at Petersburg.

Trenches Near Crater
March 2nd, 1865.

BROTHER JOHN:

Something is about to happen. I know not what. Nearly every one who will express an opinion says Gen'l Lee is about to evacuate Petersburg. The authorities are having all the cotton, tobacco &c. moved out of the place as rapidly as possible. This was commenced about the 22nd of February. Two thirds of the Artillery of our Division has been moved out. The Reserved Ordnance Train has been loaded up and is ready to move at any time. I think Gen'l Lee expects a hard fight on the right and has ordered all this simply as a precautionary measure. Since my visit to the right I have changed my opinion about the necessity for the evacuation of Petersburg. If it is evacuated Johnson's Division will be in a bad situation for getting out. Unless we are so fortunate as to give the Yankees the slip many of us will be captured. I would regret very much to have to give up the old place. The soiled and tattered Colors borne by our skeleton Regiments is sacred and dear to the hearts of every man, No one would exchange it for a new flag. So it is with us. I go down the lines, I see the marks of shot and shell, I see where fell my comrades, the Crater, the grave of fifteen hundred Yankees, when I go to the rear I see little mounds of dirt some with headboards, some with none, some with shoes protruding, some with a small pile of bones on one side near the end showing where a hand was left uncovered, in fact everything near shows desperate fighting. And here I would rather "fight it out." If Petersburg and Richmond is evacuated —from what I have seen & heard in the army—our cause will be hopeless. It is useless to conceal the truth any longer. Many of our people at home have become so demoralized that they write to their husbands, sons and brothers that desertion *now* is not *dishonorable*. It would be impossible to keep the army from straggling to a ruinous extent if we evacuate. I have just received an order from Wise to carry out on picket tonight a rifle and ten rounds of Cartridges to shoot men when they desert. The men seem to think desertion no crime & hence never shoot a deserter when he goes over—they always shoot but never hit. I am glad to say that we have not had but four desertions from our Reg't to the enemy. I enjoyed my trip to the right very much indeed. Saw Royall, Cooke, Satterwhite, Dr. & John Cannady, Prof. Wingate & the "immortal T. H. P." Cooke's Brig can scarcely be said to be in service. They are in the pride, pomp & circumstance of a glorious war. Had no idea that any of the army of N. V. was doing so well. Saw 12th Regt Va. Infantry yesterday. It had only about two hundred men & I feel sure that you could not two hundred officers—no not one hundred—out of Johnson's Division who would look as neat & as clean. I felt ashamed to go among such a neat bandbox crowd as Cooke's Brig was. Prof. W. & T. H. P. assisted by Dr. Cannady were trying to "fland" some sliding elders. Sliding Elders had decided advantage in position. Sorry I did not see Baldy Williams. Did not see the Parson. I sent you this morning "Five months in a Yankee prison" by a Petersburg Militiaman.

Write soon.

Yours truly

L. R. MILLS

WASHINGTON, D.C., MARCH 1865

Abraham Lincoln: Second Inaugural Address

President Lincoln delivered his Second Inaugural Address from the East Portico of the Capitol to an audience of thirty to forty thousand people, including thousands of African Americans. After Chief Justice Salmon P. Chase administered the oath of office, Lincoln leaned forward and kissed the Bible, which was opened to Isaiah 5:27–28. In a letter to New York Republican leader Thurlow Weed on March 15, Lincoln would write that he expected the address "to wear as well as—perhaps better than—any thing I have produced; but I believe it is not immediately popular. Men are not flattered by being shown that there has been a difference of purpose between the Almighty and them. To deny it, however, in this case, is to deny that there is a God governing the world. It is a truth which I thought needed to be told; and as whatever of humiliation there is in it, falls most directly on myself, I thought others might afford for me to tell it."

Fellow Countrymen: March 4, 1865

At this second appearing to take the oath of the presidential office, there is less occasion for an extended address than there was at the first. Then a statement, somewhat in detail, of a course to be pursued, seemed fitting and proper. Now, at the expiration of four years, during which public declarations have been constantly called forth on every point and phase of the great contest which still absorbs the attention, and engrosses the energies of the nation, little that is new could be presented. The progress of our arms, upon which all else chiefly depends, is as well known to the public as to myself; and it is, I trust, reasonably satisfactory and encouraging to all. With high hope for the future, no prediction in regard to it is ventured.

On the occasion corresponding to this four years ago, all thoughts were anxiously directed to an impending civil-war. All dreaded it—all sought to avert it. While the inaugeral address was being delivered from this place, devoted altogether to *saving* the Union without war, insurgent agents were in the city seeking to *destroy* it without war—seeking to dissolve the Union, and divide effects, by negotiation. Both parties deprecated war; but one of them would *make* war rather than let the nation survive; and the other would *accept* war rather than let it perish. And the war came.

One eighth of the whole population were colored slaves, not distributed generally over the Union, but localized in the Southern part of it. These slaves constituted a peculiar and powerful interest. All knew that this interest was, somehow, the cause of the war. To strengthen, perpetuate, and extend this interest was the object for which the insurgents would rend the Union, even by war; while the government claimed no right to do more than to restrict the territorial enlargement of it. Neither party expected for the war, the magnitude, or the duration, which it has already attained. Neither anticipated that the *cause* of the conflict might cease with, or even before, the conflict itself should cease. Each looked for an easier triumph, and a result less fundamental and astounding. Both read the same Bible, and pray to the same God; and each invokes His aid against the other. It may seem strange that any men should dare to ask a just God's assistance in wringing their bread from the sweat of other men's faces; but let us judge not that we be not judged. The prayers of both could not be answered; that of neither has been answered fully. The Almighty has His own purposes. "Woe unto the world because of offences! for it must needs be that offences come; but woe to that man by whom the offence cometh!" If we shall suppose that American Slavery is one of those offences which, in the providence of God, must needs come, but which, having continued through His appointed time, He now wills to remove, and that He gives to both North and South, this terrible war, as the woe due to those by whom the offence came, shall we discern therein any departure from those divine attributes which the believers in a Living God always ascribe to Him? Fondly do we hope—fervently do we pray—that this mighty scourge of war may speedily pass away. Yet, if God wills that it continue, until all the wealth piled by the bond-man's two hundred and fifty years of unrequited toil shall be sunk, and until every drop of blood drawn with the lash, shall be paid by another drawn with the sword, as was said three thousand years ago, so still it must be said "the judgments of the Lord, are true and righteous altogether."

With malice toward none; with charity for all; with firmness in the right, as God gives us to see the right, let us strive on to finish the work we are in; to bind up the nation's wounds; to care for him who shall have borne the battle, and for his widow, and his orphan—to do all which may achieve and cherish a just, and a lasting peace, among ourselves, and with all nations.

“A SACRED EFFORT”:
WASHINGTON, D.C., MARCH 1865

Frederick Douglass: from Life and Times of Frederick Douglass

Frederick Douglass, America's leading black abolitionist, was among those who heard Lincoln give his Second Inaugural Address. In his autobiography *Life and Times of Frederick Douglass* (1881), he would write that it “sounded more like a sermon than a state paper.” From the beginning of the war, Douglass had called for immediate emancipation and the arming of black troops, and had denounced Lincoln for his attempts to conciliate southern and border state slaveowners and for advocating the colonization of freed slaves. He later praised the Emancipation Proclamation and helped recruit for the Massachusetts 54th Infantry (in which two of his sons served), but criticized the President for failing to provide black soldiers with equal pay and protection from Confederate retribution. After meeting with Lincoln at the White House in August 1863 and August 1864, Douglass began to respect the President for his steadfastness on emancipation and willingness to rethink his positions. In *Life and Times* he would praise Lincoln for having “conducted the affairs of the nation with singular wisdom, and with absolute fidelity to the great trust confided in him. A country redeemed and regenerated from the foulest crime against human nature that ever saw the sun!” In his autobiography Douglass remembered his attempt to defy tradition and attend the inaugural reception in 1865.

In the evening of the day of the inauguration, another new experience awaited me. The usual reception was given at the executive mansion, and though no colored persons had ever ventured to present themselves on such occasions, it seemed now that freedom had become the law of the republic, now that colored men were on the battle-field mingling their blood with that of white men in one common effort to save the country, it was not too great an assumption for a colored man to offer his congratulations to the President with those of other citizens. I decided to go, and sought in vain for some one of my own color to accompany me. It is never an agreeable experience to go where there can be any doubt of welcome, and my colored friends had too often realized discomfiture from this cause to be willing to subject themselves to such unhappiness; they wished me to go, as my New England colored friends in the long-ago liked very well to have me take passage on the first-class cars, and be hauled out and pounded by rough-handed brakemen, to make way for them. It was plain, then, that some one must lead the way, and that if the colored man would have his rights, he must take them; and now, though it was plainly quite the thing for me to attend President Lincoln's reception, "they all with one accord began to make excuse." It was finally arranged that Mrs. Dorsey should bear me company, so together we joined in the grand procession of citizens from all parts of the country, and moved slowly towards the executive mansion. I had for some time looked upon myself as a man, but now in this multitude of the élite of the land, I felt myself a man among men. I regret to be obliged to say, however, that this comfortable assurance was not of long duration, for on reaching the door, two policemen stationed there took me rudely by the arm and ordered me to stand back, for their directions were to admit no persons of my color. The reader need not be told that this was a disagreeable set-back. But once in the battle, I did not think it well to submit to repulse. I told the officers I was quite sure there must be some mistake, for no such order could have emanated from President Lincoln; and if he knew I was at the door he would desire my admission. They then, to put an end to the parley, as I suppose, for we were obstructing the doorway, and were not easily pushed aside, assumed an air of politeness, and offered to conduct me in. We followed their lead, and soon found ourselves walking some planks out of a window, which had been arranged as a temporary passage for the exit of visitors. We halted so soon as we saw the trick, and I said to the officers: "You have deceived me. I shall not go out of this building till I see President Lincoln." At this moment a gentleman who was passing in recognized me, and I said to him: "Be so kind as to say to Mr. Lincoln that Frederick Douglass is detained by officers at the door." It was not long before Mrs. Dorsey and I walked into the spacious East Room, amid a scene of elegance such as in this country I had never witnessed before. Like a mountain pine high above all others, Mr. Lincoln stood, in his grand simplicity, and *home-like beauty*. Recognizing me, even before I reached him, he exclaimed, so that all around could hear him, "Here comes my friend Douglass." Taking me by the hand, he said, "I am glad to see you. I saw you in the crowd to-day, listening to my inaugural address; how did you like it?" I said, "Mr. Lincoln, I must not detain you with my poor opinion, when there are thousands waiting to shake hands with you." "No, no," he said, "you must stop a little, Douglass; there is no man in the country whose opinion I value more than yours. I want to know what you think of it?" I replied, "Mr. Lincoln, that was a sacred effort." "I am glad you liked it!" he said; and I passed on, feeling that any man, however distinguished, might well regard himself honored by such expressions, from such a man.

It came out that the officers at the White House had received no orders from Mr. Lincoln, or from any one else. They were simply complying with an old custom, the outgrowth of slavery, as dogs will sometimes rub their necks, long after their collars are removed, thinking they are still there. My colored friends were well pleased with what had seemed to them a doubtful experiment, and I believe were encouraged by its success to follow my example. I have found in my experience that the way to break down an unreasonable custom, is to contradict it in practice. To be sure in pursuing this course I have had to contend not merely with the white race, but with the black. The one has condemned me for my presumption in daring to associate with them, and the other for pushing myself where they take it for granted I am not wanted. I am pained to think that the latter objection springs largely from a consciousness of inferiority, for as colors alone can have nothing against each other, and the conditions of human association are founded upon character rather than color, and character depends upon mind and morals, there can be nothing blameworthy in people thus equal in meeting each other on the plane of civil or social rights.

"WE HAVE WORK FAITHFUL": NORTH CAROLINA, MARCH 1865

Roanoke Island Freedmen to Abraham Lincoln and to Edwin M. Stanton

In February 1862 the Union army captured Roanoke Island in North Carolina. Hundreds of slaves fled to the island during the following year, and in May 1863 the military established a freedmen's colony on the northern end of the island designed to "train and educate" the former slaves "for a free and independent community." By 1865 the settlement had a church, several schools, a sawmill, and about 3,900 residents, who grew food on one-acre family plots. Despite the hopes of Captain Horace James, the Congregational army chaplain from Massachusetts who served as its superintendent, the colony was unable to become self-sufficient. Most of the adult freedmen either served in the U.S. Colored Troops or worked away from the island as military laborers, leaving the women and children in the settlement dependent on army rations for food. The protests addressed to Lincoln and Stanton on March 9, 1865, were presented to the War Department in Washington on April 6 by Richard Boyle, a black schoolteacher on the island, and were probably drafted by him. They were forwarded to Horace James, who, in a letter sent to an officer of the Freedmen's Bureau on July 10, 1865, denied there was any danger of starvation in the colony. "The truth is *they have had too much* given them," James wrote. He described the freed people who protested their treatment as "persons to be treated like children, who do not know when they are well used, and whose complaints should influence us but a little, while we do for them that which we know will promote their best good. Those who come most in contact with the negros in the work of doing them good, *seldom win their gratitude*—" Over the next two years most of the freed people would leave Roanoke Island, and in 1867 the colony was formally decommissioned.

Roanoke Island N.C march 9th 1865.

Mr President Dear Sir We Colored men of this Island held a meeting to consult over the affairs of our present conditions and our rights and we find that our arms are so Short that we cant doe any thing with in our Selves So we Concluded the best thing we could do was to apply to you or Some of your cabinets we are told and also we have read that you have declared all the Colored people free bothe men and woman that is in the Union lines and if that be so we want to know where our wrights is or are we to be Stamp down or troden under feet by our Superintendent which he is the very man that we look to for assistents, in the first place his Proclamation was that no able boded man was to draw any rations except he was at work for the Government we all agreed to that and was willing to doe as we had done for $10,00 per month and our rations though we Seldom ever get the mony

the next thing he said that he wanted us to work and get our living as White men and not apply to the Government and that is vry thing we want to doe, but after we do this we cant satisfie him Soon as he Sees we are trying to Support our Selves without the aid of the Government he comes and make a Call for the men, that is not working for the Government to Goe away and if we are not willing to Goe he orders the Guards to take us by the point of the bayonet, and we have no power to help it we know it is wright and are willing to doe any thing that the President or our head Commanders want us to doe but we are not willing to be pull and haul a bout so much by those head men as we have been for the last two years and we may say Get nothing for it, last fall a large number of we men was Conscript and sent up to the front and all of them has never return Some Got Kill Some died and When they taken them they treated us mean and our owners ever did they taken us just like we had been dum beast

We Colored people on Roanok Island are willing to Submit to any thing that we know the President or his cabinet Say because we have Got since enough to believe it is our duty to doe every thing we Can doe to aid Mr Lyncoln and the Government but we are not willing to work as we have done for Chaplain James and be Troden under foot and Get nothing for it we have work faithful Since we have been on the Island we have built our log houses we have Cultivate our acre of Ground and have Tried to be less exspence to the Government as we Possible Could be and we are yet Trying to help the Government all we Can for our lives those head men have done every thing to us that our masters have done except by and Sell us and now they are Trying to Starve the woman & children to death cutting off they ration they have Got so now that they wont Give them no meat to eat, every ration day beef & a little fish and befor the Ten days is out they are going from one to another Trying to borrow a little meal to last until ration day Mr Streeter will just order one barrell of meet for his fish men and the others he Gives nothing but beaf but we thank the Lord for that if we no it is the President or the Secretarys orders this is what want to know whoes orders it is, one of our minister children was fool to ration house and Sent off and his father working three days in every week for his ration

Roanoke Island N.C march 9th 1865

we have appeal to General Butler and Genl Butler wrote to Capt James to do Better and Capt James has promies to do Better and instead of doing better he has done worst and now we appeal to you which is the last resort and only help we have got, feeling that we are entily friendless, on the Island there numrous of Soldiers wives and they Can hardly get any rations and some of them are almost starving

we dont exspect to have the same wrights as white men doe we know that are in a millitary country and we exspect to obey the rules and orders of our authories and doe as they say doe, any thing in reason we thank God and thank our President all of his aids for what has been done for us but we are not satisfide with our Supertendent nor the treatement we receives now we want you to send us answer what to depen upon let it be good or bad and we will be Satisfide Respectifully yours

Roanoke Island N.C.

Roanoke Island N.C March 9th 1865

we want to know from the Secretary of War has the Rev Chaplain James which is our Superintendent of negros affairs has any wright to take our boy Children from us and from the School and Send them to newbern to work to pay for they ration without they parent Consint if he has we thinks it very hard indeed he essued a Proclamation that no boys Should have any rations at 14 years old well we thought was very hard that we had to find our boy Children to Goe to School hard as times are, but rather then they Should Goe without learning we thought we would try and doe it and say no more a bout it and the first thing we knowed Mr Stereeter the Gentlemen that ration the Contrabands had Gone a round to all the White School-Teachers and told them to Give the boys orders to goe and get they ration on a Cirtain day so the negros as we are Call are use to the Cesesh plots Suspicion the Game they was Going to play and a Greate many never Sent they Children. So Some twenty or twenty-five went and Mr Streeter Give them they rations and the Guard march them down to the head quarters and put them on board the boat and carried them to newbern here is woman here on the Island which their husbands are in the army just had one little boy to help them to cut & lug wood & to Goe arrand for them Chaplain James has taken them and sent them away Some of these little ones he sent off wasen oer 12 years olds. the mothers of Some went to Chaplain and Grieved and beg for the little boys but he would not let them have them we want to know if the Prisident done essued any ration for School boys if he dont then we are satisfide we have men on the Island that Can Support the boys to Goe to School but here are Poor woman are not able to do it So the orphans must Goe without they learning that all we can say a bout the matter

the next is Concerning of our White Soldiers they Come to our Church and we treat them with all the Politeness that we can and Some of them treats us as though we were beast and we cant help our Selves Some of them brings Pop Crackers and Christmas devils and throws a mong the woman and if we Say any thing to them they will talk about mobin us. we report them to the Capt he will Say you must find out Which ones it was and that we cant do but we think very hard it they put the pistols to our ministers breast because he Spoke to them about they behavour in the Church, the next is Capt James told us When he got the mill built he would let us have plank to buil our houses we negroes went to work and cut and hewd the timber and built the mill under the northern men derection and now he Charges us 3 and 4 dollars a hundred for plank and if we Carry 3 logs to the mill he takes 2 and

Gives us one. that is he has the logs haul and takes one for hauling and one for Sawing and we thinks that is to much Without he paid us better then he does. and the next thing is he wont allow a man any ration While he is trying to buil him Self a house. to live in and how are negroes to live at that rate we Cant See no way to live under Such laws, Without Some Altiration

Roanoke Island N.C. March 9th 1865

here is men here that has been working for the last three year and has not been paid for it. they, work on the forts and Cut spiles and drove them and done any thing that they was told to do Capt James Came on the Island Jan. 1864 and told they men that he had made all the matters wright a bout they back pay and now says he I want all of you men that has due bills to carry them to Mr Bonnell at head quarters and all them has not got no paper to show for they work I will make them Swear and kiss the Bibel and the men done just as he told them and he told us that he had made out the rolls and sent them up to Washington City and now he says that money is all dead So we are very well Satisfide just So we know that he has never received it for our head men has fool us so much just because they think that we are igorant we have lost all Confidince in them. so all we wants is a Chance and we can Get a living like White men we are praying to God every day for the war to Stop So we wont be beholding to the Government for Something to Eat Yours Respectfully

Roanoke Island.

"THE DEATH FLURRY OF A WHALE": NEW YORK, MARCH 1865

George Templeton Strong: Diary, March 10, 1865

On March 6 Strong wrote that "all New York seemed in the streets, at the windows, or on the housetops" as the city held a seven-mile-long procession to celebrate recent Union victories. "All this extravagant, exuberant rejoicing frightens me," he noted. "It seems a manifest omen of mishap." Four days later Strong was encouraged by reports of desertions from Lee's army and by the Confederate debate over arming slaves.

March 10. . . . Richmond newspapers are in a special spasm of fury beyond any fit they have yet suffered. We must not attach too much weight to what these sensitive, excitable, high-toned, chivalric creatures rave when in nervous exaltation, whether arising from patriotic or from alcoholic stimulus. But this particular paroxysm certainly resembles the death flurry of a whale. The editorial utterances are violent, desperate, incoherent, hurried, and objectless. They amount in substance to this, that there is somewhere a class of "whipped seceders" and "whipped croakers" who desire subjugation and have an appetite for infamy—that these caitiffs want Davis to abdicate, and their pressure is sufficient to make it worthwhile to expend much bad language on them—that they will not succeed in these base designs, because Southerners never, never, *never* will be slaves, and because "our women" ought to take up their broomsticks and drive these wretches into the James River, and so on. There are certainly signs in Secessia of incipient decomposition. The rebellion has, at the very least, another year's fight in it, but it may die of inward disease within thirty days. I trust it will not die too soon and that it will be killed, not merely "kilt." I long for peace, but only for a durable peace, of material that will wear. John Bright writes

F. M. Edge that he hopes our war will not end till its work is done, and he sees the case aright.

The rebel hosts continue to be seriously drained by desertion. Not less than fifty deserters have taken refuge within Grant's lines every day for many weeks past, and their average number is probably nearer one hundred than fifty. Companies come in, led by their company officers. All tell the same story of compulsory service, hardships, failure of pay and of clothing and of rations, and of general despondency. The Confederacy has "gone up," they say. "We all know it, and we know it is useless to fight any longer." Lee's soldiers would throw away their arms and disband tomorrow if they dared, and so on. Such statements made by deserters are worth much "less than their face." But when made by hundreds, and corroborated by the actual desertion of thousands, at imminent risk of life and with certain and conscious loss of honor, they are worth a great deal. It is likely, moreover, that for every rebel who flees within our lines, two flee the other way and take sanctuary in the hill country or the "piney woods," supporting themselves by levying contributions on all and sundry as sovereign powers so far as their own personal sovereignty can be made practically available, and thus carrying out the doctrine of secession to its ultimate results. Many counties of Virginia, the Carolinas, and the Gulf States are said to swarm with these banditti, and they are admitted to be even more savage and reckless than the vandal hordes of the North.

The Rebel Congress seems to have reconsidered its refusal to arm the slaves and to have decided, reluctantly, and by a very close vote, that there is no help for it and that Cuffee must be conscripted and made to fight for his chivalric master. So much for the visions of glory the South saw in 1860. This sacrifice of the first principles of the Southern social system is a confession of utter exhaustion; a desperate remedy and a most dangerous experiment. And the experiment is tried at least a year too late. It will take six months to drill and equip any considerable *corps d'Afrique*, and Sherman, Sheridan, Thomas, and Grant are likely, with God's blessing, to give rebellion its death blow within that time.

But the measure has its immediate effects. It disgusts and alienates many slaveholders and many fanatical theorists about slavery, and it is received as an affront by the rebel rank and file—an affront that justifies desertion. They will feel it not only as an affront, but as a disheartening surrender of the principle for which they have fought. They learn that niggers are now to be armed and put into the field as the allies of Southern gentlemen; "that it will depend on the nigger's pluck and muscle and endurance how far he is to share with white men the glory of upholding the Southern cause. It will depend on that and nothing else. Moreover, he is to be rewarded for good service by freedom." But the first of all Southern axioms has been for thirty years past that freedom was a punishment to the slave, servitude his normal condition, and that he loved and looked up to and depended on his owner as a good dog does on his master, and that he despised and rejected emancipation just as a good dog would dislike being discharged from his duty of guardianship and kicked into the street to get his own living as best he could.

MARCHING THROUGH THE CAROLINAS: NORTH CAROLINA, MARCH 1865

Alpheus S. Williams to His Daughter

After the destruction of Columbia, Sherman's army of 60,000 men moved north again and reached Laurel Hill, North Carolina, on March 8. Its objective was Goldsboro, where Sherman planned to join up with 30,000 Union troops advancing from the North Carolina coast under John M. Schofield. Sherman's march into North Carolina was opposed by about 20,000 Confederates led by Joseph E. Johnston, whom Jefferson Davis had reluctantly restored to command on February 25. Union Brigadier General Alpheus S. Williams, the commander of the Twentieth Corps, wrote to his daughter about the campaign in the Carolinas.

Fayetteville, North Carolina, Mar. 12, 1865.

My Dear Daughter:

After long and weary marches we entered this town yesterday. A gunboat came up this morning by which I am enabled to send you a line in pencil. As soon as we get our "base," or if we linger here long enough, I will copy my journal to this point.

Our campaign has been more arduous, weather worse, and roads infamously worse than on the Georgia campaign. We have had but little fighting, however, so far, the enemy always easily driven away from the strongest positions. He has evidently been confounded by the audacity of our movements. We swept through South Carolina, the fountain-head of rebellion, in a broad, semi-circular belt, sixty miles wide, the arch of which was the capital of the state, Columbia. Our people, impressed with the idea that every South Carolinian was an arrant Rebel, spared nothing but the old men, women, and children. All materials, all vacant houses, factories, cotton-gins and presses, everything that makes the wealth of a people, everything edible and wearable, was swept away. The soldiers quietly took the matter into their own hands. Orders to respect houses and private property not necessary for the subsistence of the army were not greatly heeded. Indeed, not heeded at all. Our "bummers," the dare-devils and reckless of the army, put the flames to everything and we marched with thousands of columns of smoke marking the line of each corps. The sights at times, as seen from elevated ground, were often terribly sublime and grand; often intensely painful from the distressed and frightened condition of the old men and women and children left behind.

We saw no young men, save the deformed, the sick or wounded, and deserters (pretty numerous). Everybody else had been forced into the service, even to decrepit old men of sixty and upwards, lots of whom came to us to be paroled or to be sent home. Boys deserted to us, not over thirteen years old. The "Confederacy" has literally gathered its infancy and aged, its first and second childhood. If it fails now, all material for reinforcing its armies is gone, unless, indeed, they can make fighting men out of the Negroes.

Our line of march has been across the largest rivers, the broadest swamps, and the muddiest creeks of the state. I think I am within bounds in saying that this corps has corduroyed over a hundred miles of road. For the last fifty miles we have traveled over a shell of quicksand which would not bear up a horse, and through which a wagon would cut to the box. The country was much poorer than I expected to find. Even respectable houses are very rare, and superior ones rarer. The soil, never very fertile, is worn out. The people left at home, mainly sickly-looking and grossly ignorant. How even the politicians of South Carolina can boast a superiority over our hardy and industrious Northern people is more than I can imagine. Everything in that state presents evidence of decay and retrogradation. There is nothing new, nothing that looks flourishing, and the people look like "fossil remains."

So far into North Carolina the country, if possible, is worse and the people worser! This town, you know, is at the navigable headwaters of the Cape Fear River, and is second only to Wilmington in population. One of the largest U.S. Arsenals is here, which the Rebs. have used as their largest. Only one U.S. Arsenal stolen by Rebeldom now remains to them, that at Augusta. Our march in the rear of Charleston made necessary the evacuation of the first fort upon which the Rebels fired, and Wilmington and all their seaports follow as we interpose between them and their interior communications. How much more effectual this has proved than all the costly attempts to take these places from the sea front!

I suppose we shall move on tomorrow or next day. Gen. Sherman announces that we have new duties before us. I have no doubt that his great objective point is Richmond, but we shall probably halt this side to replenish and refit our army on the Charleston and Savannah Railroad. I received a letter from Rene of January 24th and Minnie's journal to January 17th. This is the last I have had from home. It was a pleasant surprise, brought to us from a rear corps.

I will write you again if I have time. We are sixty miles from Goldsboro and shall probably halt there for some days, if we get it, as I doubt not. Love to uncles and aunts and cousins, and believe me as ever,

Your Affectionate Father,
A.S.W.

P.S. My health has been and is excellent. No exposure seems to affect me.

LAND AND VOTES:
WASHINGTON, D.C., MARCH 1865

Charles Sumner to John Bright

A leading Radical Republican, Massachusetts senator Charles Sumner led a filibuster in late February 1865 that prevented the seating of senators representing the Louisiana state government supported by President Lincoln. Sumner, who believed that Congress should play the leading role in reconstruction, opposed restoring representation to southern states that denied black men the vote and failed to guarantee the equality of all persons before the law. He wrote about the challenges of reconstruction to his English friend John Bright, a prominent reformer, orator, and member of parliament who was one of the staunchest supporters of the Union cause in Great Britain.

---

private

Washington 13th March '65

Dear Mr Bright,

I have yr good & most suggestive letter. I concur in it substantially. A practical difficulty is this; can Emancipation be carried out without using the lands of the slave-masters. We must see that the freedmen are established on the soil & that they may become proprietors.

From the beginning I have regarded confiscation only as ancillary to Emancipation. The great plantations, which have been so many nurseries of the rebellion, must be broken up, & the freedmen must share the pieces.

It looks as if we were on the eve of another agitation. I insist that the rebel States shall not come back except on the footing of the Decltn of Indep. with all persons equal before the law, & govt. founded on the consent of the governed. In other words there shall be no discrimination on account of color. If *all* whites vote, then must all blacks; but there shall be no limitation of suffrage for one more than the other.

It is sometimes said "what—let the freedmen yesterday a slave vote?" I am inclined to think that there is more harm in refusing than in conceding the franchise. It is said that they are as intelligent as the Irish just arrived.

But the question has become immensely practical in this respect. Without their votes, we cannot establish stable govts. in the rebel states. Their votes are as necessary as their musquets. Of this I am satisfied. Without them, the old enemy will reappear &, under the forms of law, take possession of the govts.—choose magistrates & officers—&, in alliance with the Northern democracy, put us all in peril again, postpone the day of tranquility, & menace the national credit by assailing the national debt. To my mind, the nation is now bound by self-interest—aye, *self-defence*—to be thoroughly just.

The Declaration of Indep. has pledges which have never been redeemed. We must redeem them, at least as regards the rebel states which have fallen under our jurisdiction.

Mr Lincoln is slow in accepting truths. I have reminded him that if he would say the word we might settle this question promptly & rightly. He hesitates.

Meanwhile I felt it my duty to oppose his scheme of govt. in Louisiana, which for the present is defeated in Congress. Chief Justice Chase yesterday pronounced an opinion of the Sup. Ct declaring the whole scheme "illegal & void" from the beginning; so that it fares no better in court than in Congress. Mr Chase & myself have always concurred in opinion on this question. With the habit of deference here to the Sup. Ct. I anticipate much from this opinion. Substantially it affirms the conclusion which I adopted three years ago, sometimes called "the territorial theory."

That has been much misunderstood in Europe. It has been supposed sometimes as a menace of subjugation. Nothing further from my mind—at least in any offensive sense. I felt that the rebel region must for a while pass under the *jurisdiction of Congress*, in order to set up the necessary safeguards for the future; & I have labored to this end.

Nothing has been heard of Sherman for weeks,—but Mr Stanton has no anxiety about him. He will re-appear in North Carolina. Grant is very cheerful. But for the moment the curtain is down. It may lift any day.

I send you the Resolutions on Reciprocity & Lake Armaments,

as they passed the House, & as amended by me. The Italics are mine; & that is the form adopted.

You will see from the date of the House Resolution on Armaments how long I held it back. I was unwilling to take the step, until the outrages on the Lakes seemed to shew its necessity.

I came into the proposition to give the notice to terminate the Reciprocity Treaty, because I was satisfied that we could not negotiate for its modification, on a footing of equality unless our hands were untied. You will see this in my speech. I make this remark in reply to yr suggestion on the subject.

Congress has separated in good humor, without anxiety for the future, & indeed confident that we are on the verge of peace. My desire is that England should do something to take out the bitterness from the American heart—before the war closes. Help. I owe Cobden, & shall write him next.

Ever Yours, Charles Sumner

"GIVE ME A THOUSAND": KENTUCKY, MARCH 1865

Frances Johnson: Statement Regarding Her Whipping and Escape

Public outrage in the North over the expulsion of black refugees from Camp Nelson, Kentucky, in November 1864 (see pp. 486–88 in this volume) led Congress to pass a joint resolution on March 3, 1865, that emancipated the wives and children of black soldiers. The law was widely ignored by slaveowners in Kentucky, where the legislature had rejected ratification of the Thirteenth Amendment on February 24. In late March, Frances Johnson, the wife of a Union soldier, testified in a sworn statement about her attempt to secure freedom for herself and her children.

Camp Nelson Ky 25th March 1865

Personally appeared before me J M Kelley Notary Public in and for the County of Jessamine State of Kentucky Frances Johnson a woman of color who being duly sworn according to law doth depose and say—

I am the wife of Nathan Johnson a soldier in Company F. 116th U.S.C. Infty. I have three children and with them I belonged to Matthias Outon Fayette County Ky. My husband who belonged to Mary Outon Woodford Co. Ky enlisted in the United States service at Camp Nelson Ky. in May 1864. The day after my husband enlisted my master knew it and said that he (my husband) and all the "niggers" did mighty wrong in joining the Army. Subsequent to May 1864 I remained with my master until forced to leave on account of the cruel treatment to which I was subjected. On Wednesday March 8th 1865, my masters son Thomas Outon whipped me severely on my refusing to do some work which I was not in a condition to perform. He beat me in the presence of his father who told him (Thos Outon) to "buck me and give me a thousand" meaning thereby a thousand lashes. While beating me he threw me on the floor and as I was in this prostrate and helpless condition he continued to whip me endeavoring at one time to tie my hands and at another time to make an indecent exposure of my person before those present. I resisted as much as I could and to some extent thwarted his malignant designs. In consequence of this whipping suffered much pain in my head and sides. The scar now visible on my neck was inflicted at that time. After such treatment I determined to leave my master and early on the following morning—Thursday March 9″ 1865 I stealthly started for Lexington about seven miles distant where my sister resided. On my arrival there I was confined on account of sickness produced by the abuse I had received from my masters son as aforementioned.

During Friday March 10″ 1865 I sought a lodging for myself and children— Towards evening I found one and about 7 o'clock at night I left for my masters intending to take my children away. About 9. O'clock I arrived there much fatigued, went to the Cabin where my children were, no one but the colored folks knowing that I was present, got my children with the exception of one that was too sick to move, and about 10″ o'clock P.M. started for a neighboring Cabin where we remained during the night. At day break next morning I started for Lexington. My youngest child was in my arms, the other walked by my side. When on the Pike about a mile from home I was accosted by Theophilus Bracey my masters son-in-law who told me that if I did not go back with him he would shoot me. He drew a pistol on me as he made this threat. I could offer no resistance as he constantly kept the pistol pointed at me. I returned with him to his (Bracys) house carrying my children as before. I remained at Bracys all day. My sick child was moved there during the day. I tried to find some chance of running away but Bracey was watching me. He took my eldest child (about seven years of age) and kept her as an Hostage. I found I could not get away from Bracey's with my children, and determined to get away myself hoping by this means to obtain possession of them afterwards. I knew Bracey would not give me my children or allow me to go away myself so at daybreak on the following morning Sunday March 12″ I secretly left Bracey's, took to the woods in order to elude pursuit, reached Lexington and subsequently arrived at Camp Nelson. My children are still held by Bracey. I am anxious to have them but I am afraid to go near them knowing that Bracey would not let me have them and fearing least he would carry out his threat to shoot me. And further the deponent saith not

her
(Signed) Frances × Johnson
mark

Clarissa Burdett: Statement Regarding Her Whipping and Escape

Like Frances Johnson, Clarissa Burdett was the wife of a Union soldier who suffered violence at the hands of a Kentucky slaveowner. Slavery would remain legal in Kentucky and in Delaware until the ratification of the Thirteenth Amendment was completed in December 1865.

Camp Nelson Ky 27th of March 1865

Personally appeared before me J M Kelley Notary Public in and for the County of Jessamine State of Kentucky Clarissa Burdett a woman of color who being duly sworn according to law doth despose and say

I am a married woman and have four children. My husband Elijah Burdett is a soldier in the 12″ U.S.C.H. Arty. I and my children belonged to Smith Alford Garrard County Ky. When my husband enlisted my master beat me over the head with an axe handle saying as he did so that he beat me for letting Ely Burdett go off. He bruised my head so that I could not lay it against a pillow without the greatest pain. Last week my niece who lived with me went to Camp Nelson. This made my master very angry and last monday March 20″ 1865 he asked me where the girl had gone. I could not tell him He then whipped me over the head and said he would give me two hundred lashes if I did not get the girl back before the next day. On Wednesday last March 22″ he said that he had not time to beat me on Tuesday but now he had time and he would give it to me. He then tied my hands threw the rope over a joist stripped me entirely naked and gave me about three hundred lashes. I cried out. He then caught me by the throat and almost choked me then continued to lash me with switches until my back was all cut up. The marks of the switches are now very visible and my back is still very sore. My master was a very cruel man and strongly sympathizes with the rebels.

He went with the Rebel General Bragg when the latter retreated from the State. He took me and my children to Beans Station and send the parents and two sisters of my niece to Knoxville where he sold them. After he whipped me on Wednesday last he said he would give me until next morning to bring the girl back, and if I did not get her back by that time he would give me as much more. I knew that I would be whipped so I ran away. My master frequently said that he would be jailed before one of his niggers would go to Camp. I therefore knew he would not permit any of my children to come with me. So when I ran away I had to leave my children with my master. I have four children there at present and I want to get them but I cannot go there for them knowing that master who would whip me would not let any of my children go nor would he suffer me to get away

her
(Signed) Clarissa Burdett
mark

"AWAITING MY FATE": VIRGINIA, APRIL 1865

John B. Jones: Diary, April 2, 1865

By the spring of 1865 Lee's army of about 60,000 men held a line that extended for thirty-seven miles from east of Richmond to southwest of Petersburg. Lee knew that he could not defend his position indefinitely against the 100,000 Union troops opposing him, and made plans to join Johnston in North Carolina and undertake an offensive against Sherman. In an attempt to open an escape route to the west for his army, Lee attacked Fort Stedman, a Union strongpoint east of Petersburg, on March 25, hoping that its loss would force Grant to shorten his lines west of the city. The attack failed, costing the Confederates about 3,000 men killed, wounded, or captured. Grant then directed Major General Philip H. Sheridan to turn Lee's western flank. After heavy fighting at Dinwiddie Court House and White Oak Road on March 31, Sheridan advanced with 22,000 men on Five Forks, a crossroads about twelve miles southwest of Petersburg. The junction was defended by a force of 10,000 under Major General George E. Pickett, who had been ordered by Lee to hold the position "at all hazards." On the afternoon of April 1 Sheridan's troops broke the Confederate lines at Five Forks and captured 2,500 prisoners. Grant then ordered a general assault on the Petersburg defenses at dawn on April 2. Within hours Lee had telegraphed the Confederate War Department that both Petersburg and Richmond would have to be abandoned that night. John B. Jones wrote in his diary about the evacuation of the Confederate capital.

APRIL 2D.—Bright and beautiful. The tocsin was sounded this morning at daybreak, and the militia ordered to the fortifications, to relieve some regiments of Longstreet's corps, posted on this side of the river. These latter were hurried off to Petersburg, where a battle is impending, I suppose, if not in progress.

A street rumor says there was bloody fighting yesterday a little beyond Petersburg, near the South Side Road, in which Gen. Pickett's division met with fearful loss, being engaged with superior numbers. It is said the enemy's line of intrenchments was carried once or twice, but was retaken, and remained in their hands.

I hear nothing of all this at the department; but the absence of dispatches there is now interpreted as bad news! Certain it is, the marching of veteran troops from the defenses of Richmond, and replacing them hurriedly with militia, can only indicate an emergency of alarming importance. A decisive struggle is probably at hand—and may possibly be in progress while I write. Or there may be nothing in it—more than a precautionary concentration to preserve our communications.

Mrs. Davis sold nearly all her movables—including presents—before leaving the city. She sent them to different stores.

An intense excitement prevails, at 2 P.M. It pervaded the churches. Dr. Hoge intermitted his services. Gen. Cooper and the President left their respective churches, St. James's and St. Paul's. Dr. Minnegerode, before dismissing his congregation, gave notice that Gen. Ewell desired the local forces to assemble at 3 P.M.—and afternoon services will not be held. The excited women in this neighborhood say they have learned the city is to be evacuated to-night.

No doubt our army sustained a serious blow yesterday; and Gen. Lee may not have troops sufficient to defend both the city and the Danville Road at the same time.

It is true! The enemy have broken through our lines and attained the South Side Road. Gen. Lee has dispatched the Secretary to have everything in readiness to *evacuate the city to-night.* The President told a lady that Lieut.-Gen. Hardee was only twelve miles distant, and might get up in time to save the day. But then Sherman must be in *his* rear. There is no wild excitement—*yet.* Gen. Kemper was at the department looking for Gen. Ewell, and told me he could find no one to apply to for orders. The banks will move to-night. Eight trains are provided for the transportation of the archives, etc. No provision for civil employees and their families.

At 6 P.M. I saw the Hon. James Lyons, and asked him what he intended to do. He said many of his friends advised him to leave, while his inclination was to remain with his sick family. He said, being an original secessionist, his friends apprehended that the Federals would arrest him the first man, and hang him. I told him I differed with them, and believed his presence here might result in benefit to the population.

Passing down Ninth Street to the department, I observed quite a number of men—some in uniform, and some of them officers—hurrying away with their trunks. I believe they are not allowed to put them in the cars.

The Secretary of War intends to leave at 8 P.M. this evening. The President and the rest of the functionaries, I suppose, will leave at the same time.

I met Judge Campbell in Ninth Street, talking rapidly to himself, with two books under his arm, which he had been using in his office. He told me that the chiefs of bureaus determined which clerks would have transportation—embracing only a small proportion of them, which I found to be correct.

At the department I learned that all who had families were advised to remain. No compulsion is seen anywhere; even the artisans and mechanics of the government shops are left free to choose—to go or to stay.

A few squads of local troops and reserves—guards—may be seen marching here and there. Perhaps they are to burn the tobacco, cotton, etc., if indeed anything is to be burned.

Lee must have met with an awful calamity. The President said to several ladies to-day he had hopes of Hardee coming up in time to save Lee—else Richmond must succumb. He said he had done his best, etc. to save it. Hardee is distant two or three days' march.

The negroes stand about mostly silent, as if wondering what will be their fate. They make no demonstrations of joy.

Several hundred prisoners were brought into the city this afternoon—captured yesterday. Why they were brought here I am at a loss to conjecture. Why were they not paroled and sent into the enemy's lines?

At night. All is yet quiet. No explosion, no conflagration, no riots, etc. How long will this continue? When will the enemy come?

It was after 2 o'clock P.M. before the purpose to evacuate the city was announced; and the government had gone at 8 P.M.! Short notice! and small railroad facilities to get away. All horses were impressed.

There is a report that Lieut.-Gen. A. P. Hill was killed, and that Gen. Lee was wounded. Doubtless it was a battle of great magnitude, wherein both sides had all their forces engaged.

I remain here, broken in health and bankrupt in fortune, awaiting my fate, whatever it may be. I can do no more. If I could, I would.

Sallie Brock: from *Richmond During the War*

Widespread looting broke out in Richmond on the night of April 2 as hungry residents broke into warehouses in search of food. "The most revolting revelation," LaSalle Pickett (George E. Pickett's wife) later wrote, "was the amount of provisions, shoes and clothing which had been accumulated by the speculators who hovered like vultures over the scene of death and desolation." Amid the chaos Lieutenant General Richard S. Ewell, Richmond's military commander, ordered the destruction of the city's stockpiles of tobacco and cotton to prevent them from falling into Union hands. Sallie Brock, a Virginia native whose father owned a hotel in Richmond, described the fall of the city in a memoir published in 1867 under the pseudonym "a Richmond Lady." Brock's narrative of the evacuation draws heavily on the account presented in *The Last Year of the War* (1866) by Edward A. Pollard, the associate editor of the *Richmond Examiner*.

EVACUATION OF RICHMOND—BURNING OF THE CITY.

THE MORNING of the 2d of April, 1865, dawned brightly over the capital of the Southern Confederacy. A soft haze rested over the city, but above that, the sun shone with the warm pleasant radiance of early spring. The sky was cloudless. No sound disturbed the stillness of the Sabbath morn, save the subdued murmur of the river, and the cheerful music of the church bells. The long familiar tumult of war broke not upon the sacred calmness of the day. Around the War Department, and the Post Office, news gatherers were assembled for the latest tidings, but nothing was bruited that deterred the masses from seeking their accustomed places in the temples of the living God. At St. Paul's church the usual congregation was in attendance. President Davis occupied his pew.

It was again the regular monthly return for the celebration of the sacrament of the Lord's Supper. The services were progressing as usual, no agitation nor disturbance withdrew the thoughts from holy contemplation, when a messenger was observed to make his way up the aisle, and to place in the hands of the President a sealed package. Mr. Davis arose, and was noticed to walk rather unsteadily out of the church. An uneasy whisper ran through the congregation, and intuitively they seemed possessed of the dreadful secret of the sealed dispatch—the unhappy condition of General Lee's army and the necessity for evacuating Richmond. The dispatch stated that this was inevitable unless his lines could be reformed before eight o'clock that evening.

At the Second Presbyterian Church, Dr. Hoge, who had received information of the dire calamity impending over us, told his congregation of our situation, and the probability that never again would they meet there for worship, and in the thrilling eloquence of which he is so truly the master, bade them farewell.

The direful tidings spread with the swiftness of electricity. From lip to lip, from men, women, children and servants, the news was bandied, but many received it at first, as only a "Sunday sensation rumor." Friend looked into the face of friend to meet only an expression of incredulity; but later in the day, as the truth, stark and appalling, confronted us, the answering look was that of stony, calm despair. Late in the afternoon the signs of evacuation became obvious to even the most incredulous. Wagons were driven furiously through the streets, to the different departments, where they received as freight, the archives of the government, and carried them to the Danville Depot, to be there conveyed away by railroad.

Thousands of the citizens determined to evacuate the city with the government. Vehicles commanded any price in any currency possessed by the individual desiring to escape from the doomed capital. The streets were filled with excited crowds hurrying to the different avenues for transportation, intermingled with porters carrying huge loads, and wagons piled up with incongruous heaps of baggage, of all sorts and descriptions. The banks were all open, and depositors were busily and anxiously collecting their specie deposits, and directors were as busily engaged in getting off their bullion. Millions of dollars of paper money, both State and Confederate, were carried to the Capitol Square and buried.

Night came on, but with it no sleep for human eyes in Richmond. Confusion worse confounded reigned, and grim terror spread in wild contagion. The City Council met, and ordered the destruction of all spirituous liquors, fearing lest, in the excitement, there would be temptation to drink, and thus render our situation still more terrible. In the gutters ran a stream of whiskey, and its fumes filled and impregnated the air. After night-fall Richmond was ruled by the mob. In the principal business section of the city they surged in one black mass from store to store, breaking them open, robbing them, and in some instances (it is said) applying the torch to them.

In the alarm and terror, the guards of the State Penitentiary fled from their posts, and numbers of the lawless and desperate villains incarcerated there, for crimes of every grade and hue, after setting fire to the workshops, made good the opportunity for escape, and donning garments stolen wherever they could get them, in exchange for their prison livery, roamed over the city like fierce, ferocious beasts. No human tongue, no pen, however gifted, can give an adequate description of the events of that awful night.

While these fearful scenes were being enacted on the streets, in-doors there was scarcely less excitement and confusion. Into every house terror penetrated. Ladies were busily engaged in collecting and secreting all the valuables possessed by them, together with cherished correspondence, yet they found time and presence of mind to prepare a few comforts for friends forced to depart with the army or the government. Few tears were shed; there was no time for weakness or sentiment. The grief was too deep, the agony too terrible to find vent through the ordinary channels of distress. Fathers, husbands, brothers and friends clasped their loved ones to their bosoms in convulsive and agonized embraces, and bade an adieu, oh, how heart-rending!*—perhaps, thought many of them, forever.

At midnight the train on the Danville Railroad bore off the officers of the Government, and at the same hour many

*At eleven o'clock on that night, Colonel ——, on General ——'s staff, came into the city and was married. In a few moments he left his bride, in the terrible uncertainty of ever again meeting.

persons made their escape on the canal packets, and fled in the direction of Lynchburg.

But a still more terrible element was destined to appear and add to the horrors of the scene. From some authority—it seems uncertain what—an order had been issued to fire the four principal tobacco warehouses. They were so situated as to jeopardize the entire commercial portion of Richmond. At a late hour of the night, Mayor Mayo had dispatched, by a committee of citizens, a remonstrance against this reckless military order. But in the mad excitement of the moment the protest was unheeded. The torch was applied, and the helpless citizens were left to witness the destruction of their property. The rams in the James River were blown up. The "Richmond," the "Virginia" No. 2 and the "Beaufort" were all scattered in fiery fragments to the four winds of heaven. The noise of these explosions, which occurred as the first grey streaks of dawn broke over Richmond, was like that of a hundred cannon at one time. The very foundations of the city were shaken; windows were shattered more than two miles from where these gunboats were exploded, and the frightened inhabitants imagined that the place was being furiously bombarded. The "Patrick Henry," a receiving-ship, was scuttled, and all the shipping at the wharves was fired except the flag-of-truce steamer "Allison."

As the sun rose on Richmond, such a spectacle was presented as can never be forgotten by those who witnessed it. To speed destruction, some malicious and foolish individuals had cut the hose in the city. The fire was progressing with fearful rapidity. The roaring, the hissing, and the crackling of the flames were heard above the shouting and confusion of the immense crowd of plunderers who were moving amid the dense smoke like demons, pushing, rioting and swaying with their burdens to make a passage to the open air. From the lower portion of the city, near the river, dense black clouds of smoke arose as a pall of crape to hide the ravages of the devouring flames, which lifted their red tongues and leaped from building to building as if possessed of demoniac instinct, and intent upon wholesale destruction. All the railroad bridges, and Mayo's Bridge, that crossed the James River and connected with Manchester, on the opposite side, were in flames.

The most remarkable scenes, however, were said to have occurred at the commissary depot. Hundreds of Government wagons were loaded with bacon, flour and whiskey, and driven off in hot haste to join the retreating army. In a dense throng around the depot stood hundreds of men, women and children, black and white, provided with anything in which they could carry away provisions, awaiting the opening of the doors to rush in and help themselves. A cascade of whiskey streamed from the windows. About sunrise the doors were thrown open to the populace, and with a rush that seemed almost sufficient to bear off the building itself, they soon swept away all that remained of the Confederate commissariat of Richmond.

By this time the flames had been applied to or had reached the arsenal, in which several hundred car loads of loaded shell were left. At every moment the most terrific explosions were sending forth their awful reverberations, and gave us the idea of a general bombardment. All the horrors of the final conflagration, when the earth shall be wrapped in flames and melt with fervent heat, were, it seemed to us, prefigured in our capital.

At an early hour in the morning, the Mayor of the city, to whom it had been resigned by the military commander, proceeded to the lines of the enemy and surrendered it to General Godfrey Weitzel, who had been left by General Ord, when he withdrew one-half of his division to the lines investing Petersburg, to receive the surrender of Richmond.

As early as eight o'clock in the morning, while the mob held possession of Main street, and were busily helping themselves to the contents of the dry goods stores and other shops in that portion of the city, and while a few of our cavalry were still to be seen here and there in the upper portions, a cry was raised: "The Yankees! The Yankees are coming!" Major A. H. Stevens, of the Fourth Massachusetts Cavalry, and Major E. E. Graves, of his staff, with forty cavalry, rode steadily into the city, proceeded directly to the Capitol, and planted once more the "Stars and Stripes"—the ensign of our subjugation—on that ancient edifice. As its folds were given to the breeze, while still we heard the roaring, hissing, crackling flames, the explosions of the shells and the shouting of the multitude, the strains of an old, familiar tune floated upon the air—a tune that, in days gone by, was wont to awaken a thrill of patriotism. But now only the most bitter and crushing recollections awoke within us, as upon our quickened hearing fell the strains of "The Star Spangled Banner." For us it was a requiem for buried hopes.

As the day advanced, Weitzel's troops poured through the city. Long lines of negro cavalry swept by the Exchange Hotel, brandishing their swords and uttering savage cheers, replied to by the shouts of those of their own color, who were trudging along under loads of plunder, laughing and exulting over the prizes they had secured from the wreck of the stores, rather than rejoicing at the more precious prize of freedom which had been won for them. On passed the colored troops, singing, "John Brown's body is mouldering in the grave," etc.

By one o'clock in the day, the confusion reached its height. As soon as the Federal troops reached the city they were set to work by the officers to arrest the progress of the fire. By this time a wind had risen from the south, and seemed likely to carry the surging flames all over the northwestern portion of the city. The most strenuous efforts were made to prevent this, and the grateful thanks of the people of Richmond are due to General Weitzel and other officers for their energetic measures to save the city from entire destruction.

The Capitol Square now presented a novel appearance. On the south, east, and west of its lower half, it was bounded by burning buildings. The flames bursting from the windows, and rising from the roofs, were proclaiming in one wild roar their work of destruction. Myriads of sparks, borne upward by the current of hot air, were brightening and breaking in the dense smoke above. On the sward of the Square, fresh with the emerald green of early spring, thousands of wretched creatures, who had been driven from their dwellings by the devouring flames, were congregated. Fathers and mothers, and weeping, frightened children sought this open space for a breath of fresh air. But here, even, it was almost as hot as a furnace. Intermingled with these miserable beings were the Federal troops in their garish uniform, representing almost every nation on the continent of Europe, and thousands of the *Corps d'Afrique*.

All along on the north side of the Square were tethered the horses of the Federal cavalry, while, dotted about, were seen the white tents of the sutlers, in which there were temptingly displayed canned fruits and meats, crackers, cheese, etc.

The roaring, crackling and hissing of the flames, the bursting of shells at the Confederate Arsenal, the sounds of instruments of martial music, the neighing of the horses, the shoutings of the multitude, in which could be distinctly distinguished the coarse, wild voices of the negroes, gave an idea of all the horrors of Pandemonium. Above all this scene of terror, hung a black shroud of smoke through which the sun shone with a lurid angry glare like an immense ball of blood that emitted sullen rays of light, as if loth to shine over a scene so appalling.

Remembering the unhappy fate of the citizens of Columbia and other cities of the South, and momentarily expecting pillage, and other evils incidental to the sacking of a city, great numbers of ladies sought the proper military authorities and were furnished with safeguards for the protection of themselves and their homes. These were willingly and generously furnished, and no scene of violence is remembered to have been committed by the troops which occupied Richmond.

Throughout the entire day, those who had enriched themselves by plundering the stores were busy in conveying off their goods. Laughing and jesting negroes tugged along with every conceivable description of merchandise, and many an astute shopkeeper from questionable quarters of Richmond thus added greatly to his former stock.

The sun had set upon this terrible day before the awful reverberations of exploding shells at the arsenal ceased to be heard over Richmond. The evening came on. A deathlike quiet pervaded the late heaving and tumultuous city, broken only by the murmuring waters of the river. Night drew her sable mantle over the mutilated remains of our beautiful capital, and we locked, and bolted, and barred our doors; but sleep had fled our eyelids. All night long we kept a fearful vigil, and listened with beating heart and quickened ears for the faintest sound that might indicate the development of other and more terrible phases of horror. But from all these we were mercifully and providentially spared.

We will just here notice the range and extent of the fire which had in the afternoon literally burned itself out. From an authentic account we copy at length:

> "It had consumed the very heart of the city. A surveyor could scarcely have designated the business portion of the city more exactly than did the boundaries of the fire. Commencing at the Shockoe warehouse the fire radiated front and rear, and on two wings, burning down to, but not destroying, the store No. 77 Main street, south side, halfway between Fourteenth and Fifteenth Streets, and back to the river through Cary and all the intermediate streets. Westward on Main the fire was stayed on Ninth Street, sweeping back to the river. On the north side of Main, the flames were stayed between Thirteenth and Fourteenth streets. From this point the flames raged on the north side of Main up to Eighth Street, and back to Bank Street.
>
> "Among some of the most prominent of the buildings destroyed were the Bank of Richmond, Traders' Bank, Bank of the Commonwealth, Bank of Virginia, Farmers' Bank, all of the banking houses, the American Hotel, the Columbian Hotel, the Enquirer building, on Twelfth Street, the Dispatch office and job-rooms, corner of Thirteenth and Main Streets, all that block of buildings known as Belvin's Block, the Examiner office, engine and machinery rooms, the Confederate Post Office Department building, the State Court House, a fine old building on the Capitol Square at its Franklin Street entrance, the Mechanics' Institute, vacated by the Confederate War Department, and all the buildings on that Square up to Eighth Street, and back to Main Street, the Confederate Arsenal, and the Laboratory on Seventh Street.
>
> "The streets were crowded with furniture and every description of wares, dashed down and trampled in the mud, or burned where it lay. All the government stores were thrown open, and what could not be gotten off by the government was left to the people.
>
> "Next to the river the destruction of property was fearfully complete. The Danville and Petersburg Railroad depots, and the buildings and shedding attached, for the distance of half-a-mile from the north side of Main Street to the river, and between Eighth and Fifteenth Streets, embracing upwards of twenty blocks, presented one waste of smoking ruins, blackened walls, and solitary chimneys."

Except the great fire in New York, in 1837, there is said never to have been so extensive a conflagration on this continent as the burning of Richmond on that memorable day.

Upon reaching the city, General Weitzel established his headquarters in the Hall of the State Capitol, previously occupied by the Virginia House of Delegates. He immediately issued an order for the restoration of quiet, and intended to allay the fears and restore confidence and tranquillity to the minds of the inhabitants. General Shepley was appointed Military Commander of Richmond, and Lieutenant-Colonel Fred L. Manning was made acting Provost Marshal.

General Shepley issued an order which protected the citizens from insult and depredation by the Federal soldiers, and which also included a morbidly sensitive clause in deprecation of insult to the "flag," calculated rather to excite the derision than the indignation of the conquered inhabitants.

The scenes of this day give rise to many reflections, the most of which are too deeply painful to dwell upon. The spirit of extortion, the wicked and inordinate greed of mammon which sometimes overclouds and overules all the nobler instincts of humanity, are strikingly illustrated by a single incident in this connection. A lady passed up Franklin Street early on the morning of the 3d of April, and held in her hand a small phial in which there was about a table spoonful of paregoric. "This," said she, "I have just purchased on Main Street, at ——'s drug store. Richmond is in flames, and yet for this spoonful of medicine for a sick servant I had to pay five dollars."

An hour had not passed when the fire consumed the establishment of the extortionate vender of drugs. This incident points a moral which all can apply. Riches take to themselves wings, and in a moment least expected elude our grasp. Many who shirked the conscription, who made unworthy use of exemption bills, for the purpose of heaping up and watching their ill-gotten treasures, saw them in a single hour reduced to ashes and made the sport of the winds of heaven. Truly man knoweth not what a day may bring forth.

"GLORIA IN EXCELSIS DEO": NEW YORK, APRIL 1865

George Templeton Strong: Diary, April 3, 1865

George Templeton Strong recorded the jubilation that greeted the news of the fall of Richmond in New York City. Strong would travel to the former Confederate capital three weeks later on behalf of the U.S. Sanitary Commission, which had opened an office in Richmond. After walking through the "burned district, a wide area of ruin still smoking," he visited the commission's office and found it "crowded with applicants, mostly women in black, with baskets. They were receiving Northern charity with little shew of gratitude, much as a hungry, sulky, ill-conditioned hound accepts a bone—uncertain whether to gnaw the donation or to bite the fingers of the donor. The women were arrogant and sour, but there were poor little children with wan faces and pitiful stories of sick mothers and of privation and misery endured for months. We decided to stop these issues pursuant to the resolutions adopted last week. It seems hard and cruel, but providing tea and sugar for sick rebels is no part of our legitimate work, and it strengthens Southerners in their delusions about their own supreme dignity and the duty of Yankees to take care of them."

April 3. Petersburg and Richmond! *Gloria in excelsis Deo.* New York has seen no such day in our time nor in the old time before us. The jubilations of the Revolutionary War and the War of 1812 were those of a second-rate seaport town. This has been metropolitan and worthy an event of the first national importance to a continental nation and a cosmopolitan city.

The morning papers disclosed nothing decisive. There were two short despatches from City Point giving later news of yesterday's great battle, which looked well, but I omnibussed downtown expecting only to learn during the day more positively that the South Side Railroad was cut; that Lee had returned to his entrenchments badly punished, and that it was confidently expected that he would have to evacuate them at some future period.

Walking down Wall Street, I saw something on the *Com-*

mercial Advertiser bulletin board at the corner of Pine and William Streets and turned off to investigate. I read the announcement "Petersburg is taken" and went into the office in quest of particulars. The man behind the counter was slowly painting in large letters on a large sheet of brown paper another annunciation for the board outside: "Richmond is"— "What's that about Richmond?" said I. "Anything more?" He was too busy for speech, but he went on with a capital C, and a capital A, and so on, till I read the word *CAPTURED*!!! Finding that this was official, I posted up to Trinity Church to tell the sexton to suggest to Vinton to ask the Rector's permission to set the chimes going (which was duly done). When I came back, all William Street in front of the *Advertiser* office was impenetrably crowded, and people were rushing together in front of the Custom House (the *ci-devant* Merchants' Exchange), where Prosper M. Wetmore and Simeon Draper were getting up a meeting on the spur of the moment.

An enormous crowd soon blocked that part of Wall Street, and speeches began. Draper and the Hon. Moses Odell and Evarts and Dean (a proselyte from Copperheadism) and the inevitable Wetmore, and others, severally had their say, and the meeting, organized at about twelve, did not break up, I hear, till four P.M. Never before did I hear cheering that came straight from the heart, that was given because people felt relieved by cheering and hallooing. All the cheers I ever listened to were tame in comparison, because seemingly inspired only by a design to shew enthusiasm. These were spontaneous and involuntary and of vast "magnetizing" power. They sang "Old Hundred," the Doxology, "John Brown," and "The Star-Spangled Banner," repeating the last two lines of Key's song over and over, with a massive roar from the crowd and a unanimous wave of hats at the end of each repetition. I think I shall never lose the impression made by this rude, many-voiced chorale. It seemed a revelation of profound national feeling, underlying all our vulgarisms and corruptions, and vouchsafed to us in their very focus and centre, in Wall Street itself.

I walked about on the outskirts of the crowd, shaking hands with everybody, congratulating and being congratulated by scores of men I hardly know even by sight. Men embraced and hugged each other, *kissed* each other, retreated into doorways to dry their eyes and came out again to flourish their hats and hurrah. There will be many sore throats in New York tomorrow. My only experience of a people stirred up to like intensity of feeling was at the great Union meeting at Union Square in April, 1861. But the feeling of today's crowd was not at all identical with that of the memorable mass-meeting four years ago. It was no less earnest and serious, but it was founded on memories of years of failure, all but hopeless, and on the consciousness that national victory was at last secured, through much tribulation. . . .

After dinner to the Union League Club. Vast crowd, enthusiasm, and excitement. Meeting organized upstairs, Captain Marshall in the chair, and "a few remarks" made by a score of people. Honest, downright old Judge Vanderpoel was very good. "Gentlemen," said the judge, "I tell you that for years before this rebellion, we at the North lived under the tyranny of the slaveholders. I see now that when I was in Congress, almost every important vote I gave was dictated by them and given under the plantation lash. I confess it with shame, and humbly ask pardon of this meeting and of all my fellow-countrymen."

Hamilton Fish was at the Club—I never saw him there before—beaming and gushing, and shaking everybody's hands with fervor. Two years ago he talked nothing but discouragement and practical disloyalty. But (as Sydney Smith irreverently said of bishops), "If you want to know which way the wind blows, throw up Hamilton Fish."

It seems like a Fourth of July night—such a fusillade and cannonade is going on. Thus ends a day *sui generis* in my life. We shall long remember that the first troops to enter Richmond were niggers of Weitzel's corps. It is a most suggestive fact. It's said there were abundant signs of Union feeling in the city. Lee, Davis, & Co. are supposed to be making for Burke's Junction. Lynchburg or Danville is doubtless their proposed harbor of refuge. May Sheridan's cavalry be fresh enough to deal with them according to the example of Blücher after Waterloo. The government of the "Confederate States" has become nomadic. Its capitol and its departments of state and of war are probably in a dirty, damaged, worn-out railroad car, and its "seat of government" probably rests on the saddle which Jeff Davis bestrides.

"THIS PEERLESS COMRADE": VIRGINIA, APRIL 1865

William Gordon McCabe to Mary Pegram

William Pegram left the University of Virginia law school in 1861 to join the Confederate army and became the commander of the Purcell artillery battery in March 1862. Assigned to the Light Division led by A. P. Hill, he distinguished himself at Mechanicsville by keeping his battery in action after losing two-thirds of his guns and half of his men and horses. Pegram fought in every major engagement of the Army of Northern Virginia and became one of its most famous artillery officers, in part because his severe near-sightedness made him wear gold-rimmed spectacles even in battle. Promoted to battalion command in 1863, he remained hopeful about the Confederacy's prospects even after his older brother, Brigadier General John Pegram, was killed at Hatcher's Run on February 6, 1865. Writing to his sister Mary on March 14, he contrasted the "fine spirits & condition" of Lee's army with the "croakers & cowards" in Richmond who spread harmful rumors "conceived in their craven hearts." On April 1 Pegram and his close friend and adjutant, Captain William Gordon McCabe, were at Five Forks with six guns from their battalion. McCabe wrote to Mary Pegram about her brother's fate.

Bivouac in Amelia County. April 4th. 1865. Tuesday morning.
My dear Miss Mary,

I wrote two letters to Major Pegram in regard to the death of our dearest Colonel, but I fear neither will reach you, as Richmond has been evacuated. Unfortunately I sent in the last one a piece of his hair, as the opportunity seemed such a sure one. Mr Taylor, of Amelia promised to take it, & they all knew you & your mother so well & manifested such interest about it, that I reckoned very surely on its reaching you. Life is so uncertain now that I wish to tell you every circumstance concerning the death of our precious boy, as I was the only person with him when he put on immortality. On Saturday morning last at the Five (5) Forks near Mrs. Gillem's the enemy commenced pressing us, & our guns became engaged. He & I, as usual, were together, & our forces soon repelled the feeble demonstration of the enemy. We laid down together at the foot of a tree & he was sleeping, when a fierce assault was made on our centre where we had three (3) guns. I awakened him & we both mounted our horses & rode down among the guns, which were posted on the infantry line of battle. The enemy were now within 30 yds. of the guns & the fire terrific beyond description. I remember distinctly the sweet serenity of his face as he rode calmly to the very front. His last order was "Fire your canister low" & in a minute afterwards he fell from his saddle, shot through the left arm & side. He cried out, "Oh! Gordon I'm mortally wounded, take me off the field." I called the ambulance corps, sent him off, gave his last order to the Batteries, & then ran to where he was. At that time the enemy had gotten in our rear & our men were rapidly falling back. They cried out to me that we would be taken, but I put him in the ambulance & we drove through two parallel lines-of-battle of the enemy. Happily night put an end to the pursuit. Oh! dear Miss Mary, I am so thankful that I was with him then. I made him put his head on my arm & put the other one under his body to prevent the jolting of the ambulance, & we rode so for ten miles. When we were bringing him off the field, he took my hand & said, "Tell my mother & sisters that I commend them to God's protection." He was in great pain, & the Dr. gave him morphine. While in the ambulance I held him in my arms & prayed for him & kissed him over & over again. Once when I prayed that his life might be spared, he said, "If it is God's will to take me, I am perfectly resigned. I only wish life for my mother's & sisters' sake." He said several times—"Give my love to mother & both sisters & tell them I thought of them in my last moments." Once when in my agony I cried out—"My God, my God, why hast Thou forsaken me," he said quickly—"Don't say that, Gordon, it is'nt right." One thing I love to dwell upon. I bent over him & kissed him & said, calling him by his name for the first time in my life, "Willie, I never knew how much I loved you until now." He pressed my hand & answered, "But I did." Without ceasing, except when I lost my voice in tears, I prayed for him, for comfort for body & soul, & he would simply say "*Amen.*" I carried him to Ford's Depot, on the S. S. R.R. to a Mr.

Pegram's & procured a bed for him. We got there about 10 o'clock at night & about 12 the Yankees advanced & I was left alone with him. I sent off our horses, sabres, & spurs, as I did n't want them to fall into the hands of the enemy. He had been suffering very greatly & begged me for more morphine. I made the Dr give me some, with directions about using it, & he soon told me that he was better. I fixed his head easily & he fell asleep, never more to speak to me. Oh! that terrible night. All alone with him & another Col. mortally wounded, feeling utterly wretched in my impotence to help him, tho' I dressed his wound as well as I knew how, cut off from our own forces, & momentarily expecting the enemy to come & perhaps to remain deaf to my entreaties to remain with him. Dear Miss Mary, I could only watch & pray. He fell into a stupour about 2 o'clock. I could only sit by him & moisten his lips & smooth his hair & kiss him & call him a thousand fond names though he never heard me. At A.M. Sunday morning, he died without a struggle. I helped myself to dig his grave, so fearful was I that the Yankees would get his body. I buried him at Mr Pegram's in the back yard & read the service over him, as I knew he would have desired it. After he was dead, I cut off a piece of his hair for you & one for myself, & laid him out in uniform. Oh! what a splendid soldier he looked. Mr. Pegram promised me faithfully that he wd. have a fence built around the grave. He & his wife were very kind. I threw myself on their charity as I had n't a cent in the world. As soon as I had buried him, I jumped on a horse I found there & made my escape, after being fired on three or four times by their picket. And now my heart, as yours, is left unto me desolate. I will never admit that anybody loved him more than I did. This peerless comrade, my darling Willie, who was with me always, who read with me, prayed with me, slept with me, is at rest. On this terrible retreat I have talked with his spirit hour after hour, & the men, who always saw us riding together, have been very kind to me in my grief. God help us all. Remember that I will always do you any service to the measure of my life.

Your friend,

W. Gordon McCabe

OCCUPYING RICHMOND: VIRGINIA, APRIL 1865

Thomas Morris Chester to the Philadelphia Press

On the morning of April 3 Major General Godfrey Weitzel, the commander of the Twenty-fifth in the Army of the James, occupied Richmond with a regiment of black cavalry and two infantry divisions, one made up of white soldiers and the other of U.S. Colored Troops. Weitzel's men spent the day fighting fires and restoring order in the city. The following day they were surprised by the unexpected arrival of President Lincoln, who had been visiting Grant's headquarters at City Point, Virginia, since March 24. Despite Stanton's fears for his safety, Lincoln resolved to go to the captured city and telegraphed the Secretary of War: "I will take care of myself." Thomas Morris Chester had been sending dispatches to the *Philadelphia Press* from the Army of the James since August 1864. He was the only black correspondent to report on the war for a major daily newspaper.

HALL OF CONGRESS

RICHMOND, APRIL 4, 1865.

Seated in the Speaker's chair, so long dedicated to treason, but in the future to be consecrated to loyalty, I hasten to give a rapid sketch of the incidents which have occurred since my last despatch.

To Major General Godfrey Weitzel was assigned the duty of capturing Richmond. Last evening he had determined upon storming the rebel works in front of Fort Burnham. The proper dispositions were all made, and the knowing ones retired with dim visions of this stronghold of treason floating before them. Nothing occurred in the first part of the evening to awaken suspicion, though for the past few days it has been known to the authorities that the rebels, as I informed you, were evacuating the city. After midnight explosions began to occur so frequently as to confirm the evidence already in possession of the General-in-chief, that the last acts of an outgeneralled army were in course of progress. The immense flames curling up throughout the rebel camps indicated that they were destroying all that could not be taken away.

The soldiers along the line gathered upon the breastworks to witness the scene and exchange congratulations. While thus silently gazing upon the columns of fire one of the monster rams was exploded, which made the very earth tremble. If there was any doubt about the evacuation of Richmond that report banished them all. In a very few moments, though still dark, the Army of the James, or rather that part of it under General Weitzel, was put in motion.

It did not require much time to get the men in light-marching order. Every regiment tried to be first. All cheerfully moved off with accelerated speed. The pickets which were on the line during the night were in the advance.

Brevet Brigadier General Draper's brigade of colored troops, Brevet Major General Kautz's division, were the first infantry to enter Richmond. The gallant 36th U. S. Colored Troops, under Lieutenant Colonel B. F. Pratt, has the honor of being the first regiment. Captain Bicnnef's company has the pride of leading the advance.

The column having passed through Fort Burnham, over the rebel works, where they were moving heavy and light pieces of artillery, which the enemy in his haste was obliged to leave behind, moved into the Osborn road, which leads directly into the city.

In passing over the rebel works, we moved very cautiously in single file, for fear of exploding the innumerable torpedoes which were planted in front. So far as I can learn none has been exploded, and no one has been injured by those infernal machines. The soldiers were soon, under engineers, carefully digging them up and making the passage way beyond the fear of casualties.

Along the road which the troops marched, or rather double quicked, batches of negroes were gathered together testifying by unmistakable signs their delight at our coming. Rebel soldiers who had hid themselves when their army moved came out of the bushes, and gave themselves up as disgusted with the service. The haste of the rebels was evident in guns, camp equipage, telegraph wires, and other army property which they did not have time to burn.

When the column was about two miles from Richmond General Weitzel and staff passed by at a rapid speed, and was hailed by loud cheering. He soon reached the city, which was surrendered to him informally at the State House by Mr. Joseph Mayo, the mayor. The General and staff rode up Main street amid the hearty congratulations of a very large crowd of colored persons and poor whites, who were gathered together upon the sidewalks manifesting every demonstration of joy.

There were many persons in the better-class houses who were peeping out of the windows, and whose movements indicated that they would need watching in the future. There was no mistaking the curl of their lips and the flash of their eyes. The new military Governor of Richmond will, no doubt, prove equal to such emergencies.

When General Draper's brigade entered the outskirts of the city it was halted, and a brigade of Devin's division, 24th Corps, passed in to constitute the provost guard. A scene was here witnessed which was not only grand, but sublime. Officers rushed into each other's arms, congratulating them upon the peaceful occupation of this citadel. Tears of joy ran down the faces of the more aged. The soldiers cheered lustily, which were mingled with every kind of expression of delight. The citizens stood gaping in wonder at the splendidly-equipped army marching along under the graceful folds of the old flag. Some waved their hats and women their hands in token of gladness. The pious old negroes, male and female, indulged in such expressions: "You've come at last"; "We've been looking for you these many days"; "Jesus has opened the way"; "God bless you"; "I've not seen that old flag for four years"; "It does my eyes good"; "Have you come to stay?"; "Thank God", and similar expressions of exultation. The soldiers, black and white, received these assurances of loyalty as evidences of the latent patriotism of an oppressed people, which a military despotism has not been able to crush.

Riding up to a group of fine looking men, whose appearance indicated that they would hardly have influence enough to keep them out of the army, I inquired how it was they were not taken away with the force of Lee. They replied that they had hid themselves when the rebel army had evacuated the city, and that many more had done likewise, who would soon appear when assured that there was no longer any danger of falling into the power of the traitorous army.

These scenes all occurred at the terminus of Osborn road, which connects with the streets of the city, and is within the municipal limits. There General Draper's brigade, with the gallant 36th U.S.C.T.'s drum corps, played "Yankee Doodle" and "Shouting the Battle Cry of Freedom," amid the cheers of the boys and the white soldiers who filed by them. It ought to be stated that the officers of the white troops were anxious to be the first to enter the city with their organizations, and so far succeeded as to procure an order when about three miles, distant, that General Draper's brigade should take the left of the road, in order to allow those of the 24th Corps, under General Devin, to pass by. General Draper obeyed the order, and took the left of the road in order to let the troops of Devin go by, but at the same time ordered his brigade on a double-quick, well knowing that his men would not likely be over taken on the road by any soldiers in the army. For marching or fighting Draper's 1st Brigade, 1st Division, 25th Corps, is not to be surpassed in the service, and the General honors it with a pride and a consciousness which inspire him to undertake cheerfully whatever may be committed to his execution. It was his brigade that nipped the flower of the Southern army, the Texas Brigade, under Gary, which never before last September knew defeat. There may be others who may claim the distinction of being the first to enter the city, but as I was ahead of every part of the force but the cavalry, which of necessity must lead the advance, I know whereof I affirm when I announce that General Draper's brigade was the first organization to enter the city limits. According to custom, it should constitute the provost guard of Richmond.

Kautz's division, consisting of Draper's and Wild's brigades, with troops of the 24th Corps, were placed in the trenches around the city, and Thomas' brigade was assigned to garrison Manchester. Proper dispositions have been made of the force to give security, and, soldier-like, placed the defences of the city beyond the possibility of a surprise.

As we entered all the Government buildings were in flames, having been fired by order of the rebel General Ewell. The flames soon communicated themselves to the business part of the city; and continued to rage furiously throughout the day. All efforts to arrest this destructive element seemed for the best part of the day of no avail. The fire department of Richmond rendered every aid, and to them and the co-operate labors of our soldiers belongs the credit of having saved Richmond from the devastating flames. As it is, all that part of the city lying between Ninth and Fourteenth streets, between Main street and the river inclusive, is in ruins. Among the most prominent buildings destroyed are the rebel War Department, Quartermaster General's Department, all the buildings with commissary stores, Shockoe's and Dibbrel's warehouses, well stored with tobacco, *Dispatch* and *Enquirer* newspaper buildings, the court house, (Guy) House, Farmers' Bank, Bank of Virginia, Exchange Bank, Tracers' Bank, American and Columbia hotels, and the Mayo bridge which unites Richmond with Manchester. The buildings of the largest merchants are among those which have been reduced to ashes.

The flames, in spreading, soon communicated to poor and rich houses alike. All classes were soon rushing, into the streets with their goods, to save them. They hardly laid them down before they were picked up by those who openly were plundering everyplace where anything of value was to be obtained. It was retributive justice upon the aiders and abettors of treason to see their property fired by the rebel chiefs and plundered by the people whom they meant to forever enslave. As soon as the torch was applied to the rebel storehouses, the negroes and poor whites began to appropriate all property, without respect to locks or bolts. About the time our advance entered the city the tide of this inadmissible confiscation was at its highest ebb. Men would rush to the principal stores, break open the doors, and carry off the contents by the armful.

The leader of this system of public plundering was a colored man who carried upon his shoulder an iron crow-bar, and as a mark of distinguishment had a red piece of goods around his waist which reached down to his knees. The mob, for it could not with propriety be called anything else, followed him as their leader; moved on when he advanced, and rushed into every passage which was made by the leader with his crow-bar. Goods of every description were seized under these circumstances and personally appropriated by the supporters of an equal distribution of property. Cotton goods in abundance, tobacco in untold quantities, shoes, rebel military clothing, and goods and furniture generally were carried away by the people as long as any thing of value was to be obtained. As soon as Gen. Ripley was assigned to provost duty, all plundering immediately ceased, the flames were arrested, and an appearance of recognized authority fully sustained. Order once more reigns in Richmond. The streets were as quiet last night as they possibly could be. An effective patrolling and provost guard keeps everything as quiet as can be expected.

The F. F. V.'s have not ventured out of their houses yet, except in a few cases, to apply for a guard to protect their property. In some cases negroes have been sent to protect the interest of these would-be man sellers. It is pleasant to witness the measured pace of some dark sentinel before the houses of persons who, without doubt, were outspoken rebels until the Union army entered the city, owing the security which they feel to the vigilance of the negro guard.

When the army occupied the city there were innumerable inquiries for Jeff Davis, but to all of which the answer was made that he went off in great haste night before last, with all the bag and baggage which he could carry. The future capital of the Confederacy will probably be in a wagon for the facilities which it affords to travel. Jeff's mansion, where he lived in state, is now the headquarters of Gen. Weitzel.

Brigadier General Shepley has been appointed Governor of Richmond, and has entered upon the arduous duties of the office. A better selection could not have been made.

It is due to Major Stevens, of the 4th Massachusetts Cavalry, provost marshal, on the staff of Gen. Weitzel, to give him credit for raising the first colors over the State House. He hoisted a couple of guidons, in the absence of a flag, which excited prolonged cheering. Soon after General Shepley's A. D. C. raised the first storm flag over the Capitol. It is the acme standard which General Shepley laid a wager would wave over the St. Charles Hotel in the beginning of the rebellion, and he also laid another that it would be hoisted over Richmond, both of which he has had the satisfaction of winning.

During the early part of the day a number of rebel officers were captured at the Spottswood House, where they were drinking freely. They belonged to the navy, the last of which disappeared in smoke, excepting a few straggling officers and men. These fellows, when arrested, did not wish to walk through the street under a guard, but solicited the favor of being permitted to go to the provost marshal in a carriage. Their impudence was received as it deserved, with suppressed contempt.

On Sunday evening, strange to say, the jails in this place were thrown open, and all runaway negroes, those for sale and those for safe keeping were told to hop out and enjoy their freedom. You may rely upon it that they did not need a second invitation. Many of these persons will have no difficulty in convincing themselves that they were always on the side of the Union and the freedom of the slave. Great events have a wonderful influence upon the minds of guilty, trembling wretches.

When the rebels blew up the magazine in the vicinity of French Garden Hill, the people were not informed of the fact. Some of them knew it, but the great body of those in the vicinity were ignorant of what was taking place. The result was that quite a number were killed. Nearly if not quite all the paupers in the poor house—the numbers not being large—which was very near the magazine, were instantly killed also.

The fire is still burning, but not too much damage.

HALL OF CONGRESS

RICHMOND, APRIL 6, 1865.

The exultation of the loyal people of this city, who, amid the infamy by which they have been surrounded, and the foul misrepresentations to allure them from their allegiance, have remained true to the old flag, is still being expressed by the most extravagant demonstrations of joy. The Union element in this city consists of negroes and poor whites, including all that have deserted from the army, or have survived the terrible exigencies which brought starvation to so many homes. As to the negroes, one thing is certain, that amid every disaster to our arms, amid the wrongs which they daily suffered for their known love for the Union, and amid the scourging which they received for trying to reach our army and enlist under our flag, they have ever prayed for the right cause, and testified their devotion to it in ten thousand instances, and especially in aiding our escaped prisoners to find our lines when to do so placed their own lives in peril.

The great event after the capture of the city was the arrival of President Lincoln in it. He came up to Rocket's wharf in one of Admiral Porter's vessels of war, and, with a file of sailors for a guard of honor, he walked up to Jeff Davis' house, the headquarters of General Weitzel. As soon as he landed the news sped, as if upon the wings of lightning, that "Old Abe," for it was treason in this city to give him a more respectful address, had come. Some of the negroes, feeling themselves free to act like men, shouted that the President had arrived. This name having always been applied to Jeff, the inhabitants, coupling it with the prevailing rumor that he had been captured, reported that the arch-traitor was being brought into the city. As the people pressed near they cried "Hang him!" "Hang him!" "Show him no quarter!" and other similar expressions, which indicated their sentiments as to what should be his fate. But when they learned that it was President Lincoln their joy knew no bounds. By the time he reached General Weitzel's headquarters, thousands of persons had followed him to catch a sight of the Chief Magistrate of the United States. When he ascended the steps he faced the crowd and bowed his thanks for the prolonged exultation which was going up from that great concourse. The people seemed inspired by this acknowledgment, and with renewed vigor shouted louder and louder, until it seemed as if the echoes would reach the abode of those patriot spirits who had died without witnessing the sight.

General Weitzel received the President upon the pavement, and conducted him up the steps. General Shepley, after a good deal of trouble, got the crowd quiet and introduced Admiral Porter, who bowed his acknowledgments for the cheering with which his name was greeted. The President and party entered the mansion, where they remained for half an hour, the crowd still accumulating around it, when a headquarters' carriage was brought in front, drawn by four horses, and Mr. Lincoln, with his youngest son, Admiral Porter, General Kautz, and General Devin entered. The carriage drove through the principal streets, followed by General Weitzel and staff on horseback, and a cavalry guard. There is no describing the scene along the route. The colored population was wild with enthusiasm. Old men thanked God in a very boisterous manner, and old women shouted upon the pavement as high as they had ever done at a religious revival. But when the President passed through the Capitol yard it was filled with people. Washington's monument and the Capitol steps were one mass of humanity to catch a glimpse of him.

It should be recorded that the Malvern, Admiral Porter's flag-ship, upon which the President came; the Bat, Monticello, Frolic, and the Symbol, the torpedo-boat which led the advance and exploded these infernal machines, were the first vessels to arrive in Richmond.

Nothing can exceed the courtesy and politeness which the whites everywhere manifest to the negroes. Not even the familiarity peculiar to Americans is indulged in, calling the blacks by their first or Christian names, but even masters are addressing their slaves as "Mr. Johnson," "Mrs. Brown," and "Miss Smith." A cordial shake of the hand and a gentle inclination of the body, approaching to respectful consideration, are evident in the greetings which now take place between the oppressed and the oppressor.

Masters are looking through the camps of our colored troops to find some of their former slaves to give them a good character. The first night our troops quartered in the city this scene was enacted in Gen. Draper's brigade limits, his being the first organization to enter the city. His troops now hold the inner lines of works. The rapid occupation of the city cut off the retreat of many rebels, who are daily being picked up by the provost guard.

Every one declares that Richmond never before presented such a spectacle of jubilee. It must be confessed that those who participated in this informal reception of the President were mainly negroes. There were many whites in the crowd, but they were lost in the great concourse of American citizens of African descent. Those who lived in the finest houses either stood motionless upon their steps or merely peeped through the window-blinds, with a very few exceptions. The Secesh-inhabitants still have some hope for their tumbling cause.

The scenes at the Capitol during the day are of a very exciting character. The offices of General Shepley, the Military

Governor, and Colonel Morning, the Provost Marshal General, are besieged by crowds, mostly poor people, with a small sprinkling of respectability, upon every kind of pretext. They want protection papers, a guard over their property, to assure the authorities of their allegiance, to take the oath, to announce that they are paroled prisoners and never have been exchanged, and don't desire to be, and innumerable other circumstances to insure the protection of the military authorities.

The people of Richmond, white and black, had been led to believe that when the Yankee army came its mission was one of plunder. But the orderly manner in which the soldiers have acted has undeceived them. The excitement is great, but nothing could be more orderly and decorous than the united crowds of soldiers and citizens.

The Capitol building all day yesterday from the moment we took possession was surrounded by a crowd of hungry men and women clamoring for something to eat. The earnestness of their entreaties and looks showed that they were in a destitute condition. It was deemed necessary to station a special guard at the bottom of the steps to keep them from filling the building. These suffering people will probably be attended to in a day or so in that bountiful manner which has marked the advance of the Union armies.

I visited yesterday (Tuesday) several of the slave jails, where men, women, and children were confined, or herded, for the examination of purchasers. The jailors were in all cases slaves, and had been left in undisputed possession of the buildings. The owners, as soon as they were aware that we were coming, opened wide the doors and told the confined inmates they were free. The poor souls could not realize it until they saw the Union army. Even then they thought it must be a pleasant dream, but when they saw Abraham Lincoln they were satisfied that their freedom was perpetual. One enthusiastic old negro woman exclaimed: "I know that I am free, for I have seen Father Abraham and felt him."

When the President returned to the flag-ship of Admiral Porter, in the evening, he was taken from the wharf in a cutter. Just as he pushed off, amid the cheering of the crowd, another good old colored female shouted out, "Don't drown, Massa Abe, for God's sake!"

The fire, which was nearly extinguished when I closed my last despatch, is entirely so now. Thousands of persons are gazing hourly with indignation upon the ruins. Gen. Lee ordered the evacuation of the city at an hour known to the remaining leaders of the rebellion, when Gens. Ewell and Breckinridge, and others, absconded, leaving orders with menials, robbers, and plunderers, kept together during the war by the "cohesive power of public plunder," to apply the torch to the different tobacco warehouses, public buildings, arsenals, stores, flour mills, powder magazines, and every important place of deposit. A south wind prevailed, and the flames spread with devastating effect. The offices of the newspapers, whose columns have been charged with the foulest vituperation against our Government, were on fire; two of them have been reduced to ashes, another one injured beyond repair, while the remaining two are not much damaged. Every bank which had emitted the spurious notes of the rebels was consumed to ruins. Churches no longer gave audience to empty prayers, but burst forth in furious flames. Magazines exploded, killing the poor inhabitants. In short, Secession was burnt out, and the city purified as far as fire could accomplish it.

As I informed you in a previous despatch, the Union soldiers united with the citizens to stay the progress of the fire, and at last succeeded, but not until all the business part of the town was destroyed.

About three o'clock on Monday morning the political prisoners who were confined in Castle Thunder, and the Union prisoners who were in Libby, were marched out and driven off. Some of our officers escaped and were kindly cared for by the good Union folks of this city. The rebels also gathered together as many colored persons as possible, and were forcing them ahead with drawn sabres, but before they were out of the city Spear's cavalry came down upon them, rescued the negroes, and captured seventeen of the Johnnies, with their horses.

Yesterday afternoon I strolled through Castle Thunder, where so many Union men have suffered every species of meanness and tyranny which the rebels could invent. The only thing that attracted especial attention was the large number of manacles which were for the benefit of the prisoners. This place has been so often described, that it would be unnecessary to weary the reader again. The Castle is empty at present, and is in charge of Capt. Mattison, 81st New York Volunteers, who, by the way, is a very accommodating officer. The Hotel de Libby is now doing a rushing business in the way of accommodating a class of persons who have not heretofore patronized that establishment. It is being rapidly filled with rebel soldiers, detectives, spies, robbers, and every grade of infamy in the calendar of crime. The stars and stripes now wave gracefully over it, and traitors look through the same bars behind which loyal men were so long confined.

Quite a large number of rebels were brought into the city last night. I did not for a certainty learn whether they were captured, or deserted from a bad cause—most probably the latter.

Lieut. Gen. Grant will arrive in this city tomorrow, and will doubtless receive an ovation equal to President Lincoln's.

SOUTHERN "ARROGANCE AND FOLLY":
WASHINGTON, D.C., APRIL 1865

Gideon Welles: Diary, April 7, 1865

After abandoning Richmond and Petersburg, Lee marched west with about 40,000 men, hoping to evade his Union pursuers and reach Johnston's army in North Carolina. His army reached Amelia Court House, about thirty-five miles northwest of Petersburg, on April 4, having lost thousands of hungry, exhausted, and demoralized men along the way to straggling and desertion. When Lee discovered that Sheridan had blocked his planned route into North Carolina, he was forced to continue heading west toward Lynchburg. On April 6, Union troops led by Sheridan closed in on the rear of the Confederate column at Sailor's Creek and captured more than 6,000 prisoners, including eight generals. Watching the fighting from a nearby hill, Lee exclaimed, "My God! Has the army been dissolved?" In his message reporting the victory, Sheridan wrote, "If the thing is pressed I think Lee will surrender." Lincoln then telegraphed Grant: "Let the *thing* be pressed." With the end of the war seemingly close, Secretary of the Navy Gideon Welles reflected on its origins.

April 7, Friday. We have word that Sheridan has had a battle with a part of Lee's army, has captured six Rebel generals and several thousand prisoners. His dispatch intimates the almost certain capture of Lee.

In the closing up of this Rebellion, General Grant has [ ] proved himself a man of undoubted military talent and genius. Those who have doubted and hesitated must concede him great capacity as a general. His demonstrations and movements have been masterly. The persistency which he has exhibited is as much to be admired as any quality in his character. He is regardless of life.

It is desirable that Lee should be captured. He, more than any one else has the confidence of the Rebels, and can, if he escapes, and is weak enough to try to continue hostilities, rally for a time a brigand force in the interior. I can hardly suppose he would do this, but he has shown great weakness, and his infidelity to the country which educated, and employed, and paid him betrays gross ingratitude. His true course would be to desert the country he has betrayed, and never return.

Memo. This Rebellion which has convulsed the nation for four years, threatened the Union and caused such sacrifice of blood and treasure may be traced in a great degree to the diseased imagination of certain South Carolina gentlemen, who some thirty and forty years since studied Scott's novels, and fancied themselves cavaliers, imbued with chivalry, a superior class, not born to labor but to command, brave beyond mankind generally, more intellectual, more generous, more hospitable, more liberal than others. Others of their countrymen who did not own slaves, and who labored with their own hands, who depended on their own exertions for a livelihood, who were mechanics, traders and tillers of the soil were, in their estimate, inferiors who would not fight, were religious and would not gamble, moral and would not countenance duelling, were serious and minded their own business, economical and thrifty, which was denounced as mean and miserly. Hence the chivalrous Carolinian affected to, and actually did, hold the Yankee in contempt.

The women caught the contagion. They were to be patriotic, Revolutionary matrons and maidens. They admired the bold, dashing, swaggering, licentious, boasting, chivalrous slave-master who told them he wanted to fight the Yankee but could not kick and insult him into a quarrel. And they disdained and despised the pious, peddling, plodding, persevering Yankee who would not drink, and swear, and fight duels.

The speeches and letters of James Hamilton and his associates from 1825 forward will be found impregnated with the romance and poetry of Scott, and they came ultimately to believe themselves a superior and better race.

Only a war could wipe out this arrogance and folly which had through party and sectional instrumentalities been disseminated through a large portion of the South. Face to face in battle and in field, they learned their own weakness and misconception of the Yankee character. Without self-assumption of superiority, the Yankee was proved to be as brave, as generous, as humane, as chivalric as the vaunting and superficial Carolinian to say the least. Their ideal, however in Scott's pages of Marmion, Ivanhoe, etc., no more belonged to the Sunny South the punky Palmetto than to other sections less arrogant and presuming but more industrious and frugal.

SURRENDER TERMS: VIRGINIA, APRIL 1865

Ulysses S. Grant to Robert E. Lee

Grant's aggressive pursuit of Lee neared its end on April 8 when Union cavalry blocked the road to Lynchburg near Appomattox Court House. The next morning the Army of Northern Virginia soon found itself surrounded on three sides. When Lee realized that his army was trapped, he told his aides "there is nothing left for me to do but to go and see General Grant, and I would rather die a thousand deaths." The two generals met on the afternoon of April 9 in the parlor of the McLean House, Lee wearing a full dress uniform with sword and Grant a private's uniform with a lieutenant general's shoulder straps. On March 3 Lincoln had responded sternly to an overture from Lee about negotiating peace "by means of a military convention," ordering Grant "not to decide, discuss, or confer upon any political question" with the Confederate commander. Subsequently, when Grant, Sherman, and Lincoln had conferred at City Point on March 28, the President expressed a desire to have the Confederate armies receive lenient terms of capitulation. With these indications in mind, Grant wrote out his surrender terms.

Appomattox C. H. Va.
Apl. 9th 1865

GEN. R. E. LEE,
COMD.G C. S. A.
GEN.

In accordance with the substance of my letter to you of the 8th inst. I propose to receive the surrender of the Army of N. Va. on the following terms: towit:

Rolls of all the officers and men to be made in duplicate One copy to be given to an officer designated by me, the other to be retained by such officer or officers as you may designate. The officers to give their individual paroles not to take up arms against the Government of the United States until properly exchanged and each company or regimental commander sign a like parole for the men of their commands.

The Arms, Artillery and public property to be parked and

stacked and turned over to the officer appointed by me to receive them. This will not embrace the side Arms of the officers nor their private horses or baggage.—This done each officer and man will be allowed to return to their homes not to be disturbed by United States Authority so long as they observe their parole and the laws in force where they may reside.

Very respectfully
U. S. GRANT Lt. Gn

Robert E. Lee: General Orders No. 9

Lee read Grant's terms and remarked that in the Confederate army soldiers serving in the cavalry and the artillery owned their own horses. Grant did not revise his written terms, which addressed only horses owned by officers, but told Lee that he would permit paroled soldiers to take their own horses and mules home with them. He also gave orders for the surrendered Confederates to be fed from Union army rations. Lee signed a letter accepting Grant's terms, and the two men parted. As news of the surrender spread, the Union artillery began firing a one-hundred-gun salute that Grant immediately ordered silenced. "The Confederates were now our prisoners," he would write in his memoirs, "and we did not want to exult over their downfall." Thousands of men cheered Lee and reached out to touch him as he rode through the Confederate ranks on his horse Traveller. The next day Lee issued a farewell message to his army that was initially drafted by one of his senior aides, Lieutenant Colonel Charles Marshall. Having given his parole, Lee left Appomattox Court House on April 11 and returned to his home in Richmond.

GENERAL ORDER, NO. 9

Headquarters, Army of Northern Virginia
April 10, 1865

After four years of arduous service, marked by unsurpassed courage and fortitude, the Army of Northern Virginia has been compelled to yield to overwhelming numbers and resources.

I need not tell the brave survivors of so many hard fought battles, who have remained steadfast to the last, that I have consented to the result from no distrust of them.

But feeling that valor and devotion could accomplish nothing that would compensate for the loss that must have attended the continuance of the contest, I determined to avoid the useless sacrifice of those whose past services have endeared them to their countrymen.

By the terms of the agreement officers and men can return to their homes and remain until exchanged. You will take with you the satisfaction that proceeds from the consciousness of duty faithfully performed, and I earnestly pray that a Merciful God will extend to you His blessing and protection.

With an increasing admiration of your constancy and devotion to your country, and a grateful remembrance of your kind and generous considerations for myself, I bid you all an affectionate farewell.

R. E. Lee
Genl

LINCOLN'S ASSASSINATION: WASHINGTON, D.C., APRIL 1865

Elizabeth Keckly: from Behind the Scenes

Lincoln returned to Washington from City Point on April 9, Palm Sunday, the day Lee surrendered to Grant. Two days later the President spoke to a large crowd from a window in the White House. After saying that "the surrender of the principal insurgent army" gave "hope of a righteous and speedy peace," Lincoln devoted most of his speech to the problems of reconstruction. Defending at length his support for the new government in Louisiana, which was opposed by Charles Sumner and other Radical Republicans (see pp. 629–31 in this volume), he cited its adoption of a free-state constitution, ratification of the Thirteenth Amendment, and creation of public schools for black and white children. Regarding the failure of the Louisiana government to extend the franchise to black men, Lincoln stated that "I would myself prefer that it were now conferred on the very intelligent, and on those who serve our cause as soldiers." It was his first public endorsement of black suffrage. Listening in the audience was John Wilkes Booth. "This means nigger citizenship," Booth said. "Now, my God, I'll put him through." Elizabeth Keckly was a former slave who had become a successful Washington dressmaker and a confidante of Mary Todd Lincoln. She wrote about the President's speech on April 11 and the days that followed in her 1868 memoir, *Behind the Scenes, or, Thirty Years a Slave, and Four Years in the White House.*

I HAD never heard Mr. Lincoln make a public speech, and, knowing the man so well, was very anxious to hear him. On the morning of the Tuesday after our return from City Point, Mrs. Lincoln came to my apartments, and before she drove away I asked permission to come to the White House that night and hear Mr. Lincoln speak.

"Certainly, Lizabeth; if you take any interest in political speeches, come and listen in welcome."

"Thank you, Mrs. Lincoln. May I trespass further on your kindness by asking permission to bring a friend with me?"

"Yes, bring your friend also. By the way, come in time to dress me before the speaking commences."

"I will be in time. You may rely upon that. Good morning," I added, as she swept from my room, and, passing out into the street, entered her carriage and drove away.

About 7 o'clock that evening I entered the White House. As I went up-stairs I glanced into Mr. Lincoln's room through the half-open door, and seated by a desk was the President, looking over his notes and muttering to himself. His face was thoughtful, his manner abstracted, and I knew, as I paused a moment to watch him, that he was rehearsing the part that he was to play in the great drama soon to commence.

Proceeding to Mrs. Lincoln's apartment, I worked with busy fingers, and in a short time her toilette was completed.

Great crowds began to gather in front of the White House, and loud calls were made for the President. The band stopped playing, and as he advanced to the centre window over the door to make his address, I looked out, and never saw such a mass of heads before. It was like a black, gently swelling sea. The swaying motion of the crowd, in the dim uncertain light, was like the rising and falling of billows—like the ebb and flow of the tide upon the stranded shore of the ocean. Close to the house the faces were plainly discernible, but they faded into mere ghostly outlines on the outskirts of the assembly; and what added to the weird, spectral beauty of the scene, was the confused hum of voices that rose above the sea of forms, sounding like the subdued, sullen roar of an ocean storm, or the wind soughing through the dark lonely forest. It was a grand and imposing scene, and when the President, with pale face and his soul flashing through his eyes, advanced to speak, he looked more like a demi-god than a man crowned with the fleeting days of mortality.

The moment the President appeared at the window he was greeted with a storm of applause, and voices re-echoed the cry, "A light! a light!"

A lamp was brought, and little Tad at once rushed to his father's side, exclaiming:

"Let me hold the light, Papa! let me hold the light!"

Mrs. Lincoln directed that the wish of her son be gratified, and the lamp was transferred to his hands. The father and son standing there in the presence of thousands of free citizens, the one lost in a chain of eloquent ideas, the other looking up into the speaking face with a proud, manly look, formed a beautiful and striking tableau.

There were a number of distinguished gentlemen, as well as ladies, in the room, nearly all of whom remarked the picture.

I stood a short distance from Mr. Lincoln, and as the light from the lamp fell full upon him, making him stand out boldly in the darkness, a sudden thought struck me, and I whispered to the friend at my side:

"What an easy matter would it be to kill the President, as he stands there! He could be shot down from the crowd, and no one be able to tell who fired the shot."

I do not know what put such an idea into my head, unless it was the sudden remembrance of the many warnings that Mr. Lincoln had received.

The next day, I made mention to Mrs. Lincoln of the idea that had impressed me so strangely the night before, and she replied with a sigh:

"Yes, yes, Mr. Lincoln's life is always exposed. Ah, no one knows what it is to live in constant dread of some fearful tragedy. The President has been warned so often, that I tremble for him on every public occasion. I have a presentiment that he will meet with a sudden and violent end. I pray God to protect my beloved husband from the hands of the assassin."

Mr. Lincoln was fond of pets. He had two goats that knew the sound of his voice, and when he called them they would come bounding to his side. In the warm bright days, he and Tad would sometimes play in the yard with these goats, for an hour at a time. One Saturday afternoon I went to the White House to dress Mrs. Lincoln. I had nearly completed my task when the President came in. It was a bright day, and walking to the window, he looked down into the yard, smiled, and, turning to me, asked:

"Madam Elizabeth, you are fond of pets, are you not?"

"O yes, sir," I answered.

"Well, come here and look at my two goats. I believe they are the kindest and best goats in the world. See how they sniff the clear air, and skip and play in the sunshine. Whew! what a jump," he exclaimed as one of the goats made a lofty spring.

"Madam Elizabeth, did you ever before see such an active goat?" Musing a moment, he continued: "He feeds on my bounty, and jumps with joy. Do you think we could call him a bounty-jumper? But I flatter the bounty-jumper. My goat is far above him. I would rather wear his horns and hairy coat through life, than demean myself to the level of the man who plunders the national treasury in the name of patriotism. The man who enlists into the service for a consideration, and deserts the moment he receives his money but to repeat the play, is bad enough; but the men who manipulate the grand machine and who simply make the bounty-jumper their agent in an outrageous fraud are far worse. They are beneath the worms that crawl in the dark hidden places of earth."

His lips curled with haughty scorn, and a cloud was gathering on his brow. Only a moment the shadow rested on his face. Just then both goats looked up at the window and shook their heads as if they would say "How d'ye do, old friend?"

"See, Madam Elizabeth," exclaimed the President in a tone of enthusiasm, "my pets recognize me. How earnestly they look! There they go again; what jolly fun!" and he laughed outright as the goats bounded swiftly to the other side of the yard. Just then Mrs. Lincoln called out, "Come, Lizabeth; if I get ready to go down this evening I must finish dressing myself, or you must stop staring at those silly goats."

Mrs. Lincoln was not fond of pets, and she could not understand how Mr. Lincoln could take so much delight in his goats. After Willie's death, she could not bear the sight of anything he loved, not even a flower. Costly bouquets were presented to her, but she turned from them with a shudder, and either placed them in a room where she could not see them, or threw them out of the window. She gave all of Willie's toys—everything connected with him—away, as she said she could not look upon them without thinking of her poor dead boy, and to think of him, in his white shroud and cold grave, was maddening. I never in my life saw a more peculiarly constituted woman. Search the world over, and you will not find her counterpart. After Mr. Lincoln's death, the goats that he loved so well were given away—I believe to Mrs. Lee, *née* Miss Blair, one of the few ladies with whom Mrs. Lincoln was on intimate terms in Washington.

During my residence in the Capital I made my home with Mr. and Mrs. Walker Lewis, people of my own race, and friends in the truest sense of the word.

The days passed without any incident of particular note disturbing the current of life. On Friday morning, April 14th—alas! what American does not remember the day—I saw Mrs. Lincoln but for a moment. She told me that she was to attend the theatre that night with the President, but I was not summoned to assist her in making her toilette. Sherman had swept from the northern border of Georgia through the heart of the Confederacy down to the sea, striking the death-blow to the rebellion. Grant had pursued General Lee beyond Richmond, and the army of Virginia, that had made such stubborn resistance, was crumbling to pieces. Fort Sumter had fallen;—the stronghold first wrenched from the Union, and which had braved the fury of Federal guns for so many years, was restored to the Union; the end of the war was near at hand, and the great pulse of the loyal North thrilled with joy. The dark war-cloud was fading, and a white-robed angel seemed to hover in the sky, whispering "Peace—peace on earth, good-will toward men!" Sons, brothers, fathers, friends, sweethearts were coming home. Soon the white tents would be folded, the volunteer army be disbanded, and tranquillity again reign. Happy, happy day!—happy at least to those who fought under the banner of the Union. There was great rejoicing throughout the North. From the Atlantic to the Pacific, flags were gayly thrown to the breeze, and at night every city blazed with its tens of thousand lights. But scarcely had the fireworks ceased to play, and the lights been taken down from the windows, when the lightning flashed the most appalling news over the magnetic wires. "The President has been murdered!" spoke the swift-winged messenger, and the loud huzza died upon the lips. A nation suddenly paused in the midst of festivity, and stood paralyzed with horror—transfixed with awe.

Oh, memorable day! Oh, memorable night! Never before was joy so violently contrasted with sorrow.

At 11 o'clock at night I was awakened by an old friend and neighbor, Miss M. Brown, with the startling intelligence that the entire Cabinet had been assassinated, and Mr. Lincoln shot, but not mortally wounded. When I heard the words I felt as if the blood had been frozen in my veins, and that my lungs must collapse for the want of air. Mr. Lincoln shot! the Cabinet assassinated! What could it mean? The streets were alive with wondering, awe-stricken people. Rumors flew thick and fast, and the wildest reports came with every new arrival. The words were repeated with blanched cheeks and quivering lips. I waked Mr. and Mrs. Lewis, and told them that the President was shot, and that I must go to the White House. I could not remain in a state of uncertainty. I felt that the house would not hold me. They tried to quiet me, but gentle words could not calm the wild tempest. They quickly dressed themselves, and we sallied out into the street to drift with the excited throng. We walked rapidly towards the White House, and on our way passed the residence of Secretary Seward, which was surrounded by armed soldiers, keeping back all intruders with the point of the bayonet. We hurried on, and as we approached the White House, saw that it too was surrounded with soldiers. Every entrance was strongly guarded, and no one was permitted to pass. The guard at the gate told us that Mr. Lincoln had not been brought home, but refused to give any other information. More excited than ever, we wandered down the street. Grief and anxiety were making me weak, and as we joined the outskirts of a large crowd, I began to feel as meek and humble as a penitent child. A gray-haired old man was passing. I caught a glimpse of his face, and it seemed so full of kindness and sorrow that I gently touched his arm, and imploringly asked:

"Will you please, sir, to tell me whether Mr. Lincoln is dead or not?"

"Not dead," he replied, "but dying. God help us!" and with a heavy step he passed on.

"Not dead, but dying! then indeed God help us!"

We learned that the President was mortally wounded—that he had been shot down in his box at the theatre, and that he was not expected to live till morning; when we returned home with heavy hearts. I could not sleep. I wanted to go to Mrs. Lincoln, as I pictured her wild with grief; but then I did not know where to find her, and I must wait till morning. Never did the hours drag so slowly. Every moment seemed an age, and I could do nothing but walk about and hold my arms in mental agony.

Morning came at last, and a sad morning was it. The flags that floated so gayly yesterday now were draped in black, and hung in silent folds at half-mast. The President was dead, and a nation was mourning for him. Every house was draped in black, and every face wore a solemn look. People spoke in subdued tones, and glided whisperingly, wonderingly, silently about the streets.

About eleven o'clock on Saturday morning a carriage drove up to the door, and a messenger asked for "Elizabeth Keckley."

"Who wants her?" I asked.

"I come from Mrs. Lincoln. If you are Mrs. Keckley, come with me immediately to the White House."

I hastily put on my shawl and bonnet, and was driven at a rapid rate to the White House. Everything about the building was sad and solemn. I was quickly shown to Mrs. Lincoln's room, and on entering, saw Mrs. L. tossing uneasily about upon a bed. The room was darkened, and the only person in it besides the widow of the President was Mrs. Secretary Welles, who had spent the night with her. Bowing to Mrs. Welles, I went to the bedside.

"Why did you not come to me last night, Elizabeth—I sent for you?" Mrs. Lincoln asked in a low whisper.

"I did try to come to you, but I could not find you," I answered, as I laid my hand upon her hot brow.

I afterwards learned, that when she had partially recovered from the first shock of the terrible tragedy in the theatre, Mrs. Welles asked:

"Is there no one, Mrs. Lincoln, that you desire to have with you in this terrible affliction?"

"Yes, send for Elizabeth Keckley. I want her just as soon as she can be brought here."

Three messengers, it appears, were successively despatched for me, but all of them mistook the number and failed to find me.

Shortly after entering the room on Saturday morning, Mrs. Welles excused herself, as she said she must go to her own family, and I was left alone with Mrs. Lincoln.

She was nearly exhausted with grief, and when she became a little quiet, I asked and received permission to go into the Guests' Room, where the body of the President lay in state.

When I crossed the threshold of the room, I could not help recalling the day on which I had seen little Willie lying in his coffin where the body of his father now lay. I remembered how the President had wept over the pale beautiful face of his gifted boy, and now the President himself was dead. The last time I saw him he spoke kindly to me, but alas! the lips would never move again. The light had faded from his eyes, and when the light went out the soul went with it. What a noble soul was his—noble in all the noble attributes of God! Never did I enter the solemn chamber of death with such palpitating heart and trembling footsteps as I entered it that day. No common mortal had died. The Moses of my people had fallen in the hour of his triumph. Fame had woven her choicest chaplet for his brow. Though the brow was cold and pale in death, the chaplet should not fade, for God had studded it with the glory of the eternal stars.

When I entered the room, the members of the Cabinet and many distinguished officers of the army were grouped around the body of their fallen chief. They made room for me, and, approaching the body, I lifted the white cloth from the white face of the man that I had worshipped as an idol—looked upon as a demi-god. Notwithstanding the violence of the death of the President, there was something beautiful as well as grandly solemn in the expression of the placid face. There lurked the sweetness and gentleness of childhood, and the stately grandeur of god-like intellect. I gazed long at the face, and turned away with tears in my eyes and a choking sensation in my throat. Ah! never was man so widely mourned before. The whole world bowed their heads in grief when Abraham Lincoln died.

Returning to Mrs. Lincoln's room, I found her in a new paroxysm of grief. Robert was bending over his mother with tender affection, and little Tad was crouched at the foot of the bed with a world of agony in his young face. I shall never forget the scene—the wails of a broken heart, the unearthly shrieks, the terrible convulsions, the wild, tempestuous outbursts of grief from the soul. I bathed Mrs. Lincoln's head with cold water, and soothed the terrible tornado as best I could. Tad's grief at his father's death was as great as the grief of his mother, but her terrible outbursts awed the boy into silence.

Sometimes he would throw his arms around her neck, and exclaim, between his broken sobs, "Don't cry so, Mamma! don't cry, or you will make me cry, too! You will break my heart."

Mrs. Lincoln could not bear to hear Tad cry, and when he would plead to her not to break his heart, she would calm herself with a great effort, and clasp her child in her arms.

Every room in the White House was darkened, and every one spoke in subdued tones, and moved about with muffled tread. The very atmosphere breathed of the great sorrow which weighed heavily upon each heart. Mrs. Lincoln never left her room, and while the body of her husband was being borne in solemn state from the Atlantic to the broad prairies of the West, she was weeping with her fatherless children in her private chamber. She denied admittance to almost every one, and I was her only companion, except her children, in the days of her great sorrow.

"A FEARFUL, GIGANTIC CRIME": NEW YORK, APRIL 1865

George Templeton Strong: Diary, April 15, 1865

After the fall of Richmond, John Wilkes Booth abandoned his plan to abduct Lincoln and resolved instead to simultaneously assassinate the president, vice president, and secretary of state. On the night of April 14, Good Friday, as Lincoln watched *Our American Cousin* in Ford's Theatre, Booth shot him in the head, then jumped down onto the stage, shouted "Sic semper tyrannis," and escaped. At the same time Booth's fellow conspirator Lewis Powell, a former Confederate soldier, used a ruse to enter the house of Secretary of State William H. Seward, who was recovering from a serious carriage accident on April 5. Powell severely beat Seward's son Frederick with a revolver that broke apart, then used a bowie knife to slash Seward, his son Augustus, a male army nurse, and a state department messenger before fleeing. Seward's life was saved by a heavy neck brace that protected him when Powell tried to cut his throat. The plot to assassinate Vice President Andrew Johnson at his hotel failed when George Atzerodt, another conspirator, lost his nerve and fled. George Templeton Strong recorded the reaction in New York to the attacks in Washington.

April 15, SATURDAY. Nine o'clock in the morning. *LINCOLN AND SEWARD ASSASSINATED LAST NIGHT! ! ! !*

The South has nearly filled up the measure of her iniquities at last! Lincoln's death not yet certainly announced, but the one o'clock despatch states that he was then dying. Seward's side room was entered by the same or another assassin, and his throat cut. It is unlikely he will survive, for he was suffering from a broken arm and other injuries, the consequence of a fall, and is advanced in life. Ellie brought this news two hours ago, but I can hardly *take it in* even yet. *Eheu* A. Lincoln!

I have been expecting this. I predicted an attempt would be made on Lincoln's life when he went into Richmond; but just now, after his generous dealings with Lee, I should have said the danger was past. But the ferocious malignity of Southerners is infinite and inexhaustible. I am stunned, as by a fearful personal calamity, though I can see that this thing, occurring just at this time, may be overruled to our great good. Poor Ellie is heartbroken, though never an admirer of Lincoln's. We shall appreciate him at last.

Up with the Black Flag now!

Ten P.M. What a day it has been! Excitement and suspension of business even more general than on the 3rd instant. Tone of feeling very like that of four years ago when the news came of Sumter. This atrocity has invigorated national feeling in the same way, almost in the same degree. People who pitied our misguided brethren yesterday, and thought they had been punished enough already, and hoped there would be a general amnesty, including J. Davis himself, talk approvingly today of vindictive justice and favor the introduction of judges, juries, gaolers, and hangmen among the dramatis personae. Above all, there is a profound, awe-stricken feeling that we are, as it were, in immediate presence of a fearful, gigantic crime, such as has not been committed in our day and can hardly be matched in history.

Faulkner, one of our Kenzua directors, called for me by appointment at half-past nine, and we drove to the foot of Jane Street to inspect apparatus for the reduction of gold ore by amalgamation, which he considers a great improvement on the machinery generally used for that purpose. Returned uptown and saw Bellows to advise about adjournment of our Sanitary Commission meeting next week. Thence to Wall Street. Immense crowd. Bulletins and extras following each other in quick, contradictory succession. Seward and his Fred had died and had not. Booth (one of the assassins, a Marylander, brother of Edwin Booth) had been taken and had not. So it has gone on all day. Tonight the case stands thus:

Abraham Lincoln died at twenty-two minutes after seven this morning. He never regained consciousness after the pistol ball fired at him from behind, over his wife's shoulder, entered his brain. Seward is living and may recover. The gentleman assigned to the duty of murdering him did his butchery badly. The throat is severely lacerated by his knife, but it's believed that no arteries are injured. Fred Seward's situation is less hopeful, his skull being fractured by a bludgeon or sling shot used by the same gentleman. The attendant who was stabbed, is dead. (Is not.)

The temper of the great meeting I found assembled in front of the Custom House (the old Exchange) was grim. A Southerner would compare it with that of the first session of the Jacobins after Marat's death. I thought it healthy and virile. It was the first great patriotic meeting since the war began at which there was no talk of concession and conciliation. It would have endured no such talk. Its sentiment seemed like this: "Now it is plain at last to everybody that there can be no terms with the woman-flogging aristocracy. Grant's generous dealing with Lee was a blunder. The *Tribune's* talk for the last fortnight was folly. Let us henceforth deal with rebels as they deserve. The rose-water treatment does not meet their case." I have heard it said fifty times today: "These madmen have murdered the two best friends they had in the world!" I heard of three or four men in Wall Street and near the Post Office who spoke lightly of the tragedy, and were instantly set upon by the bystanders and pummelled. One of them narrowly escaped death. It was Charles E. Anderson, brother of our friend Professor Henry James Anderson, father of pretty Miss Louisa. Moses H. Grinnell and the police had hard work to save him. I never supposed him a secessionist.

To Trinity Church vestry meeting, specially called, at half-past three at the rebuilt vestry office, corner Fulton and Church. A series of resolutions was read, drawn by the Rector. They were masculine and good, and they were passed *nem. con.*, though Verplanck and Tillou were in their seats—Copperheads both. I looked at the record of our action when Washington died sixty-six years ago. It was a mere resolution that the church and chapels be put in mourning. Our resolutions of today went, naturally, much further. I record to the credit of Gouverneur Ogden, whom I have always held cold-hearted and selfish, that he broke down in trying to read these resolutions, could not get beyond the first sentence, and had to hand them back to the Rector. There was a little diversity of opinion whether we should put our chancel into mourning tomorrow, being Easter Sunday, or postpone it a day longer. We left it to the Rector's discretion. No business was done today. Most shops are closed and draped with black and white muslin. Broadway is clad in "weepers" from Wall Street to Union Square. At 823 with Agnew, Bellows, and Gibbs. George Anthon dined here; with him to Union League Club. Special meeting and dense, asphyxiating crowd. Orations by George Bancroft and by the Rev. (Presbyterian) Thompson of the Tabernacle. Both good; Thompson's very good. "When A. Johnson was sworn in as President today," said the Rev. Thompson, "the Statue of Liberty that surmounts the dome of the Capitol and was put there by Lincoln, looked down on the city and on the nation and said, 'Our Government is unchanged—it has merely passed from the hands of one man into those of another. Let the dead bury their dead. Follow thou Me.'" Burnside tells me this morning that he ranks Johnson very high.

Jeff Davis has at last issued a manifesto. It is from Danville, before Lee's surrender and is full of fight.

THE PRESIDENT'S DEATHBED: WASHINGTON, D.C., APRIL 1865

Gideon Welles: Diary, April 18, 1865

By 1865 Seward and Gideon Welles were the only members of Lincoln's original cabinet still serving in the administration. Sometimes called "Father Neptune" by Lincoln, Welles had successfully presided over the wartime expansion and modernization of the U.S. Navy. He recorded his recollections of the assassination and its immediate aftermath on April 18, the day before funeral services were held for the President in the White House. John Wilkes Booth would be fatally wounded by Union troops near Port Royal, Virginia, on April 26. Eight defendants were convicted by a military commission for conspiring with Booth, and four of them—Lewis Powell, George Atzerodt, David Herold, and Mary Surratt—were hanged on July 7, 1865. Although the prosecution alleged that Jefferson Davis and several Confederate agents in Canada had conspired in the assassination, they presented no evidence beyond the testimony of three unreliable witnesses. While Booth may have told Confederate agents about his plan to abduct Lincoln, most historians believe he was the sole instigator of the assassination plot.

I had retired to bed about half-past ten on the evening of the 14th of April, and was just getting asleep when my wife said some one was at our door. Sitting up in bed I heard some one twice call to John, my son whose sleeping room was directly over the front. I arose at once and raised a window, when my messenger James called to me that Mr. Lincoln the President had been shot, and that Secretary Seward and his son, Assistant Secretary Frederick Seward, were assassinated. James was much alarmed and excited. I told him his story was very incoherent and improbable, that he was associating men who were not together and liable to attack at the same time. Where, I inquired, was the President when shot? James said he was at Ford's Theatre on 10th Street. Well, said I Secretary Seward is an invalid in bed in his house on 15th Street. James said he had been there, stopped in at the house to make inquiry before alarming me.

I immediately dressed myself, and against the earnest remonstrance and appeals of my wife went directly to Mr. Seward's. James accompanied me. As we were crossing 15th Street, I saw four or five men in earnest consultation under the lamp on the corner by St. John's Church. Before I had got half across the street, the lamp was suddenly extinguished and the knot of persons rapidly dispersed. For a moment and but a moment I was disconcerted to find myself in darkness but recollecting that it was late and about time for the moon to rise, I proceeded on, not having lost five steps, merely making a pause without stopping. Hurrying forward into 15th Street I found it pretty full of people especially near the residence of Secretary Seward, where there were many soldiers as well as citizens already gathered.

Entering the house I found the lower hall and office full of persons, and among them most of the foreign legations, all anxiously inquiring what truth there was in the horrible rumors afloat. I replied that my object in calling was to ascertain the facts. Proceeding through the hall to the stairs, I found one, and I think two of the servants there checking the crowd. They were frightened and appeared relieved to see me. I hastily asked what truth there was in the story that an assassin or assassins had entered the house and assaulted the Secretary. I was assured that it was true, and that Mr. Frederick was also badly injured. They wished me to go up, but no others. At the head of the first stairs I met the elder Mrs. Seward or her sister I think who desired me to proceed up. On reaching the third story I met Mrs. Frederick Seward who, although evidently distressed, was, under the circumstances exceedingly composed. I inquired for the Secretary's room which she pointed out—the southwest room. As I entered, I met Miss Fanny Seward with whom I exchanged a single word, and proceeded to the foot of the bed. Dr. Verdi and I think two others were there. The bed was saturated with blood. The Secretary was lying on his back, the upper part of his head covered by a cloth, which extended down over his eyes. His mouth was open, the lower jaw dropping down. I exchanged a few whispered words with Dr. V. Secretary Stanton who came almost simultaneously with me spoke in a louder tone. We almost immediately withdrew and went into the adjoining front room, where lay Frederick Seward on his right side. His eyes were open but he did not move them, nor a limb, nor did he speak. Doctor White told me he was unconscious and more dangerously injured than his father.

As we descended the stairs, I asked Stanton what he had heard in regard to the President that was reliable. He said the President was shot at Ford's Theatre, that he had seen a man who was present and witnessed the occurrence. I remarked that I would go immediately to the White House. Stanton told me the President was not there but was down at the theatre. Then, said I let us go immediately there. He said that was his intention, and asked me, if I had not a carriage, to go with him.

In the lower hall we met General Meigs, whom he requested to take charge of the house, and to clear out all who did not belong there. General Meigs requested Stanton not to go down to 10th Street, others remonstrated against his going. Stanton I thought hesitated. I remarked that I should go immediately, and I thought it his duty also. He said he should certainly go, but the remonstrants increased and gathered round him. I remarked that we were wasting time, and pressing through the crowd entered the carriage and urged Stanton, who was detained after he had placed his foot on the step. I was impatient. Stanton, as soon as he had seated himself, said the carriage was not his. I said that was no objection. He invited Meigs to go with us, and Judge Cartter of the Supreme Court mounted with the driver. At this moment Major Eckert rode up on horseback and protested vehemently against Stanton's going to 10th Street—said he had just come from there, that there were thousands of people of all sorts there and he considered it very unsafe for the Secretary of War to expose himself. I replied that I knew not where he would be safe, and the duty of both of us was to attend the President immediately. Stanton concurred. Meigs called to some soldiers to go with us, and there was one on each side of the carriage. The streets were full of people. Not only the sidewalk but the carriage-way was to some extent occupied, all or nearly all hurrying towards 10th Street. When we entered that street we found it pretty closely packed.

The President had been carried across the street from the

theatre, to the house of a Mr. Peterson. We entered by ascending a flight of steps above the basement and passing through a long hall to the rear the President lay extended on a bed breathing heavily. Several surgeons were present, at least six, I should think more. Among them I was glad to observe Dr. Hall, who, however soon left. I inquired of one of the Surgeons Dr. H., I think, the true condition of the President and was told he was dead to all intents, although he might live three hours or perhaps longer.

The giant sufferer lay extended diagonally across the bed which was not long enough for him. He had been stripped of his clothes. His large arms, which were occasionally exposed were of a size which one would scarce have expected from his spare appearance. His slow, full respiration lifted the clothes. His features were calm and striking. I had never seen them appear to better advantage than for the first hour, perhaps, that I was there. After that his right eye began to swell and became discolored.

Senator Sumner was there, I think, when I entered. If not he came in soon after, as did Speaker Colfax, Mr. Secretary McCulloch and the other members of the Cabinet, with the exception of Mr. Seward. A double guard was stationed at the door and on the sidewalk, to repress the crowd which was excited and anxious.

The room was small and overcrowded. The surgeons and members of the Cabinet were as many as should have been in the room, but there were many more, and the hall and other rooms in the front or main house were full. One of them was occupied by Mrs. Lincoln and her attendants. Mrs. Dixon and Mrs. Kinney came about twelve o'clock. About once an hour Mrs. Lincoln would repair to the bedside of her dying husband and remain until overcome by her emotion.

A door which opened upon a porch or gallery, and the windows were kept open for fresh air. The night was dark, cloudy and damp, and about six it began to rain. I remained until then without sitting or leaving, when, there being a vacant chair at the foot of the bed, I occupied for nearly two hours, listening to the heavy groans, and witnessing the wasting life of the good and great man who was expiring before me.

About 6 A.M. a fainting sickness came over me and for the

first time since entering the room, a little past eleven, I left it and the house, and took a short walk in the open air. It was a dark and gloomy morning, and rain set in before I returned to the house, some fifteen minutes. Large groups of people were gathered every few rods, all anxious and solicitous. Some one stepped forward as I passed, to inquire into the condition of the President, and to ask if there was no hope. Intense grief exhibited itself on every countenance when I replied that the President could survive but a short time. The colored people especially—and there were at this time more of them perhaps than of whites—were painfully affected.

Returning to the house, I seated myself in the back parlor where the Attorney-General and others had been engaged in taking evidence concerning the assassination. Stanton, and Speed, and Usher were there, the latter asleep on the bed—there were three or four others also in the room. While I did not feel inclined to sleep as did many, I was somewhat indisposed and had been for several days—the excitement and atmosphere from the crowded rooms oppressed me physically.

A little before seven, I went into the room where the dying President was rapidly drawing near the closing moments. His wife soon after made her last visit to him. The death struggle had begun. Robert, his son stood at the head of the bed and bore himself well, but on two occasions gave way to overpowering grief and sobbed aloud, turning his head and leaning on the shoulder of Senator Sumner. The respiration became suspended at intervals, and at length entirely ceased at twenty-two minutes past seven.

A prayer followed from Dr. Gurley; and the Cabinet, with the exception of Mr. Seward and Mr. McCulloch immediately thereafter assembled in the back parlor, from which all other persons were excluded, and signed a letter which had been prepared by Attorney-General Speed to the Vice President, informing him of the event, and that the government devolved upon him.

Mr. Stanton proposed that Mr. Speed, as the law officer, should communicate the letter to Mr. Johnson with some other member of the Cabinet. Mr. Dennison named me. I saw that it disconcerted Stanton, who had expected and intended to be the man and to have Speed associated with him. As I was disinclined personally to any effort for myself I therefore named Mr. McCulloch as the first in order after the Secretary of State.

I arranged with Speed with whom I rode home for a Cabinet meeting at twelve meridian at the room of the Secretary of the Treasury, in order that the government should experience no detriment, and that prompt and necessary action might be taken to assist the new Chief Magistrate in promoting the public tranquillity. We accordingly met at noon. Mr. Speed reported that the President had taken the oath which was administered by the Chief Justice, and had expressed a desire that affairs should proceed without interruption. Some discussion took place as to the propriety of an inaugural address, but the general impression was that it would be inexpedient. I was most decidedly of that opinion.

President Johnson, who was invited to be present, deported himself with gentlemanly and dignified courtesy, and on the subject of an inaugural was of the opinion that his acts would best disclose his policy. In all essentials it would be the same as that of the late President. He desired the members of the Cabinet to go forward with their duties without any interruption. Mr. Hunter, Chief Clerk of the State Department was designated to act *ad interim* as Secretary of State. I suggested Mr. Speed, but I saw it was not acceptable in certain quarters. Stanton especially expressed a hope that Hunter should be assigned.

A room for the President as an office was proposed, and Mr. McCulloch offered the adjoining room. I named the State Department as appropriate and proper until there was a Secretary of State, or so long as the President wished, but objections arose at once. The papers of Mr. Seward would be disturbed—it would be better here, etc., etc. Stanton I saw had a purpose.

On returning to my house the morning of Saturday, I found Mrs. Welles who had been confined to the house from indisposition for a week had been twice sent for by Mrs. Lincoln and had yielded, and imprudently gone, although the weather was inclement. She remained at the Executive Mansion through the day.

For myself, wearied, shocked, exhausted but not inclined to sleep, the day passed off strangely.

On Sunday the 16th the President and Cabinet met by agreement at 10 A.M. at the Treasury. The President was half an hour behind time. Stanton was more than an hour later and brought with him papers, and had many suggestions relative to our measures before the Cabinet at our last meeting with President Lincoln. The general policy of the treating the Rebels and the Rebel States was fully discussed. President Johnson is not disposed to treat treason lightly, and the chief Rebels he would punish with exemplary severity.

Stanton has divided his original plan and made the reestablishing of State government applicable to North Carolina, leaving Virginia which has a loyal government and governor, to arrange that matter of election to which I had excepted, but elaborating it for North Carolina and the other States.

Being at the War Department Sunday evening, I was detained conversing with [ ] and finally Senator Sumner came in. He was soon followed by Gooch and Dawes of Massachusetts and some two or three other general officers also came in. Stanton took from his table in answer to an inquiry from some one, his document which had been submitted to the Cabinet and which was still a Cabinet measure.

It was evident the gentlemen were there by appointment and that I came as an intruder. Stanton did not know how to get rid of me and supposed I was there by arrangement; I felt embarrassed and was very glad after he had read to them his first programme for Virginia, and had got about half through with the other, when a line was brought me at this time by the messenger, giving me an opportunity to leave.

On Monday the 17th I was actively engaged in bringing forward business issuing orders, and arranging for the funeral solemnities of President Lincoln. Secretary Seward and his son continue in a low condition, and Mr. Fred Seward's life is precarious.

Tuesday, 18. Details in regard to the funeral, which takes place on the 19th, occupied general attention and little else was done at the Cabinet meeting. From every part of the country comes lamentation. Every house, almost, has some drapery, especially the homes of the poor. Profuse exhibition is displayed on the public buildings and the houses of the wealthy, but the little black ribbon or strip of black cloth from the hovel of the poor negro or the impoverished white is more touching.

I have tried to write something consecutively since the horrid transactions of Friday night, but I have no heart for it, and the jottings down are mere mementos of a period, which I will try to fill up when more composed, and I have some leisure or time for the task.

Sad and painful, wearied and irksome, the few preceding incoherent pages have been written for future use, for they are fresh in my mind and may pass away with me but cannot ever be forgotten by me.

A POLITICAL AGREEMENT: NORTH CAROLINA, APRIL 1865

William T. Sherman to Ulysses S. Grant or Henry W. Halleck

After fighting an inconclusive battle with Joseph E. Johnston at Bentonville, North Carolina, on March 19–21, Sherman had reached Goldsboro on March 23, establishing a supply line to the coast and joining up with Union forces under John M. Schofield. His army remained at Goldsboro for nearly three weeks, resting and resupplying, while Johnston held Smithfield twenty-five miles to the northwest. Sherman resumed the offensive on April 10, advancing toward Raleigh with 89,000 men while Johnston withdrew with about 20,000 troops toward Greensboro. By the time Union forces occupied Raleigh on April 13, both commanders had learned of Lee's surrender at Appomattox. Convinced that continued fighting would be futile, Johnston wrote to Sherman proposing a cease-fire and the opening of peace negotiations. The two commanders met near Durham Station on April 17, shortly after Sherman learned of Lincoln's assassination. Although Sherman had telegraphed Grant that he would offer Johnston the same terms given to Lee and "be careful not to complicate any points of civil policy," he changed his position once the talks began. Concerned about the prospect of prolonged guerrilla warfare, Sherman offered political concessions in return for the surrender of all the remaining Confederate armies. On April 18 the opposing commanders signed their "basis of agreement," which Sherman sent to Washington by courier along with an accompanying letter.

Headquarters, Military Division
of the Mississippi,
In the Field, Raleigh N.C.,
April 18, 1865.

Lt. Genl. U. S. Grant, or Maj. Gen. Halleck,
Washington D.C.
General,

I enclose herewith a copy of an agreement made this day between Gen. Joseph E. Johnston and myself which if approved by the President of the United States will produce Peace from the Potomac and the Rio Grande. Mr. Breckinridge was present at our conference in his capacity as Major General, and satisfied me of the ability of General Johnston to carry out to the full extent the terms of this agreement, and if you will get the President to simply endorse the copy, and commission me to carry out the terms I will follow them to the conclusion.

You will observe that it is an absolute submission of the Enemy to the lawful authority of the United States, and disperses his armies absolutely, and the point to which I attach most importance is that the dispersion and disbandment of these armies is done in Such a manner as to prevent their breaking up into Guerilla Bands. On the other hand we can retain just as much of an army as we please. I agreed to the mode and manner of the surrender of arms set forth, as it gives the States the means of repressing Guerrillas which we could not expect them to do if we stript them of all arms.

Both Generals Johnston & Breckinridge admitted that Slavery was dead and I could not insist on embracing it in such a paper, because it can be made with the states in detail. I know that all the men of substance south sincerely want Peace and I do not believe they will resort to war again during this century. I have no doubt that they will in the future be perfectly subordinate to the Laws of the United States.

The moment my action in this matter is approved, I can spare five Corps and will ask for orders to leave Gen. Schofield here with the 10th Corps and to march myself with the 14, 15, 17, 20 and 23d Corps, via Banksville, and Gordonsville to Frederick or Hagerstown there to be paid and mustered out. The question of Finance is now the chief one and every soldier & officer not needed should be got home at work. I would like to be able to begin the march north by May 1. I urge on the part of the President speedy action as it is important to get the Confederate Armies to their homes as well as our own. I am with great respect yr. obt. Servant

William T. Sherman
Maj. Gen. Comdg.
(Copy)

Memorandum or basis of agreement, made this 18th day of April, A.D. 1865, near Durham's Station in the State of

North Carolina, by and between General Joseph E. Johnston, commanding the Confederate army, and Major General William T. Sherman, commanding the Army of the United States in North Carolina, both present:

First: The contending armies now in the field to maintain the "*status quo*," until notice is given by the commanding General of any one to its opponent, and reasonable time, say forty-eight hours, allowed.

Second: The Confederate armies now in existence to be disbanded and conducted to their several State capitals, then to deposit their arms and public property in the State Arsenal: and each officer and man to execute and file an agreement to cease from acts of war, and to abide the action of both State and Federal authority. The number of arms and munitions of war to be reported to the Chief of Ordnance at Washington City, subject to the future action of the Congress of the United States, and in the meantime to be used solely to maintain peace and order within the borders of the States respectively.

Third: The recognition by the Executive of the United States of the several State Governments, on their officers and Legislatures taking the oaths prescribed by the Constitution of the United States: and where conflicting State Governments have resulted from the war, the legitimacy of all shall be submitted to the Supreme Court of the United States.

Fourth: The re-establishment of all the Federal Courts in the several States, with powers as defined by the Constitution and laws of Congress.

Fifth: The people and inhabitants of all the States to be guaranteed, so far as the Executive can, their political rights and franchises, as well as their rights of person and property as defined by the Constitution of the United States and of the States respectively.

Sixth: The Executive authority of the Government of the United States not to disturb any of the people by reason of the late war, so long as they live in peace and quiet, abstain from acts of armed hostility, and obey the laws in existence at the place of their residence.

Seventh: In general terms, the war to cease: a general

amnesty so far as the Executive of the United States can command, on condition of the disbandment of the Confederate armies, the distribution of the arms, and the resumption of peaceful pursuits by the officers and men hitherto composing said armies.

Not being fully empowered by our respective principals to fulfil these terms, we individually and officially pledge ourselves to promptly obtain the necessary authority and to carry out the above programme.

(signed) W. T. Sherman	(signed) J. E. Johnston
Maj. Genl. Com'd'g	General Comg.
Army U.S. in N.C.	C.S. Army in N.C.

compared with the original in my possession and hereby certified.

W. T. Sherman
Maj. Gen. Comdg.

"IT IS ALL MURDER": LOUISIANA, APRIL 1865

Sarah Morgan: Diary, April 19, 1865

Reactions to Lincoln's assassination varied widely among white Southerners. Sherman wrote that when Joseph E. Johnston learned of the President's death during their meeting on April 17, he "admitted that the act was calculated to stain his cause with a dark hue, and he contended that the loss was most serious to the People of the South, who had begun to realize that Mr. Lincoln was the best friend the South had." Amid the ruins of Columbia, South Carolina, Emma LeConte responded differently, writing on April 21: "Hurrah! Old Abe Lincoln has been assassinated! It may be abstractly wrong to be so jubilant, but I just can't help it. After all the heaviness and gloom of yesterday this blow to our enemies comes like a gleam of light. We have suffered till we feel savage. There seems no reason to exult, for this will make no change in our position—will only infuriate them against us. Never mind, our hated enemy has met the just reward of his life." The daughter of a prominent Baton Rouge lawyer, Sarah Morgan had reluctantly moved with her sister and widowed mother to Union-occupied New Orleans in April 1863. Two of her brothers had died in January 1864, one while serving with Lee's army in Virginia and the other in a Union prison camp in Ohio.

April 19th. 1865. No. 211. Camp St.

"All things are taken from us, and become portions and parcels of the dreadful past."

My life change, changes. I let it change as God will, feeling he doeth all things well. Sister has gone to Germany with Charlotte, Nellie, and Lavinia to place them at school, probably at Brussels. Mother and I have taken her place with the five remaining children. I am nominally housekeeper; that is to say I keep the keys in my pocket, and my eyes on the children, and sit at the head of the table. But I dont order dinner, for which I am thankful; for I would not be able to name a single article, if my reputation depended on the test. Of course I have a general idea that soup, roast, baked and boiled meats are eaten, but whether all the same day, or which to be chosen, I could not decide, nor as to the kind of animal or fish. So the cook does that, though I am trying to observe every day what he provides, in order to perfect myself in the mystery.

In five days, I have twice been heart-broken about making Brother's coffee too strong. He will not complain, and I would still be ignorant of the error if I had not accidently observed the untouched cup after he left the table, and discovering the mistake by tasting punished myself by drinking every drop of the bitter draught. Mem. To-morrow if I fail, drink it until I learn the exact proportion.

Thursday the 13th, came the dreadful tidings of the surrender of Lee and his army on the 9th. Every body cried, but I would not, satisfied that God will still save us, even though all should apparently be lost. Followed at intervals of two or three hours by the announcement of the capture of Richmond, Selma, Mobile, and Johnson's army, even the staunchest Southerners were hopeless. Every one proclaimed Peace, and the only matter under consideration was whether Jeff. Davis, all politicians, every man above the rank of Captain in the army, and above that of Lieutenant in the navy, should be hanged immediately, or *some* graciously pardoned. Henry Ward Beecher humanely pleaded mercy for us, supported by a small minority. Davis and all leading men *must* be executed; the blood of the others would serve to irrigate the country. Under this lively prospect, Peace! blessed Peace! was the cry. I whispered "Never! let a great earthquake swallow us up first! Let us leave our land and emigrate to any desert spot of the earth, rather than return to the Union, even as it Was!"

Six days this has lasted. Blessed with the silently obstinate disposition, I would not dispute, but felt my heart swell repeating "God is our refuge and our strength, a very present help in time of trouble," and could not for an instant believe this could end in our overthrow.

This morning when I went down to breakfast at seven, Brother read the announcement of the assassination of Lincoln and Secretary Seward. "Vengence is mine; I will repay, saith the Lord." This is murder! God have mercy on those who did it! A while ago, Lincoln's chief occupation was thinking what death, thousands who ruled like lords when he was cutting logs, should die. A moment more, and the man who was progressing to murder countless human beings, is interrupted in his work by the shot of an assassin. Do I justify this murder? No! I shudder with horror, wonder, pity and fear, and then feeling that it is the salvation of all I love that has been purchased by this man's crime, I long to thank God for those spared, and shudder to think that that is rejoicing against our enemy, being grateful for a fellow-creature's death. I am not! Seward was ill—dying—helpless. This was dastard murder. His throat was cut in bed. Horrible!

Charlotte Corday killed Marat in his bath, and is held up in history as one of Liberty's martyrs, and one of the heroines of her country. To me, it is all Murder. Let historians extol blood shedding; it is woman's place to abhor it. And because I know that they would have apotheosized any man who had crucified Jeff Davis, I abhor this, and call it foul murder, unworthy of our cause—and God grant it was only the temporary insanity of a desperate man that committed this crime! Let not his blood be visited on our nation, Lord!

Across the way, a large building undoubtedly inhabited by officers is being draped in black. Immense streamers of black and white hang from the balcony. Down town, I understand all shops are closed, and all wrapped in mourning. And I hardly dare pray God to bless us, with the crape hanging over the way. It would have been banners, if our president had been killed, though! Now the struggle will be desperate, awful, short. Spare Jimmy, dear Lord! Have mercy on us as a people!

And yet what was the song of Deborah, when she hammered a nail in the head of the sleeping Sisera? Was she not extolled for the treacherous deed? What was Miriam's song over the drowning Egyptian? "Our enemies are fallen, fallen!" Was not Judith immortalized for delivering her people from the hands of a tyrant? "Pour le salut de ma patree—!"

Where does patriotism end, and murder begin? And considering that every one is closely watched, and that five men have been killed this day for expressing their indifference on the death of Mr Lincoln, it would be best to postpone this discussion.

Robert E. Lee to Jefferson Davis

Ten days after attributing the surrender of his army to "overwhelming numbers and resources" in General Orders No. 9 (pp. 673–74 in this volume), Lee offered a different explanation for his defeat in a letter to Jefferson Davis. Writing to the Confederate president, now in Charlotte, North Carolina, Lee reflected on the "moral condition" of his troops while arguing against a resort to partisan warfare. In a memoir drafted in 1897–99, Edward Porter Alexander, the longtime artillery commander in Longstreet's corps, recounted a conversation he had with Lee at Appomattox on the morning of April 9, 1865. Alexander recalled urging Lee to order his men to "scatter in the woods & bushes" and then carry on the war, either with Johnston in North Carolina or in their home states. Lee responded that the "men would have no rations & they would be under no discipline. They are already demoralized by four years of war. They would have to plunder & rob to procure subsistence. The country would be full of lawless bands in every part, & a state of society would ensue from which it would take the country years to recover." Lee told Alexander that "as for myself, while you young men might afford to go to bushwhacking, the only proper & dignified course for me would be to surrender myself & take the consequences of my actions." Deeply moved by his commander's arguments, Alexander had surrendered with the rest of the army. (While it is unlikely that he remembered his conversation with Lee verbatim, it is probable that Alexander's account reflects Lee's views at the time.)

Richmond, Virginia
April 20, 1865

Mr. President:

The apprehensions I expressed during the winter, of the moral condition of the Army of Northern Virginia, have been realized. The operations which occurred while the troops were in the entrenchments in front of Richmond and Petersburg were not marked by the boldness and decision which formerly characterized them. Except in particular instances, they were feeble; and a want of confidence seemed to possess officers and men. This condition, I think, was produced by the state of feeling in the country, and the communications received by the men from their homes, urging their return and the abandonment of the field. The movement of the enemy on the 30th March to Dinwiddie Court House was consequently not as strongly met as similar ones had been. Advantages were gained by him which discouraged the troops, so that on the morning of the 2d April, when our lines between the Appomattox and Hatcher's Run were assaulted, the resistance was not effectual: several points were penetrated and large captures made. At the commencement of the withdrawal of the army from the lines on the night of the 2d, it began to disintegrate, and straggling from the ranks increased up to the surrender on the 9th. On that day, as previously reported, there were only seven thousand eight hundred and ninety-two (7892) effective infantry. During the night, when the surrender became known, more than ten thousand men came in, as reported to me by the Chief Commissary of the Army. During the succeeding days stragglers continued to give themselves up, so that on the 12th April, according to the rolls of those paroled, twenty-six thousand and eighteen (26,018) officers and men had surrendered. Men who had left the ranks on the march, and crossed James River, returned and gave themselves up, and many have since come to Richmond and surrendered. I have given these details that Your Excellency might know the state of feeling which existed in the army, and judge of that in the country. From what I have seen and learned, I believe an army cannot be organized or supported in Virginia, and as far as I know the condition of affairs, the country east of the Mississippi is morally and physically unable to maintain the contest unaided with any hope of ultimate success. A partisan war may be continued, and hostilities protracted, causing individual suffering and the devastation of the country, but I see no prospect by that means of achieving a separate independence. It is for Your Excellency to decide, should you agree with me in opinion, what is proper to be done. To save useless effusion of blood, I would recommend measures be taken for suspension of hostilities and the restoration of peace.

I am with great respect, yr obdt svt

R. E. Lee

Genl

Jefferson Davis to Varina Howell Davis

Jefferson Davis and his cabinet had left Richmond by train on the night of April 2 and arrived in Danville, Virginia, along the North Carolina border the following day. On April 4 he issued an address to "the People of the Confederate States of America" asserting that the fall of Richmond left the Army of Northern Virginia "free to move from point to point and strike in detail the detachments and garrisons of the enemy, operating on the interior of our own country, where supplies are more accessible, and where the foe will be far removed from his own base and cut off from all succor in case of reverse, nothing is now needed to render our triumph certain but the exhibition of our own unquenchable resolve. Let us but will it, and we are free." Davis left Danville on April 10 and went by train to Greensboro, North Carolina, where he reluctantly agreed to let Johnston open negotiations with Sherman before departing for Charlotte on April 15. Traveling by horseback because of Union cavalry raids against the railroad, he reached his destination four days later. When he wrote to his wife, who had left Richmond with their four children on March 30, Davis was uncertain as to her whereabouts, but correctly surmised that she was staying in Abbeville, South Carolina.

Charlotte N. C 23 April 65

MY DEAR WINNIE

I have been detained here longer than was expected when the last telegram was sent to you. I am uncertain where you are and deeply felt the necessity of being with you if even for a brief time, under our altered circumstances. Gov. Vance and Genl. Hampton propose to meet me here and Genl. Johnston sent me a request to remain at some point where he could readily communicate with me. Under these circumstances I have asked Mr. Harrison to go in search of you and to render you such assistance as he may. Your Brother William telegraphed in reply to my inquiry that you were at Abbeville and that he would go to see you. My last despatch was sent to that place and to the care of Mr. Burt. Your own feelings will convey to you an idea of my solicitude for you and our family, and I will not distress by describing it.

The dispersion of Lee's army and the surrender of the remnant which remained with him destroyed the hopes I entertained when we parted. Had that army held together I am now confident we could have successfully executed the plan which I sketched to you and would have been to-day on the high road to independence. Even after that disaster if the men who "straggled" say thirty or forty thousand in number, had come back with their arms and with a disposition to fight we might have repaired the damage; but all was sadly the reverse of that. They threw away theirs and were uncontrollably resolved to go home. The small guards along the road have sometimes been unable to prevent the pillage of trains and depots.

Panic has seized the country. J. E. Johnston and Beauregard were hopeless as to recruiting their forces from the dispersed men of Lee's army and equally so as to their ability to check Sherman with the forces they had. Their only idea was to retreat of the power to do so they were doubtful and subsequent desertions from their troops have materially diminished their strength and I learn still more weakend their confidence.

The loss of arms has been so great that should the spirit of the people rise to the occasion it would not be at this time possible adequately to supply them with the weapons of War.

Genl. Johnston had several interviews with Sherman and agreed on a suspension of hostilities, and the reference of terms of pacification. They are secret and may be rejected by the Yankee govt.—to us they are hard enough, though freed from wanton humiliation and expressly recognizing the state governments, and the rights of person and property as secured by the Constitutions of the U. S. and the several states. Genl. Breckenridge was a party to the last consultation and to the agreement. Judge Reagan went with him and approved the agreement though not present at the conference.

Each member of the Cabinet is to give his opinion in writing to day, 1st upon the acceptance of the terms, 2d upon the mode of proceeding if accepted. The issue is one which it is very painful for me to meet. On one hand is the long night of oppression which will follow the return of our people to the "Union"; on the other the suffering of the women and children, and courage among the few brave patriots who would still oppose the invader, and who unless the people would rise en masse to sustain them, would struggle but to die in vain.

I think my judgement is undisturbed by any pride of opinion or of place, I have prayed to our heavenly Father to give me wisdom and fortitude equal to the demands of the position in which Providence has placed me. I have sacrificed so much for the cause of the Confederacy that I can measure my ability to make any further sacrifice required, and am assured there is but one to which I am not equal, my Wife and my Children. How are they to be saved from degradation or want is now my care. During the suspension of hostilities you may have the best opportunity to go to Missi. and thence either to sail from Mobile for a foreign port or to cross the river and proceed to Texas, as the one or the other may be more practicable. The little sterling you have will be a very scanty store and under other circumstances would not be counted, but if our land can be sold that will secure you from absolute want. For myself it may be that our Enemy will prefer to banish me, it may be that a devoted band of Cavalry will cling to me and that I can force my way across the Missi. and if nothing can be done there which it will be proper to do, then I can go to Mexico and have the world from which to choose a location. Dear Wife this is not the fate to which I invited when the future was rose-colored to us both; but I know you will bear it even better than myself and that of us two I alone will ever look back reproachfully on my past career.

I have thus entered on the questions involved in the future to guard against contingencies, my stay will not be prolonged a day beyond the prospect of useful labor here and there is every reason to suppose that I will be with you a few days after Mr. Harrison arrives.

Mrs Omelia behaved very strangely about putting the things you directed—Robt says she would not permit to pack, that she even took groceries out of the mess chest when he had put a small quantity there. Little Maggie's saddle was concealed and I learned after we left Richmond was not with the saddles and bridles which I directed to be all put together. At the same time I was informed that your saddle had been sent to the Saddlers and left there. Every body seemed afraid of connexion with our property and your carriage was sent to the Depot to be brought with me. a plea was made that it could not go on the cars of that train but should follow in the next, specific charge and promise was given but the carriage was left. The notice to leave was given on Sunday, but few hours were allowed and my public duties compelled to rely on others, count on nothing as saved which you valued except the bust and that had to be left behind.

Mrs. Omelia said she was charged in the event of our having to leave, to place the valuables with the Sisters and that she would distribute every thing. I told her to sell what she could, and after feeling distrust asked Mrs. Grant to observe her; and after that became convinced that she too probably under the influence of her husband was afraid to be known as having close relations with us.

Kiss Maggie and the children many times for me. The only yearning heart in the final hour was poor old Sara wishing for "Pie cake", and thus I left our late home. No bad preparation for a search for another. Dear children I can say nothing to them, but for you and them my heart is full my prayers constant and my hopes are the trust I feel in the mercy of God.

Farewell my Dear; there may be better things in store for us than are now in view, but my love is all I have to offer and that has the value of a thing long possessed and sure not to be lost. Once more, and with God's favor for a short time only, farewell—

YOUR HUSBAND

"SOMETHING THAT HAUNTED US": VIRGINIA, APRIL 1865

Stephen Minot Weld to Hannah Minot Weld

For many of the young men who came of age during the war, soldiering came to seem their only way of life. "We expect to make this our trade for we have become fitted for nothing else now," wrote Samuel Selden Brooke, a company commander in the 47th Virginia Infantry, in March 1864. Lieutenant Colonel Stephen Minot Weld had been captured at the battle of the Crater in Petersburg on July 30, 1864, while leading the 56th Massachusetts Infantry. Weld was imprisoned in Columbia, South Carolina, until December, when he was paroled and sent north. Exchanged in March 1865, he rejoined his regiment in Virginia on April 4. He wrote to his older sister about Lee's surrender.

CITY POINT, *April* 24, 1865.

DEAR HANNAH,—I received several letters from you last night, several of them complaining of my short letters and my want of enthusiasm for Lee's surrender. To tell the truth, we none of us realize even yet that he has actually surrendered. I had a sort of impression that we should fight him all our lives. He was like a ghost to children, something that haunted us so long that we could not realize that he and his army were really out of existence to us. It will take me some months to be conscious of this fact.

In regard to the brevity of my epistle, I can only say that I have nothing to tell about.

I have got a splendid mule, which I am going to take home with me, if I can. He is the finest animal I have ever seen.

Last Thursday we received orders to move to City Point, and from there to Washington. Part of our corps has already moved and we are waiting for transportation. We shall probably move to-morrow, having reached here yesterday afternoon. Last Wednesday, the day before we moved, I went up to General Miles's headquarters. First I went to Second Corps headquarters and then with Charlie Whittier to General Miles's. While there, about forty negroes came in from Danville. General Miles ordered the band out, and told the negroes that he would hang every one who would not dance. About seven refused to dance, saying they were church members. The rest went at it tooth and nail, gray-headed old men and young boys. I never laughed so hard in my life. From General M.'s we went to General Barlow's, who commands the 2d Division. We amused ourselves with a galvanic battery which General B. has for his health. From there we went to General Meade's headquarters, where I had a very pleasant talk with General M. Saw Theodore Lyman, who is probably home by this time. He was very kind to me indeed, and gave me several articles of clothing which were very acceptable. Had a very nice time there indeed, and had a very pleasant reception from the staff. When my men saw me on my arrival, they gave me 9 cheers and then 9 more, etc., etc. I tell you this because you asked me.

We had quite hard marching, making 63 miles in a little over 3 days. The story is that we are going to Texas, that we are to be sent home for 6 months to be disbanded by that time, in case we are not wanted, etc., etc. No one seems to know what we are going to do. If we have a good camp in or near Washington, perhaps I will let you come down there.

“WHAT WERE WE FIGHTING FOR”: NORTH CAROLINA, APRIL–MAY 1865

Samuel T. Foster: Diary, April 18–May 4, 1865

Following the costly battle of Franklin, Captain Samuel T. Foster of the 24th Texas Cavalry (dismounted) had advanced with the Army of Tennessee to the outskirts of Nashville, where the Confederates were decisively defeated on December 15–16, 1864. Foster and his men had then retreated through bitter cold, freezing rain, and snow into northern Mississippi, where in January 1865 General John B. Hood resigned his command. At the end of January the remnants of the Army of Tennessee began moving to the Carolinas, and on March 20 Foster joined Johnston's forces at Smithfield, North Carolina. Foster's company was camped near Greensboro when Johnston and Sherman signed their agreement on April 18. He recorded in his diary the hopes, fears, and bizarre rumors that swept through their camp as Johnston's army confronted "the new order of things," which in many respects would not be as severe as Foster and his fellow soldiers feared. Despite their apprehensions, Confederate veterans would not have their lands confiscated, nor would they endure lifelong disenfranchisement.

APRIL 18

Still in camp. More clothing issued today, but still not enough. Had Battalion drill today just to see if the men would drill.

Various reports afloat in camp. Some say the surrender is already made— But there is so much news that there is no importance attached to anything we hear— Late this evening an order comes from Genl Johnson which is read out to all the troops announcing that an Armistice has been agreed upon by the commanders of the two armies, but not for the purpose of surrendering this army— This seems to satisfy everybody. Lees men from Va. are passing us every day—one at the time— Every man for himself. It is also reported that Genl [ ] is south of us with 10,000 mounted infantry—which have been sent down there by Genl Grant from his Army since Lees surrender—

APRIL 19,

Moved ½ mile today and camp in regular order to remain until the armistice ends. We hear it reported on very good authority that the President of the U S Mr Lincoln was killed a few nights ago in Washington, and that about the same time Seward was shot at and mortally wounded.

It is also reported that the United States has recognized the Confederacy, and agrees to give us all our rights (and slavery) if we will help them to fight all their enemies whatsoever.

Another report is we go back into the Union and free all the slaves in —— years—some fill up the blank with 5 years some 10 and some 20 and so on. All hands talking politics and making peace.

Soon after we arrive at our new camp today some of our men found two barrels of Old Apple brandy burried under the root of an old pine tree that had blown down. One barrel of it was brought to Our Brigade and tapped— Every one helped themselves, and of course some get funny, some get tight some get gentlemanly drunk and some get dog drunk, of this latter class are all the officers from our Maj up. Kept up a noise nearly all night, but no one gets mad—all in a good humor.

APRIL 20th

We are still in camp passing rumors from one Brigade to another all day— Some say that the thing is settled and some say that the difficulty has hardly begun yet—so it goes.

APRIL 21st 1865

Rumor today says we are to go back into the Union, but as that is not the kind of news we want to hear, we don't believe a word of it. What have we been fighting all these years for? Oh no—no more Union for us.

APRIL 22

Rumor says (this morning) that we will start for home in course of the next 10 days, and the rumor comes or purports to come from those that ought to know.

Later in the day the report is that we go to fighting again, that Genl Johnson can't make any terms but submission re-union free negroes &c, and we have been fighting too long for that.

I have not seen a man today but says fight on rather than submit.

APRIL 23 *Sunday*

We have moved camp today 6 or 7 miles, and are nearer Greensboro.

I have been out Visiting this evening and find that we are in a quaker settlement. Considerable talk about the peace question—Rumor says the Yankee Army is being fed from our Comissary to keep them from living off the citizens.

Plenty rumors of the French and the U.S.' going to war. If that is true then we will have recognition or nothing.

APR 24

All very quiet today. No rumors from any source that can be relied upon.

Some think that the big war is about to commence, a war of some Magnitude. France Austria Mexico and the Confederacy on one side, against England Russia and the U S' on the other, and the great battle ground will be in the Confederacy. One plan is for the Confederacy to go back into the Union, then France will declare war with the U S' and land her troops on the C S' Coast where they will have no opposition, and as the French Army advances through the C S' the people will take the oath of Allegiance to France, and our soldiers will enlist under French colors & so on.

APRIL 25

This morning an order is read to the command from Genl Cheatham saying "that Sherman has notified Johnson that the armistice will end and hostilities begin tomorrow 26th inst. at 11 Oclock A.M." At this announcement every body seems gloomy and despondent.

The supposition is that as we can't run out of this place we must fight out. We had talked peace so long in camp and had made so many calculations how we were going home &c that it is up hill business to go to fighting again. We have been very loose in discipline here of late, but that will all come out right in a few days of hard marching and some fighting.

Late in the evening the rumor is that another flag-of-truce has gone to Genl. Sherman, and our fate depends upon the answer. Should it come back before 11 Oclock tomorrow, we may not move yet awhile or we may go double quick.

April 26th

Ordered to be ready to move at 11 O'Clock today, but whether we move or not depends upon the answer to the new propositions sent by the flag-of-truce yesterday.

Andy Johnson the *now* President of the U S' (no kin to the General) sent back the peace papers sent by Sherman as agreed upon between him and Genl Johnson. Not signed by him nor accepted, as a settlement of the war questions at all. —Saying "that the rebellion must be crushed by the force of Arms, and all the prominent men concerned put to death, and the rest banished or made slaves."

At 12 Noon we move out and travel 10 or 12 miles in a westerly direction and camp. Some say we are to remain here tomorrow.

April 27

No move today. This evening Muster Rolls are made out and all hands including officers and men draw 1.25 in silver—the first silver larger than a dime I have seen in a long while.

Just before night the following order from Head Qurs is read

Hd Qurs Army of Tenn
near Greensboro N C
April 27 1865

Genl order
NO 18

By the terms of a military convention made on the 26th inst. by Maj. Gen. W. T. Sherman U S A. and Gen. J. E. Johnson C. S. A. the officers and men of this army are to bind themselves not to take up arms against the U. S.' until properly relieved from that obligation, and shall receive guarantees from the U. S.' officers against molestation by the U. S.' authorities, so long as they observe that obligation, and the laws in force where they reside.

For these objects a duplicate muster roll will be immediately made, and after distribution of the necessary papers, the troops will march under their officers to their respective States, and there be disbanded, all retaining their personal property. The object of this convention is pacification to the extent of the authority of the commanders who made it.

Events in Va. which broke every hope of success by war imposed on its General the duty of sparing the blood of this gallant army, and saving the country from further desolation and the people from ruin.

J E Johnson
General

APRIL 28th

We had a dreadful night, all hands up and talking over the situation. They go over the war again, count up the killed and wounded, then the results obtained— It is too bad! If crying would have done any good, we could have cried all night.

Just to think back at the beginning of this war—and see the young men in the bloom of life—the flower of the country—Volunteering to defend their country from the Yankee hosts, who were coming to desolate their homes. Men who shut their stores and warehouses, stoped their plows, droped the axe, left their machinery lying idle, closed their law offices, churches banks and workshops; and all fall into line to defend the country.

Now where are they. As for our own Company, Regt. and Brgd.—they can be found at Ark. Post, at the prison cemetery of Camp Springfield Ill. at Chickamauga—at Missionary Ridge—at New Hope Church 27 May 64 at Atlanta Aug 22/64 at Jonesboro Ga at Franklin and Nashville Tenn. Dec/64 and there find the remains of as noble men, and as kind hearted faithful friends as ever trod the face of the earth.

And those men who fell in 1864 even in Dec. 64 sacrificed their lives as freely as did the very first that fell in the war. There was no cooling down, no tapering off, no lukewarmness in those men, but they would brave danger when ordered as fearless of Yankee bullets as if they no power to hurt them. At Franklin Tenn. Dec 1st or Nov 30/64 was the most wholesale butchery of human lives ever witness by us. Those brave men had been taught by Genl Johnson to fear nothing when he made a fight, and expecting the same thing of Hood, were betrayed into a perfect slaughter pen.

Who is to blame for all this waste of human life? It is too bad to talk about. And what does it amount to? Has there been anything gained by all this sacrifice? What were we fighting for, the principles of slavery?

And now the slaves are all freed, and the Confederacy has to be dissolved. We have to go back into the Union. Ah! there is the point. Will there ever be any more Union, as there once was?

April 29th

Men still talking politics, but it is over and over the same thing, with the same regrets for our loss, and end with the same "What does it amount to?"

Later in the day the talk is about going home, by what route, and whether we will have to walk all the way &c &c.

Men are beginning to realize their situation, and are talking about going home to Texas. Our guns have all been turned in, to our own Ordnance officers. And we suppose to save us from further humiliation there has not been a Yank in sight of us yet.

Our Muster rolls went up yesterday for paroles, which will be here tomorrow or next day.

April 30th

It seems curious that mens minds can change so sudden, from opinions of life long, to new ones a week old.

I mean that men who have not only been taught from their infancy that the institution of slavery was right; but men who actually owned and held slaves up to this time,—have now changed in their opinions regarding slavery, so as to be able to see the other side of the question,—to see that for man to have property in man was wrong, and that the "Declaration of Independence meant more than they had ever been able to see before. That all men are, and of right ought to be free" has a meaning different from the definition they had been taught from their infancy up,—and to see that the institution (though perhaps wise) had been abused, and perhaps for that abuse this terrible war with its results, was brought upon us as a punishment.

These ideas come not from the Yanks or northern people but come from reflection, and reasoning among ourselves.

This evening a circular from Head Qurs. announce that Rev. J B McFerrin Our Army Chaplain will preach his farewell sermon to the Texas and Ark. troops tomorrow at 10 O'Clock AM.

MAY 1st 1865

Have just heard the best sermon that it has ever been our good fortune to hear before. Rev. J B McFerrin preached to us out in the open woods, the men sitting on the ground, and the preacher holding one book while the other is on the ground.

His text is Revelations 11th Chapter, and the latter part of the 10th verse "Be thou faithful unto death, and I will give thee a Crown of life—" The congregation joined in the singing with their whole souls and for prayer all without an exception knelt down, and for the sermon it held those rough weatherbeaten soldiers spell bound for more than an hour by the eloquence of the preacher— It was a time long to be remembered.

In the evening we receive our parols, which read as follows—

Greensborough
North Carolina
May 2nd 1865

In accordance with the terms of the military convention entered into on the twenty-sixth day of April 1865 between General Joseph E. Johnson Commanding the Confederate Army: and Major General W. T. Sherman, Commanding the United States Army in North Carolina, S T Foster Company "I" Granburys Brigade Consolidated, has given his solemn obligation not to take up arms against the Government of the United States until properly released from this obligation; and is permitted to return to his home, not to be disturbed by the United States Authorities so long as he observes this obligation and obey the laws in force where he may reside

S M Litchee
Maj & CM U.S.A.
Special Commission

W. A. Ryan
Lieut Col. C S A
Commanding

MAY 3rd

After turning in our guns, and getting our parols, we feel relieved. No more picket duty, no more guard duty, no more fighting, no more war. It is all over, and we are going home. HOME after an absence of four years from our families and friends.

Actually going to start home tomorrow or perhaps this morning.

Left our camp surenough at 9 A.M. Came 10 miles, crossed the R.R. at Thomasville, and came 12 miles further towards Salisbury making 22 miles today, and all hands very tired.

MAY 4th

Came to Salisbury today—traveled 20 miles. The Confederate Army will go to pieces here. The South Carolina and Georgia Alabama and Missippi troops will march on foot directly home. The Tennessee Arkansas and Texas troops will turn west from here and cross over the Blue Ridge into East Tennessee, and there take the R.R. for Chattanooga and to Nashville where *we* will take a steamboat for N. O. provided the Yanks will give us transportation.

We are getting accostomed to the new order of things, but there is considerable speculation as to what will be done with us.

Some think that all the officers will be courtmartialed. Some think they will be banished out of the country.

Nearly every one deplores the death of Lincoln and believes that he would have been the best man for us now.

That things would have been different if he had lived. Some go so far as to say that perhaps we were wrong, and that the negroes ought to have been freed at the start off. While others are still not whiped and evince a determination to fight it out some way, or leave the country, rather than go back into the Union, and be ruled by them; and have to be ground to death by being robbed of all our negroes, and lands and other property—not allowed to Vote nor hold office any more.

We do not suppose, nor expect to be allowed to vote any more, as long as we live. We also expect that all the lands in the Confederacy, will be taken away from the white people to pay their war expenses then given in small 160 acre lots to the negroes.

Ellen Renshaw House: Diary, May 2, 1865

Ellen Renshaw House had settled in Eatonton in central Georgia several months after the Union army expelled her from Knoxville for her Confederate sympathies. A visitor from nearby Milledgeville told House on April 21 that Lee had surrendered, a report she initially refused to believe. Two days later she conceded its validity, writing, "We have depended too much on Gen Lee too little on God, & I believe God has suffered his surrender to show us he can use other means than Gen Lee to affect his ends." By May 2 she had still not received definitive news regarding Johnston's surrender. When the Johnston-Sherman agreement reached Washington on April 21, President Johnson and the cabinet had immediately rejected it and sent Grant to North Carolina to obtain Johnston's capitulation on terms similar to those given to Lee. Johnston complied, and on April 26 surrendered all Confederate forces in the Carolinas, Georgia, and Florida. In the summer of 1865, House returned to Tennessee and was reunited with her beloved younger brother, John Moore House, after his release from the Union prison camp on Johnson's Island in Lake Erie. Her happiness at his return was cut short in November when "Johnnie" was killed by robbers near Nashville, a victim of the widespread lawlessness that would afflict much of the South in the aftermath of the war.

May 2. Tuesday. I have been in such a state for the last week I could not write. We have heard a thousand rumors. First that we would be recognized, then that we were going back into the Union. I would not believe the last for a long time, but I am obliged to. Oh! how humiliating. Gen Johnston has surrendered, or rather Gen Sherman and himself have had a conference in which it was agreed that Gen Johnston's men should be marched to their respective states and disbanded. We to go back into the Union with all our former rights &c. Gen Johnston was so completely surrounded that he was compelled to succumb. We have heard so many reports. First that the French have taken New Orleans. That we are to have armed intervention. That Kirby Smith has been reenforced by one hundred thousand French. That there is a French fleet off New York, and I dont know what else.

Lieut Thomas and Capt Robinson called this afternoon, both very blue. How can a true Southerner be any thing else. Yesterday there was a large picnic at Jenkins Mill, neither of us went. I do not think this is any time for picnics &c. Tonight there is to be a dance at Mr Buddins—a Union man. What the young men and girls can be thinking of to go there at such a time I cannot imagine. Almost all the young men have returned. I never saw so many in as small a place.

"HE BEHAVED SO BRAVE": WASHINGTON, D.C., MAY 1865

Walt Whitman: from Specimen Days

Walt Whitman left Brooklyn and traveled to northern Virginia in December 1862 when he learned that his brother George, a captain in the 51st New York Infantry, had been wounded at Fredericksburg. After discovering that his brother's wound was slight, Whitman accompanied a group of wounded soldiers to Washington. He stayed in the capital for most of the remainder of the war, visiting military hospitals while working as a government clerk. In his book of prose remembrance, *Specimen Days* (1882), Whitman included a letter he sent to the mother of a Union soldier who had been wounded near Petersburg in the last weeks of the war. In an earlier passage in *Specimen Days* he wrote about the fatally wounded soldiers who never reached hospitals and were never buried in marked graves: "No history ever—no poem sings, no music sounds, those bravest men of all—those deeds. No formal general's report, nor book in the library, nor column in the paper, embalms the bravest, north or south, east or west. Unnamed, unknown, remain, and still remain, the bravest soldiers. Our manliest—our boys—our hardy darlings; no picture gives them. Likely, the typic one of them (standing, no doubt, for hundreds, thousands,) crawls aside to some bush-clump, or ferny tuft, on receiving his death-shot—there sheltering a little while, soaking roots, grass and soil, with red blood—the battle advances, retreats, flits from the scene, sweeps by—and there, haply with pain and suffering (yet less, far less, than is supposed,) the last lethargy winds like a serpent round him—the eyes glaze in death—none recks—perhaps the burial-squads, in truce, a week afterwards, search not the secluded spot—and there, at last, the Bravest Soldier crumbles in mother earth, unburied and unknown."

DEATH OF A PENNSYLVANIA SOLDIER.

Frank H. Irwin, company E, 93d Pennsylvania—died May 1, '65—My letter to his mother.—Dear madam: No doubt you and Frank's friends have heard the sad fact of his death in hospital here, through his uncle, or the lady from Baltimore, who took his things. (I have not seen them, only heard of them visiting

Frank.) I will write you a few lines—as a casual friend that sat by his death-bed. Your son, corporal Frank H. Irwin, was wounded near fort Fisher, Virginia, March 25th, 1865—the wound was in the left knee, pretty bad. He was sent up to Washington, was receiv'd in ward C, Armory-square hospital, March 28th—the wound became worse, and on the 4th of April the leg was amputated a little above the knee—the operation was perform'd by Dr. Bliss, one of the best surgeons in the army—he did the whole operation himself—there was a good deal of bad matter gather'd—the bullet was found in the knee. For a couple of weeks afterwards he was doing pretty well. I visited and sat by him frequently, as he was fond of having me. The last ten or twelve days of April I saw that his case was critical. He previously had some fever, with cold spells. The last week in April he was much of the time flighty—but always mild and gentle. He died first of May. The actual cause of death was pyæmia, (the absorption of the matter in the system instead of its discharge.) Frank, as far as I saw, had everything requisite in surgical treatment, nursing, &c. He had watches much of the time. He was so good and well-behaved and affectionate, I myself liked him very much. I was in the habit of coming in afternoons and sitting by him, and soothing him, and he liked to have me—liked to put his arm out and lay his hand on my knee—would keep it so a long while. Toward the last he was more restless and flighty at night—often fancied himself with his regiment—by his talk sometimes seem'd as if his feelings were hurt by being blamed by his officers for something he was entirely innocent of—said, "I never in my life was thought capable of such a thing, and never was." At other times he would fancy himself talking as it seem'd to children or such like, his relatives I suppose, and giving them good advice; would talk to them a long while. All the time he was out of his head not one single bad word or idea escaped him. It was remark'd that many a man's conversation in his senses was not half as good as Frank's delirium. He seem'd quite willing to die—he had become very weak and had suffer'd a good deal, and was perfectly resign'd, poor boy. I do not know his past life, but I feel as if it must have been good. At any rate what I saw of him here, under the most trying circumstances, with a painful wound, and among strangers, I can say that he behaved so brave, so composed, and so sweet and affectionate, it could not be surpass'd. And now like many other noble and good men, after serving his country as a soldier, he has yielded up his young life at the very outset in her service. Such things are gloomy—yet there is a text, "God doeth all things well"—the meaning of which, after due time, appears to the soul.

I thought perhaps a few words, though from a stranger, about your son, from one who was with him at the last, might be worth while—for I loved the young man, though I but saw him immediately to lose him. I am merely a friend visiting the hospitals occasionally to cheer the wounded and sick.

W. W.

“HEROES OF THE SUBLIMEST CONFLICT”:
MAY 1865

New York Herald: *The Grandest Military Display in the World*

May 24, 1865

On May 4 Lieutenant General Richard Taylor surrendered all Confederate forces in Alabama, Mississippi, and eastern Louisiana. Jefferson Davis was captured by Union cavalry near Irwinville, Georgia, on May 10, ending his hopes of reaching Texas. With the war almost over, the Union celebrated its victory by staging a Grand Review of the Armies in Washington on May 23 and 24. Over the course of two days about 150,000 men from the Army of the Potomac and the Armies of the Tennessee and Georgia marched along Pennsylvania Avenue from the Capitol to the White House. At the start of the procession they passed a large banner hung across the northwest corner of the Capitol that read: “The Only National Debt We Can Never Pay, Is The Debt We Owe To The Victorious Soldiers.” Tens of thousands of citizens watched and cheered. “God Bless them all,” wrote Benjamin Brown French, the commissioner of public buildings for the District of Columbia, “I saw them depart for the war, and my eyes moistened with grief, as I thought how many of them would never return! I have seen many of them come back—brave veterans who have fought and bled to defend the liberties for which their fathers fought so well, and my eyes moistened with joy to think that they were on their way *home*.” The *New York Herald* had become one of the most widely circulated newspapers in the country under its founding editor James Gordon Bennett. Although the *Herald* had criticized Lincoln for much of his administration, the newspaper had remained neutral in the 1864 election. On May 24 the *Herald* hailed the triumph of the Union armies and commented on the international significance of their victory.

Yesterday the magnificent review at Washington began. The vast army of two hundred thousand American soldiers commenced to pass before the President and the Lieutenant General. The scenes and incidents will be found fully described in our news columns. Washington was of course crowded with strangers from all parts of the Union, and their cheers expressed to the brave veterans the gratitude which the country feels toward them for its preservation. There have been many grand military displays in the past; but never before has there been one as grand as this. The number of soldiers in line is immense. Neither Napoleon nor Wellington ever saw so many veterans in one army at one time. When Napoleon reviewed his army of two hundred thousand men, at the opening of his first Russian campaign, many of his soldiers were young conscripts, fresh from the farm and the counter. The great Russian army, reviewed by the Duke of Wellington after the capitulation of Paris in 1814, numbered only one hundred and sixty thousand. But our army—which is, in fact but part of our force, since the commands of Thomas, Schofield, Curtis, Ord, Canby, Foster and others are not represented—is composed entirely of veterans, and is quite two hundred thousand strong.

It is not mere numbers, however, which make this display at Washington so grand. The immensity of the numbers has its effect, because we have never seen anything like it in this country before. General Grant gives us a faint idea of this immensity when he says that it will take this army two days to cross the Long Bridge. McClellan's reviews were small compared to this, and the long processions which we get up here in the metropolis in honor of distinguished visitors sink into insignificance. But this review is a review of triumph. The troops which file before the thousands of spectators at Washington are not going into a war, and are not preparing for battle. They have come out of the war triumphant, and all their battles are over. Leading them we see Peace and Victory hand in hand. The gallant conquerors of many a hard fought field are going home to share the blessings they have won for the nation. They are not only heroes, but they are the heroes of the sublimest conflict in all history. They have been battling for that great principle of democracy for which so many valiant martyrs in former times have fallen in vain, and they have secured the perpetuity of that Union upon which the hopes of all oppressed of all climes and countries depend. They are the champions of free governments throughout the world. The applause which greets them comes not from the Washington crowds alone, nor from the millions of their fellow citizens in all the States; but we can hear it ringing across the Atlantic, echoed alike from the Alps and the Andes, and swelled by the majestic chorus of republican voices from Mexico to Denmark. From one end of the world to the other the people thank our soldiers for having conquered in the people's cause.

Two hundred thousand American soldiers are marching on through Washington to-day. Every regiment, brigade and division has its proud record, which spectators eagerly recall. Those fine fellows fought at Antietam, and those at Atlanta. Here are the men who held Lee in a vice, and yonder come Sherman's legions, who passed like a sword through the vitals of the rebellion. We leave to our correspondents the grateful task of noting the achievements of the troops in line, and pause to ask ourselves where their march is to end? They are going home; but will they stay there long? With one-quarter of the number Scott captured Mexico. With one-half of that tremendous army Canada would be ours. With such a body of veterans our generals could humble the pride of combined Europe. Where will their grand march end? This is a question which no one can answer now. One thing is, nevertheless, sure. These thousands of soldiers may fight no more; their remaining years may be passed in quiet usefulness, at their homes; one by one they may pass away, honored and beloved by all, like the patriots of the Revolution; scattered far and wide, their bodies may rest sweetly beneath the flowers and the grasses; but all this while their souls and those of their slain comrades will be marching on. On—till thrones shake and crumble at the sound of their coming, and are crushed beneath their steady tramp. On—till the people everywhere rise and demand their liberties with invincible voices. On—till no despot tyrannizes over his fellow men, and no aristocracy lords it over the down-trodden masses. On—till every nation is a republic, and every man a freeman. On—till the soldiers of Grant, Sherman and Sheridan have saved the world as they have saved the Union. On, and on, and on!

THE GRAND REVIEW:
WASHINGTON, D.C., MAY 1865

Lois Bryan Adams to the Detroit Advertiser and Tribune

Lois Bryan Adams described the Grand Review for her readers in Michigan in dispatches that appeared on May 29 and 31. In her second letter Adams observed that the only black troops who marched on either day of the celebration were pioneers attached to Sherman's army. Although some abolitionists protested that the U.S. Colored Troops had been excluded from the Grand Review as the result of a deliberate slight, there were no black regiments assigned to the Army of the Potomac or to the Armies of the Tennessee and Georgia, and the black troops from the Army of the James were about to embark for Texas. Black soldiers had participated in the inaugural parade in March and in Lincoln's funeral procession on April 20, and the presence in the review of black pioneers who had built roads and bridges for Sherman's army was celebrated by the abolitionist newspaper *The Liberator.*

Letter from Washington

REVIEW OF THE ARMIES MARCHING HOME

Washington, May 24, 1865

For two days past Washington has done nothing but watch our national heroes marching home. The display, though embracing but comparatively a small portion of the entire army of the Union, has been a very grand one indeed. The manner of the review was not such as would permit of military evolutions by the troops; it was simply a street parade, and as such only limited numbers of the immense masses passing by could be seen from any one point. The best view was from the head of Pennsylvania Avenue, where it bends to the north past the Treasury building. Standing there and looking towards the Capitol, the scene was a most grand and imposing one. As far as the eye could reach on either hand, the sidewalks were densely crowded with spectators, and every window and balcony and even the roofs and the trees along the way were full. As brigade after brigade swept up the noble avenue with their war-worn flags and inspiring music, they were welcomed with cheers and songs, the waving of flags and handkerchiefs, and now and then a showering of bouquets and wreaths of evergreens and beautiful flowers. Many of the Generals had their horses' necks wreathed with garlands, the gifts of grateful hands along the way.

The children of the public schools dressed in uniform white, with black sashes, assembled at the Capitol and greeted the troops with songs and flowers. Everywhere, through all the grand pageant, blended with the symbols of rejoicing were to be seen also the emblems of mourning for the dead President—he who so longed to see this day, and was caught up out of our sight before it came. All the National flags about the city were at half-mast and heavily draped with black, and every ensign, banner and battle-flag in the passing regiments had crape upon it, while mourning badges were worn by all the officers and very many of the soldiers.

Immense temporary pavilions built in front of the White House and occupying all the broad pavements on either side of the avenue, were handsomely decorated, and filled by Government dignitaries and officials, from the President down, together with Foreign Ministers, attaches, etc., and here also was stationed Lieut. Gen. Grant, before whom these two grand armies passed in review. Standing back of these, almost hidden by the dense foliage of the great trees around it, the White House with its tall pillars still shrouded in black, was desolate and silent as a tomb. It was as if life and death, joy and sorrow had met, and hope had crowned them together with victory and peace and the bloom of spring.

The entire of yesterday was occupied with the passage of Sheridan's cavalry and the 9th, 5th, and 2d Army Corps, together with artillery and engineer corps. Sheridan of course was not here, as he has gone to crush out the one head of the hydra yet alive, in Texas; but his gallant troopers, under command of our own brave Custer, were wildly cheered as they swept up the avenue. Indeed, all were cheered, as they well deserved to be; but, oh, how poor, how empty does all this pageantry and cheering seem, compared with what we owe to these bronzed and war-torn veterans. Shouts and songs and fading flowers seem almost like mockery when offered to such men who have accomplished a work so grand, and yet what else had these gratified crowds to offer?

Sherman's magnificent army passed through the city today. It was worth a lifetime of common events to witness a sight like this. If your Northern doughfaces and copperheads could but look in the iron faces of these men, as they come up in their mighty strength, they would easily understand why chivalry begged for peace and then took to its heels, in petticoats, at their approach. Grinding between the upper and nether millstone wouldn't have been a circumstance to the pulverizing all secession would have got, if it had not crumbled in pieces and scattered just as it did. No one can look at troops like these without feeling sure that an enemy's country, through which they have once marched, must be pretty thoroughly conquered. They are not the men to march without a purpose, and certainly not the ones to leave till that purpose is accomplished.

There were some particulars about this army, and some little incidents, which I will try to gather up this afternoon, and give you in my next.

L.

Letters from Washington

THE GRAND REVIEW | AN ENGLISHMAN'S OPINION | CITIZEN SOLDIERS | SOUTH CAROLINA'S PUNISHMENT | SHERMAN'S MEN | GRANT'S IRISH BRIGADE | SERENADE TO GOV. CRAPO AND SENATOR CHANDLER | MICHIGAN'S RECORD, ETC.

From Our Own Correspondent
Washington, May 27, 1865

For twelve hours, from 9 till 3 o'clock on Tuesday, and the same on Wednesday, we stood at the head of Pennsylvania Avenue and watched the moving masses of men crowned with glittering steel as they came pouring around and down the slopes of Capitol Hill and went rolling on like a mighty river past the stand where the great review took place. It was, without doubt, the grandest military pageant ever witnessed upon the American continent. I overheard an Englishman speaking of it, and he said, "I have witnessed military reviews in England and France, and other parts of Europe, but never saw anything that could equal this. I only wish John Bull at home could see what we see here today." There was an emphasis in the tone that gave a peculiar force to the words; coming from English lips, too, it seemed to mean something, especially when it was added, "And to think that this is not more than one-third of the Union army! and the grandeur of it all is that these men are citizens."

Yes; there is where foreigners see the grandeur, if we do not. These are all citizens who know the value of their country and their Government; they saw the danger menacing both, they made heroes of themselves, they have averted the danger, have given a progressive interpretation to the old Constitution, and are now quietly disbanding to go home and be citizens again. The heroes made by Kings and Emperors are not to be compared with these.

I remember in the early part of the war there was a great anxiety on the part of many as to what should be done with the soldiers after the war was over. But even the most anxious need have no uneasiness on that score; the soldiers will take care of themselves just as well as they did before the war, and better too, many of them. I have talked with hundreds of them, and the universal expression is one of joy at the prospect of going home—home to their families, their farms, and their workshops. Home is the first word they speak in connection with their discharge from service. Our soldiers don't know what "demoralization" means. They had something dearer than life to fight for; they fought, and won, and are now going home to enjoy the peaceful fruits of their victory.

Some of Sherman's men who had fallen out of the ranks from weariness yesterday, came and stood beside us and told us of the hollowness of the Confederate shell through which they had been marching. They said that if ever there was a thoroughly whipped and conquered people it was the Southern rebels; and, said one, "South Carolina is, as it deserves to be, the most completely humbled and desolated spot in all rebeldom. We had no friends there, and we made the country support us. I think it will be some time before that State will want to set up for herself against the Union again!"

It is impossible to describe the feeling of these men towards their commander. They speak of Sherman as a beloved and indulgent father. "There's no place this side of Tophet," said one, "that Sherman's boys wouldn't take if he asked them to; and I reckon they'd go clean that out if he said so!"

The troops came up the broad avenue in splendid marching order, 26 abreast, each corps of infantry followed by its artillery, the shining brass pieces and wicked steel rifled guns, each drawn by eight stout horses, and their accompanying caissons the same. These cannon, which have been talking thunder to the rebels so long, looked peaceful and innocent enough now, and many of them were wreathed with evergreens and garlands of flowers.

One peculiarity of Sherman's army was the great numbers of heavily packed mules between the divisions, and the long train of loaded army wagons, and the promiscuous masses following in the rear. Most of those leading or riding the mules were contrabands of all ages, from little boys to old men; one black woman was among them. But what created great amusement among the thousands of spectators were the roosters perched on tops of the mule-packs and seeming to enjoy the display as much as anybody. They looked around with great apparent satisfaction on the laughing, clapping, shouting crowd, and every now and then answered the cheers by flapping their wings and crowing triumphantly as they "went marching on." They evidently understood that there was victory to be celebrated and that they were expected to do their part; and they did it. In one instance there was a beautiful white goat, a pet of some good soldier boy, standing on one of the mule-packs eating from a pannier as contentedly as if born to ride horseback and live on rations.

No colored troops were on review either day, except the few with Sherman's army who were attached to the Pioneer corps and armed with picks and shovels. The black soldiers are still in the field, in the army of the James, or at the West and Southwest.

The Irish Brigade, under Grant, the first day made a fine appearance, every soldier in it having a sprig of green box in his cap. Looking over and down the long columns, the effect was very pleasing. The green flag of Erin was carried beside the national colors, and the tattered battle flags give token of the hard service they had seen.

The weather for the grand review could not have been finer. For a week or more past there had been a constant succession of thunderstorms, day and night; so that when it did clear off the atmosphere was pure and fresh and cool. Both days were perfectly delightful, with clear blue skies, bright sunshine, and sweet invigorating airs.

Hundreds of Michigan people have been here to witness the spectacle. It was chronicled on Monday that Gov. Crapo and staff, Senator Chandler, and others were in town, and on the evening of that day they were serenaded by the band of the Michigan Cavalry Brigade. The Governor was called out and made a patriotic speech. Senator Chandler also spoke, and the band were handsomely entertained at the Governor's rooms.

This cavalry brigade, comprising the 6th, 7th, 1st, and 5th Michigan cavalry, was commanded by Col. Peter Stagg, of Trenton, Mich. He was a Colonel day before yesterday, but is a Brigadier General now, having been promoted since the review.

It was amusing yesterday to hear the little boys as they ran up and down among the crowds on the side-walks, crying "Photographs of Jeff. Davis trying to escape in his wife's clothes."

Here, if ever, from the scene in the avenue on one hand, to the pictured masquerade on the other, the oft talked-of "step from the sublime to the ridiculous" was a visible, tangible reality.

But the splendid pageant of the day passed on, and as the sun went down the armies of the Union spread their tents on the hills and along the valleys, around about the capital they have guarded so long and so well. The city, with its 70,000 visitors, seemed as quiet as ordinarily, save the serenading bands, with their pleasant music at the hotels, where their Generals were quartered.

Today the boys in blue have taken the city by storm. They are everywhere, seeing the sights and making the most of Washington while the opportunity lasts.

L.

"ALL SLAVES ARE FREE": TEXAS, JUNE 1865

Gordon Granger: General Orders No. 3

On May 26 General Edmund Kirby Smith surrendered all Confederate forces west of the Mississippi. Major General Gordon Granger arrived in Galveston on June 18 and issued General Orders No. 3 the following day. His order enforcing the Emancipation Proclamation brought freedom to about 250,000 slaves in Texas and became the basis for the African American holiday of Juneteenth.

HEADQUARTERS DISTRICT OF TEXAS,
Galveston, Tex., June 19, 1865.

GENERAL ORDERS,
No. 3.

The people of Texas are informed that, in accordance with a proclamation from the Executive of the United States, all slaves are free. This involves an absolute equality of personal rights and rights of property between former masters and slaves, and the connection heretofore existing between them becomes that between employer and hired labor. The freedmen are advised to remain quietly at their present homes and work for wages. They are informed that they will not be allowed to collect at military posts and that they will not be supported in idleness either there or elsewhere.

By order of Major-General Granger:

F. W. EMERY,
Major and Assistant Adjutant-General.

CHRONOLOGY

BIOGRAPHICAL NOTES

NOTE ON THE TEXTS

NOTES

INDEX

Chronology March 1864–June 1865

1864 Union Brigadier General Judson Kilpatrick abandons cavalry raid aimed at freeing prisoners of war held in Richmond, Virginia, on March 1 and retreats toward Union lines. Richmond newspapers publish documents found during the Kilpatrick raid on the body of Union Colonel Ulric Dahlgren outlining plans to kill Jefferson Davis and burn Richmond, March 5 (Kilpatrick will deny any knowledge of alleged plot). The same day, Secretary of the Treasury Salmon P. Chase ends his undeclared challenge to the renomination of President Abraham Lincoln by announcing that he is not a candidate for president. Major General Ulysses S. Grant and President Lincoln meet for the first time on March 8 at the White House. Grant receives his commission as lieutenant general the next day, and is named general-in-chief of the armies of the United States on March 10. Union expedition in Louisiana led by Major General Nathaniel P. Banks and Rear Admiral David P. Porter begins advance up the Red River toward Shreveport, March 12, and occupies Alexandria, March 15. Arkansas unionists vote 12,177–266 in favor of a constitutional amendment abolishing slavery in the state, March 14–16. Confederate cavalry commander Major General Nathan Bedford Forrest leads raid from northern Mississippi into West Tennessee and southwestern Kentucky, March 15–May 5. Grant discusses plans for the spring campaign with Major General William T. Sherman, his successor as overall Union commander in the western theater, in Nashville and Cincinnati, March 17–20. Major General Frederick Steele leaves Little Rock, Arkansas, with 6,800 Union troops on March 23 and begins advance on Shreveport from the north. Altercation between Union soldiers on furlough and antiwar Copperheads in Charleston, Illinois, on March 28 results in riot in which six soldiers and three civilians are killed.

In letter to Sherman on April 4, Grant outlines plan for spring campaign involving simultaneous Union offensives with the objective of decisively defeating the two main

Confederate armies. Sherman will move against the Army of Tennessee in northern Georgia, led by General Joseph E. Johnston, while Grant will make his headquarters in the field with the Army of the Potomac, commanded by Major General George G. Meade, and direct its operations against the Army of Northern Virginia, led by General Robert E. Lee. The Army of the Potomac's offensive against Lee will be supported by Major General Benjamin F. Butler, who will move up the James River toward Richmond, and Major General Franz Sigel, who will advance south through the Shenandoah Valley. (Grant's plan for Banks to lead an expedition in the spring against Mobile, Alabama, will be abandoned due to the Red River campaign.) Convention in Louisiana approves on April 6 a new state constitution abolishing slavery. U.S. Senate approves Thirteenth Amendment to the Constitution abolishing slavery by 38–6 vote on April 8. The same day, Major General Richard Taylor defeats the vanguard of Banks's army at Sabine Crossroads near Mansfield, Louisiana, and drives it back several miles to Pleasant Hill. Although fighting at Pleasant Hill on April 9 is tactically inconclusive, Banks abandons advance on Shreveport and begins retreat to Alexandria. Confederate troops led by Forrest capture Union outpost at Fort Pillow, Tennessee, on April 12 and kill hundreds of black soldiers who are trying to surrender. News of the massacre causes widespread outrage in the North. Steele's expedition in southern Arkansas occupies Camden on April 13. Grant orders general prisoner exchanges suspended on April 17 until the Confederates treat black and white prisoners equally and recognize the validity of the surrender terms given to the Confederate garrisons at Vicksburg and Port Hudson in July 1863. Confederates capture Plymouth, North Carolina, and take 2,500 Union prisoners, April 17–20. Corps commanded by Lieutenant General James Longstreet rejoins Lee's army near Gordonsville, Virginia, on April 22 after serving in East Tennessee since September 1863. Retreating forces under Banks reach Alexandria, April 25–26, where low water in the Red River threatens to strand the Union gunboat flotilla. Confederate destruction of Union supply columns at Poison Spring, April 18, and Marks's Mill, April 25, forces Steele to abandon expedition against Shreveport. Union forces evacuate Camden on April 26 and fight rear-guard action at Jenkins's Ferry, April 30, as they retreat across the Saline River toward Little Rock. (Evidence indicates that some black troops killed Confederate prisoners at Jenkins's Ferry in retaliation for the murder of black soldiers and fugitive slaves at Poison Spring and Marks's Mill.)

On May 4 the Army of the Potomac begins crossing the Rapidan River in Virginia east of Lee's camps and advances into the Wilderness of Spotsylvania, an area of scrub woods and dense undergrowth. Butler sails up the James River on May 5 with 30,000 men and begins landing at Bermuda Hundred, a peninsula between the James and Appomattox rivers south of Richmond and north of Petersburg. Lee moves his army of 66,000 men into the Wilderness to engage the Union forces, which total about 120,000. Two days of intense fighting in the Wilderness, May 5–6, end in a stalemate after the Union loses more than 17,000 men killed, wounded, or missing, and the Confederates 11,000. Both armies move southeast toward Spotsylvania Court House on May 7. Sherman begins his campaign in northern Georgia on May 7 by advancing toward Dalton along the railroad line from Chattanooga to Atlanta. His command of about 100,000 men, divided among the Army of the Cumberland (Major General George H. Thomas), the Army of the Tennessee (Major General James B. McPherson), and the Army of the Ohio (Major General John M. Schofield), is opposed by General Joseph E. Johnston, who commands about 50,000 men (later reinforced to 60,000) in the Army of Tennessee. While Thomas and Schofield probe the Confederate defenses on Rocky Face Ridge west of Dalton, Sherman sends McPherson on a flanking march to the south toward the railroad at Resaca. Lee's troops reach crossroads at Spotsylvania Court House ahead of Union forces on May 8 and the two armies begin fighting there. Butler advances toward Petersburg on May 9, but then withdraws to prepare for movement toward Richmond. Union assault at Spotsylvania on May 10 fails to break the Confederate line. Major General J.E.B. Stuart, the commander of Lee's cavalry since 1862, is fatally wounded on May 11 at Yellow Tavern near Richmond while fighting a cavalry raid led by Major General Philip H. Sheridan. Union assault on "Mule Shoe" salient at Spotsylvania, May 12, captures several thousand Confederate prisoners but fails to achieve a decisive break in Lee's lines. The same day, Butler begins advance from Bermuda Hundred toward the southern defenses of Richmond at Drewry's Bluff. Johnston abandons Dalton, Georgia, on the night of May 12 and retreats to Resaca. Banks evacuates Alexandria, Louisiana, on May 13 after the Union gunboat flotilla escapes down the Red River. Johnston retreats from Resaca on May 15 after two days of fighting around the town. Union army of 9,000 men led by Franz Sigel is defeated at New Market in the Shenandoah Valley on May 15 by force of 5,000 Confederates led by Major General John C. Breckinridge that includes local militia and more than two hundred Virginia Military Institute cadets. General Pierre G. T. Beauregard defeats Union forces at Drewry's Bluff on May 16, causing Butler to retreat to Bermuda Hundred and entrench his position. Failure of Sigel's and Butler's offensives allows reinforcements to reach Lee. Union assault against the base of the "Mule Shoe" salient is repulsed on May 18. Johnston retreats to strong defensive position at Allatoona Pass, Georgia, May 19–20. Banks retreats across Atchafalaya Bayou in southern Louisiana on May 20, ending Red River campaign. Grant abandons Union positions at Spotsylvania, May 20–21, and moves southeast toward the North Anna River, ending battle in which about 18,000 Union and 12,000 Confederate soldiers are killed, wounded, or missing. Lee reaches North Anna before Grant but is unable to prevent Union troops from crossing the river on May 23. Sherman moves away from the Chattanooga–Atlanta railroad on May 23 in attempt to turn Johnston's southern flank. Union forces encounter strongly entrenched Confederate position south of the North Anna River on May 24. Sherman's flanking maneuver results in heavy fighting at New Hope Church, May 25, and Pickett's Mill, May 27. Grant's troops cross the Pamunkey River, May 27–28, and occupy crossroads at Cold Harbor nine miles east of Richmond on May 31. Coalition of abolitionists and War Democrats hold Radical Democracy convention in Cleveland on May 31 and nominate Major General John C. Frémont for president.

Fighting at Cold Harbor on June 1 is inconclusive. Grant orders general assault against Lee's defensive line on June 3 that is repulsed with the loss of 7,000 Union soldiers killed, wounded, or missing, while Confederate casualties total about 1,500. National Union convention, coalition of Republicans and War Democrats meeting in

Baltimore, nominates Lincoln for president on nearly unanimous first ballot on June 8 and chooses Democrat Andrew Johnson, the military governor of Tennessee, as its vice presidential candidate. After maneuvering back to the Chattanooga–Atlanta railroad line, Sherman resumes his advance on June 10. With a force of 3,500 men, Forrest defeats 8,500 Union troops led by Brigadier General Samuel G. Curtis at Brice's Crossroads in northern Mississippi, June 10. Major General David Hunter, Sigel's replacement as Union commander in the Shenandoah Valley, occupies Lexington on June 11 and burns Virginia Military Institute the following day. Grant withdraws from Cold Harbor on June 12 and begins moving the Army of the Potomac toward the James River. (From May 4 to June 12 the Army of the Potomac lost about 55,000 men killed, wounded, or missing, while losses in the Army of Northern Virginia are estimated at about 33,000 men.) Union troops begin crossing the James on June 14. Lincoln signs legislation on June 15 that partially redresses grievances of black soldiers regarding their unequal pay. The same day, the House of Representatives defeats passage of the Thirteenth Amendment, 93–65. Union troops assault Petersburg, June 15–18, capturing several defensive positions but failing to take the city itself despite their superior numbers. Grant decides not to launch any further frontal assaults on the city, and Union troops begin to entrench east and southeast of Petersburg. Hunter advances on railroad junction at Lynchburg, Virginia, June 17–18, then retreats into West Virginia when he encounters reinforcements sent by Lee from the Army of Northern Virginia. After a week of skirmishing and maneuvering in northern Georgia, Johnston retreats to defensive line anchored on Kennesaw Mountain, June 18. U.S.S. *Kearsarge* sinks the Confederate commerce raider C.S.S. *Alabama* off Cherbourg, France, on June 19. Union forces make unsuccessful attempt to cut Weldon Railroad linking North Carolina with Petersburg, June 21–24. Confederate troops under Lieutenant General Jubal A. Early begin advancing north through the Shenandoah Valley toward Maryland. Sherman orders unsuccessful frontal assault on Confederate positions at Kennesaw Mountain, June 27. Congress repeals Fugitive Slave Act on June 28 (legislation passed in March 1862 had already prohibited the Union military from returning fugitive slaves). Lincoln accepts Chase's resignation as secretary of the treasury on June 30 and names William P. Fessenden as his replacement.

Sherman turns southern flank of the Confederate position at Kennesaw Mountain on July 2, forcing Johnston to retreat to the Chattahoochee River. Congress passes Wade-Davis reconstruction bill, July 2. Lincoln pocket-vetoes the bill on July 4 and recommits himself to the "Ten Percent Plan" for reconstruction he first put forward in December 1863. The same day, Lincoln signs bill abolishing the $300 commutation fee paid by drafted men to avoid military service (the legislation allows the fee to be paid by conscientious objectors, and continues to permit the hiring of substitutes). Early crosses the Potomac in western Maryland with 14,000 men, July 5–6, and moves toward Washington. Sherman sends troops across the Chattahoochee upriver from Johnston's defensive position, July 8. Johnston abandons the western bank of the Chattahoochee, July 9, and falls back to Peachtree Creek on the north side of Atlanta. Early defeats Major General Lew Wallace at the battle of Monocacy, July 9. As reinforcements from the Army of the Potomac arrive by water in Washington, Early's troops skirmish with Union defenders at Fort Stevens on the northern outskirts of Washington, July 11–12. Early withdraws from the capital and retreats across the Potomac on July 14. Union force of 14,000 men led by Major General Andrew J. Smith defeats 9,500 Confederates under the command of Lieutenant General Stephen D. Lee and Forrest at Tupelo, Mississippi, July 14–15. (Fighting at Brice's Crossroads and Tupelo helps prevent Forrest from raiding the Nashville–Chattanooga railroad that supplies Sherman's army in Georgia.) Davis removes Johnston from command of the Army of Tennessee on July 17 and replaces him with Lieutenant General John B. Hood. (From May 4 to July 17 Sherman's troops lose about 22,000 men killed, wounded, or missing, and Johnston's about 14,000.) Jefferson Davis meets in Richmond with two unofficial Union envoys on July 17 and tells them that the Confederacy will only negotiate peace once its independence is recognized. Lincoln issues call for 500,000 volunteers on July 18, with unfulfilled quotas to be met by a draft held on September 5. The same day, Lincoln writes a safe-conduct for Confederate agents in Canada in which he states his willingness to negotiate peace on the basis of reunion and emancipation. Hood unsuccessfully attacks Sherman's forces south of Peachtree Creek on July 20. Confederate agents in Canada release letter to the press on July 21 denouncing Lincoln's peace terms. Hood orders assault on Union forces east of Atlanta, July 22, that is repulsed with the loss of 5,500 Confederate and 3,700 Union soldiers killed, wounded, or missing. Union forces are defeated at Kernstown in the Shenandoah Valley, July 24. Hood attacks Union positions west of Atlanta at Ezra Church on July 28 and is again repulsed. Sherman entrenches his army to the east, north, and west of Atlanta and begins shelling Hood's positions. Grant sends Union troops across the James River at Deep Bottom, July 27–29, to draw Confederate reserves away from Petersburg by threatening attack on Richmond from the southeast. Union engineers explode mine beneath strongpoint at Petersburg on July 30, creating breach in Confederate line that Union troops are unable to exploit. Battle of the Crater costs the Union 3,800 men killed, wounded, or missing, including about 1,300 men from the U.S. Colored Troops, while Confederate losses total about 1,500. Cavalry from Early's command raid Chambersburg, Pennsylvania, on July 30 and demand $100,000 in gold as compensation for destruction of property in the Shenandoah Valley carried out on Hunter's orders. They then burn much of the town when its residents fail to pay.

In North Carolina, Governor Zebulon B. Vance, a critic of the Davis administration who supports continued fighting for Confederate independence, wins reelection on August 4, defeating peace candidate William W. Holden, 57,873–14,432. Union squadron led by Rear Admiral David G. Farragut forces passage between Forts Morgan and Gaines and defeats Confederate flotilla in Mobile Bay, August 5, closing off the main Confederate port on the Gulf of Mexico. Grant appoints Sheridan to command Union forces in the Shenandoah Valley, August 7. Second Union offensive at Deep Bottom, August 14–20, draws Confederate reserves away from Petersburg and allows Union forces to cut the Weldon Railroad at Globe Tavern, August 18–21. Forrest raids Memphis on August 21. Lincoln writes private memorandum on August 23 acknowledging that he will probably not win reelection. Union attempt to destroy the Weldon Railroad below Globe Tavern is defeated at Reams Station on August 25. The same day, Sherman begins moving his army south of Atlanta in order to cut the railroad line to Macon. Democratic national convention in Chicago adopts platform calling for an immediate armistice, August 30, and nominates Major General George B. McClellan for president, August 31. Sherman's forces cut the Atlanta–Macon railroad, August 31, and repulse a Confederate counterattack at Jonesboro, August 31–September 1.

Hood abandons Atlanta on September 1 and retreats to Lovejoy's Station twenty miles south of the city. Union troops enter Atlanta September 2. (From July 18 to September 2 Sherman's troops lose about 15,000 men killed, wounded, or missing, and Hood's about 17,000.) Confederate cavalry raider Brigadier General John Hunt Morgan is killed by Union troops at Greeneville, Tennessee, September 4. Unionist voters approve the new Louisiana state constitution abolishing slavery, 6,836–1,566, on September 5. Sherman orders the evacuation of the remaining civilian population of Atlanta, September 7, causing outrage in the Confederacy. McClellan accepts Democratic nomination, September 8, but repudiates platform plank calling for immediate armistice. Confederate Major General Sterling Price invades southeastern Missouri on September 19 with 12,000 men and advances toward St. Louis. Sheridan defeats Early at Winchester, September 19, and Fisher's Hill, September 22. Union troops seize livestock and burn barns, mills, and warehouses in the Shenandoah Valley, a major source of food and fodder for the Confederate armies. Frémont announces his withdrawal from the presidential contest on September 22. Lincoln replaces conservative Montgomery Blair as postmaster general with William Dennison as conciliatory gesture to Radical Republicans, September 23. Forrest raids Union outposts and railroads in northern Alabama and Middle Tennessee, September 24–October 6, but fails to reach the Nashville–Chattanooga rail line. Price unsuccessfully attacks Union outpost at Pilot Knob, Missouri, September 27. The same day, Confederate guerrillas led by William (Bloody Bill) Anderson kill and mutilate 146 Union soldiers, some of them unarmed, at Centralia, Missouri. Hood crosses Chattahoochee River southwest of Atlanta, September 28–29, and advances toward Atlanta–Chattanooga railroad in attempt to cut Sherman's supply line and force him to retreat from Georgia. In the battle of New Market Heights,

September 29–30, Union troops attacking north of the James River capture Fort Harrison but are unable to break through the inner Richmond defenses. At Peebles Farm, September 30–October 2, Union forces extend their trench line south of Petersburg closer to the Boydton Plank Road, a major Confederate supply route into the city.

Price occupies Union, Missouri, forty miles from St. Louis, October 1–3, then abandons plans to take the city and turns westward. Hood destroys several miles of track along the Chattanooga–Atlanta railroad, October 2–4, but is repulsed by the Union garrison at Allatoona Pass, October 5, as Sherman pursues him with most of his army. In battle of the Darbytown Road, October 7, Union troops repulse Lee's attempt to regain the ground lost outside Richmond in late September. U.S.S. *Wachusett* captures Confederate commerce raider *Florida* in port of Salvador, Brazil, October 7. Chief Justice of the U.S. Supreme Court Roger B. Taney, the author of the *Dred Scott* decision, dies October 12. Maryland voters approve constitution abolishing slavery, 30,174–29,799, October 12–13. Union assault on new Confederate defensive line near the Darbytown Road is repulsed on October 13. Hood continues offensive against the Chattanooga–Atlanta railroad, capturing Dalton, Georgia, on October 13 and destroying more track before moving his army west toward northern Alabama. Forrest begins raid into West Tennessee, October 16. Early mounts a successful surprise attack with 21,000 men on Sheridan's army of 32,000 at Cedar Creek on October 19. Sheridan rides to the battlefield from Winchester, rallies his troops, and directs counterattack that routs Early's forces and gives the Union control of the northern Shenandoah Valley. Confederate commerce raider *Shenandoah*, purchased as merchant ship in Great Britain, is commissioned off Madeira in the North Atlantic, October 19. Band of Confederate raiders rob three banks in St. Albans, Vermont, of $200,000 on October 19 before escaping back into Canada. Sherman halts his pursuit of Hood at Gaylesville, Alabama, on October 21. Price is defeated by Union forces at Westport, Missouri, October 23, and Mine Creek, Kansas, October 25. Confederate guerrilla leader "Bloody Bill" Anderson is killed by Union cavalry near Albany, Missouri, October 27. Union offensives east of Richmond at the Darbytown Road and Fair

Oaks and southwest of Petersburg at Hatcher's Run fail to gain ground, October 27–28. Sherman leaves Gaylesville, October 28, and returns to Georgia. Hood reaches Tuscumbia, Alabama, October 31, and begins gathering supplies for invasion of Middle Tennessee. Union forces retake Plymouth, North Carolina, October 31.

Sherman sends 25,000 troops north to help Major General George H. Thomas defend Tennessee against Hood's anticipated invasion. Price escapes into Indian Territory, November 7. In message to the Confederate Congress on November 7, Jefferson Davis suggests that arming slaves may become necessary if the Confederacy is to survive. Lincoln is reelected on November 8, winning 55 percent of popular vote and 212 of 233 electoral votes. Republicans also gain forty-three seats in the House of Representatives and defeat the reelection bid of New York governor Horatio Seymour, a leading anti-administration Democrat. Forrest returns from West Tennessee raid and joins Hood's army at Florence, Alabama, on November 14. Sherman leaves Atlanta on November 16 after destroying railroads, factories, and part of the city, and with army of 60,000 men begins march across Georgia that advances along front 50–60 miles wide. Hood leaves Florence, Alabama, with 38,000 men on November 21 and begins invasion of Tennessee. Sherman's troops capture Milledgeville, the Georgia state capital, on November 23. U.S. attorney general Edward Bates resigns on November 24 and is replaced by James Speed. After several months of escalating violence between whites and Indians in Colorado and western Kansas, Union Colonel John M. Chivington leads Colorado militia in attack on Indian village at Sand Creek in eastern Colorado on November 29, in which more than 150 Southern Cheyenne and Arapaho men, women, and children are killed and mutilated. Hood outflanks Union position at Columbia, Tennessee, on November 29, but fails to prevent Major General John M. Schofield from retreating past his army at Spring Hill and reaching Franklin. On November 30 Hood orders series of frontal assaults on the Union lines at Franklin that cost the Confederates 6,200 men killed, wounded, or missing, and the Union 2,300. Schofield withdraws after the battle and joins Thomas at Nashville.

Hood reaches vicinity of Nashville on December 2 and entrenches south of the city. In his annual message to Congress, December 6, Lincoln urges the House to promptly pass the Thirteenth Amendment. The same day, he nominates, and the Senate confirms, Salmon P. Chase as chief justice of the Supreme Court. Sherman reaches outskirts of Savannah, Georgia, on December 10 and captures Fort McAllister on December 13, opening supply line to naval vessels offshore. In battle of Nashville, December 15–16, Union force of 55,000 men under Thomas defeats Hood's army and forces it to retreat into northern Mississippi. Confederate losses in the fighting are about 6,000 men killed, wounded, or missing, while Union losses total about 3,000. Confederate troops evacuate Savannah, December 20, and Union forces occupy the city the next day. Expedition led by Major General Benjamin F. Butler and Rear Admiral David D. Porter unsuccessfully attacks Fort Fisher, North Carolina, December 24–25. (The fort commands the entrance to Wilmington, the last remaining Confederate deep-water port on the Atlantic coast.)

1865 At Grant's request, Lincoln relieves Butler on January 8. Grant names Brigadier General Alfred H. Terry as army commander of renewed attack on Fort Fisher. State convention in Missouri votes 60–4 in favor of the immediate abolition of slavery, January 11. Tennessee convention approves constitutional amendment abolishing slavery, January 13. Second Union expedition captures Fort Fisher, January 13–15. After consulting with Secretary of War Stanton, Sherman issues Special Field Orders No. 15 on January 16, reserving coastal strip thirty miles wide from Charleston, South Carolina, to the St. John's River in Florida for the settlement of freed people. Confederate Congress passes bill on January 23 creating position of general-in-chief of the Confederate armies. U.S. House of Representatives approves the Thirteenth Amendment, 119–56, on January 31. (Although Delaware, Kentucky, New Jersey, and Mississippi will vote against ratification, the Thirteenth Amendment is approved by twenty-seven states, included eight former members of the Confederacy, by December 6, 1865, and on December 18 Secretary of State Seward will declare its ratification complete.)

On February 1 Boston lawyer John S. Rock becomes the first black man admitted to the bar before the U.S. Supreme Court. Sherman leaves Savannah and begins advance into South Carolina, February 1, inflicting greater destruction on private homes and property than in Georgia. Lincoln and Seward hold unsuccessful negotiations with Confederate peace commissioners Alexander H. Stephens, Robert M. T. Hunter, and John A. Campbell on the *River Queen* in Hampton Roads, February 3. Renewed Union offensive at Hatcher's Run southwest of Petersburg, February 5–7, forces Lee to further extend his already overstretched lines. James A. Seddon resigns as Confederate secretary of war on February 6 and is replaced by John C. Breckinridge. The same day, Davis appoints Lee as general-in-chief (Lee remains commander of the Army of Northern Virginia). Sherman's army enters Columbia, South Carolina, February 17. On the night of February 17 fire destroys much of the city while Union soldiers engage in widespread looting. Confederates evacuate Charleston on February 18 (among the Union troops who occupy the city are former slaves from the region now serving in the 21st U.S. Colored Infantry). On February 20 the Confederate House of Representatives approves bill, 40–37, authorizing the Confederate army to enlist slaves with the permission of their masters, but without providing for their emancipation. Tennessee unionists approve, 25,293–48, amendment to the state constitution abolishing slavery, February 22. The same day, Union troops capture Wilmington. Davis reluctantly restores Joseph E. Johnston to command of the Army of Tennessee, which is being sent to the Carolinas to oppose Sherman, February 24.

Sheridan's cavalry routs the remnants of Early's command at Waynesboro, Virginia, March 2, ending organized fighting in the Shenandoah Valley. On March 3 Lincoln signs bill creating the Bureau of Refugees, Freedmen, and Abandoned Lands, as well as legislation emancipating enslaved family members of black soldiers and giving black troops full back pay. Lincoln is inaugurated for his second term on March 4. Hugh McCulloch replaces William P. Fessenden as U.S. secretary of the treasury. Confederate Senate approves bill for arming slaves, 9–8, March 8. Sherman occupies Fayetteville, North Carolina, on March 11. Johnston attacks the left wing of Sherman's army near Bentonville on March 19 with force of 21,000 men and is repulsed. After withdrawing behind entrenchments on March 20, Johnston retreats to Smithfield on the night of March 21. Sherman enters Goldsboro on March 23 and joins up with Union forces under Schofield that had advanced from the coast. Lee launches unsuccessful assault on Fort Stedman, Union strongpoint east of Petersburg, on March 25. Major General Edward R. S. Canby begins siege of Spanish Fort, Confederate strongpoint on the eastern side of Mobile Bay, March 27. Grant orders Sheridan to lead major offensive west of Petersburg, resulting in heavy fighting at Dinwiddie Court House and White Oak Road on March 31.

Sheridan overruns the Confederate positions at Five Forks west of Petersburg on April 1, capturing 2,500 prisoners. Grant orders general assault on the Petersburg defenses at dawn on April 2. Attack breaks Confederate lines and forces Lee to evacuate Petersburg and Richmond on the night of April 2. (Fighting at Petersburg and Richmond costs the Union about 42,000 men killed, wounded, or missing from June 1864 to April 1865, and the Confederates about 28,000.) Davis and his cabinet flee by train to Danville, Virginia, as fires set by retreating Confederate troops cause extensive destruction in the city. Union cavalry captures Selma, Alabama, on April 2. Lincoln tours Richmond on April 4. Lee's army retreats westward to Amelia Court House on April 4. Unable to secure needed supplies and finding his planned route to North Carolina blocked by Union troops, Lee continues retreating to the west. Pursuing Union forces capture more than 6,000 prisoners at Sailer's Creek, Virginia, on April 6. After his retreat is blocked by Union troops at Appomattox Court House, Lee surrenders to Grant on April 9. The same day, Union troops storm Fort Blakely near Mobile. Sherman resumes offensive in North Carolina, April 10. Union cavalry captures Montgomery, Alabama, on April 12, the same day that Confederate forces abandon Mobile. Sherman occupies Raleigh on April 13. While watching a performance of *Our American Cousin* at Ford's Theatre in Washington on April 14, Lincoln is shot by actor John Wilkes Booth, who flees the theater. At the same time, Secretary of State Seward is seriously wounded by Booth's co-conspirator Lewis Powell. Lincoln dies on the morning of April 15 and Andrew Johnson is sworn in as president. Sherman and Johnston meet near Durham Station, North Carolina, on April 18 and sign agreement providing military and political terms for the surrender of the remaining Confederate armies. Lincoln funeral train leaves Washington on April 21 and is viewed by millions as it makes its way to Illinois. The same day, Johnson and the cabinet reject the Sherman-Johnston agreement. Johnston surrenders Confederate forces in the Carolinas, Georgia, and Florida on April 26 on terms similar to those given to Lee. The same day, Booth is killed by Union troops near Port Royal, Virginia. (Powell and three other convicted conspirators are hanged on July 7.) Steamship *Sultana* explodes and burns in the Mississippi near Memphis, April 27, killing 1,600–1,800 people, mostly released Union prisoners of war.

Lincoln is buried in Springfield, Illinois, on May 4. The same day, Lieutenant General Richard Taylor surrenders Confederate forces in Alabama, Mississippi, and eastern Louisiana to Major General Edward R. S. Canby on May 4. Union cavalry capture Jefferson Davis near Irwinville, Georgia, on May 10 and take him as a prisoner to Fort Monroe, Virginia. The same day, Confederate guerrilla leader William Quantrill is fatally wounded by Union troops near Bloomfield, Kentucky. In the Grand Review of the Union Armies, May 23–24, about 150,000 men from the Army of the Potomac and Sherman's armies march through Washington. Surrender terms for the Confederate Trans-Mississippi department are negotiated in New Orleans on May 26. Unaware of the Confederate surrenders, the commerce raider *Shenandoah* begins capturing and burning American whaling ships in the Sea of Okhotsk on May 29. (After making its final capture in the Bering Sea on June 28, the *Shenandoah* ceases hostilities and sails into Liverpool, England, on November 7.) Johnson issues proclamation on amnesty and pardon on May 29 and begins establishing new state governments in the South on terms Radical Republicans consider too lenient.

Confederate General Edmund Kirby Smith signs Trans-Mississippi surrender agreement on June 2. Major General Gordon Granger arrives in Galveston and issues General Orders No. 3 on June 19, proclaiming the end of slavery in Texas.

The official records of the U.S. War Department recorded the deaths of 360,000 Union soldiers during the war, including 110,000 in battle or from battle wounds and 250,000 from disease and other non-battle causes. Confederate deaths were estimated in the late nineteenth century at 258,000, including 94,000 battle deaths and 164,000 non-battle deaths. Many records of Confederate battle losses are missing or incomplete, and the assumption underlying the estimate for Confederate non-battle deaths—that Confederate soldiers died from disease at the same rate as Union soldiers—has been challenged. In the late twentieth century, total civilian deaths in the war, primarily from disease and malnutrition, were estimated at 50,000. A new study of census records published in 2011 by the demographic historian J. David Hacker estimated that the war caused the death of 752,000 American men from 1861 to 1870.

Biographical Notes

Charles Francis Adams (August 18, 1807–November 21, 1886) Born in Boston, Massachusetts, the son of John Quincy Adams and Louisa Johnson Adams and grandson of John and Abigail Adams. Graduated from Harvard in 1825. Admitted to the bar in 1829. Married Abigail Brown Brooks the same year. Served as a Whig in the Massachusetts house of representatives, 1841–43, and in the state senate, 1844–45. Vice-presidential candidate of the Free Soil Party in 1848. Edited *The Works of John Adams* (1850–56). Served in Congress as a Republican, 1859–61. As U.S. minister to Great Britain, 1861–68, helped maintain British neutrality in the Civil War. Served as the U.S. representative on the international arbitration tribunal that settled American claims against Great Britain for losses caused by Confederate commerce raiders built in British shipyards, 1871–72. Edited the *Memoirs of John Quincy Adams* (1874–77). Died in Boston.

Charles Francis Adams Jr. (May 27, 1835–March 20, 1915) Born in Boston, Massachusetts, brother of Henry Adams, son of lawyer Charles Francis Adams and Abigail Brooks Adams, grandson of John Quincy Adams, great-grandson of John Adams. Graduated Harvard College, 1856. Read law in Boston and passed bar, 1858. Commissioned first lieutenant, 1st Massachusetts Cavalry, December 1861. Served at Hilton Head, South Carolina, 1862, and with the Army of the Potomac, 1862–63, including Antietam and Gettysburg campaigns; promoted to captain, October 1862. Commanded detached company on guard service at Army of the Potomac headquarters, spring 1864. Commissioned as lieutenant colonel of the 5th Massachusetts Cavalry, a black regiment, in July 1864, and as its colonel, February 1865; the regiment guarded Confederate prisoners at Point Lookout, Maryland, until March 1865, when it was sent to Virginia. Left army and married Mary Ogden in November 1865. Served on Massachusetts Railroad Commission, 1869–79. President of Union Pacific Railroad, 1884–90. Published series of historical works, including *Three Episodes of Massachusetts History* (1892) and biographies of Richard Henry Dana (1890) and Charles Francis Adams (1900). Died in Washington, D.C.

Henry Adams (February 16, 1838–March 27, 1918) Born in Boston, Massachusetts. Brother of Charles Francis Adams Jr., son of lawyer Charles Francis Adams and Abigail Brooks Adams, grandson of John Quincy Adams, great-grandson of John Adams. Graduated Harvard

1858; studied law in Berlin and Dresden until 1860. Served as secretary to father while Charles Francis Adams served in Congress, 1860–61, and as U.S. minister to Great Britain, 1861–68. Reported British reaction to the American Civil War as anonymous London correspondent of *The New York Times*, 1861–62. Returned to Washington, D.C., in 1868 to work as journalist. Appointed assistant professor of history at Harvard (1870–77); assumed editorship of *North American Review* (1870–76). Married Marion Hooper in 1872. Published *The Life of Albert Gallatin* (1879), biography; *Democracy* (1880), a novel that appeared anonymously; *John Randolph* (1882), a biography; *Esther* (1884), a novel that appeared pseudonymously; *History of the United States during the Administrations of Thomas Jefferson and James Madison* (1889–91); *Mont-Saint-Michel and Chartres: A Study of Thirteenth-Century Unity* (1904); *The Education of Henry Adams* (1907). Died in Washington.

Lois Bryan Adams (October 14, 1817–June 28, 1870) Born in Whitestown, New York, the daughter of a carpenter. Family moved in 1823 to Michigan Territory and settled near Ypsilanti, then moved to the Constantine area in 1835. Attended White Pigeon Academy, branch of the University of Michigan, in 1839. Married James R. Adams, a newspaper editor, in 1841. Moved to Kentucky after her husband died of consumption in 1848, and taught school for three years before returning to Michigan in 1851. Began writing for the monthly (later weekly) *Michigan Farmer* and for the *Detroit Advertiser and Tribune*. Moved to Detroit in 1853 to work on the *Michigan Farmer*, and became its copublisher in 1854 and household editor in 1856. Sold her interest in the publication in 1861. Published *Sybelle and Other Poems* (1862). Moved to Washington, D.C., in 1863 to take post as clerk in the recently formed Department of Agriculture and became assistant to the director of the agricultural museum. Volunteered during the war for the Michigan Soldiers' Relief Association while contributing columns to the *Detroit Advertiser and Tribune*. Continued work at the Department of Agriculture after the war. Died in Washington, D.C.

Henry Robinson Berkeley (March 27, 1840–January 16, 1918) Born in Hanover County, Virginia, the son of a farmer. Studied at the Hanover Academy, 1859–61. Enlisted in the Hanover artillery company in May 1861. Sent home in October 1861 to recover from typhoid fever. Returned to duty in March 1862. Saw action in the siege of Yorktown and at Glendale. Joined Kirkpatrick's Battery in Nelson's Battalion after the Hanover company disbanded in October 1862. Fought at Fredericksburg, Gettysburg, the Wilderness, Spotsylvania, Cold Harbor, Monocacy, Kernstown, Winchester, Fisher's Hill, and Cedar

Creek. Captured at Waynesboro, Virginia, March 2, 1865. Held as prisoner of war at Fort Delaware until June 20, 1865, when he was released after taking oath of allegiance. Became tutor and schoolteacher in Loudoun County, Virginia. Moved to Orange County, Virginia, in 1882. Married his cousin Anna Louisa Berkeley in 1883. Bought farm near Orange Court House in 1886 and operated school there until 1900. Retired from teaching in 1904. Died in Orange County, Virginia.

Edgeworth Bird (July 21, 1825–January 11, 1867) Born William Edgeworth Bird in Hancock County, Georgia, the son of a planter. Graduated from Georgetown College in 1844. Married Sarah Baxter in 1848. Lived on Granite Farm, a cotton plantation four miles east of Sparta, Georgia. Ran unsuccessfully as secessionist for the Georgia convention held in January 1861. Became captain of Company E, 15th Georgia Infantry, in the summer of 1861. Seriously wounded at Second Manassas on August 30, 1862. Returned to duty in March 1863 as quartermaster of Benning's Brigade in Hood's (later Field's) Division. Served at Gettysburg, Chickamauga, Knoxville, the Wilderness, Cold Harbor, and in the defense of Richmond. Appointed in September 1864 to board handling claims made for the loss of slaves used as laborers by the Confederate army. Returned to Granite Farm in early 1865. Died in Hancock County, Georgia.

John Wilkes Booth (May 10, 1838–April 26, 1865) Born on a farm near Bel Air, Maryland, the son of well-known actor Junius Booth. Raised on farm and in Baltimore. Educated at Milton Academy in Cockeysville and St. Timothy's Hall in Catonsville. Began acting career in Baltimore in 1855. Became a member of the nativist Know-Nothing movement. Continued acting in Philadelphia and Richmond. A strong supporter of slavery, Booth joined Virginia militia company that helped guard the execution of John Brown at Charles Town in December 1859. Began touring the country as a leading man in 1860. Ended professional acting career in May 1864, although he would later appear in benefit performance of *Julius Caesar* with his brothers Edwin and Junius. Began enlisting conspirators in plot to abduct President Lincoln and exchange him for Confederate prisoners of war. Met with Confederate agents in Montreal in October 1864 and may have taken money from them. (Booth told his sister Asia in November 1864 that he smuggled quinine into the Confederacy.) Decided after the fall of Richmond to assassinate Lincoln, Secretary of State Seward, and Vice President Johnson. Shot Lincoln in Washington on April 14 and escaped through Maryland into Virginia, where he was killed by Union soldiers at the Garrett farm near Port Royal on April 26, 1865.

Thomas Bramlette (January 3, 1817–January 12, 1875) Born in Cumberland County, Kentucky. Studied law and was admitted to the Kentucky bar in 1837. Married Sallie Travis in 1837. Elected as Whig to the state house of representatives and served one term, 1841–42. Appointed commonwealth's attorney for the eighth district, 1849–51. Moved to Adair County in 1852. Elected judge for the sixth district and served 1856–61. At the outbreak of the war Bramlette opposed both secession and the neutrality policy of Governor Beriah Magoffin. Raised and led the 3rd Kentucky Infantry, August 1861–July 1862. Appointed as U.S. district attorney for Kentucky by Lincoln in February 1863. Elected governor as a Union Democrat in August 1863 and served from September 1863 until September 1867. Opposed enlistment of black troops and suspension of the writ of habeas corpus in Kentucky. Practiced law in Louisville after leaving office. Married Mary Adams in 1874 after the death of his first wife. Died in Louisville.

Charles Harvey Brewster (October 10, 1833–October 7, 1893) Born in Northampton, Massachusetts. Educated in Northampton public schools. Worked as a store clerk. Voted for Lincoln in the 1860 election. Enlisted in 10th Massachusetts Infantry in April 1861 and commissioned as second lieutenant in December 1861. Served at Camp Brightwood outside Washington, D.C., until April 1862, when his regiment was sent to the Peninsula. Saw action in the siege of Yorktown, Fair Oaks, Oak Grove, and Malvern Hill. Promoted to first lieutenant in September 1862 and made regimental adjutant in December 1862. Saw action at Chancellorsville, Rappahannock Station, the Wilderness, Spotsylvania, North Anna, and Cold Harbor. Mustered out in June 1864 when his regiment completed its three-year term of service. Commissioned as captain and served as recruiter of black troops in Norfolk, Virginia, from July to November 1864, when he resigned from the army and returned to Northampton. Married Anna Williams in 1868. Opened sash, door, and paint store, then began successful florist business. Died onboard ship in New York harbor.

Sallie Brock (March 18, 1831–March 22, 1911) Born Sarah Ann Brock in Madison County, Virginia, the daughter of a hotel owner. Moved with her family to Richmond in 1858. Began working as a tutor in King and Queen County, Virginia, in 1860, but returned to Richmond in 1861 and remained there for the duration of the war. Moved to New York City in 1865. Published *Richmond During the War: Four Years of Personal Observations* (1867). Edited *The Southern Amaranth* (1869), a collection of poetry about the Confederacy and the war, and published a novel, *Kenneth, My King* (1873). Married Richard F. Putnam in 1882. Died in Brooklyn.

Clarissa Burdett A slave from Garrard County, Kentucky, who escaped to Camp Nelson in March 1865 and sought help in freeing her four children. Her husband, Elijah Burdett, was a soldier in the 12th U.S. Colored Heavy Artillery.

C. Chauncey Burr (1815–May 1, 1883) Born Charles Chauncey Burr in Maine. Studied law and passed bar. Edited quarterly magazine *The Nineteenth Century* in Philadelphia, 1848–52, which included reform and antislavery material. Helped care for Edgar Allan Poe when Poe collapsed in Philadelphia in 1849, and wrote article defending his reputation in 1852. Married Celia Kellum in 1851. Edited and published newspaper *Daily National Democrat* in New York, 1851–54. Managed lecture tours of Lola Montez in the United States, Ireland, and Great Britain, 1857–60 (the claim that he ghosted her lectures and autobiography is disputed). Edited *The Old Guard*, 1862–69, monthly magazine published in New York that defended slavery and secession and supported the Peace Democrats. Published *The History of the Union and the Constitution* (1862) and *Notes on the Constitution of the United States* (1864). Remained active in Democratic politics and journalism after the war. Died in West Hoboken, New Jersey.

Benjamin F. Butler (November 5, 1818–January 11, 1893) Born in Deerfield, New Hampshire, the son of a merchant. Graduated from Waterville (now Colby) College in 1838. Admitted to the bar in 1840 and began practicing law in Lowell, Massachusetts. Married Sarah Hildreth in 1844. Served as a Democrat in the Massachusetts house of representatives, 1853, and in the Massachusetts senate, 1859. Commissioned as brigadier general of Massachusetts militia in April 1861 and as major general of U.S. volunteers in May 1861. Led occupation of Baltimore in May 1861 before becoming commander at Fort Monroe, Virginia. Commanded troops that captured Fort Hatteras, North Carolina, in August 1861. Military governor of New Orleans, May–December 1862. Commanded the Army of the James in Virginia, 1864. Relieved of command by Ulysses S. Grant after his failed assault on Fort Fisher, North Carolina, in December 1864. Served in Congress as a Republican, 1867–75 and 1877–79, and was one of the House managers at the impeachment trial of Andrew Johnson in 1868. Elected governor of Massachusetts as a Democrat and served one-year term in 1883. Presidential candidate of the Greenback and Anti-Monopolist parties in 1884. Died in Washington, D.C.

J.F.J. Caldwell (September 19, 1837–February 3, 1925) Born in Newberry, South Carolina, the son of a lawyer, and later named James Fitz James Caldwell. Graduated from South Carolina College in 1857. Studied law in Charleston and was admitted to bar. Spent two years traveling in Europe before returning to South Carolina in early 1861. Enlisted as private in 3rd South Carolina Infantry and served until after the First Manassas campaign, when he was discharged because of illness. Joined Company B, 1st South Carolina Infantry, in April 1862 and became aide to its commander, Colonel Daniel H. Hamilton. Saw action at Mechanicsville, Gaines's Mill, Second Manassas, Antietam, and Fredericksburg. Served as brigade ordnance officer before returning to duty as lieutenant in 1st South Carolina in early 1863. Fought at Chancellorsville and was wounded at Gettysburg on July 1, 1863. Saw action at the Wilderness, Spotsylvania, North Anna, Cold Harbor, the first battle of Weldon Railroad, First Deep Bottom, and Second Deep Bottom, where he was wounded on August 16, 1864. Returned to duty in late November 1864 and served as brigade staff officer. Fought at White Oak Road and Sutherland's Station before surrendering at Appomattox. Published *The History of a Brigade of South Carolinians, known first as "Gregg's," and subsequently as "McGowan's Brigade"* (1866). Practiced law in Newberry and served as bank director and as trustee of the University of South Carolina. Married Rebecca Connor in 1875. Published *The Stranger* (1907), novel set in South Carolina during Reconstruction. Died in Newberry.

George E. Chamberlin (June 30, 1838–August 22, 1864) Born in Lyndon, Vermont. Graduated from Dartmouth College in 1860, studied law in St. Louis, and graduated from Harvard Law School in 1862. Commissioned as major in the 11th Vermont Infantry in August 1862. Served in fortifications defending Washington, D.C. Regiment renamed the 1st Vermont Heavy Artillery in December 1862. Married Adelia Gardiner in October 1863. After his regiment was sent to fight as infantry with the Army of the Potomac, saw action at Spotsylvania, Cold Harbor, and in the first battle of Weldon Railroad. Promoted to lieutenant colonel. Returned to Washington, D.C., in July when regiment was sent to help defend the capital against raid led by Lieutenant General Jubal A. Early. Wounded in skirmish at Charles Town, West Virginia, on August 21, 1864, and died at Sandy Hook, Maryland, the following day.

Salmon P. Chase (January 13, 1808–May 7, 1873) Born in Cornish, New Hampshire, the son of a farmer. After the death of his father in 1817, he was raised in Worthington, Ohio, by his uncle, Philander Chase, an Episcopal bishop. Graduated from Dartmouth College in 1826. Read law in Washington with Attorney General William Wirt and was admitted to the bar in 1829. Established law practice in Cincinnati, Ohio, in 1830. Married Catherine Jane Garniss, 1834; after her death, Eliza Ann Smith, 1839; and after Smith's death, Sarah Bella Dunlop Ludlow, 1846. Began defending fugitive slaves and those who aided them in 1837. Became a leader in the antislavery Liberty Party and campaigned for the Free Soil ticket in 1848. Served in the U.S. Senate as a Free Soil Democrat, 1849–55. Republican governor of Ohio, 1856–60. Candidate for the Republican presidential nomination in 1860. Won election to the U.S. Senate in 1860, but resigned in March 1861 to become secretary of the treasury. Helped found national banking system and successfully financed Union war effort. Resigned June 29, 1864, after making unsuccessful attempt to challenge Lincoln for the Republican nomination. Appointed chief justice of the U.S. Supreme Court on December 6, 1864, and served until his death. Upheld Radical Reconstruction measures and presided over the 1868 Senate impeachment trial of President Andrew Johnson. Died in New York City.

Thomas Morris Chester (May 11, 1834–September 30, 1892) Born in Harrisburg, Pennsylvania, the son of a restaurant owner. Parents were abolitionists active in the local black community. Attended Allegheny Institute, 1850–52. Became advocate for African American emigration to Liberia. Attended Alexander High School in Monrovia, Liberia, 1853–54. Returned to United States and attended Thetford Academy in Vermont, 1854–56. Visited Liberia 1856–58, 1858–59, and 1860–62, teaching school in Robertsport and Monrovia and publishing newspaper *Star of Liberia*. Recruited in Pennsylvania in 1863 for the 54th and 55th Massachusetts regiments. Made lecture tour in Britain in support of the Union cause, 1863–64. Began reporting on U.S. Colored Troops serving with the Army of the James for the *Philadelphia Press* in August 1864, becoming the first black war correspondent for a major American daily newspaper. Covered the fall of Richmond and Lincoln's visit to the city. Returned to Harrisburg in the summer of 1865 and joined the Equal Rights League, which campaigned against racial discrimination in the North. Made lecture tour of Britain and Europe, 1866–67, and visited Russia. Studied law in London, 1867–70, and was called to the English bar. Returned to the United States and went to Louisiana in 1871. Wounded during altercation between Republican factions in New Orleans, January 1, 1872. Admitted to the Louisiana bar in 1873. Served as brigadier general of Louisiana militia, 1873–76, and superintendent of public education for a district outside New Orleans, 1875–76. Married Florence Johnson. Practiced law in Louisiana and Pennsylvania. Settled in New Orleans in 1888. Died in Harrisburg.

Achilles V. Clark (March 13, 1842–July 29, 1874) Born in Henry County, Tennessee. College student and slaveowner at the start of the war. Enlisted in the Confederate 20th Tennessee Cavalry in early 1864. Promoted to sergeant and then lieutenant. Returned to Henry

County after the war and settled in Paris. Married Mary Elizabeth Wilson in 1866. Died in Nashville.

Clement C. Clay (December 13, 1816–January 3, 1882) Born in Huntsville, Alabama, the son of a lawyer who later served as governor of Alabama and as a U.S. senator. Graduated from the University of Alabama, 1834. Received law degree from the University of Virginia, 1839. Began legal practice in Huntsville in 1840. Married Virginia Tunstall in 1843. Served in state legislature, 1842, 1844, and 1845. Judge of the Madison County court, 1846–48. Served in the U.S. Senate as a Democrat, 1853–61, and in the Confederate senate, 1862–64. Confederate agent in Canada, May 1864–January 1865. Surrendered at Macon, Georgia, on May 11, 1865, after being accused of complicity in the assassination of President Lincoln. Imprisoned without trial at Fort Monroe until his release in April 1866. Returned to Alabama and practiced law in Jackson County. Died in Madison County, Alabama.

Howell Cobb (September 7, 1815–October 9, 1868) Born in Jefferson County, Georgia, the son of a wealthy cotton planter. Graduated from The University of Georgia and married Mary Ann Lamar in 1834. Admitted to the bar in 1836. Served as solicitor general of the western judicial district of Georgia, 1837–41. Elected to Congress as a Democrat and served 1843–51 and 1855–57. Supported Compromise of 1850 as Speaker of the House, 1849–51. Governor of Georgia, 1851–53. Secretary of the treasury in the Buchanan administration from March 1857 until December 1860, when he resigned and called for the immediate secession of Georgia. President of the Provisional Confederate Congress, February 1861–February 1862. Commissioned as brigadier general in February 1862. Led brigade in Seven Days' Battles and at Crampton's Gap. Promoted to major general in 1863. Commanded Georgia state troops, 1863–65. Practiced law in Macon after the war. Died in New York City.

James A. Connolly (March 8, 1838–December 15, 1914) Born in Newark, New Jersey, the son of a tanner. Moved with family around 1850 to Chesterville, Ohio. Graduated from Selby Academy in Chesterville and studied law. Admitted to the bar in 1859 and served as assistant clerk of the Ohio state senate, 1859–60. Moved to Charleston, Illinois, in 1860. Mustered into service as major of the newly formed 123rd Illinois Infantry in September 1862. Fought at Perryville. Married Mary Dunn, sister of the judge with whom he had read law, in February 1863. Fought at Milton (Vaught's Hill) and Chickamauga. Joined staff of the Third Division, Fourteenth Corps, commanded by Brigadier General Absalom Baird. Served at Chattanooga, in the

Atlanta campaign, and in Sherman's marches through Georgia and the Carolinas. Helped escort Abraham Lincoln's body to Springfield. Returned to law practice in Charleston before moving to Springfield in 1886. Served in Illinois house of representatives, 1872–76, as U.S. attorney for the Southern District of Illinois, 1876–85 and 1889–94, and as a Republican congressman, 1895–99. Died in Springfield.

Maria Lydig Daly (September 12, 1824–August 21, 1894) Born Maria Lydig in New York City, the daughter of a wealthy grain merchant and landowner. Married Judge Charles P. Daly of the New York Court of Common Pleas, the son of poor Irish immigrants, in 1856 despite opposition from many members of her family who objected to his Catholicism and family background. Supported the Woman's Central Association of Relief during the Civil War and visited sick and wounded soldiers. Died at her country home in North Haven, New York.

Charles A. Dana (August 8, 1819–October 17, 1897) Born in Hinsdale, New Hampshire, the son of a merchant. Worked as clerk in uncle's store in Buffalo, New York, 1831–39. Studied at Harvard, 1839–41. Lived at Brook Farm, utopian community in West Roxbury, Massachusetts, 1841–46. Wrote for the *Boston Daily Chronotype*, 1844–46. Married Eunice MacDaniel in 1846. Hired by Horace Greeley as city editor of the *New-York Daily Tribune* in 1847. Reported for the *Tribune* from France and Germany, 1848–49. Served as managing editor of the *Tribune*, 1849–62, and helped make it one of the most widely circulated antislavery newspapers in the country. Began working for the War Department, and was sent to Grant's headquarters in the spring of 1863 to report on his conduct to Lincoln and Secretary of War Stanton. Gained Grant's confidence and wrote reports that reassured the administration. Served as assistant secretary of war, January 1864–July 1865. Editor of the *Chicago Daily Republican*, 1865–67. Wrote campaign biography *The Life of Ulysses S. Grant* (1868) with James H. Wilson. Editor of the *New York Sun*, 1868–97. Supported Horace Greeley, the Liberal Republican candidate, against Grant in 1872 and followed independent course in politics afterward. Published *The Art of Newspaper Making* (1895). Memoir *Recollections of the Civil War* (1898), published posthumously, was based in part on interviews journalist Ida M. Tarbell conducted with Dana in 1896. Died in Glen Cove, New York.

Henry Winter Davis (August 16, 1817–December 30, 1865) Born in Annapolis, Maryland, the son of an Episcopal minister. Graduated from Kenyon College in 1837. Studied law at the University of Virginia. Began legal practice in Alexandria, Virginia, 1840. Married

Constance Gardiner in 1845. Moved to Baltimore, 1850. Elected to Congress as an American (Know-Nothing) and served 1855–61. Married Nancy Morris in 1857 after the death of his first wife. Opposed secession in Maryland. Defeated for reelection but returned to Congress as an Unconditional Unionist, 1863–65. Served on the Select Committee on Rebellious States and coauthored the Wade-Davis reconstruction bill in 1864. Defeated for reelection. Died in Baltimore.

Jefferson Davis (June 3, 1808–December 6, 1889) Born in Christian (now Todd) County, Kentucky, the son of a farmer. Moved with his family to Mississippi. Graduated from West Point in 1828 and served in the Black Hawk War. Resigned his commission in 1835 and married Sarah Knox Taylor, who died later in the year. Became a cotton planter in Warren County, Mississippi. Married Varina Howell in 1845. Elected to Congress as a Democrat and served 1845–46, then resigned to command a Mississippi volunteer regiment in Mexico, 1846–47, where he fought at Monterrey and was wounded at Buena Vista. Elected to the Senate and served from 1847 to 1851, when he resigned to run unsuccessfully for governor. Secretary of war in the cabinet of Franklin Pierce, 1853–57. Elected to the Senate and served from 1857 to January 21, 1861, when he withdrew following the secession of Mississippi. Inaugurated as provisional president of the Confederate States of America on February 18, 1861. Elected without opposition to six-year term in November 1861 and inaugurated on February 22, 1862. Captured by Union cavalry near Irwinville, Georgia, on May 10, 1865. Imprisoned at Fort Monroe, Virginia, and indicted for treason. Released on bail on May 13, 1867; the indictment was dropped in 1869 without trial. Published *The Rise and Fall of the Confederate Government* in 1881. Died in New Orleans.

John Q. A. Dennis A freed slave from Worcester County, Maryland, who was living in Boston in 1864 when he wrote to Secretary of War Stanton seeking help in freeing his three children.

Frederick Douglass (February 1818–February 20, 1895) Born Frederick Bailey in Talbot County, Maryland, the son of a slave mother and an unknown white man. Worked on farms and in Baltimore shipyards. Escaped to Philadelphia in 1838. Married Anna Murray, a free woman from Maryland, and settled in New Bedford, Massachusetts, where he took the name Douglass. Became a lecturer for the American Anti-Slavery Society, led by William Lloyd Garrison, in 1841. Published *Narrative of the Life of Frederick Douglass, An American Slave* (1845). Began publishing *North Star*, first in a series of antislavery newspapers, in Rochester, New York, in 1847. Broke with Garrison and became an ally of Gerrit Smith, who advocated an antislavery interpretation of the Constitution and participation in electoral politics. Published *My Bondage and My Freedom* (1855). Advocated emancipation and the enlistment of black soldiers at the outbreak of the Civil War. Met with Abraham Lincoln in Washington in August 1863 and August 1864, and wrote public letter supporting his reelection in September 1864. Continued his advocacy of racial equality and women's rights after the Civil War. Served as U.S. marshal for the District of Columbia, 1877–81, and as its recorder of deeds, 1881–86. Published *Life and Times of Frederick Douglass* (1881). After the death of his wife Anna, married Helen Pitts in 1884. Served as minister to Haiti, 1889–91. Died in Washington, D.C.

Samuel Francis Du Pont (September 27, 1803–June 23, 1865) Born in Bergen Point, New Jersey, the son of a former French diplomat. Moved with family to Delaware, where his uncle had founded the Du Pont gunpowder works. Appointed a midshipman in the U.S. Navy in 1815. Promoted to lieutenant, 1826. Married first cousin Sophie Madeleine du Pont in 1833. Promoted to commander, 1842. Commanded sloop *Cyane* along the Pacific coast during the Mexican War. Promoted to captain, 1855, and flag officer, September 1861. Led South Atlantic blockading squadron in capture of Port Royal, South Carolina, in November 1861. Appointed rear admiral, 1862. Failed to capture Charleston in April 1863 while leading fleet of seven ironclad monitors. Relieved of command in July 1863 at his request. Died in Philadelphia.

Catherine Edmondston (October 10, 1823–January 3, 1875) Born Catherine Ann Devereux in Halifax County, North Carolina, the daughter of a plantation owner. Married Patrick Edmondston in 1846. Lived on Looking Glass plantation in Halifax County. Published pamphlet *The Morte d'Arthur: Its Influence on the Spirit and Manners of the Nineteenth Century* (1872), in which she accused the Union army of barbarism. Died in Raleigh.

David G. Farragut (July 5, 1801–August 14, 1870) Born James Glasgow Farragut at Campbell's Station, near Knoxville, Tennessee, the son of a naval officer. After his mother's death in 1808 he was adopted by David Porter, a naval officer, and became foster brother to his son David D. Porter (later a Union rear admiral). Appointed midshipman in the U.S. Navy, 1810. Changed his name to David. Served in the War of 1812 under Porter's command on frigate *Essex* until the ship's capture off Chile in March 1814. Married Susan C. Marchant in 1823 and settled in Norfolk, Virginia. Promoted to lieutenant, 1825, and commander, 1843. After the death of his first wife, married Virginia Loyall in 1843. Assigned to blockade duty during the

U.S.-Mexican War. Promoted to captain in 1855 while serving as commander of the Mare Island navy yard in Vallejo, California. Remained loyal to the Union when Virginia seceded, and was appointed commander of the West Gulf Blockading Squadron in January 1862. Forced passage of the lower Mississippi and captured New Orleans, April 24–25, 1862. Promoted to newly created rank of rear admiral, July 1862. Commanded squadron in the Union victory at Mobile Bay, August 5, 1864. Promoted to vice admiral in 1864 and admiral in 1866. Remained on active duty until his death in Portsmouth, New Hampshire.

Charles B. Fisher (c. 1839–January 27, 1903) Born in Alexandria, Virginia. Worked as a bookbinder. Enlisted in U.S. Navy in Boston, January 1862. Served on the steam sloop U.S.S. *Kearsarge* as landsman (apprentice seaman), officers' cook, and steward. Discharged November 1864. After the war, formed and led "Butler's Zouaves," the first black militia in the District of Columbia. Died in Washington, D.C.

Wilbur Fisk (June 7, 1839–March 12, 1914) Born in Sharon, Vermont, the son of a farmer. Family moved to Lowell, Massachusetts, in 1852 to work in woolen mills, then returned to Vermont in 1854 and settled on farm in Tunbridge. Worked as hired farm laborer and taught in local schools. Enlisted in September 1861 in Company E, 2nd Vermont Infantry. Contributed regular letters under the name "Anti-Rebel" to *The Green Mountain Freeman* of Montpelier from December 11, 1861, to July 26, 1865. Saw action in the siege of Yorktown and in the Seven Days' Battles. Hospitalized with severe diarrhea in Washington, D.C., in early September 1862. Recovered in convalescent camp in Fairfax, Virginia, then went absent without leave and married Angelina Drew of Lawrence, Massachusetts, in February 1863. Returned to regiment in March 1863 and served at Chancellorsville, Gettysburg, Rappahannock Station, Mine Run, the Wilderness, Spotsylvania, North Anna, Cold Harbor, and Petersburg. Sent with regiment in July 1864 to help defend the capital against Jubal Early's Washington raid. Served in the Shenandoah Valley at Winchester, Fisher's Hill, and Cedar Creek before returning to Petersburg siege lines in December 1864. Detached for guard duty at Sixth Corps hospital at City Point, Virginia, in January 1865, and served there for remainder of the war. Rejoined family, who had moved to Geneva, Kansas, and worked on farm. Licensed as Congregational preacher in 1874, and the following year became pastor of a church in Freeborn, Minnesota, where he served until his retirement in 1909. Following the death of his first wife in 1898, married Amanda Dickerson Dickey in 1909. Died in Geneva, Kansas.

Samuel W. Fiske (July 23, 1828–May 22, 1864) Born in Shelburne, Massachusetts. Graduated from Amherst College in 1848. Taught school, studied for three years at Andover Theological Seminary, then returned to Amherst in 1853 as a tutor. Traveled in Europe and the Middle East. Published *Dunn Browne's Experiences in Foreign Parts* (1857), travel letters written to the *Springfield Republican* under a nom de plume. Became pastor of the Congregational church in Madison, Connecticut, in 1857. Married Elizabeth Foster in 1858. Became second lieutenant in the 14th Connecticut Infantry in August 1862. Signing himself Dunn Browne, wrote weekly letters to the *Springfield Republican* describing campaigns and camp life (collected in 1866 under the title *Mr. Dunn Browne's Experiences in the Army*). Served at Antietam and Fredericksburg. Promoted to captain in early 1863. Captured at Chancellorsville on May 3, 1863, was paroled in late May and exchanged in June. Served at Gettysburg. Wounded in the battle of the Wilderness on May 6, 1864, and died in Fredericksburg, Virginia.

Eugene Forbes (May 14, 1833–February 7, 1865) Born in Trenton, New Jersey. Worked as a printer. Served in the 3rd New Jersey Militia, April–August 1861. Enlisted for three years in Company B, 4th New Jersey Infantry, in fall 1861. Captured along with most of his regiment at Gaines's Mill. Held at the Libby prison and Belle Isle camp in Richmond before being exchanged in August 1862. Saw action at Second Bull Run, Crampton's Gap, and Fredericksburg, and guarded supply trains at Chancellorsville and Gettysburg. Reenlisted in 1864 and promoted to sergeant. Captured in the Wilderness on May 6, 1864. Imprisoned in stockades at Andersonville, Georgia, May 24–September 12, and Florence, South Carolina, from September 15 until his death on February 7, 1865. His diary was saved by a fellow prisoner and printed at Trenton in 1865.

Samuel T. Foster (November 9, 1829–January 8, 1919) Born in Union District (county), South Carolina. Moved with family to Hallettsville, Lacava County, Texas, in 1847. Married Mary Ham in 1855 and began practicing law. Moved in 1859 to Oakville and was appointed chief justice of the Live Oak County court in 1860. Mustered into Confederate service in April 1862 as first lieutenant, Company H, 24th Texas Cavalry. Regiment was sent to Arkansas in summer of 1862 and dismounted. Captured at surrender of Fort Hindman, Arkansas, January 11, 1863. Imprisoned at Camp Chase, Columbus, Ohio. Exchanged in May 1863. Posted with his regiment to the Army of Tennessee. Promoted to captain. Commanded company in the Tullahoma campaign and at Chickamauga. Wounded at Chattanooga. Returned to duty in March 1864 and led company during the Atlanta campaign and the invasion of Tennessee. Fought at Franklin before being wounded outside Nashville on December 13, 1864. Retreated into northern Mississippi. Joined Joseph E. Johnston's army in North Carolina in March 1865, and surrendered with Johnston's forces on April 26, 1865. Returned to Oakville. Served in Texas house of representatives in 1866. Moved to Corpus Christi in 1868 and became manager for a general merchandising and banking house. Moved to Laredo in 1880. Served as commissioner for the U.S. District Court for the Western (later Southern) District of Texas. After the death of his first wife, married Bettie Moore in 1897. Died in Laredo.

Garrison Frazier (1797–?) Born into slavery in Granville County, North Carolina. Became a Baptist minister around 1830. Bought his and his wife's freedom for $1,000 in 1856. Lived in Savannah, Georgia, in 1865.

Henry Highland Garnet (December 23, 1815–February 13, 1882) Born in Kent County, Maryland, the son of slaves. Family escaped in 1824 and settled in New York City, taking the name Garnet. Graduated from the Oneida Institute in Whitesboro, New York, in 1839. Served as pastor of the Liberty Street Presbyterian Church in Troy, New York, 1840–48. Underwent leg amputation in 1840 as the result of an earlier injury. Became active in the antislavery Liberty Party and a leading advocate of abolishing the property qualification that prevented most black men from voting in New York State. Attended National Negro Convention held in Buffalo in 1843, where his call for violent resistance to slavery was opposed by Frederick Douglass. Taught school in Geneva, New York, 1848–49. Toured Great Britain and Ireland as an antislavery speaker, 1850–53. Served as a Presbyterian missionary in Jamaica, 1853–56, and as pastor of the Shiloh Presbyterian Church in New York City, 1856–64. Founded African Civilization Society in 1858 to promote cotton cultivation by African American colonists in the Niger valley. Helped recruit black troops and aided victims of the New York draft riots in 1863. Became pastor of the Fifteenth Street Presbyterian Church in Washington, D.C., in 1864. Delivered sermon in the House of Representatives in 1865 to celebrate congressional approval of the Thirteenth Amendment. President of Avery College in Allegheny, Pennsylvania, 1868–70, then returned to Shiloh Church. Appointed U.S. minister to Liberia in 1881 and died there shortly after his arrival.

John White Geary (December 30, 1819–February 8, 1873) Born near Mount Pleasant, Pennsylvania, the son of a schoolmaster. Studied at Jefferson College. Taught school and worked as surveyor and railroad engineer. Studied law and was admitted to the Pennsylvania bar.

Married Margaret Logan in 1843. Appointed lieutenant colonel of the 2nd Pennsylvania Infantry in January 1847 and fought at La Hoya, Chapultepec, and Garita de Belen. Promoted to colonel, November 1847. Served as postmaster of San Francisco, 1849, and as its mayor, 1850–51. Returned to Pennsylvania in 1852 to practice law. Appointed governor of Kansas Territory in July 1856. Resigned in March 1857 after coming into conflict with proslavery settlers. After the death of his first wife, married Mary Henderson in 1858. Appointed colonel of the 28th Pennsylvania Infantry in June 1861. Became commander of a brigade posted on the upper Potomac in September 1861, and was wounded in skirmishes at Bolivar Heights, October 1861, and Leesburg, March 1862. Commissioned as a brigadier general, April 1862. Seriously wounded at Cedar Mountain, August 1862. Returned to duty in late September 1862 and was given command of the Second Division, Twelfth Corps. Led division at Chancellorsville, where he was again wounded, and at Gettysburg. Sent with his division to Tennessee in October 1863. Fought at Wauhatchie, where his eighteen-year-old son Edward, an officer in the division, was killed, and at Chattanooga. Division became part of the Twentieth Corps, April 1864. Served in the Atlanta campaign, the march to Savannah, and the march through the Carolinas. Elected governor of Pennsylvania as a Republican, 1866, and served two terms, 1867–73. Died in Harrisburg, Pennsylvania.

James R. Gilmore (September 10, 1822–November 16, 1903) Born in Boston, Massachusetts. Established successful cotton and shipping business in New York City. Proprietor of *Continental Monthly*, 1862–64. Under the penname Edmund Kirke, published *Among the Pines, or South in Secession-time* (1862) and *My Southern Friends* (1863). Accompanied Colonel James F. Jaquess on unofficial peace mission to Richmond in July 1864. Writing as Edmund Kirke, published *Down in Tennessee, and back by way of Richmond* (1864), *Among the Guerillas* (1866), *Patriot Boys and Prison Pictures* (1866), and *On the Border* (1867). Married Laura Edmonds. Resumed business career in 1873. Under his own name, published *The Life of James A. Garfield* (1880). Retired from business in 1883. Published *The Rear-Guard of the Revolution* (1886), *John Sevier as a Commonwealth-Builder* (1887), *The Advance-Guard of Western Civilization* (1888), *A Mountain-White Heroine* (1889), *The Last of the Thorndikes* (1889), and *Personal Recollections of Abraham Lincoln and the Civil War* (1898). Died in Glen Falls, New York.

Gordon Granger (November 6, 1822–January 10, 1876) Born in Joy, Wayne County, New York. Graduated from West Point in 1845 and commissioned as second lieutenant. Fought at Cerro Gordo, Contreras, Churubusco, and Chapultepec in the war with Mexico. Served in

Washington and Oregon, 1849–51, and Texas and New Mexico, 1852–60. Promoted to first lieutenant, 1852, and captain, 1861. Fought at Wilson's Creek as a brigade staff aide. Commissioned as colonel of the 2nd Michigan Cavalry in September 1861. Promoted to brigadier general, March 1862, and led cavalry division in John Pope's Army of the Mississippi at New Madrid, Island No. 10, and the advance on Corinth. Promoted to major general. Commanded Union troops in Kentucky and Middle Tennessee, October 1862–June 1863, and defended Franklin, Tennessee, against Confederate cavalry raids. Led Reserve Corps of the Army of the Cumberland in the Tullahoma campaign and at Chickamauga, where he reinforced George H. Thomas and helped hold the Union left. Commanded Fourth Corps of the Army of the Cumberland at Chattanooga and in the relief of Knoxville. Led army detachment that captured Forts Gaines and Morgan in Mobile Bay, August 1864. Commanded Union forces in western Florida and southern Alabama, September 1864–February 1865. Led Thirteenth Corps in Mobile campaign, March–April 1865. Commanded District of Texas, June–August 1865. Mustered out of volunteer service in 1866 and served as colonel in the postwar army. Married Maria Letcher in 1867. Commanded District of New Mexico, 1871–73 and 1875–76. Died in Santa Fe, New Mexico Territory.

Ulysses S. Grant (April 22, 1822–July 23, 1885) Born in Point Pleasant, Ohio, the son of a tanner. Graduated from West Point in 1843. Served in the U.S.-Mexican War, 1846–48, and promoted to first lieutenant in 1847. Married Julia Dent in 1848. Promoted to captain, 1854, and resigned commission. Worked as a farmer, real estate agent, and general store clerk, 1854–61. Commissioned colonel, 21st Illinois Volunteers, June 1861, and brigadier general of volunteers, August 1861. Promoted to major general of volunteers, February 1862, after victories at Forts Henry and Donelson. Defeated Confederates at Shiloh, April 1862, and captured Vicksburg, Mississippi, July 1863. Promoted to major general in the regular army, July 1863, and assigned to command of Military Division of the Mississippi, covering territory between the Alleghenies and the Mississippi, October 1863. Won battle of Chattanooga, November 1863. Promoted to lieutenant general, March 1864, and named general-in-chief of the Union armies. Accepted surrender of Robert E. Lee at Appomattox Court House, April 9, 1865. Promoted to general, July 1866. Served as secretary of war ad interim, August 1867–January 1868. Nominated for president by the Republican Party in 1868. Defeated Democrat Horatio Seymour, and won reelection in 1872 by defeating Liberal Republican Horace Greeley. President of the United States, 1869–77. Made world tour, 1877–79. Failed to win Republican presidential nomination, 1880. Worked on Wall Street, 1881–84, and was financially ruined when private banking firm of Grant & Ward collapsed. Wrote *Personal Memoirs of U.S. Grant*, 1884–85, while suffering from throat cancer, and completed them days before his death at Mount McGregor, New York.

John Chipman Gray (July 14, 1839–February 25, 1915) Born in Brighton, Massachusetts, the son of a merchant and iron manufacturer. Educated at Boston Latin School. Graduated from Harvard College in 1859 and from Harvard Law School in 1862. Commissioned as second lieutenant in the 41st Massachusetts Infantry, October 1862. Served as an aide to Brigadier General George H. Gordon in Virginia, South Carolina, Florida, and Arkansas, 1862–64. Appointed judge advocate for the Department of the South in the fall of 1864 and served until the end of the war. Founded successful law practice with John Codman Ropes in 1865. Married Anna Lyman Mason, 1873. Lecturer at Harvard Law School, 1870–75, Story Professor of Law, 1875–83, and Royall Professor of Law, 1883–1913. Published *Restraints on the Alienation of Property* (1883), *The Rule against Perpetuities* (1886), and *The Nature and Sources of the Law* (1909). Died in Boston.

Horace Greeley (February 3, 1811–November 29, 1872) Born in Amherst, New Hampshire, the son of a farmer. Learned printing trade in Vermont, upstate New York, and Pennsylvania. Moved to New York City in 1831. Founded and edited weekly *New Yorker*, 1834–41. Married Mary Cheney in 1836. Edited Whig campaign newspapers *Jeffersonian*, 1838, and *Log Cabin*, 1840. Founded *New York Tribune*, 1841, and used it to advocate for social reforms and antislavery positions. Served in Congress, 1848–49. Active in Whig and Republican politics. Nominated for president by the Liberal Republicans and the Democrats in 1872, but was defeated by Ulysses S. Grant. Died in New York City.

Cornelia Hancock (February 8, 1840–December 31, 1927) Born in Hancock's Bridge, near Salem, New Jersey, the daughter of a Quaker fisherman. Educated in Salem schools. Brother and several cousins enlisted in Union army in 1862. Traveled to Gettysburg with her brother-in-law Dr. Henry T. Child in July 1863 and served as volunteer nurse in Second Corps and general army hospitals until September. Volunteered as nurse at the Contraband Hospital for escaped slaves in Washington, D.C., October 1863–February 1864, and at army hospitals in Virginia at Brandy Station, February–April 1864; Fredericksburg and White House, May–June 1864; and City Point, June 1864–May 1865. Founded the Laing School for freed slaves in

Pleasantville, South Carolina, in 1866 with funds from the Freedmen's Bureau and donations from the Philadelphia Yearly Meeting of the Society of Friends. Resigned as principal in 1875 and returned to Philadelphia. Visited England and studied efforts to help the poor in London. Helped found the Philadelphia Society for Organizing Charitable Relief in 1878 and the Children's Aid Society of Philadelphia in 1882. Engaged in philanthropic work in the Sixth Ward and in "Wrightsville," a slum neighborhood in South Philadelphia. Retired in 1914 to Atlantic City, New Jersey, where she died.

Mathella Page Harrison A resident of Clarke County, Virginia, in 1864. Her husband was a slaveholding physician and farmer.

John Hay (October 8, 1838–July 1, 1905) Born in Salem, Indiana, the son of a doctor. Family moved to Warsaw, Illinois. Graduated from Brown University in 1858. Studied law in office of his uncle in Springfield, Illinois. Traveled to Washington in 1861 as assistant private secretary to Abraham Lincoln, serving until early in 1865. First secretary to American legation in Paris, 1865–67; chargé d'affaires in Vienna, 1867–68; and legation secretary in Madrid, 1868–70. Published *Castilian Days* (1871) and *Pike County Ballads and Other Pieces* (1871). Married Clara Louise Stone in 1874. Served as assistant secretary of state, 1879–81. Political novel *The Bread-Winners*, an attack on labor unions, published anonymously in 1884. In collaboration with John G. Nicolay, wrote *Abraham Lincoln: A History* (10 volumes, 1890) and edited *Complete Works of Abraham Lincoln* (2 volumes, 1894). Ambassador to Great Britain, 1897–98. Served as secretary of state in the administrations of William McKinley and Theodore Roosevelt, 1898–1905. Among first seven members elected to American Academy of Arts and Letters in 1904. Died in Newbury, New Hampshire.

Jim Heiskell (1848–June 14, 1886) A slave who escaped from his loyalist owner in Knoxville in March 1864 and was freed by the Union army. Later worked as a barber in Knoxville, where he died.

James P. Holcombe (September 20, 1820–August 22, 1873) Born in Powhatan County, Virginia, the son of a physician. Attended Yale and the University of Virginia. Married Anne Watts, 1841. Practiced law for several years in Cincinnati, Ohio, and published several books on legal subjects. Professor of law at the University of Virginia, 1851–61. Prominent advocate of secession in the Virginia convention. Member of the Confederate house of representatives, 1862–64. Served as Confederate agent in Canada, March–September 1864. Opened private school in Bedford County, Virginia, in 1866. Died in Capon Springs, West Virginia.

Ellen Renshaw House (August 10, 1843–May 19, 1907) Born in Savannah, Georgia, the daughter of a customs collector. Moved with family to Marietta in 1848 and to Knoxville around 1860. Expelled from Knoxville by the Union army in April 1864 as a Confederate sympathizer. Lived in Abingdon, Virginia, and Eatonton, Georgia, before returning to Knoxville in June 1865. Married James Fletcher in 1867. Died while visiting family in South Carolina.

Harriet Ann Jacobs (1813–March 7, 1897) Born in Edenton, North Carolina, the daughter of slaves. After the death of her mother in 1819, she was raised by her grandmother and her white mistress, Margaret Horniblow, who taught her to read, write, and sew. In 1825 Horniblow died, and Jacobs was sent to the household of Dr. James Norcom. At sixteen, to escape Norcom's repeated sexual advances, Jacobs began a relationship with a white lawyer, Samuel Tredwell Sawyer (later a member of the U.S. House of Representatives), with whom she had two children, Joseph (b. 1829) and Louisa Matilda (b. 1833). In 1835, Jacobs ran away and spent the next seven years hiding in a crawl space above her freed grandmother's storeroom. In 1842, she escaped to New York City, where she was reunited with her children. Worked as a nurse for the family of Nathaniel Parker Willis; moved to Boston in 1843 to avoid recapture by Norcom. Moved to Rochester in 1849, where she became part of a circle of abolitionists surrounding Frederick Douglass. In 1852, Cornelia Grinnell Willis, second wife of Nathaniel Parker Willis, purchased Jacobs's manumission. Published *Incidents in the Life of a Slave Girl, Written by Herself* pseudonymously in 1861. From 1862 to 1868 engaged in Quaker-sponsored relief work among former slaves in Washington, D.C.; Alexandria, Virginia; and Savannah, Georgia. She then lived with her daughter in Cambridge, Massachusetts, and in Washington, D.C., where she died.

Louisa M. Jacobs (1833–April 5, 1917) Born in Edenton, North Carolina, the daughter of Harriet Jacobs and Samuel Tredwell Sawyer. In 1835 she was sold by Dr. James Norcom to her father, who took her to Washington, D.C., and then sent her to Brooklyn to work as a maid for his cousins. Rescued in 1844 by her mother and lived with her in Boston. Attended Young Ladies' Domestic Seminary in Clinton, New York. Lived with her mother at Idlewild, the home of Nathaniel Parker Willis in Cornwall-on-Hudson, New York, and in Brooklyn and Boston. With her mother, established schools for freed people in Alexandria, Virginia, in 1864 and Savannah, Georgia, in 1865. Toured upstate New York as speaker for the Equal Rights Association. Taught school in Washington, D.C. Lived in Cambridge, Massachusetts, 1868–77. Returned to Washington in 1877. Taught in the Industrial School at Howard University and later worked at the National Home for the Relief of Destitute Colored Women and Children. Died in Cambridge, Massachusetts.

Frances Johnson A slave from Fayette County, Kentucky, who escaped to Camp Nelson in March 1865 and sought help in freeing her three children. Her husband, Nathan Johnson, was a soldier in the 116th U.S. Colored Infantry.

John B. Jones (March 6, 1810–February 4, 1866) Born in Baltimore, Maryland. Lived in Kentucky and Missouri as a boy. Married Frances Custis in 1840. Became editor of the *Saturday Visitor* in Baltimore, 1841. Published several novels, including *Wild Western Scenes* (1841), *The War Path* (1858), and *Wild Southern Scenes* (1859). Established weekly newspaper *Southern Monitor* in Philadelphia, 1857. Fearing arrest as a Confederate sympathizer, Jones moved in 1861 to Richmond, Virginia, where he worked as a clerk in the Confederate War Department. Died in Burlington, New Jersey, shortly before the publication of *A Rebel War Clerk's Diary.*

George W. Julian (May 5, 1817–July 7, 1899) Born near Centreville, Indiana, the son of a farmer. Attended common schools, studied law, and was admitted to the Indiana bar in 1840. Married Anne Elizabeth Finch in 1845. Elected as a Whig to the Indiana house of representatives and served 1845–46. Attended convention in Buffalo, New York, that founded Free Soil party in 1848. Elected to Congress as a Free Soiler and served 1849–51. Free Soil candidate for vice president in 1852. Attended first Republican national convention in Philadelphia, 1856. Served in Congress as a Republican, 1861–71. A member of the Joint Committee on the Conduct of the War, Julian later helped prepare the articles of impeachment against President Johnson. After the death of his first wife, married Laura Giddings, daughter of abolitionist congressman Joshua Giddings, in 1863. Supported Horace Greeley, the Liberal Republican nominee, against Grant in 1872 and later became a Democrat. Advocated woman suffrage. Practiced law in Washington, D.C., 1879–84, and served as surveyor general of New Mexico Territory, 1885–89. Published *Political Recollections, 1840 to 1872* (1884) and *The Life of Joshua R. Giddings* (1892). Died in Irvington, Indiana.

Jane Kamper A slave from Talbot County, Maryland, who fled with her children to Baltimore in November 1864.

Robert Garlick Hill Kean (October 7, 1828–June 13, 1898) Born in Caroline County, Virginia, the son of a schoolmaster and farmer. Graduated from the University of Virginia in 1850 and studied law. Began legal practice in Lynchburg in 1853. Married Jane Randolph in

1854. Enlisted in 11th Virginia Infantry and fought at First Manassas. Commissioned as captain in February 1862 and assigned to the staff of Brigadier General George W. Randolph, his wife's uncle. Randolph was appointed Confederate secretary of war in March 1862, and in April Kean became the head of the Bureau of War, where he served for the remainder of the war. Retreated with other members of the Confederate War Department to Charlotte, North Carolina, after the fall of Richmond. Left Charlotte on April 26, 1865, and returned to Virginia. Resumed his law practice in Lynchburg. After the death of his first wife, married Adelaide Prescott in 1874. Died in Lynchburg.

Elizabeth Keckly (February 1818–May 26, 1907) Born Elizabeth Hobbs in Dinwiddie County, Virginia, the daughter of Agnes Hobbs, a slave, and her owner, Armistead Burwell. Worked from an early age as a house servant. Moved to Hillsborough, North Carolina, in 1835 with family of Robert Burwell, Armistead's son. Forced into a sexual relationship by Alexander Kirkland, a white neighbor, and gave birth to a son, George, in 1839. Returned to Dinwiddie County in 1842 and worked in household of Hugh Garland, Armistead Burwell's son-in-law. Moved to St. Louis with the Garland family in 1847. Became successful dressmaker. Married James Keckly, a black man from Virginia, in 1852. Using $1,200 borrowed from her clients, bought her and her son's freedom in 1855. Separated from her husband and moved to Washington, D.C., in 1860. Began making dresses for Mary Lincoln in 1861 and became her close friend and confidante. Her son, George Kirkland, enlisted as a white man in the 1st Missouri Light Artillery and was killed at Wilson's Creek in August 1861. Founded the Contraband Relief Association in 1862 to assist former slaves in Washington. Published memoir *Behind the Scenes, or, Thirty Years a Slave and Four Years in the White House* (1868); its appearance caused Mary Lincoln to break off their friendship. Moved to Xenia, Ohio, in 1892 to teach in the Department of Sewing and Domestic Science Arts at Wilberforce University. Returned to Washington and lived in the National Home for the Relief of Destitute Colored Women and Children. Died in Washington, D.C.

Emma LeConte (December 10, 1847–March 2, 1932) Born in Liberty County, Georgia, the daughter of a chemist and geologist. Lived in Athens, 1852–56, while father taught at The University of Georgia. Family moved to Columbia, South Carolina, when father became professor at South Carolina College. Educated at home in Greek, Latin, French, German, and mathematics. Witnessed burning of Columbia in February 1865. Married Farish Furman in 1869 and moved to farm near Milledgeville, Georgia. Assumed management of the farm after her husband died in 1883. Moved to Macon early in the twentieth century. Died in Macon, Georgia.

Elizabeth Blair Lee (June 20, 1818–September 13, 1906) Born in Frankfort, Kentucky, daughter of journalist Francis Preston Blair and Elizabeth Gist Blair, sister of Montgomery Blair (postmaster general, 1861–64) and Frank Blair (a Union major general, 1862–65). Moved with family in 1830 to Washington, D.C., where her father edited the *Globe* and advised Andrew Jackson. Educated at boarding school in Philadelphia. Married naval officer Samuel Phillips Lee, a cousin of Robert E. Lee, in 1843. Became board member and active patron of the Washington City Orphan Asylum in 1849. Lived in Washington and at the Blair estate in Silver Spring, Maryland. Died in Washington.

Robert E. Lee (January 19, 1807–October 12, 1870) Born in Westmoreland County, Virginia, the son of Revolutionary War hero Henry "Light-Horse Harry" Lee and Ann Carter Lee. Graduated from West Point in 1829. Married Mary Custis, great-granddaughter of Martha Washington, in 1831. Served in the U.S.-Mexican War, and as superintendent of West Point, 1852–55. Promoted to colonel in March 1861. Resigned commission on April 20, 1861, after declining offer of field command of the Federal army. Served as commander of Virginia military forces, April–July 1861; commander in western Virginia, August–October 1861; commander of the southern Atlantic coast, November 1861–March 1862; and military advisor to Jefferson Davis, March–May 1862. Assumed command of the Army of Northern Virginia on June 1, 1862, and led it until April 9, 1865, when he surrendered to Ulysses S. Grant at Appomattox. Named general-in-chief of all Confederate forces, February 1865. Became president of Washington College (now Washington and Lee), September 1865. Died in Lexington, Virginia.

Francis Lieber (March 18, 1798–October 2, 1872) Born Franz Lieber in Berlin, Prussia. Fought in the Prussian army in the Waterloo campaign and was seriously wounded at Namur. Imprisoned for four months for antigovernment activities in 1819. Received degree in mathematics from Jena in 1820. Studied at Dresden, then served briefly as volunteer in the Greek War of Independence in 1822. Left Greece and traveled to Rome, where the Prussian ambassador, the historian Barthold Niebuhr, encouraged him to publish a book on his experiences in Greece (it appeared in 1823). Returned to Berlin in 1823 and continued his study of mathematics. Arrested in 1824 and imprisoned for six months for alleged subversion. Fled to England in 1826. Immigrated to Boston in 1827, where he served as director of a newly established gymnasium and swimming school. After the gymnasium venture failed, edited the *Encyclopaedia Americana*, published successfully in thirteen volumes, 1829–33. Married Mathilda Oppenheimer in 1829. Moved to Philadelphia in 1834 and published a constitution and plan of education for Girard College. Accepted a chair in history and political economy at South Carolina College (later University of South Carolina) in Columbia in 1835. Published numerous books and essays on law, government, and politics, including *Legal and Political Hermeneutics* (1837), *Manual of Political Ethics* (1838–39), and *On Civil Liberty and Self-Government* (1853). Resigned position in South Carolina in 1855. Appointed professor of history and political science at Columbia College in New York in 1857. During the Civil War one of his sons was killed fighting for the Confederacy in 1862, while his other two sons fought for the Union, one of them losing an arm at Fort Donelson. Became adviser to Henry W. Halleck on the laws of war. Wrote *A Code for the Government of Armies*, issued in revised form by the Union War Department as General Orders No. 100 in April 1863. Became professor at Columbia Law School in 1865. Helped gather and preserve the records of the Confederate government. Appointed in 1870 to commission settling claims arising from the U.S.-Mexican War. Died in New York City.

Abraham Lincoln (February 12, 1809–April 15, 1865) Born near Hodgenville, Kentucky, the son of a farmer and carpenter. Family moved to Indiana in 1816 and to Illinois in 1830. Settled in New Salem, Illinois, and worked as a storekeeper, surveyor, and postmaster. Served as a Whig in the state legislature, 1834–41. Began law practice in 1836 and moved to Springfield in 1837. Married Mary Todd in 1842. Elected to Congress as a Whig and served from 1847 to 1849. Became a public opponent of the extension of slavery after the passage of the Kansas-Nebraska Act in 1854. Helped found the Republican Party of Illinois in 1856. Campaigned in 1858 for Senate seat held by Stephen A. Douglas and debated him seven times on the slavery issue; although the Illinois legislature reelected Douglas, the campaign brought Lincoln national prominence. Received Republican presidential nomination in 1860 and won election in a four-way contest; his victory led to the secession of seven southern states. Responded to the Confederate bombardment of Fort Sumter by calling up militia, proclaiming the blockade of southern ports, and suspending habeas corpus. Issued preliminary and final emancipation proclamations on September 22, 1862, and January 1, 1863. Appointed Ulysses S. Grant commander of all Union forces in March 1864. Won reelection in 1864 by defeating Democrat George B. McClellan. Died in Washington, D.C., after being shot by John Wilkes Booth.

Theodore Lyman (August 23, 1833–September 9, 1897) Born in

Waltham, Massachusetts, the son of a wealthy merchant and textile manufacturer. Graduated from Harvard in 1855. Studied natural history with Louis Agassiz after graduation. Traveled to Florida in 1856 to collect marine specimens for the Harvard Museum of Comparative Zoology. Graduated from Lawrence Scientific School at Harvard in 1858. Married Elizabeth Russell, a cousin of Robert Gould Shaw, in 1858. Traveled in Europe, 1861–63. Joined staff of George G. Meade in September 1863 with rank of lieutenant colonel and served until Lee's surrender. Returned to home in Brookline, Massachusetts, and resumed work at Museum of Comparative Zoology. Served in Congress as an independent, 1883–85. Retired from scientific work in 1887 due to failing health. Died in Brookline.

William Gordon McCabe (August 4, 1841–June 1, 1920) Born in Richmond, Virginia, the son of an Episcopal minister. Educated at Hampton Academy. Entered University of Virginia in 1860. Contributed poems, essays, and stories to the *Southern Literary Messenger.* Enlisted as private in the 3rd Company, Richmond Howitzer Battalion in May 1861. Commissioned as first lieutenant of artillery, May 1862. Served in Richmond defenses with the 19th Battalion, Virginia Heavy Artillery (Atkinson's), and as adjutant of Lightfoot's Artillery Battalion, 1862–63. Assigned to staff of Brigadier General Roswell S. Ripley during the siege of Charleston Harbor, August–October 1863. Returned to Richmond defenses in the fall of 1863. Became ordnance officer, and later adjutant, of field artillery battalion commanded by William Pegram and saw action at the Wilderness, Spotsylvania, Cold Harbor, and in the Petersburg campaign. Founded University School preparatory academy in Petersburg in 1865. Married Jane Osborne in 1867. Contributed poems, essays, and historical articles to newspapers and magazines in the United States and Britain. Published *A Grammar of the Latin Language* (1884), *Caesar's Gallic War* (1886), and *Virginia Schools Before and After the Revolution* (1890). Moved school to Richmond in 1895 and closed it when he retired as headmaster in 1901. After the death of his first wife, married Gallena Cary in 1915. Died in Richmond.

George B. McClellan (December 3, 1826–October 29, 1885) Born in Philadelphia, the son of a surgeon. Graduated from West Point in 1846. Served in the U.S.-Mexican War. Resigned from the army in 1857 to become chief engineer of the Illinois Central Railroad. Became president of the Ohio & Mississippi Railroad in 1860. Married Ellen Marcy, 1860. Appointed major general in the regular army, May 1861. Commanded offensive that drove Confederate troops from western Virginia, July 1861. Assumed command of the Military Division of the Potomac on July 25, 1861, following the Union defeat at First Bull

Run. Served as general-in-chief of the Union armies, November 1861–March 1862. Commanded the Army of the Potomac on the Peninsula, in the Second Bull Run campaign, and at Antietam. Relieved of command by President Lincoln on November 7, 1862. Nominated for president by the Democratic Party in 1864, but was defeated by Lincoln. Governor of New Jersey, 1878–81. Died in Orange, New Jersey.

Judith W. McGuire (March 19, 1813–March 21, 1897) Born Judith White Brockenbrough near Richmond, Virginia, the daughter of a judge. Married John P. McGuire, an Episcopalian rector, in 1846. Moved to Alexandria in 1852 when husband became principal of the Episcopal High School of Virginia. Fled Alexandria in May 1861 and settled in Richmond in February 1862. Worked as a clerk in the Confederate commissary department, November 1863–April 1864. Published *Diary of a Southern Refugee, During the War* (1867). Kept a school with her husband in Essex County in the 1870s. Published *General Robert E. Lee: The Christian Soldier* (1873). Died in Richmond.

Benjamin F. McIntyre (September 15, 1827–November 7, 1910) Born in Adams County, Ohio. Educated in public schools. Moved to Maysville, Kentucky, in 1849. Married Emeline Williams in 1850. Moved to Keokuk, Iowa, in 1856. Worked as a carpenter and undertaker. Enlisted in the 19th Iowa Infantry in August 1862 as first sergeant. Served in southern Missouri and northern Arkansas, September 1862–May 1863, and fought at Prairie Grove. Promoted to second lieutenant in January 1863. Sent with regiment to Vicksburg in mid-June and served in siege until Confederate surrender on July 4, 1863. Remained in Mississippi until late July, when the 19th Iowa was posted to Louisiana. Escaped capture at battle of Sterling's Plantation, where more than 200 men from his regiment were taken prisoner on September 29, 1863. Served in force that occupied Brownsville, Texas, November 1863–July 1864. Promoted to first lieutenant in August 1864. Posted to Fort Barrancas near Pensacola, Florida, August–December 1864. Served at Fort Gaines at the entrance to Mobile Bay and in southeastern Mississippi, December 1864–March 1865. Saw action in the siege of Spanish Fort near Mobile, March 27–April 8, 1865. Remained at Mobile after the Confederate surrender until July 1865, when his regiment was mustered out. Returned to Keokuk and worked as carpenter and builder. Died in Lee County, Iowa.

Alexander McKinley (September 10, 1817–August 24, 1874) Born in Philadelphia, Pennsylvania. Graduated from the University of

Pennsylvania in 1835. Admitted to Philadelphia bar in 1844. Practiced law with William B. Reed and served as his secretary when Reed was U.S. minister to China, 1857–58. Served as civilian secretary to Samuel Francis Du Pont, commander of the South Atlantic Blockading Squadron, 1861–63, and to David G. Farragut, 1864–65. Died in Philadelphia.

Mary S. Mallard (June 12, 1835–August 31, 1889) Born in Liberty County, Georgia, the daughter of the Rev. Charles C. Jones, a Presbyterian clergyman and plantation owner. Attended seminary in Philadelphia, 1850–52. Married Robert Q. Mallard, a Presbyterian clergyman, in 1857. Lived in Walthourville, Georgia, 1857–63, and Atlanta, 1863–64. Moved to New Orleans in 1866. Died in Marietta, Georgia.

Herman Melville (August 1, 1819–September 28, 1891) Born in New York City, the son of a merchant. Educated at schools in New York City and in upstate New York. Worked as bank clerk, bookkeeper, and schoolteacher. Sailed for Pacific on whaling ship in 1841 and returned in 1844 on frigate *United States*. Published *Typee* (1846) and *Omoo* (1847), fictionalized accounts of his experiences in the South Seas. Married Elizabeth Shaw in 1847. Published *Mardi* (1849), *Redburn* (1849), *White-Jacket* (1850), *Moby-Dick* (1851), *Pierre; or, The Ambiguities* (1852), *Israel Potter* (1855), *The Piazza Tales* (1856), and *The Confidence-Man* (1857). Visited Union troops in Virginia in spring 1864. Published poetry collection *Battle-Pieces and Aspects of the War* (1866). Worked as customs inspector in New York City, 1866–85. Published long poem *Clarel* (1876) and two small books of poetry, *John Marr and Other Sailors* (1888) and *Timoleon* (1891). Died in New York City, leaving *Billy Budd, Sailor*, in manuscript.

Joseph Miller (1819–January 6, 1865) A slave from Lincoln County, Kentucky, who enlisted in the 124th U.S. Colored Infantry in October 1864. His wife, Isabella, and their four children accompanied him to Camp Nelson. Died at Camp Nelson, Kentucky.

Luther Rice Mills (August 17, 1840–August 18, 1920) Born in Halifax County, Virginia, the son of a Baptist minister and plantation owner. Graduated from Wake Forest College in 1861. Enlisted in the 26th Virginia Infantry and was eventually commissioned as second lieutenant. Served at Gloucester Point, Virginia, during winter of 1861–62. Posted with regiment to Chaffin's Bluff on the James River near Richmond in May 1862, and remained there through the summer of 1863, seeing no action. Sent with regiment to Charleston, South Carolina, in September 1863. Returned to Virginia in May 1864 and fought at Bermuda Hundred and in the defense of

Petersburg. Wounded in the battle of the Crater. Returned to duty and commanded a company of sharpshooters. Captured during retreat to Appomattox. Released on June 19, 1865, after taking oath of allegiance. Professor of mathematics at Wake Forest College, 1867–1907, and bursar of the college, 1876–1907. Married Anna Lewis in 1869. Died in Wake Forest, North Carolina.

Sarah Morgan (February 28, 1842–May 5, 1909) Born in New Orleans, the daughter of a lawyer. Family moved in 1850 to Baton Rouge, where father served as a judge. Spent war with widowed mother and sisters in Baton Rouge, in the countryside near Port Hudson, and in Union-occupied New Orleans. Two of her brothers died of illness in January 1864 while serving in the Confederate army. Moved with mother to brother's plantation near Columbia, South Carolina, in 1872. Began writing editorials for the Charleston *News and Courier* in 1873 as "Mr. Fowler." Married Francis Warrington Dawson, editor of the *News and Courier*, in 1874. Husband killed in 1889 by doctor who had been paying unwanted attentions to family's governess. Moved in 1899 to Paris, where her son lived. Published *Les Aventures de Jeannot Lap*, version of Brer Rabbit stories, in 1903. Died in Paris.

John S. Mosby (December 6, 1833–May 30, 1916) Born in Powhatan County, Virginia, the son of slave-owning farmer. Family moved in 1841 to large farm near Charlottesville. Entered the University of Virginia in 1850. Dismissed in 1853 after shooting a fellow student who was trying to beat him. Convicted of unlawful shooting and served seven months of one-year sentence before being pardoned in December 1853. Studied law and was admitted to the Virginia bar in 1855. Established practice in Howardsville, Virginia, and married Pauline Clarke in 1856. Moved to Bristol, Tennessee, in 1858. Voted for Stephen A. Douglas in the 1860 presidential election. Enlisted in the 1st Virginia Cavalry in 1861. Served as a scout for Confederate cavalry commander J.E.B. Stuart, 1861–62. With the support of Stuart, organized a small detachment of partisan rangers in northern Virginia in January 1863 and began raiding Union outposts and supply wagons in Fairfax, Prince William, Fauquier, and Loudoun counties. Commissioned as major in March 1863. Command designated as 43rd Battalion, Virginia Cavalry, in June 1863. Scouted for Stuart during the Gettysburg campaign and raided Union supply lines during the 1864 Shenandoah Valley campaign. Wounded in August 1863, September 1864, and December 1864. Promoted to lieutenant colonel, January 1864, and to colonel, December 1864. Disbanded his command on April 21, 1865. Practiced law in Warrenton, Virginia, 1865–76. Angered many former Confederates by supporting Ulysses S.

Grant in the 1872 presidential election. Served as U.S. consul in Hong Kong, 1878–85. Attorney for the Southern Pacific Railroad in San Francisco, 1885–1901. Investigated land fraud for the Department of the Interior in Colorado, Nebraska, and Alabama, 1901–4. Assistant attorney at the Department of Justice in Washington, D.C., 1904–10. Published *Mosby's War Reminiscences and Stuart's Cavalry Campaigns* (1887) and *Stuart's Cavalry in the Gettysburg Campaign* (1908). Died in Washington, D.C.

Henry Nutt (June 25, 1811–December 18, 1881) A successful merchant and distillery owner in New Hanover County, North Carolina, who owned thirty-eight slaves in 1850. Promoted the clearing and dredging of the Cape Fear River at Wilmington. Served as director of the Wilmington and Manchester Railroad after the war.

Robert Patrick (December 24, 1835–December 8, 1866) Born in East Feliciana Parish, Louisiana. Family moved in 1842 to Clinton, Louisiana, where father worked as a court clerk. Attended local schools. Worked as bookkeeper before becoming a deputy sheriff in 1860. Enlisted in the 4th Louisiana Infantry in May 1861. Served as quartermaster and commissary clerk. Saw action at Shiloh. Posted to Port Hudson, October 1862–April 1863. Served with Joseph E. Johnston's army during the Vicksburg campaign. Posted to garrison in Mobile, then served as brigade quartermaster clerk during the Atlanta campaign. Accompanied the Army of Tennessee through northern Georgia and Alabama, October–November 1864, then remained in northern Mississippi when Hood invaded Tennessee. Served in South Carolina at the end of the war. Returned to his position as deputy sheriff. Died in East Feliciana Parish.

William Pegram (June 29, 1841–April 2, 1865) Born in Richmond, Virginia, the son of a banker. Studied law at the University of Virginia, 1840–41. Appointed second lieutenant in the Purcell artillery battery, May 1861. Saw action at First Manassas. Promoted to captain in March 1862 and appointed battery commander. Fought at Mechanicsville, Gaines's Mill, Malvern Hill, Cedar Mountain, Second Manassas, Antietam, Fredericksburg, and Chancellorsville in A. P. Hill's Light Division. Promoted to major and became commander of an artillery battalion commander in Hill's Third Corps. Fought at Gettysburg. Promoted to lieutenant colonel in February 1864. Led battalion in the Wilderness, Spotsylvania, Cold Harbor, and in the battles near Petersburg. Promoted to colonel in February 1865. Fatally wounded at the battle of Five Forks, April 1, 1865. Died in Dinwiddie County, Virginia.

Horace Porter (April 15, 1837–May 29, 1921) Born in Huntingdon,

Pennsylvania, the son of an iron manufacturer who served as governor, 1839–45. Attended Lawrence Scientific School at Harvard. Graduated from West Point in 1860. Commissioned as first lieutenant in May 1861. Served as ordnance officer in the Sea Islands, October 1861–July 1862, and saw action at Fort Pulaski and Secessionville. Posted to the Army of the Potomac, July–September 1862. Served as chief ordnance officer of the Army of the Ohio, September 1862–January 1863, and of the Army of the Cumberland, January–November 1863. Assigned to ordnance bureau in Washington, D.C., November 1863–April 1864. Appointed as aide to Ulysses S. Grant in April 1864 with rank of lieutenant colonel, and remained with him for the rest of the war. Served as aide to Grant in the postwar army, 1865–69, and as his personal secretary in the White House, 1869–73. Moved to New York City, became vice president of the Pullman Car Company, and invested in several other railroad ventures, 1873–97. Published *Campaigning with Grant* (1897). U.S. ambassador to France, 1897–1905, and delegate to the Hague peace conference, 1907. Died in New York City.

Stephen Dodson Ramseur (May 31, 1837–October 20, 1864) Born in Lincolnton, North Carolina, the son of a merchant. Attended Davidson College, 1853–55. Graduated West Point in 1860. Resigned from the U.S. Army in April 1861. Commissioned as major and served with 1st North Carolina Artillery near Norfolk, Virginia. Appointed colonel of the 49th North Carolina Infantry in April 1862. Led regiment at Malvern Hill, where he was severely wounded. Promoted to brigadier general in November 1862. Returned to duty in January 1863 as brigade commander. Led North Carolina brigade in Rodes's Division, Second Corps, Army of Northern Virginia, at Chancellorsville and Gettysburg. Married Ellen Richmond in October 1863. Commanded brigade at the Wilderness, Spotsylvania, and North Anna. Promoted to major general and assigned command of Early's Division in the Second Corps. Led division at Cold Harbor, Monocacy, Winchester, Fisher's Creek, and Cedar Creek, where he was mortally wounded and captured on October 19, 1864. Died the following day at Union headquarters near Meadow Mills, Virginia.

Spottswood Rice (November 20, 1819–October 31, 1907) Born into slavery in Madison County, Missouri, Sold in 1843 to Benjamin Lewis, a tobacco farmer in Howard County, Missouri. Married Arry Ferguson in 1844 (marriage was officially recorded in 1864). Separated from his wife and children, who lived on another plantation. Escaped in February 1864 and enlisted in the 67th U.S. Colored Infantry. Reunited with his family, he lived in St. Louis after the war. Became a minister in the African Methodist Episcopal Church in 1874. Founded

Grant Chapel in Albuquerque, New Mexico, in 1882. After his first wife died, married Eliza Lightner in 1888. Moved to Colorado Springs, where he founded Payne Chapel. Died in Colorado Springs, Colorado.

William T. Sherman (February 8, 1820–February 14, 1891) Born in Lancaster, Ohio, the son of an attorney. Graduated from West Point in 1840. Served in Florida and California, but did not see action in the U.S.-Mexican War. Married Ellen Ewing in 1850. Promoted to captain; resigned his commission in 1853. Managed bank branch in San Francisco, 1853–57. Moved in 1858 to Leavenworth, Kansas, where he worked in real estate and was admitted to the bar. Named first superintendent of the Louisiana State Seminary of Learning and Military Academy at Alexandria (now Louisiana State University) in 1859. Resigned position when Louisiana seceded in January 1861. Commissioned colonel, 13th U.S. Infantry, May 1861. Commanded brigade at First Bull Run, July 1861. Appointed brigadier general of volunteers, August 1861, and ordered to Kentucky. Assumed command of the Department of the Cumberland, October 1861, but was relieved in November at his own request. Returned to field in March 1862 and commanded division under Ulysses S. Grant at Shiloh. Promoted major general of volunteers, May 1862. Commanded corps under Grant during Vicksburg campaign, and succeeded him as commander of the Army of the Tennessee, October 1863, and as commander of the Military Division of the Mississippi, March 1864. Captured Atlanta, September 1864, and led march through Georgia, November–December 1864. Marched army through the Carolinas and accepted the surrender of Confederate General Joseph E. Johnston at Durham Station, North Carolina, April 26, 1865. Promoted to lieutenant general, 1866, and general, 1869, when he became commander of the army. Published controversial *Memoirs of General W. T. Sherman* (1875, revised 1886). Retired from army in 1884 and moved to New York City. Rejected possible Republican presidential nomination, 1884. Died in New York City.

Kate Stone (May 8, 1841–December 28, 1907) Born Sarah Katherine Stone in Hinds County, Mississippi, the daughter of a plantation owner. Family moved to plantation in Madison Parish, Louisiana, thirty miles northwest of Vicksburg. Educated at boarding school in Nashville. Two of her five brothers died while serving in the Confederate army in 1863. Family fled plantation in March 1863 during the Vicksburg campaign and went to eastern Texas. Returned to plantation in November 1865. Married Henry Bry Holmes in 1869. Founded local chapter of the United Daughters of the Confederacy. Died in Tallulah, Louisiana.

John H. Stringfellow (November 14, 1819–July 24, 1905) Born in Culpeper County, Virginia. Educated at Columbian College, Washington, D.C. Received medical degree from the University of Pennsylvania in 1845. Moved to Carrollton, Missouri, that same year and married Ophelia Simmons. Practiced in Platte City and Brunswick, Missouri. Moved to Kansas Territory in 1854 and helped found town of Atchison. Founded the proslavery *Atchison Squatter Sovereign* and served as speaker of the house of representatives in the first Kansas territorial legislature. Led proslavery militia in the sack of Lawrence, Kansas, in May 1856. Returned to Virginia in 1858. Served as surgeon in Confederate army hospitals throughout the war. Practiced medicine in Atchison, Kansas, 1871–76, before moving to St. Joseph, Missouri, where he died.

George Templeton Strong (January 26, 1820–July 21, 1875) Born in New York City, the son of an attorney. Graduated from Columbia College in 1838. Read law in his father's office and was admitted to the bar in 1841. Joined father's firm. Married Ellen Ruggles in 1848. Served on Columbia board of trustees and as vestryman of Trinity Episcopal Church. Helped found the U.S. Sanitary Commission, June 1861, and served as its treasurer through the end of the war; also helped found the Union League Club of New York in 1863. Died in New York City.

Charles Sumner (January 6, 1811–March 11, 1874) Born in Boston, Massachusetts, the son of a lawyer. Graduated from Harvard College in 1830 and from Harvard Law School in 1833. Practiced law in Boston and became active in social reform movements. Unsuccessful Free Soil candidate for Congress in 1848. Elected to the U.S. Senate as a Free Soiler in 1851. Badly beaten with a cane on the Senate floor by South Carolina congressman Preston Brooks on May 22, 1856, two days after delivering his antislavery speech "The Crime Against Kansas." Reelected as a Republican in 1857, but did not regularly return to his seat in the Senate until December 1859; reelected in 1863 and 1869. Chairman of the Senate Foreign Relations Committee, 1861–71. Supported Radical Reconstruction and the rights of blacks after the war. Married Alice Mason Hooper in 1866. Joined Liberal Republicans in opposing reelection of President Grant in 1872. Died in Washington, D.C.

Richard Taylor (January 27, 1826–April 12, 1879) Born near Louisville, Kentucky, the son of army officer and future president Zachary Taylor. Graduated from Yale College in 1845. Managed father's cotton plantation in Jefferson County, Mississippi, 1848–49. Inherited sugar plantation in St. Charles Parish, Louisiana, after President

Taylor's death in 1850. Married Louise Marie Myrthé Bringier, 1851. Served in the Louisiana senate, 1856–61. Commissioned as colonel of the 9th Louisiana Infantry, July 1861. Promoted to brigadier general, October 1861. Commanded the Louisiana Brigade in the Shenandoah Valley campaign of 1862. Promoted to major general, July 1862, and assigned command of the District of Western Louisiana, August 1862. Defeated General Nathaniel P. Banks in the Red River campaign in Louisiana, March–May 1864. Promoted to lieutenant general, May 1864. Commanded the Department of Alabama, Mississippi, and Eastern Louisiana from September 1864 to May 4, 1865, when he surrendered at Citronelle, Alabama. Active in the postwar Democratic Party in Louisiana. *Destruction and Reconstruction: Personal Experiences of the Late War* published posthumously in 1879. Died in New York City.

Lorenzo Thomas (October 26, 1804–March 2, 1875) Born in New Castle, Delaware. Graduated from West Point in 1823. Served as quartermaster in the Second Seminole War, 1836–37, and as staff officer in the U.S.-Mexican War. Chief of staff to General-in-Chief Winfield Scott, 1853–61. Served as adjutant-general of U.S. Army, March 1861–March 1863. Promoted to brigadier general in August 1861. Assigned by Secretary of War Stanton to recruit and organize black troops in the Mississippi Valley, March 1863–October 1865. Returned to duty as adjutant-general and made inspection tour of national cemeteries. Appointed secretary of war by President Andrew Johnson on February 21, 1868, but was unable to serve because Stanton refused to surrender the office. Retired from the army in February 1869. Died in Washington, D.C.

Robert Toombs (July 2, 1810–December 15, 1885) Born in Wilkes County, Georgia, the son of a cotton planter. Studied at The University of Georgia. Graduated from Union College in Schenectady, New York, in 1828. Studied law at the University of Virginia. Began legal practice in Washington, Georgia, in 1830, and married Julia DuBose in the same year. Led company of Georgia militia in 1836 during the Creek War, but saw no action. Served in the Georgia house of representatives, 1837–40 and 1842–43. Elected to Congress as a Whig and served 1845–53. Supported the Compromise of 1850. Elected to the U.S. Senate as member of the Constitutional Union party and served 1853–61. Supported immediate secession at the Georgia convention in 1861. Member of the Provisional Confederate Congress, February 1861–February 1862. Confederate secretary of state, February–June 1861. Commissioned as brigadier general, July 1861. Led brigade in the Seven Days and at Antietam, where he was wounded. Resigned commission in March 1863 and became a leading public critic of the Davis administration. Served as inspector general of the Georgia militia, 1864. Fled his home in May 1865 to avoid arrest and made his way to Cuba and then France. Returned to the United States in 1867 and reestablished law practice. Delegate to the 1877 Georgia constitutional convention. Died in Washington, Georgia.

Clement L. Vallandigham (July 29, 1820–June 17, 1871) Born in New Lisbon, Ohio, the son of a Presbyterian minister. Attended New Lisbon Academy and Jefferson College in Washington, Pennsylvania. Served as principal of Union Academy in Snow Hill, Maryland, 1838–40. Returned to Ohio in 1840 to study law. Admitted to bar in 1842. Served as a Democrat in the Ohio house of representatives, 1845–46. Married Louisa Anna McMahon in 1846. Moved in 1847 to Dayton, where he practiced law and edited the *Dayton Western Empire*, 1847–49. Served in Congress, 1858–63, and became a leading "Peace Democrat" opposed to emancipation and the continued prosecution of the war. Arrested in Dayton on May 5, 1863, and tried before military commission for expressing "disloyal sentiments and opinions." Expelled across lines into Confederate-held territory in Tennessee. Made his way to Canada in June 1863 after receiving Democratic nomination for governor of Ohio and campaigned from exile, but was defeated in October 1863. Returned to United States in June 1864 and helped draft peace platform adopted by Democratic national convention in August. Resumed law practice. Accidentally shot himself on June 16, 1871, while demonstrating to other attorneys how his client's alleged victim could have accidentally shot himself during an altercation (his client was later acquitted). Died the following day in Lebanon, Ohio.

Benjamin F. Wade (October 27, 1800–March 2, 1878) Born in Feeding Hills, Massachusetts, the son of a farmer. Moved with family to Andover, Ohio, in 1821. Worked as a laborer on the Erie Canal, taught school, and studied medicine in Albany, New York, before being admitted to the Ohio bar in 1828. Served in Ohio senate as a Whig, 1837–38 and 1841–42. Married Caroline Rosekrans, 1841. Judge of circuit court of common pleas, 1847–51. Served in the U.S. Senate as a Whig and then as a Republican, 1851–69. Chairman of the Joint Committee on the Conduct of the War, 1861–65. Co-sponsored the Wade-Davis Bill on Reconstruction, 1864, which was pocket-vetoed by President Lincoln. Elected president pro tempore of the Senate in 1867, he would have succeeded Andrew Johnson as president had Johnson been convicted during his impeachment trial. Unsuccessful candidate for Republican vice-presidential nomination in 1868. Died in Jefferson, Ohio.

Stephen Minot Weld (January 4, 1842–March 16, 1920) Born in

Jamaica Plain, Massachusetts, the son of a schoolmaster. Graduated from Harvard in 1860. Served as civilian aide in Port Royal expedition in 1861. Commissioned as second lieutenant in the 18th Massachusetts Infantry in January 1862. Served on staff of Brigadier General Fitz John Porter, commander of the Fifth Corps, during the Peninsula campaign. Captured at Gaines's Mill and exchanged in early August. Served as aide to Porter at Second Bull Run and Antietam. Testified at Porter's court-martial in December 1862. Served on staff of the Engineer Brigade of the Army of the Potomac at Chancellorsville. Joined staff of Major General John Reynolds, commander of the First Corps, in May 1863. Served at Gettysburg on July 1, 1863, before accompanying Reynolds's body to Philadelphia. Appointed lieutenant colonel of the 56th Massachusetts Infantry in August 1863. Led regiment at the Wilderness, Spotsylvania, North Anna, Cold Harbor, and Petersburg. Promoted to colonel. Captured in the battle of the Crater, paroled in December 1864, and exchanged in March 1865. Returned to Massachusetts and became a successful cotton broker and horticulturalist. Married Eloise Rodman in 1869 and, after her death, Susan Waterbury in 1904. Privately published *War Diary and Letters of Stephen M. Weld* (1912). Died in Boca Grande, Florida.

Gideon Welles (July 1, 1802–February 11, 1878) Born in Glastonbury, Connecticut, the son of a merchant. Educated in Vermont at the American Literary, Scientific, and Military Academy (now Norwich University). Editor of the *Hartford Times*, 1826–36. Served as a Democrat in the Connecticut house of representatives, 1827–35. Married Mary Hale in 1835. Postmaster of Hartford, 1836–41. Served as chief of the bureau of provisions and clothing in the navy department, 1846–49. Helped organize Republican Party in Connecticut. Wrote for the *Hartford Evening Press*, the *New York Evening Post*, and other Republican newspapers. Secretary of the navy in the Lincoln and Andrew Johnson administrations, 1861–69. Died in Hartford.

Walt Whitman (May 31, 1819–March 26, 1892) Born in Huntington Township, New York, the son of a farmer and carpenter. Moved with family to Brooklyn in 1823. Learned printing trade at Brooklyn newspapers. Taught school on Long Island, 1836–38. Became freelance journalist and printer in New York and Brooklyn. Published first edition of *Leaves of Grass* in 1855 (revised editions appeared in 1856, 1860, 1867, 1870, 1881, and 1891). Traveled to northern Virginia in December 1862 after learning that his brother George had been wounded at Fredericksburg. Became volunteer nurse in Washington, D.C., army hospitals. Published *Drum-Taps* and *Sequel to Drum-Taps* in 1865. Worked as clerk at the Interior Department, 1865, and the office of the attorney general, 1865–73. Published prose recollections of his war experiences in *Memoranda During the War* (1875) and *Specimen Days and Collect* (1882). Died in Camden, New Jersey.

Rachel Ann Wicker (August 1840–1910) Born in Urbana, Ohio. Married William Leroy Walker in 1858. Her husband enlisted in the 55th Massachusetts Infantry in June 1863 and survived the war. Died in Piqua, Ohio.

Edward A. Wild (November 25, 1825–August 28, 1891) Born in Brookline, Massachusetts, the son of a physician. Graduated from Harvard in 1844 and from Jefferson Medical College in Philadelphia in 1846. Began homeopathic practice in Brookline, 1847. Traveled in Europe, 1849–50. Married Frances Ellen Sullivan in 1855. Volunteered as surgeon with the Turkish army during the Crimean War, 1855–56, and served in the Caucasus. Returned to Brookline in 1857 and resumed practice. Mustered in as captain of Company A, 1st Massachusetts Volunteers, in May 1861. Fought at Blackburn's Ford, First Bull Run, Yorktown, and Williamsburg, and was wounded at Oak Grove. Appointed colonel of the 35th Massachusetts Infantry, August 1862. Wounded at South Mountain, September 14, 1862, and lost his left arm. Commissioned brigadier general in April 1863 and spent the remainder of the war recruiting and commanding black troops. Began recruiting "African Brigade" at New Bern, North Carolina, May 1863. Led brigade during siege of Charleston Harbor, August–October 1863. Assigned command of the U.S. Colored Troops at Norfolk, Virginia, and led them on raid into eastern North Carolina, December 1863. Commanded First Brigade, Third Division, Eighteenth Corps, Army of the James, April–June 1864, holding outposts along the James River and then fighting at Petersburg. Found guilty at court-martial of disobeying orders, but verdict was overturned. Recruited at Fort Monroe, July–October 1864. Commanded First Division in the Twenty-fifth Corps, January–March 1865, and the Second Brigade of the First Division, March–April 1865. Helped occupy Richmond. Supervisor of the Freedmen's Bureau in Macon, Georgia, June–September 1865. Became involved in silver-mining ventures in Nevada, Colorado, and Canada. Traveled to Colombia in 1891 to help survey railroad route. Died in Medellín, Colombia.

Frank Wilkeson (March 8, 1848–April 22, 1913) Born in Buffalo, New York, the son of a lawyer and iron manufacturer who later reported on the Civil War for the *New-York Daily Tribune* and the *New York Times*. After his older brother Bayard was killed at Gettysburg, he enlisted in the 11th New York Light Artillery Battery during the winter of 1863–64. Saw action at the Wilderness, Spotsylvania, North Anna, Cold Harbor, and Petersburg. Commissioned as second lieutenant in the 4th U.S. Artillery in June 1864. Served in Washington defenses during Early's raid, and helped guard Confederate prisoners in Elmira, New York, before being posted to northern Alabama and East Tennessee in the spring of 1865. Worked as mining engineer in Pennsylvania. Married Mary Crouse in 1869. Moved to cattle ranch and wheat farm in Gypsum, Kansas, in 1871. Helped survey possible railroad route through the North Cascades. Wrote for newspapers and magazines about hunting, fishing, and ranching. Published *Recollections of a Private in the Army of the Potomac* (1887). Lived in Washington and Kansas. Died in Chelan, Washington.

Alpheus S. Williams (September 20, 1810–December 21, 1878) Born in Deep River, Connecticut, the son of a manufacturer. Graduated from Yale College in 1831. Admitted to the bar in 1834. Moved to Detroit in 1836, where he practiced law and joined the local militia company. Married Jane Hereford Pierson in 1839; she died in 1848. Served as probate judge of Wayne County, 1840–44, and published the *Detroit Daily Advertiser*, 1843–48. Commissioned as brigadier general of volunteers in August 1861. Commanded brigade in the Army of the Potomac, October 1861–March 1862. Led a division in the Shenandoah Valley campaign and at Cedar Mountain and Second Bull Run. Assumed temporary command of Twelfth Corps at Antietam following the death of General Mansfield. Commanded division at Chancellorsville and was temporary commander of the Twelfth Corps at Gettysburg. Sent with his division in September 1863 to Tennessee, where they guarded railroads. Served in the Atlanta campaign and commanded the Twentieth Corps in the march through Georgia and the Carolinas. Mustered out on January 15, 1866. Served as U.S. minister to San Salvador, 1866–69. Returned to Detroit. Married Martha Ann Tillman in 1873. Elected to Congress as a Democrat and served from 1875 until his death in Washington, D.C.

William Winters (1830–April 8, 1864?) Born in Connecticut. Married Harriet J. Smith in Cincinnati, Ohio, in 1853. Moved to Hawes Creek Township in Bartholomew County, Indiana, where he worked as a saddle and harness maker. Enlisted in Company I, 67th Indiana Infantry, in August 1862. Taken prisoner along with his regiment when the Union garrison at Munfordville, Kentucky, surrendered on September 17, 1862. Returned to Indiana after being paroled the day after his capture. Exchanged in late November 1862. Regiment joined Sherman's expedition against Vicksburg. Saw action at Chickasaw Bayou. Served as hospital attendant during expedition to capture Arkansas Post and in army camps near Vicksburg. Saw action at Port Gibson, Champion Hill, Big Black River, and in the siege of Vicksburg. Sent with regiment to southern Louisiana in August 1863 and to Matagorda Bay, Texas, in December. Returned to southern Louisiana in February 1864 and served in Red River campaign. Missing in action and presumed killed in the battle of Sabine Crossroads.

Susan C. Woolker Lived in Hillsdale, North Carolina, in 1864. Her husband served in the Confederate army.

Note on the Texts

This volume collects nineteenth- and early twentieth-century writing about the Civil War, bringing together public and private letters, newspaper and magazine articles, pamphlets, memoranda, speeches, journal and diary entries, proclamations, messages, addresses, military orders, legal statements, poems, sermons, and excerpts from memoirs written by participants and observers and dealing with events in the period from March 1864 to June 1865. Most of these documents were not written for publication, and most of them existed only in manuscript form during the lifetimes of the persons who wrote them. With seven exceptions, the texts presented in this volume are taken from printed sources. In cases where there is only one printed source for a document, the text offered here comes from that source. Where there is more than one printed source for a document, the text printed in this volume is taken from the source that appears to contain the fewest editorial alterations in the spelling, capitalization, paragraphing, and punctuation of the original. In seven instances where no printed sources (or no complete printed sources) were available, the texts in this volume are printed from manuscripts.

This volume prints texts as they appear in the sources listed below, but with a few alterations in editorial procedure. The bracketed conjectural readings of editors, in cases where original manuscripts or printed texts were damaged or difficult to read, are accepted without brackets in this volume when those readings seem to be the only possible ones; but when they do not, or when the editor made no conjecture, the missing word or words are indicated by a bracketed two-em space, i.e., [   ]. In cases where a typographical error or obvious misspelling in manuscript was marked by earlier editors with "[*sic*]," the present volume omits the "[*sic*]" and corrects the typographical error or slip of the pen. In some cases, obvious errors were not marked by earlier editors with "[*sic*]" but were printed and then followed by a bracketed correction; in these instances, this volume removes the brackets and accepts the editorial emendation. Bracketed editorial insertions used in the source texts to identify persons or places, to expand contractions and abbreviations, or to clarify meaning, have been deleted in this volume. In instances where canceled, but still legible, words were printed in the source texts with lines through the deleted material, or where canceled words were printed and indicated with an asterisk, this volume omits the canceled words.

In *The Papers of Jefferson Davis*, material that was written in interlined form in manuscript is printed within diagonal marks; this volume prints the interlined words and omits the diagonals. *The Papers of Jefferson Davis* prints two portions of a sentence in the letter written by Davis to Varina Howell Davis on April 23, 1865, as canceled material because they were crossed out in the manuscript. This volume prints "and after" and "bly under the the influence of her husband was afraid to be known as having close relations with us" (see page 708.12–15 in this volume) without cancellation marks because they were crossed out by someone other than Davis. Similarly, *Inside Lincoln's White House: The Complete Civil War Diary of John Hay* (1997), edited by Michael Burlingame and John R. Turner Ettlinger, prints as canceled material a paragraph that was crossed out in the manuscript of the November 11, 1864, entry, describing William H. Seward's anger at the newspaper editor John W. Forney (page 461.26–29 in this volume). This volume prints the paragraph without cancellation marks because it is likely that it was crossed out by someone other than Hay, possibly after his death.

The selections from the diary of Gideon Welles, the secretary of the navy in the Lincoln administration, are taken from *Diary of Gideon Welles* (1960), edited by Howard K. Beale. Welles kept a diary during the Civil War that he extensively revised from 1869 to his death in 1878. The revised text was published in 1911 as *Diary of Gideon Welles*, edited by his son Edgar T. Welles with the assistance of John Morse Jr. and Frederick Bancroft. In the 1960 edition, Beale presented the text of the 1911 edition while printing deleted material from the original diary in the margins and using brackets, italics, strike-through lines, and other editorial markings to indicate the differences between the original version of the diary and the revised text. The texts of the selections from the Welles diary printed in this volume are taken from the 1960 edition and incorporate the changes indicated by Beale in order to present a clear text of the diary as originally written by Welles during the Civil War. In two instances, emendations made by Welles while revising his diary have been accepted in this volume as corrections of slips of the pen: at 690.30, "that there thousands" becomes "that there were thousands," and at 691.27, "but there many more" becomes "but there were many more."

An error in the letter written by John H. Stringfellow to Jefferson Davis on February 8, 1865, is treated as a slip of the pen and corrected in this volume, even though it was not corrected in *Freedom: A Documentary History of Emancipation, 1861–1867, Series II: The Black Military Experience*: at 577.1, "furnishishing" becomes "furnishing." Six slips of the pen in documents printed from manuscript sources are also corrected: at 303.19, "my innermost heat" becomes "my innermost heart"; at 304.5–6, "they would they would harm" becomes "they would harm"; at 304.12, "Hood's army is stregthening" becomes "Hood's army is strengthening"; at 304.37–38, "there is retribution atlast" becomes "there is retribution at last"; at 306.1, "but I has not been given us" becomes "but it has not been given us"; at 512.31, "is calculated to to increase them" becomes "is calculated to increase them."

The following is a list of the documents included in this volume, in the order of their appearance, giving the source of each text. The most common sources are indicated by these abbreviations:

CWAL	*The Collected Works of Abraham Lincoln*, ed. Roy P. Basler (8 vols., New Brunswick, N.J.: Rutgers University Press, 1953). Copyright © 1953 by the Abraham Lincoln Association. Used by permission of the Abraham Lincoln Association.
Foster	*One of Cleburne's Command: The Civil War Reminiscences and Diary of Capt. Samuel T. Foster, Granbury's Texas Brigade, CSA*, ed. Norman D. Brown (Austin: University of Texas Press, 1980). Copyright © 1980 by the University of Texas Press.
Freedom: Destruction	*Freedom: A Documentary History of Emancipation, 1861–1867. Series I, Volume I: The Destruction of Slavery*, ed. Ira Berlin, Barbara J. Fields, Thavolia Glymph, Joseph P. Reidy, Leslie S. Rowland (New York: Cambridge University Press, 1985.) Copyright © 2010 by Cambridge University Press. Used by permission of Cambridge University Press.
Freedom: Lower South	*Freedom: A Documentary History of Emancipation, 1861–1867. Series I, Volume III: The Wartime Genesis of Free Labor: The Lower South*, ed. Ira Berlin, Thavolia Glymph, Steven F. Miller, Joseph P. Reidy, Leslie S. Rowland, Julie Saville (New York: Cambridge University Press, 1993). Copyright © 1993 by Cambridge University Press. Used by permission of Cambridge University Press.
Freedom: Military	*Freedom: A Documentary History of Emancipation, 1861–1867. Series II: The Black Military Experience*, ed. Ira Berlin (Cambridge and New York: Cambridge University Press, 1982). Copyright © 2010 by Cambridge University Press. Used by permission of Cambridge University Press.
Freedom: Upper South	*Freedom: A Documentary History of Emancipation, 1861–1867. Series I, Volume II: The Wartime Genesis of Free Labor: The Upper South*, ed. Ira Berlin, Steven F. Miller, Joseph P. Reidy, Leslie S. Rowland (New York:

Cambridge University Press, 1993). Copyright © 1993 by Cambridge University Press. Used by permission of Cambridge University Press.

OR — *The War of the Rebellion: A Compilation of the Official Records of the Union and Confederate Armies* (128 vols., Washington, D.C.: Government Printing Office, 1880–1901).

PUSG — *The Papers of Ulysses S. Grant*, ed. John Y. Simon (31 vols. to date, Carbondale: Southern Illinois University Press, 1967–2009). Volume 10 (1982), Volume 11 (1984), Volume 14 (1985). Copyright © 1982, 1984, 1985 by The Ulysses S. Grant Association. Used by permission of The Ulysses S. Grant Association.

SCW — *Sherman's Civil War: Selected Correspondence of William T. Sherman, 1860–1865*, ed. Brooks D. Simpson and Jean V. Berlin (Chapel Hill: The University of North Carolina Press, 1999). Copyright © 1999 by The University of North Carolina Press. Used by permission of the publisher, www.uncpress.unc.edu.

Strong — George Templeton Strong, *Diary of the Civil War, 1860–1865*, ed. Allan Nevins (New York: The Macmillan Publishing Company, 1962), 481–83. Reprinted with permission of Scribner, a Division of Simon & Schuster, Inc., from *The Diary of George Templeton Strong* edited by Allan Nevins and Milton Halsey Thomas. Copyright © 1952 by The Macmillan Publishing Company; copyright renewed © 1980 by Milton Halsey Thomas. All rights reserved.

Welles — *Diary of Gideon Welles*, volume II, ed. Howard K. Beale (New York: W. W. Norton & Company, Inc., 1960). Copyright © 1960 by W. W. Norton & Company, Inc.

WPREL — *The Wartime Papers of Robert E. Lee*, ed. Clifford Dowdey and Louis H. Manarin (Boston: Little, Brown, 1961). Copyright © 1961 by Commonwealth of Virginia. Used by permission of Little, Brown and Company. All rights reserved.

Catherine Edmondston: Diary, March 8, 1864. *"Journal of a Secesh Lady": The Diary of Catherine Ann Devereux Edmondston, 1860–1866*, ed. Beth G. Crabtree and James W. Patton (Raleigh: North Carolina Division of Archives and History, 1979), 536–38. Copyright © 1979 by the North Carolina Division of Archives and History. Used by permission.

Ellen Renshaw House: Diary, March 9–11, March 19, 1864. *A Very Violent Rebel: The Civil War Diary of Ellen Renshaw House*, ed. Daniel E. Sutherland (Knoxville: University of Tennessee Press, 1996), 112–14, 117–18. Copyright © 1996 by The University of Tennessee Press/Knoxville. Ellen Renshaw House's diary, Copyright © 1996 by Ellen Allran and Victoria Guthrie. Used by permission of the University of Tennessee Press.

Scientific American: New Rolling Mills in Pittsburgh. *Scientific American*, March 26, 1864.

Harriet Ann Jacobs and Louisa M. Jacobs to Lydia Maria Child, March 26, 1864. *The Harriet Jacobs Family Papers*, vol. II, ed. Jean Fagan Yellin (Chapel Hill: The University of North Carolina Press, 2008), 558–61. Copyright © 2008 Jean Fagan Yellin. Used by permission of the publisher.

Jim Heiskell: Statement Regarding His Escape from Slavery, March 30, 1864. *Freedom: Destruction*, 320–22.

Susan C. Woolker to Zebulon B. Vance, April 3, 1864. *North Carolina Civil War Documentary*, ed. W. Buck Yearns and John G. Barrett (Chapel Hill: The University of North Carolina Press, 1980), 262–63. Copyright © 1980 by The University of North Carolina Press. Used by permission of the publisher, www.uncpress.unc.edu.

Ulysses S. Grant to William T. Sherman, April 4, 1864. *PUSG*, vol. 10, 251–53.

William Winters to Harriet Winters, April 4, 1864. *The Musick of the Mocking Birds, the Roar of the Cannon: The Civil War Diary and Letters of William Winters*, ed. Steven E. Bloodworth (Lincoln: University of Nebraska Press, 1998), 121–22. Copyright © 1998 by University of Nebraska Press. Used by permission of the publisher.

Wilbur Fisk to *The Green Mountain Freeman*, April 7, 1864. *Hard Marching Every Day: The Civil War Letters of Private Wilbur Fisk, 1861–1865*, ed. Emil and Ruth Rosenblatt (Lawrence: University Press of Kansas, 1992), 205–8. Copyright © 1983, 1992 by Emil Rosenblatt. Used by permission of the University Press of Kansas.

Ellen Renshaw House: Diary, April 8, 1864. *A Very Violent Rebel: The Civil War Diary of Ellen Renshaw House*, ed. Daniel E. Sutherland (Knoxville: University of Tennessee Press, 1996), 127–28. Copyright © 1996 by The University of Tennessee Press/Knoxville. Ellen Renshaw House's diary, Copyright © 1996 by Ellen Allran and Victoria Guthrie. Used by permission of the University of Tennessee Press.

Lois Bryan Adams to the *Detroit Advertiser and Tribune*, April 9, 1864. Lois Bryan Adams, *Letter from Washington, 1863–1865*, ed. Evelyn Leasher (Detroit: Wayne State University Press, 1999), 102–7. Copyright © 1999 by Wayne State University Press.

Achilles V. Clark to Judith Porter and Henrietta Ray, April 14, 1864. John Cimprich and Robert C. Mainfort Jr., "Fort Pillow Revisited: New Evidence About an Old Controversy," *Civil War History*, vol. 28, no. 4, December 1982, 297–99. Copyright © 1982 by Kent State University Press.

Robert E. Lee to Jefferson Davis, April 15, 1864. *WPREL*, 699–700.

The New York Times: The Black Flag. *The New York Times*, April 16, 1864.

Abraham Lincoln: Address at Baltimore Sanitary Fair, April 18, 1864. *CWAL*, vol. VII, 301–3.

R.H.C. to *The Christian Recorder*. *The Christian Recorder*, April 30, 1864.

Gideon Welles: Diary, May 3, 5–6, 1864. *Welles*, vol. 2, 23–24, 24–25.

Petition from the Slaveholders of Randolph County, Alabama, May 6, 1864. *Freedom: Destruction*, 756–58.

Samuel W. Fiske to the *Springfield Republican*, May 3, 1864. *Mr. Dunn Browne's Experiences in the Army: The Civil War Letters of Samuel W. Fiske*, ed. Stephen W. Sears (New York: Fordham University Press, 1998), 245–49. Copyright © 1998 by Stephen W. Sears. Used by permission of Fordham University Press.

Theodore Lyman: Journal, May 4–7, 1864. *Meade's Army: The Private Notebooks of Lt. Col. Theodore Lyman*, ed. David W. Lowe (Kent, Ohio: Kent State University Press, 2007), 130–44. Copyright © 2007 by Kent State University Press. Used by permission of the publisher.

Wilbur Fisk to *The Green Mountain Freeman*, May 9, 1864. *Hard Marching Every Day: The Civil War Letters of Private Wilbur Fisk, 1861–1865*, ed. Emil and Ruth Rosenblatt (Lawrence: University Press of Kansas, 1992), 214–18. Copyright © 1983, 1992 by Emil Rosenblatt. Used by permission of the University Press of Kansas.

J.F.J. Caldwell: from *The History of a Brigade of South Carolinians*. J.F.J. Caldwell, *The History of a Brigade of South Carolinians, known first as "Gregg's," and subsequently as "McGowan's Brigade"* (Philadelphia: King & Baird, 1866), 127–36.

Horace Porter: from *Campaigning with Grant*. Horace Porter, *Campaigning with Grant* (New York: The Century Co., 1897), 78–79.

Herman Melville: The Armies of the Wilderness. (1863–4.) Herman Melville, *Battle-Pieces and Aspects of the War* (New York: Harper & Brothers, 1866), 93–104.

Ulysses S. Grant to Edwin M. Stanton and Henry W. Halleck, May 11, 1864. *PUSG*, vol. 10, 422–23.

Charles Harvey Brewster to Martha Brewster, May 11, 1864; to Mary Brewster, May 13, 1864; and to Martha Brewster, May 15, 1864. *When This Cruel War Is Over: The Civil War Letters of Charles*

Harvey Brewster, ed. David W. Blight (Amherst: The University of Massachusetts Press, 1992), 292–300. Copyright © 1992 by Historic Northampton.

J.F.J. Caldwell: from *The History of a Brigade of South Carolinians.* J.F.J. Caldwell, *The History of a Brigade of South Carolinians, known first as "Gregg's," and subsequently as "McGowan's Brigade"* (Philadelphia: King & Baird, 1866), 140–47.

Edward A. Wild to Robert S. Davis, May 12, 1864. *Freedom: Destruction*, 95–97.

James A. Connolly to Mary Dunn Connolly, May 15, 20, 1864. "Major James Austin Connolly," *Transactions of the Illinois State Historical Society for the Year 1928* (Springfield: Illinois State Historical Library, 1928), 331–32. Used by permission of the Abraham Lincoln Presidential Library and Museum.

Alpheus S. Williams to Mary Williams, May 20, 1864. *From the Cannon's Mouth: The Civil War Letters of Alpheus S. Williams*, ed. Milo M. Quaife (Detroit: Wayne State University Press, 1959), 307–9.

Richard Taylor: General Orders No. 44, May 23, 1864. *The New York Times*, May 20, 1879.

Samuel T. Foster: Diary, May 23–28, 1864. *Foster*, 80–89.

Charles Harvey Brewster to Mary Brewster, May 23, 1864; to Martha Brewster, May 24, 1864; and to Mattie Brewster, May 26, 1864. *When This Cruel War Is Over: The Civil War Letters of Charles Harvey Brewster*, ed. David W. Blight (Amherst: The University of Massachusetts Press, 1992), 300–8. Copyright © 1992 by Historic Northampton.

Eugene Forbes: Diary, May 24–27, 1864. *Death Before Dishonor: The Andersonville Diary of Eugene Forbes, 4th New Jersey Infantry*, ed. William B. Styple (Kearny, N.J.: Belle Grove Publishing Company, 1995), 53–56.

Charles Francis Adams Jr. to Charles Francis Adams, May 29, 1864. Manuscript, Adams Family Papers, Massachusetts Historical Society. Used by permission.

Lorenzo Thomas to Henry Wilson, May 30, 1864. *Freedom: Military*, 530–31.

Cornelia Hancock to Ellen Hancock Child, May 28, May 31–June 3, 1864. *Letters of a Civil War Nurse: Cornelia Hancock, 1863–1865*, ed. Henrietta Stratton Jaquette (Lincoln: University of Nebraska Press, 1998), 91–97.

Frank Wilkeson: from *Recollections of a Private Soldier in the Army of the Potomac.* Frank Wilkeson, *Recollections of a Private Soldier in the Army of the Potomac* (New York: G. P. Putnam's Son, 1887), 128–39, 149–52.

Maria Lydig Daly: Diary, June 8, 1864. Maria Lydig Daly, *Diary of a Union Lady, 1861–1865*, ed. Harold Earl Hammond (New York: Funk & Wagnalls, 1962), 298–300. Copyright © 1962 by Funk and Wagnalls Company, Inc.

Robert Patrick to Alonzo Lewis, June 9, 1864. *Reluctant Rebel: The Secret Diary of Robert Patrick, 1861–1865*, ed. F. Jay Taylor (Baton Rouge: Louisiana State University Press, 1959), 180–82. Copyright © 1959 by Louisiana State University Press. Used by permission of the publisher.

Judith W. McGuire: Diary, June 11, 1864. Judith W. McGuire, *Diary of a Southern Refugee, during the war*, 3rd edition (Richmond, Va.: J. W. Randolph & English, Publishers, 1889), 276–80.

Charles Harvey Brewster to Mattie Brewster, June 11, 1864. *When This Cruel War Is Over: The Civil War Letters of Charles Harvey Brewster*, ed. David W. Blight (Amherst: The University of Massachusetts Press, 1992), 314–16. Copyright © 1992 by Historic Northampton.

Charles Francis Adams to Charles Francis Adams Jr., June 17, 1864. Manuscript, Adams Family Papers, Massachusetts Historical Society. Used by permission.

Charles B. Fisher: Diary, June 19–21, 1864. *Diary of Charles B. Fisher*, ed. Paul E. Sluby, Sr., and Stanton L. Wormley (Washington, D.C.: Columbian Harmony Society, 1983), 83–91. Copyright © 1983 by Charles B. Fisher III and the Columbian Harmony Society.

Wilbur Fisk to *The Green Mountain Freeman*, June 19, 1864. *Hard Marching Every Day: The Civil War Letters of Private Wilbur Fisk, 1861–1865*, ed. Emil and Ruth Rosenblatt (Lawrence: University Press of Kansas, 1992), 229–32. Copyright © 1983, 1992 by Emil Rosenblatt. Used by permission of the University Press of Kansas.

Stephen Minot Weld to Stephen Minot Weld Sr., June 21, 1864. *War Diary and Letters of Stephen Minot Weld, 1861–1865* (Cambridge, Mass.: The Riverside Press, 1912), 317–19.

George E. Chamberlin to Ephraim Chamberlin, June 27, 1864. *Letters of George E. Chamberlin, Who Fell in the Service of His Country near Charlestown, Va., August 21st, 1864*, ed. Caroline Chamberlin Lutz (Springfield, Ill.: H. W. Rokker, 1883), 338–42.

Eugene Forbes: Diary, June 13–30, 1864. *Death Before Dishonor: The Andersonville Diary of Eugene Forbes, 4th New Jersey Infantry*, ed. William B. Styple (Kearny, N.J.: Belle Grove Publishing Company, 1995), 69–80.

William T. Sherman to Ellen Ewing Sherman, June 30, 1864. *SCW*, 659–61.

Horace Greeley to Abraham Lincoln, July 7, 1864. Manuscript, Abraham Lincoln Papers, Library of Congress.

John White Geary to Mary Geary, July 8, 1864. *A Politician Goes to War: The Civil War Letters of John White Geary*, ed. William Alan Blair (University Park, Pa.: The Pennsylvania State University Press, 1995), 184–86. Copyright © 1995 by The Pennsylvania State University. Used by permission of The Pennsylvania State University Press.

Abraham Lincoln: Proclamation Concerning Reconstruction, July 8, 1864. *CWAL*, vol. VII, 433–34.

Abraham Lincoln to Horace Greeley, July 9, 1864. *CWAL*, vol. VII, 435.

Eugene Forbes: Diary, July 11, 1864. *Death Before Dishonor: The Andersonville Diary of Eugene Forbes, 4th New Jersey Infantry*, ed. William B. Styple (Kearny, N.J.: Belle Grove Publishing Company, 1995), 85–87.

Henry Robinson Berkeley: Diary, July 4–13, 1864. *Four Years in the Confederate Artillery: The Diary of Private Henry Robinson Berkeley*, ed. William H. Runge (Chapel Hill: The University of North Carolina Press, 1961), 85–88. Copyright © 1961 by The Virginia Historical Society. Used by permission of The Virginia Historical Society.

Lois Bryan Adams to the *Detroit Advertiser and Tribune*, July 13, 15, 1864. Lois Bryan Adams, *Letter from Washington, 1863–1865*, ed. Evelyn Leasher (Detroit: Wayne State University Press, 1999), 174–77. Copyright © 1999 by Wayne State University Press.

Ulysses S. Grant to Henry W. Halleck, July 14, 1864. *PUSG*, vol. 11, 242–43.

Charles A. Dana to Ulysses S. Grant, July 15, 1864. *OR*, series 1, vol. 37, part 2, 332.

Abraham Lincoln, Offer of Safe Conduct for Peace Commissioners, July 18, 1864. *CWAL*, vol. VII, 451.

Clement C. Clay and James P. Holcombe to Horace Greeley, July 21, 1864. *The New York Times*, July 22, 1864.

James R. Gilmore to the *Boston Evening Transcript*. *Boston Evening Transcript*, July 22, 1864.

Henry Robinson Berkeley: Diary, July 14–24, 1864. *Four Years in the Confederate Artillery: The Diary of Private Henry Robinson Berkeley*, ed. William H. Runge (Chapel Hill: The University of North Carolina Press, 1961), 85–88. Copyright © 1961 by The Virginia Historical Society. Used by permission of The Virginia Historical Society.

Samuel T. Foster: Diary, July 18–23, 1864. *Foster*, 105–15.

John Q. A. Dennis to Edwin M. Stanton, July 26, 1864. *Freedom: Destruction*, 386.

Benjamin McIntyre: Diary, July 29, 1864. *Federals on the Frontier: The Diary of Benjamin F. McIntyre, 1862–1864*, ed. Nannie M. Tilley

(Austin: University of Texas Press, 1963), 380–82. Copyright © 1963, renewed 1991 by Nannie M. Tilley. Used by permission of the University of Texas Press.

David G. Farragut, General Orders Nos. 10 and 11, July 12 and 29, 1864. *Official Records of the Union and Confederate Navies in the War of the Rebellion*, series 1, vol. 21 (Washington: Government Printing Office, 1906), 397–98.

Stephen Minot Weld: Diary, July 30, 1864, and Memoir from 1912. *War Diary and Letters of Stephen Minot Weld, 1861–1865* (Cambridge, Mass.: The Riverside Press, 1912), 352–57.

William Pegram to Virginia Johnson Pegram, August 1, 1864. "'The Boy Artillerist': Letters of Colonel William Pegram, C.S.A.," ed. James I. Robertson Jr., *The Virginia Magazine of History and Biography*, vol. 98, no. 2, April 1990, 242–45. Copyright © 1990 by The Virginia Historical Society. Used by permission of The Virginia Historical Society.

C. Chauncey Burr: Editor's Table. *The Old Guard*, August 1864.

Edgeworth Bird to Sallie Bird, August 4, 1864. Manuscript, Hargrett Rare Book and Manuscript Library, University of Georgia.

Benjamin F. Wade and Henry Winter Davis: To the Supporters of the Government. *New-York Daily Tribune*, August 5, 1864.

Robert Garlick Hill Kean: Diary, August 7, 1864. *Inside the Confederate Government: The Diary of Robert Garlick Hill Kean*, ed. Edward Younger (New York: Oxford University Press, 1957), 168–70. Copyright © 1957 by Oxford University Press. Used by permission of Oxford University Press, USA.

Mathella Page Harrison: Diary, August 17, 1864. Typescript, Albert and Shirley Small Special Collections Library, University of Virginia.

Abraham Lincoln: Memorandum on Probable Failure of Reelection, August 23, 1864. *CWAL*, vol. VII, 514.

Benjamin F. Butler to Robert Ould, August 27, 1864. *OR*, series 2, vol. 7, 687–91.

Robert Toombs to Alexander H. Stephens, August 30, 1864. *The Correspondence of Robert Toombs, Alexander H. Stephens, and Howell Cobb*, ed. Ulrich B. Phillips (Washington, D.C.: American Historical Association, 1913), 651–52.

Platform of the Democratic National Convention, August 30, 1864. *Official Proceedings of the Democratic National Convention, held in 1864 at Chicago* (Chicago: The Times Steam Book and Job Printing House, 1864), 27.

James R. Gilmore: Our Visit to Richmond. *The Atlantic Monthly*, September 1864.

Robert E. Lee to Jefferson Davis, September 2, 1864. *WPREL*, 847–50.

Spottswood Rice to His Children and to Kitty Diggs, September 3, 1864. *Freedom: Military*, 689–90.

Gideon Welles: Diary, September 3, 1864. *Welles*, vol. 2, 135–36.

Thomas Bramlette to Abraham Lincoln, September 3, 1864. *Freedom: Destruction*, 604–6.

Clement L. Vallandigham to George B. McClellan, September 4, 1864. Manuscript, George B. McClellan Papers, Library of Congress.

Kate Stone: Diary, September 5, 1864. *Brokenburn: The Journal of Kate Stone, 1861–1868*, ed. John Q. Anderson (Baton Rouge: Louisiana State University Press, 1955), 194–99. Copyright © 1989 by Louisiana State University Press. Used by permission of Louisiana State University Press.

George Templeton Strong: Diary, September 5–8, 1864. *Strong*, 481–83.

George B. McClellan to the Democratic Nomination Committee, September 8, 1864. *The Civil War Papers of George B. McClellan: Selected Correspondence, 1860–1865*, ed. Stephen W. Sears (New York: Ticknor & Fields, 1989), 595–96. Copyright © 1989 by Stephen W. Sears. Used by permission of the Houghton Mifflin Harcourt Publishing Company. All rights reserved.

James A. Connolly to Mary Dunn Connolly, September 11, 1864. "Major James Austin Connolly," *Transactions of the Illinois State Historical Society for the Year 1928* (Springfield: Illinois State Historical Library, 1928), 360–62. Used by permission of the Abraham Lincoln Presidential Library.

William T. Sherman to James M. Calhoun and Others, September 12, 1864. *SCW*, 707–9.

Rachel Ann Wicker to John A. Andrew, September 12, 1864. *Freedom: Military*, 402–3.

Alexander McKinley to Samuel Du Pont, September 18, 1864. *Samuel Francis Du Pont: A Selection from His Civil War Letters*, vol. III, ed. John D. Hayes (Ithaca, N.Y.: Cornell University Press, 1969), 381–87. Copyright © 1969 by Eleutherian Mills-Hagley Foundation. Reprinted courtesy of Hagley Museum and Library.

Henry Robinson Berkeley: Diary, September 19, 1864. *Four Years in the Confederate Artillery: The Diary of Private Henry Robinson Berkeley* (Chapel Hill: The University of North Carolina Press, 1961), 96–99. Copyright © 1961 by The Virginia Historical Society. Used by permission of The Virginia Historical Society.

Jefferson Davis, Speech at Macon, September 23, 1864. *The Papers of Jefferson Davis, Volume 11: September 1864–May 1865*, ed. Lynda Lasswell Crist, Barbara J. Rozek, and Kenneth H. Williams (Baton Rouge: Louisiana State University Press, 2003), 61–63. Copyright

© 2003 by Louisiana State University Press. Used by permission of the publisher.

Elizabeth Blair Lee to Samuel Phillips Lee, September 24, 1864. *Wartime Washington: The Civil War Letters of Elizabeth Blair Lee*, ed. Virginia Laas (Urbana: University of Illinois Press, 1990), 281–83. Copyright © 1991 by the Board of Trustees of the University of Illinois. Used by permission from the Blair and Lee Family Papers, Manuscripts Division, Department of Rare Books and Special Collections, Princeton University Library.

Jefferson Davis, Speech at Columbia, October 4, 1864. *The Papers of Jefferson Davis, Volume 11: September 1864–May 1865*, ed. Lynda Lasswell Crist, Barbara J. Rozek, and Kenneth H. Williams (Baton Rouge: Louisiana State University Press, 2003), 82–88. Copyright © 2003 by Louisiana State University Press. Used by permission of the publisher.

Address of the Colored National Convention, October 6, 1864. *Proceedings of the National Convention of Colored Men, Held in the City of Syracuse, N.Y., October 4, 5, 6 and 7, 1864* (Boston: Geo. C. Rand & Avery, 1864), 44–62.

William T. Sherman to Ulysses S. Grant, October 9, 1864. *SCW*, 731.

Stephen Dodson Ramseur to Ellen Richmond Ramseur, October 10, 1864. *The Bravest of the Brave: The Correspondence of Stephen Dodson Ramseur*, ed. George G. Kundahl, 286–88. Copyright © 2010 by The University of North Carolina Press. Used by permission of the publisher, www.uncpress.unc.edu.

John B. Jones: Diary, October 10–13, 1864. J. B. Jones, *A Rebel War Clerk's Diary at the Confederate States Capital*, vol. II (Philadelphia: J. B. Lippincott & Co., 1866), 302–6.

Samuel Francis Du Pont to William King Hall, October 13, 1864. *Samuel Francis Du Pont: A Selection from His Civil War Letters*, vol. III, ed. John D. Hayes (Ithaca, N.Y.: Cornell University Press, 1969), 401–6. Copyright © 1969 by Eleutherian Mills-Hagley Foundation. Reprinted courtesy of Hagley Museum and Library.

Catherine Ann Devereux Edmondston: Diary, October 18, 1864. *"Journal of a Secesh Lady," The Diary of Catherine Ann Devereux Edmondston*, ed. Beth G. Crabtree and James W. Patton (Raleigh: North Carolina Division of Archives and History, 1979), 623–24. Copyright © 1979 by the North Carolina Division of Archives and History. Used by permission.

Francis Lieber: Lincoln or McClellan. Francis Lieber, *Lincoln or McClellan, Appeal to the Germans in America* (New York: Loyal Publication Society, 1864), 1–8.

George Templeton Strong: Diary, November 9, 1864. *Strong*, 511–12.

John Hay: Diary, November 11, 1864. *Inside Lincoln's White House: The Complete Civil War Diary of John Hay*, ed. Michael Burlingame and John R. Turner Ettlinger (Carbondale and Edwardsville: Southern Illinois University Press, 1997), 247–49. Copyright © 1997 by the Board of Trustees, Southern Illinois University. Used by permission of Southern Illinois University Press.

John S. Mosby to Philip H. Sheridan, November 11, 1864. *OR*, series 1, vol. 43, pt. 2, 920.

Jane Kamper: Statement Regarding Her Emancipation, November 14, 1864. *Freedom: Upper South*, 519.

Maria Lydig Daly: Diary, November 15, 1864. *Diary of a Union Lady, 1861–1865*, ed. Harold Earl Hammond (New York: Funk & Wagnalls, 1962), 312–14. Copyright © 1962 by Funk and Wagnalls Company, Inc.

James A. Connolly: Diary, November 17–23, 1864. "Major James Austin Connolly," *Transactions of the Illinois State Historical Society for the Year 1928* (Springfield: Illinois State Historical Library, 1928), 401–8. Used by permission of the Abraham Lincoln Presidential Library.

Henry Adams to Charles Francis Adams Jr., November 25, 1864. *The Letters of Henry Adams*, vol. I, ed. J. C. Levenson, Ernest Samuels, Charles Vandersee, Viola Hopkins Winner (Cambridge: The Belknap Press of Harvard University Press, 1982), 458–59. Copyright © 1982 by the Massachusetts Historical Society. Reprinted courtesy of the Adams Family Papers, Massachusetts Historical Society. Used by permission.

John Wilkes Booth: "To whom it may concern," November 1864. "*Right or Wrong, God Judge Me": The Writings of John Wilkes Booth*, ed. John Rhodehamel and Louise Taper (Urbana and Chicago: University of Illinois Press, 1997), 124–27. Copyright © 1997 by the Board of Trustees of the University of Illinois.

Joseph Miller: Statement Regarding His Family, November 26, 1864. *Freedom: Military*, 269–71.

Samuel T. Foster: Diary, November 30–December 1, 1864. *Foster*, 147–51.

Abraham Lincoln, Annual Message to Congress, December 6, 1864. *CWAL*, vol. VIII, 136–53.

Henry Nutt to Zebulon B. Vance, December 12, 1864. Manuscript, Zebulon B. Vance Papers, State Archives of North Carolina, Raleigh, North Carolina. Used by permission of the State Archives of North Carolina.

John Chipman Gray to John C. Ropes, December 14, 1864. *War Letters, 1862–1865, of John Chipman Gray and John Codman Ropes*, ed.

Worthington Chauncey Ford (Boston: Houghton Mifflin Company, 1927), 425–29.

John White Geary to Mary Geary, December 17, 1864. *A Politician Goes to War: The Civil War Letters of John White Geary*, ed. William Alan Blair (University Park, Pa.: The Pennsylvania State University Press, 1995), 217–18. Copyright © 1995 by The Pennsylvania State University. Used by permission of The Pennsylvania State University Press.

Mary S. Mallard: Journal, December 17–21, 1864. *The Children of Pride: A True Story of Georgia and the Civil War*, abridged edition, ed. Robert Manson Myers (New Haven, Conn.: Yale University Press, 1984), 510–15. Copyright © 1972, 1984 by Robert Manson Myers.

Harper's Weekly: Retaliation. *Harper's Weekly*, January 7, 1865.

Howell T. Cobb to James A. Seddon, January 8, 1865. *OR*, series 4, vol. 3, 1009–10.

Catherine Ann Devereux Edmondston: Diary, January 9, 1865. *"Journal of a Secesh Lady": The Diary of Catherine Ann Devereux Edmondston*, ed. Beth G. Crabtree and James W. Patton (Raleigh: North Carolina Division of Archives and History, 1979), 652–55. Copyright © 1979 by the North Carolina Division of Archives and History. Used by permission.

Petition of the Colored Citizens of Nashville to the Union Convention of Tennessee, January 9, 1865. *Freedom: Military*, 811–16.

Robert E. Lee to Andrew Hunter, January 11, 1865. *OR*, series 4, vol. 3, 1012–13.

Meeting of Colored Ministers with Edwin M. Stanton and William T. Sherman, January 12, 1865. *Freedom: Lower South*, 332–37.

William T. Sherman: Special Field Orders No. 15, January 16, 1865. *Freedom: Lower South*, 338–40.

Thirteenth Amendment to the Constitution of the United States, January 31, 1865. *The Debate on the Constitution: Part Two: January to August 1788*, ed. Bernard Bailyn (New York: The Library of America, 1993), 957.

George Julian: Journal, February 1, 1865. "George Julian's Journal—The Assassination of Lincoln," *Indiana Magazine of History*, vol. XI, no. 4, December 1915, 327.

Robert Garlick Hill Kean: Diary, February 5, 1865. *Inside the Confederate Government: The Diary of Robert Garlick Hill Kean*, ed. Edward Younger (New York: Oxford University Press, 1957), 194–98. Copyright © 1957 by Oxford University Press. Used by permission of Oxford University Press, USA.

John H. Stringfellow to Jefferson Davis, February 8, 1865. *Freedom: Military*, 291–95.

Henry Highland Garnet: A Memorial Discourse, February 12, 1865. *A Memorial Discourse by Rev. Henry Highland Garnet, delivered in the hall of the House of representatives, Washington City, D.C. on Sabbath, February 12, 1865* (Philadelphia: Joseph M. Wilson, 1865), 69–91.

Emma LeConte: Diary, February 17–18, 1865. Manuscript, Emma LeConte Diary, #420-z, Southern Historical Collection, The Wilson Library, The University of North Carolina at Chapel Hill.

Luther Rice Mills to John Mills, March 2, 1865. George D. Harmon, "Letters of Luther Rice Mills—A Confederate Soldier," *The North Carolina Historical Review*, vol. IV, no. 3, July 1927, 307–8. Published by the North Carolina Historical Commission. Used by permission of the North Carolina Office of Archives and History.

Abraham Lincoln, Second Inaugural Address, March 4, 1865. *CWAL*, vol. VIII, 332–33.

Frederick Douglass: from *Life and Times of Frederick Douglass. Life and Times of Frederick Douglass* (Hartford, Conn.: Park Publishing Co., 1882), 443–45.

Roanoke Island Freedmen to Abraham Lincoln, March 9, 1865. *Freedom: Upper South*, 231–35.

George Templeton Strong: Diary, March 10, 1865. *Strong*, 563–64.

Alpheus S. Williams to His Daughter, March 12, 1865. *From the Cannon's Mouth: The Civil War Letters of Alpheus S. Williams*, ed. Milo M. Quaife (Detroit: Wayne State University Press, 1959), 373–75.

Charles Sumner to John Bright, March 13, 1865. *The Selected Letters of Charles Sumner*, vol. II, ed. Beverly Wilson Palmer (Boston: Northeastern University Press, 1990), 273–74. Copyright © 1990 by Beverly Wilson Palmer; copyright © 1990 by University Press of New England, Lebanon, N.H. Used by permission.

Frances Johnson: Statement Regarding Her Whipping and Escape, March 25, 1865. *Freedom: Military*, 694–95.

Clarissa Burdett: Statement Regarding Her Whipping and Escape, March 27, 1865. *Freedom: Destruction*, 615–16.

John B. Jones: Diary, April 2, 1865. J. B. Jones, *A Rebel War Clerk's Diary at the Confederate States Capital*, vol. II (Philadelphia: J. B. Lippincott & Co., 1866), 465–67.

Sallie Brock: from *Richmond During the War*. Sallie Brock Putnam, *Richmond During the War: Four Years of Personal Observation* (New York: G. W. Carleton & Co., 1867), 362–71.

George Templeton Strong: Diary, April 3, 1865. *Strong*, 573–76.

William Gordon McCabe to Mary Pegram, April 4, 1865. *Ham Chamberlayne—Virginian: Letters and Papers of an Artillery Officer in the War for Southern Independence 1861–1865*, ed. C. G. Chamberlayne (Richmond, Va.: Dietz Printing Co., 1932), 317–19. Copyright © 1932 by C. G. Chamberlayne.

Thomas Morris Chester to the *Philadelphia Press*, April 4 and 6, 1865. *Thomas Morris Chester, Black Civil War Correspondent: His Dispatches from the Virginia Front*, ed. R.J.M. Blackett (Baton Rouge: Louisiana State University Press, 1989), 288–99. Copyright © 1989 by Louisiana State University Press. Used by permission of the publisher.

Gideon Welles: Diary, April 7, 1865. *Welles*, vol. 2, 276–78.

Ulysses S. Grant to Robert E. Lee, April 9, 1865. *PUSG*, vol. 14, 373–74.

Robert E. Lee, April 10, 1865. *WPREL*, 934–35.

Elizabeth Keckly: from *Behind the Scenes*. Elizabeth Keckly, *Behind the Scenes, or, Thirty Years a Slave, and Four Years in the White House* (New York: G. W. Carleton & Co., 1868), 174–93.

George Templeton Strong: Diary, April 15, 1865. *Strong*, 582–84.

Gideon Welles: Diary, April 18, 1865. *Welles*, vol. 2, 283–92.

William T. Sherman to Ulysses S. Grant or Henry Halleck, April 18, 1865. *SCW*, 863–65.

Sarah Morgan: Diary, April 19, 1865. *Sarah Morgan: The Civil War Diary of Sarah Morgan*, ed. Charles East (Athens: The University of Georgia Press, 1991), 605–8. Copyright © 1991 by The University of Georgia Press. Used by permission of The University of Georgia Press.

Robert E. Lee to Jefferson Davis, April 20, 1865. *WPREL*, 938–39.

Jefferson Davis to Varina Howell Davis, April 23, 1865. *The Papers of Jefferson Davis, Volume 11: September 1864–May 1865*, eds. Lynda Lasswell Crist, Barbara J. Rozek, and Kenneth H. Williams (Baton Rouge: Louisiana State University Press, 2003), 557–60. Copyright © 2003 by Louisiana State University Press. Used by permission of the publisher.

Stephen Minot Weld to Hannah Weld, April 24, 1865. *War Diary and Letters of Stephen Minot Weld, 1861–1865* (Cambridge, Mass.: The Riverside Press, 1912), 396–98.

Samuel T. Foster: Diary, April 17–May 4, 1865. *Foster*, 164–74.

Ellen Renshaw House: Diary, May 2, 1865. *A Very Violent Rebel: The Civil War Diary of Ellen Renshaw House*, ed. Daniel E. Sutherland (Knoxville: The University of Tennessee Press, 1996), 163. Copyright © 1996 by The University of Tennessee Press/Knoxville. Ellen Renshaw House's diary, Copyright © 1996 by Ellen Allran and Victoria Guthrie. Used by permission of The University of Tennessee Press.

Walt Whitman: from *Specimen Days*. Walt Whitman, *Specimen Days & Collect* (Philadelphia: Rees Walsh & Co., 1882–83), 71–72.

New York Herald: The Grandest Military Display in the World. *New York Herald*, May 24, 1865.

Lois Bryan Adams to the *Detroit Advertiser and Tribune*, May 24, 27, 1865. Lois Bryan Adams, *Letter from Washington, 1863–1865*, ed. Evelyn Leasher (Detroit: Wayne State University Press, 1999), 263–68. Copyright © 1999 by Wayne State University Press.

Gordon Granger, General Orders No. 3, June 19, 1865. *OR*, series 1, vol. 48, pt. 2, 929.

This volume presents the texts of the printings and manuscripts chosen as sources here but does not attempt to reproduce features of their typographic design or physical layout. In the texts that have been printed from manuscript, the beginnings of sentences have been capitalized and punctuation at the end of sentences and closing quotation marks have been supplied. The texts are printed without other alteration except for the changes previously discussed and for the correction of typographical errors. Spelling, punctuation, and capitalization are often expressive features, and they are not altered, even when inconsistent or irregular. The following is a list of typographical errors corrected, cited by page and line number: 4.6, Dahlgreen's; 52.30, it's; 54.17, thu; 54.18, butched; 111.1, Spotylvania; 114.12, it as; 147.27, arms. three; 153.1, presssing; 169.30, graounds; 170.31, trops; 170.35–36, demonstate; 172.19, staied; 174.40, dosen; 197.13, that it; 199.28, rife; 206.22–23, fore castle; 207.27, perfactly; 213.36, work of; 227.15, their one; 273.14, runing; 300.7, cotemporary; 322.23, in every; 323.1, Caster; 337.29, well; 364.10, Spotswood; 366.19, assured; 400.25, enemy It; 404.38 Cooperheads,; 405.15, enemies—"; 408.17, power If; 461.34, things.; 491.7, and and; 499.5, $1,740,690 489 49.; 491.7, and and; 503.27, pension, rolls,; 504.1, $4,505,616,92; 516.33, be to; 549.20, whey; 552.9, grave.; 558.25, Jan., 12,; 563.24, as soon as soon; 579.30, outly,; 581.31, of if; 614.2, altogether"; 617.4, exclaimed. so; 633.25, mad; 633.28, before I; 646.7, calvary; 654.24, protection. He; 654.28, resigned." I; 654.29, sake. He; 662.22, to much; 694.37, al most,; 697.27, 17 20; 707.32, arrives; 708.14, know; 713.33, A.M. At; 713.34, despondent.; 720.28, humilating; 722.36, seem.

Notes

In the notes below, the reference numbers denote page and line of this volume (the line count includes headings, but not rule lines). No note is made for material included in the eleventh edition of *Merriam-Webster's Collegiate Dictionary.* Biblical references are keyed to the King James Version. Quotations from Shakespeare are keyed to *The Riverside Shakespeare*, ed. G. Blakemore Evans (Boston: Houghton Mifflin, 1974). Footnotes and bracketed editorial notes within the text were in the originals. For further historical and biographical background, references to other studies, and more detailed maps, see James McPherson, *Battle Cry of Freedom: The Civil War Era* (New York: Oxford University Press, 1988); *Encyclopedia of the American Civil War: A Political, Social, and Military History*, edited by David S. Heidler and Jeanne T. Heidler (New York: W. W. Norton, 2002); *The Library of Congress Civil War Desk Reference*, edited by Margaret E. Wagner, Gary W. Gallagher, and Paul Finkelman (New York: Simon & Schuster, 2002); and Aaron Sheehan-Dean, *Concise Historical Atlas of the U.S. Civil War* (New York: Oxford University Press, 2008).

2.1 Lieut. Pollard] First Lieutenant James Pollard of New Kent County, whose military service ended when he lost a leg in the fighting at Nance's Shop southeast of Richmond on June 24, 1864.

3.15–16 Dahlgren . . . the Commodore] Ulric Dahlgren (1842–1864) was the son of Rear Admiral John A. Dahlgren (1809–1870), commander of the South Atlantic Blockading Squadron, 1863–65.

3.17 infamous attempt . . . whole city] Union artillery based on the islands of Charleston Harbor had been intermittently shelling the city of Charleston since August 1863.

3.27–28 Punic Faith] Proverbially, an untrustworthy oath, having the character of treachery attributed to the Carthaginians by the Romans.

3.30 marked D] Edmondston placed newspaper clippings regarding the Kilpatrick-Dahlgren raid in another part of her journal.

4.22 Will] House's brother William McLean House (1834–1884).

4.31 sister] Frances Renshaw House (1832–1923).

5.19 Johnnie] House's brother John Moore House (1844–1865), a prisoner on Johnson's Island who had been captured at Chattanooga in November 1863.

5.25 Gen Carters] Brigadier General Samuel P. Carter (1819–1891) was the Union provost marshal at Knoxville.

7.1 Admiral Renshaw] House's uncle, Francis B. Renshaw (1815–1867), a commander in the Confederate navy, had resigned his commission as a lieutenant in the U.S. Navy in 1861.

7.3 (Gen C) is an old navy officer] Carter had joined the navy in 1840 and held a commission as a lieutenant commander while serving in the Union army.

7.31 Gen Longstreet] After his failure to capture Knoxville in November 1863, Lieutenant General James Longstreet (1821–1904) had retreated into northeast Tennessee.

8.2–3 Mrs Brownlow] Eliza O'Brien Brownlow (1819–1914), the wife of William G. Brownlow (1805–1877), a prominent Knoxville unionist.

12.32 Chas. Sumner] See Biographical Notes.

14.19–20 vote to abolish slavery in Virginia] A constitutional convention called by the unionist "Restored Government" of Virginia met in Alexandria on February 13, 1864, and voted to abolish slavery on March 10.

15.12–13 rank of second-lieutenant . . . conferred] Massachusetts governor John A. Andrew (1818–1867) commissioned Sergeant Stephen A. Swails (1832–1900) of the 54th Massachusetts Infantry as a second lieutenant on March 11, 1864. Because of opposition from the War Department, Swails was not mustered in as an officer until January 17, 1865.

15.17–18 "a man's a man for a' that."] See Robert Burns, "For A' That and A' That" (1795).

15.19–20 emigrants returned from Hayti] President Lincoln had signed a contract on December 31, 1862, with Bernard Kock, a cotton trader who proposed to transport 5,000 freed slaves to Île à Vache, a small uninhabited island off the southwest coast of Haiti. In April 1863 a ship carried 453 former slaves from Fort Monroe, Virginia, to the island, where attempts to establish a cotton plantation failed. Of the colonists, 88 died of hunger and disease, 73 fled to the Haitian mainland, and 292 returned to the United States on the relief ship *Marcia Day*, which docked at Alexandria on March 20, 1864.

15.29 the Massachusetts Cavalry] The 5th Massachusetts Cavalry, a black regiment.

15.30 Mr. Downing . . . Mr. Remond] Black abolitionists George T. Downing (1819–1903) of Rhode Island and Charles L. Remond (1810–1873) of Massachusetts.

21.26–29 Banks . . . Steele] Major General Nathaniel P. Banks (1816–1894) commanded the Department of the Gulf, December 1862–May 1864. Major General Frederick Steele (1819–1868) commanded the Department of Arkansas, January–December 1864. For the Red River campaign, see the headnote on page 24 of this volume, and the Chronology, March–May 1864.

22.4–7 Gilmore . . . W. F. Smith] Major General Quincy A. Gillmore (1825–1888), commander of the Tenth Corps in South Carolina, who would join the Army of the James for the spring offensive; Major General Benjamin F. Butler (1818–1893), commander of the Army of the James; Major General William F. Smith (1824–1903), who would lead the Eighteenth Corps in the Army of the James.

22.9 Burnsides Corps] The Ninth Corps, commanded by Major General Ambrose Burnside (1824–1881).

22.11–13 Sigel . . . Crook] Major General Franz Sigel (1824–1902), commander of the Department of West Virginia; Major General Edward O. C. Ord (1818–1883); Brigadier General William W. Averell (1832–1900); Brigadier General George Crook (1828–1890).

30.14–19 "Far better die . . . and fame."] Cf. the final stanza of "The Call of Kansas" by the Reverend John Pierpont (1785–1866), published in the *New-York Daily Tribune* on July 30, 1856: "Far better fall, in such a strife, / Than still to Slavery's claims concede: / Than crouch beneath her frown, for life, / Far better on the field to bleed. / To live thus is a life-long shame! / To die thus, victory and fame!"

32.23 Schofield] Major General John M. Schofield (1831–1906), commander of the Army of the Ohio.

34.32 Reverdy Johnson] Johnson (1796–1876) repesented Maryland in the Senate as a Whig, 1845–49, and as a Democrat, 1863–68.

34.34–35.1 George Thompson] Thompson, a prominent British abolitionist (1804–1878), was on his third and final lecture tour of the United States.

37.14 Senators Hale and Clark] John P. Hale (1806–1873) represented New Hampshire in the Senate as a Free Soiler, 1847–53, and as a Republican, 1855–65; Daniel Clark (1809–1891) was a Republican senator from New Hampshire, 1857–66.

37.17–18 Powell . . . McDougal] Lazarus W. Powell (1812–1867), Democratic senator from Kentucky, 1859–65; Willard Saulsbury Sr. (1820–1892), Democratic senator from Delaware, 1859–71; James Alexander McDougall (1817–1867), Democratic senator from California, 1861–67; Garrett Davis (1801–1872), Unionist and later Democratic senator from Kentucky, 1861–65, 1865–72.

38.15 vote of 37 to 6!] The vote was 38–6.

38.22–23 "'Twere worth . . . at their array."] Cf. Sir Walter Scott, *The Lady of the Lake* (1810), canto 6, stanza 15: "'Twere worth ten years of peaceful life, / One glance at their array!"

39.13 Howard] Jacob M. Howard (1805–1871), Republican senator from Michigan, 1862–71.

42.31 Col. Bell] Tyree H. Bell (1815–1902) commanded a brigade in Forrest's Cavalry Corps.

43.14–15 Major Boothe . . . Major Bradford] Lionel F. Booth (1838–1864) commanded the 1st Battalion of the Sixth U.S. Colored Heavy Artillery; William F. Bradford (c. 1832–1864) commanded the 13th Tennessee Cavalry, which he had organized at Union City in the fall of 1863.

43.34 Capt. Wilson] J. Cardwell Wilson (c. 1839–1864) led Company F of the Confederate 20th Tennessee Cavalry.

45.19–22 the 8th Corps . . . Rappahannock] The Eighth Corps had not been moved to the Rappahannock front.

45.23 Lt Col Mosby] John S. Mosby (1833–1916); see Biographical Notes.

45.24–25 11th & 12th Corps, consolidated . . . Burnside] The Eleventh and Twelfth Corps of the Army of the Cumberland were consolidated into the Twentieth Corps in April 1864 and remained in the western theater.

46.8 Beauregard] General Pierre G. T. Beauregard (1818–1893) commanded the troops defending Charleston, South Carolina.

46.12 Genl Buckner] Major General Simon B. Buckner (1823–1914) commanded the Department of East Tennessee. His headquarters were at Bristol on the Tennessee-Virginia border.

48.27–28 Capt. BRADFORD . . . REVEL] Captain Theodorick F. Bradford, Major Bradford's brother, and Second Lieutenant John C. Barr (1837–1864) of Company D were killed during the attack on the fort. Lieutenant Wilson of Company A, Lieutenant Cordy B. Revelle of Company E, and Lieutenant John C. Akerstrom, the post quartermaster, were killed after surrendering.

48.30 Capt. POSTON and Lieut. LYON] Captain John L. Poston of Company E was captured but escaped in November 1864. There is no record of a Lieutenant Lyon in the 13th Tennessee Cavalry; the dispatch may be referring to First Lieutenant Nicholas Logan of Company C, who was taken prisoner and died on June 6, 1864.

48.31 Capt. YOUNG] While a Confederate prisoner, Captain John T. Young (d. 1915) of the 24th Missouri signed an affidavit stating that he had seen "no ill-treatment of the wounded on the evening of the battle or the next morning," though he later recanted, saying the statement had been "extorted from me while under duress."

48.33 Maj. BRADFORD . . . has been killed] Bradford was murdered by Confederate soldiers near Brownsville, Tennessee, on April 14, 1864.

49.3–4 Capt. PORTER . . . Adjt. LEMMING] Captain John H. Porter (or Potter) was shot in the head and died on June 21, 1864. Lieutenant Henry Lippett died on April 18, 1864. Adjutant Mack J. Leming, or Lemming, survived.

49.6 Parrotts] Muzzle-loading artillery with rifled barrels, named after their designer, Robert Parker Parrott (1804–1877), superintendent of the West Point Iron and Cannon Foundry.

49.36 Gen. LEE] Major General Stephen D. Lee (1833–1908), the Confederate cavalry commander in Mississippi, was not at Fort Pillow.

50.1 Gen. CHALMERS] Brigadier General James Ronald Chalmers (1831–1898) commanded the First Division of Forrest's Cavalry Corps.

50.25 Col. REED] Lieutenant Colonel Wyly M. Reed of the 5th Mississippi Cavalry.

51.13–14 soldiers . . . pass through Baltimore] Four soldiers from the 6th Massachusetts Infantry were killed by a pro-secessionist mob while passing through Baltimore on April 19, 1861.

55.30 Wagoner . . . Milliken's bend] Black soldiers had fought at Fort Wagner, South Carolina, July 18, 1863; Port Hudson, Louisiana, May 27, 1863; and at Milliken's Bend, Louisiana, June 7, 1863.

55.34 New York, the *July riots!*] At least eleven African American men were lynched during the draft riots in New York City, July 13–17, 1863.

55.38 "Legrees;"] Simon Legree, cruel slave owner in *Uncle Tom's Cabin* (1852) by Harriet Beecher Stowe.

57.26–27 committee from Congress . . . soon report.] The Joint Committee reported to Congress on May 5, 1864, that the Confederates had massacred three hundred Union soldiers at Fort Pillow after the garrison had surrendered.

58.1 Mrs. W and Edgar] Mary Jane Hale Welles (1817–1886) and Edgar Thaddeus Welles (1843–1914).

58.3 Tom] Thomas Gideon Welles (1846–1892).

58.24 Seward . . . Chase] William H. Seward (1801–1872), secretary of state, 1861–69; Edwin M. Stanton (1814–1869), secretary of war, 1862–68; Salmon P. Chase (1808–1873), secretary of the treasury, 1861–64.

58.28 Mr. Bates and Mr. Blair] Edward Bates (1793–1869), attorney general, 1861–64; Montgomery Blair (1813–1883), postmaster general, 1861–64.

65.11 Senator Wilson] Henry Wilson (1812–1875), Republican senator from Massachusetts, 1855–73, was chairman of the Committee on Military Affairs.

66.13 Gen. Halleck] Major Henry W. Halleck (1814–1872), chief of staff of the Union army, 1864–65.

67.29 Meade's] Major General George G. Meade (1815–1872), commander of the Army of the Potomac, 1863–65.

69.8 the General] Meade.

69.17 withdrawal from Mine Run. *Sapristi*] Meade had crossed the Rapidan on November 26, 1863, in an attempt to turn Lee's right flank. After deciding not to attack the Confederate positions along Mine Run on November 30, Meade withdrew the Army of the Potomac back across the Rapidan on December 1. *Sapristi*: French: Good heavens!

69.19 Griffin] Brigadier General Charles Griffin (1825–1867), commander of the First Division of the Fifth Corps.

69.21 Gregg] Brigadier General David M. Gregg (1833–1916) led the Second Division of the Army of the Potomac's Cavalry Corps, commanded by Major General Philip H. Sheridan.

71.5 Duff & old Jerry Dent] Lieutenant Colonel William L. Duff (1822–1894) and Lieutenant Colonel Frederick T. Dent (1820–1892) were aides to Grant. Dent was a West Point classmate of Grant's and his brother-in-law.

71.7–8 Gen. Seymour . . . Olustee] Brigadier General Truman Seymour (1824–1891) commanded the Second Brigade, Third Division, Sixth Corps. While commanding Union forces in northern Florida, Seymour had been defeated at the battle of Olustee, February 20, 1864.

71.16–18 Torbert . . . Wilson] The three divisions of Sheridan's cavalry corps were commanded by Brigadier General Alfred T. A. Torbert (1833–1880), Brigadier General David M. Gregg (see note 69.21), and Brigadier General James H. Wilson (1837–1925).

72.15–16 Bill Thorndike . . . Robinson] William Thorndike (1835–1887), who had graduated from Harvard a year before Lyman, had served as the surgeon of the 39th Massachusetts Infantry since November 1863. Brigadier General John C. Robinson (1817–1897) commanded the Second Division of the Fifth Corps.

72.18 Wright] Brigadier General Horatio G. Wright (1820–1899) commanded the First Division of the Sixth Corps.

72.23 Getty] Brigadier General George W. Getty (1819–1901) led the Second Division of the Sixth Corps.

72.36–37 Crawford's . . . Gen. Eustis] Brigadier General Samuel W. Crawford (1829–1892) commanded the Third Division of the Fifth Corps; Brigadier General Henry L. Eustis (1819–1911) led the Fourth Brigade, Second Division, Sixth Corps.

72.40 Hill] Lieutenant General Ambrose Powell Hill (1825–1865) commanded the Third Corps in the Army of Northern Virginia.

73.7 Wadsworth] Brigadier General James S. Wadsworth (1807–1864) commanded the Fourth Division of the Fifth Corps.

73.20 Joe Hayes . . . Dalton] Colonel Joseph Hayes (1835–1912), commander of the 18th Massachusetts Infantry, and Surgeon Edward Dalton (1834–1872), medical inspector of the Army of the Potomac, were both Harvard classmates of Lyman.

73.25–26 mustering officer, Geo. Barnard] Captain George M. Barnard Jr. (1835–1898), the officer responsible for maintaining the muster rolls (personnel records) in Griffin's division.

73.27 Ewell] Lieutenant General Richard S. Ewell (1817–1872) led the Second Corps of the Army of Northern Virginia until May 27, 1864, when he fell seriously ill with dysentery. He was replaced by Major General Jubal A. Early (1816–1894).

73.31 Rawlins] Brigadier General John A. Rawlins (1831–1869), Grant's chief of staff.

73.37 Bartlett] Brigadier General Joseph J. Bartlett (1834–1893) led the Third Brigade, First Division, Fifth Corps.

74.6 Wheaton] Brigadier General Frank Wheaton (1833–1903) led the First Brigade, Second Division, Sixth Corps.

74.16 Maj. Mundy] Major Charles Mundee (1826–1871), assistant adjutant general on Getty's staff.

74.18–19 Gen. Gibbon . . . Gen. Mott] Brigadier General John Gibbon (1827–1896) commanded the Second Division of the Second Corps; Brigadier General Gershom Mott (1822–1884) led the Fourth Division of the Second Corps.

74.22–23 Maj. Mitchell] Major William Mitchell (1836–1883), an aide on Hancock's staff.

74.27 Prince . . . Carr] Brigadier General Henry Prince (1811–1892) commanded the division from July 1863 to March 1864. He was succeeded by Brigadier General Joseph B. Carr (1828–1895), who held the position for a little more than a month owing to procedural difficulties with his promotion to brigadier general.

74.29–30 breaking up of the Third Corps] The First and Third Corps were broken up in March 1864 when the Army of the Potomac was reorganized into three infantry corps.

74.32–33 reduced to a brigade . . . Battle of Hatcher's Run] On May 13 the two infantry brigades that composed Mott's division were assigned to the Third Division, Second Corps. They were later consolidated into a single brigade, commanded by Colonel Robert McAllister (1813–1891), that fought with distinction at the battle of Hatcher's Run, February 5–7, 1865.

74.35 Carroll's & Hays's] Colonel Samuel S. Carroll (1832–1893) led the Third Brigade, Second Division, Second Corps, and Brigadier General Alexander Hays (1819–1864) commanded the Second Brigade, Third Division, Second Corps.

75.18 Duane] Major James C. Duane (1824–1897), chief engineer on Meade's staff.

75.22–23 Capt. Hutton of B's staff] Captain Charles G. Hutton (d. 1900) was an aide on the staff of Ambrose Burnside, the commander of the Ninth Corps.

76.2–3 no command over Gen. Burnside] Burnside, who outranked Meade, reported directly to Grant until May 23, 1864, when he was placed under Meade's command.

76.13 Birney] Major General David B. Birney (1825–1864) led the Third Division of the Second Corps.

76.27 Webb's brigade] Brigadier General Alexander S. Webb (1835–1911) led the First Brigade, Second Division, Second Corps.

76.29 Abbott] Major Henry Livermore Abbott (1842–1864) of the 20th Massachusetts Infantry.

76.30 Stevenson] Brigadier General Thomas G. Stevenson (1836–1864) led the First Division of the Ninth Corps.

76.33 Charlie Mills . . . Stevie Weld] Lieutenant Charles J. Mills (1841–1865), an adjutant general on Stevenson's staff; Lieutenant Colonel Stephen M. Weld, see Biographical Notes.

76.35 Barlow's] Brigadier General Francis C. Barlow (1834–1896) led the First Division of the Second Corps.

77.6 *Longstreet's Corps*] James Longstreet, commander of the First Corps of the Army of Northern Virginia, had rejoined Lee's army in April 1864 after serving in northern Georgia and East Tennessee since September 1863.

77.9 Macy] Colonel George N. Macy (1837–1875), who had lost his left hand at Gettysburg, was the commander of the 20th Massachusetts Infantry.

77.14 Maj. Angel] Major Ashbel W. Angel (c. 1838–1884), a topographical engineer with the Second Corps.

77.15 Maj. Norval] Major John M. Norvell (1834–1922).

78.7 brigade of raw "Veterans"] The First Brigade of Stevenson's division contained three Massachusetts infantry regiments, the 56th, 57th, and 59th, that had been organized in early 1864. Their soldiers were a mixture of reenlisted veterans, mostly from nine-month service regiments, and conscripts.

78.8 Col. Griswold] Colonel Charles E. Griswold (1834–1864), commander of the 56th Massachusetts Infantry.

78.9 Col. Bartlett] Colonel William F. Bartlett (1840–1876), commander of the 57th Massachusetts Infantry.

78.18 Gen. Patrick] Brigadier General Marsena R. Patrick (1811–1888) was provost marshal of the Army of the Potomac, commanding a brigade of three infantry and one cavalry regiments.

78.25 Comstock] Lieutenant Colonel Cyrus B. Comstock (1831–1910), a member of Grant's staff.

79.7 Potter] Brigadier General Robert B. Potter (1829–1887) led the Second Division of the Ninth Corps.

79.13 Flint] Captain Edward A. Flint (1832–1886) of the 1st Massachusetts Cavalry returned to the Wilderness in May 1865 and later shared with Lyman his impressions of the battlefield.

79.21 Cope] Captain Emmor B. Cope (1834–1927), a topographical engineer.

79.32 Macy] See note 77.9.

80.20 Major Hancock] Major John Hancock (1830–1912) was an aide to Brigadier General Francis Barlow and brother of Second Corps commander Winfield Scott Hancock.

80.25 Saunders] Captain William W. Sanders (1839–1883), a mustering officer on Meade's staff.

80.32 Capt. Beaumont . . . Lt. Col. Kent] Captain Eugene B. Beaumont (1837–1916) was an aide on the staff of Major General John Sedgwick. Lieutenant Colonel Jacob Kent (1835–1918) was Sedgwick's inspector general.

80.36 Gen. M] Meade.

80.37 Upton . . . Shaler] Colonel Emory Upton (1839–1881) commanded the Second Brigade, First Division, Sixth Corps, and Brigadier General Alexander Shaler (1827–1911) led the Fourth Brigade, First Division, Sixth Corps.

81.4 Capt. Cadwalader] Captain Charles E. Cadwalader (1839–1907), a member of Meade's staff.

81.10 Edw. Johnson's division] The engagement was fought with the Confederate brigade commanded by Brigadier General Robert D. Johnston (1837–1919), part of the division led by Major General Jubal Early in the Second Corps of the Army of Northern Virginia.

81.11 Ricketts] Brigadier General James B. Ricketts (1817–1887) was commander of the Third Division of the Sixth Corps.

81.23 Col. Walker] Lieutenant Colonel Francis A. Walker (1840–1897) was Hancock's chief of staff.

81.25 Washburn] Elihu B. Washburne (1816–1887), Grant's political patron since 1861, was a Whig, and then a Republican, congressman from northwestern Illinois, 1853–69. He later served as U.S. minister to France, 1869–77.

81.37–38 Ferrero's negro div.] Brigadier General Edward Ferrero (1831–1899) was commander of the Fourth Division of the Ninth Corps; both of its infantry brigades were composed entirely of black troops.

82.16 Capt. Martin] Captain Augustus P. Martin (1835–1902).

83.4 "Rosie"] Lieutenant Frederick Rosenkrantz, a courier on General Meade's staff.

83.6 Mr. Dana, Asst. Sec. of War] Charles A. Dana; see Biographical Notes.

83.13–14 McGregor . . . Associated Press] William D. McGregor (1826–1907).

83.15 Mimi] Lyman's wife, Elizabeth Russell Lyman (1836–1911).

84.20 the General] Meade.

86.25 hop poles] Tall poles, usually fifteen feet or more in height, on which hop plants are trained.

90.33 Rev. Mr. Mullaly . . . Orr] Francis P. Mulally was chaplain of the 1st (Orr's) Regiment, South Carolina Rifles, commanded by Lieutenant Colonel George Miller.

91.13 Heth's division] Major General Henry Heth (1825–1899) led one of the four divisions in A. P. Hill's Third Corps.

91.23–25 First regiment . . . Fourteenth Regiment] All of the regiments were from South Carolina.

91.27 Lane's and Thomas's brigades] Brigadier General James H. Lane (1833–1907) led a brigade of five North Carolina infantry regiments, and Brigadier General Edward L. Thomas (1825–1898) commanded a brigade of four Georgia regiments; both brigades served in Major General Cadmus M. Wilcox's division.

92.22 Lieut. Col. Shooter] Lieutenant Colonel Washington P. Shooter (1837–1864).

93.3 Gen. McGowan] Brigadier General Samuel McGowan (1819–1897).

93.5–6 Capt. L. C. Haskell . . . Lieut. G. A. Wardlaw] Alexander C. Haskell (1839–1910) and George A. Wardlaw, quartermaster of the 1st South Carolina Infantry.

93.9–10 Scales' brigade] Brigadier General Alfred M. Scales (1827–1892) led a brigade composed of five North Carolina regiments in Wilcox's Division.

94.18–19 Kershaw's . . . Anderson's divisions] Brigadier General Joseph B. Kershaw (1822–1894) and Major General Charles W. Field (1828–1892) led divisions in Longstreet's First Corps. Brigadier General Richard H. Anderson (1821–1879) commanded a division in Hill's Third Corps.

94.31 still no Blucher] The timely arrival of Field Marshal Gebhard von Blücher's Prussian army at Waterloo on the evening of June 18, 1815, resulted in the defeat of Napoleon's army.

95.4–5 *the War Horse!*] Longstreet was sometimes referred to as "Lee's War Horse."

96.10 Poague's artillery] Lieutenant Colonel William T. Poague (1835–1914) commanded an artillery battalion in Hill's Third Corps.

96.27 McLaws', afterwards Kershaw's division] Major General Lafayette McLaws (1821–1897) had fallen out with Longstreet in December 1863 and been replaced as division commander by Kershaw.

97.7 Nance . . . Doby] Colonel James D. Nance (1837–1864), commander of the 3rd South Carolina Infantry; Lieutenant Colonel Franklin Gaillard (1829–1864), commander of the 2nd South Carolina Infantry; and Captain Alfred E. Doby, an aide to Kershaw, were killed in the fighting on May 6, 1864.

97.20–22 Longstreet . . . Brigadier-General Jenkins] Both Longstreet and Micah Jenkins (1835–1864), a brigade commander in Field's Division, were accidentally shot by Confederate soldiers.

104.20 Paran] In Genesis 21:21, the wilderness dwelling place of the outcast Ishmael.

105.22 Lord Fairfax's parchment deeds] In 1719, Thomas, sixth Lord Fairfax of Cameron (1693–1781), had inherited title to more than five million acres of land in Virginia, including the Northern Neck, the land between the Rappahannock and Potomac Rivers.

106.29 Mosby's prowling men] See headnote, page 463 of this volume.

107.31 Stonewall had charged] Confederate Lieutenant General Thomas J. (Stonewall) Jackson led a successful attack against the Union right flank on May 2, 1863, during the battle of Chancellorsville. He was mortally wounded that night when his own men accidentally opened fire on his returning scouting party.

109.2 *Pillar of Smoke*] See Exodus 13:21.

109.6 Sabæan lore] The surviving inscriptions of the Sabæans of Yemen, the biblical Sheba, have proved difficult to read and interpret.

112.28–30 Lt Ashley . . . Lt Eldridge] First Lieutenant William A. Ashley (1828–1864) of Company I; First Lieutenant Edward H. Graves (c. 1839–1880) of Company K, who was severely wounded in the abdomen; Lieutenant Alfred W. Midgley (1838–1864) of Company H, who died from his wounds on May 12; First Lieutenant L. Oscar Eaton of Company F was severely wounded in the leg; Second Lieutenant Simeon N. Eldridge of Company E was wounded in the arm. Graves, Eaton, and Eldridge were mustered out on July 1, 1864.

113.5 Capt Shurtleff] Captain Flavel Shurtleff (1829–1910) commanded Company H of the 10th Massachusetts Infantry.

113.26 the 2nd RI] The 2nd Rhode Island Infantry.

115.12 Sedgwick was killed] Major General John Sedgwick (1813–1864) was killed by a sharpshooter at Spotsylvania on May 9, 1864. He was succeeded as Sixth Corps commander by Horatio G. Wright.

115.17 Colonel Edwards] Colonel Oliver Edwards (1835–1904) had previously commanded the 37th Massachusetts Infantry.

115.18 Neil] Brigadier General Thomas H. Neill (1826–1885) had replaced Getty as commander of the Second Division, Sixth Corps.

115.22 Gen Augur] Major General Christopher C. Augur (1821–1898) commanded the Twenty-second Corps at Washington, D.C. The report of his arrival was unfounded.

115.25–26 the 57th Veterans of Mass] See note 78.7.

116.9 Bill Robinson] Captain William B. Robinson of the 5th Vermont Infantry Regiment was wounded twice at the Wilderness, and discharged in August 1864.

117.7 Col P] Lieutenant Colonel Joseph B. Parsons (1828–1906) of Northampton commanded the 10th Massachusetts Infantry.

117.17–18 Maj Gen Johnson + 2 Brig Generals] Major General Edward Johnson (1816–1873), a division commander in the Second Corps, and Brigadier General George H. Steuart (1828–1903), one of Johnson's brigade commanders. Both men were exchanged on August 3, 1864.

117.26–29 Capt Weatherill . . . Lieut Munyan] Captain James H. Weatherell (1826–1864) of Company C died from his wounds on June 20; Captain Edwin L. Knight of Company E was wounded in the left side, but lived until 1909; Captain Eben M. Johnson of Company K was slightly wounded in the hand; Captain Homer G. Gilmore of Company D was severely wounded in the leg, but lived until 1908; Captain George W. Bigelow of Company F was wounded on the side of the head, but survived and was still living in 1909; Major Dexter F. Parker (1828–1864) was shot in the right arm and died from complications after amputation on May 30, 1864; Alanson E. Munyan, a first lieutenant in Company H from Northampton, died from his wounds on May 21, 1864.

119.22 Sidney Williams] First Sergeant Sydney S. Williams (1837–1916), another Northampton resident, was taken prisoner on May 12 and was held at Andersonville, Georgia, and Florence, South Carolina, before escaping on September 19. He was recaptured but then made a successful escape in February 1865. Brewster married his sister, Anna B. Williams, in 1868.

119.35 Gen Shermans . . . Gen Butler] Union forces captured Tunnel Hill and Dalton in northern Georgia, May 7–11, 1864. The report that Butler had captured Petersburg, Virginia, was incorrect.

121.23 the Gazzette] The Northampton, Massachusetts, *Daily Hampshire Gazette.*

121.31 Thomas] Brewster's brother-in-law, Thomas Boland.

123.22 Maj. Gen. Rodes] Major General Robert E. Rodes (1829–1864) commanded a division in the Second Corps of the Army of Northern Virginia.

125.3–4 General Abner Perrin] Brigadier General Abner M. Perrin (1827–1864) commanded an Alabama brigade in Anderson's Division, Third Corps.

125.16–17 Colonel Brockman . . . Colonel J. N. Brown] Colonel Benjamin T. Brockman (1831–1864), commander of the 13th South Carolina Infantry, died of his wounds on June 8, 1864; Colonel Joseph N. Brown (1832–1921).

125.24 Harris] Nathaniel H. Harris (1834–1900) commanded a brigade in Anderson's Division, Third Corps.

127.18 Lieutenant Carlisle] First Lieutenant John W. Carlisle (1827–1914) commanded Company C of the 13th South Carolina Infantry.

129.21–22 this tree, . . . twenty-two inches in diameter!] The stump of this tree is in the collection of the National Museum of American History of the Smithsonian Institution in Washington, D.C.

129.36 Longstreet's corps] The First Corps had been led by Richard H. Anderson since May 7.

131.10 Capt. Eagle] Captain Clifford F. Eagle (1845–1938) commanded Company B of the 1st U.S. Colored Infantry.

131.26–28 Major Cook . . . Capt. Choate] Major John B. Cook (c. 1839–?), Sergeant Henry Harris (c. 1843–?), Captain Francis C. Choate (1832–1881).

133.33 Judah] Brigadier General Henry Moses Judah (1821–1866) commanded the Second Division, Twenty-third Corps, Army of the Ohio.

134.6 Hooker] Major General Joseph Hooker (1814–1879) commanded the Twentieth Corps, Army of the Cumberland.

135.34 "Rosinante"] In *Don Quixote* (1605–15), Rocinante, a worn-out workhorse, is the hero's steed.

138.10 Butterfield] Major General Daniel Butterfield (1831–1901) commanded the Third Division of the Twentieth Corps, Army of the Cumberland.

138.12 Stanley] Major General David S. Stanley (1828–1902) commanded the First Division of the Fourth Corps, Army of the Cumberland.

138.16–17 Capt. Simonson, Lt. Morrison] Captain Peter Simonson (1804–

1864), commander of the 5th Indiana Light Artillery, known as Simonson's Battery, was killed at Pine Mountain, Georgia, on June 16; First Lieutenant Alfred Morrison (1836–1901).

138.23 Gen. Howard] Major General Oliver Otis Howard (1830–1909).

142.6–7 Genl Granbury] Brigadier General Hiram B. Granbury (1831–1864).

142.7 Col Wilkes] Colonel Franklin C. Wilkes (c. 1822–1881) commanded the 24th Texas Cavalry Regiment (Dismounted) in Granbury's Brigade.

145.37 Genl Hardee] Lieutenant General William J. Hardee (1815–1873) commanded the First Corps of the Army of Tennessee.

150.34 Lt. Bartlett] First Lieutenant Edwin B. Bartlett (1839–1864) of Company B in the 10th Massachusetts Infantry was shot through the head and killed on May 22.

154.13 Stewart Campbell] Stuart Campbell, Brewster's first cousin, lived in western Virginia and served in the Confederate army.

154.17–18 Major Parker . . . Lieut Graves] See notes 117.26–29 and 112.28–30.

154.20–22 Artemas Ward . . . wrong in the newspapers.] Artemas Ward was the pen name of American humorist Charles Farrar Browne (1834–1867). The quip has also been ascribed to Lord Byron.

158.25 Capt Shaw of the 2nd RI] Captain John P. Shaw (1834–1864).

158.33 Capt Bishop] Captain Willard I. Bishop (1837–1911), commanding Company A of the 10th Massachusetts Infantry, had been injured in the eye by a pine tree limb and was mustered out on July 1, 1864.

158.35 Lt Cottrell] Mark H. Cottrell was first lieutenant in Company D of the 10th Massachusetts Infantry.

159.11–13 Captain Haydens leg . . . Mr. Joel Hayden] Captain Joseph L. Hayden, the commander of Company H of the 37th Massachusetts Infantry, was discharged for disability on September 22, 1864. Joel Hayden (1798–1873) of Williamsburg, Massachusetts, just north of Northampton, was lieutenant governor of Massachusetts, 1863–66, and the proprietor of a large brass works factory in Haydenville. The reference may be to him, or to his son of the same name.

159.14 Joe + Sid Bridgeman] Brothers Joseph C. Bridgman (1831–1910) and Sidney E. Bridgman (1827–1906) were booksellers in Northampton who traveled to Fredericksburg as representatives of the U.S. Christian Commission, an organization that provided supplies, medical services, and religious material to Union soldiers.

159.18 Veteran Volunteers] Veterans who had reenlisted.

162.30 Lieuts. Flannery and Heston] Lieutenants David Flannery and Joseph S. Heston of the 4th New Jersey Infantry were exchanged in March 1865.

163.26 John] Adams's brother John Quincy Adams II (1833–1894), who was serving on the staff of Massachusetts governor John A. Andrew.

165.31 McClellan . . . McDowell] Brigadier General Irvin McDowell (1818–1885) had been defeated at the first battle of Bull Run, July 21, 1861, and replaced as commander of what became the Army of the Potomac by Major General George B. McClellan (see Biographical Notes). Promoted to major general the following year, McDowell was defeated at Second Bull Run, August 28–30, 1862, while commanding the Third Corps of the Army of Virginia. He was relieved of command and held no further field assignments during the war.

166.20 Humphreys] Major General Andrew A. Humphreys (1810–1883), chief of staff of the Army of the Potomac, July 1863–November 1864.

167.40 your negotiation] In the spring of 1864, Charles Francis Adams Sr. had become involved in an abortive effort to explore possible peace terms with the Confederate government through an intermediary, American businessman Thomas Yeatman (1828–1880). The attempt ended when Yeatman failed to make his way to Richmond.

170.20–22 bridge at Moscow . . . regiment of blacks] The 61st U.S. Colored Infantry defended the bridge at Moscow, Tennessee, against a raid by Forrest's cavalry on December 4, 1863.

170.29 Forrest attacked Paducah] Forrest raided the town of Paducah, Kentucky, on March 25–26, 1864, but was unable to capture Fort Anderson, an outpost defended by 665 Union soldiers, including 274 men from the 8th U.S. Colored Heavy Artillery.

172.14 Mrs. Lee] Mary W. Lee (c. 1819–?), nurse with the Army of the Potomac.

172.33 Capt. Harris] Captain Isaac Harris (1838–1907) of Brooklyn, New York, an assistant superintendent with the U.S. Sanitary Commission.

173.29 Georgy Willets] Georgiana Willets (1840–1912), nurse with the Army of the Potomac.

174.21 Dr. Dudley] Dr. Frederick Dudley (1842–1923), a Union army surgeon with whom Hancock may have been romantically involved during the war.

176.6 Dr. Aiken] Dr. John Aiken (1838–1866), surgeon attached to the 71st Pennsylvania Infantry. His death was attributed to a disease contracted while serving with the army in August 1864.

179.20 Spencer carbine] A lever-action repeating rifle that held seven rounds in a tube magazine.

182.18 the Red Division] The First Division, Second Corps, commanded by Brigadier General Francis C. Barlow (1834–1895). Its standard featured a red three-leaf clover on a white field.

183.4–6 Twenty minutes . . . ten-thousand of our men] Union losses at Cold Harbor on June 3, 1864, totaled about 7,000 men killed, wounded, or missing.

184.7–8 The army . . . refused to obey] The claim that Union soldiers refused en masse to advance at Cold Harbor on the afternoon of June 3 was first made by William Swinton (1833–1892), a war correspondent for *The New York Times*, in his book *Campaigns of the Army of the Potomac* (1866). It is not known to be supported by contemporaneous letters, diaries, or narratives.

189.17 Badeau] Colonel Adam Badeau (1831–1895) was military secretary on Grant's staff. He wrote several books after the war, including *Military History of Ulysses S. Grant* (1881) and *Grant in Peace: From Appomattox to Mount McGregor* (1887), and assisted Grant in the preparation of his memoirs until the two men had a falling-out in May 1885.

189.24 Wadsworth, Sedgwick, Rice] Brigadier General James Wadsworth, commanding the Fourth Division, Fifth Corps, was fatally wounded in the Wilderness on May 6 and died in a Confederate field hospital on May 8; Major General John Sedgwick was killed by a sharpshooter at Spotsylvania on May 9; Brigadier General James C. Rice (1828–1864), commanding the Second Brigade, Fourth Division, Fifth Corps, was wounded at Spotsylvania on May 10 and died later that day after his leg was amputated.

189.28 Saturday last] June 4, 1864.

189.29 the Judge] Daly's husband, Charles P. Daly.

189.34–190.1 Women's Patriotic League . . . Luxuries] Daly was president of the Women's Patriotic Association for Diminishing the Use of Imported Luxuries, which was organized in New York on May 16, 1864. The organization was dedicated to stemming the drain of specie overseas by curtailing imports of "silks, satins, velvets, laces, jewelry, ribbons, trimmings, carpets, mirrors, and other imported luxuries."

190.7 Miss Mary Hamilton . . . Miss Schuyler] Mary M. Hamilton (1828–1877), granddaughter of Alexander Hamilton, served on the association's committee on manufactures. Louisa Lee Schuyler (1837–1926), Mary M. Hamilton's niece and later stepdaughter, was a key figure in the Woman's Central Association of Relief, an auxiliary of the U.S. Sanitary Commission.

191.35–192.1 sees the beam . . . mote in his own!"] Cf. Matthew 7:3–5.

194.11 General Pemberton] Captured at Vicksburg when he surrendered the city on July 4, 1863, and exchanged on October 13, Major General John C. Pemberton (1814–1881) had resigned as a general officer on May 9, 1864, and offered to serve as a private. Jefferson Davis instead recommissioned him as a lieutenant colonel on May 12.

194.20 General Quarles] Brigadier General William A. Quarles (1825–1893) commanded a brigade in Walthall's Division, Third Corps, Army of Tennessee.

195.19 General Warren] Major General Gouverneur K. Warren (1830–1882) commanded the Fifth Corps, Army of the Potomac.

195.23 "Haw's Shop"] Confederate and Union cavalry had fought for eight hours near Haw's Shop in Hanover County, Virginia, on May 28, 1864. The battle, in which the Union lost 365 men killed, wounded, or missing, and the Confederates 378, ended in a Confederate retreat.

196.11 her little son] Willoughby Newton (1856–1923).

196.13 Captain Newton] Captain William Brockenbrough Newton (1832–1863) of the 4th Virginia Cavalry was killed at Raccoon Ford, Virginia, on October 11, 1863.

197.20–21 our nephew, J. P., . . . General W. H. F. Lee] Jefferson Phelps (1834–?) of the 9th Virginia Cavalry; Major General William Henry Fitzhugh Lee (1837–1891), Robert E. Lee's son, commanded a cavalry division in the Army of Northern Virginia.

197.25 General Ferrara] See note 81.37–38.

198.12 the Libby] Prison for Union officers established in a Richmond warehouse formerly used by Libby & Sons, a ship-provisioning company.

200.35–36 18th . . . Smiths] On Grant's orders, the Eighteenth Corps, led by Major General William F. Smith (1824–1903), had been detached from the Army of the James and transported by water to reinforce the Army of the Potomac. The corps began disembarking at White House Landing on the Pamunkey on May 30 and had fought at Cold Harbor.

202.13 write the date] Adams wrote to his son on the eighty-ninth anniversary of the battle of Bunker Hill, June 17, 1775.

202.23 "I tremble for my country . . . God is just."] From *Notes on the State of Virginia* (1785), query XVIII.

204.1 "Jesurun has waxed fat"] See Deuteronomy 32:15.

204.1–2 octogenarian leader . . . Maurepas] Henry John Temple, third Viscount Palmerston (1784–1865), prime minister of Great Britain, 1859–65; Jean-Frédéric Phélypeaux, Comte de Maurepas (1701–1781), adviser to Louis XV and Louis XVI.

206.4 the Captain] Captain John A. Winslow (1811–1873).

206.26–27 wounding Capt. Semmes] Semmes (1809–1877) was not wounded during the battle.

208.38 down 200 fathoms] In 1984 the French navy discovered the wreck of the *Alabama* in about 200 feet of water seven miles off the coast.

213.28 Burnside's negroes] The black troops who fought at Petersburg in mid-June 1864 were from the Third Division of Smith's Eighteenth Corps.

214.35 Chaplain Hunter] The Reverend William H. Hunter, a Methodist minister from Baltimore, was born into slavery in Raleigh, North Carolina, in 1831.

219.28 Lieutenant-Colonel Benton] Lieutenant Colonel Reuben C. Benton (1830–1895) had resigned after contracting a malarial fever.

219.29 Colonel Warner] Colonel James M. Warner (1836–1897) had been wounded at Spotsylvania on May 18 and sent home to convalesce. He returned to duty on July 8 as a brigade commander.

219.31–32 Garton Branch and Petersburg Railroad] More commonly known as the Weldon Railroad.

219.35 Captain M.] Captain Edwin J. Morrill (1834–1864) of St. Johnsbury had enlisted in August 1862.

219.36 Lieutenant-Colonel P.] Lieutenant Colonel Samuel E. Pingree (1832–1922) of the 3rd Vermont Infantry. As the corps officer of the day, Pingree commanded the advance detachments from the 4th Vermont and 11th Vermont that formed the brigade skirmish line on June 23. Pingree escaped capture and was mustered out on July 27, 1864. He later served as governor of Vermont, 1884–86.

219.37 Major F] Major Charles K. Fleming (1831–1919) was captured on June 23, 1864, and held in a military prison in Columbia, South Carolina, before being paroled on February 28, 1865.

220.5 two hundred and seventy-five prisoners] A total of 407 officers and enlisted men from the Vermont Brigade were captured on June 23, 1864, including 267 men from the 11th Vermont Infantry and 140 from the 4th Vermont Infantry. Of the 407, two officers were killed trying to escape, while 224 of the enlisted men died either while being held as prisoners of war or shortly after their release.

220.6 Second-Lieutenant Sherman] Merritt H. Sherman (1842–1864) of Company C.

220.8 Captain M. and Lieutenant R.] Morrill was wounded while trying to escape on June 29 and died the following day. Lieutenant Lester S. Richards (1825–1910) was paroled on March 1, 1865.

220.10–11 Totten . . . Lincoln] Forts in the Washington, D.C., fortifications.

220.31 Carrie] Chamberlin's younger sister, Caroline.

222.19 Belle Island] Belle Isle, in the James River at Richmond, Virginia, was used as a prison camp for Union enlisted men, June–September 1862 and May 1863–October 1864.

222.25–27 "As ye do . . . to you again."] Cf. Matthew 7:2 and 7:12 and Luke 6:31.

223.23 57-3] Beginning in April 1864, camp administrators divided Andersonville's prisoners into detachments of 270 men each for the purpose of calling the roll and distributing rations. Each detachment was divided into three ninety-man squads, and each squad into five eighteen-man messes.

224.3–4 Gaines' Mill] Most the 4th New Jersey Infantry was surrounded and captured at the battle of Gaines's Mill on June 27, 1862. The battle of Cold Harbor was fought near the Gaines's Mill battlefield.

224.10 Gen. Winder] Brigadier General John H. Winder (1800–1865) had administered the Libby and Belle Isle prisons as provost marshal of Richmond, 1861–64. He arrived at Andersonville on June 16 and personally supervised the camp until July 26, when he was given responsibility for all prison camps in Georgia and Alabama. In November 1864, Winder was placed in charge of all prison camps east of the Mississippi, a position he held until his death from a heart attack on February 7, 1865.

225.12 Capt. Wurtz] Swiss-born Captain Henry H. Wirz (1823–1865) was commandant of Andersonville from April 1864 until his arrest by Union forces in May 1865. He stood trial on multiple charges relating to his administration of the camp, including murder, and was hanged on November 10, 1865, the only Confederate officer executed for war crimes committed during the Civil War.

226.7 Fort Darling] Union name for the Confederate fortifications on Drewry's Bluff overlooking the James River south of Richmond.

226.10 Kilpatrick] Brigadier General Hugh Kilpatrick (1836–1881) had been wounded at Resaca on May 13, 1864, while leading a cavalry division in the Army of the Cumberland. He returned to his command in late July 1864.

229.17 Col. Ewing . . . wounded] Lieutenant Colonel Charles Ewing (1841–1872), the commander of the 4th New Jersey Infantry, was discharged as a result of his wound.

232.22 Mary Ewing] Mary Gillespie Ewing (1832–1880) was the wife of Philomen Ewing (1820–1896), Sherman's brother-in-law.

232.23 the new baby] Charles Sherman, born on June 11, would die on December 4, 1864.

232.34 the Kilkenny Cats] Cats who according to an Irish tradition fought each other so fiercely that in the end nothing but their tails was left of either of them.

233.37 Lancaster] In Ohio.

235.35 A. H. Stephens] Confederate vice president Alexander H. Stephens (1812–1883) had approached Fort Monroe in Virginia on a Confederate flag of truce boat on July 4, 1863, and requested safe passage to Washington in an attempt to open peace negotiations. Lincoln and his cabinet refused to receive him, and Stephens returned to Richmond.

236.7–8 momentous election . . . North Carolina] See Chronology, August 4, 1864.

240.4 Pisgah] See Deuteronomy 3:27.

244.13–14 Foster . . . James Island] The assault ordered by Major General John G. Foster (1823–1874), commander of the Department of the South, was repulsed on July 3, 1864. James Island was one of many low-lying islands near Charleston, South Carolina.

247.29–30 Gen Gordon's Division] Major General John B. Gordon (1832–1904) commanded a division in the Second Corps of the Army of Northern Virginia.

248.18–19 Mr. Gilmer] Thomas W. Gilmer (1834–1869), a Presbyterian, was chaplain in Lieutenant Colonel William Nelson's artillery battalion.

249.7–8 Capt. Carpenter's Battery] Captain John C. Carpenter (1839–1912) led the artillery battery attached to the 27th Virginia Infantry.

251.12–13 'a little more slumber . . . hands to sleep,'] Cf. Proverbs 6:10.

252.1–2 "the thunder . . . the shouting."] Cf. Job 39:25.

253.37–38 "little foxes." . . . spoiling the grapes] Cf. Song of Solomon 2:15.

256.12 Mr. Dana] See Biographical Notes.

256.14 Hunter] Major General David Hunter (1802–1886), commander of the Department of West Virginia.

256.15 19th Corps] A detachment from the Nineteenth Corps in the Gulf that was originally intended to reinforce the Army of the James was sent to Washington during Early's raid.

256.20 the road] The railroad.

256.22 Wright] Major General Horatio Wright, commander of the Sixth Corps.

256.26 Col. Comstock] See note 78.25.

261.8 JACOB THOMPSON] Jacob Thompson (1810–1885) was the senior Confederate agent in Canada, 1864–65. He had served as a Democratic congressman from North Carolina, 1839–51, and as secretary of the interior, 1857–61.

262.24–27 "No bargaining . . . sued for mercy."] A close paraphrase of a passage from a speech given in Congress on August 2, 1861, by Pennsylvania Republican Thaddeus Stevens (1792–1868).

264.31 Gov. Yates] Richard Yates (1815–1873), Republican governor of Illinois, 1861–65.

264.33–34 Pittsburg Landing] A northern name for the battle of Shiloh.

265.1 General Rosecrans's] Major General William S. Rosecrans (1819–1898) commanded the Army of the Cumberland, October 1862–October 1863.

265.25–26 Sanders-Greeley negotiation] George N. Sanders (1812–1873) of Kentucky, one of the Confederate agents in Canada, had served as U.S. consul-general in London, 1853–54.

265.28 Sidney Howard Gay] Gay (1814–1888) was managing editor of the *New-York Daily Tribune*, 1862–67.

267.26–27 Canby's . . . Gen. Hunter's] In addition to his own Sixth Corps, which had been sent from the Army of the Potomac, the force that Wright led from Washington in pursuit of Early included a detachment from the Nineteenth Corps led by Brigadier General William H. Emory (1811–1887). Emory's detachment had originally been sent from the Military Division of West Mississippi, commanded by Major General Edward R. S. Canby (1811–1873), to reinforce the Army of the James, but had been diverted to the defense of Washington. Major General Lew Wallace commanded the Eighth Corps, and Major General David Hunter (1802–1886) led the Army of West Virginia.

268.15 Ramseur] Brigadier General Stephen D. Ramseur (1837–1864). See Biographical Notes.

273.7 Cheatham] On July 19, Major General Benjamin F. Cheatham (1820–1886) had assumed command of Second Corps when Hood was elevated to replace Johnston. Command of Cheatham's Division was assigned to Brigadier General George E. Maney (1826–1901).

275.31 Genl Walker] Major General William H. T. Walker (1816–1864) led a division in the First Corps of the Army of Tennessee.

280.19 the Mustang] A coastal steamer that had been commandeered by Union forces when they occupied Brownsville.

280.20 Col Day] Colonel Henry M. Day (1827–1900).

282.13 Gen Herron] Major General Francis J. Herron (1837–1902), commander of the Union forces in Texas.

282.23 Col Bruce] Lieutenant Colonel John Bruce (1832–1901) led the 19th Iowa Infantry.

282.25 Col Dye] Colonel William M. Dye (1831–1899) of the 20th Iowa Infantry.

285.20 all obstructions.] After this sentence, the text printed in *The Life of David Glasgow Farragut* includes the following sentence: "The Admiral will endeavor to remove the others before the day of attack, as he thinks they support that which will otherwise sink, and at least to destroy them for guides to the demons who hope to explode them."

285.25 the enemy's] In *The Life of David Glasgow Farragut*, "their." The text printed in *The Life of David Glasgow Farragut* also included a postscript: "P.S.— Carry low steam. D. G. F."

286.35–36 Colonel Marshall . . . Colonel Gould] Colonel Elisha G. Marshall (1829–1883) was wounded and captured during the battle of the Crater; Brigadier General William F. Bartlett (1840–1876), leading the First Brigade, had lost his left leg at Yorktown in April 1862, and would lose his cork prosthesis at the Crater; Colonel Jacob P. Gould (1822–1864), leading the 59th Massachusetts Infantry, was wounded and died on August 22.

287.8 Ledlie] Brigadier General James H. Ledlie (1832–1882), commander of the First Division, Ninth Corps.

287.38 Captain Fay] Captain Wilson W. Fay (d. 1922), of Company D, 56th Massachusetts Infantry.

288.3 Captain Amory] Captain Charles B. Amory (1841–1919) of the 24th Massachusetts Regiment was Bartlett's adjutant. He was captured with Bartlett, whom he had helped off the field after his cork leg was shattered. Amory described his experience of the "great disaster" of the battle of the Crater in *A Brief Record of the Army Life of Charles B. Amory, Written for His Children* (1902).

290.18–20 nine regiments . . . left alive.] Four out of the six regimental commanders in Weld's brigade were killed or mortally wounded in the battle of the Crater.

291.28–29 Cousin Dick's batty] Captain Richard G. Pegram (1829–1896) led an artillery battery in Branch's artillery battalion.

291.33 Mahone] On May 7, 1864, Brigadier General William Mahone (1826–1895) had assumed command of Anderson's Division of the Third Corps.

292.36 Sharpsburg] A southern name for the battle of Antietam.

293.6–7 Beauregard's] Beauregard had defended Petersburg against the initial Union assaults in mid-June 1864 with forces not assigned to the Army of Northern Virginia.

293.39 Col. McIntosh] Lieutenant Colonel David G. McIntosh (1836–1919). He married Virginia Pegram on November 8, 1865.

295.12 Pope . . . Hooker] Major General John Pope (1822–1892), commander of the Army of Virginia, was defeated at Second Bull Run in August 1862; Burnside led the Army of the Potomac to defeat at Fredericksburg in December 1862; Hooker lost the battle of Chancellorsville in May 1863.

296.2–3 Said Napoleon . . . left."] As recorded by his nephew, Charles-Louis Napoleon Bonaparte, the future Napoleon III, in *Des Idées Napoléoniennes. On the Opinions and Policy of Napoleon* (1840).

300.12–13 *Oderint dum metuant*] Latin: Let them hate, so long as they fear. The phrase, attributed to the poet Lucius Accius, was said to be a favorite of the emperor Caligula.

300.15 Minos or Æacus] Legendary kings who in Greek mythology were judges in the underworld.

300.20 Gideon J. Tucker] Tucker (1826–1899) was secretary of state of New York, 1858–59, and surrogate of New York County, 1863–69. He co-founded the *New York Daily News* in 1855.

300.34 Elijah F. Purdy] Purdy (1796–1866) was a banker and member of the Tammany Hall political organization.

303.13 Sallie's letter] Bird's daughter Saida (Sallie) Bird (1848–1922) regularly corresponded with her father.

304.15–16 Iverson . . . Lieut Genl S. D. Lee] Brigadier General Alfred Iverson (1829–1911) commanded the Confederate cavalry force that captured Stoneman near Hillsboro, Georgia, on July 31, 1864. Lieutenant General Stephen D. Lee (1833–1908) commanded the Second Corps, Army of Tennessee.

304.37 Chambersburg] See Chronology, July 30, 1864.

305.39 Cook's battalion] Major Ferdinand W. C. Cook, a firearms manufacturer in Athens, led the battalion of the Georgia State Guard charged with protecting the city. He was killed in action on December 11, 1864.

309.12–13 Gen. Banks . . . Senator Doolittle] Nathaniel P. Banks was commander of the Department of the Gulf, headquartered in New Orleans; James R. Doolittle (1815–1897), Republican senator from Wisconsin, 1857–69.

310.36 Banks's defeat] In the Red River campaign.

310.38 Gen. Banks's proclamation] Addressed to "The People of Louisiana," the proclamation, issued on January 11, 1864, announced that elections for governor and other state offices would be held on February 22.

311.17–18 failure of a military . . . Florida] The Union defeat at Olustee, Florida, on February 20, 1864.

312.13 The Supreme Court has formally declared] In *Luther v. Borden* (1849), a case that grew out of an 1841–42 rebellion against the government of Rhode Island led by Thomas W. Dorr (1805–1854). Stymied in his efforts to reform Rhode Island's government as a legislator, Dorr organized the People's Party, which held a convention and drafted a new constitution that instituted universal male suffrage. When Dorr was elected governor under the new constitution, the established state government declared martial law and jailed Dorr and many of his supporters, including Martin Luther. Luther appealed his arrest by state official Luther M. Borden on the grounds that the original, or charter, government of Rhode Island had been rendered illegal by the new constitution. Called upon to decide which government was legitimate, the

Court ruled it was a political question to be decided by Congress and not the judiciary.

315.5 MICHAEL HAHN] Hahn (1830–1886) was elected governor of Louisiana on February 22, 1864, and served until March 4, 1865, when he resigned.

319.10–12 Mr. G. A. Trenholm . . . imbroglio] Citing irreconcilable differences with the Confederate Congress, Treasury Secretary Christopher G. Memminger (1803–1888) resigned on June 15, 1864. Wealthy cotton broker George A. Trenholm (1807–1876) and two other individuals declined Jefferson Davis's offer of the post, before Trenholm finally accepted it on July 18.

319.12–13 Bragg . . . in the South] Jefferson Davis's military advisor at Richmond since February 1864, Major General Braxton Bragg (1817–1876) had been sent by Davis to Atlanta on July 9 to assess the military situation in Georgia and evaluate the candidates to replace Johnston.

320.12 the Secretary] James Seddon (1815–1880) was the Confederate secretary of war, 1862–65.

320.26 Jack Mosby] See Biographical Notes.

321.2–3 Mosby . . . executed *ten*] There is no record of Mosby engaging in the retaliatory executions described by Kean here. Mosby did order the hanging of seven Union prisoners on November 6, 1864, in retaliation for the killing of seven of his men (see pp. 463–64 in this volume).

321.5 his] The enemy's.

321.12 Gold 252] That is, on the New York gold exchange $252 of paper money (greenbacks) would buy $100 in gold. (In the first four months after the passage of the Legal Tender Act in February 1862, the highest greenback price for $100 in gold was $106.)

323.1 Custer] Brigadier General George Armstrong Custer (1839–1876) commanded a cavalry brigade in Sheridan's Army of the Shenandoah.

325.24 Major Mulford] Major John E. Mulford (1829–1908).

333.16 Linton] Lieutenant Colonel Linton Stephens (1823–1872), commander of the 15th Georgia Infantry, was Stephens's half brother.

334.2 Wheeler] Major General Joseph Wheeler (1836–1906), commander of the cavalry corps in the Army of Tennessee.

334.13 Bragg's worthless pets] General Braxton Bragg (1817–1876) had commanded the Army of Tennessee, November 1862–December 1863.

334.30 Kirby Smith . . . Dick Taylor] Lieutenant General Edmund Kirby Smith (1824–1893) commanded the Trans-Mississippi Department; Lieutenant General Richard Taylor (1826–1879) commanded the Department of Alabama and East Mississippi.

334.34 Gov. Lubbock] Francis Lubbock (1815–1905), governor of Texas, 1861–63.

338.13–14 "Down in Tennessee."] *Down in Tennessee, and Back By Way of Richmond* (1864).

341.27–28 our glorious Massachusetts General] Benjamin F. Butler.

341.33–34 hang them higher than Haman] See Esther 7:9.

342.36 Foster] Brigadier General Robert S. Foster (1834–1903) led the Third Brigade of the First Division, Tenth Corps, Army of the James.

345.32 J. P. Benjamin] Judah P. Benjamin (1811–1884) served as Confederate secretary of state, 1862–65.

346.23–25 Headley's "History," . . . a complete set of the "Rebellion Record,"] J. T. Headley, *The Great Rebellion: A History of the Civil War in the United States* (2 vols., 1863); Benson J. Lossing, *Pictorial Field Book of the American Revolution* (2 vols., 1855); James Parton, *General Butler in New Orleans* (1864); Horace Greeley, *The American Conflict: A History of the Great Rebellion in the United States of America, 1860–'64* (1864); Frank Moore, editor, *The Rebellion Record: A Diary of American Events* (12 vols., 1861–68), of which seven volumes had been published by July 1864.

348.19–20 President of the . . . Franklin Pierce] Davis was secretary of war in the Pierce administration, 1853–57.

352.36–37 Mr. Ashley's Reconstruction Bill] James M. Ashley (1824–1896) was a Republican congressman from Ohio, 1859–69. Ashley introduced a reconstruction bill in December 1863 that authorized the president to appoint provisional military governors in the rebelling states. The governors would organize elections for state constitutional conventions in which suffrage would be extended to black men but denied to those who had fought against the Union or held office in a secessionist government. The bill was tabled in February 1864.

356.31 "Ephraim is joined . . . alone,"] See Hosea 4:17.

356.34 Castle Thunder] Confederate prison in Richmond used to house political prisoners and suspected spies.

360.24 the reserve force] The Confederate reserve force was made up of white males aged 17–18 and 45–50.

363.18 mary] Born in 1852, Mary Rice married a man named Bell in 1882. In 1937, at the age of 85, Mary Bell was interviewed in St. Louis by the Federal Writers' Project of the Works Progress Administration for their collection of narratives by former slaves. Bell concluded her life story by saying: "I love a man who will fight for his rights, and any person who wants to be something."

365.24–25 Military Commandant . . . important election] An election was held in the second appellate district of Kentucky on August 1, 1864, for judge of the state court of appeals. In an attempt to secure the seat for the Unconditional Unionist candidate, Brigadier General Stephen G. Burbridge (1831–1894), the Union commander in Kentucky, ordered county sheriffs on July 29 to remove the name of Alvin Duvall (1813–1891), the incumbent since 1856, from the poll books. Union Democrats in the district then rallied behind George Robertson (1790–1874), a former chief justice of the court of appeals, who was elected on August 1.

365.29–30 necessary trade . . . restrictions] On August 12, 1864, Burbridge required all persons shipping goods or produce in Kentucky to obtain special permits and take loyalty oaths.

366.6 Genl Payne] Brigadier General Eleazer A. Paine (1815–1882) had assumed command of the District of Western Kentucky on July 19, 1864. After levying a $100,000 tax on suspected Confederate sympathizers in his district, Paine expelled twenty-three prominent citizens from Paducah and confiscated their property. Brigadier General Henry Prince (1811–1892), the Union commander at Columbus, Kentucky, wrote to Grant on August 16 about the expulsions, and detailed two instances "well and thoroughly known to me" in which Paine had men publicly killed "in semblance of an execution, without authority of law or any proper justification." On September 4, Grant ordered Halleck to remove Paine from western Kentucky. "He is not fit to have a command where there is a single solitary family within reach favorable to the Government," Grant wrote. "He will do to put in an intensely disloyal district to scourge the people but even then it is doubtful whether it comes within the bounds of civilized warfare to use him." Paine was replaced on September 11, 1864, and received no other command before resigning his commission in 1865.

366.7–8 Genl Payne . . . Cunningham] Lieutenant Colonel Richard D. Cunningham of the 8th U.S. Colored Heavy Artillery had led his troops on a raid from Paducah up the Ohio River to Union County on June 7, 1864, and seized a steamboat carrying 158 slaves. Le Roy Fitch, a Union naval officer serving on the Ohio, wrote to his superior on June 11 that Cunningham's troops had "gone on shore to conscript every negro they could find. These negroes, it is reported, were sent on shore armed and without an officer with them, entered private houses, broke open the doors, and entered ladies' bedrooms before they were up, insulted women, and plundered and searched generally."

368.12 Raymond] See headnote on page 324 of this volume.

371.12 Capt. Lea] Joseph C. Lea (1841–1904), Confederate guerrilla leader in Louisiana who had previously fought with William Quantrill in Missouri and participated in the August 1863 raid on Lawrence, Kansas.

371.14 Col. Parsons] Colonel William H. Parsons (1826–1907) led a Texas cavalry brigade that fought in Louisiana and Arkansas.

371.24 ruthless destruction of Floyd and Pin Hook] In retaliation for raids made by Lea's guerrillas on Union-held plantations, a detachment of 230 men from the 3rd U.S. Colored Cavalry burned the villages of Pin Hook and Floyd on August 30, 1864.

372.4 Corps D'Afrique] In May 1863, Major General Nathaniel P. Banks had announced plans to organize a "Corps d'Afrique" of eighteen black regiments in Louisiana. The name was later used by both northerners and southerners to refer to black troops in general.

373.12 Hardee is said to be killed] An incorrect report.

373.15–20 *Georgia* . . . British colors.] Confederate agents had purchased the British steamer *Japan* in 1863 and commissioned it at sea as the commerce raider *Georgia*. After capturing nine American ships, the *Georgia* was decommissioned as a warship in Liverpool on May 10, 1864, and subsequently sold to a British merchant. The ship was seized off the coast of Portugal on August 15, 1864, by the U.S.S. *Niagara* and taken to Boston, where a federal court condemned it as a lawful prize on account of its previous belligerent status.

373.21 Agnew] Cornelius R. Agnew (1830–1888), an ophthalmologist, was surgeon general of New York state, 1859–62, and served on the executive committee of the Sanitary Commission.

374.3–8 Is all our travail . . . effeminate peace?] *1 Henry VI* , V.v.102–7.

374.11 Belmont tells Charley] New York financier August Belmont (1813–1890) was chairman of the Democratic National Committee; Charles E. Strong (1824–1897) was Strong's cousin and law partner.

374.18 Major Halpine (Miles O'Reilly)] Charles G. Halpine (1829–1868), Irish-born journalist and poet who while serving on Halleck's staff published humorous topical articles under the name of "Miles O'Reilly," a purported private in the 47th New York Infantry.

374.19 Jem Brady] James Topham Brady (1815–1869), a prominent New York trial lawyer.

375.3 "Knights of the Golden Circle"] A secret society founded in the 1850s to promote the creation of a "golden circle" of slaveholding states surrounding the Gulf of Mexico and the Caribbean. During the Civil War, Union authorities alleged that it was a predecessor of various Copperhead secret societies, including the Organization of American Knights and the Sons of Liberty.

375.15–18 Fuller . . . we were prosperous."] Thomas Fuller, *Mixt Contemplations in Better Times* (1660), xvi.

375.20 Blake] Charles F. Blake (1834–1881), a New York patent lawyer.

375.26–27 George H. Pendleton] Pendleton (1825–1889) was a Democratic congressman from Ohio, 1857–65.

375.38–39 *noscitur . . . ab ipso*] Latin: He who is not known in himself is known by the company he keeps.

375.40 *Worthies of England*] By Thomas Fuller (1608–1661), published posthumously in 1662.

376.3–4 Sue for bondage, yielding . . . as they're insolent and base.] See William Cartwright (1611–1643), *The Siege, or Love's Convert*, I.i.

379.30 Horatio Seymour] Seymour (1810–1886) was the Democratic governor of New York, 1853–54 and 1863–64.

380.35 Brig. Gen. Govan] Daniel C. Govan (1829–1911) commanded a brigade in Patrick Cleburne's Division in the First Corps of the Army of Tennessee.

381.21 Capt. A——] John W. Acheson (1837–1872), a cousin of Baird from Washington, Pennsylvania, served as an assistant adjutant general on Baird's staff.

389.16 Captain Drayton] Captain Percival Drayton (1812–1865) commanded Farragut's flagship, the U.S.S. *Hartford*.

389.18–19 gone down in the *Locus Point*] The Union steamship *Locust Point* collided with the steamship *Matanzas* and sank off Absecon, New Jersey, on July 3, 1864, with the loss of seventeen lives.

389.20 Fox's fast *Eutaw* class] Gustavas V. Fox (1821–1883) was first assistant secretary of the navy. Commissioned on July 2, 1863, the U.S.S. *Eutaw* was a steam gunboat capable of making ten knots.

389.21 Corbin] Captain Thomas G. Corbin (1820–?) of the U.S.S. *Augusta* had departed Hampton Roads on July 5, 1864, to escort the monitor *Tecumseh* to the Gulf of Mexico where it was to join Farragut's squadron. The *Augusta* experienced engine trouble and only made it as far as Pensacola.

390.2 Captain Jenkins] Captain Thornton A. Jenkins (1811–1893), commanding the U.S.S. *Richmond*, was fleet captain of Farragut's squadron.

391.14–16 *Tecumseh* . . . sunk] The explosion and sinking killed 94 members of the ship's crew.

393.16 Mississippi monitors] The monitors *Chickasaw* and *Winnebago* had been built in Missouri for service on the Mississippi River.

393.19 Admiral Buchanan] Admiral Franklin Buchanan (1800–1874) commanded the Confederate squadron at Mobile from his flagship, the ironclad *Tennessee*, and suffered a fractured right leg before surrendering. He was exchanged on March 7, 1865.

393.20 Captain Le Roy] William E. LeRoy (1818–1888), commander of the 11-gun steam sloop *Ossipee*.

394.4 Commander Johnston] James D. Johnston (c. 1817–1896) was commander of the *Tennessee.*

394.7–8 "Get thee behind me, Satan."] Matthew 16:23.

394.8–10 Captain Heywood . . . *Merrimack* rammed her] Buchanan had commanded the Confederate ironclad *Virginia* (formerly the U.S.S. *Merrimack*) when it rammed and sank the U.S.S. *Cumberland* at Hampton Roads on March 8, 1862. Captain Charles Heywood (1839–1915) served aboard the *Cumberland* as the commander of its marine detachment.

394.29–32 (Anderson) . . . surrender] Colonel Charles D. Anderson (c. 1827–1901) surrendered over 800 men and 26 guns.

394.34 General Granger] Major General Gordon Granger (1822–1876), the commander of the Reserve Corps of the Department of the Gulf, led the Union land forces in the battle of Mobile Bay.

395.1 General Page] Brigadier General Richard L. Page (1807–1901).

395.2 The result] Fort Morgan surrendered on August 23.

395.7 General Canby] Major General Edward Richard S. Canby (1817–1873), commander of the Military Division of West Mississippi.

396.26 Vaughan] Brigadier General John C. Vaughan (1824–1875) led a brigade in Breckenridge's Division, Second Corps, Army of Northern Virginia.

396.30–31 Capt. Massie] Captain John L. Massie (1838–1864) led a company of Virginia Light Artillery in Nelson's battalion. He was fatally wounded on September 23.

396.32 Capt. Milledge] Captain John Milledge Jr. led a company of Georgia Light Artillery in Nelson's battalion.

397.10 Rodes] See note 123.22. Rodes was struck in the back of the head by a shell fragment.

397.20–21 Capt. Kirkpatrick] Captain Thomas J. Kirkpatrick (1829–1897) led a company of Virginia Light Artillery in Nelson's battalion.

398.20 Gen. Ramseur] Brigadier General Stephen D. Ramseur. See Biographical Notes.

400.7 Gen. Polk] Lieutenant General Leonidas Polk (1806–1864) had been killed by an artillery projectile at Pine Mountain, Georgia, on June 14, 1864, while commanding the Third Corps of the Army of Tennessee. Polk had joined Johnston in northern Georgia in May, bringing three infantry divisions with him from Alabama.

400.22–23 "Let the dead bury the dead."] Matthew 8:22.

400.26 said that I had abandoned Georgia] Joseph E. Brown (1821–1894), governor of Georgia, 1857–65, and a bitter political opponent of Davis, had issued an address to the state militia on July 9 that began: "A late correspondence with the President of the Confederate States satisfies my mind that Georgia is to be left to her own resources."

400.28 Walker . . . Gen. Stephen D. Lee] Major General William H. T. Walker (1816–1864), commander of a division that was transferred to Hardee's First Corps of the Army of Tennessee in December 1863, was killed during the battle east of Atlanta on July 22. Lieutenant General Stephen D. Lee was transferred from Mississippi to lead the Second Corps of the Army of Tennessee on July 26.

401.18 Butler the Beast] Davis had issued a proclamation on December 23, 1862, outlawing Benjamin F. Butler as "a felon, deserving of capital punishment," for his actions as the Union commander of occupied New Orleans.

404.2 the Frémont controversy] The Blair family had initially supported the appointment of Major General John C. Frémont as Union commander in Missouri in July 1861, but then became highly critical of his leadership and sought his removal. After Lincoln relieved Frémont on November 2, 1861, many Radical Republicans in Congress sought his exoneration and restoration to command. When Frank and Montgomery Blair testified against Frémont before the Joint Committee on the Conduct of the War in February 1862, Frémont responded by giving the *New-York Daily Tribune* a letter Montgomery Blair had written to him on August 24, 1861, in which the postmaster general criticized Lincoln for being inclined "to the feeble policy of Whigs." Blair offered his resignation from the cabinet, but Lincoln refused to accept it. Frank Blair then denounced "the paralyzing influence" of Frémont's "imbecility" in a speech to Congress on March 7. Despite the opposition of the Blairs, Lincoln chose to conciliate the Radicals by appointing Frémont to command in western Virginia on March 11, 1862.

404.27–29 its highest honor . . . my ambition for him] Francis Preston Blair hoped that his son Montgomery would be chosen to replace Chief Justice Roger B. Taney, who was known to be in declining health. (Taney died on October 12, 1864.)

405.12 Betty] Elizabeth Blair (1841–1872), Montgomery Blair's daughter.

405.19 Blair] Francis Preston Blair Lee (1857–1944), the only child of Elizabeth Blair Lee and Samuel Phillips Lee.

406.11 Your Mayor] Thomas Jefferson Goodwyn (1800–1877), a physician who had served in the 1860 secession convention, was elected mayor of Columbia in 1863.

407.14–15 Israelites . . . flesh pots] See Exodus 16:3.

407.25 we sent commissioners] Davis had sent three commissioners to

Washington on February 27, 1861, in an attempt to gain recognition of southern independence. They were never officially received by the Lincoln administration, but did exchange messages with Secretary of State Seward through intermediaries. The commissioners left Washington on April 11 after it became clear that the administration would attempt to resupply Fort Sumter.

407.28–29 Vice-President . . . refused a passport] See note 235.35.

407.40–408.1 our stocks . . . foreign market] Confederate cotton bonds were traded in the European financial markets.

409.6 plan of negociation by States] The idea that peace could be negotiated by a convention of the states had been endorsed by Alexander H. Stephens in a public letter written on September 22, 1864.

411.10 Gov. Strong, of Massachusetts] During the War of 1812, Massachusetts governor Caleb Strong, a Federalist who opposed the war, refused to order the Massachusetts militia into federal service, arguing that only the governor of a state, and not the president, had the authority to call out its militia.

417.38–418.1 "Anti-slavery Standard," . . . "Liberator"] *The National Anti-Slavery Standard* (1840–70), official weekly newspaper of the National Anti-Slavery Society, and *The Liberator* (1831–65), abolitionist newspaper founded and edited by William Lloyd Garrison.

419.31–32 interpreted by Judge Taney] Chief Justice Roger B. Taney (1777–1864), in the opinion for the Court in the *Dred Scott* case in 1857.

421.25 a few weeks ago . . . Seward] Seward spoke in Auburn, New York, on September 3.

429.7–10 the late Bishop Hughes . . . Governor Seymour] John Joseph Hughes (1797–1864), Roman Catholic archbishop of New York, 1850–64, was a supporter of the war and opponent of abolitionism. On July 17, 1863, the last day of the New York draft riots, Hughes spoke from the balcony of his residence to a crowd of several thousand people and appealed for the restoration of peace and order. As reported in the *New York Herald*, he began his speech by saying: "Men of New York: They call you rioters but I cannot see a rioter's face among you [applause]. I call you men of New York, not gentlemen, because gentlemen is so threadbare a term that it means nothing positive [applause]." Horatio Seymour (1810–1886), the Democratic governor of New York, 1863–64, who had repeatedly criticized the draft as unconstitutional, addressed as "My friends" a crowd gathered outside of City Hall on the morning of July 14, the second day of the riots.

434.16 Mr. S.] Ramseur's lifelong friend David Schenck (1835–1902), who had married Ramseur's sister Sarah (Sallie) in 1859. He edited and published *Sketches of Maj.-Gen. Stephen Dodson Ramseur*, a collection of tributes in prose and verse, in 1892.

434.17 Charley] Ramseur's brother, Charles R. Ramseur (1847–?).

434.32–33 the issue of your confinement] Ramseur had married his cousin Ellen Richmond (1840–1900) on October 28, 1863, and their only child, Mary Dodson Ramseur (1864–1935), was born on October 11, 1864. Before his death on October 20, Ramseur learned that his wife had given birth, but did not know the name or the sex of the baby.

435.35 Colonel Frank Huger] Lieutenant Colonel Frank Huger (1837–1897) led Huger's Artillery Battalion in the First Corps of the Army of Northern Virginia in the 1864 spring campaign and the siege of Petersburg.

435.40 Nous verrons!] French: We shall see!

436.5 Dr. David] Ramseur's brother, Dr. David P. Ramseur (1839–1905), a surgeon who served with the 14th North Carolina Infantry.

436.7 Caleb . . . Mr. H.] Lieutenant Caleb Richmond, one of Ramseur's cousins, whom Ramseur had placed on his staff as an aide. The Reverend Ephraim H. Harding (1832–1923), chaplain of the 45th North Carolina Infantry, was Ramseur's confidant and frequent courier.

437.25 Gen. W. M. Gardner . . . Gen. Winder's place] Brigadier General William M. Gardner (1824–1901) had replaced Winder (see note 224.10) as superintendent of Richmond prisons.

437.26 exempts] Men who had been exempted from conscription on account of their occupation.

437.30–31 Gov. Brown . . . State militia] Joseph E. Brown (1821–1894), governor of Georgia, 1857–65; Major General Howell Cobb (1815–1868) was the commander of the Georgia state troops.

438.5 Gen. Taylor is the President's kinsman] Jefferson Davis had married Sarah Knox Taylor (1813/14–1835), Richard Taylor's sister, on June 17, 1835. Sarah Davis died of malaria on September 15, 1835, at Brierfield, Davis's plantation on the Mississippi forty miles south of Vicksburg.

438.27 Gen. Barton] Brigadier General Seth M. Barton (1829–1900) commanded a brigade that served in the southern Richmond defenses as part of the division led by Brigadier General George Washington Custis Lee (1832–1913), Robert E. Lee's son.

439.5 *detailed* men] Soldiers who had been detailed to noncombat positions.

439.17 Judge Campbell, and Mr. Kean] John A. Campbell (1811–1889) was the Confederate assistant secretary of war, 1862–65. He had previously served as an associate justice of the U.S. Supreme Court, 1853–61. For Robert Garlick Hill Kean, see Biographical Notes.

440.27 Field's] See note 94.18–19.

440.35 Gov. Smith] William Smith (1797–1887) was governor of Virginia,

1846–49 and 1864–65. He had led a regiment, and then a brigade, in the Army of Northern Virginia, 1862–63, and saw action at the Seven Days, Antietam, Chancellorsville, and Gettysburg before resigning his commission as a major general.

442.27 Goodenough] James G. Goodenough (1830–1875), a gunnery expert and captain in the Royal Navy, had served on the China station with Du Pont and Hall. He was sent to America in 1863 to observe the war.

442.30 Foote] Rear Admiral Andrew H. Foote (1806–1863) had died on his way to take command of the South Atlantic Blockading Squadron. The command went instead to Rear Admiral John A. Dahlgren (see note 3.15–16).

443.16 Rodgers] John Rodgers II (1812–1882) had served as Du Pont's aide at Port Royal Sound in 1861. Promoted to captain, he commanded the ironclad monitor U.S.S. *Weehawken* during Du Pont's unsuccessful attack on the fortifications guarding Charleston Harbor on April 7, 1863.

444.1 La Vendée] Region of west-central France, scene of a revolt against the French revolutionary government, 1793–96, that resulted in 60,000 to 200,000 deaths.

444.4–5 Pélissier in Algeria] Colonel Amable Jean-Jacques Pélissier (1794–1864), a French commander in Algeria, gave orders on June 18, 1845, to set fires that suffocated more than five hundred Kabyle men, women, and children who had taken refuge in a series of caves near Mostaganem. The incident stirred indignation in Europe, but the French government rewarded Pélissier with successive promotions, later conferring on him the title Duke of Malakoff for his military accomplishments in the Crimean War.

444.21–22 a clever antislavery novel] Harriet Beecher Stowe's *Uncle Tom's Cabin* (1852).

444.23–27 Lord Brougham . . . land were assembled.] At the opening session of the International Statistical Congress in London in 1860, with Prince Albert in attendance, Lord Brougham, the presiding officer, publicly drew the attention of George Dallas (1792–1864), the U.S. minister to Great Britain, to the presence of abolitionist Martin Delany (1812–1885). When Dallas refrained from acknowledging him, Delany reportedly responded: "I pray your Royal Highness will allow me to thank his lordship, who is always a most unflinching friend of the negro, for the observation he has made, and I assure your Royal Highness and his lordship that I also am a man."

445.7 poor creature Semmes] See headnote, page 205 of this volume.

446.2–4 The Secretary of War . . . now in arms] John Buchanan Floyd (1806–1863), secretary of war, 1857–60, became a brigadier general in the Confederate army, 1861–62, and later a major general of the Virginia militia, before he succumbed to illness in 1863; Howell Cobb (see note 437.30–31), secretary of the treasury, 1857–60, became president of the provisional

Confederate Congress, 1861–62, before being commissioned a brigadier general in the Confederate army; and Jacob Thompson (see note 261.8).

446.14 Gallic gentleman . . . freaky personage.] Possibly a reference to Henri Mercier (1816–1886), the French minister to the United States from July 1860 to December 1863, who was considered by many northerners to be sympathetic to the Confederacy.

446.36 Sir Michael Seymour] Admiral Sir Michael Seymour (1802–1887) was commander-in-chief of the East Indies and China Station, 1856–59.

447.12 landsmen] Novice seamen.

449.3 cheif engineer] Lieutenant John R. Meigs (1841–1864), the son of Quartermaster General Montgomery C. Meigs, was killed near Dayton, Virginia, on October 3 after he encountered three Confederate cavalry scouts. His death was attributed to guerrilla "bushwhacking," and more than twenty houses were burned in retaliation.

449.34 "too old a bird . . . such chaff."] Variant of a proverb dating at least to the fifteenth century.

450.26–27 letter of Alexander H. Stephens . . . Judge Advocate Holt] Stephens's public letter was written on September 22, 1864, and reprinted in *The New York Times* on October 16. Joseph Holt (1807–1894), the judge advocate general of the Union army, submitted a lengthy report to Stanton on October 8 regarding the subversive activities of the Organization of American Knights, the Sons of Liberty, and other Copperhead secret societies.

452.13 old hero told South Carolina] In his Nullification Proclamation, issued on December 10, 1832.

452.18–19 Pumpernickel sovereignties . . . "Algerine states,"] Allusions to Germany's division into many autonomous petty states. Although nominally under the authority of the Ottoman Sultan, the regencies of Algiers, Tunis, and Tripolitania were in fact each ruled independently by a pasha or dey.

455.5 Ostend proclamation] The result of a meeting in 1854 at Ostend, Belgium, attended by the U.S. ministers to Spain, Great Britain, and France, the Ostend Manifesto argued for the purchase of Cuba from Spain and proposed annexation by force if Spain refused. It was widely understood as an attempt to acquire slaveholding territory beyond the continental United States.

455.16 the opinion which his Attorney-General . . . gave] Attorney General Jeremiah S. Black (1810–1883) submitted his opinion on secession and coercion to Buchanan on November 20, 1860, for the President's use in drafting his annual message to Congress. In his conclusion, Black argued that the "right of the General Government to preserve itself in its whole constitutional vigor by repelling a direct and positive aggression upon its property or its officers, cannot be denied. But this is a totally different thing from an offensive war to punish the people for the political misdeeds of their State Government, or to prevent a threatened violation of the Constitution or to enforce an acknowledgment that the Government of the United States is supreme. The States are colleagues of one another, and if some of them shall conquer the rest and hold them as subjugated provinces, it would totally destroy the whole theory upon which they are now connected."

458.11–12 *VICTORIA! Te Deum . . . Deo!*] Latin: Victory! We praise thee, O God; we acknowledge thee to be God . . . Praise God!

458.18–19 McClellanized are Missouri, . . . New Jersey.] Lincoln won in Missouri.

458.21–22 *Subversi sunt . . . vehementibus*] Exodus 15:10: "They sank as lead in the mighty waters."

458.30 Belmont . . . Barlow] August Belmont (see note 374.11); New York lawyer Samuel L. M. Barlow (1826–1889).

459.2 *Fuit* McClellan, Napoleoniculus] Latin: This was McClellan, the Little Napoleon.

459.20 presence of General Butler] Butler was sent to New York City with 5,000 troops to maintain order on election day. His soldiers remained on their transport ships during the voting.

459.22 George Anthon] Schoolmaster George C. Anthon (1821–1870), a close friend of the Strongs.

459.24–25 William E. Dodge . . . James Brooks] Republican William E. Dodge (1805–1883) and Democrat James Brooks (1810–1873), candidates in the New York Eighth Congressional District. Dodge successfully challenged the election results and was seated in Congress in April 1866.

459.28 sure that Seymour is beaten!] Seymour lost to the Union candidate, Reuben E. Fenton (1819–1885), by 8,293 votes.

460.8 Nicolay] John G. Nicolay (1832–1901), secretary to Abraham Lincoln, 1860–65.

460.10–11 Wentworth . . . and Moulton at Large] Republicans John Wentworth (1815–1888), John F. Farnsworth (1820–1897), Elihu Washburne (see note 81.25), Burton C. Cook (1819–1894), Ebon C. Ingersoll (1831–1879), Abner C. Harding (1807–1874), Shelby M. Cullom (1829–1914), Henry P. H. Bromwell (1823–1903), Andrew J. Kuykendall (1815–1891), and Samuel W. Moulton (1821–1905).

460.12 Thornton . . . and Marshall] Democrats Anthony Thornton (1814–1904), William R. Morrison (1824–1909), Lewis W. Ross (1812–1895), and Samuel S. Marshall (1821–1890).

461.24 Forney] John W. Forney (1817–1881), editor of the *Philadelphia Press* and the *Washington Chronicle*.

461.28 President . . . two last Serenades] Lincoln had spoken to well-wishers at the White House on November 8 and 10.

461.35 Raymond] Henry J. Raymond (see headnote, page 324 of this volume) had narrowly won election to Congress as the Union candidate in the New York Sixth District. Raymond believed that members of rival Republican factions employed in patronage jobs at the New York Custom House had worked to defeat him.

466.9 *Vox Populi, vox Dei*] Latin: The voice of the people is the voice of God.

466.18 Beecher] Henry Ward Beecher (1813–1887), prominent pastor of Plymouth Congregational Church in Brooklyn, New York.

466.29 Theodore Fay] Fay (1807–1898) was secretary of the U.S. legation in Berlin, 1837–53, and the U.S. minister to Switzerland, 1853–61. He was a prolific author whose novels included *Norman Leslie* (1835) and *Hoboken: A Romance* (1843).

467.12 the Judge] Daly's husband, Charles P. Daly.

467.17 Darley and his wife] Artist and book illustrator Felix O. C. Darley (1822–1888) and his wife, Jenny Colburn Darley.

467.18–19 doppelkümmel] A liqueur made with caraway, cumin, or fennel.

467.24 "Chancellor Kent,"] Charles P. Daly was writing a biography (never completed) of jurist and legal scholar James Kent (1763–1847), New York state chancellor, 1814–23.

467.29 Mr. Field] The Reverend Henry M. Field (1822–1907), publisher of *The Evangelist*, a "religious and family paper."

467.34 Baron Gerolt] Friedrich von Gerolt (1797–1879), Prussian minister to the United States, 1844–71.

468.25 Capt. Acheson] See note 381.21.

469.30 a son who is a colonel] Colonel Charles T. Zachry (1828–1906), the son of James B. Zachry, led the 27th Georgia Infantry.

475.5–6 Colonel Poe . . . Captain Buttrick] Colonel Orlando M. Poe (1832–1895) and Captain Edward K. Buttrick of the 31st Wisconsin Infantry.

476.16 Kilpatrick] See note 226.10.

477.11–13 Davis' . . . Slocum's] Brigadier General Jefferson C. Davis (1828–1879) led the Fourteenth Corps. During the march through Georgia and the Carolinas, Major General Henry W. Slocum (1827–1894) commanded the left wing of Sherman's army, which consisted of the Fourteenth and Twentieth Corps.

477.33 “Oglethorpe”] James Oglethorpe (1696–1785), social reformer and investigator of prison abuses who was granted a royal charter in 1732 to establish the colony of Georgia.

479.21–22 (In the words of your Master.)] See page 259 in this volume.

484.30–31 The Chief . . . be relieved.] Charles Francis Adams (1807–1886) would serve as U.S. minister to Great Britain until May 1868.

491.3 Gen Pat Cleburn . . . Gen Granbury] Both Major General Patrick R. Cleburne (1828–1864), Foster’s division commander, and Brigadier General Hiram Granbury (1831–1864), his brigade commander, were killed at Franklin.

491.27–28 Col. Young . . . Hickox] Lieutenant Colonel Robert B. Young (1828–1864) of the 10th Texas Infantry was Granbury’s chief of staff. Major William A. Taylor (1832–1891) was held in an officers’ prison at Johnson’s Island, Ohio, until June 1, 1865. Like Foster, Lieutenant Alfred Hickox was an officer in Company H of the 24th Texas Cavalry.

492.22–23 “Vengeance is mine . . . the Lord”] Cf. Romans 12:19.

493.17 Mexico continues . . . civil war] Between the imperialist forces of Maximilian (1832–1867), who had been installed by the French as emperor of Mexico in June 1864, and the republican supporters of President Benito Juárez (1806–1872).

493.24–26 the difficulties . . . inter-oceanic transit route] General Máximo Jerez (1818–1881) staged a revolt in 1863 against the Nicaraguan government of Tomás Martínez (1820–1873) that was suppressed in 1864.

493.34–494.1 a claims convention] Addressing long-standing U.S. claims arising out of an 1856 riot in Panama, then a province of Colombia.

494.7 Aves Island claim] The claim was made by a group of Boston merchants for losses suffered when their guano mining operation on Aves Island in the Caribbean was confiscated by the Venezuelan navy in 1854. The Venezuelan government agreed in 1859 to pay $130,000 over a six-year period in return for the merchants dropping their claim to the uninhabited island.

494.14–15 threatened war between Peru and Spain] A fatal altercation between Peruvian landowners and Spanish immigrants at Talambo in August 1863 led to the Spanish navy seizing the Chinchas Islands off Peru in April 1864. Under a treaty signed in January 1865, Peru agreed to pay three million pesos in compensation for the return of the islands. Public outrage in Peru caused the agreement to be rejected, and in 1866, Peru and Chile fought a brief naval war with Spain.

494.23–24 seizure of the cargo . . . in 1821] During the Chilean War of Independence, Chilean forces seized $70,400 in silver from an American merchant ship captain in southern Peru, claiming that it was Spanish property. Acting as an international arbiter, King Leopold I of Belgium settled the dispute on May 15, 1863, by awarding the American claimants $42,400, which was paid by the Chilean government in April 1864.

495.20–24 representative in Egypt . . . the successor] William S. Thayer (1830–1864), the American consul general in Egypt since 1861, died in April 1864. Francis Dainese, the acting consul, then became involved in a dispute with the Egyptian authorities over damage to a water aqueduct allegedly caused by an American citizen, and eventually broke off relations with the government in Cairo. Relations were restored when Thayer's replacement, Charles Hale (1831–1888), took up his post in the fall of 1864.

495.27 The rebellion . . . has at last been suppressed] The Taiping Rebellion ended with the fall of the rebel capital Nanking (Nanjing) in July 1864.

496.32–33 political difficulties . . . Brazilian and British ports] The U.S.S. *Wachusett* had captured the Confederate commerce raider *Florida* in the neutral port of Salvador, Brazil, on October 7, 1864, causing a protest by the Brazilian government. British authorities had protested when the U.S.S. *Tioga* anchored in the Bimini roadstead in the Bahamas without official permission on April 12, 1864.

497.1–2 the claims . . . in Oregon] These claims by British companies were first recognized by the United States in the 1846 treaty with Great Britain that resolved the Oregon boundary dispute. The claims were settled when the United States made payments of $325,000 in 1870 and 1871.

497.6–7 recent assaults and depredations] Confederate raiders based in Canada attempted on September 19, 1864, to capture the gunboat U.S.S. *Michigan* and use it to free the Confederate prisoners held on Johnson's Island in Lake Erie. The Confederates were able to seize two ferryboats, but abandoned their plan to board the *Michigan* after realizing that its crew had been alerted. On October 19, 1864, a band of Confederate raiders crossed the Canadian border and robbed three banks in St. Albans, Vermont, killing one citizen and escaping back into Canada with $200,000.

497.26–27 The act passed . . . encouragement of emigration] Passed on July 4, 1864, the act established a commissioner of immigration within the State Department and authorized labor contracts under which emigrants could pledge up to twelve months of their future wages to pay for transportation.

501.18 creating the new rank of vice-admiral] Congress established the rank on December 21, 1864.

504.9–10 Agricultural Department . . . energetic and faithful head] Isaac Newton (1800–1867), commissioner of agriculture, 1862–67. (The first secretary of agriculture with cabinet rank was appointed in 1889.)

504.15 The war continues.] Surviving autograph fragments indicate that the message from this point on was Lincoln's own composition. The preceding parts were probably written by the various members of the cabinet, with the likely exception of the opening paragraph.

514.2 *John C. Ropes*] Ropes (1836–1899) was unable to serve in the army because of a childhood spinal injury. He later formed a law partnership with John Chipman Gray and published several works of military history, including *The Army under Pope* (1881) and *The Story of the Civil War* (2 vols., 1894–98). His brother, First Lieutenant Henry Ropes (1839–1863), fought with the 20th Massachusetts Infantry at Fair Oaks, the Seven Days' Battles, Antietam, Fredericksburg (December 1862 and May 1863), and Gettysburg, where he was killed by the premature explosion of a Union shell.

515.1 General Hatch] Brigadier General John P. Hatch (1822–1901) commanded the Coast Division in the Department of the South.

515.2 General Foster's wound] Foster had been wounded in the leg in the battle of Molino del Ray, on September 8, 1847. The same leg was seriously injured when his horse fell in East Tennessee on December 23, 1863.

515.5–6 Grahamville, . . . considerable loss] Union casualties in the fighting near Grahamville, South Carolina, on November 30, 1864, were reported as 88 men killed, 623 wounded, and 43 missing.

515.12 General Potter] Formerly Foster's chief of staff, Brigadier General Edward E. Potter (1823–1889) had assumed command of the First Brigade of the Coast Division on November 28, 1864.

515.20 Colonel Hartwell] Colonel Alfred S. Hartwell (1836–1912) of the 55th Massachusetts Infantry led the Second Brigade of the Coast Division.

515.25 General Howard's] During the march through Georgia and the Carolinas, Major General Oliver Otis Howard (1830–1909) commanded the right wing of Sherman's army, which consisted of the Fifteenth and Seventeenth Corps.

515.34 General Hazen] Major General William B. Hazen (1830–1887) led the Second Division, Fifteenth Corps.

516.30 *Punch*] Weekly English humor magazine founded in 1841.

517.3 Hardie] Lieutenant General William J. Hardee.

518.3 General Saxton] Brigadier General Rufus Saxton (1824–1908) commanded the District of Beaufort in the Department of the South.

519.19 discern the signs of the times] See Matthew 16:3.

521.1 John Brooks] A black man from Georgia, Brooks escaped and made his way north to Pennsylvania in March 1865.

524.33–34 Colonel Jones." . . . Mary Ruth] Mallard's brother, Lieutenant Colonel Charles C. Jones (1831–1893), a Confederate artillery officer, and Mallard's niece, Mary Ruth Jones (1861–1934).

526.32–33 Brother Charlie . . . mayor] Charles C. Jones was mayor of Savannah, 1860–61.

526.39 Liberty Independent Troop] Mounted militia organized in Liberty County, Georgia, in 1778.

537.28–30 two Union officers . . . two rebel officers] On July 6, 1863, Confederate authorities selected by lot Henry Sawyer and John Flinn, two Union captains held in Libby Prison in Richmond, and announced that they would be executed in retaliation for the deaths of Captain William Francis Corbin and Lieutenant Thomas Jefferson McGraw, who had been shot as spies on May 15, 1863, after being captured within the Union lines in northern Kentucky while secretly recruiting for the Confederate army. President Lincoln responded on July 15 by declaring that if Sawyer and Flinn were executed, the Union would retaliate by hanging Brigadier General William Henry Fitzhugh Lee (1837–1891), Robert E. Lee's son, who had been captured by Union cavalry in Virginia on June 26. The threatened executions were not carried out, and on March 14, 1864, Sawyer, Flinn, and Brigadier General Neal Dow were exchanged for Lee and another Confederate officer who had been held as a hostage, Captain Robert H. Tyler.

537.32–33 trenches before Charleston . . . release of Union officers] In June 1864, Major General Samuel Jones (1819–1887), the Confederate commander in South Carolina, attempted to deter the further shelling of Charleston by having fifty Union officers imprisoned in an area of the city within the range of Union artillery. Major General John G. Foster retaliated by having fifty Confederate officers sent from Fort Delaware and held on Morris Island in Charleston Harbor. During the summer of 1864 another 900 Union prisoners were sent to Charleston as Confederate authorities tried to reduce the number of prisoners who could potentially be freed by Union cavalry raids in Georgia. Foster then responded by having another 600 Confederate officers sent to Morris Island, where they were imprisoned in an open-air stockade near Fort Wagner. When the Union prisoners at Charleston were moved inland in October 1864, Foster sent the Confederate officers on Morris Island to Fort Pulaski in Georgia.

541.12 "Out of the abundance . . . mouth speaketh,"] Cf. Luke 6:45.

543.2–3 short distance of Ft Fisher] The sidewheel steamer *Louisiana* was loaded with 215 tons of gunpowder and detonated about 600 yards from the fort at 1:46 A.M. on December 24, 1864.

543.16 Gen D H Hill] Major General Daniel H. Hill (1821–1889) was placed in command of the Confederate forces at Augusta, Georgia, on January 21, 1865. Hill (no relation to A. P. Hill) had commanded a division in the Seven Days' Battles and Antietam and a corps at Chickamauga.

543.21 Christmas gift to Mr. Lincoln] Sherman had sent a telegram to President Lincoln from Savannah on December 22, 1864, that read: "I beg to present you as a Christmas gift the City of Savannah with 150 heavy guns & plenty of ammunition & also about 25,000 bales of cotton."

543.34 demonstration on Gordonsville] Union cavalry advanced on the rail junction at Gordonsville, Virginia, on December 23, 1864, but then retreated after discovering that the town was defended by two infantry brigades.

544.1 haslets] Hog viscera.

544.37 Motley's "United Netherlands"] John Lothrop Motley (1814–1877), *History of the United Netherlands* (2 vols. 1860). The final two volumes were published in 1867.

545.12 stabbing as Joab] See 2 Samuel 3:27.

545.13 Ld Bacon's Essays] Francis Bacon, *The Essays, or Counsels, Civill and Morall* (1597–1625).

545.26–27 "there is nothing . . . sun."] Ecclesiastes 1:9.

548.39–549.1 *Felix Grundy . . . Foster*] Felix Grundy (1777–1840) served in the Senate, 1829–38 and 1839–40, and as attorney general, 1838–39; John Bell (1796–1869) served in the Senate, 1847–59; Hugh L. White (1773–1840) served in the Senate, 1825–40; Cave Johnson (1793–1866) was postmaster general, 1845–49; Ephraim H. Foster (1794–1854) served in the Senate, 1838–39 and 1843–45.

549.2 *Gen. William Carroll* . . . Aaron V. Brown] William Carroll (1788–1844), governor of Tennessee, 1821–27 and 1829–35; Samuel Houston (1793–1863), governor of Tennessee, 1827–29; and Aaron V. Brown (1795–1859), governor of Tennessee, 1845–47.

563.36–37 the Act of Congress] An act adopted on July 4, 1864, permitting Union agents to recruit black men in the South and credit their numbers against northern draft quotas.

570.22–23 Mr. Chase . . . Mrs. Sprague] Salmon P. Chase had been nominated and confirmed as chief justice of the U.S. Supreme Court on December 6, 1864. Kate Chase Sprague (1840–1899), the wife of Rhode Island senator William Sprague, was the chief justice's daughter.

571.8 Doctor Rock] Boston abolitionist, physician, and lawyer John S. Rock (1825–1866) was the first black man to be admitted to the bar of the Supreme Court. His admission was sponsored by Senator Charles Sumner.

571.10 the old Dred Scott judges] James M. Wayne (1790–1867), associate justice, 1835–67; John Catron (1786–1865), associate justice, 1837–65; Samuel Nelson (1792–1873), associate justice, 1845–73; and Robert C. Grier (1794–1870), associate justice, 1846–70, had all voted in the majority in *Dred Scott* v. *Sandford* (1857).

572.33 Major Eckert] Major Thomas T. Eckert (1825–1910), superintendent of the War Department telegraph office, 1862–66.

573.16 the secret committee] While serving in Congress together in 1847–48, Lincoln and Stephens had been members of a committee that worked to secure the Whig nomination for Zachary Taylor.

573.18–19 'sleeping together' . . . Botts and Tyler] John Minor Botts (1802–1869), a Whig congressman from Virginia, 1839–43 and 1847–49, and vice president–elect John Tyler had shared a bed in an overcrowded hotel in Washington, D.C., while attending the inauguration of President William Henry Harrison in 1841.

574.28–31 Mr. Hunter's . . . *story* of the pigs.)] On June 7, 1865, the Augusta, Georgia, *Chronicle and Sentinel* printed what it described as "the history" of the Hampton Roads conference "as nearly as we can remember it from the statement of Mr. STEPHENS to us, directly after his return." The *Chronicle and Sentinel* reported that when Robert M. T. Hunter "said something about the inhumanity of leaving so many poor old negroes and young children destitute, by encouraging the able-bodied negroes to run away, and asked what are they—the helpless—to do?" Lincoln responded by saying, "that reminded him of an old friend in Illinois, who had a crop of potatoes and did not want to dig them. So he told a neighbor that he would turn in his hogs and let them dig them for themselves. But, said the neighbor, the frost will soon be in the ground, and when the soil is hard frozen, what will they do then? To which the worthy farmer replied, '*let 'em root!*'" In his memoir *Six Months at the White House with Abraham Lincoln* (1866), the painter Francis B. Carpenter recorded how the President had retold the story of the hogs to him shortly after the conference. In Carpenter's version, Lincoln told the story after Hunter warned that "both blacks and whites would starve" throughout the South if slavery were ended.

575.10–11 the President] Jefferson Davis.

585.23–28 "Thus man devotes . . . inflicted on a beast."] See William Cowper (1731–1800), *The Task* (1785), book 2, lines 20–25.

585.31 Anathema-maranatha.] See 1 Corinthians 16:22, where these words, one Greek, often used in excommunications, the other Syriac, meaning "the Lord cometh" (i.e., to take vengeance), are invoked as a curse.

586.37–38 "Proud Nimrod . . . his prey was man."] Alexander Pope, "Windsor Forest" (1713), lines 61–62.

587.17 Mahomet] Muhammad.

589.19–20 "*Therefore all things . . . the prophets.*"] Matthew 7:12.

589.23 "Sages who wrote . . . bled."] William Marsden (1754–1836), "What Is Time?" line 6.

589.31 higher than Haman] See Esther 7:9.

590.8–10 "There is preparing . . . a total emancipation."] See *Notes on the State of Virginia*, Query XVIII: "The spirit of the master is abating, that of the slave rising from the dust, his condition mollifying, the way I hope preparing, under the auspices of heaven, for a total emancipation, and that this is disposed, in the order of events, to be with the consent of the masters, rather than by their extirpation."

590.13–16 "It is among . . . not be wanting."] Cf. Washington's August 4, 1797, letter to Lawrence Lewis: "I wish from my Soul that the Legislature of this State could see the policy of a gradual abolition of Slavery; It might prevt much future mischief."

590.22–23 Giddings . . . Lovejoy] Joshua R. Giddings (1795–1864), congressman from Ohio, 1838–42 and 1842–59, was an outspoken opponent of slavery; Owen Lovejoy (1811–1864), abolitionist who served as a Republican congressman from Illinois, 1857–64. His brother, Elijah Lovejoy (1802–37), a newspaper editor, was killed by a proslavery mob in Alton, Illinois.

590.28 POPE LEO X testifies] Leo X issued a papal bull criticizing the enslavement of American Indians in 1514.

590.30 PATRICK HENRY said] Cf. Henry's January 13, 1773, letter to John Alsop: "I believe a time will come when an opportunity will be afforded to abolish this lamentable evil. Everything we can do, is to improve it, if it happens in our day; if not, let us transmit to our descendants, together with our slaves, a pity for their unhappy lot, and an abhorrence of Slavery."

590.33 LAFAYETTE proclaimed] In the second number of *The Liberator*, January 8, 1831, William Lloyd Garrison quoted Lafayette as having said: "While I am indulging in my views of American prospects, and American liberty, it is mortifying to be told that in that very country, a large portion of the people are slaves! It is a dark spot on the face of the nation. Such a state of things cannot always exist."

590.36 JONATHAN EDWARDS declared] Jonathan Edwards the Younger (1745–1801), son of the famous theologian, was himself a theologian and minister. In *The Injustice and Impolicy of the Slave Trade*, a sermon preached in New Haven on September 15, 1791, before the annual meeting of the Connecticut Society for the Promotion of Freedom, Edwards said that "to hold a man in a state of slavery, who has a right to his liberty, is to be every day guilty of robbing him of his liberty, or of manstealing."

591.21–23 "Whoso stealeth . . . be put to death."] See Exodus 21:16.

591.37 Balak] King of Moab; see Numbers 22–24.

592.1–2 Chatham, . . . Curran,] William Pitt, Earl of Chatham (1708–1778), British statesman; Edmund Burke (1729–1797), British orator and essayist; Granville Sharp (1735–1813), William Wilberforce (1759–1833), and Thomas Clarkson (1760–1846), leaders of the British antislavery movement; John Philpot Curran (1750–1817), Irish lawyer and statesman.

592.16 Morrises, and Bokers] George Pope Morris (1802–1864), newspaper publisher and popular poet; George Henry Boker (1823–1890), author of *Poems of the War* (1864) and a founder of the Union League Club.

593.11–18 "Down let the shrine . . . from heaven."] John Greenleaf Whittier, "Expostulation" (1834), lines 105–112.

594.3–4 "Bound on . . . little known,"] William Cowper, "Human Frailty," lines 17–18.

595.32–33 "*that they go forward.*"] See Exodus 14:15.

596.4–33 "Hear ye not . . . close to thee!"] "Exodus," by Adeline Dutton Train Whitney (1824–1906), first published anonymously in the April 1862 number of the *Atlantic Monthly*.

598.3 *Emma LeConte: Diary*] LeConte wrote her diary in pencil on "pieces of brownish Confederate letter paper," and later copied it into a notebook at the time of her marriage in 1869. The text printed here is taken from the 1869 notebook. Some of the sheets of the original diary have survived, and a collation of the two texts shows that LeConte made significant revisions in wording while copying the original. An example of these changes is presented in the note below.

598.37–599.6 How long is . . . reigning up town.] In the original diary, this appears as: "How long is this distress of mind to continue? It is now about 11 o'clock and it is the longest morning I ever passed. I threw myself on the bed without undressing, late last night—or rather early this morning feeling that if I did not take some rest I would be sick. It was some time before I could sleep as every now and then a cannon report would break the stillness. So in spite of my heavy eyelids I lay awake thinking of the dreadful possibility of the town being shelled in the night and also of the tumult I knew was reigning up town."

599.14 Jane . . . Henry] Slaves who worked as servants in the LeConte household.

600.1 Sallie] Sarah Elizabeth LeConte (1850–1915), Emma LeConte's younger sister.

600.11 Carrie] Caroline Eaton LeConte (1863–1946), Emma LeConte's youngest sister.

600.15 the mayor] See note 406.11.

600.23 Aunt Josie's, Miss Mary] Eleanor Josephine Graham LeConte (1824–1894), the wife of John LeConte (1818–1891), and her sister, Mary A. Graham (d. 1890).

601.1–2 Col Stone] Colonel George A. Stone (1833–1901) commanded the Third Brigade, First Division, Fifteenth Corps.

601.11 Wheeler's command] Major General Joseph Wheeler (1836–1906) led a Confederate cavalry corps during Sherman's march through the Carolinas.

601.38 Howards and Logans] Major General Oliver Otis Howard (1830–1909) commanded the right wing of Sherman's army, which consisted of the Fifteenth and Seventeenth Corps. Major General John A. Logan (1826–1886) commanded the Fifteenth Corps.

602.1–2 Slocum's . . . Davis'] See note 477.11–13.

602.14–15 Gen Hampton] Lieutenant General Wade Hampton (1818–1902), a wealthy South Carolina plantation owner, had recently been appointed commander of Confederate cavalry in South Carolina. Hampton had previously led the cavalry corps of the Army of Northern Virginia, May 1864–January 1865.

604.11 Mary Ann] A slave who worked as a servant in the LeConte household. She and Henry were married.

604.25 Dr Thomson] Andrew W. Thomson (1827–1881) was the surgeon in charge of the Second North Carolina Hospital, which was housed on the South Carolina College campus.

606.35 Poor father! . . . he hears] Joseph LeConte (1823–1901) and his brother John left Columbia on February 16 with several wagons carrying household belongings and Niter Bureau property. They encountered soldiers from the left wing of Sherman's army, who took their food and destroyed the wagons. Joseph LeConte returned to Columbia and was reunited with his family on February 24, 1865.

609.30 our Division] Johnson's Division, led by Major General Bushrod R. Johnson (1817–1880), part of the Fourth Corps of the Army of Northern Virginia, commanded by Lieutenant General Richard H. Anderson (1821–1879).

610.22 Wise] Mills served in a brigade commanded by Brigadier General Henry A. Wise (1806–1876), the former governor of Virginia, 1856–60.

610.28 Cooke] First Lieutenant Charles M. Cooke (1844–1920), the adjutant of the 55th North Carolina Infantry, had attended Wake Forest College with Mills.

610.29 Dr. & John Cannady] Isaac G. Cannady, assistant surgeon of the 55th North Carolina Infantry, and Sergeant John P. Cannady, who served in Company K. Both men surrendered at Appomattox.

610.30 Cooke's Brig] The 55th was one of five North Carolina regiments in an infantry brigade commanded by Brigadier General John R. Cooke (1833–1891). It was assigned to the division led by Major General Henry Heth (1825–1899), part of the Third Corps of the Army of Northern Virginia.

613.22–23 let us . . . judged.] Cf. Matthew 7:1; Luke 6:37.

613.25–27 "Woe unto . . . the offence cometh!"] Matthew 18:7.

614.1–2 "the judgments . . . altogether!"] See Psalms 19:9.

616.12–13 "they all with . . . make excuse."] See Luke 14:18.

616.13 Mrs. Dorsey] Louise Tobias Dorsey, the free-born wife of Thomas J. Dorsey, a former slave who had established a successful catering business in Philadelphia.

620.6 Mr Streeter] Holland Streeter, a former butcher from Lowell, Massachusetts, who had originally been hired by Horace James to oversee shad fisheries on the island, became the assistant superintendent of the colony in October 1864. He was accused in June 1865 of profiting from the illegal sale of rations intended for distribution to the colonists. On July 24, 1865, a military commission convicted Streeter of embezzlement and fraud and sentenced him to three months' hard labor and a $500 fine (the prison sentence was later remitted).

620.14 General Butler] Major General Benjamin F. Butler (1818–1893) commanded the Department of Virginia and North Carolina, November 1863–January 1865.

623.33 John Bright] A prominent orator and reformer who served in the House of Commons, 1843–89, John Bright (1811–1889) was a leading British advocate of the Union cause.

624.1 F. M. Edge] Frederick Milnes Edge (1830–?), a British journalist, pamphleteer, and supporter of the Union cause. In 1862, Edge had accompanied the Army of the Potomac in the Peninsula campaign as a correspondent for the London *Morning Star*.

627.2 "bummers,"] Soldiers detailed to foraging parties.

628.10 Rene . . . Minnie's] Williams's daughters, Irene Williams (1843–1907) and Mary Williams (1846–1935).

629.17 yr good & most suggestive letter] In a letter written on February 17, 1865, Bright advised that reconstruction should be based on the abolition of slavery, a generous amnesty policy, limited confiscation of southern land, the exclusion of Confederate leaders from federal or state office, and the nullification of Confederate debts.

630.19–20 govt. in Louisiana . . . defeated in Congress] On February 24, 1865, the Senate began debating a resolution recognizing the legitimacy of the reconstruction government in Louisiana. Sumner engaged in a successful filibuster against the measure, and on February 27 the Senate voted, 34–12, to postpone further consideration of the resolution.

630.20–22 Chief Justice Chase . . . "illegal & void"] In a letter to Bright written on March 18, 1865, Sumner explained that he had initially misunderstood Chase's ruling in *United States v. Alexander*, a case arising from the seizure of cotton by the Union navy during the 1864 Red River campaign.

The chief justice had subsequently explained to him that the Court had not ruled on "the validity of the La. govt., but only on the validity of proceedings in certain parts of the state."

630.28 "the territorial theory."] Sumner had argued in 1862 that the seceding states should be treated as federal territories over which Congress had complete jurisdiction.

630.39 Resolutions on Reciprocity & Lake Armaments,] The Senate had voted on January 12, 1865, to terminate the Reciprocity Treaty of 1854, liberalizing trade between the United States and Canada, and on January 18 to terminate the Rush-Bagot Treaty of 1817, limiting naval armaments on the Great Lakes and Lake Champlain.

631.3–4 the date . . . held it back] Concerned about the activities of Confederate agents in Canada, the House of Representatives voted on June 20, 1864, to end the Great Lakes naval agreement. As chairman of the Foreign Relations Committee, Sumner had delayed Senate consideration of the measure.

631.5 outrages on the Lakes] See note 497.6–7.

631.16 Cobden] Richard Cobden (1804–1865), a British reformer who served in Parliament, 1841–57 and 1859–65, was a supporter of the Union and a friend and political ally of John Bright.

635.15 U.S.C.H. Arty.] United States Colored Heavy Artillery.

636.1–2 Rebel General Bragg . . . the State] After the inconclusive battle of Perryville, October 8, 1862, General Braxton Bragg abandoned his invasion of Kentucky and retreated into Tennessee.

637.32 the South Side Road] The Southside Railroad, which connected Petersburg with Lynchburg in western Virginia.

638.9–10 Mrs. Davis . . . leaving the city] Varina Howell Davis left Richmond on March 30, 1865.

638.12 Dr. Hoge . . . Gen. Cooper] Moses Hoge (1818–1889), pastor of the Second Presbyterian Church of Richmond; General Samuel Cooper (1798–1876), adjutant general of the Confederate army.

638.14 Dr. Minnegerode] Charles Minnegerode (1814–1894), rector of St. Paul's Episcopal Church in Richmond.

638.15 Gen. Ewell] Lieutenant General Richard S. Ewell (1817–1872) had commanded the Department of Richmond since June 13, 1864.

638.21 Danville Road] The Richmond & Danville Railroad.

638.23–24 the Secretary] Confederate Secretary of War John C. Breckinridge (1821–1875).

638.25 Lieut.-Gen. Hardee] Lieutenant General William J. Hardee

(1815–1873) commanded a corps in the Army of Tennessee. At the beginning of April 1865 his corps was camped near Smithfield, North Carolina.

638.28 Gen. Kemper] Major General James L. Kemper (1823–1895) commanded the Reserve Forces of Virginia, made up of men aged 17–18 and 45–50, as well as men aged 18–46 who had been exempted from army service to work in munitions manufacture.

638.33 Hon. James Lyons] James Lyons (1801–1882), a Richmond attorney who served in the Confederate Congress, 1862–64.

639.8 Judge Campbell] John A. Campbell (1811–1889), associate justice of the U.S. Supreme Court, 1853–61, and Confederate assistant secretary of war, 1862–65.

639.38–39 A. P. Hill . . . Lee] Hill was killed on the morning of April 2, 1865, but Lee was not wounded.

643.37–38 Colonel —— . . . his bride] Lieutenant Colonel Walter H. Taylor (1838–1916), an assistant adjutant general on Robert E. Lee's staff, married Ellen Selden Saunders (1840–1916).

644.8 Mayor Mayo] Joseph C. Mayo (1795–1872), mayor of Richmond, 1853–65 and 1866–68.

644.22 receiving-ship] A vessel where new recruits were sent to await their service assignments.

645.23–24 General Godfrey Weitzel . . . General Ord] Major General Godfrey Weitzel (1835–1884) commanded the Twenty-fifth Corps in the Army of the James; Major General Edward O. C. Ord (1818–1883) had replaced Benjamin F. Butler as commander of the Army of the James on January 8, 1865.

645.25 one-half of his division] Ord had sent the Twenty-fourth Corps, i.e, one half of the Army of the James, to the Petersburg front.

645.32–33 Major A. H. Stevens . . . Major E. E. Graves] Atherton H. Stevens Jr. (1824–1872); Emmons E. Graves (1843–1891).

646.7 Long lines of negro cavalry] From the 5th Massachusetts Cavalry, commanded by Colonel Charles Francis Adams Jr.

648.2–3 an authentic account] Edward A. Pollard, *The Last Year of the War* (1866).

649.8–9 General Shepley . . . Lieutenant-Colonel Fred L. Manning] Brigadier General George F. Shepley (1819–1878), chief of staff of the Twenty-fifth Corps, Army of the James; Frederick L. Manning (1837–?), provost marshal of the Army of the James.

649.13–14 morbidly sensitive clause . . . "flag,"] In his order of April 3, 1865, Shepley stated: "No treasonable or offensive expressions insulting the flag, the cause or the armies of the Union will hereafter be allowed."

649.34–35 man knoweth not . . . bring forth.] Cf. Proverbs 27:1.

650.28 City Point] City Point, Virginia, a port on the James River where Grant had made his headquarters during the siege of Petersburg.

651.11 Vinton] Francis Vinton (1809–1872), assistant minister of Trinity Church.

651.16 Prosper M. Wetmore . . . Simeon Draper] Wetmore (1798–1876) was a merchant active in Democratic politics; Draper (1804–1866) was collector of customs at New York, 1864–65, and had served as chairman of the state Republican Party, 1860–62.

651.19–20 Hon. Moses Odell and Evarts] Odell (1818–1866) was a Democratic congressman from New York, 1861–65; William Evarts (1818–1901), a New York attorney who later served as U.S. attorney general, 1868–69, as secretary of state, 1877–81, and as a Republican senator from New York, 1885–91.

652.12–14 Captain Marshall . . . Judge Vanderpoel] Charles Henry Marshall (1792–1865), a merchant and retired sea captain; Aaron Vanderpoel (1799–1870), a judge of the New York Superior Court, 1842–50, had served in Congress as a Jacksonian Democrat, 1833–37 and 1839–41.

652.22 Hamilton Fish] Fish (1808–1893) had been a Whig congressman, 1843–45, governor of New York, 1849–50, and a U.S. senator, 1851–57. He later served as secretary of state, 1869–77.

652.25 Sydney Smith] English essayist (1771–1845).

653.24 Major Pegram] William Pegram's surviving brother, Major James West Pegram (1839–1881), who served on Ewell's staff.

654.32–33 "My God, . . . forsaken me,"] Matthew 27:46.

655.9 another Col. mortally wounded] Colonel Joshua H. Hudson (1832–1909), commander of the 26th South Carolina Infantry, survived the wound he received at Five Forks.

656.26 Fort Burnham] After capturing Fort Harrison on September 29, 1864, the Union army renamed the strongpoint after Brigadier General Hiram Burnham (1814–1864), who had been killed during the assault. The fort was about seven miles southeast of Richmond.

657.15–19 Brevet Brigadier General Draper . . . Captain Bicnnef] Colonel Alonzo Draper (1835–1865) commanded the First Brigade, First Division, Twenty-fifth Corps; Brigadier General August Kautz (1828–1895) commanded the First Division, Twenty-fifth Corps; Benjamin F. Pratt (1824–1890) led the 36th U.S. Colored Infantry in the First Brigade; Captain Francis A. Bicknell (1844–?) commanded Company A of the 36th U.S. Colored Infantry.

658.16 Devin's] Brigadier General Charles Devens (1820–1891) commanded the Third Division, Twenty-fourth Corps, Army of the James. The

Third Division had remained north of the James River when the remainder of the Twenty-fourth Corps was sent to the Petersburg front in late March 1865.

659.23–24 Texas Brigade, under Gary] In the battle of New Market Heights (or Chaffin's Farm), September 29, 1864, Draper's brigade of U.S. Colored Troops captured a position held by Gregg's Brigade, composed of the 1st, 4th, and 5th Texas and 3rd Arkansas infantry regiments. The Texas Brigade, which had been one of the most renowned formations in the Army of Northern Virginia since the Seven Days' Battles, was led during the battle by Colonel Frederick S. Bass (1831–1897) of the 1st Texas Infantry. Brigadier General John Gregg (1828–1864), the brigade's commander, was in overall command of the Confederate forces defending New Market Heights, which also included a brigade of dismounted cavalry led by Brigadier General Martin W. Gary (1831–1881). At the time of New Market Heights, Draper's brigade was designated the Second Brigade, Third Division, Eighteenth Corps. It lost 477 men killed, wounded, or missing in the battle.

659.32 Wild's] Brigadier General Edward A. Wild (1825–1891) led the Second Brigade, First Division, Twenty-fifth Corps.

659.34 Thomas' brigade] Brigadier General Henry G. Thomas (1837–1897) led the Third Brigade, First Division, Twenty-fifth Corps.

661.5 Gen. Ripley] Colonel Edward H. Ripley (1839–1915) led the First Brigade, Third Division, Twenty-fourth Corps.

661.11 F.F.V.' s] First Families of Virginia.

663.6 Admiral Porter's] Rear Admiral David D. Porter (1813–1891) commanded the North Atlantic Blockading Squadron, 1864–65.

663.37 his youngest son] Thomas (Tad) Lincoln (1853–1871).

663.38 General Devin] Devens (see note 658.16).

665.1 Colonel Morning] Manning (see note 649.8–9).

665.24 yesterday (Tuesday)] April 4, 1865.

666.7–8 "cohesive power of public plunder"] The origin of this phrase is attributed to a speech in the Senate by John C. Calhoun on May 27, 1836: "A power has risen up in the government greater than the people themselves, consisting of many and various and powerful interests, combined into one mass, and held together by the cohesive power of the vast surplus in the banks."

666.33 Spear's cavalry] Colonel Samuel P. Spear (1815–1875) commanded the Second Brigade, Cavalry Division, Army of the James.

667.2 Capt. Mattison] Lucius V. S. Mattison (1842–1910).

667.15 Lieut. Gen. Grant . . . tomorrow] Grant was in the field with the Army of the Potomac on April 7, 1865, as it pursued Lee's retreating army.

669.30 James Hamilton] James Hamilton Jr. (1786–1857), governor of South Carolina, 1830–32, and a leading proponent of nullification.

670.2–3 Marmion, Ivanhoe] *Marmion: A Tale of Flodden Field* (1808), *Ivanhoe: A Romance* (1819).

678.27 Willie's death] William Wallace (Willie) Lincoln (1850–1862), the Lincolns' third son, had died in the White House on February 20, 1862, probably from typhoid fever.

678.38 Mrs. Lee, *née* Miss Blair] Elizabeth Blair Lee (1818–1906); see Biographical Notes.

679.2 Mr. and Mrs. Walker Lewis] Walker Lewis worked for the government as a messenger and steward; Virginia Lewis was a seamstress.

681.18 Mrs. Secretary Welles] Mary Jane Hale Welles (1817–1886).

682.32 Robert] Robert Todd Lincoln (1843–1926), the Lincolns' oldest son.

684.29 Ellie] Ellen Ruggles Strong (1825–1888), Strong's wife.

684.30 *Eheu*] Latin: Alas.

685.19 Faulkner . . . Kenzua] Hiram D. Faulkner, who served with Strong on the board of directors of the Kenzua Petroleum Company.

685.24 Bellows] Henry Bellows (1814–1882), a Unitarian pastor from New York City, helped found the U.S. Sanitary Commission in 1861 and served as its president throughout the war.

685.27 his Fred] Frederick W. Seward (1830–1915), assistant secretary of state, 1861–69, recovered from his wounds.

686.19–20 Professor Henry James Anderson . . . Moses H. Grinnell] Anderson (1799–1875) was professor of mathematics and astronomy at Columbia, 1825–43, and a trustee of the college, 1851–75; Grinnell (1803–1877), a merchant and banker, had served in Congress as a Whig, 1839–41.

686.26 Verplanck and Tillou] Gulian Verplanck (1786–1870), a lawyer who had served in Congress, 1825–33, and in the state senate, 1838–41; Francis R. Tillou (c. 1795–1865), an attorney who served as recorder of New York City, 1852–54.

686.31 Gouverneur Ogden] Ogden (1809–1884) was an attorney and trustee of Columbia College.

686.40 823 . . . Gibbs] 823 Broadway, the headquarters of the U.S. Sanitary Commission; Oliver Wolcott Gibbs (1822–1908), professor of chemistry at the Free Academy (later City College of New York), 1849–63, and at Harvard, 1863–87, and a member of the executive committee of the Sanitary Commission.

687.2–3 George Bancroft . . . Rev. (Presbyterian) Thompson] Bancroft

(1800–1891), author of *History of the United States* (1854–78); Joseph Parrish Thompson (1819–1879), pastor of the Broadway Tabernacle, 1845–71.

687.10 Let the dead bury their dead.] Cf. Matthew 8:22.

687.11 Burnside] Ambrose Burnside, who had been sent on indefinite leave in August 1864 following the Union defeat in the battle of the Crater.

687.13 Jeff Davis . . . Danville] See headnote, page 705 in this volume.

688.24 John, my son] John Arthur Welles (1849–1883).

689.26 elder Mrs. Seward or her sister] Frances Miller Seward (1805–1865), who died on June 21, 1865, after years of poor health; Lazette Miller Worden (1803–1875).

689.28 Mrs. Frederick Seward] Anna Wharton Seward (1836–1919).

689.31–32 Miss Fanny Seward] Frances Adeline Seward (1844–1866), the daughter of William H. Seward and Frances Miller Seward.

689.33 Dr. Verdi] Tullio Verdi (1829–1902).

690.14 General Meigs] Brigadier General Montgomery C. Meigs (1816–1892), quartermaster general of the U.S. Army, 1861–82.

690.26 Judge Cartter] David Cartter (1812–1887), chief justice of the Supreme Court of the District of Columbia, 1863–87.

690.27 Major Eckert] See note 572.33.

691.1 Mr. Peterson] William Petersen (1816–1871), a tailor, lived in the house with his family and several boarders.

691.5–6 Dr. Hall] James Crowdhill Hall (1805–1880).

691.19 Senator Sumner] See Biographical Notes.

691.20–21 Speaker Colfax, Mr. Secretary McCulloch] Schuyler Colfax (1823–1885), Republican congressman from Indiana, 1855–69, Speaker of the House, 1863–69, and vice president of the United States, 1869–73; Hugh McCulloch (1808–1895), secretary of the treasury, 1865–69 and 1884–85.

691.29–30 Mrs. Dixon . . . Mrs. Kinney] Elizabeth Cogswell Dixon (1819–1871) and her sister Mary Cogswell Kinney (1814–1877). Elizabeth Dixon was a friend of Mary Lincoln and the wife of James Dixon, a Republican senator from Connecticut.

692.13 the Attorney General] James Speed (1812–1887) served as attorney general, 1864–66.

692.15 Usher] John Palmer Usher (1816–1889), secretary of the interior, 1863–65.

692.29 Dr. Gurley] Phineas Gurley (1816–1868), pastor of the New York Avenue Presbyterian Church in Washington, D.C.

692.38 Mr. Dennison] William Dennison Jr. (1815–1882), postmaster general, 1864–66.

693.22 Mr. Hunter] William Hunter (1805–1886), chief clerk of the Department of State, 1852–66, and second assistant secretary of state, 1866–86.

694.12 Virginia which has a loyal government] The unionist "Restored Government" of Virginia was established in Wheeling in June 1861. When West Virginia was admitted as a state on June 20, 1863, Governor Francis H. Pierpont (1814–1899) had relocated his government to Alexandria, where it exercised authority over areas occupied by Union forces.

694.17 Gooch and Dawes] Daniel Wheelwright Gooch (1820–1891), Republican congressman from Massachusetts, 1858–65 and 1873–75; Henry L. Dawes (1816–1903), Republican congressman from Massachusetts, 1857–75, and U.S. senator, 1875–93.

694.30 his son] Major Augustus Seward (1826–1876) had been wounded during the assassination attempt.

697.1–2 Mr. Breckinridge] Major General John C. Breckinridge (1821–1875) served as Confederate secretary of war, February 6–May 10, 1865. Sherman would only meet with him in his capacity as a Confederate officer because of the Union policy prohibiting any recognition of the Confederate government.

697.25 Gen. Schofield] Brigadier General John M. Schofield (1831–1906), commanding general, Army of the Ohio, 1864–65, and of the Department of North Carolina, 1865.

700.23–24 "All things . . . the dreadful past."] See Alfred Tennyson, "Choric Song of the Lotos-Eaters" (1832), lines 46–47.

700.26–27 Sister . . . Lavinia] Morgan's sister-in-law, Beatrice Ford Morgan (1826–1905), and her three oldest children, Charlotte (1853–1884), Nellie (1855–?), and Lavinia (1857–?).

700.28–29 five remaining children] The five youngest children of Beatrice Ford Morgan and Philip Hickey Morgan (1825–1900), Morgan's half brother.

701.31–32 "God is our refuge . . . trouble,"] See Psalm 46:1.

701.36–37 "Vengence . . . the Lord."] Cf. Romans 12:19.

702.26 Spare Jimmy] Morgan's brother, James Morris Morgan (1845–1928), served as midshipman in the Confederate navy, 1861–65, and later published a memoir, *Recollections of a Rebel Reefer* (1917).

702.27–28 Deborah . . . Sisera] See Judges 4:2–3.

702.29–30 Miriam . . . fallen, fallen!"] See Exodus 15:20–21.

702.31 Judith] See the Book of Judith.

702.32 "Pour le salut de ma patree—!"] French: To save my country.

705.27 Gov. Vance] Zebulon B. Vance (1830–1894), governor of North Carolina, 1862–65 and 1877–79, and a Democratic U.S. senator, 1879–94.

705.31 Mr. Harrison] Burton Harrison (1838–1904), private secretary of Jefferson Davis, 1862–65.

705.35 Mr. Burt] Armistead Burt (1802–1883), Democratic congressman from South Carolina, 1843–53.

706.6 executed the plan] For Lee's army to join Johnston's forces in North Carolina and defeat Sherman.

706.15 Beauregard] General Pierre G. T. Beauregard (1818–1893) was serving as Johnston's second in command.

706.33 Judge Reagan] John H. Reagan (1818–1905), a former Texas district court judge, served as Confederate postmaster general, 1861–65.

706.35 member of the Cabinet . . . opinion] The Confederate cabinet unanimously recommended that Davis accept the terms negotiated by Johnston and Sherman. Davis agreed to do so, although he correctly anticipated that President Johnson would reject the agreement.

707.33 Mrs Omelia] Mary O'Melia (c. 1822–1907) was the Davises' housekeeper in Richmond.

707.36 Little Maggie's] Davis's daughter, Margaret Howell Davis (1855–1909).

708.12 Mrs. Grant] Ann Elizabeth Crenshaw Grant (1826–1901), a close friend and neighbor of Varina Howell Davis in Richmond.

708.15 Maggie] Margaret Howell (1842–1930), younger sister of Varina Howell Davis.

709.32 General Miles] Brigadier General Nelson Miles (1839–1925) commanded the First Division, Second Corps.

709.34 Charlie Whittier] Lieutenant Colonel Charles A. Whittier (1840–1908), a Harvard classmate of Weld's, served on the staff of the Sixth Corps, 1863–64, and the Second Corps, 1865.

710.5 Barlow's] Brigadier General Francis C. Barlow (1834–1896) had commanded the First Division, Second Corps, until August 17, 1864, when he went on sick leave. Barlow rejoined the Army of the Potomac on April 6, 1865, and was assigned command of the Second Division, Second Corps.

710.9 Theodore Lyman] See Biographical Notes.

713.30–31 Genl Cheatham] Major General Benjamin F. Cheatham commanded a division in the Army of Tennessee at the time of its surrender.

715.32 Atlanta Aug 22/64] The battle east of Atlanta was fought on July 22, 1864.

717.10 Rev. J B McFerrin] John B. McFerrin (1807–1887), a Methodist minister from Nashville, served as a chaplain with the Army of Tennessee, 1863–65.

717.18–19 Revelations IIth . . . 10th verse] Revelation 2:10.

718.25 N. O.] New Orleans.

720.37 Kirby Smith] See note 334.30.

723.3 fort Fisher, Virginia] A large Union earthwork south of Petersburg built after the battle of Peebles Farm, September 30–October 2, 1864.

723.8 Dr. Bliss] D. Willard Bliss (1825–1889), chief surgeon of Armory Square Hospital, 1862–65.

729.38 our own brave Custer] Brigadier General George Armstrong Custer had spent part of his youth in Michigan, and had led a brigade composed of the 1st, 5th, 6th, and 7th Michigan cavalry regiments, June 1863–September 1864.

733.3 The Irish Brigade] The Second Brigade, First Division, Second Corps, commanded by Colonel Robert Nugent (1824–1901).

733.16–17 Gov. Crapo . . . Senator Chandler] Henry H. Crapo (1804–1869), Republican governor of Michigan, 1865–69; Zachariah Chandler (1813–1879), Republican senator from Michigan, 1857–75.

733.23 Col. Peter Stagg] Stagg (1836–1884) commanded the Michigan cavalry brigade in the Shenandoah Valley and the Appomattox campaign, October 1864–May 1865.

733.29–30 Jeff. Davis . . . wife's clothes."] Jefferson Davis was wearing his wife's cloak and shawl when he was captured by Union cavalry near Irwinville, Georgia, on May 10, 1865.

733.32–33 "step from . . . ridiculous"] In *Histoire de l'Ambassade dans le Grand-Duché de Varsovie en 1812* (1815), Dominique de Pradt (1759–1837) quotes Napoleon as saying after his retreat from Moscow: "Du sublime au ridicule, il n'y a qu'un pas" (There is only one step from the sublime to the ridiculous).

Index

This book is set in 10 point ITC Galliard Pro, a face designed for digital composition by Matthew Carter and based on the sixteenth-century face Granjon. The paper is acid-free lightweight opaque and meets the requirements for permanence of the American National Standards Institute. The binding material is Brillianta, a woven rayon cloth made by Van Heek–Scholco Textielfabrieken, Holland. Composition by Dedicated Book Services. Printing and binding by Edwards Brothers Malloy, Ann Arbor. Designed by Bruce Campbell.

THE LIBRARY OF AMERICA SERIES

The Library of America fosters appreciation and pride in America's literary heritage by publishing, and keeping permanently in print, authoritative editions of America's best and most significant writing. An independent nonprofit organization, it was founded in 1979 with seed funding from the National Endowment for the Humanities and the Ford Foundation.

1. Herman Melville: *Typee, Omoo, Mardi*
2. Nathaniel Hawthorne: *Tales and Sketches*
3. Walt Whitman: *Poetry and Prose*
4. Harriet Beecher Stowe: *Three Novels*
5. Mark Twain: *Mississippi Writings*
6. Jack London: *Novels and Stories*
7. Jack London: *Novels and Social Writings*
8. William Dean Howells: *Novels 1875–1886*
9. Herman Melville: *Redburn, White-Jacket, Moby-Dick*
10. Nathaniel Hawthorne: *Collected Novels*
11. Francis Parkman: *France and England in North America*, vol. I
12. Francis Parkman: *France and England in North America*, vol. II
13. Henry James: *Novels 1871–1880*
14. Henry Adams: *Novels, Mont Saint Michel, The Education*
15. Ralph Waldo Emerson: *Essays and Lectures*
16. Washington Irving: *History, Tales and Sketches*
17. Thomas Jefferson: *Writings*
18. Stephen Crane: *Prose and Poetry*
19. Edgar Allan Poe: *Poetry and Tales*
20. Edgar Allan Poe: *Essays and Reviews*
21. Mark Twain: *The Innocents Abroad, Roughing It*
22. Henry James: *Literary Criticism: Essays, American & English Writers*
23. Henry James: *Literary Criticism: European Writers & The Prefaces*
24. Herman Melville: *Pierre, Israel Potter, The Confidence-Man, Tales & Billy Budd*
25. William Faulkner: *Novels 1930–1935*
26. James Fenimore Cooper: *The Leatherstocking Tales*, vol. I
27. James Fenimore Cooper: *The Leatherstocking Tales*, vol. II
28. Henry David Thoreau: *A Week, Walden, The Maine Woods, Cape Cod*
29. Henry James: *Novels 1881–1886*
30. Edith Wharton: *Novels*
31. Henry Adams: *History of the U.S. during the Administrations of Jefferson*
32. Henry Adams: *History of the U.S. during the Administrations of Madison*
33. Frank Norris: *Novels and Essays*
34. W.E.B. Du Bois: *Writings*
35. Willa Cather: *Early Novels and Stories*
36. Theodore Dreiser: *Sister Carrie, Jennie Gerhardt, Twelve Men*

37a. Benjamin Franklin: *Silence Dogood, The Busy-Body, & Early Writings*

37b. Benjamin Franklin: *Autobiography, Poor Richard, & Later Writings*

38. William James: *Writings 1902–1910*
39. Flannery O'Connor: *Collected Works*
40. Eugene O'Neill: *Complete Plays 1913–1920*
41. Eugene O'Neill: *Complete Plays 1920–1931*
42. Eugene O'Neill: *Complete Plays 1932–1943*
43. Henry James: *Novels 1886–1890*
44. William Dean Howells: *Novels 1886–1888*
45. Abraham Lincoln: *Speeches and Writings 1832–1858*
46. Abraham Lincoln: *Speeches and Writings 1859–1865*
47. Edith Wharton: *Novellas and Other Writings*
48. William Faulkner: *Novels 1936–1940*
49. Willa Cather: *Later Novels*
50. Ulysses S. Grant: *Memoirs and Selected Letters*
51. William Tecumseh Sherman: *Memoirs*
52. Washington Irving: *Bracebridge Hall, Tales of a Traveller, The Alhambra*
53. Francis Parkman: *The Oregon Trail, The Conspiracy of Pontiac*
54. James Fenimore Cooper: *Sea Tales: The Pilot, The Red Rover*
55. Richard Wright: *Early Works*
56. Richard Wright: *Later Works*
57. Willa Cather: *Stories, Poems, and Other Writings*
58. William James: *Writings 1878–1899*
59. Sinclair Lewis: *Main Street & Babbitt*
60. Mark Twain: *Collected Tales, Sketches, Speeches, & Essays 1852–1890*
61. Mark Twain: *Collected Tales, Sketches, Speeches, & Essays 1891–1910*
62. *The Debate on the Constitution: Part One*
63. *The Debate on the Constitution: Part Two*
64. Henry James: *Collected Travel Writings: Great Britain & America*
65. Henry James: *Collected Travel Writings: The Continent*

66. *American Poetry: The Nineteenth Century*, Vol. 1
67. *American Poetry: The Nineteenth Century*, Vol. 2
68. Frederick Douglass: *Autobiographies*
69. Sarah Orne Jewett: *Novels and Stories*
70. Ralph Waldo Emerson: *Collected Poems and Translations*
71. Mark Twain: *Historical Romances*
72. John Steinbeck: *Novels and Stories 1932–1937*
73. William Faulkner: *Novels 1942–1954*
74. Zora Neale Hurston: *Novels and Stories*
75. Zora Neale Hurston: *Folklore, Memoirs, and Other Writings*
76. Thomas Paine: *Collected Writings*
77. *Reporting World War II: American Journalism 1938–1944*
78. *Reporting World War II: American Journalism 1944–1946*
79. Raymond Chandler: *Stories and Early Novels*
80. Raymond Chandler: *Later Novels and Other Writings*
81. Robert Frost: *Collected Poems, Prose, & Plays*
82. Henry James: *Complete Stories 1892–1898*
83. Henry James: *Complete Stories 1898–1910*
84. William Bartram: *Travels and Other Writings*
85. John Dos Passos: *U.S.A.*
86. John Steinbeck: *The Grapes of Wrath and Other Writings 1936–1941*
87. Vladimir Nabokov: *Novels and Memoirs 1941–1951*
88. Vladimir Nabokov: *Novels 1955–1962*
89. Vladimir Nabokov: *Novels 1969–1974*
90. James Thurber: *Writings and Drawings*
91. George Washington: *Writings*
92. John Muir: *Nature Writings*
93. Nathanael West: *Novels and Other Writings*
94. *Crime Novels: American Noir of the 1930s and 40s*
95. *Crime Novels: American Noir of the 1950s*
96. Wallace Stevens: *Collected Poetry and Prose*
97. James Baldwin: *Early Novels and Stories*
98. James Baldwin: *Collected Essays*
99. Gertrude Stein: *Writings 1903–1932*
100. Gertrude Stein: *Writings 1932–1946*
101. Eudora Welty: *Complete Novels*
102. Eudora Welty: *Stories, Essays, & Memoir*
103. Charles Brockden Brown: *Three Gothic Novels*
104. *Reporting Vietnam: American Journalism 1959–1969*
105. *Reporting Vietnam: American Journalism 1969–1975*
106. Henry James: *Complete Stories 1874–1884*
107. Henry James: *Complete Stories 1884–1891*
108. *American Sermons: The Pilgrims to Martin Luther King Jr.*
109. James Madison: *Writings*
110. Dashiell Hammett: *Complete Novels*
111. Henry James: *Complete Stories 1864–1874*
112. William Faulkner: *Novels 1957–1962*
113. John James Audubon: *Writings & Drawings*
114. *Slave Narratives*
115. *American Poetry: The Twentieth Century*, Vol. 1
116. *American Poetry: The Twentieth Century*, Vol. 2
117. F. Scott Fitzgerald: *Novels and Stories 1920–1922*
118. Henry Wadsworth Longfellow: *Poems and Other Writings*
119. Tennessee Williams: *Plays 1937–1955*
120. Tennessee Williams: *Plays 1957–1980*
121. Edith Wharton: *Collected Stories 1891–1910*
122. Edith Wharton: *Collected Stories 1911–1937*
123. *The American Revolution: Writings from the War of Independence*
124. Henry David Thoreau: *Collected Essays and Poems*
125. Dashiell Hammett: *Crime Stories and Other Writings*
126. Dawn Powell: *Novels 1930–1942*
127. Dawn Powell: *Novels 1944–1962*
128. Carson McCullers: *Complete Novels*
129. Alexander Hamilton: *Writings*
130. Mark Twain: *The Gilded Age and Later Novels*
131. Charles W. Chesnutt: *Stories, Novels, and Essays*
132. John Steinbeck: *Novels 1942–1952*
133. Sinclair Lewis: *Arrowsmith, Elmer Gantry, Dodsworth*
134. Paul Bowles: *The Sheltering Sky, Let It Come Down, The Spider's House*
135. Paul Bowles: *Collected Stories & Later Writings*
136. Kate Chopin: *Complete Novels & Stories*
137. *Reporting Civil Rights: American Journalism 1941–1963*
138. *Reporting Civil Rights: American Journalism 1963–1973*
139. Henry James: *Novels 1896–1899*
140. Theodore Dreiser: *An American Tragedy*
141. Saul Bellow: *Novels 1944–1953*
142. John Dos Passos: *Novels 1920–1925*

143. John Dos Passos: *Travel Books and Other Writings*
144. Ezra Pound: *Poems and Translations*
145. James Weldon Johnson: *Writings*
146. Washington Irving: *Three Western Narratives*
147. Alexis de Tocqueville: *Democracy in America*
148. James T. Farrell: *Studs Lonigan: A Trilogy*
149. Isaac Bashevis Singer: *Collected Stories I*
150. Isaac Bashevis Singer: *Collected Stories II*
151. Isaac Bashevis Singer: *Collected Stories III*
152. Kaufman & Co.: *Broadway Comedies*
153. Theodore Roosevelt: *The Rough Riders, An Autobiography*
154. Theodore Roosevelt: *Letters and Speeches*
155. H. P. Lovecraft: *Tales*
156. Louisa May Alcott: *Little Women, Little Men, Jo's Boys*
157. Philip Roth: *Novels & Stories 1959–1962*
158. Philip Roth: *Novels 1967–1972*
159. James Agee: *Let Us Now Praise Famous Men, A Death in the Family*
160. James Agee: *Film Writing & Selected Journalism*
161. Richard Henry Dana, Jr.: *Two Years Before the Mast & Other Voyages*
162. Henry James: *Novels 1901–1902*
163. Arthur Miller: *Collected Plays 1944–1961*
164. William Faulkner: *Novels 1926–1929*
165. Philip Roth: *Novels 1973–1977*
166. *American Speeches: Part One*
167. *American Speeches: Part Two*
168. Hart Crane: *Complete Poems & Selected Letters*
169. Saul Bellow: *Novels 1956–1964*
170. John Steinbeck: *Travels with Charley and Later Novels*
171. Capt. John Smith: *Writings with Other Narratives*
172. Thornton Wilder: *Collected Plays & Writings on Theater*
173. Philip K. Dick: *Four Novels of the 1960s*
174. Jack Kerouac: *Road Novels 1957–1960*
175. Philip Roth: *Zuckerman Bound*
176. Edmund Wilson: *Literary Essays & Reviews of the 1920s & 30s*
177. Edmund Wilson: *Literary Essays & Reviews of the 1930s & 40s*
178. *American Poetry: The 17th & 18th Centuries*
179. William Maxwell: *Early Novels & Stories*
180. Elizabeth Bishop: *Poems, Prose, & Letters*
181. A. J. Liebling: *World War II Writings*
182s. *American Earth: Environmental Writing Since Thoreau*
183. Philip K. Dick: *Five Novels of the 1960s & 70s*
184. William Maxwell: *Later Novels & Stories*
185. Philip Roth: *Novels & Other Narratives 1986–1991*
186. Katherine Anne Porter: *Collected Stories & Other Writings*
187. John Ashbery: *Collected Poems 1956–1987*
188. John Cheever: *Collected Stories & Other Writings*
189. John Cheever: *Complete Novels*
190. Lafcadio Hearn: *American Writings*
191. A. J. Liebling: *The Sweet Science & Other Writings*
192s. *The Lincoln Anthology: Great Writers on His Life and Legacy from 1860 to Now*
193. Philip K. Dick: *VALIS & Later Novels*
194. Thornton Wilder: *The Bridge of San Luis Rey and Other Novels 1926–1948*
195. Raymond Carver: *Collected Stories*
196. *American Fantastic Tales: Terror and the Uncanny from Poe to the Pulps*
197. *American Fantastic Tales: Terror and the Uncanny from the 1940s to Now*
198. John Marshall: *Writings*
199s. *The Mark Twain Anthology: Great Writers on His Life and Works*
200. Mark Twain: *A Tramp Abroad, Following the Equator, Other Travels*
201. Ralph Waldo Emerson: *Selected Journals 1820–1842*
202. Ralph Waldo Emerson: *Selected Journals 1841–1877*
203. *The American Stage: Writing on Theater from Washington Irving to Tony Kushner*
204. Shirley Jackson: *Novels & Stories*
205. Philip Roth: *Novels 1993–1995*
206. H. L. Mencken: *Prejudices: First, Second, and Third Series*
207. H. L. Mencken: *Prejudices: Fourth, Fifth, and Sixth Series*
208. John Kenneth Galbraith: *The Affluent Society and Other Writings 1952–1967*
209. Saul Bellow: *Novels 1970–1982*
210. Lynd Ward: *Gods' Man, Madman's Drum, Wild Pilgrimage*
211. Lynd Ward: *Prelude to a Million Years, Song Without Words, Vertigo*
212. *The Civil War: The First Year Told by Those Who Lived It*
213. John Adams: *Revolutionary Writings 1755–1775*
214. John Adams: *Revolutionary Writings 1775–1783*
215. Henry James: *Novels 1903–1911*
216. Kurt Vonnegut: *Novels & Stories 1963–1973*

217. *Harlem Renaissance: Five Novels of the 1920s*
218. *Harlem Renaissance: Four Novels of the 1930s*
219. Ambrose Bierce: *The Devil's Dictionary, Tales, & Memoirs*
220. Philip Roth: *The American Trilogy 1997–2000*
221. *The Civil War: The Second Year Told by Those Who Lived It*
222. Barbara W. Tuchman: *The Guns of August & The Proud Tower*
223. Arthur Miller: *Collected Plays 1964–1982*
224. Thornton Wilder: *The Eighth Day, Theophilus North, Autobiographical Writings*
225. David Goodis: *Five Noir Novels of the 1940s & 50s*
226. Kurt Vonnegut: *Novels & Stories 1950–1962*
227. *American Science Fiction: Four Classic Novels 1953–1956*
228. *American Science Fiction: Five Classic Novels 1956–1958*
229. Laura Ingalls Wilder: *The Little House Books, Volume One*
230. Laura Ingalls Wilder: *The Little House Books, Volume Two*
231. Jack Kerouac: *Collected Poems*
232. *The War of 1812: Writings from America's Second War of Independence*
233. *American Antislavery Writings: Colonial Beginnings to Emancipation*
234. *The Civil War: The Third Year Told by Those Who Lived It*
235. Sherwood Anderson: *Collected Stories*
236. Philip Roth: *Novels 2001–2007*
237. Philip Roth: *Nemeses*
238. Aldo Leopold: *A Sand County Almanac & Other Writings on Ecology and Conservation*
239. May Swenson: *Collected Poems*
240. W. S. Merwin: *Collected Poems 1952–1993*
241. W. S. Merwin: *Collected Poems 1996–2011*
242. John Updike: *Collected Early Stories*
243. John Updike: *Collected Later Stories*
244. Ring Lardner: *Stories & Other Writings*
245. Jonathan Edwards: *Writings from the Great Awakening*
246. Susan Sontag: *Essays of the 1960s & 70s*

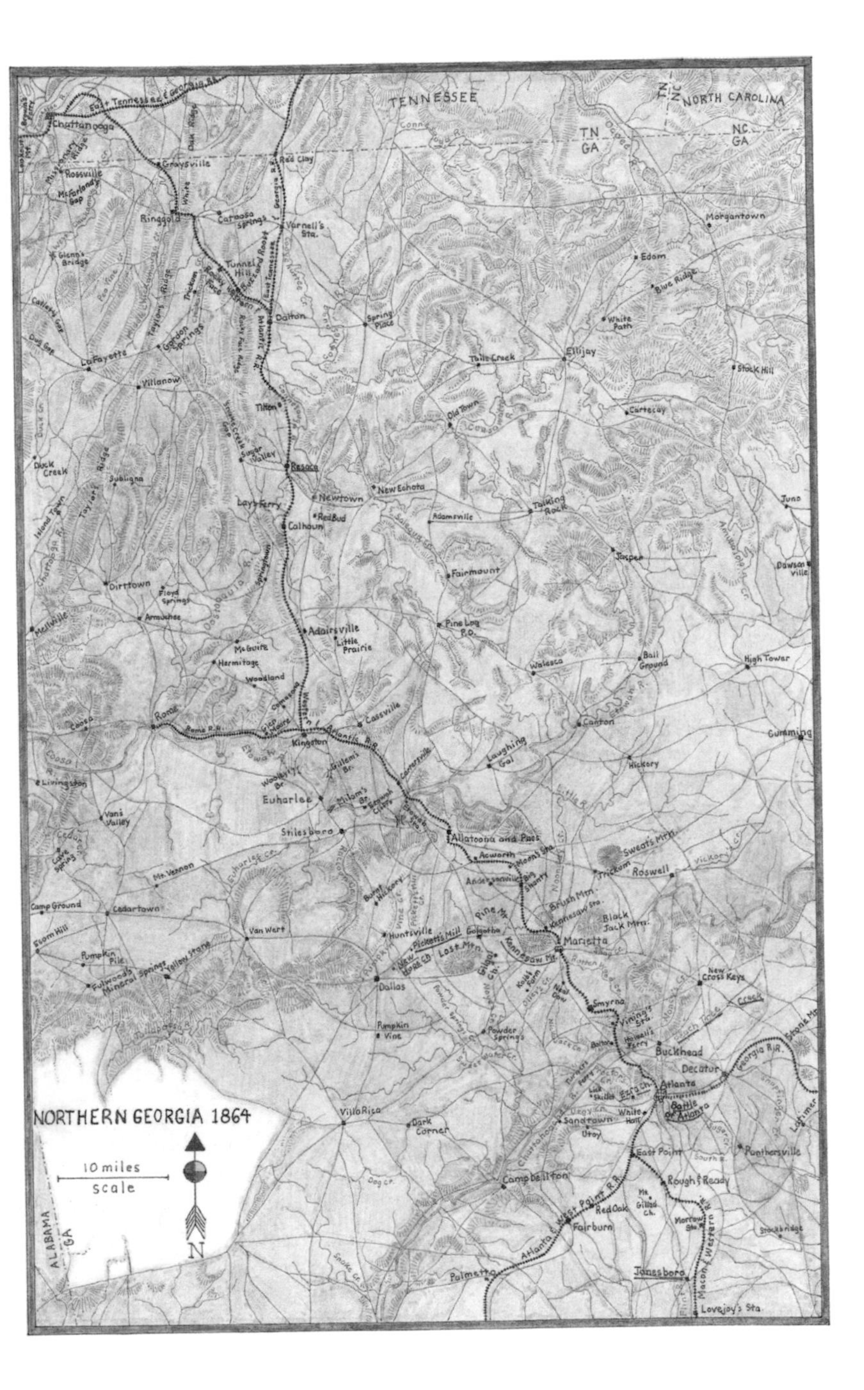
NORTHERN GEORGIA 1864
10 miles
scale
N
TENNESSEE
NORTH CAROLINA
TN
GA
NC
GA
ALABAMA
GA
Chattanooga
Missionary Ridge
Rossville
McFarland's Gap
Graysville
Ringgold
Red Clay
Catoosa Springs
Varnell's Sta.
Tunnel Hill
Dalton
Spring Place
LaFayette
Gordon Springs
Villanow
Tilton
Resaca
Sugar Valley
Lay's Ferry
Newtown
New Echota
Calhoun
Red Bud
Adamsville
Talking Rock
Jasper
Fairmount
Dirttown
Floyd Springs
Armuchee
Adairsville
Little Prairie
Pine Log P.O.
McGuire
Hermitage
Woodland
Waleska
Ball Ground
High Tower
Rome
Kingston
Cassville
Canton
Cumming
Cartersville
Laughing Gal
Hickory
Euharlee
Stilesboro
Allatoona and Pass
Acworth
Sweat's Mtn.
Roswell
Trickum
Big Shanty
Brush Mtn.
Kennesaw Sta.
Black Jack Mtn.
Cedartown
Van Wert
Huntsville
Pickett's Mill
New Hope Ch.
Lost Mtn.
Pine Mt.
Marietta
Kennesaw Mt.
Dallas
Smyrna
New Cross Keys
Pumpkin Vine
Powder Springs
Buckhead
Decatur
Atlanta
Battle of Atlanta
Georgia R.R.
Villa Rica
Dark Corner
Sandtown
Utoy
White Hall
East Point
Panthersville
Campbellton
Rough & Ready
Red Oak
Fairburn
Atlanta & West Point R.R.
Macon & Western R.R.
Palmetto
Jonesboro
Lovejoy's Sta.
Morgantown
Edom
Blue Ridge
White Path
Ellijay
Talls Creek
Stock Hill
Old Town
Cartecay
Juno
Dawsonville
Duck Creek
Subligna
Melville
Coosa
Livingston
Vans Valley
Cave Spring
Mt. Vernon
Camp Ground
Esom Hill
Pumpkin Pile
Fulwood's Mineral Springs
Yellow Stone
Stockbridge

Harrisonburg
Keezletown
McGaheysville
Conrad's Store
Blue Ridge Mtns.
Bluff Mtn.
Robertsons R.
Madison C.H.
North R.
Mt. Crawford
Cross Keys
South Fork Shenandoah R.
Swift Run Gap
Wolftown
Port Republic
Middle R.
Stanardsville
Mt. Sidney
Weyers Cave
Fort Defiance
Piedmont
New Hope
Browns Gap
Staunton
Lewis Cr.
Jarman's Gap
Barboursville
Liberty Mills
Fishersville
Waynesborough
Charlottesville
South West Mtns.
Orange And Alexandria R.R.
Rockfish Gap
Stuart's Draft
Carters Mtn.
Rivanna R.
Green Mtns.
Rockfish R.
Palmyra C.H.
Hardware River
Scottsville
Lovingston
Howardsville
canal
Warminster
New Canton
New Market
Randolph's Cr.
Slate R.
Physic Springs
Greenway
Willis R.
Maysville C.H.
Amherst C.H.
Buffalo Ridge
Duguidsville
canal
Rock Island Cr.
Bent Cr.
Cairo
New Store
Willis R.
Curdsville
Piney Mt.
Elk Cr.
Lynchburg
New Hope Ch.
Planterstown
Cumberland Church
High Bridge
Appomattox C.H.
Appomattox R.
Walkers Church
Prospect Sta.
Appomattox Station
Sailor's Creek
Evergreen Sta.
Farmville
Rice's Sta.
Pamplin's Sta.
South Side R.R.
Hampden Sydney College
Briery R.
Bush R.
Sandy R.
Prince Edward C.H.
Buffalo R.
Chickentown
Shattersburg
10 miles
scale
EASTERN VIRGINIA
1864~1865
N